LISTENING
TO
AMERICAN
JEWS

"We print typos which do not obscrue the meaning."

SH'MA

Library of Congress Cataloging-in-Publication Data

Listening to American Jews

1. Judaism — United States. 2. Judaism — 20th century.
3. Judaism and social problems. 4. Jews — United
States — Attitudes toward Israel. 5. Israel and the
Diaspora. I. Oppenheim, Carolyn Toll.
BM2O5.L56   1987   296'.O973   87-19268
ISBN 1-55774-OO4-6
ISBN O-55774-OO2-X (pbk.)

Printed in Israel

Adama Books, 306 West 38 Street, New York, New York 10018

LISTENING TO AMERICAN JEWS

Sh'ma 1970-1987

edited by *Carolyn Toll Oppenheim*

ADAMA BOOKS

Acknowledgments

Many people were instrumental in making this book possible and we gratefully acknowledge their contributions. Thanks to all the authors who granted permission to reprint their articles. The author identifications which appear here are those that followed the essays at the time they were written.   We apologize for those that are no longer applicable and to the authors we could not find.

A special thanks to Esther Cohen, Susan Nover, and June Evers of Adama Books for their support and encouragement on this project.

We are indebted to our administrator, Alicia Seeger, who tied all the ends together to see the book through, and who has been a backbone of Sh'ma for many years.

We are indebted to Miriam Weintraub of Weinglas Graphic Services, Inc. for her considerable help with design and layout.

Thanks, too, to former assistant editors Rabbis Mark Golub and Margaret Wenig and to Dan Dorfman, Joan Friedman, Debra Hachen, Jeffrey Salkin, Ruth Sohn and Yoel Kahn who worked as assistants to the editor and helped with the selection of the articles that appear here.

A special thanks to Jerrold Oppenheim who kept two little girls fed and occupied for many weekends and school vacations while their mother sat engrossed in 17 years of Sh'ma.

שמע   Join us now   שמע

I wish to subscribe to Sh'ma
enelosed is a check for:
[   ] 10 issues for $6 (new subscribers only)
[   ] 2 years for $22

name _____

street _____

city & state _____ zip _____

Sh'ma   Box 567   Port Washington, NY 11050

Introduction

Sh'ma,
A Bold Experiment in
American Jewish Journalism

by *Carolyn Toll Oppenheim*

"For this is not the liberty which we can hope, that no grievance ever should arise in the Commonwealth, that let no man in this world expect; but when complaints are freely heard, deeply considered, and speedily reformed, then is the utmost bound of civil liberty attained that wise men look for."
(John Milton, *Areopagitica*, 1644.)

"I believe that no society is good and can be healthy without freedom for dissent and for creative independence."
(I.F. Stone, July 1963).

"Criticism is the lifeblood of modern thought.... We need public criticism if only so that honest men will feel more at home among us."
(Eugene B. Borowitz, *Sh'ma 1/1, Nov. 1970.)*

One day early in 1971 someone changed my life by thrusting a copy of *Sh'ma* into my hands. Until then I had never imagined it possible to combine my two deepest commitments: Judaism and critical journalism. If anything, they had been in deep conflict. I was a young reporter working for the *Chicago Tribune,* having just returned from Israel and meetings with the then-fledgling Israeli peace and civil rights movement. The gap between Israeli press coverage of alternative viewpoints and the propaganda that passed for news in the American Jewish press heightened my disappointment with American Jewish life.

The principal preoccupation of every idealistic young American journalist in the 1970's was how to achieve democracy in the media. Only two years before, the 1968 Democratic convention had been a watershed for most working journalists. When Chicago's notorious Mayor Daley had ordered his police to fire on radical demonstrators, hardly a newspaper editor in the country would believe his own staffers' reports. Nor would they print the truth until the next day when their own reporters were vindicated by footage on the television networks.

The outrage created by this climate of censorship fueled a nationwide movement of alternative magazines in which reporters had space to write the stories suppressed by editors shielding too many sacred cows. These reviews spawned a decade of investigative journalism culminating in the Watergate exposé. The first of these was the *Chicago Journalism Review*, of which I was an active participant. We exposed corruption — deals between public officials and real estate or other business interests — which we had not been permitted to write for the newspapers where we worked. Our *Journalism Review* examined the workings of censorship in the four daily newspapers of Chicago. These stories were scrutinized by volunteer editors applying high standards of journalistic ethics and professionalism before publication. The journalism reviews took pains to distinguish themselves from what they considered "ideological, radical rags" among the alternative media of the late '60's and early '70's.

Where was the Jewish Equivalent?

Sh'ma read like a Jewish journalism review, with its dedication to freedom of expression. For instance, there were articles taking the Jewish establishment to task for suppressing open criticism and for its silence about the My Lai massacre of Vietnamese civilians by American troops during the Vietnam war (Frimer, Chapter 9). I read my first piece on Jewish feminism in *Sh'ma* — Deborah Miller's "Equal Only When Obligated," (Chapter 5) and was amazed such thoughts had only occurred to me in a secular and not a Jewish context. (How many people had heard of Jewish feminism in 1971, two years before the first Jewish women's conference and a year before the first woman rabbi was ordained?) Seymour Siegel's reassessment of the Jewish community's traditional position on church-state separation over aid to religious schools (Chapter 9) and the debate that followed were intriguing. The candor of Balfour Brickner's account of his dilemma between his Zionism and liberal politics (Chapter 10) was something I had never read in an American Jewish publication. It broke my stereotype that those involved in organized Jewish life had none of the moral conflicts of the Jews who chose the arena of secular, progressive politics.

These articles hooked me into a regular subscription. But I knew I'd found my Jewish niche in *Sh'ma* when I read Borowitz's "In the Beginning" (Chapter 1) welcoming Jews to share their different viewpoints and confront one another in *Sh'ma*: "Criticism is the life-blood of modern thought," he wrote. "It is our only strong genre of ethics. But not in the Jewish community. Neither books nor ideas are permitted to be strongly contested; institutions and their leaders are always beyond public judgment. We must not give aid and comfort to the anti-Semite, Jewish or not. One who does not wish to join the conspiracy has little place in Jewish things — and then we wonder why intellectuals, who are nothing if not critics, have little use for our community style. We need public criticism if only so that honest men will feel more at home among us. That must include not only criticism of the opinions expressed in these pages but of the entire enterprise as a whole. Candor need not mean cruelty; bluntness does not require boorishness, yet they are the risks. Despite them we must dispense with the old, protective etiquette of Jewish communal discourse. That is why I have created this journal as a private project, unbeholden to any established institution. Writers may say what they wish here, from whatever point of view they believe is valuable. Articles will be accepted — and letters are welcomed from those who wish a shorter format — solely in terms of whether, within this broad purview, I believe they make a contribution to the ongoing debate. . . ."

Remembering the Jewish Arguing of Yore

Sh'ma's honesty and lively controversy also filled me with nostalgia for the Jewish world of my childhood where my love of Judaism and critical journalism took root, a world that does not exist any more and, indeed, was dying even as I was growing up in the late 1940's and early 1950's.

My parents had a stormy intermarriage of ideologies. My mother, inclined to religious observance and *Shabbat*, struggled with my father, an agnostic and Workmen's Circle Yiddishist. My grandparents' kitchen tables were the battlegrounds for the diverse religious and political viewpoints of all our family: Zionism, Socialism, secular *Yiddishkeit*, Orthodoxy, Conservative and even Reform. My anti-Zionist secular-Socialist grandfather threatened to cast his daughter out if she left for Palestine to join a *kibbutz* in 1940. My aunt rebelled against him by marrying an Orthodox man instead. Today her four grown children live in Israel and send their collective 15 children to Israeli religious schools. Another cousin, a deeply nationalistic, anti-religious Labor Zionist left the U.S. in 1945 to join a secular *kibbutz* and refused to ever visit his family in the United States in protest against what he considered the materialism of American Jewish values. Yet another cousin, a Conservative rabbi, became a vocal opponent of the ordination of women by the Jewish Theological Seminary. In my world, Jews cared deeply about their viewpoints. Nothing else seemed more exciting than being Jewish, with its exotic clash of freely flowing ideas. *Sh'ma* evoked the spirit of this community.

The Bonds Good Talk Creates

Sh'ma also reminded me of the intimate feeling of the Yiddish press my family all read, regardless of persuasion, particularly the *Forverts,* the *Jewish Daily Forward*, where writers conversed with readers and each other and were concerned with the personal experiences of the readers. The *Forward*, under the stewardship of editor Abraham Cahan, brought the work of serious intellectuals to the lay people, and the writings of the lay people to the intellectuals through the famous *Bintel Brief* (a bunch of letters) column. In a similar way, the impressive array of well known Jewish intellectuals who serve *Sh'ma* as contributing editors take part in rich dialogue with ordinary Jews through the letters, which make up such large sections of each *Sh'ma* issue. Ordinary Jews may tell their own stories — in letter or article form — as well as respond to or criticize a contributing editor.

The personal stories about Jewish life between 1970 and 1985 in *Sh'ma* are as important historically as the published collected columns of the *Bintel Brief*. We look back nostalgically to the *Forward* letters like the one from "a socialist and a free-thinker" agonizing over whether it is "hypocritical to say *Kaddish* on a *yortzayt* for a dead parent." The next generation may well feel similarly about our period of Jewish history when reading Sharon Strassfeld's rage (Chapter 6) at a Jewish community for pinning guilt on young Jewish mothers for wanting careers and feeling reluctant to have third children in today's economy. Or the wonderfully poignant story of the tensions at a modern family's *seder* table (Shafton, Chapter 11) may evoke nostalgia for the 80's.

As Cahan used the *Forward* in its early years, Borowitz seemed to be using *Sh'ma* to build a new Jewish community committed to the principles of free speech and open discussion. Both were willing to antagonize some intellectuals because they cared more about free speech than ideology.

Another American Jewish editor, Henry Hurwitz of the Menorah Journal (1915-1964) used a publication to build a Jewish community and encouraged open criticism and self examination of American Jewish life. He, too, did not fear to step on toes. But his publication, essentially a product of Jewish academics and Harvard-trained intellectuals, seemed to me a much narrower community than that of *Sh'ma*.

What other magazine today than *Sh'ma* — Jewish or otherwise — would publish articles by two opposing writers representing the most extreme positions on the farthest ends of the spectrum? *Sh'ma* published a piece by Meir Kahane, claiming democracy and Jewish tradition are in fundamental conflict, as well as an article by Henry Schwarzschild, resigning as *Sh'ma* contributing editor and announcing his withdrawal from all Jewish organizations which did not renounce the State of Israel following its invasion of Lebanon (both in Chapter 10). These articles were not published for sheer sensationalism; both writers spoke from the depths of their love of the people Israel, a unifying editorial theme of *Sh'ma*. *These articles contributed to the complexity of where such love could take one's thoughts.*

How the Readers Shape the Journal

My move to New York granted me the opportunity to participate more fully in the *Sh'ma* community as a Fellow for three years (1982-85). Fellows played an interesting role in the work of *Sh'ma*. We met periodically with the Assistant to the Editor—usually a rabbinical student—and the Editor to brainstorm story ideas and suggest writers we might help solicit for articles. We were each assigned a contributing editor to telephone all year—to prod to write articles and to critique the current issues with suggestions for new stories. We all did brief book reviews. Each year the Fellows struggled to develop funny ideas for Purim, when an entire issue of *Sh'ma* is devoted to humor, usually parodies. There are two Purim pieces in Chapter 12. Also, the humorous article by William Wallen in Chapter 11 captures the tone of a typical Purim piece as well as makes a wry commentary on the life of young, single Jewish urban professionals today.

The Fellows' diversity reflected the richly varied views of *Sh'ma*. One year's group included, among others, a Yale undergraduate and a retired Anti-Defamation League director; a young Orthodox mother of five from Brooklyn; a middle-aged rabbinical student who was the mother of grown children; a Russian refusenik turned Conservative rabbinical student; an Orthodox Jew who was a New York State Court judge; and me. We were each encouraged to suggest a theme for an issue which we would produce: find its authors, solicit the articles, and follow up until publication. My first issue was a round-table discussion among politically left-wing Jews about why they felt alienated from organized Jewish life. Another issue I suggested was on Jewish intra-marriage. The stories of tensions within Ashkenazi-Sephardic or Reform-Orthodox marriages were juicy reminiscences many—including myself—could resonate to. A third issue my husband and I both contributed to was entirely devoted to the phenomemon of homelessness and the Jewish community's response.

In that issue, a hard-hitting piece by Margaret Holub (Chapter 4) chided the Jewish community for taking large contributions from Jewish businessmen whose "flagrant business and political practices...increase the numbers and the suffering of the homeless." Holub, who was recently ordained a rabbi by the Hebrew Union College-Jewish Institute of Religion, called such contributions "blood money" and hoped that some day Jewish communities would turn back such funds to the givers.

Change and Continuity over the Years

Interestingly, although *Sh'ma* had originally been most notable for such outspoken articles on major social issues, the magazine did not escape the national trend of turning inward from larger societal concerns to more specifically Jewish issues affecting the entire Jewish community. This has been a source of continuing worry to Borowitz.

On *Sh'ma's* fifth anniversary, he wrote: "Despite my devotion to the Jewish community, its ethics and its spirituality, I am somewhat troubled that *Sh'ma* is largely inner-directed these days. I hope we shall soon again see that our Jewish imperatives lead us to take an active responsibility for America's destiny and the world's."

The feisty journalism reviews, too, after a few years of hard-nosed exposés, moved into a period of reflection about the nature of journalism and society. Muckraking journalists turning inward triggered a national dialogue about their profession. After the Watergate success, the journalists had less reason to be angry at the establishment media which had responded to their criticisms. More of their energies turned to achieving personal success. By 1980 the reviews were gone.

There the similarity between *Sh'ma* and the journalism reviews ends. *Sh'ma* is alive and well after 17 years, with a solid circulation of three times its original 2,000 subcriptions. And *Sh'ma's* reputation is growing.

Sh'ma has been building its own institution in these years: a democratic, Jewish forum. The letters from the readers, in Chapter 12, are a good sample of that forum. Here, readers debate with writers, everything from the nature of Jewish powerlessness, to the morality of fleeing from neighborhoods when Blacks move in, to the proper role of Jews in American political campaigns. There are letters about Downs Syndrome Children and the Jewish community, about the image of Jews on television sit-coms, and about the good or bad service on El-Al airlines!

Even when it is successful, *Sh'ma* can never self-destruct, as did the journalism reviews. They were gadflies, critiquing another institution for which they claimed no responsibility. When they succeeded in transforming the object of their criticism, their purpose for coming into being had been accomplished. *Sh'ma's* goal is not merely to critique the Jewish community, but to set an example in its own pages of how that community might develop. It is this sense of responsibility — for the larger world and the Jewish world — that is the key to *Sh'ma's* staying power.

An Odd "Pulpit"; an Unconventional Rabbi

The driving force behind that sense of purpose is Borowitz, the Editor with a commitment to build a new Jewish community in which thoughtful critics can play a major role. Luckily for *Sh'ma*, Borowitz is also blessed with the gift of excellent management skills. He has made intelligent business decisions in the interests of keeping *Sh'ma* modest and independent; he takes very little salary for himself or his employees (usually one rabbinical student assistant and a wonderful administrator, Mrs. Alicia Seeger). Yet he devotes enormous time and energy to keeping the publication thriving and meeting new challenges.

That sense of responsibility, which keeps Borowitz committed to *Sh'ma* long after others might have wearied of the project, is reflected in the articles, even when the writers seem especially self-absorbed in Jewish issues. Some of what seems like inner-directedness is not. Jewish affairs are no longer so parochial as they once were before Jewish issues moved to the foreground of contemporary events. In the past 17 years we have been deprived of the luxury of sitting safely on the sidelines where we could view world history from a Jewish perspective and debate our own history with only each other. Increasingly we are sharing in that history ourselves. Jewish issues are so frequently the major events on the front pages of our newspapers: the controversies surrounding Israel, Bitburg, Waldheim, Lebanon, Leon Klinghoffer, Farrakhan, the Wall Street insider trading scandals, the Iran-Contra scandals and Baby M, to name just a few.

In the way he guides our Jewish discussions about these events, Borowitz can be compared to the 19th century Yiddish writer I.L. Peretz, who was also a cultural leader concerned with the rebuilding of an idealistic Jewish community in Warsaw, as Jews were pouring out of the rural towns. "All of us can be criticized publicly, especially the writer," Peretz once said, "for he speaks to the public and therefore belongs to the public. It used to be said that the work and not the author should be criticized. But the public has the right to demand from time to time that the supplicant remove his prayer shawl so that it can see who prays in its behalf and who blows the shofar for it."

Speak — but Know Others will Respond

In sharing his personal dissent on Israeli policy (Chapter 10), Borowitz opened himself up to public criticism from the very thinkers he eagerly courts as writers in *Sh'ma* — the religious right, the modern Orthodox, and the political conservatives. Articles in Chapter 10 by Kraus and Wigoder strongly take issue with him, as he had invited writers to do.

Such polemical pieces as these, or the more extreme views of Kahane and Henry Schwarzschild, have value beyond the spice they bring to the publication. For example, in the early years Henry Siegman wrote a scathing criticism of his Orthodox rabbinical colleagues' silence about Vietnam, provoking a rash of responses from fellow Orthodox clergy — a group normally less forthcoming with pieces for *Sh'ma* than others. We readers became privy to a debate that was otherwise kept under wraps, giving us useful insight into the pulls and tugs within that community on responding to American political issues. Two pieces from that debate by Frimer and Berman (Chapter 9) go into considerably more depth than the original article which prompted theirs.

Such many-faceted debates offer the opportunity to apply a distinctly Jewish kind of thinking to contemporary social and political problems, an original of *Sh'ma*. As Dan Dorfman writes (in Chapter 11), "Jewish thought is more subtle, more sensitive, and even more realistic than what most of us derive from Western thought. . . . Each situation we face has its own peculiar combination of considerations, factors, and values that come into play. Hard and fast, writ-in-stone rules rigidly applied in all situations do not yield accurate perceptions or provide reliable guidance." It is the strength of this particular Jewish system of thought about issues which has sustained the *Sh'ma* enterprise, whereas the journalism review movement — with its rigid western view of good guys and bad guys — could only have run its course.

Is this Book, then, the Highlights of Sh'ma?

The very nature of this process of Jewish debate made the task of culling the "best" articles from 17 years of *Sh'ma* for this anthology a nearly impossible task. For what was "best" about *Sh'ma*, to me, was never the individual article, but the dialectic created by a series of responses and counter-reponses and letters and adding pieces of the puzzle until we saw a topic in all its complexity. The debates on the Baby M case in Chapter 7 and the role and nature of the Jewish family in Chapter 4 give some of the flavor of a real *Sh'ma* free-for-all. To accurately reproduce such a forum would require the addition of half a dozen reader responses and responses to the responses with the original articles.

However, this does not make the endeavor to do an anthology of *Sh'ma* an impossible task. As a devoted reader of *Sh'ma* and a journalist, I was delighted to be offered the opportunity. The articles in this volume are a *forshpeis*, an appetizer, of the *Sh'ma* experience. The past 17 years have been witness to some extraordinary social and political turmoil and *Sh'ma* has had lengthy colloquia on all of these topics and more: the civil rights and women's movements, the black power movement, the war in Vietnam and the success of the American anti-war movement; the homosexual and handicapped rights movements, the Yom Kippur war, the rise of Gush Emunim and the West Bank settlements, the rise to power of Begin, the Israeli invasion of Lebanon, the Jewish feminist movement, the ordination of the first Reform woman rabbi, the decision to ordain the first Conservative woman rabbi, the growth from no women in the rabbinate to more than 100, the Reform movement's vote on patrilineal descent, the rise of a vocal Israel peace movement, Watergate, the rise of international terrorism, Reagan, Reaganism and Reagonomics.

The selections of the articles in this book are an attempt to touch on some of the highlights of these discussions to illustrate the breadth of *Sh'ma's* scope. A prospective reader of *Sh'ma* should get an idea, from this anthology, of the range of topics covered. Subscribers who have not saved their copies might enjoy reminiscing over old times. In order to hit the highlights, enormous quantities of excellent material had to be left out.

The Eternal Amid the Ephemeral

Some of the sections read like diaries of the discussions which took place about events as they were unfolding. Chapter 5 documents the emergence of Jewish women bringing the strength of the secular women's movement into the Jewish community. Chapter 6 chronicles some of the contemporary experimentation with and debate over new birth rituals for our daughters. Chapter 7 relates the ongoing dialogue in the Jewish community about the impact of new medical technologies on birth and death — do we use amniocentesis for our pregnancies, do we abort handicapped fetuses, do we use mechanical life support systems to extend our lives when we are terminally ill? Future readers may be intrigued when reading Chapter 3 to find the personal story of a remarkable "righteous gentile" who was honored by the State of Israel for saving many Jewish children from death. This chapter also includes a rich discussion among theologians about how they view the Covenant in the aftermath of the Holocaust. Readers will be moved and relieved to read the anguish of two important writers about the prominent role of Jews in the New York City corruption scandals in Chapter 4. Chapter 9 contains a strong claim that Sanctuary for Central Americans is inherently a Jewish issue by a Rabbi who led his congregation to declare sanctuary.

A Forum for People like Stone and Arendt

Borowitz seems to have the same kind of zeal to crusade for free speech and the same persistence that drove the well-known muckracking American journalist I.F. Stone to keep publishing his now famous *I. F. Stone's Weekly* newsletter throughout the dark McCarthy years of the 1950's. Stone became the mentor of the generation of young journalists who founded the journalism reviews and the decade of investigative journalism. Carl Bernstein, of the Woodward and Bernstein journalist team of Watergate fame, had been Stone's protegé. In March 1971, when *Sh'ma* was less than a year old, an organization of young journalists honored "Izzie" Stone in New York at the first annual MORE Journalism Review convention.

Ironically, although American McCarthyism had not succeeded in silencing Izzie, Jewish cencorship had. Writing in the *New York Review of Books* in 1978 in "Confessions of a Jewish Dissident," Stone claimed he was boycotted and blackballed by the Jewish establishment organizations because he wrote about his support for a bi-national state in his book *Underground to Palestine* (interviews with Holocaust surviviors on ships breaking through the British blockade to the Palestine mandate, written on assignment for *P. M.* newspaper in 1946. Izzie said he did all the interviews in Yiddish).

When Izzie published this story, I felt sad that a superb journalist who had been one of my inspirations had never had a forum in which I could know his Jewish perspectives. I could have learned from his views of Jewish affairs and from other Jews' debates with him. I had a similar reaction to the storm of protest about Hannah Arendt's criticism of Jews and Israel which followed her reportage of the 1961 Eichmann trial, in Israel, for the *New Yorker* magaine. Widely respected by scholars for her political philosophy, she was invisible to us as a Jewish critic. Her virtual excommunication from Jewish life following the ugly response to her Eichmann stories robbed us all of the value of her critique for the dialectic process.

Welcoming the Thoughtful "Stranger"

Yet a third major American Jewish intellectual found himself silenced within the Jewish community. Seymour Melman, Columbia University professor, who is widely regarded as the preeminent specialist on conversion from a military to peacetime economy, and a longtime national co-chairman of SANE Nuclear Policy, told his Jewish story on the occasion of receiving the first annual Abraham Joshua Heschel Peace Award from the Jewish Peace Fellowship in 1983. A nationally prominent academic and peace activist, Melman was always considered to be a secular, unaffiliated Jew—even when he worked with Rabbi Heschel and the Clergy and Laity Concerned in opposition to the Vietnam war.

In a touching speech, Melman shared his Jewish history and his eventual separation from any communal Jewish life. A Zionist in college, Melman spent a year on a *kibbutz* in Palestine in 1939 and became enthusiastic about a bi-national solution. Upon returning to the U.S. he edited a journal of Arab-Jewish Cooperation and did much public speaking. It was during this period—up to the early 1950's—that he felt himself "frozen out" from speaking engagements and publications. He was chastised by members of his Zionist organization for continuing to express his viewpoint even after the declaration of the state.

These intellectuals—all of whom cared deeply about the fate of Jews and the health of society—were lost to the Jewish public forum. I cannot help but wonder what the texture of Jewish thought and debate might be today if *Sh'ma* had been around for them, and solicited their views and responses. An abridgement of Melman's address was published in *Sh'ma* (see Chapter 11). Since it was founded, *Sh'ma* has offered a home to concerned, Jewish critics of all stripes to voice their positions and engage fellow Jews in debate. This anthology is a sample of that process. May *Sh'ma* live 120 years!

Contents

III. THE PUZZLES AND FASCINATIONS OF JEWISH LIFE

11. The Varieties of Jewish Experience

I

IN A REFLECTIVE MOOD

1.

The View from Sh'ma

At the beginning
Eugene B. Borowitz

In self-certain eras magazines were inaugurated with declarations of principle. Sh'ma is the child of troubled times so it has a different character. For example, its contributing editors differ radically on many matters: belief, politics, duty, social values, to mention a few. They probably could not agree on a substantive program this magazine ought to foster. If they are unanimous on anything, it is on their individual freedom. They do not want me or anyone else to presume to speak for them. They will speak for themselves and then, attach their names. Otherwise, they take no responsibility for opinions expressed in Sh'ma's pages.

I too speak only for myself. Yet I think it may be of help to say what brought me to start Sh'ma. I feel called by a problem and commanded to do something about it.

The problem is society. It always has been, as the Bible and rabbinic literature indicate. Yet only a few years ago men of culture sought to ignore its ugly realities and, by retreating to a rich inner life, save their soul. What was then psychologizing and romanticism, *The Power of Positive Thinking* and *Franny and Zooey,* has now shown its degenerate tendency in the ego-centricity of psychedelic faddism and drug abuse.

Man's emotions need expression. His consciousness needs expansion far beyond what technical reason has shrunk it to. But psychology can no longer claim priority in fostering human welfare. What society projects upon the individual has clearly become the single greatest source of continuing, changeable evil that we know. We must do something

about it not because we cannot ignore the many problems, once so carefully hidden from us, nor even because the suffering has intensified in recent years. The degradation is intolerable because it is unnecessary and we cannot, Eichmann-like, be morally content to do the bidding of the old order.

Were we cowardly enough to ignore what is happening, we would be denounced by our students or our children. Radicals, liberals, conservatives, they keep wanting to know what we are doing about mankind. They will no longer give much respect or confer significant leadership **upon people without a social concern. They prefer honest error in the service of man to selfish wisdom. They are making harsh demands and they are right.**

But what shall we do?
In the New Deal days men were confident they could solve most social problems. Most men today, I among them, are not. We do not even know how much amelioration is possible without creating new difficulties. But that humility is not to be identified with a retreat to depending on God for everything. We wrong each other in a thousand ways but we are also capable of changing cholera from a plague to a problem. There is much we can do. At the least, we can talk to one another and, by showing such humanity, make what is insoluble less terrifying. If we could also learn to listen to one another, particularly when we are in fundamental disagreement, we might thereby give a sign of how society can become community.

An equally powerful drive bringing me to this magazine is my trust in the Jewish tradition. In all its variegation it taught our forefathers how to face life realistically and yet ennoble it. As I see what my Jewishness has meant to my life, I know it has something fundamentally significant to say about what man and society ought to be today. I think I have always believed that but as I have seen the growing collapse of the old, accepted value systems in America, that feeling has become more intensified and self-conscious. In a world where espousing pagan a-morality is almost a pre-requisite for status, the virtues of being Jewish have become very precious. So I would like to see what my Jewish set toward things discloses about my duties in contemporary society.

Surprisingly enough here too there are few certainties. However, two of the dogmas of my youth seem quite shattered. The first was that Judaism was really only ethics and the second, that modern Jewish social responsibility was essentially liberal politics.

The identification of Judaism with Kantian style ethics is not so much false as obsolete. I do not feel I have to prove to society that Jews have universal human concerns. I am rather quite concerned to understand what it means that I and many others still want to be Jews. Had we not learned from the neo-Kantian teachers of previous generations how deep the universal ethical passion was embedded in Jewish practice, I doubt that a magazine of this sort could have been conceived.

Finding a greater sense of commandment

But if the effective range of our Jewish duty has been shaped by the old ethical emphasis, it nonetheless far transcends it. My loyalty to the Jewish people and the Jewish tradition is of the essence, not secondary in my Jewishness. They certainly do not require continual ethical apology. So my concern with the affairs and failures of the Jewish community is as natural to me as is my involvement with the problems of mankind. I imagine that the precise implications of these commitments, when they conflict, will often be argued about here. And that is a good indication of the fragmented sort of existence most Jews lead today.

Yet even the ethical aspect of Judaism is by no means clear or well-defined. Despite a century and a half of boasting about the superiority of the ethics of Judaism, not more than two or three serious books have been written on the topic. With regard to social ethics, we are even poorer. Only the second volume of Moritz

Lazarus' *Ethics of Judaism* deals with it but in a way that is of such minimal continuing interest that it has never been translated.

We are in a somewhat better situation as far as specific issues are concerned. Here, though we must generally work by analogy or extrapolation, there is often direct halakhic material available. Yet full-scale, modern studies of the range and development of Jewish opinion, like Feldman's on birth control, are quite rare. Other journals exist for such scholarly work. Sh'ma will confront the issues rather than study the sources. But each author will bring his own Jewish learning and experience to bear on his theme. In that living confrontation all of us can learn a good deal about the modern scope and content of Jewish duty.

That leads to the other aspect of our uncertainty. We cannot simply identify liberal politics as the social imperative of Judaism. For some Jews the old liberalism is an excuse for procrastination and an evasion of the root difficulties. For other Jews the primary obligation of our community is to keep healthy and stable that democratic process upon which our existence in America depends. Today **Jewish values imply different social strategy to different people. Instead of a relatively widespread, unlegislated but conventional agreement as to what modern Jews ought to do, the best guidance Judaism might offer to us is a vigorous dialectic of opinion.**

Creating a dialogue in difference

Such a clash of views might be useful if it does not remain sporadic and private rather than continuing and public. If we can draw thoughtful people to this forum they will learn as well as teach the community If we cannot have common answers, if we must live with the anxiety of alternatives, then let us at least know what the various views entail and what seem their major drawbacks. There is something quite traditional in encouraging such a dialectic as the instrument for fostering Jewish wisdom.

As I see it, then, Sh'ma is more identifiable in method than results, in approach than conclusions, in process than outcomes .

Some simple corollaries would seem to flow from that: a concern for realism and criticism.

To speak only about what is good and positive about us, worse to confine oneself to the conventionally acceptable topics and rhetoric is in effect, to protect the old patterns of inequality. Modern conservatism like modern radicalism is most effective when it stops trying to be nice and helps us face the realities. It is important to talk freely about what actually moves men and institutions: sex and money, ego and power. I believe it would help the Jewish community greatly if for a change we could speak about our leaders and organizations by name and not by suffocating euphemisms.

Criticism is the life-blood of modern thought. It is our only strong genre of ethics. But not in the Jewish community. Neither books nor ideas are permitted to be strongly contested; institutions and their leaders are always beyond public judgment. We must not give aid and comfort to the anti-semite, Jewish or not. One who does not wish to join the conspiracy has little place in Jewish things—and then we wonder why intellectuals, who are nothing if not critics, have little use for our community style. We need public criticism if only so that honest men will feel more at home among us. That must include not only criticism of the opinions expressed in these pages but of the enterprise as a whole. Candor need not mean cruelty; bluntness does not require boorishness, yet they are the risks. Despite them we must dispense with the old, protective etiquette of Jewish communal discourse.

Founding an unestablishedment

That is why I have created this journal as a private project, unbeholden to any established institution. Writers may say what they wish here, from whatever point of view they believe is valuable. Articles will be accepted—and letters are welcomed from those who wish a shorter format—solely in terms of whether, within this broad purview, I believe they make a contribution to the ongoing debate. I am therefore particularly grateful to my friends in Port Washington and elsewhere, and to those of Arnold J. Wolf in Chicago, whose contributions have made Sh'ma possible. They have not sought control or *kavod*. They have only asked me to do what intellectual Jews always said they wanted to do. By such trust, they have increased the sense of high responsibility with which this venture begins. I do not know whether it can succeed. I know it has to

be tried. As the utterly realistic Psalm 90 puts it: Be pleased with us, Adonai, our God, and give our work more lasting value than we have. Yes, make it of some lasting worth.

What we learned from the 1970's

At Sh'ma's *annual meeting of the contributing editors last June, a symposium was held on the implications of the past decade on Jewish life. Opening, prepared remarks were made by Nora Levin, Arnold Jacob Wolf, and David Novak. A lively discussion followed. As we now wind up the 1970's and move forward into a new decade, we would like to share with you the highlights of last spring's exchange. Although recent world events have been such that if the symposium were held today it would undoubtedly include additional material, the contents of the June discussion remain current and provocative.*

Nora Levin

The most shocking development for some of us during the seventies has been a growing realization that the establishment of the state of Israel has not, as we had believed, created general Jewish security or provided the sole answer to Jewish survival. This, despite the fact that for American Jewry, the Jewish state has had an extraordinarily positive emotional and psychological effect, one that has been stirring, inspiring, and strengthening. It has created a force around which most American Jews have rallied and thus expressed their pride and solidarity. And it has also enabled us to become more assertive politically. But in a very fundamental sense Israel has also had certain de-stabilizing effects on Jewish life. Israel is in the center of a global fire-storm because of the oil crisis, the OPEC cartel, the deep, pervasive, ceaseless Arab hostility, and the intensification of anti Semitism in the Arab world, the third world and in the communist world. In American liberal circles there is the notion that Israel is an oppressive state and whatever our counter-arguments, this image has not gone away.

A fundamental re-examination of Zionism as an ideology and a strategy for Jewish survival has been and is essential, but most American Jews have resisted this re-thinking and continue to use slogans and assumptions of a simpler past. The old Zionist rejection of *Galut* (Exile) and the Israeli contempt for it need a fresh analysis. We must find the necessary balance between our two needs. On one hand we need to develop an autonomous Jewish culture in America with our own interests, perspectives and philosophy — without guilt. On the other hand we need to develop an understanding of Israel as a nation-state with a different dynamic and different perspectives from our own. We must recognize Israel as a vital force in Jewish life, but not necessarily *the central one,* the one which defines the totality of Jewish cultural and political-ideological values. Pre-state Zionism is no longer valid either for Israel or American Jewry.

This change has wrenched us out of old and familiar reactions and is very disturbing, but why should American Jews be more comfortable about Jewish dilemmas than other Jewries? Historically, we have always been faced with nearly insoluble problems. Criticism of Israel is still viewed as a kind of treachery, but this cannot continue as we view the Jewish state, "our" state, taking un-Jewish turns: leaving the social gap festering, arming Somoza, planting settlements on the West Bank and planning to annex it, radicalizing the once bright "bridge-to-peace" — the Arabs of Israel. To some of us, the Begin government is taking a self-destructive course. How can we refrain from criticizing it?

. . . One of the horns of our dilemma, of course, is the growing isolation of Israel, the fear that American Jewry alone can be counted on to support it and must not seem to falter. But if Israel was created to serve *all* Jews, and if Israel's policies and decisions affect the lives of diaspora Jews, our involvement in Israel's affairs seems inescapable. The mechanism for this involvement is as yet undeveloped, largely because of American Jewry's lesser position in the "partnership" and our inhibitions about interfering in Israel's sovereignty. At the same time, the global complications that I have touched on have diminished the leverage, the true sovereignty possible to Israel. Rather, Israel is increasingly becoming the whipping boy of the Arab world and the Soviet Union, and a counter to be pressured and maneuvered by the United States. Israel is only partially able, if not entirely incapable of protecting the interests and lives of Jews living in other countries.

American Jews have begun to feel uneasy about these fissures and conflicts but continue to submerge them and acquiesce in decisions of the Israeli government. But this cannot last. We have got to face the real world. Israel's national interests may be at odds with those of the United States, creating increasing tensions and conflicts, for which an imaginative American Jewish leadership and informed American Jewry are vital. I see few signs of such a leadership today . . .

We Must Respond to Soviet Anti-Semitism

One conflict which disturbs me very much is the ugly argument over *aliyah* of Soviet Jews. Although consciousness of Russian Jewry and its struggle has increased, and activity in behalf of refuse-niks has been effective, these efforts, it seems to me, have been very narrowly defined, largely on behalf *only* of those Jews planning to go to Israel. Israel and Soviet Jewry councils are generally not concerned with the fate of Jews who want to, or have to, remain in the Soviet Union. Moreover, although there is plenty of documentation regarding anti-Semitism in the Soviet Union, and the absence of opportunities for Jews there to learn about Judaism and Jewish life, there is no effort as far as I can determine, on the part of American Jewish leadership to combat official and unofficial Soviet anti-Semitism. . . I myself have written to all of the national defense organizations in America to ask what they are doing specifically, besides making studies of anti-Semitism, to deal with the reality of anti-Semitism and I have yet to hear from a single one. How can American Jewry do nothing about Soviet anti-Semitism? On this issue, is the non-policy a reflection of Israel's decision regarding priorities which, in turn, reflect *her* needs, rather than an authentic, responsible analysis by American Jews? Is not anti-Semitism as much a violation of human rights as barriers to emigration?

. . . And We Must Respond to Soviet Refugees

The issue of the so-called drop-outs — a very offensive term — is another issue on which we differ. Here, too, Soviet Jewry Councils seem to be echoing the Israeli position; in America, only HIAS seems to be vigorously defending its (and the American Jewish) traditional position of the right of Jews to go — and be helped — where they choose . . . The argument that Israel often uses, namely, that the Soviet Union will stop granting visas to Israel if Soviet Jews continue to go to the United States instead of Israel is not a legitimate threat. Permission to go to Israel is the only way a Jew can leave the Soviet Union . . . Even non-Jews have used this channel.

the best synagogue is in the heart

Related to this question are the prevailing feelings regarding Russian Jews who come to the United States. The attitudes are often quite negative. Social agencies are conscientious about helping them settle; employment and family agencies have their specific professional functions, but they have little understanding of the culture out of which Soviet Jews have come, and no knowledge or interest or professional skill as to how to guide them into meaningful American *Jewish* life or experiences. There are some signs that Russian Jews are starting to organize their own movements which have relevance to them. In Philadelphia there is a very interesting new connection being made between newcomers from the Soviet Union and survivors of the Holocaust. Two years ago I would have said this was impossible because the gap there was so enormous. Now this seems to be a very encouraging link-up. However, the numbers involved are very small. If a more conscious effort is not devoted to helping Russian Jews find satisfying and interesting activities in American Jewish life they will be another of our lost generations, another wasted valuable human resource.

In the past, American Jews have been deeply involved in general political and social questions such as civil rights, civil liberties, black rights, public housing and busing, but in recent years we have become almost entirely preoccupied with questions of Jewish security — for Israel and the rest of us. In the 1980's these will still be serious problems but perhaps we shall see a broader agenda. There is already some Jewish inter-

vention in behalf of the "boat people", and some involvement in the struggle against nuclear power and the contaminated planet. But social and political issues no longer seem to excite us . .

Young Jews Are Cause For Optimism

Within American Jewry, the good news is to be found among some young Jews of the third or fourth generation, some of whom are here tonight. They seem much more self-confident about their Jewishness than we did at their age — they have fewer complexes. One of the most amazing things I have seen is this throw-away prepared by Sharon Kaplan Wallace, a young candidate for the Philadelphia City Council. On the front of it is a picture of a *matzah;* most of the material inside deals with her own Jewish background which she describes glowingly and without any inhibition whatsoever . . . I have been very excited by the surge of activity and vigor among young Jews (and a few middle aged) in the Conference for Alternatives in Jewish Education. The *havurah* movement seems to be alive and well and spreading. The Reconstructionist College in Philadelphia is growing and attracting a steadily growing student body and lay support. There is more Jewish vitality on campuses than for a very long time. There are many Judaic programs on university campuses. The involvement of Jewish women in Jewish institutional life and their growing acceptance in important synagogue roles is very heartening. Jewish scholarship in America is coming of age — it needs no apologies.

These creative changes demonstrate that there is an immense well of originality and independent energy within American Jewry. We need no longer exist in Israel's shadow culturally, but can move forward toward the making of a Jewish culture of our own. . .

In the blackness of spreading anti-Semitism, I see one small light, some movement in Jewish-Christian understanding as a result of the study of the Holocaust. I have found many Christians who are deeply anguished over the consequences of Christian anti-Semitism who have committed themselves, personally and professionally, to work that requires Christians to confront the history of Christian anti-Semitism and to view Jewish history and Jewish faith as authentic, separate and distinct from any Christian expectations, deserving respect and understanding.

Whether this activity can offset the enormous increase in anti-Semitism elsewhere in the world is problematic, but I feel that we all must work as if it can and will.

Arnold Jacob Wolf

I want to be rather more personal than Nora, if I may, and I guess even less optimistic. When I looked over the things that I have written and thought about in the last ten years, I was surprised and frightened to see how often I was right. Twenty years ago I started a project on the Holocaust which was the first in the country — also the first project in the *havurah* movement — and we memorialized and studied the Holocaust for a weekend every year. It was one of Elie Wiesel's first appearances and a very important break-through. I have now come out the other end. Having been one of the first to believe in the importance of thinking about and experiencing the Holocaust, I am now convinced that most of what has been done about it has been the wrong thing, the wrong time, by the wrong people for the wrong purpose. Again I was right about Cambodia when I said that Nixon and Kissinger were not only mistaken but criminal. I think if nothing else the Shawcross book proves that to be right. I was right about the college students. I wrote about them so early that I could publish the same article in the *New York Times* three years later and still be accurate if depressing. I was right about the peace initiative from Egypt about which I published in *Sh'ma* just days before Sadat came to Jerusalem. I felt this partly because I'd been in Egypt and it seemed obvious to me that this had to be coming soon though my correspondents didn't think so.

The real question is not so much whether I was right but why. I think there are some answers, one of them *not* being that I'm more brilliant than most of the people who didn't agree with me, but that I had better teachers than they did. From birth I had Felix Levy as a teacher, from the age of eighteen I had Abraham Heschel as a teacher, and from very little after that I had Martin Buber as a teacher — mostly through his books but also on several important occasions in person. And one of my fears for the next generation is that you don't have teachers like that because there aren't any. The influence of these people was simply over-powering in my life as it cannot be

for anybody who comes at a later time in history. And if you see what they said, you will see where I got it.

Our Starting Point Is Our Teachers

The agenda of Martin Buber is still absolutely current. Every issue that Nora mentioned is in his books and treated presciently. Heschel was a little more restrained but talked about these things where he didn't write about them. He certainly knew as very few people did what was going on not just in the civil rights movement but in Jewish circles themselves and in intellectual life in general. And my uncle and teacher, Felix Levy, who was of course much less well known, was at least a generation ahead of his time. And it is from these people that I learned. I said nothing that was not simply an extrapolation of what they had taught me.

I was also very fortunate in colleagues, particularly Gene, and Steve Schwarzschild who have been my intimate friends for over thirty-five years now. With them everything that is said between us is often in an exchange of letters which cross in the mail. We are saying the same thing about the same issue even when we haven't talked about it before. That doesn't mean we always agree or disagree. But what we have learned from each other is, again, exceedingly precious and I think almost unheard of in this century. And I have also had the benefit of my family who argue well and constantly. We often come out at very different points but they keep me from making some bad mistakes. I take all of these three very seriously — teachers, colleagues and family. I do not think without them it is possible to be right about things, whatever that means.

The question then for me is, since I am vindicated by history, why don't I feel better about it? And I don't. Why is there no satisfaction, even grim satisfaction, if nothing else at having over and over again been ahead of other people in pointing out what was going to be important to our community? I'm not sure that I know the answer to that except that it's very definitely the case. I happened a few days ago to read a letter of Heinrich Mann's in which he says the same thing. Having been right about Hitler and the whole period of the Nazis, having had the world come over to his view, he reached a state of what he called in French — the letter was in French — *indifference.* Something very much like that is happening to me. There is no pleasure, no *elan* in being right. It does not lead to anything. It is in some ways the most discouraging of all possible outcomes. I do not mean reward, you understand. It is not that I wasn't recognized as a prophet. If your teachers are Buber and Heschel and Felix Levy, you don't expect reward. You know in advance that's not in the cards. In fact, you'd be very frightened if there were any organizational honors forthcoming. It's something deeper than that. It is not something that people have not done, but that *I* have not done.

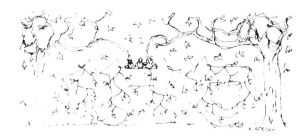

Judaism and Humanism Increasingly Clash

What for the future, is a terrible collision between what we have believed and what the Jews believe — what *we* Jews believe. Between what may be called humane values and what are now construed almost everywhere as Jewish values. I'll give you a few symptoms of this terrible conflict which I see on the horizon and of which Nora has already spoken about in some particulars. It is no accident that on the same Sunday there is an anti-nuclear demonstration and a parade for Israel; or that different people go to those two; and will increasingly drop one of these two issues. Those of us who have tried to keep together particularism in universalism or

our concerns as Jews and our concerns as human beings, and, in some way, still try to validate one with the other, are finding it technically impossible to do and increasingly difficult to assert.

The leader of the student struggle for Soviet Jewry at Yale, a brilliant young man named Matthew, had the very good idea of becoming a leader also in Amnesty International, which is very important for the Jewish Soviet movement as well as the whole Soviet dissident movement. He went to a meeting and he found, as he came back to tell me, almost in tears: the Israelis are supporting Somoza — is that true? For two or three hours I tried to defuse him and tried to explain away a terrible fact, "Yes, probably because the Americans want them to; I don't know why else." Here was a young man deeply concerned with Jewish values being confronted with the fact that the Jewish issue throws him into the wrong camp on some very important occasions, Somoza being only the least of them.

I was in Israel the very week that they raised the South African mission to an embassy while all the world was doing something else. Affirmative action is another relevant case. It is not simply that the Jewish organizations were on the side of Bakke. It is, I believe, technically true now that almost all the Jewish organizations and almost all Jewish individuals, on "Jewish" grounds are against any useful affirmative action. That's the kind of collision which frightens me terribly.

Can We Balance Both Sides Much Longer?

I could give many other examples, but the attempt which I think was characteristic of *Sh'ma* perhaps more than anywhere else, of balancing both sides, is now coming apart. The great tragedy of Breira was not that we were prematurely right – and I think we were right – I think now we seem to everyone to have been right. The tragedy is that it was impossible even to think about those issues for almost all American Jews, on "Jewish" grounds. What I foresee in Israel is that they cannot ever accept — perhaps even for good reason — the possibility of a Palestinian state, and that refusal means increasing terrorism, increasing repression and a replication in detail of the South African experience. That is what is coming. How does one who believes what I believe possibly reconcile himself to that? What do you do about that?

Perhaps that is what leads to *indifference.* You simply cannot deal with it coherently and keep your sanity. The representative Jew of the present day for me is Yeshia Lebovitz, an Orthodox Jewish scientist at the Hebrew University who has seen the inhumanity of the Jews and is furious and prophetic — perhaps more like Cassandra than like Isaiah. To read him is to experience again the terror of being a Jew in a world in which being a Jew often means being what you don't want to be. Humanism and Judaism, humane values, liberal values and "Jewish" positions are increasingly at odds. About this tragedy I welcome your advice and your consolation.

David Novak

The previous two speakers, Nora and Arnold, have alluded to a problem that I would like to discuss in a bit more detail because I think that it colored the entire period of the 1970's and will, to even a greater extent, color the 1980's. It is the relationship between Israeli Jewry and non-Israeli Jewry — American Jewry in particular — but not exclusively American Jewry.

I always thought that somehow, beneath the surface, there was a recognition by Israelis that the Jewish people transcended the political issues of the state of Israel. That was continually belied by experience. Granted the Israelis whom I met during the 1970's, were mostly people who were not terribly reflective or people who had undergone intense experiences and therefore considered the state of Israel to be the be-all and end-all of the existence of the Jewish people. I recall one saying that there is no such thing as *Galut.* According to him, the Jews who are living in the *Galut* are living an unreal existence!

For Too Many The Golah Has No Validity
To speak personally, this past week I had what

for me was a devastating experience because it belied my expectations. One of the truly great scholars of the state of Israel happened to visit my community for four days. Professor Ephraim Urbach, is a man of tremendous Jewish learning, he's certainly steeped in European culture and he is a deeply committed Israeli. (As many of you know he was actually a candidate for the presidency of Israel.) In public and also in private conversation where we spoke in Hebrew, there was basically a notion, a mind-set, that was no different than the most uneducated, parochial Israeli. When he was asked by a colleague of mine, "Professor, do you negate the *Golah* (lit. Exile; fig., Jewish life outside of Israel)?" He indicated to us that the *Golah* is a contradiction in Jewish terms; that we cannot affirm its existence in any way. I was almost embarrassed to throw Talmudic texts at him which contradict him. (Who am I to throw Talmudic texts at Ephraim Urbach?) So I said to him, "Professor, then obviously your view of the *Golah* is a sort of an Aristotelian view in that the *Golah* at best is a potential for the state of Israel: either a potential to send money or a potential for *aliyah,* but there is no chance of a viable Jewish life in the *Golah.*" He affirmed that.

Now it seems to me that this has been the mind-set of virtually every Israeli that I have had contact with from very parochial sabras to people of broad culture, broad learning, both humanistic and Jewish. I don't think we can continue in that posture in the 1980's. One of the problems which has been a historical one in our relationship with the state of Israel is that every time we have just about reached the point where we can discuss these issues, there's another crisis and who's in the mood to do it?

Israel and Diaspora are Both Vital
The relationship of American Jewry to the state of Israel has been a festering problem in Zionist ideology, and I consider myself a Zionist. Zionist ideology told us continually – Nora alluded to it – that the state of Israel is the solution to the Jewish problem, and what we have discovered for better or for worse (maybe it's better to have this kind of problem) is that the state of Israel is the Jewish problem. It is the only Jewish problem in the full sense — at least the only Jewish problem that is being discussed. It seems to me that what is called for is the assumption that this type of a relationship where Israel is the actuality; and we *Golah* Jews simply exist as something to feed into it.

This assumption has been bought by the majority of American Jews, where we had hoped, and still hope, that the state of Israel would be a vitalizing factor in Jewish existence. This assumption has been a negative factor especially in American Jewish life. There are American Jews in all positions — and especially important positions – who basically don't believe the Jewish life outside the state of Israel is possible in some sort of independent posture. This has had an extremely negative effect on funding for Jewish education on all sorts of other things.

It can be put another way. After the emotional investment in Israel, there just doesn't seem to be time or energy for much of anything else. Most of us would agree that the state of Israel plays a very important indeed crucial role in our Jewish life one that excludes the viability of a Jewish life outside of Israel. That type of thinking should be called what it is: pseudo-Messianism. I think there's a pseudo-Messianism which regards everything outside of Israel as *Golah* and obviulsy if the *Golah* is what is outside of Israel then the *Geulah,* Redemption, is inside of Israel. Now it seems to me that that's a false assumption on Jewish grounds. I'm glad Arnold mentioned Martin Buber, because I consider Buber's most important book, though it is the least read of all of his books, *Israel and Palestine,* (now retitled by Schocken). In the first line of that book, he said that anybody who considers Zion to be simply a political idea doesn't know what it means.

Jewish Universalism Exists on Two Levels

I think that our agenda in the 1980's is going to have to reaffirm Jewish universalism. It will be Jewish universalism on two levels: number one is that the reality of the Jewish people and Judaism transcends the political borders even of a Jewish state, the state of Israel. It's a time for us to revitalize, certainly among Jewish intellectuals, the thinking of Yehezkel Kaufman who negated Jewish particularism of the present type in his book *Golah ve'Nekhar,* Exile and Alienation. He certainly was a Jewish nationalist, but he also affirmed Jewish universalism. We need a similar view, one which deals with the Jewish people as a universal entity which has a political factor , but which is not reducible to the political structure of the state of Israel. Within that Jewish universalism, I think that we also have to discover humanistic models in the Jewish tradition which enable us, on Jewish grounds, to participate in

the social movements of our day critically. I think that one of the problems of the '60's was that many Jews were uncritical in their social involvements. They simply affirmed whatever was *au courant*.

I consider a total and complete rethinking of our relationship with the state of Israel to be the main agenda of the 1980's. And if that alone happens, if that is one benefit of the peace, or at least a lessening of the danger of hostilities, then I think that we're in for a very exciting decade in Jewish life.

After fifteen years—my world
Michael Wyschogrod

During the fifteen years that have passed since *Sh'ma* was born, much has changed both in the world and my perception of the world.

I now consider the danger of nuclear war the greatest danger hanging over our heads. It is ironic that the greatest danger facing Jews today is not a specifically Jewish one. Jews are so accustomed to being singled out for persecution and destruction that it is understandably difficult for them to entertain the possibility that the greatest catastrophe in Jewish history might be an event in which Jews are just incidental participants. I am not sure I know what we (Jews and non-Jews) must do to avert this danger. But I am sure that we should be spending the largest part of our time and energy thinking of ways to awaken governments and peoples to this unspeakable peril. I cannot understand why so little attention is paid to this problem.

In 1970, Jews were just coming down from the high precipitated by the Six Day War. The 1973 war brought us back to reality again and this has been with us ever since. I am now less inclined to believe in the possibility of a ''solution'' to the Arab-Israeli problem than before. In fact, the very conviction that a solution is possible may be causing considerable damage. The Middle East is just not an area where solutions happen. The Iraq-Iran war has been dragging on for four years with close to a million dead so far. Lebanon is in worse shape than ever. Bloodletting may just be a way of life in the Middle East and the very conviction that

MICHAEL WYSCHOGROD *teaches and leads the work in philosophy at Baruch College, C. U. N. Y., and is a founding Contributing Editor of Sh'ma.*

a solution is around the corner may only encourage people fighting for lost causes to fight even harder. A more realistic level of expectations may not only avert much disappointment but also avert such adventures as the Israeli action in Lebanon which was probably, in part, caused by the Western idea that a "solution" to the Lebanese problem was possible.

Our Fellow Jews, Abroad and Here

Which brings me to the situation of Soviet Jewry. Anatoly Sharansky has now been in prison over eight years and we have accepted it. Of course, we have not liked it. There have been rallies and advertisements, the U.S. and other governments have been influenced to raise the matter at meetings with Soviet officials and so on. But Sharansky is still rotting in prison. And as things look now, we will not do very much more no matter how long he rots in Soviet prisons. I find this situation unacceptable. I do not know how to get Sharansky (with whom I spent a day in Moscow in 1976) out of prison. But I do know that it is our duty to try harder, until it hurts. It is not our duty to get him out of prison. But it is our duty to hurt ourselves trying to get him out of prison. That is the only measure of our commitment that counts. Everything else is cheap. I would very much like to talk to people who have some sympathy for what I have just said.

Looking at the Jewish religious scene in this country, I am deeply disturbed by developments in the Conservative movement. Until recently, there were three branches of Judaism in this country. While for a long time Conservative Judaism has been taking liberties with *halacha* that I could not approve, one still had the feeling that the movement was anchored in loyalty to Torah. In spite of everything, it was not difficult to distinguish it from Reform Judaism. This is becoming far less the case. While the boundary between Reform and Conservatism has not yet been totally eliminated, it has certainly been made less sharp. The die was cast, I think, when Conservatism joined Reform in the campaign to maintain Israeli recognition of non-Orthodox conversions. If Conservative Judaism is willing to recognize Reform conversions, then will it not very soon also embrace the Reform position on patrilineal transmission of Judaism? If so, the fusion of the two movements cannot be too far in the future.

The absorption of Conservative Judaism by Reform would be a major step toward the polarization of the Jewish people into a segment committed to To-

rah in the traditional sense and one eager to shape a new Judaism unhindered by the tradition. This can only lead to tragic results.

The Fresh Pain of Exile

I am beginning to entertain the idea that the most significant fact of Jewish history since 1948 is the refusal of the vast majority of the Jews of the free world to settle in Israel. It may just be possible that by not choosing *aliyah*, we are passing a death sentence on Israel. Even if, in theory, a vital diaspora Judaism is possible under present circumstances when every Jew who wishes to settle in Israel can do so, given the realities of the situation in the Middle East, an influx of 6-8 million Jews into the land may be the only way of maintaining the Jewishness of the country. The refusal of the Jews of the free world to vote for Israel with their feet is an immensely significant decision, probably symptomatic of a serious erosion of the Jewish will to live

It is, of course, always possible to rewrite Judaism by eliminating the sense of exile and the hope and will to return to the land from which our ancestors were evicted. But that is tampering with the soul of the faith. To consider oneself permanently American by nationality and Jewish by religion is to bring Judaism to its conclusion. But this is, in fact, what most of us have done. And I am speaking here, first and foremost, about myself. I have certainly not done any of this consciously. If asked, I would certainly say that I am in exile in the U. S. and argue vehemently against those who would deny this. But is all this not simply cheap talk? Whatever my mouth says, my actions prove that I do not consider Israel my homeland. And this causes me no end of anguish. □

After fifteen years—my mind

Seymour Siegel

It is hard to believe that fifteen years have already passed since *Sh'ma* was founded. These have been fateful years indeed for all of us. As I look back now on the decade and a half since our first issue I believe that my mind has changed in two directions. In the political realm I have definitely be-

SEYMOUR SIEGEL *teaches Jewish theology and ethics at the Jewish Theological Seminary. He is a founding Contributing Editor of* Sh'ma.

come more *right wing*. In the religious realm my mind has become more *left wing*.

What that means practically is that where political and social issues are concerned, I tend more than usual to favor the conservative position. At the present time that means alignment with the Reagan administration and its policies. In domestic matters that involves reliance on the free enterprise tradition. In foreign affairs it means maintenance of a strong national defense against the Soviets, especially through the maintenance of nuclear armaments so that there is maintained a rough parity with the Soviets. And in social issues it involves emphasis on traditional values such as the value of human life; the introduction of a religious dimension in the common life of the nation (that is, an abandonment of a rigid and unyielding attitude toward the church-state issue); support of a close scrutiny of programs designed to help the underprivileged; and a strict enforcement of standards of fairness in employment (that is, no preferential treatment of "minorities"). In short, an endorsement of the rightward direction of the contemporary political climate.

Fifteen years ago I felt myself to be much more insistent on halachic conformity. Though I welcome the traditional emphasis in the Reform movement, I realize that halachic rigidity should not be seen as an end in itself but as a means toward increased Jewishness, spirituality and humaneness. It is clear to me now that insistence on halachic norms which leads to human difficulty and self satisfied "hardness of heart" is not very Jewish, or even halachic in the deepest and most profound sense.

Two Cases Requiring Renewal

I suppose the factor that has been most important in the development of my thinking in this matter has been the emergence of the women's movement in Jewish life, especially at the Jewish Theological Seminary. Try as one would, I am convinced that strict adherence to the demands of *halacha* would not permit the important changes in synagogue life which the past period has brought about. I am not bothered by that now. For it is clear in my mind, at least, that if strict halachic conformance frustrates our highest and best human instincts, then the halachic considerations should be secondary and yield to ethics and *menshlichkeit*.

Just this past week, in the State of Israel, I saw a dramatic example of this. The Ethiopian Jews, a proud and beautiful tribe of our people, have been sorely vexed because the rabbinic authorities in Israel have expressed doubts about their halachic integrity and demand a *pro forma* religious ritual before the Ethiopians can be accepted as full Jews. The recent immigrants have rejected this demand with vigor, dignity and determination. I say, "More power to them!"

When *halacha* functions as it always had, to sensitize people to the Divine, then it has some claim to call itself "divine." When Jewish law makes us insensitive, less human and more prone to withhold human rights from our fellowmen, then it has lost its claim to primacy in Jewish life.

I have cited two examples where this is the case—women's rights and the status of hitherto cast off tribes. Many more examples could be cited. This is not the place or the time to compile such a list. But I hope my point is clear. Halacha *is a means, not an end in itself.* The means should be judged by the ends.

So my thinking on this matter has moved towards the left.

The Basis for the Paradox

Now I am sure the reader is asking, "Is this not inconsistent? How can a person move toward the right in politics and toward the left in religious matters?"

I have searched my mind to find some common thread to account for the seemingly contradictory direction of my thinking. The answer at which I arrived is: *realism.*

The besetting error of liberal political thinking is the tendency to see issues in non-realistic terms. To make real and meaningful political choices is to make choices between real alternatives, not desired alternatives. You choose between real options; not imagined or idealized ones. Thus, for example, it is, of course, right and moral to oppose racial discrimination in South Africa. But a sudden transition to "one man, one vote," it is clear to sober observers, would mean chaos, dictatorship and worse suffering. So the more realistic moralist would seek options other than the trendy sloganeering of the liberals.

The same is true regarding the halachic problems facing us. It is not the exact halachic norms that should be primary but the goals of the Law, indeed of Judaism, which are to follow the *derekh Hashem* (the way of the Lord), *laasot tzedakah umishpat* (to do righteousness and justice).

As many of my friends know, I write these lines recuperating from a hospital stay. My remarks therefore, are partial and slightly undeveloped. But I do hope the trend of my thought is clear enough to indicate the direction of my mind in these crucial and troubling times. □

After fifteen years—my view

Eugene B. Borowitz

My biggest surprise—and disappointment—over the past fifteen years has been American Jewish liberalism's inability to reestablish its intellectual foundations. The same, largely aging voices sound the old battle cries to oppose the conservatives' lively defense of old structures and traditional values.

This general American phenomenon has hit the Jewish community with special impact because of our fresh interest in Jewish authenticity. Liberals are asked, "What's Jewish about your liberal, universalistic concern?" Or, "Is it good for the Jews?" And if by that is meant what's good for the State of Israel, harsh ethical consequences can follow: guns over butter, cold-war over detente, and reserving our political clout for pro-Israel, anti-Arab issues. Liberals have tried to make a case for both/and but the political atmosphere of our time has made their position difficult to hold consistently.

If, too, halachic texts are demanded to authenticate a position, then liberalism can only offer wisps of tradition. Jewish law, like all law, is essentially conservative—though one may marvel that, since its classic texts originate in times of economic scarcity and Jewish oppression, it has its undoubted liberal currents. Jewish liberalism, we need to remember, arose as a result of the Emancipation. It begins from the faith that the grant of equality, for all its limits, lays a new commandment on Jews. Having full democratic rights, we should manifest an expanded social horizon, and having economic strength, we should manifest substantial mutuality. But quoting the Prophets has limited validity in what we know to be a rabbinic religion.

The Philosophical Credibility Gap

Despite these intellectual difficulties, the most American Jews have not become socially conserva-

EUGENE B. BOROWITZ, *was the principal founder of* Sh'ma *and has been its Editor since its inception. But like all its other writers he speaks only for himself.*

tive (thus, perhaps, teaching thinkers some greater humility). Immediately after the last presidential election Jewish rightists began lamenting the stubborn insistence of American Jews on voting as liberals. And individual issues, like Vietnamese boat people, nuclear disarmament and sanctuary (see the next number of *Sh'ma*) can still generate considerable activism. In the face of this recidivism, conservatives console themselves with the statistics showing Jewish college students have moved to the right. Liberals retort that they know the syndrome. Their own trendy youthful activism has turned into yuppiedom and suburbanitis but the basic American Jewish liberal orientation has refused to die.

As I read it, this gap between commitment and theory testifies to the reality of an underlying insight which awaits conceptualization. If young religious liberals today devote themselves to action rather than theorizing, they have good Jewish warrant for so doing. But our community will long retain its strong ethical thrust if we do not explicate its grounds.

Such a new ethics of Jewish liberalism must confront two nettlesome questions: how and on what grounds should we define Jewish duty today when we find *halacha* inadequate to our deepest sense of Covenant responsibility? and what imperative impels us to do this Jewish duty? The one question forces us to confront how we might extend classic *halacha*, the other, what we believe about God. No wonder most thinkers find it difficult to offer a fresh philosophy of Jewish obligation. Having, myself, frequently written about these matters in *Sh'ma* and elsewhere (e.g., "The Autonomous Jewish Self," *Modern Judaism*, Feb., 1984) let me now rather look toward the future and make some comments about the prospects of the social right.

The Waning Appeal of Social Conservatism

Though my hopes in this regard have been thwarted several times already, I am now reasonably well convinced that conservatism's greatest influence has passed. In part such ebbing of power befalls all cultural movements. They are most appealing as critics of past excesses. So conservatism's greatest strength has been its telling critique of liberalism's failures. But many of those lessons have now been learned. Today, I find liberals cautious about their goals, realistic about costs and appropriately sceptical about theories of how to cure social problems. So familiarity and cooptation have made conservatism less exciting than it was.

Then too, as they have sought to articulate a program of their own, conservatives have lost their image of moral superiority. There is something mean-spirited about a tax program that gives the rich greater advantage while the deficit budget increases the holes in the safety net for the poor. Does respect for life indeed mean denying abortions to rape or incest victims because their unwanted pregnancies are not life threatening? Does the circulation of sexually explicit material cause such character damage that we should risk a return to the banning of books like James Joyce's *Ulysses*? Surely Jerry Falwell scaled some peak of spiritual hubris when he recently traveled to South Africa to give it spiritual sanction—and that at a time when the egregiousness of *apartheid* had become so apparent that even our conservative Secretary of State publicly denounced it.

Facing the Excesses of the Right

However, the most significant reason for the move to the center has been the growing evidence of humane conservatism's easy slide into rightist fanaticism. It is easiest to see as the religious roots of the right begin producing extremism. Gush Emunim once inspired much admiration in world Jewry; most of it has evaporated as an increasingly provocative assertion of Jewish rights culminated in efforts, under the guise of self defense, to blow up Arab buses at rush hour. Less dramatically, our Jewish turn from an American culture going pagan toward *halacha* has stalled as the sages, instead of displaying flexibility on women's rights in Judaism have instead challenged the feminist's motives.

I cannot help but see this as a logical development of the religious position involved. If God gave the Law and established the proper instrument for its exposition, then believers will necessarily use terms like development, evolution and creativity quite differently than do liberals. For where the fundamentals of the faith are at stake, including who may explicate the Law and how, God must be defended at all cost. It makes no difference that no specific, classic text prohibits the modern aberration suggested—even with their terseness of expression, the sages could hardly have listed all the abominations promoted by the contemporary love of license. By goyish standards, some sacrifice of self is called for. But has it not been this very will to sacrifice that has kept Judaism alive? and is not this devotion to Jewishness, so appallingly absent in many of the non-Orthodox, that made the traditional alternative so attractive?

I think that states one great source of Orthodoxy's fresh appeal—but it also indicates its accompanying problem. How much sacrifice? Rejecting American self-indulgence for the worth that comes with Jewish self discipline is initially appealing. But what if, in due course, it also entails giving up the right to think and will freely we so intimately associate with human dignity? Is our humanity found essentially in living God's Law as enunciated by our sages and not equally in utilizing mind and heart to determine personally what God wants of one, a member of the Jewish people? And what about the further entailment, that sacrificing our right of conscience implies that others ought to do the same, thus vitiating the grounds for democracy?

The Return of the Repressed Self

From such ruminations, I believe, arises the glimmering intuition that orthodoxies are a dangerous therapy for a self and society sick of freedom. Law and authority promise to contain the waywardness that turned the liberation of autonomy into individual and social excess. With rationality and culture no longer able to provide convincing limits to our self-defeating experimentation, we hope orthodoxies will. Only, it turns out, the creative power of the self cannot long be denied. We see it emerging on two levels in contemporary Orthodoxy, masked as objectivity, to be sure, but identifiable as self-determination and as subjectivity.

Consider for a moment the pluralism inherent in *halacha*, a feature of which we are often reminded these days and one of which all Jews have reason to be proud. Learned non-Orthodox views to the side, how should a Jew respond to the variety of instruction available? Thus, shall we give credence to Eliezer Waldenberg who permits the abortion of a thalidomide affected fetus when almost all other authorities forbid it? Or shall we listen to Yehudah Perilman's lonely voice authorizing postcoital contraception in the case of a raped but nonetheless healthy mother? (Abortion has no support at all.) Hearing a diversity of voices, any caring Jew must then ask how one can tell which voice speaks authentically.

As a result, since one intends to abide by *halacha*, one goes about picking and choosing among *poskim* until one finds one who agrees with one's own conscience. It is the covert Orthodox equivalent of *The Jewish Catalog*. (And not entirely our idea as indicated by the maxim: *a yid gefint sich an etzah*, "a Jew'll find a way out.") Such shopping for rulings makes the self, not God (via the *posek*), the final authority —the very heresy of liberal Judaism.

Subjectivity in the Halachic Process

A similar issue arises in trying to understand why *poskim* read and combine the same texts in such differing ways. Why do some of them come to quite individual conclusions? To be sure, their texts, their times, their community, their halachic peer group, all channel their rulings. So much might be "objective." But why do they see just this in their texts, times, community and peers? And their personal form of piety. Some may say, in faith, Judaism teaches that is how God instructs us. But one might agree that God works through persons and mean that to say that who the sage is will powerfully affect his rulings. Conceal it as one will under layers of institutionalized erudition and piety, the creativity of the self still operates. Law arises first in the independent will responding to God in Covenant—that seems undeniably obvious to the modern eye. To trust the sages, in this view, is not merely to entrust one's self to God but, to a considerable extent, to the person of this or that sage. In many instances that is a fulfillment—and thus the appeal of contemporary Orthodoxy in its several forms of withdrawal from contemporary fashion. But, I contend, the rest of us increasingly realize that "many instances" is too small a promise to warrant a surrender of the self.

If, for all our loyalty to tradition, the exercise of our full intellectual and spiritual individuality so significantly shapes our religious lives, should we not now openly acknowledge that fact? and should we not then seek to determine what, in extending the chain of tradition, might constitute a proper Jewish self today?

The Realism Behind the Abstraction

Those of us who are liberals have an immediate political reason for wanting to know about the ultimate place of conscience in Orthodoxy. We wonder: are the modernist, quasi-democratic readings of *halacha* only temporary accommodations made by those seeking to make their discipline attractive to the sceptical? or are the restrictive, anti-democratic ones only the exceptional products of zeal for God? In brief, what might we expect if Orthodoxy came to full political power in the State of Israel or had equivalent sway in American Jewish life?

I see some such aggregate of understanding slowly arising among many who have hoped to remedy the failures of liberalism by social conservatism and a turn to Orthodoxy. And in this shift toward what we might yet freely create out of devotion to the Covenant if not the *halacha*, I also see our community's greatest hope. □

LYNNE AVADENKA, *of Oak Park, Mich., did the drawings for this issue.*

2.
Of Jewish Philosophy and Mysticism

Abraham joshua heschel, model

Eugene B. Borowitz

Perhaps mourning makes me exaggerate but I think it is the simple truth to say that Abraham Heschel was the most important American Jew of the past generation. Before him all our models of modern Jewishness distorted what we dimly sensed the organic wholeness of the modern Jew ought to be. In him, finally, it all came together in a model of persuasive authenticity.

We had long known ethical types who did wonderful things for mankind but seemed not to love their own as much as their neighbors. The secularists wrote Yiddish or built the State of Israel dreaming that language or land were enough to nurture all the recesses of the Jewish soul. Our learned men applied critical methods to Bible and History and Literature and showed us what it meant to end up believing in change and footnotes and little else. The organization men considered their conventions and resolutions contemporary Sinaitic assemblies, complete with thunderous authority and Torah-for-the-masses. The religious figures defended the Law against the impious Jews; or justified the Jews against a petrified Law; or used the Law (deviant) to change the Law (practical) against the Law (traditional). They talked to us of Discipline, Tradition, Values, Peoplehood, Survival — anything but God — anything but a God who might arouse, inspire or even overwhelm us by His presence. And without a God to command, *mitzvot* became options and Jews became non-observant. I exaggerate, I suppose, but, then again, I mourn.

He showed us a jewish heart
Amidst all these many post-World War II Jews and Judaisms Abraham Heschel appeared, *sui generis.* Where the Litvaks or the Germans or the pseudo-

Germans had come to the university sensibility with a cold *Mitnagdic* (rationalist/legalist) Judaism, Heschel brought a glowing Hasidic faith to his Berlin studies. Unlike Buber, his Hasidism was first-hand, a matter of cradle-songs and family association, not the acquired mysticism of a *fin-de-siecle* intellectual. What he learned in Europe he brought to America and adapted to our naturalist mentality. So when he spoke to all the scientific, psychological, sociological, philosophic

Abraham Joshua Heschel, 1907-1972

17

anti-religious theses which were the unspoken dogmas of our secular education, we could hear him answer not only out of Jewish learning but out of a Jewish soul. We responded to his teaching warmly for we were sick of Judaism as Kant or Dewey or watered-down Freud and we sought a Judaism that knew God wants the heart and not just the head.

We could not have listened to him so carefully had he not shown us what we also knew must somehow be true, that a Jewish heart is responsive to the needs even of the uncircumcised. The Law does not command Jewish involvement in the causes of Blacks and there is almost no Jewish precedent for taking action against the gentile Sovereign so he may know his war is far more evil than any good that could possibly derive from it. But Abraham Heschel knew that the same sense of Jewish duty which kept him an observant Jew now made participation in American public struggles a simple *mitzvah*. So when we heard of him parading or proclaiming in some human cause, we knew he was as truly Jewish there as he was when waxing eloquent over Soviet Jewry or the State of Israel. He was the whole Jew we had been searching for.

His greatest gift: a presence that strengthened us
Losing such a man would make any time a bad time. But ours is a particularly bad time for we seem to be forgetful of his teaching. As the world has grown more vicious we have cultivated Jewish cynicism and hardened our Jewish hearts. Of course we shall be sensitive to the cries of the *goyim* but we do not propose to do much about them — they are many and we are few; they are strong and we are weak; they hate us and we must take care of ourselves first. Besides, we are tired; and only human; and entitled to enjoy ourselves a little; and have already made our contribution to humanity. On every side, despite the model of Abraham Heschel, Jews are busy building a psychic ghetto.

I do not mourn that Abraham Heschel leaves behind no school of Heschelians to advance and amplify his ideas. His blend of Hasidic immanentism and existentialist anti-naturalism was simply unique to his life and person. Rather I mourn our fall from his stature and I am grieved that in our new-found littleness we shall not have his noble presence to enlarge and uplift us. Woe to the generation that has lost its teacher! Woe, woe to the generation that neglects his instruction!

I and thou — an intellectual experience
Leon Sol Wieseltier

It was Martin Buber who initiated me and many of my peers into the world of the spirit. He provided the dearly sought terms with which we formulated our most difficult questions and commitments. The concern and understanding which pervade his works revealed for us possibilities within Judaism which we had not been taught but which our century demanded. Certainly the teachings of Buber which most deeply influenced us were the formulation of the dialogical relationship and the appreciation of *Chasidism*. But these do not exhaust Buber's legacy; they are both in fact grounded in a more overwhelming truth, and that is *Buber's powerful commitment to the actuality of the world*. "Faith is not a feeling in the soul of man but an entrance into reality, an entrance into the *whole* reality without reduction or curtailment. This thesis is simple but it contradicts the usual way of thinking." Such a presupposition was by no means common sense; had it only been so! It is a stubborn refusal to be distracted from reality, to be seduced by power or theory away from concrete situations which relentlessly confront us. Buber's dedication to the real is uncompromising and is, I think, the greatest challenge that he proposes.

The rejection of mystical union
The description of reality as the condition of spiritual meaning stands as a consciously marked departure from the religious traditions. Both Christianity and the Eastern traditions belong for Buber to "the abysmal history of deactualization." Both annul the temporal in favor of the eternal, the transient in favor of the immutable, the immanent in favor of the transcendent. Both refuse to admit the ultimacy of finitude. This refusal comes in the form of mysticism. Johanine Christianity declares that "I and the Father are One;" the Buddhist endeavors to lose the self by its deification and absorption. Such "doctrines of immersion" carry the I beyond itself, beyond the Thou, beyond the world. Human fulfillment is achieved at the price of the human. Responsibility is only to self and to God, and succeeds with its own cancellation. Unity is thirsted for, but no such unity is to be found in the world.

The temptation to unity is a powerful one. The young Buber felt it strongly, and in his early work grappled with its possible realization. But it is a temptation which he resisted, and for ethical motives. For if the world is real, then existence is an ethical project. Only the faith which takes the present seriously is concerned with justice. We encounter the concreteness of the everyday in the person of the other, who demands not individual fulfillment but responsibility. It is responsibility which is the final term of Buber's theology of immanence. The mystic seeks unity, but "in lived actuality there is no unity of being. Actuality is to be found only in effective activity." The rejection of mystical union is thus simultaneously the recognition of the other who remains separate.

Reconciling the contraries of being

It is often asserted that the experience of the Holocaust has made theodicy a renewed priority for Jewish thought, and it seems strange that there is no extensive treatment of suffering in Buber. But one will not find such a theodicy in Buber because Buber has understood that theodicy is ultimately theory, but suffering is real. The response to evil must be as real as evil itself — that is, the response to evil is moral action. Suffering is not to be understood but eliminated. And the meaning of history is found in niether reflection nor faith, but in "living action and suffering itself, in the unreduced immediacy of the moment. Only he reaches the meaning who stands firm, without holding back or reservation, before the whole might of reality and answers it in a living way."

Unlike Maimonides, that other great advocate of immanent religious meaning, Buber's immanence is never a reductive naturalism. Dialogue is an act which negotiates irreducible distances, and as movement it carries itself forward to transcendence and encounters the living God. "Extended, the lines of relationship intersect in the Eternal Thou." God is addressed, and only addressed: prayer is the bond through which God and myself became agents in one universe. God enters my world, and transforms it; I approach God, but as myself. Such a relationship respects the identity of the human and the identity of the Divine. Trancendence and immanence are not, then, incompatible, but rather coexist, and this coexistence is the structure of reality. History, neither God's autobiography nor my own, is the development of this coexistence in time.

Buber's theism is essentially paradoxical — it is directed to a transcendence which insists upon the essential being of immanence — and is thereby a significant resolution of traditional theological dilemmas. In dialogue God and man, the contraries of being, exist together and exist apart. God is both near and far.

At the very heart of Buber's thought lies the primal fact of creation — for what is the miracle of creation if not the created being, the being who was once not-being but who now meaningfully perseveres in existence and challenges his Creator?

The thrust of Buber's theism is, then, towards a faith that "leaves out nothing, leaves nothing behind, comprehends all — all the world — in comprehending the Thou, gives the world its due and truth, has nothing beside God but grasps everything in Him. One does not find God if one leaves the world." Faith in God need not be at the expense of the world, indeed, it must not be, for the world and I exist with God. Faith is grounded precisely in a world real enough to compel both God and man. This is Buber's legacy: that we can be with God as men, that our human existence is not the obstacle but the condition for the spiritual life.

Buber's thought: profoundly jewish

The rejection of mysticism, the ethical encounter with the Thou, the theology of coexistence, are all responses to Buber's acute sensitivity of the significance of being human. But all that we have said could have been expressed by saying that Buber's thought originates from the basic impulse of Judaism itself, and that is *Judaism's radical realism.* Judaism can be an *orach chaim,* a way of life, because it begins with the faith that there is ultimate meaning to our existence in this world. Deny this premise, and Judaism becomes an arbitrary series of empty forms, But accept it, and Judaism appears as the way in which man can express before God his courage to be himself. Unlike so many other creeds, Judaism has never caviled at finitude. And if it is therefore a 'this-worldly' religion, it is so only before God, its Revealer. Put simply — and this should be developed more completely — Judaism is a faith for men who seek human meaning. Buber is thus profoundly Jewish, for the promise of his thought, like the promise of Judaism, is the promise of existence itself.

We today are experiencing the pains of a realization which has been long overdue: the realization of our own limits. We have been deceived by our control of nature into acting as its lord. The scientific conceit, still the mind's most powerful weapon for health and peace, has nonetheless tempted us to alter the order of things. For too long our project has been to become God. But our spirit remains human, despite all our pretensions, and we are slowly arriving at the bounds of our humanity. We are not God because though, like Him, we can kill, we cannot, like Him, create. Ours can only be human creations, conceived in humility and at the mercy of time. Our concern for history must be a concern for immediate justice. In other words, we must begin again to find meaning in finitude.

Our limits are not confining, they are defining; they are not conditions of failure, but they, *and they alone,* are conditions of fulfillment. Buber's mentor Feuerbach said that "dread of limitation is dread of existence." Buber teaches that existence is not to be dreaded but sanctified. And the alternative to the intoxicating tyranny of science is not an equally intoxicating flight into a seductive transcendence; nor is the hegemony of the heart any more just than the hegemony of the mind. Buber speaks out of our tradition and demands that we confront our shared limits and thereby achieve justice. As souls before God in a world racked by cruelty and death, we had best heed his words.

Bringing our neshama closer to god

Charles Roth

What I write here may come across as nonsense or very strange at best for those who would try to absorb it with the mind only. These views come mainly from experience so the best thing to do is to read quickly before the mind has a chance to catch up.

I'd like to begin with a response that Reb Yaakov Yitzchak, the Seer of Lublin, gave a disciple who asked to be shown one general way in the service of God. "One way is through teaching, another through prayer, another through fasting and another through, eating. Everyone should carefully observe which way his heart draws him and then choose this way with all his strength."

My way is not the same from day to day and this is as it should be for me. My way is attempting to function in day to day living from a place within me that accepts just what happens to me without resistance. This is not a moral position for which I strive, but hopefully results if I am connected with my inner self — my *neshama,* which, the Talmud teaches us, is actually a part of God.

My way accepts the *yetzer hara* as being synonymous with my ego, which wages a continuous battle with my *neshama.* (Wishful thinking; often my *neshama* is nowhere to be heard from and my ego rules unchallenged; just ask my kids or the people at the office.)

Good Intentions have Value only when Actualized
My way is based heavily on the point to be learned

from a story told by that beautiful Hasidic Master, Reb Haim Sanzer. "What would you do if you found a bag of gold coins?" he asked one. "I'd return it to the rightful owner as the Torah says," was the reply. "You're a fool," responded Reb Haim. And to a second who said he would take the money for himself he said "You are a thief." Then he asked a third who replied "Rebbe, how do I know where my *neshama* will be when I find the coins. If it is connected with the *Rebono shel olam* at that time it will be like second nature to return the money, but if my *neshama* is far away at that time I'll grab the money for myself." "Those are good words!" cried the Rebbe. "You are a true sage."

This story may be understood in this way. When we borrow from a bank and promise to pay back we get immediate cash in exchange for the promise. Likewise, when we promise or commit ourselves to be a good Jew, a Liberal, a Conservative, a Zionist, a good husband, a true friend, etc. . . , we must be getting some kind of immediate gratification for the promise we make. This ego-gratification may be from others or from our own selves.

What I learn from Reb Haim is that I am what I do and not what I believe in, or what I commit myself to, and least of all what I claim "my way" is. Judaism is more meaningful as a tool or vehicle for aliveness and for actualization than as a group to belong to or with which to identify.

My way is accepting the Kabbalistic definition of *Teshuva* as '*Tshuv Heh*' or returning to God in your next action if you have turned away from him in your last.

Letting my Connection to God Replace my Ego
My way is to try to make a *shidach* between the appropriate action and each minute of life, but to accept myself without regret if I don't. The good *shidach* is the one prompted by a source other than ego.

My ways are best achieved through *davening* (prayer), Torah study and Hasidic stories. I believe that the strength of the Hasidic tale is that the Rebbe shares the energies he generates when he internalizes the point of the tale he is telling. These energies I believe remain connected with the words in the story whether told by Hasidim in *sh'tiblach* or on the pages of books of Hasidic tales.

My way is to live in *D'vakut* (connection to God) not because it is the right way, but because my experience tells me that it is sweeter than the desires of ego which are insatiable, while in *D'vakut* the opposite is true. To believe in the right way is a pitfall. Right is right only until it becomes important and if *D'vakut* becomes important that simply means that the ego has taken over. Importance exists only in the mind, while *D'vakut* is achieved only through experience. (That's why the Kabbalah must remain secret lest it be taken over by the "other side.")

Just think of how much importance we have in Jewish life today and you'll quickly see which side is running things.

And when I am able to act from that place of connectedness my actions come from the side of *Hessed* – Love – even if I have to spank a child or stand up to kill another. The hate and hostility that we generate is never brought about by what confronts us no matter how evil. It is brought about from a source within us when at that moment our *neshama* is far from the *rebono shel olam*.

What has mysticism to do with judaism?
Cynthia Ozick

One winter morning in my early teens I had what may perhaps have been a Genuine Mystical Experience. I used to ride the Pelham Bay line of the Lexington Avenue subway on my way to Hunter High, then at East 68th Street. It was a straight ride on the local, and since I got on at the first stop, I always easily found a corner seat for reading, dreaming, or doing my Latin. One day, having overslept, afraid of being late for school, I left my usual train and crossed the platform at 125th Street to take the express. This meant that I had to stand, a small and skinny kid crushed in the merciless convulsion of the morning mob. And I still had my Latin to do. Pressed on all sides, hanging as if on the rack with one hand, my schoolbag squeezed between my ankles, my left hand mired in Cicero, my knees forced up against the ersatz-silk-stocking knees (this was wartime, and nylon belonged to the military) of the immortal woman seated before me, I was all at once lifted out of that time and place and given access to Everything.

I suddenly Understood. I was in possession. I Knew. The sensation lasted only a second, but in that instant some gap into the secret innerness of the universe was opened to me, and I could penetrate, with perfect clarity, into the Why of all things.

My Period of Immersion in the "Mystical"
The astonishing moment passed. There I was, an adolescent in a subway mob once again; but different somehow. I was stunned. I stood paralyzed, trying in desperation to retrieve what I had just experienced: not the experience itself – already that seemed hopeless – but its blazing spill of universal knowledge. I ransacked myself for even a shadow, even a sliver, of that knowledge; not for its method or its source, not for the impossible renewal of the spell, but for a return of a fraction of what I had just learned. I had the crazy sense of having turned, out of the blue, into a bewildered amnesiac, grieved by loss. Enlightenment had slipped off and could not be summoned again.

From that moment on I began to take note of mysticism. An uncle who was a poet sent me to William James' *Varieties of Religious Experience*. I became interested in "revelation," "epiphany," "the Oversoul." I bathed in the Romantic poets, as much for their claims of transcendence as for the lyrical ecstasies every literary adolescent uncovers in Blake, Shelley, Keats, Coleridge, Wordsworth. In college I wrote an undergraduate thesis on the "monistic and mystical" elements in these poets. I took a course or two in comparative religion and afterward began systematic readings, which lasted for years, in Hinduism, Buddhism, Zen, Tao, and related streams. This was well before, I ought to add, there was any popular or cultic interest in Oriental religions.

After Scripture, Mysticism is Definitely unJewish
When I became – intellectually, morally, responsibly – an adult Jew, I grew out of all that, almost by definition. The vision of the Ineffable All that I had had in the subway did not in any way touch on my

thoroughly conscious Jewish identity. What it *did* touch was the narcissism that may be normal in adolescents, but is nonsensical in adults.

It would be a mistake to insist that mysticism is un-Jewish. God spoke to Abraham, the first Jew, and afterward to Moses; if this means Abraham and Moses were mystics, then Scripture is thick with mystical precedents. The dispute, then, is not with Scripture, and not with the readers of Scripture, pious or otherwise, but with the post-Biblical practitioners of a so-called Jewish mysticism. The gargantuan monument of Gershom Scholem's work, when one has scaled even a little of it, demonstrates that there has always been mysticism among Jews; but that is something different from the claim (though Scholem makes it) that mysticism, when we get past Scripture, is Jewish.

Mysticism Leads Away from Communal Responsibility
What is the case to be made against mysticism, as a view tending to lead away from Jewishness? A skeletal adumbration:

1. Narcissism. Singularity. Emphasis on the private experience. The Godhead is apprehended through subjective means. Emphasis away from the communal. The loneliness of the mystic.

2. The frequent puncture of the uncertain membrane or curtain separating the "mystical" from the unashamedly magical. Devices, practices, disciplines to induce the mystical "state." A tendency toward the occult, the "spirit" world, angels, demons, visionary beings of every kind. All of this explicitly proscribed by Moses.

3. A tendency to pantheism. If the Godhead is felt to invade the self, if the Godhead is felt to be indistinguishable from, to be *in,* the self, then the Divine infuses all things. Creator and creation are one. But Jewish thought explicitly separates the Maker from the made. Pantheism is incorrigibly unJewish.

4. Diminishing of the ethical. The obvious corollary of monism, narcissism, and emphasis on the experiential as opposed to the societal. Personal longing for the Divine contact becomes more significant than deed. But Jewishness demands deed; *mitzvah* is imperative, and is itself a form of worship of the Divine.

Jewish Holiness Comes Through our Unique Covenant
5. The link with other mystical systems. The Covenantal idea sets Israel apart, to make a *goy kadosh,* a holy people. The Covenant is uniquely Jewish; the Commandments, though inherited by other peoples, are in origin uniquely Jewish. Mystical ideas are, like having a pair of feet, humanly universal, and are not especially Jewish. Certain hasidic notions and certain Taoist aphorisms are practically interchangeable. Mysticism is a commonplace, however "special" it may feel itself to be; the Covenant can't be found anywhere else.

6. The emphasis on the carnal and the material (despite the seeming devotion to the "spirit," the invisible, the ineffable). The Divine infusion always claims its vessel. Incarnation inevitably follows, turning God (in the way of pantheism or trinitarianism) into crudest matter or flesh. (Cf. the materialist *klipot* of *kabbala.*)

The Jewish way is to feel responsible to the Creator, not to fancy you own a piece of the Creator, or that the Creator inhabits you; to be responsible to your fellow-creatures, not to be lifted above them by special intuitive or magical gifts of Divine apprehension; to express the Covenantal relationship by fellow-feeling in peoplehood, in duty, and in deed, not to blur it, evade it, or make it secondary to subjective longings; to distinguish between the holy and the profane, not to wash away the holy by finding it everywhere in a great flood of undifferentiated and ubiquitous magical appearance; to attempt to control the self, not to follow the unyoked self's demand for equation with the forces of the universe.

Mystical practice leads directly and inexorably to idolatry; and in most cases is indistinguishable from it.

Copyright© 1978 by Cynthia Ozick

The prophet and mystic in each of us
Lawrence Kushner

Ms. Ozick is right (*Sh'ma* 8/148) that Mysticism (in some of its forms) is dangerous, prone to narcissism and contrary to some forms of Judaism as it is currently taught in many schools. And we should be grateful to her for reminding us that any movement for religious renewal must be especially vigilant. On the other hand her argument is so insulting and categorical that I cannot help but wonder just who or what she is mad at.

It could hardly be Isaac Luria, the Baal Shem Tov, Nachman of Bratzlav or Martin Buber. Whatever their excesses may have been we cannot call them "dangerous," "anti-communal," "un-Jewish" or (even worse) "idolatrous." Nor could it be the few neo-hippies and chronic members of the latest fad cult of our generation. Whatever their piety or folly they are hardly serious heirs of the Covenant. One gets the uneasy sensation that anyone who has encountered the mystery of holiness and refused to dismiss it as adolescent or irrelevant is the "enemy" of all that is good and Judaism. It is in hopes therefore of saving a lot of these "heretics" that I submit some additional dimensions of Mysticism which Ms. Ozick has overlooked.

Mysticism is not a religion. It is a way of being religious, a response to the Holy which lies at one end of a spectrum. On one side there stands the prophetic. Here one is painfully aware of the abyss between man and God. Our inadequacy is compared with His expectations. Our corruption of His world is seen against how God must feel. Prophecy's impulse is to bridge the gap by ever calling attention to it. On the other side of the spectrum is Mysticism. Here one seeks to realize God by constantly being close to him. We do not seek to supplant, overpower or confuse ourselves with the Light of the *Ayn Sof,* (God, the Limitless) we wish merely to BE IN it. Some can BE IN a congregation, sunlight, darkness or snow and be aware of their fullness and furthermost extremities without confusing their identity with the One in which they are. Here one RETURNS to God, not by going up and out but down and within. The gap is bridged by ignoring it.

A Mature Personality has Many Aspects
No one is at one end or the other. And that is because no mystic can hear the voice without a bit of the prophet just as no prophet can speak the voice without a bit of the mystic. Such is the nature of the human soul. And such is the task of religion: To mediate between the two. Or, as Arnold Jacob Wolf has taught me, to make it possible at least to withstand them. Either extreme is as dangerous as it is indispensable to a mature religious personality and a vibrant religious community. After all, sometimes those who began by listening for the voice have instead spoken it — Heschel did march to Selma with Martin Luther King — even as those who began by trying to repair the world (a Mystical term in Judaism) turned also, like Rav Kook, to mystical search. Or, to put it another way, Mysticism is not necessarily exclusive of other religious responses. Akiva, Nachmanides, Karo and the Vilna Gaon were ALSO mystics. And their generations, fortunately for us, realized that there were some things it is neither possible nor worthwhile to change about people. God cries, scolds and demands. God also whispers, coos and sings. And for this reason there are many ways to serve the King and Queen.

Mysticism Reminds Us that All is Not Black or White
But perhaps the most serious issue Ms. Ozick raises, albeit with more than enough anger, one too long in need of serious attention, is why are so many people now talking about mysticism. Even a superficial reading of Jewish history could detect a pattern in the half a dozen or so flowerings of the spiritual. Mysticism seems to have arisen in times of over glorified rationality. Times of intense concern with doing at the expense of being. Times of great concentrations of communal power. Times after a great trauma. Times like the present.

In such days another response is heard, one which returns ecclesiastical power back to each individual and sends each soul out again into the fields in search of ultimate spiritual truths. It breaks away the centuries of pious crust which form around holy acts. It is the only mode of awareness able to convince a rationality which knows only "yes" or "no" that there can be something in between. For this reason, flowerings of the mystical invariably revitalize not only the tradition but the community as well.

We seem to spend all our days talking about what we are doing to the world and what the world is doing to us. Instead of why we bother or whose voice we have heard. The result, indeed, is that the most wealthy, rational, powerful and organized (which some misunderstand as communal) generation of Jews in history is also the most secular, boring and empty. It is hardly surprising that the tiny melody of spiritual search should be heard again from the tents of Jacob.

CHARLES ROTH *is developing a form of Hasidic meditation for the general Jewish public.*

CYNTHIA OZICK, *whose most recent book was* Bloodshed and Other Novellas, *took time out from working on a new novel to do this article for us.*

LAWRENCE KUSHNER *is the rabbi of Congregation Beth El in Sudbury, Massachusetts and has recently published an American Jewish mystical work,* Honey From The Rock.

LEON SOL WIESELTIER *is studying philosophy at Columbia University.*

3.

The Holocaust, Our Continuing Trauma

The holocaust as a "subject"

Earl L. Dachslager

Much has been written about the Holocaust and much more, no doubt, will be written in the future. According to the Yad Vashem Bibliographical Series (No. 12), up through 1971 around 6,000 books, articles, essays, reviews, collections, anthologies have been published in English (including translations) that deal with the Holocaust. This 6,000 — and the number must be nearly twice that by now — does not include the thousands of writings published in Polish, Yiddish, Hebrew, German, French, etc., etc. In short, the Holocaust has become a subject, something to be written about, a huge — some might say bloated — corpus of philosophical, historical, personal, critical, sociological, fictional, theological, political, psychological writings intended (or at least available) to be studied, analyzed, criticized, and reviewed.

The purpose of this enormous body of writing is fairly obvious: it is a way of commemorating the event itself, of not allowing what happened to be misunderstood or forgotten, even — perhaps especially — by those who would most like to misunderstand or forget. Beyond that, and perhaps most importantly, it is a way of reminding the world that contrary to what we have been told for the past 2,000 years, it is not the Jews who all along have been the infidels, but the Gentiles.

To Speak the Unspeakable We Make it into a Subject
All of this, again, would seem to be obvious. What is perhaps less obvious, and less well understood, is *how* this enormous body of writing has come into being. Given its purpose — the need to make the world remember and understand what happened — and given the nature of the event itself, how have we managed to produce (thus far) a multi-volume bibliography of writings on the Holocaust? How, indeed, have we made a subject *at all* out of what is over and over again said to be unspeakable and undescribable? The answer is that we have done it by transforming in some way, or ways, the chaos and mystery of the actual experience to the order and logic of language. We have, in a literal sense, *subjected* it to our understanding. The Holocaust had to become a subject, similar to any other event which is capable and needful of verbal explication, narration, and commentary. Otherwise it would disappear.

Since the Holocaust is an event in history, the problem here, and the potential danger, comes precisely from accepting it and treating it as any other historical event, which means, ultimately, as a social-science subject or as "background" for fiction or poetry or whatever. Elie Wiesel has stated the danger thus:

"For today a book about the Holocaust is a book like any other, produced by literary technicians. Anyone can write it: words, words which are carefully weighed, measured, borrowed for their market value, words distorted to satisfy some sort of thirst for vanity, or intrigue, or revenge. It is as though the survivors no longer existed."

As time goes by and the survivors and their kin pass away, this danger will become more and more prevalent; for example, the day will surely come — indeed it has already started — when the Holocaust will become, at least in part, an academic subject, something to be studied for final exam purposes, a topic for dissertations, a theme for learned conferences, a device by which to publish and not to perish.

The Holocaust is Not Just Another Historical Event
This sort of subjective treatment of the Holocaust would perhaps to some degree be acceptable and even valid were the Holocaust in fact comparable to other, similar, historical events. Most Jews as well as sensitive non-Jews (perhaps I should say sensitive people),

understand that the Holocaust is *not* the same as the bombing of Dresden or Hiroshima, that Auschwitz is *not* comparable to the Japanese-American internment camps of World War Two, that the calculated murder of six-million Jews is *not* the equivalent of the deaths of millions of World War Two or Korean War or Vietnam War combatants and civilians (all of which are typical comparisons made by those who do not know what the Holocaust meant). Franklin Littell, for example, recently attacked the all-too-prevalent view of the Holocaust as simply another example of "man's inhumanity to man." According to Littell, such a response is illogical, a "non-sequitur," a "banal utterance," "a shallow escape mechanism"; in short, a failure not only to understand history but to understand the Holocaust itself.

Still, in a paradoxical way, we evidently find some comfort, even a need, to align the Holocaust with other superficially-alike events, even to respect it for its universal, as well as for its particular, causes and effects. The recognition that the Holocaust is unique and, simultaneously, treating it as something other than unique — seems understandable, even logical, when we recognize an even greater paradox which pertains to writings about the Holocaust; that is, the most effective writings may turn out to be the least effective — least because if the writing is vivid enough and potent enough the reader may well be turned away. The task facing an author writing about the Holocaust is how to write effectively without giving a negative, or unacceptable, effect. How can anyone read, say, a story about the Holocaust and *like* the story?

Readers are Turned Off when Suffering is Too Real
In his superb book, *The Holocaust and the Literary Imagination,* Lawrence Langer asks the following question pertinent to Holocaust literature (used in the strict, not general, sense): "How should art — how *can* art? — represent the inexpressibly inhuman suffering of the victims, without doing an injustice to that suffering?" This is, in truth, a pertinent question, but I would add to it: without *also* doing an injustice to the reader? It is not simply a question of making poems, stories, essays, articles, etc. out of the absolute degradation and pain of the victims but also a question of asking readers to *read* about such degradation and pain. And if the writing is too effective then, understandably, the reader may rebel — perhaps even should rebel. To my knowledge this problem is not faced — at least not to the same degree —

with writers or readers of subjects such as Hiroshima, Vietnam, the Civil War, African slavery, or any other brutal historical event. Here, if anywhere, is irrefutable proof of the uniqueness of the Holocaust. Of no other event in human history potentially describable in language does there exist as much likelihood of reader resistance as the Holocaust. Yet in spite of this uniqueness and the difficulty — if not impossibility — of truly writing about the Holocaust, there is no doubt that the great corpus of writings will continue to grow; even now it is literally impossible for one to "keep up with" Holocaust writings.

No Middle Ground Between Silence and "Subject"
This activity will continue not simply (to put it banally) because the Holocaust is there but rather because only by reducing it to a subject — to the abstract logic of language — is it possible for the Holocaust to become "speakable" and "readable" and "writable." By this means the writing, or speaking, *about* has become a surrogate for the actuality, not only, as some have argued, a cathartic device, but an actual substitute, a vicarious means of participating in Jewish history at (or on) its most meaningful level.

Looking back, it seems that this was the only thing that could have happened. Short of silence, there doesn't seem to be anything else that could be done with the Holocaust *except* to study it, read about it, talk about it, write about it, being careful, for the most part, not to encumber the reader or listener with too many or too excessively graphic details. Irving Greenberg has given us what he calls a "working principle" for discussing the Holocaust: "No statement, theological or otherwise, should be made that would not be credible in the presence of the burning children." If this principle is true, then one asks what "credible" statements *could* be made in the face of the burning children? Not many, I suspect. By this principle, how many of the millions of statements already made about the Holocaust would be, or should be, thrown into the trash? Most, probably.

Holocaust as History can be Interpreted, even Denied
The fact is that the burning children are kept in the backs, not the fronts, of our minds when we write or read or speak about the Holocaust. Again, short of silence, there doesn't seem much else that could be done with them. They are, surely, incapable of subjective, much less objective, treatment. Along these same lines, one wonders to what extent the increasingly prevalent — and so far little understood — attempts to

void the reality of the Holocaust, to disavow its very existence, have to do with its having been made a subject and, therefore, open to the possibility of debate and disapproval. If history is seen (as it frequently is) as the interpretation of the past (i.e., subject) rather than merely the actual record of the past (i.e., object), then the Holocaust, as history, opens itself to interpretation, which includes denial. And since for many, history has come to mean journalism (or vice versa) then the Holocaust becomes not merely an historical event but also a media event. I quote from a letter in the Houston *Post* (May 13, 1976):

"There were about six million Jews in all of Europe and slightly more than one million in Germany at the beginning of WWII. This big lie about six million Jews was started by the Jews and copied by the ignorant press to gain sympathy for the Israelis. Why doesn't the news media check for facts and truth?"

Here we find, in its crudest expression, the danger of giving the Holocaust the status (if that's the right word) of *subjectivity*. The Holocaust becomes one man's (or people's) *opinion* about what happened, which may or may not have anything to do with the "facts or truth." By extension, the same would hold true for the treatment of the Holocaust as a chapter in a history textbook (worse, a couple of paragraphs), a three-credit college course, an essay topic for advanced *cheder* students, a theme for sisterhoods' study groups, a lecture by an authority.

Reality Finds Expression in Carefully Chosen Words
While such activities are well-meaning and legitimate attempts to come to terms with the Holocaust, nevertheless it remains the subject and therefore capable of subjective treatment. The Holocaust thus becomes merely a point of dissension between those who believe in it (putting it that way perhaps underscores the problem) and those who don't. The cheapest use of the Holocaust that I can possibly imagine would be to have to defend its actual occurrence, yet, as we know, this is precisely something which we have had to do! I believe that, at least to some extent, this is the result of subjectifying the thing itself, of speaking and writing about it in terms similar to other subjects, even though we say it is unique, unduplicatable, incapable of being exposed by language.

Yet what is the alternative? Silence? This is obviously not possible, assuming it is desirable. Besides it is too late for silence. We have, in a real sense, talked the

Holocaust into existence (or into *an* existence), and hence to stifle the talk would mean to stifle the existence. Certainly the Holocaust defeats our comprehension and our justification. Yet, for all of that, it may be that part of the meaning of the Holocaust is our inherent necessity to verbalize it, perhaps even to debate it. I don't mean that this process is necessarily "Jewish" (although that is not without possibility), but rather that as intelligent beings any attempt to comprehend or define reality must necessarily be expressed by language and this means necessarily to treat it subjectively. The time will come — it may already have — when the real Holocaust can no longer be known, no more than the real Exodus or Masada or *shtetl*. The writing about — the thing as subject — will be all that we know of it. In the end, one can only hope that the Holocaust as subject is treated with care, understanding, and the full recognition, somehow, of the burning children.

After the holocaust, another covenant?
David W. Weiss

The incumbency of a radically new Judaic theology has been argued with growing insistence during the past thirty years. Pivotal to the claim is the imputed uniqueness of the European holocaust of 1939-1945. The horror visited on the Jewish people during these years has been, it is claimed, a wholly singular experience, and one that signals the beginning of a new era. The classic Judaic delineation of the relationship between God and the House of Israel is no longer tenable, perhaps, indeed, has not been since the destruction of the Second Temple and Jewish commonwealth. The covenant that was, or the illusion of this covenant, has been abrogated in the German death camps. What is demanded of the survivors is a new covenant, a unilateral, voluntary assertion by the House of Israel of the will to continue Jewish existence in the face of an indifferent, changeable, or non-existent diety.

I address myself not to the terrifying implications of the proposed new theology, nor make any attempt to analyze the diverse motivations of its proponents. I ask: Is the contention valid?

DAVID W. WEISS *is Chairman of the Lautenberg Center for General and Tumor Imunology at the Hebrew University, Hadassah Hospital.*

It is not, and I am at a loss to comprehend the reasoning of serious thinkers who posit the view. Perhaps I do not have the privilege of saying this. I have not experienced in my body the suffering of European Jewry—although I lived for nearly a year in Austria after the *Anschluss* until escaping, and lost all but my immediate family in the period that followed—and I may therefore lack a certain right, or authority, to speak. But then, perhaps the obligation to speak has now devolved on those not so seared, who still have speech.

The Holocaust of 1939-1945 Was Not Unique

It may be that what transpired was unprecedented in scope, setting and expectation. One would not have thought it possible that this could take place in mid-twentieth century, at the hands of a cultured nation, and to the apathy of the rest of the civilized world. But the uniqueness of even these aspects of the holocaust is debatable. A more sober estimation of the behavior of technologically advanced peoples before, during, and after the destruction of European Jewry, and in other regards, leaves less room for astonishment. Man has always given evidence of the potential of humanity and compassion, but the dominant theme of his record to the present is not undeserving of the epitomization *hominis lupus est*. The Jewish people have accepted, as part of their ancient covenant, the challenge of witness to greater possibilities.

For this we have suffered, horribly, uniquely, and repeatedly throughout post-biblical history. Whole regions have been devastated of their Jewish communities in recurrent, earlier holocausts; I employ that denotation advisedly. I doubt that the impact on individual Jew, or community, or a land of communities of devastation in the reaches all about was very different in the past than the impact now on world Jewry of ruin on a larger geographic and numerical scale. It is uncertain, too, whether the German attrition was in fact of a vastly different order proportionately than earlier desolation; there are data that suggest otherwise.

Theologically, religiously, it seems to be absurd to hold that the extirpation of Judean, Rhineland, or South-Eastern European Jewry was a more acceptable experience than what transpired between 1939 and 1945. Is the vision of an infinite God who is Guardian of Israel less shaken by the annihilation of *only* a million Jews at the hands of the Romans, of *only* several hundred thousand each by crusaders, cossacks, haidamuks, than by the six million dead in German Europe? A god who plays these odds is not the God of Judaism. And Judaism has survived until 1936, as it shall now, without denying its God and the covenant with Him.

Individuals Choose; The People May Not

Certainly, this last havoc demands a searching, penetrating reaffirmation of faith and commitment, as there have been urgent gropings for renewed meaning in the wake of earlier holocausts. The striving for new perspectives and new apperceptions is indeed constant demand of the spirit on every Jew, at all times. But a "new *covenant*", a "new *epoch*"—that is a closing of the book of Judaism. Whatever their sincerity, their love of Israel, their loyalties to Jewish practice, the prophets of the new covenant call not to a revitalization but to denial of the God of Israel and annulment of the Jew's *raison d'etre* in the world. That, too, is not unique. Not all the gropings after preceding desolation remained anchored in the covenant that is. Those that were not, led into apostate movements and disappearance.

The endeavor for new covenants today too shall fail, to be remembered as a tragic aberration. The *individual* Jew has choice before him. He can opt for the prototype antipodes of hasidism and of Sabbatean-Frankist oblivion, to add new dimensions and nuance to the mainstream of Judaism or to cut himself off. The House of Israel has no such choice. Once initiated with the Patriarchs and reconfirmed by the assembled multitudes at Sinai, the covenant is irrevocable. This is a principle of the faith of Judaism. It is put eloquently in *Midrash Rabba* on Exodus 3:14: " 'I Shall Be As I Shall Be.' R. Johanan said: 'I Shall Be As I Shall Be' to individuals, but for the community of Israel, I rule over them even if against their desire and will, even though they break their teeth, as it is said: 'As I live, saith the Lord God, surely with a mighty hand and with an outstretched arm, and with fury poured out, will I be King over you' (Ezekiel 20:33)." The commentary on the Midrash, *Matnat Kehunah*, amplifies: "The individual who desires and chooses me, to him I shall be God; and if he does not so desire, it is given him to cast off the yoke; but to the community of Israel I do not give the option of casting off the yoke of heaven."

The advocates of new covenants will not halt the salvational history of the Jewish people, but they can add to the century's attritions. They must not go unchallenged, therefore. It must be told unequivocally: They are advocates not of a reaffirmed Judaism, but of something other than the religion eternal of a God eternal.

A Perspective of Holocausts

The Jew must struggle to come to grips with ravage and loss on two distinct levels, that of the People collectively and that of the individual.

For the People, the covenant is indissoluble, and its conditions have been spelled out: "See, I have set before thee this day life and good, and death and evil... I command thee this day to love the Lord thy God, to walk in his ways, and to keep his commandments... Then thou shalt live and the Lord thy God shall bless thee in the land into which thou goest... But if thy heart turn away... and shalt worship other gods... I announce to you this day, that thou shalt surely perish, and that thou shalt not prolong your days upon the land... I call heaven and earth to witness this day against you, that I have set before thee life and death, blessing and cursing. Therefore choose life... And the Lord said to Moses, Behold, thou shalt sleep with thy fathers; and this people will... go astray after the gods of the... land into which they go... and break my covenant which I have made with them. Then... I will forsake them, and I will hide my face from them, and they shall be devoured... so that they will say on that day, are these evils not come upon us, because our God is not among us? And I will surely hide my face on that day for all the evils which they shall have perpetrated." (Deuteronomy 30:15-20; 31:16-18).

This is a clear blueprint of Jewish history, in promise and realization. The terms of the covenant are repeated, again and again, throughout Scripture and rabbinic literature, and their fulfillment is historical record. The People that chose and was chosen to bear witness to the God who is revealed in the affairs of mankind cannot survive at ease the betrayal of that God and the forcing him to turn his face. We are given the choice to make God's presence large in the world of man or to banish the *Shechinah*, but we cannot avoid the consequences of then being alone in a godless world. God's banishment paves the way to holocausts. In Jewish

mysticism, every Jew is held to be an organic member of the corpus of the *Shechinah*. No people has flourished intact for very long in the eclipse of the divine; we Jews are left especially vulnerable—but we survive, and in our pain remain incandescent.

The Covenant's Truth Remains Eternal

There is an additional stipulation in the covenant with the Jewish people: "And it shall come to pass, when all these things are come upon thee... and thou shalt return to the Lord thy God and shalt obey his voice... with all thy heart and with all thy soul; that then the Lord thy God will turn thy captivity, and have compassion upon thee, and will return, and gather thee from all the nations among whom the Lord thy God has scattered thee..." (Deuteronomy 30:1-3).

That promise, too, echoes throughout the chronicles of God's dialogue with the Jewish people. The covenant is not for review, neither is the eternity of Jewish existence. God is in exile with his people, and when they permit him, He returns from exile and with him once more the people. With Jewish justice and righteousness lies Jewish redemption. Until then, the door remains closed and the lights darkened.

The privilege of *being* a covenantal people is transcendent. The consequences of violation are agonizing. Many Jews have individually reasserted their allegiance to the collective covenant, even in bitter experience of its terms. I ask myself whether I should have the strength for such personal reassertion, had I endured them fully in my being. But I do know this: The covenant has unfolded for the people, and continues to unfold, in panlucid verity. It has not been broken by God, nor has he permitted the People to shake it off.

For the individual, the question of theodicy— the innocent who suffer, the evildoers who flourish—is ultimately the same whether suffering is in the midst of an inclusive catastrophe or in aloneness. The question to God, Why?, is the same for the first child struck down in human history and for the last to perish in Auschwitz. That is the eternal confrontation of all men with God.

R. Johanan, the *amorah* who lost his children, would visit mourners and show a bone of his tenth, last son. A mute rendering of comfort in a sharing of faith: R. Johanan remained the sage. Elishah b. Abuyah did not. Countless human beings, Jew and non-Jews, have found it possible, somehow, to take the way of Johanan, Jews even after the German visitation. That is the challenge to the individual always. For the individual Jew to whom the evidence for the being of God as Judaism has known him is too persuasive to elude, for all the suffering experienced, the seeking of new covenants is a search in the wrong dimension, a delusion. •

The covenant, a century of modernization
Eugene B. Borowitz

As they modernized, most Jews abandoned the class Jewish notion of the Covenant. Their reaction to the Kishinev massacre of 1903 makes that clear. For Biblical-rabbinic Judaism (and thus all pre-modern Judaism), the Covenant is intimately identified with God's justice. When Jews do the good, God will give them abundant blessing; when they sin God will punish them — a theme so significant, a Torah passage (Dt. 11:13-21) expounding it is the second paragraph of the full *sh'ma*. This leads to the doctrine that God employs the enemies of the Jews to punish them and bring them back to faithful observance. From the prophets through at least the Chmielnicki pogroms (1648), Jewish calamity evoked the Covenantal judgment: because of our sins, God has properly brought this evil upon us.

As Jews left the ghetto in the 19th century they gave up the notion that a tight, close, Divine Providence ordered history. Moderns no longer used God as the primary means of interpreting the world; science did that for them. And the secular perspective of the newspaper, not the literal claims of the Bible, did the same for history. When people still talked about God, they did so with a new abstractness and distance. God might still be the origin of all things, the one who set their order and the criterion of human striving, but God was no longer expected to do anything specific. Until recent decades, evolution and progress were the key terms for describing history. And the one reliable agent for historic change was humankind.

EUGENE B. BOROWITZ's *tenth book*, Liberal Judaism, *has just been published by the U.A.H.C.*

The Covenant of People as the Creator

The shift from God who acts-and-saves to self-fulfillment via politics-education-and-culture was thoroughgoing. For most Jews it was sufficient reason to surrender traditional religious belief and practice substantially if not altogether. Even today, though the foundations of confident modernism have eroded, such "salvation" as most modern Jews still hope for is sought in courses, therapies and other human strategems, not in what the Bible says God may be expected to do. Thus, insofar as they took God seriously at all, modern Jews reinterpreted the Covenant in terms of human freedom and capacity. History would be what people made of it — and considering the progress enlightened societies had made in the 19th century, the Messianic Age seemed barely beyond the horizon. The reaction of modern Jewry to the Kishinev pogroms — most particularly of those who lived in Russia — illustrates how substantially the notion of Covenantal Providence had been replaced by the notion of human self-help. There was as good as no cry that Jewish sin had brought this upon the community. Any suggestion that the Russian mobs and their governmental protectors were God's agents would have been thought ridiculous. Instead, the Russian Zionists and others called for Jewish self-defense units and the Hebrew writers decried the passivity of Jews in accepting slaughter. World Jewry turned to political action, emergency aid and rescue, not to prayer, lamentation and fast. No major, enlightened Jewish writer seriously asked where God was during the pogroms; they no longer expected God to be that involved in historic events. But they and much of the democratic world were outraged that people could so spurn the lessons of modernity and behave so vilely.

All Our Philosophers Were Humano-centric

Every major modern Jewish thinker reinforced this view of history. Surely 20th century rationalism permitted little else. In its European Jewish variety, most notably the neo-Kantianism of Hermann Cohen, God is grounding idea and moral spur, but history is only what a free humanity will make of it. In its American variety, Mordecai Kaplan's naturalism, God is essentially the projection of our human drive to self-fulfillment, hence a Divinity of limited power.

Even in the reach beyond reason to religious consciousness (of Leo Baeck), God remains what we sense behind our ethics, not an independent agent dominating history. The non-rationalisms of Franz Rosenzweig and Martin Buber do not yield a stronger view of Providence. The former denies that the Jewish people truly lives in history while the latter relegates what we call history to the realm of I-it, where God is never seen. In some ways the most telling instance is Abraham Heschel. Though his thought, for all its contemporary idiom, is nearly Orthodox, and God dominates his theology, all but a few sentences of his remarks about the Holocaust speak about human failure not God's ineffability.

The God most modern Jews heard their rabbis speaking about through late mid-century derived from these master images. They bear almost no resemblance to the "ultimate, omnipotent actor in history," that Richard Rubenstein discovered had died for him as a result of the Holocaust. Why, then, was the Jewish community disturbed during the late 1960's and early 1970's by discussions of the death of God? If they had not believed in the God whose end was now announced, why should the arguments have been so troubling?

Surely some Jews had never become as modern in their thought as they had in the Jewish life style. What remnant of belief they retained was still quite traditional, regardless of their non-observance, and now they were troubled that they might have to give up this last tie with their devout grandparents. Perhaps too, as we have often seen in trauma, some Jews reverted to an older, childhood faith in God. Neither of these explanations is very satisfying. As Elie Wiesel has pointed out, it was generally not the devout traditionalists who lost faith during the Holocaust but the liberals.

Explaining The Agnostics' Mourning

For modern Jews, that is, those who, regardless of label or synagogue affiliation, had a Covenant between a relatively shadowy, passive God and a highly active, effective human- kind, the 1960's Holocaust discussion was earth-shaking. For their modernized Covenant had been built upon faith in humanity and that "god" had now died for them. (Indeed, it took two decades for the discussion to being not because we were traumatized but because it took that long for newly affluent Americans to perceive how few of our fundamental problems we could truly solve.) I agree with Wiesel, Rubenstein, Fackenheim and Greenberg that the Holocaust forces us to rethink the Covenant. Only I deny that the Covenant most of us have been devoted to in recent decades is the Biblical-rabbinic one of pre-modern times.

Modernity replaced overwhelming faith in God with unrestricted faith in humankind, "the perfectibility of man" we called it in those sexist days. What requires reconsideration in our modernized Covenant is its near-idolatrous view of humankind. We cannot, even the best of us, collectively as well as individually, be the agents of our own fulfillment. We are, as recent decades have demonstrated, too flawed and problematic for that. But we are also not without great human power, as Zionism insisted and the State of Israel has exemplified. We therefore cannot return to the comparatively passive status of individual conscience under the class Covenant even as we can no longer take all the burden of a messianic history upon ourselves.

A chastened but not despairing humankind has therefore opened itself up afresh to God. We still cannot believe in Deuteronomy's notion of Providence but in our faith that our values are lasting and ultimately triumphant, we know ourselves not to be alone in history. God may be astoundingly inscrutable, or merely finite, but now, for all our realism, the Covenant Partner is again real and significant. And we modern Jews, at our best, seek to live that faith even as we continue to struggle to understand it. •

Our ancient covenant has been shattered
Michael Berenbaum

The Hofetz Chaim once said: "For the believer there are no questions and the unbeliever there are no answers." David Weiss has sidestepped the questions posed by the Holocaust.

He has restated the eternity of the covenant that binds God and Israel, but he has not wrestled with the fundamental question. What can we say of that covenant in the wake of Auschwitz? Need we alter our understanding? Need we rely less upon God and more upon our fellow Jews in the struggle for survival? And finally, how can we talk of God's attributes of compassion and mercy in a world of death camps?

MICHAEL BERENBAUM *teaches theology at Georgetown University and is the Opinion Page Editor of National Washington Jewish Week.*

Weiss' conclusions are expected. *Bitachon* (trust), as Zwi Werbloski so beautifully demonstrated, is central to the religious Jew's perception of the world. I concur that there are dangers in a Godless world. There is also a sense of emptiness and aloneness, a void. Jewish salvational history is jeopardized: most Jews do not live salvational history (except in its most secularized form of Israel and Zionism), and many devout Jews have politicized salvational history, identifying it with settlement of Judea and Samaria.

But in order to avoid the existential problem posed by the Holocaust, Professor Weiss is forced to deny its historical uniqueness and theological singularity. He also questions the religious integrity of unnamed thinkers who wrestle with the question of covenant after Auschwitz.

Space will not permit me to argue for the uniqueness of the Holocaust. I am uncomfortable with the term "Holocaust" — an *olah* (a sacrificial offering burnt whole unto the Lord)—
for I believe that the term softens and falsifies the impact of the event by imparting a religious meaning to the destruction. Yet the case for uniqueness is overwhelming. Divergent thinkers who disagree on many issues agree that the Holocaust was a singular and unprecedented event.

Its Uniqueness Should Not Be Denied

For Yehudah Bauer two historical elements mark the Holocaust as unique: the total planned annihilation of a people and its quasi religious-apocalyptic meaning. Forever an empiricist, Bauer argues that "to date, this has only happened to Jews." Scholars such as Uri Tal, Lucy Dawidowicz, Emil Fackenheim, and George Mossee essentially agree with his judgment. Other thinkers maintain that the inner experience of the victim and the survivor or the mechanisms and processes of destruction mark the Holocaust as unique. (Raul Hilberg, Joseph Borkin, Hannah Arendt, Lawrence Langer and Richard Rubenstein share this perspective to various degrees.)

Suffice it to say that there is credible evidence advanced by distinguished scholars to suggest that the Holocaust was unprecedented not only in scope, setting, expectation, and proportion but in intention, intensity, duration, methodology and consequences.

Professor Weiss' reasons for denying the uniqueness and offending many by using the plural, small "h" (holocausts) is religious rather than scholarly. He is not alone. Many who object to aesthetics or politics of Holocaust commemorations or the disproportionate role the Holocaust assumes in contemporary Jewish identity strike out at the concept of uniqueness instead of tackling the troubling issue more directly.

Now to the heart of the matter. One good Midrash deserves another. Moses said: "The great, powerful, and awesome God." Jeremiah came along and said: "Aliens are rampaging His Temple. Where is His awesomeness?" He no longer spoke (of God as) awesome. Daniel came along and said "His children are slaves to foreigners. Where is His power?" He no longer spoke of God as powerful.

The men of the Great Synod restored the crown to God's attributes by reinterpreting the power and the awesomeness of God. This change took time. And although the words were the same, their meaning had changed.

The Covenant Has Been Reevaluated Before

Jewish history testifies to a reinterpretation of the covenant after every transformative historical experience: the Exodus, Sinai, the destruction of the first and second temples, the defeat of 135 C.E. and the Spanish Inquisition. While the covenant may be eternal, our understanding of the covenant and hence our relationship to the God of history was changed by each of these events.

When the poet said: "The Torah was given at Sinai and returned at Lublin" or when the novelist proclaims "For the first time in Jewish history the covenant was broken... We must begin all over again..." they are reshaping the language of tradition in order to bear witness to their historical experience. Perhaps until the next Great Synod we will be unable to speak of God's power or His mercy except in the most muted of voices.

If we judge by the behavior of Jews as a people, our understanding of the covenant has changed. From Gush Emunim to Hashomer Hatzair, Jews have reentered history and are struggling for their survival by military and political means. They are no longer relying upon the promise of God's salvation, nor content to await the Messiah. Even those who profess their faith in the eternal covenant have altered the way they behave in history.

Professor Weiss does not refer to new covenantal thinkers by name. Nor can I recognize their thought from his characterizations. The men, whose writings I have read, share three essential convictions. The Holocaust has shattered the Jewish people and made it difficult to use religious language in a traditional way. Irving Greenberg's principle of truth sums it up best. "No statement, theological or otherwise, should be made that can not be said in the presence of the burning bodies of Jewish children."

Secondly, they maintain that the Holocaust has imposed new responsibilities on the Jewish people.

While I do not concur with Fackenheim's "commanding Voice of Auschwitz", he has captured the sense of obligation that the Holocaust has imposed upon the Jewish people. Thirdly, they are not closing the door on Judaism or on the Jewish witness "to something better."

With the notable exception of my teacher Richard Rubenstein, most post-Holocaust theologians believe that the reality of despair must energize us to hope. In a world of evil, we must create good. In a world without God, we must restore His image. This is neither an aberration nor a tragic path to assimilation. Rather it is the essence of the contemporary Jewish challenge; the core of our witness.

For Weiss there are no questions. Many theologians of the Holocaust have chosen to wrestle with serious questions and not to avoid them or argue that they just don't exist. •

It came to pass in those days...
Marion P. Pritchard

(A year ago, a friend who was present when Marion Pritchard received the State of Israel's Medal for the Righteous Gentile, introduced me to her. I felt immediately that she ought to share her story with the Jewish community. Though she had never done so before, she agreed to set down some of her memories for Sh'ma. *I also wrote about her to Leonard Fein, Editor of* Moment, *and he published a lengthy interview with Marion in* Moment, *Dec. 1983. That article provides a useful backdrop for the memoir she prepared for us, which follows below. Shortly after this issue appears, Marion will be traveling to the State of Israel to plant her tree in the Alley of the Righteous Gentiles at Yad Vashem in Jerusalem.—E.B.B.)*

Before the Nazi-occupation I did not have any special or close relations with Jews. Amongst the adults my parents socialized with, I cannot remember any Jews. My British-born mother really did not have any particular attitude towards Jews; she did not know any. My father was very upset with developments in Germany after Hitler came to power, and increasingly disturbed about the Dutch government's policies with regard to *not* admitting any Jew who wished to seek refuge in the Netherlands. It was very easy for many people in those days to see Hitler's ravings as just that, and not to believe that he really planned to destroy all Jews. My father did believe he had that in mind. He was a judge, he came from a long line of judges, and justice (not law and order) was very important to him. And the way Jews were being treated in Germany certainly was not just.

I was living in Nijmegen, near the German border, when the Nazis invaded Holland. May tenth was a beautiful, sunny day, it was light by four a.m. and the sky was filled with German planes. In the street were thousands of German troops on motorcycles. Our reponse was outrage, fear, and slowly, the realization that our lives had changed drastically. Of course I worried about my parents and brother in Amsterdam, and on May 15th, when I heard that we had been forced to surrender, I got on my bicycle and headed for Amsterdam. Death, destruction and German uniforms were everywhere, rumors were rife, and I was greatly relieved to find my family unharmed.

The behavior of the Germans for the first few months was—if one wanted to see it that way—reassuring. The Germans, knowing that anti-Semitism would not be popular in Holland, attempted a very unsubtle propaganda/educational approach to enlist the Dutch to help them with their plans.

An example, fairly early in the occupation, was when the movie theaters showed a movie called "The Eternal Jew." One of the instructors at the school of social work suggested we see it and write a paper on it. We went, a mixed group of Jews and Gentiles. We laughed and made remarks out loud through the whole showing. It was so unbelievably crude and scurrilous, so totally incredible that we left, feeling we had not been influenced, yet the next day one of the

Gentile students said to me: "You know, I hate to admit it, but that movie *did* affect me. For the first time I have a feeling of 'us' and 'they.' I am ashamed to admit this, and am all the more determined to help 'them,' but there is a sense of being 'different.' "

A Process of Gradual Isolation

It was but one of the hundreds of techniques the Germans used to separate Jews from Gentiles, in a country where anti-Semitism had always been minimal. Holland had welcomed the Jews who were expelled from Spain and Portugal in the sixteenth century. Though excluded from some professions, they were never made to live in ghettos, and as the centuries went on, their rights were constantly expanded until there were no barriers left. Socially they were seen differently by different segments of the Dutch community. In artistic and academic circles they were greatly respected and valued. I don't think it is coincidence that a large number of people who decided to do all they could to save Jews were artists, students, and teachers.

The first official action taken was the removal of all Jews from the civilian air-raid patrols. Many non-Jews resigned in protest, but many people took the attitude that not being allowed to serve was not so terrible, and not worth antagonizing the Germans for. This happened in July 1940. There were numerous small measures, each one by itself not seeming significant enough to the majority of people to mount any large scale protest. For instance, the decision to dispense with Jews from Public Service at first was limited to not hiring or promoting Jews, but nothing was said about firing. The first time that I remember that many people had to make an important decision was when all public servants had to sign a statement declaring whether they were Jewish or not. At the time, very few people were willing to recognize the significance of this measure, that this was but one step in the many that would follow, in order to effectively separate the Jews from the non-Jews. Far too many people signed, including some who were later to join the resistance. There were numerous such measures, the end result of which was the virtual isolation of the Jewish population. They had to live in certain prescribed areas, wear yellow stars on their outer clothing (children under six were exempt), could not shop in Gentile stores, could not use any public facilities, transportation, could not go to the movies or theatre, had to obey a curfew, and carry identity cards marked with a large J.

When the Jews were forced to wear the stars, my 12-year-old brother and his friends decided, as many adults did, briefly, to wear stars too. Some of them were severely beaten by the Nazis. My mother forbade my brother to continue to wear it, as I remember it was the cause for serious disagreement between my parents. How old is old enough to take a stand?

What Constitutes "Collaboration"?

Identifying what constituted cooperation, or collaboration with the Nazis; is a very complicated question. Betraying your Jewish neighbors for the monetary reward, joining a branch of the German Army are the obvious and simple forms of collaboration. But when all civil servants were asked to sign a statement whether they were Jewish or not, did that not turn out to be collaboration? Obeying the curfew the Germans imposed? Not acting when you saw transports of Jews being herded to the station? How about the actions of burgomasters and other Dutch government officials?

After physical attacks on Jews in the old Amsterdam Jewish quarter, a mostly working class area, during which the Jews fought back, assisted by many non-Jewish neighbors, the German authorities summoned a very prominent Amsterdam Jew, A. Asscher, and several other leaders in the Jewish community and demanded that they form a council, whose task would be to represent the Jews, and be the liaison between the German authorities and the Jewish community. Asscher and a man called Professor D. Cohen agreed to serve.

Some of the people who were asked to serve refused immediately. Some on principle, recognizing that serving on the council inevitably was, in and of itself, an act of cooperation with the Germans. Others argued long and hard with themselves, their friends and their families. The father of a girl I knew joined, genuinely believing that this form of liaison might be used to the advantage of the Jews.

The Role of the Council

One of the first tasks of the Jewish Council was to publish a Jewish Weekly Newspaper. The existing Jewish papers were forbidden to publish, and the Jewish Weekly carried all the new measures the Germans imposed daily, with editorial comments. The regular Dutch Press was discouraged from printing news of anti-Jewish measures. In numerous ways the work of the Jewish Council helped the Germans accomplish the first steps of their program, the isolation of Holland's Jewish citizens from its Gentile citizens. Still many members and employees of the Council were sincerely convinced that they were working in the best interest of their people. Cooperation? Collaboration?

Eventually, when the mass deporations started, the issue was clearly defined: it was the job of the Jewish Council to fill the quotas for deportation, first to Westerbork, a camp in the North of Holland where the Jews were assembled, and from where they were taken to the extermination camps in Poland and Germany. The council members, their families, and the council's employees and families, were the last to go. Chaos reigned at the Council offices when they had to decide.which of this in-group were "dispensable" and who were not. In the end, of course, even Cohen was sent to Theresienstadt. It is easy to condemn the man, to feel that his behavior was morally reprehensible. He saved his own skin, and that of the members of his immediate family, at the expense of others. But how many would have acted differently in his place?

When the deporations started in 1942, I spent a lot of time talking with Jewish friends about what they should do. It is much easier to deport people who go willingly than to have to use force. So the Germans would announce tht they needed x number of Jews for a transport, make all kinds of promises, "Yes, the work would be hard, but families would be allowed to stay together, etc.," whereas if they did not show up as ordered, they would be rounded up and executed. Again, people needed to believe there was hope; too many believed and went. They sometimes became angry at those of us who really believed that Hitler was out to exterminate the Jewish people, and tried to persuade them not to go willingly, but to *onderduiken*. *Onderduiken*, literally translated, means to "dive under," and many did. Some of the most famous and well-known *onderduikers* were Anne Frank and her family. *Onderduiken* was a risky business, for the people themselves as well as for those who helped them. Holland is a very small, very densely populated country, and there were few places where a family could take in one or more *onderduikers* and be reasonably confident that the neighbors would not find out. Families often had to be split up, which was heartbreaking for all involved, but safer.

Somebody might be willing to take in adults, but babies and children were much more difficult to place.

Making My Own Commitment

On the way to classes one morning I saw a truck outside a Jewish children's home. The children were orphans, ranging in age from infants to about eight years old. The Germans were loading them into a truck. They did not move very fast, were crying and upset. The Germans then just picked them up, by an arm, a leg, the hair, and flung them into the truck. I was sick with rage. As I got off my bike, two women on their way to work tried to stop them, the Germans picked them up and threw them on top of the children. That was when I decided that I would do anything I could to frustrate the execution of "the final solution." Until that time we had helped Jewish friends and acquaintances in whatever way we could, but then we formed a sort of loose organization. What we did changed with the time and the circumstances.

For instance, when the deportations started on the grand scale, there were all sorts of exemptions (at least for while). There was the Palestine stamp, the Calmeyer list, baptized Jews were exempted for a while, Jews working for the Wehrmacht, the Puttkammer list, the Buhler list and others I do not remember. Hans Calmeyer was an interesting man with whom I dealt personally several times. He was the head of the Generalkommissariat for Administration and Justice, and Jews trying to prove they should not have to be considered a full-blooded Jew had to get a statement from him that this was so. He gave everybody he could the benefit of the doubt. The first time I tried to get him to declare that a child I was trying to take care of was baptized, he told me that if I went to the minister of a church in another part of Holland, and it happened that some pages in the registry had been lost, but that the minister did remember baptizing the child, he would give me the desired piece of paper. He was, I believe, the only highly placed German official who was working against the regime as hard as he dared. How it was that he was not found out, or betrayed, I will never know. I personally felt we were wasting our time with all these lists and stamps and certificates. It was a ploy to keep the victims thinking that maybe they had a chance, where in reality most of them were not worth the paper they were written on, and were apt to be revoked and canceled at any time.

Bearing Two Babies in Five Months

I saw *onderduiken* as the most promising avenue, and worked in that area. I worked finding families who were willing to take in *onderduikers*, helping get food, clothing, etc. I remember the first time we had a Jewish newborn baby to take care of. The parents were living with a family in the center of Amsterdam. They had a good hiding place in case of a raid, but the host family was not prepared to take the risk of having the neighbors hear the crying of an infant, when there were only supposed to be the hosts—a middle-aged couple—inhabiting the house. We did not spend too much time pondering the total craziness of the fact that this five or six pounds of humanity would undoubtedly be killed or deported to be killed if it were found. The simple solution was to register it as the illegitimate child of one of us. I had three babies that way during the course of the war, even making the mistake of having two in a five month period, but fortunately nobody checked that one out. The tragedy is that I do not know what happened to two of them. We kept no written lists or records, nothing that could betray them or us. If, and of course it is a big if, the parents did survive and came back to Holland to look for their child, they may never have found it. A whole book could be written about the tragedies of some parents who came back, and whose, two, three, four, five-year-old children had become totally part of the foster family they had been placed with.

Some people had to be placed and replaced many times before a satisfactory situation could be worked out. Frustrating as it was to be turned down again and again, in all fairness it must be said that it was a very important commitment you were asking people to make. First and foremost, they were risking their lives, and those of their families, as least the adult members. In addition, having an *onderduiker* placed tremendous restrictions on the host family. You could never go away, unless you lived in an isolated situation (and there are few of those in Holland), and your guests could never leave the house. You had to be extremely careful who you invited into your house, they might betray you purposely or inadvertently. Imagine the tensions that arise, when you are sharing with an *onderduiker*, when food is very scarce and your own children are hungry.

The Challenges for Host Families

Life is not fair, and though war is a great equalizer, the wealthy who had reserves of food, or the money to buy in the black market, or a garden to grow food, were better off than the average person. Sharing tight quarters with your guests provides more potential for tension than a large house with ample privacy. A Jewish couple, expecting a baby, asked me to find a place for that baby. You can imagine what they went through in making this decision. One of my best sources of addresses was one of my high school teachers. She knew a great many people all over the country and was often able to help. She told me of a couple she knew in Rotterdam, who had four children of their own. I went to see them. They were courteous and angry. They said that Wies (my high school teacher) was really going too far. They were contributing financially to help hide Jews, they were making a certain amount of food available each month, and paying the doctor's bill for plastic surgery for several people, but asking them to take a Jewish child into their home was too much!! I listened to them for a long time, it got to be too late for me to leave (because of the curfew) so I accepted their invitation to spend the night.

The next morning they told me that they had changed their minds. They still did not like the idea, but had talked all night, and felt it was a responsibility they had to shoulder. Hopefully, it would not be for too long a time. We discussed the details. The baby was due to be born in four months. Mrs. M. would pretend to be pregnant, when the baby was born I would bring it to Rotterdam. They would register it as their child. They planned to hire a nursemaid (in addition to the governess they had for their own four children) to take care of this baby. Did I really understand what I was asking them to do? Give their own name—indeed an old highly respected Dutch name—to a Jewish baby?

Three months later I took a prematurely born, sad looking red-headed baby boy to Rotterdam. He was installed on the third floor. I stayed and took care of him for the week it took for the nursemaid they had hired to become available. Mr. and Mrs. M. barely looked at him when we arrived, and during the week I was there, never went upstairs. After that I had no contact with this situation, but about a year later I had to tell Wies that the baby's parents had been caught and deported. Mr. and Mrs. M. ended up keeping him as a member of the family. When I last heard about them, in May or June of 1945, they were talking about whether to tell him about his real origins, or whether it would be better to let him grow up thinking he was their real child.

Compassion in the Moment of Crisis

At about the same time, I took another baby to a farm in the northeast. I arrived in the village after a twelve hour trip by train that should have taken three. But desultory bombings and strafings, failure of equipment, blocked roads and bridges made many trips long and tedious in those days. A man came up to me, and said: "If you are on your way to the Gerritsen's, don't go. They are in trouble." I knew he was telling me they had been caught. The baby was hungry and exhausted, so was I. This was one placement where the guarantee had seemed a certainty, and I just wanted to drop the baby and run. The man clearly wanted no part of me or the baby, and felt he had done his duty by warning me that the family was not available (that they had been betrayed). I must have looked very pathetic because he hesitated, finally said, "Well, why don't you come to my house, you can rest, and maybe we can find some milk for the baby before you go back." He led me to a small house at the end of the village. It was warm, there were his wife and four or five children. They were clearly people of very limited financial circumstances. I fell asleep in my chair. When I woke up, his wife had taken the baby, changed it, fed it, and was telling the children that they should pray for me because I was a sinner, I had had this baby out of wedlock, could not take care of it, and that they were going to keep it. That my punishment was that I would never see my baby again. Walking me back to the station, Mr. D. apologized(!) but said that this story made it possible for them to keep the baby and protect themselves.

There was a little girl, Tinka, who was in hiding with a local physician. We were informed that the Gestapo in Amsterdam had found out about this three year old and had decided she had to be deported. First, the physician agreed that we could take her, but when we went to pick her up, his wife was too scared, they had of course already committed a crime punishable by death, by housing her, but she hoped that if they turned her over, her own children and she and her husband might be spared.

An hour later, very shortly before curfew, Karel and I went back to the house, he engaged the family in conversation at the back door, while I went in through the front door and found Tinka, who fortunately knew me, and came with me without a protest. I understand she is now a singer in East Germany.

I could go on, but these three vignettes may give you an adequate picture of the infinite variety of attitudes we met.

A Decision One Must Live With

In 1943 the half-Jewish wife of a Jewish man, a friend of some close Gentile friends of mine, decided she could not take the strain anymore, and left her husband and three small children, the youngest a week old. I was asked to take care of them until other arrangements could be made. We never made other arrangements, and I stayed with them until the end of the war. The more attached I became to them, the more scared did I become that we would be found out. One night they did come; four Germans, led by a local policeman, a Dutchman, whom I had known for years. They could not find the hiding place, and finally left. Then after we had gone back to bed and tried to sleep, the Dutchman came back, by himself. The only solution at that time, was to kill him, which I did. I have never stopped feeling guilty about that, even though under similar circumstances I would of course do it again. But the feeling is always: There should have been a better way.

Humiliation in Prison

At one point I was arrested and put in jail. This prison experience is the most difficult one to talk about, or even to remember and think about. The objective of the interrogations and accompanying mistreatment (I even now don't want to use the word "torture") was twofold it seemed. They wanted any information they thought I might have about the resistance, names of active members, plans, etc., etc. but sometimes it just seemed that they were amusing themselves with me (and with the other prisoners) to pass the time of day. My parents did not use physical punishment with their children at any age, so that being deliberately hurt by others was a totally new, humiliating and infuriating experience. The attempts to break down my resistence to telling them anything included leaving on a very bright light in the cell for days, leaving me in total darkness for long lengths of time, giving us laxatives (hidden in the food) and nothing to clean up with. Taking the toilet bucket out of the cell and giving only a toothbrush to clean up with. Causing the cells to have extremes of temperature, very hot or very cold. Taking all your clothes. There were others but even now I find it so humiliating to write about, I cannot go on.

They would promise that you would be released, or that you would be given a cup of tea, or an opportunity to shower, if you would only say "Heil Hitler" or give them this or that or the other little piece of information. Sometimes they did give you a privilege like that for no apparent reason, after that it would be even more difficult to hold out. We had established a rule of thumb to resist giving information for 24 hours. During that time anything we knew would be changed, and therefore without value.

I think that what kept me going was pride. I could not have faced myself afterwards if I had "knuckled under." I told myself I was behaving in a way my father would have approved of. I remember thinking often about Christ on the Cross, and that this was a real opportunity to follow Him. I would be letting down my friends, Jews and Gentiles alike, if I gave in. The temptation to give in was always there and was very strong. When I saw my best friend, in passing, we would whisper encouragements to each other. One night they put us in a cell together, and I found out she was using similar techniques to keep her spirits up and not to give in. We did not think we would be released, and speculated about when and which concentration camps we would be sent to. I think now that the decision I made was that they could do anything they chose with me, inflict any indignity, kill me, but they could not make me cooperate. In fact, the thought of being killed had at times its attractions. Surely I would go to Heaven, God would say I had done the right thing and I would have attained the "life hereafter" that my religion promised. I now recognize many of the elements of self-deception, childish magical thinking, omnipotence, grandiosity or what have you, but at the time my value system was pretty simple, pretty straightforwardly black and white, I knew what I had to do and tried to do it. The experience of being completely at the mercy of a torturer is unforgettable. It sets you apart from other people in the world for the rest of your life. The fear never goes away. You live with it, confront it, try to forget it, overcome it, resist it, it does not work. I live on a back road in the hills of Vermont, every time a truck comes down the road at night, I am afraid. I have to get out of bed, reassure myself that it is not stopping at the house.

How Did Fear Affect Decisions

Of course, the fear was there after we were (without any explanation) released. On the one hand the experience strengthened my conviction that the enemy was capable of all imaginable evil, and that the only important thing was to continue to resist with any tools at one's disposal. On the other hand, I wonder how much I was influenced by fear in making decisions. For instance, we would learn that the village I lived in at the time, and where I was solely responsible for three small Jewish children and their father, was to be raided that night. I knew that most of the *onderduikers* and their hosts had been informed, but nobody had contacted one particular house. Do I go out, after curfew, and risk being caught which would have left my charges in a completely vulnerable position? Or am I justified in staying with them? Am I making the decision sensibly and responsibly, or primarily from fear?

One final irony. After our work in the UNNRA operated D.P. camps, my husband started his college education at Harvard in September of 1947. I went and applied for a job with the Jewish Family and Children's Services, having heard that those D.P.s who had decided to come to the U.S. were being assisted by this agency in their adjustment to this country. I was told that the agency's philosophy did not allow the hiring of Gentile workers, so I went to another job. A year later JFCS called, and offered me a position, they did not have enough Jewish social workers who spoke Yiddish!

I did accept the position, and what I remember most is how misunderstood my clients felt by the communities in which they were living. People did not want to know about the horrors they had been through. They felt hurt and insulted at having to work out a budget and the limitations the agency set on the amount of financial support they were to receive.

So, in sum, until 1940 I had lived a very sheltered, protected life. I went to school, played field hockey, went to dances and parties, traveled a lot (with my parents) and was surrounded by many people who liked, loved, and took care of me. My exposure to "evil" was minimal, and I am sure I could not have told you what my "values" were, had you asked me at that time. My way of life, of course, changed drastically after the occupation. The Nazis were evil personified. I have tried to find a good, true answer to why I did what I did, but I am afraid that the truth is simple: I just could not have done anything else. I think I learned about the extremes we are capable of, that there are really no limits to man's inhumanity to man, but also no limits to forces of good we can mobilize. •

An appeal to jewish holocaust survivors

Harold M. Schulweis

From whatever audience we speak to about the Christian rescuers who risked life and limb to protect our hunted people in every country the Nazis occupied, Jewish survivors come forth to offer witness to their heroism. Some tell of being hidden in attics, cellars, stables, open fields; some of being fed and clothed and cared for during their illness; some of being given forged identification papers to escape the predators. The degree of risk, the duration of the rescue, the level of cooperation with neighbors, the number of Jews saved, the motivations of the acts vary—but they are all testimonies of acts of righteousness for people outside the circle of their faith.

Many survivors have lost contact with their rescuers. While some communicate with them, not a few have sought to put that chapter behind them. They fear that to awaken that memory of those days will raise the nightmares they seek to bury. Understandably they seek a moratorium from those traumatic years. Yet all of them seek ways to express their gratitude. The rescuers of these Jews came from people not of the Jewish faith, who chose to act against the common grain of narrow self-interest. The heroism of their acts was not casual or impulsive. They were life and death decisions involving their families and requiring more than a short term commitment.

Tragically, many of these non-Jewish rescuers who survived the war years were not and are not regarded as heroes by their fellow countrymen. On the contrary, they were harassed and vilified as traitors and "Jew-lovers." Herman Graebe's son was taunted by his playmates once the revelation

of his parents' saving of Jews became known. The Polish beggar, Karol Kicinski, bidding goodbye to two Jews he had hidden in place, pleaded with them "Please do not tell I saved you. I fear for my life." The late Philip Friedman, in his pioneering study *Their Brother's Keepers*, reported that 180 Christian families were being persecuted by rightist groups in Bialystock after the war for their generosity to Jews during Hitler years.

Memory must Motivate Gratitude

Today, four decades after the Holocaust, the rescuers live all over the world and in a variety of circumstances. Scattered reports inform us that many are living out their lives unbefriended, alone, in poor health and in dire economic circumstances. We have a moral mandate to lend dignity to the remaining life of these extraordinary human beings who would not join those who found reasons not to help. Jews have a unique stake in this witness. Surviving Jews possess a double memory: one of unspeakable evil and of incredible good. No scale

Facing our world . . .

can balance the two. Who can measure the quality of goodness against that of evil? The evil must be pursued and brought to the bar of justice. But the good must equally be pursued and raised to high honor. Goodness must be rewarded in this world for the sake of the rescuers and the survivors, for their children and our own. Those who protected our family during the years of unspeakable atrocity must be protected by us from poverty and neglect in our times. They must know that they are not alone.

I write to appeal to survivors who know of such men and women to come forth and testify, to tell us where the rescuers may be reached so that we may help them in their waning years. And I appeal to ''parnasim,'' supporters who can help the newly established *Foundation to Sustain the Righteous Christians*, either by financial contribution and/or by serving as friends who will make contact with the rescuers. The tragedy of the Holocaust cannot be reversed. What remains to be done is to raise the sparks of human decency out of the impenetrable darkness. There is an obligation to recognize goodness, not just with rhetoric, but through deeds of loving kindness. The Foundation is an expression of Jewish gratitude to Christians who acted with exceptional courage to save Jewish children and adults from the ravages of Nazi madness. Such human altruism must not be forgotten.

Please write to me, c/o Valley Beth Shalom, 15739 Ventura Boulevard, Encino, CA. 91436; or to Eva Fogelman, Director, c/o CUNY Graduate Center, Social Psychology Department, 33 West 42 St., New York, N.Y. 10036, to tell us of your help. (Contributions are tax-deductible.) ☐

HAROLD M. SCHULWEIS, *Founding Chairman of the Foundation, is rabbi of Valley Beth Shalom Cong. and a* Sh'ma *Contributing Editor.*

EARL L. DACHSLAGER *teaches English at the University of Houston.*

JUDITH MAY, *an historian of Jewish art and a calligrapher working in Stony Brook, N.Y.*

AL LORENZ *did the drawing on page 38.*

4.

Jewish Ethics Today: Challenges and Responses

The question of jewish ethics today

Steven S. Schwarzschild

Every body of law is posited for some specific social organism. The *Code Napoléon* addresses itself primarily to France and its citizens. American law is concerned with the United States and its people. To be sure, every social organism and some of its members enter at some time or other into various relations with other such organisms and some of their members, and, therefore, its body of law must also provide for the manner in which these relations ought to be conducted; but the laws concerning foreign relationships, abroad or at home, will necessarily and properly be a practically subsidiary - however morally significant - part of every body of law.

Mutatis mutandis, halakhah is the body of law for the Jewish polity. In bulk it is, in its social dimension, concerned with the relations of Jews among one another - whether they live in one state, in more than one state, or in none, in voluntary communities or simply as disparate individuals. *Pari passu* this body of law also has its provisions for non-Jews by themselves and especially in their relations with Jews and *vice-versa*. Thus there are "the Noachite laws," provisions for aliens, settlers, converts, etc., rules "for the sake of the paths of peace" *(mipnay darkhay shalom* - which is to be taken literally, as aiming at the highest social good, peace, and not, as it is usually vulgarized, "as a prudential tactic"), "going into the depths of (within) the line of the law," etc. These "international" stipulations, like their analogues in other legal systems, necessarily constitute a quantitatively minor portion of the entirety of *halakhah*. Depending on the conditions of Jewry in any particular period they are paid greater or lesser attention and thus expanded or left in *status quo ante*; this is

jurisprudentially and ethically relatively unimportant. What does matter ultimately, qualitatively, is whether the inter-national legislation (and its appurtenances) are rationally consistent with the domestic legislation and whether both together make for a moral, humane social and individual life.

Are modern jewish legal ethics moral or not?
Now, that there would be occasional, and sometimes even serious, inconsistencies between domestic and international legislation in the *halakhah* (or any other body of law), or at least in its interpretation and application, cannot be surprising in the least. Individual statutes and even basic constitutional provisions come into conflict with one another constantly. That is one, perhaps the most important, reason that we have courts, all the way up to a court of final appeal and interpretation, whose task it is to adjudicate between the conflicting demands not so much of different subjects of the law as of the laws themselves and to arrive at an unified, consistent, and sociomorally desirable legal system. The question is only how good, in terms of both consistency and morality, the developing system of law turns out to be.

It is certainly the case that the vast accumulated literature of Jewish ethics and law can be and often has been interpreted in a selectively restrictive and ethically ultimately self-contradictory fashion. But the opposite, expansive, philosophically and ethically ultimately convincing option is also always open - and in the end it commends itself more.

Some very few, learned, profound, and sensitive observer-analysts of Jewish law and ethics have tried for some time to raise warnings about what is happening on this score in our era. Thus the late Prof. Leon Roth wrote about "Moralization and Demoralization in Jewish Ethics" (*Judaism,* XI/4, Fall 1962) and the recently deceased Prof. Samuel Hugo Bergman about "Expansion and Contraction in Jewish Ethics" (in *The Quality of Faith*, Jerusalem' World Zionist Organization, 1970). Of the issue that they raised and which their titles outline clearly Bergman rightly said that it is "one of the most burning issues of our life." It is the issue of how, in the present era, the question of the consistency and morality of the *halakhah* and its implied ethic with respect to both Jews and non-Jews is being handled, - and both Roth and Bergman warn that in fact the ethic of the *halakhah* is increasingly being "demoralized" or "contracted."

In this context *Modern Jewish Ethics - Theory and Practice*, ed. Marvin Fox, Ohio State University Press, 1975 (but for the editor's introduction, papers and discussions at the July 1972 meeting of the Institute for Judaism and Contemporary Thought in Israel) becomes interesting. Precisely the question of contemporary Jewish moralizaiton or demoralization of Jewish (legal) ethics is raised very sharply.

One view: law demands more than letter of the law
In a contribution that is already gaining fame (1) "Does Jewish Tradition Recognize an Ethic Independent of Halakha?" Rabbi Aharon Lichtenstein, *rosh yeshivah* of Yeshivat Har Zion in Israel, with his acknowledged credentials of traditional as well as modern Jewish learning, makes essentially one point — that, according to Jewish law, to do no more than what the letter of the law requires is itself a violation of this law (i.e. "the quality of Sodom" (2) and that, to the contrary, to go "within the line of the law" (*middat chassidut* - "the quality of [selfless] righteousness") "is part of the fabric of Halakha." The interested reader should consider the full evidence and analysis as presented in this study. R. Lichtenstein's conclusion is this: "What I reject emphatically is the position that, on the one hand, defines the function and scope of Halakha in terms of the latitude implicit in current usage and yet identifies its content with the more restricted sense of the term (*halakhah*). The resulting equation of duty and *din* (statute) and the designation of supralegal conduct as purely optional or pietistic is a disservice to Halakha and ethics alike."

Despite the cogent case that he makes, R. Lichtenstein will doubtless continue to be contradicted on the usual allegedly logical ground that a supra-legal principle, such as equity, cannot, by definition, be part-and-parcel of the law. (3) But this is, despite its surface plausibility, a fallacious argument. In the first place, *lifnim mishurat hadin* is "within," not, as the usual rendering has it, "beyond" "the line of the law"; i.e., the very term indicates that we are here dealing with a dynamic function that operates within the system. In the second place, Hermann Cohen proved long ago and in a significantly different connection (*Ethik des reinen Willens*, Berlin 1904, pp. 585-589) that equity is not a factor additional to the *jus strictum* but a judgment-procedure which makes sure that the application of the law in each individual case is proper (i.e. moral); thus all of the law, statutes as well as procedures, operationalizes ethical values (*'aggadah*).

Another: law is limited, a higher ethic may exist
A contribution by Prof. Ernst Akiba Simon raises serious doubts that R. Lichtenstein's meta-halakhic ethics conforms to the sources of Tradition. In fact, the article "The Neighbor (Re'a) Whom We Shall Love" comes to the conclusion that the neighbor whom we ought to love must, according to the *halakhah*, be a Jew. Simon is, of course, deeply pained by and morally unwilling to accept this. Therefore, he appeals to "a Jewish ethic that is external to the Halakha" and tells the story of Bertha Pappenheim (incidentally, Freud's famous patient "Miss O. [3a] who, when the rabbis of Frankfurt couldn't overcome the problem of *'iagunot* (deserted wives) cried out to them: "Gentlemen, when the capitalist economy developed to the point where it was no longer possible to observe the Torah's explicit prohibition against lending money for interest your predecessors managed to find within the halakha an acceptable way to circumvent the law. From your failure to act now, I can only conclude that halakha, as you interpret it, places higher value on economic concerns than on the human needs and rights of these pathetic and unfortunate women."

Studies in ethics: no. two

If Prof. Simon's reading of the classic sources of Judaism is correct, then, of course, his appeal to an higher Jewish ethic than the *halakhah* is imperative. If, in addition, it can be shown, as would appear to be the case, that the nature of classic Judaism rules out the possibility of "an higher Jewish ethic," then anyone committed to a truly human, non-chauvinistic morality will feel compelled to turn his back - however painful this may be - on that classical Judaism. And if, furthermore, the non-classical, non-standard, "modernized" forms of Judaism present themselves, as they certainly on the whole do in our epoch, as at least as chauvinistic as Simon understands the classical form to be, then there is only one and even more drastic - and correspondingly more painful - course left open to such a person. Leo Strauss formulated this quandary with great sensitivity in a lecture which he originally gave in Jerusalem (4): "A mother loves her child because he is her own . . . But she also loves the good. All human love is subject to the law that it be both love of one's own and love of the good, and there is necessarily a tension between one's own and the good, a tension which may well lead to a break, be it only the breaking of a heart . . . The practical meaning of this idealism is that the good is of higher dignity than one's own . . . The Jewish equivalent of this relation might be said to be the relation between the Torah and Israel."

Evidence for judaism's universalist ethical stance

The present writer, to whom Ernst Simon is a lifelong teacher (while most of the other writers in *Modern Jewish Ethics* are his contemporaries and friends), must then want to hold that his teacher is mistaken.

One can, to begin with, wonder what would result if R. Lichtenstein's present thesis were confronted with Prof. Simon's. Unfortunately this confrontation does not take place within the pages of this book.

The evidence from beyond the confines of the book would be too massive and complex to be manageable here. I can cite and consider only two or three *loci classici*. One is the Rabbinic principle (5) that "the honor/dignity of all human beings (*habriyot* - not only Jews) overrides every prohibition (the weightier of the two basic types of injunctions) in the Torah." What makes this principle the graver and the more relevant to our present concern is that it is derived (Rashi etc.) from *Deut.* 22:4 (and 23:8): "If you see the ox of your brother (!) fall by the way you shall

not hide yourself" - i.e. one must not be indifferent to other people's misfortunes. The *Gemara* itself in *Meg.* 3b applies the term "brother" to all human beings. And *Tosfot ad locum* in turn goes out of its way to generalize from the specific issue being treated, the burial of unattended corpses of special Jewish concern, to "all the dead in the world." (6)

Maimonides, in his legal *Code*, "Laws of Sabbatical and Jubilee Years," 13:12f. - in a striking and authoritative place, formulates the Jewish doctrine of the universality of human brother-hood on the highest spiritual level in unsurpassable terms: "Every single man among all creatures in the world" (*kol ish ve'ish mikol ba'ay 'olam* - an extraordinary and memorable phrase) is the equal of the Levite tribe, set apart (distinguished) for the whole-hearted service of God, if he, too, "is inspired by the spirit and convinced by knowledge . . . to walk straight as God has made him and if he has broken off his neck the yoke of human calculativeness (cp. *Ecc.* 7:29) . . ." Every such human being - also Gentiles - "is sanctified as the Holy of Holies, and God will be his portion and his inheritance forever and ever . . ."

A case where morality depends on interpretation

Simon and Lichtenstein both treat one important and specific issue which casts a full light on the nature of the texts with which we are concerned and on the options for their utilization. Both adduce *Mekhilta, "mishpatim,"* (4) Prof. Simon regretfully infers from it (pp. 41ff.) that the Jewish murder of a Gentile is treated under Jewish law in a fashion that "may be less severe (than) and certainly not (so) immediate" as that of a Jew, while R. Lichtenstein clearly holds (p. 65) - I should have thought correctly - that "punishment by God" (the penalty stipulated for the former case) is, for religious people, emphatically a more severe condemnation than punishment by a merely human court (the penalty stipulated for the latter case). The Me'iri, for example, resolves the problem of "the perjured witnesses" in capital cases by precisely this consideration. (7) Which of the two juridical authorities comes into force, the human court or God, is then only a *de facto* question of the sovereignty that happens to be involved.

These two ways of reading the same text are by no means necessarily in conflict with one another. The question is only which element one wants to put the greater emphasis on and therefore, to use preferably for the purposes of ethics and legal morality.

How the "universalistic" thrust can be advanced is also cogently illustrated by a profound strain in the classical literature which condemns even Moses in the strongest possible terms for his act of killing a non-Jew (*Ex.* 2:11f.). This episode is paradigmatic not only because the status of Moses in Judaism is beyond cavil but also because his victim was a brutal taskmaster. Even so, Moses is condemned for his defensive deed by God Himself, and the halakhically significant point is made that he instituted his "cities of refuge" so that he himself could save himself there, like other unwitting murderers, from the death-penalty which would otherwise have devolved on him. (8)

The most difficult issue: human survival

The most important ethico-legal text that crops up over and over again in *Modern Jewish Ethics* and in all similar discussions is *Baba Metzia'* 62a - whether R. Akiba is right that if two men have only enough water to see one of them out of the desert, then "I am nearest to myself," or whether ben-Petura is right that both should share the same risk of death. Abner Weiss, of the Society for Justice, Ethics, and Morals of South Africa and Israel, lines up with Achad Ha'am and his late English protagonist Sir Leon Simon on the side of R. Akiba. So does Harold Fisch, of Bar-Ilan University and the Whole Land of Israel Movement. Fisch even goes so far in arguing against Ernst Simon's ethics as to impute a meaning to the term "*chessed*" ("grace"), i.e. "reciprocal obligation," entirely contrary to its historic use (9); he would use "love" as Erich Fromm condemns Freud for thinking of it - as a pie in the capitalist economy of scarcity that can be divided into only a limited number of slices. And this is then commonly declared to be the normative, authoritative halakhic standard. Somewhere in the middle of the spectrum Jakob Petuchowski, of Hebrew Union College - Jewish Institute of Religion, and Nachum Rabinovitch, of Jews' College in England, open the door increasingly wider to the option of voluntarily accepting the more altruistic ethic of ben-Petura. Lichtenstein and Simon are joined eloquently by Emmanuel Levinas and Rabbi Louis Jacobs (quoted at length by Petuchowski) in tending to identify normative Jewish ethics with ben-Petura's posture.

In fact the question of *B.M.* 62a needs to be narrowed down. The Maharsha points up that the proprietary status of the water at issue plays a decisive role. (10) If both men own it together then R. Akiba would agree with ben-Petura: one of them usurping it for himself would violate the fundamental rule that noone's blood is redder than another's (*Yoma* 2:2, *Pes.* 25b) and make himself divinely deserving of death. (11) R. Akiba's decision then applies only where one of the two men either owns the water at issue or takes prior physical possession of it, *de facto* (12) But this does not really make sense: regardless of the proprietary question, the equality of all human blood still obtains, and as for physical possession - R. Akiba's view boils down to an ultimate appeal to sheer physical superiority, which is scarcely and answer to a juridico-ethical question. Maharam Schiff, then, though in fact accepting R. Akiba's view, admits that rationally ben-Petura's should prevail. Furthermore, all would presumably have to follow ben-Petura if they cannot refute R. Lichtenstein's thesis that to act beyond the narrowest requirements of the law is itself a normative requirement of the *halakhah*.

Modern anti-semitism and modern jewish ethics

What may we conclude then at this point of our considerations? It turns out to be by no means a settled matter that Jewish ethics are essentially what Max

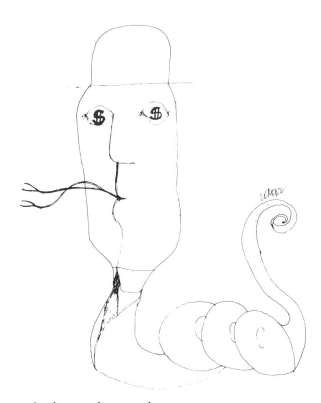

Studies in ethics: no. three

43

Weber called "*Binnenethik*.. (intra-tribal ethics); the contrary can be convincingly demonstrated. Therefore, a universalist in ethics need not dissociate himself from Jewish ethics, - though, as we are about to see more fully, it is certainly the case that in order to overcome powerful current tendencies in the restrictive direction the most energetic efforts, intellectual and practical, must be made.

The allegation that Jewish law and ethics are *Binnenethik* and that toward non-Jews Judaism prescribes a purely exploitative attitude has always been one of the chief stocks in trade of traditional antisemitism. The Christian Middle Ages were full of it, and so is modern antisemitism. How these banked fires would be stoked if one yielded to the temptation to translate and thus make accessible to a public not privy to halakhic language and dialectics some of the more chauvinistic exercises published in certain rabbinic and Zionist publications! The consequences could be disastrous. Another historical reminder may then not be amiss.

As part of the rise of the new racist-ethnic antisemitism in Germany and elsewhere in the 1870's and 1880's, Prof. August Rohling published his notorious *Der Talmudjude* in 1871. Its main thesis was that "Jews are permitted by their religion to cause, secretly or overtly, non-Jews to perish physically and morally." This triggered off a wave of arguments, books, political controversies, and court trials for decades thereafter. One of the chief Jewish scholarly and ethical by-products was Joseph S. Bloch's *Israel und die Voelker nach juedischer Lehre*, Berlin/Vienna 1922. (Its publication so much later and its English translation in 1927 by the editor of the *American Jewish Year Book* occurred in the wake of the antisemitic campaign of Henry Ford Sr., in which Rohling was resuscitated.) All of the issues broached in our present discussion were treated in its heavy bulk: chapt. 8, "Sacredness of Human Life," chapt. 19, "The Commandment to Love our Fellow-Men," etc. The essential affirmation of Bloch's book is, of course, that Judaism's authoritative ethos is universalistic and humanistic. And it is no historical coincidence that during the same years before and after 1900 the great Rabbi Elie Benamozegh published his studies on Jewish cosmopolitan ethics, every sentence of which gives passionate lie to the new chauvinism which is spreading so widely in our days.

We cannot agree to jewish chauvinism
One of the legal by-products of the Rohling episode

was a trial in Marburg, Germany in 1888, in which the question was raised before the court "whether the Law of Moses is applicable only as among Jews, that it is not applicable to Goyim, and that the latter may be robbed and deceived." Prof. de Lagarde of Goettingen (14) argued as an expert in the affirmative and Prof. Hermann Cohen of Marburg in the negative. Throughout the rest of his life Cohen had to come back to this question over and over again, not only for philosophical and ethical reasons but also in order to defend Jewry against recurring spiritual and physical attacks. As late as during World War I and shortly before his death he had to respond to the famous Protestant Bible scholar Rudolf Kittel on this score. And when Martin Buber re-issued Cohen's "Four Treatises about the Relation between Man and Man according to the Teachings of Judaism" in Berlin in 1935 (Schocken Popular Library, number 20) he stated clearly what was at stake: "It seems important to me to have this man give this testimony about this subject in this hour."

Are we to say that these men, and many others like them throughout the millenia of Jewish defenselessness, lied, or that they totally misunderstood the Judaism to which they devoted their lives, their work, and their very deaths? Are we prepared to stick with the presently ascendant Jewish ethic of chauvinistic self-service, even if or when we may some day, if not today, stand in need of moral protection at the hands of others? In 1935, in the heart of Nazi Germany, the editor of Cohen's essays on Jewish morality toward non-Jews wrote that "vulgarian antisemitism has, then and now, accused Judaism of applying its ethico-humane principles only to Jews and of commending immoral conduct toward non-Jews." Are Jews who today put forward such a thesis any the less vulgarian? (Kant had a telling phrase for this: "ethnicismus brutus") And can they expect anything but egoistic reciprocity in the future?

What about immoral acts by the israeli military?
We have almost imperceptibly moved from theoretical to political questions. This is inevitable. Also the subtitle of the book under discussion is, after all, "Theory and Practice." Its last section deals with "the contemporary situation" — which, not surprisingly, turns out to mean the State of Israel. Zvi Yaron, of the Jewish Agency, puts it quite correctly: "Israel has by now become a crucial factor in the considerations of Diaspora Jews in their thinking on the contemporary Judaism-ethics issue." And the chief question that is

here raised is military ethics, under the entrenched phrase "the purity of arms."

There is surely something frighteningly Prussian about the very phrase "the purity of arms." I cannot here unpack its very terminological implications or its historical parallels and consequences. In any case, the "doves," in this case Me'ir Pa'il, favor it. Although Pa'il reports (p. 216) that "all the quotations (cited in his article) indicate that Jewish Israeli soldiers are making their peace with the perpetration of inhumane acts towards the Arab enemy and civilian population, justifying it as an extreme requirement of national defense," also he, as a matter of fact, puts an apologetically good face on the facts. The "hawks" at best cast doubts on or even oppose the notion of "the purity of arms." Thus Milton Himmelfarb, of *Commentary* magazine, in a comment filled with the "*golus*-mentality" of servility before the State, says: "To sacrifice even survival to exaggerated moralistic sentimentality borders on idiocy." (How the Right-wingers are permitted prejudicial language!)

Some jews really say, one may kill the goyim
Since the words here cited were used, the 1973 War has occurred, and much further deterioration has set in. One of the consequences of that war was a booklet put out by the Central Command Headquarters/ Israeli Army Chaplaincy and authored by Abraham Avidan (Zamel), military rabbi of the Command, under the title *After the War: Chapters of Meditation, Rule, and Research.* One of its highlights is the rabbi's thesis that ". . . insofar as the killing of civilians is performed against the background of war, one should not, according to religious law, trust a Gentile . . . 'The best of the Gentiles you should kill.' . . ." It took an outraged article in the Mapam newspaper to have the booklet withdrawn by the army, but no principled refutation of its barbarism has been put forward, and insofar as any notice was taken of this occurrence in Jewish publications in this country at all, *tu quoque* evasions were used to muddy the waters. (*Cf.* Nathan Suesskind, "Tov Sheba-Goyim . . .," *C.C.A.R. Journal,* Spring 1976, pp. 28f. and n. 2) [14a] Whatever its administrative fate, the booklet reveals the mind-set of some of the more sophisticated religious and military personages; one can imagine, if one doesn't know, its counterpart on cruder levels of culture. Thus the question is really not one of "purity of arms" (whatever that may mean) but of the socio-political conditions which

make for or against purity of minds and morals. Lest it be thought that these basic problems arise only within a Jewish polity, I want to remind ourselves — without being able to enter into this phase of things — that the moral traffic among Jews is, of course, bilateral and multilateral. Bank affairs, businessmen in high commercial, political, and even religious places, not to speak of ideologists and propagandists, indeed even organized crime, exercise their power here and there — in local affairs, in national, foreign, and international channels.

Jewish self-interest must not destroy jewish ethics
The fact is that people who feel bound by ben-Petura or *middat chassidut* have, or logically should have, the most serious problems with contemporary Jewish institutionalized behavior and with the rationale offered for it. What is cause and what is effect in this syndrome could itself be debated: does one justify this Jewish behavior because one holds to the validity of ultimate self-interest, or does one adhere to the principle of the ultimacy of self-interest because one

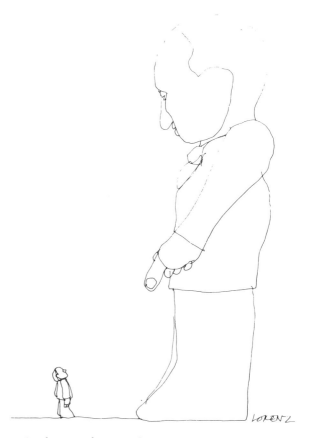

Studies in ethics: no. four

wants to justify this behavior? (We are not now raising the question whether this behavior does in fact serve real self-interest.)

When one surveys the historical and literary facts one conclusion emerges quite clearly — and not to one's surprise: the tendency to "moralize" Jewish legal ethics predominates in periods when Jews have relatively little worldly self-interest to defend and when a theory of selfless, universal morality is in fact to their interest (*pace* Nietzsche); on the other hand, when and where they do have a wordly stake — position, money, a state, etc. — then they tend to "demoralize" it and to use it to justify their self-interested behavior. This is only human, all too human. One may ask, however, whether Jewish law and ethics are supposed to be so human. Or are they not supposed to be "divine," absolute? Either way, can something be ethical if it is parochial or moral if it is egotistical?

One may also point to the fact that even in times of relative Jewish well-being there has always been at least a small minority — moralists, 'amcha, rabbis, not to speak of prophets — who proclaimed and practiced absolute, universal moral standards as over against narrowly conceived Jewish self-interest. Above all, it is simply a fact that these minorities and the ages of worldly Jewish helplessness defined, in the Talmud and its extrapolations, and for modern times the 18th and 19th centuries of Western Jewish apologetics, the nature of classical Judaism. This is why our evidence tends to come from such sources. And if a Leon Roth, say, then has to hear himself excoriated as a "*golus*-Jew" one may have to draw the consequences.

There is yet a final aspect to this problematic, which is very immediate, practical, and — let us be frank about it — extremely frightening. The boastful affirmation of the legitimacy of self-interest can, of course, easily be turned against one by someone else's self-interest. And Jewish self-interest does not, in the long run, stack up very favorably against the many other and more powerful self-interests in the world. As Rabbi J. B. Soloveitchik puts it in distinguishing the legitimacy ("sanctity") of Joshua's conquest of Palestine from that of Ezra's occupation: "that which results from the force of conquest is annulled by the force of another's conquest." (15) The validity of historic Jewish experience (as much as and more than that of others) and of its theoretical, ethical ideologization is surely undiminished — to say the least — by the events of the 20th century. All who tamper with it tamper with the very existence of the Jewish people.

The question of Jewish ethics today is the perennial question: is it to be *imitatio Dei* or individual and collective *sacro egoismo?*

Polarity in jewish ethics

Jacob B. Agus

The discussion of Jewish ethics, launched by Steven Schwarzschild (*Sh'ma*, 7/124), is a timely reminder of the need to clarify the contemporary relevance of the fundamental principles of Judaism. The fact that some of the participants in this symposium responded in tones of bitterness and belligerence indicates that a live nerve was touched. While all the discussants refer constantly to the Halachah and the "sacred tradition," they are clearly aware that they are dealing with the central issues of our time, not simply with ancient texts.

May I comment on the major points raised in this discussion:

One, the Jewish tradition contains some passages which restrict the range of moral obligation to the Jewish community as well as maxims which extend it to all men. Neither set of instructions can be disregarded in any discussion of Jewish ethics. To disregard the high principles of humanity is to remove the heart and mind of Judaism; to ignore such passages as *tov shebagoyim* ("the best of the gentiles should be murdered") and *omad vehifkir mamonom leyisroel* ("make his money available to any taker") and to pretend that they do not exist is to turn a blind eye to their potential harm, as the pamphlet by the Israeli chaplain, Rabbi Abraham Avidon, demonstrates. The many disclaimers that the term *goy,* and the terms supplied by medieval censors, do not refer to the Gentiles of our day are clouded by ambiguities and qualifications, except in the case of Meiri (*Avodah Zara* 2a, *Tosefot*). Jewish ethics is a broad spectrum of principles, not a sharply defined viewpoint. I was recently reminded of the point raised by Prof. Leon Roth in the article to which Schwarzschild refers. In keeping with the trend to emphasize Jewish "roots," a Jewish-sponsored hospital in a large city displayed in large Hebrew letters the Mishnaic saying — *"kol hamekayem nefesh ahat* meyisroel *ke-ilu kiyaim olam moleh."* (Anyone who saves one soul *of Israel,* it is as if he has saved an entire world.) The Jewish Chaplain of that hospital selected that statement simply because it is commonly known, translating it as if the restrictive word, *meyisroel,* were not there. Its occurrence in the printed version of the Babylonian Talmud was to him sufficient authority. The hospital administrators consented to remove the word, *meyisroel,* when it was pointed out to them that the Jerusalem Talmud and Maimonides offered the humanistic version of this saying. And the Hebrew inscription must be right, as well as its English translation.

Halachah not the final word in judaism

That some unethical and even ugly passages occur in the Talmud and Midrash was recognized in the early Middle Ages by Rashi and Judah Halevi and in modern times by such scholars as Rabbi Nahman Krochmal. (An interesting little book which defends this thesis from the Orthodox viewpoint and cites many authorities is Chayim Bloch's, *Veda mah shetashiv,* N.Y. 1962.)

On the other hand, no one can rightly question that beautiful and noble statements of the ethical impulse predominate in our tradition.

The priority of "the love of the good" over "the love of one's own" in Leo Straus' terms, is already affirmed in Deuteronomy 33:9 — a passage which is reflected in the Gospels (Mark 3:31-34, Mt. 12:46 — 50, Lk. 8:19-21).

Two, the Jewish tradition, taken as a whole, is far more than *Halachah.* Aside from Lichenstein's claim that the Law itself requires the dimension of *lifnim mishurat hadin* (within the line of the law), there is the whole body of biblical and Aggadic exhortations, ranging ahead of the Law. In fact, in modern times and for most modern religious Jews, *Aggadah* is more normative than *Halachah.* And *Aggadah* includes the entire range of Jewish philosophy and ethical teaching from Philo to the great philosophers of our own day. Our revered teacher and friend, Prof. Abraham J. Heschel, used to inveigh against so called "pan-halachism," the attempt to confine the whole of Judaism and Jewish experience within "the four ells of Halachah."

It has been said that the Septuagint translation of Torah as *nomos,* law, was a source of the gravest misunderstanding of Judaism, as is clearly evident in the letters of Paul. Torah is teaching; it contains laws and principles; laws become obsolete, but principles remain valid at all times. All the 613 Commandments — how few apply in our lives — are intended to train us in the love and fear of God. (Maimonides, *Guide of the Perplexed,* III, 52.) Consider Heschel's summation of the Kotzker's teaching — "a *mizvah* can become idolatry." *(Kotsk,* vol. II, p. 255).

Shared destiny lets us speak out on israel

In many areas, including relations to non-Jews, the process of *Halachah*-legislation was cut short at the time of a virtual civil war between Jews and Gentiles on the eve of The Great War (65-70c.e.) against Rome, when the Eighteen Decrees were issued. It took the initiative of an exceptional figure of authority, the younger Rabbi Judah the Patriarch, to rescind the prohibition against "Gentile oil." But even he could not go as far as he wanted. (*Avoda Zara* 37a. It is R. Yehudah Nesia, grandson of the first R. Yehudah the Patriarch. The pernicious consequence of the Halachah's distinction between the killing of a Jew and a non-Jew is illustrated in paragraph 866 of *Sefer Hasidim,* though that book is generally humanistic.)

Three, the establishment of the state of Israel cannot but lead to the emergence of new ethical problems, involving the role of government and limits on the use of power. Can one argue that American Jewish thinkers should not react to moral issues in the life of Israel? Or should they sanction, sight unseen, whatever it is that happens in Israel? Or should they employ one measure for the actions of Israeli authorities and another for all other governments? It is precisely because we, Jews, are one family that we take pride in each other's achievements and agonize over each other's failures.

If it is morally right for President Carter to call attention to the violation of human rights in the Soviet Union, because we share in the destiny and character of the society of mankind, do not we, American Jews, have the moral right and obligation, to voice our concerns regarding ethical issues in the life of Israel, because we share in the character and destiny of world Jewry?

Born and raised in Germany, Schwarzschild is naturally irritated by the Prussian sounding phrase, "purity of arms," though its intent is beyond reproach. I do not think that in Israel today there is an imminent danger of glorifying war and "the right of conquest." Our historic experience cannot be easily set aside. We recall the words of the *Mishnah,* which speaks of weapons "as a disgrace for us." (*Mishnah Shabbat* 6,4.)

Political response to ethics is out of place

Four, I share Wyschogrod's feeling that we must not assume we know the consequences of our choices in social-political affairs. The religious feeling of humble dependence is an intrinsic part of our encounter with our Creator. It serves to deter us from yielding to the fascination of "the idols of the market-place." We seek to restrain all we can influence from yielding to the lure of the preachers of futurist utopias, be they of the proletarian, racist, or technocratic variety.

But, then, how can philosophical skepticism become a stepping stone to a legalistic fundamentalism? "I need the Law to tell me . . ." he writes.

If he were to substitute the term "Judaism," the totality of Jewish teaching, for "the Law," the problematic character of what he is told to do would be evident. I respect the deep awareness of the unity of Israel's faith and destiny on the part of some of the respondents. But on what basis is this unity to be maintained? Do the needs or interests of the people determine the character of the faith? Or do the principles of faith determine the goals and policies of the people? Shall the ideal of a "holy people" be degraded to the level of "sanctified ethnicism," which is the primitive religion of the majority of the human race? Fortunately, the issues confronting us are not so stark in nature. Yet, many a colleague prefers the categories of politics to those of ethics. Let us recall that we can tell right from wrong far more surely than we can foretell the course of future events.

Fifth, to judge from some of the comments, Kant's categorical imperative is, strangely enough, anti-Jewish. Kant's views of Judaism were indeed unfair; he assumed that all of Judaism was nothing but "legislation," or *Halachah,* but this formulation of the basic law of ethics is true to one phase of Judaism, its quest of justice, as is evident in Hillel's dictum, "*mah di aloch soni . . .*" (what is hateful to you, do not do to your fellow man).

The other pole of Judaism is the quest of the "nearness of God," or "imitatio dei."

Samuelson points out that "commitment to one's own group takes precedence" over the categorical imperative. As a general rule, this principle is simply unethical. On the other hand, human rights in general are translated into specific legal obligations within states. Kant did not deny that we enter into a "social contract" with other citizens of the same state, assuming a specific pattern of duties and rights. He projected a global society of states. He assumed that states too "would act so that their action might serve as a standard of action for all states." What is "un-Jewish" about Kant's ethic and his vision of the future?

Israel has more to lose than arabs do

Samuelson's example of Jews presumably favoring each other in business is ill-chosen. What does he think of the latest project, of American antisemites, the movement to print Yellow Pages of "born again Christians," that they might favor each other in business?

I concur with the general thesis that the categorical imperative cannot be applied to groups indiscriminately; if one group's life is at stake, while its opponents stand to lose only matters of convenience, the Kantian equivalence does not apply. This is true in the case of the Israel-Arab dispute, where the people of Israel stand to lose their very life and the Jews of the world their one state, while the Palestinian Arabs stand to lose only political rights, as distinct from civic rights, in the areas presently occupied by Israeli forces. The case for Israel does not require either the repudiation of "universalism" or the dubious support of a mystical ethic exceptionalism. And the best way of reinforcing the bonds of unity between Israel and the Diaspora is to foster the spirit of critical inquiry in the light of ethical ideals.

For we are one family, a family of adults, brothers and sisters, cousins and *mehutanim* (in-laws), and relations of all sorts, scattered in different countries and thinking in different idioms, united only by a tradition, of which God is the Father and "Keneset Yisroel" is the Mother. (*Berachot* 31b.) And in this tradition ethical criticism is the one sure bond between God and man.

Within the spectrum of Judaism there is some support for the two opposite maxims — God seeks that which is right, and whatever God ordains is right. The rationalist and the mystic will choose the aspect of the tradition that favors their respective type of piety — hopefully, without derogating from the right of others to do likewise. □

Caring for disabled: halachic dilemmas
Yonah N. Fortner

Case One: Tefilin

It is axiomatic with all observant Jews that all males, having been *bar mitzvah*, are obliged to lay *tefilin* every day. I had taken a group of physically disabled young people to a community event. To my surprise, I saw a tall, bearded person, wearing the garb of a Hasidic seminarian, in earnest conversation with one of my friends. The conversation went something like this: Hasid: Do you lay *tefilin?* Friend: No, of course not. Hasid: Well, you certainly should. Friend: No way. How could I possibly put them on? Hasid: Don't you have someone who could put them on for you? Well, if I'm here to help you now, will you try?

The next thing I heard, was a loud cry for help. The leather thongs of the *shel rosh* (headpiece) had become entangled in the spokes of the wheelchair. My spastic friend, in trying to free the thongs, involved his fingers in the process. My hasidic visitor looked on as if I were the M— ha-M—, (angel of death) as I somewhat brusquely separated the thong from its housing in the phylactery. He informed me that the *tefilin* were thereby rendered unclean, while I, still freeing fingers from spokes, suggested he purchase a copy of the *Shulchan Aruch.*

SOLUTIONS. As yet, I have none, but this question is bound up with the larger one of worship services for the disabled. The religious practices of severely disabled persons are, like everything else about their lives, limited by a variety of imponderables, including stamina, attention span, diminished acuity as a result of medication, anomalies in communication skills, lack of previous opportunities for socialization of any kind, (including any previous experience with formal worship services), and fear of what others will say if they fail to "do it right."

Case Two: Shabbat

It is a few years after the end of World War II. We are on the third floor of a large Orthodox seminary in Brooklyn. It is the second day of Passover, which also happens to fall on the Sabbath. It is the end of *Musaf*, (afternoon service) and people are beginning to move from the study hall toward the stairs. Present was a Jewish League of Nations, including a large number of graduates from Volozhin, Pressburg and Skolni, three Hasidic dynasties including forty boys from Bobover, and contingents of rabbis speaking Rumanian, Spanish and Arabic.

At this point, a young lad sallies forth from the study hall, and grasps the rail, intending to start down the stairs. He tries to transfer his spare crutch from his right hand to his left. Instead, he manages to lose both. They go clattering down the first staircase, and, bouncing off the walls make their way almost to the first floor before stopping. The young man, not knowing what conduct most befits his situation, sits down on the stairs and begins to cry. *"Ni que musaf, ni que pesah"*, he mutters to himself. *"Hubiera estado mejor en Toledo."*

DIFFICULTY. Volozhin and Pressburg opine that the crutches, while not prohibited for the disabled user who owns them, are definitely off-limits to any able-bodied person who might wish to return them to the boy. "After all," they said, "he's in no danger. We'll give him his dinner in the study hall and bring the crutches up after *havdalah.*" Their leader determined that, although they could not return the crutches, they could in fact kick them off the stairs, so that people would not fall over them in the meantime.

The *Sephardim* decided that there was in all this somewhere an affront to their national honor, especially as the young man spoke such fine Spanish. For the Hasidim, however, it was three hundred years of *misnaged* (opposition) legalism all summed up in one sublime moment of indifference and evident insensitivity to the claims of humanity. "If the Talmud forbids us to taunt the lame and the impaired," they held, "so much more does it forbid us to celebrate the holiday while this young man sits crying on the stairs." And, with this, the youngest of the Bobovers, being the most nimble and the first to reach the crutches, picked them firmly in his grip and brought them to the third floor.

DIFFICULTIES. It is true that the young man's life was not threatened, and that, except in the special circumstances described, the possession, conveyance or utilization of the crutches would, indeed, have constituted a violation of the Sabbath.

More subtle are problems that arise when a disabled person using a wheelchair or crutches requires assistance on the Sabbath. An emphysema victim whose respirator has malfunctioned, asks a

Jew to operate the manual bellows while he awaits assistance. A non-Jewish person in a wheelchair finds himself hanging perilously from an electric lift gate. He asks a Jewish passerby to operate the over-ride switch that will permit him to lower himself to the ground and to safety. The passerby, aware that he is only a block away from the *shul* in which he serves as a committee member of some importance, declines to assist. The lift gives way and the disabled person is seriously injured.

Question: Can we blame an observant Jew for seeking to avoid breaking the Sabbath? After all, it would take some previous familiarity with electric lift-gates to realize that the young man really was in imminent danger— that there was, in fact, no time to go in search of a non-Jew to effect the rescue.

Truth to tell, there are so many *shailes*, (questions) in this world, and Elijah is nowhere in sight!

Case Three: Prolonged Fasting

A disabled veteran freed himself from the creche-like security of a local spinal injury facility to seek his fortune as a business management student. At our invitation, he came to hear the *Kol Nidrei* at a nearby Hillel facility which, however reluctantly, had installed a ramp for the disabled.

Like most spinal injury victims, this young man took a diuretic as part of his bladder program. Persons in this category are subject to bouts of dehydration, which lead first to nausea and rapidly thereafter to collapse. Accordingly, during a break in the service, he asked the rabbi's wife how he might obtain a glass of water. (It turned out that he could not reach the spigot himself and needed assistance.)

What he got instead of his glass of water was a sermon. Given her husband's exalted station, she told him, there was no question of allowing anyone to see *her* give him a glass of water. She suggested, furthermore, that the proper thing was for him to leave the services and, she strongly implied, he was under no obligation to return.

Like the vast majority of Jews today, this young woman was actually practicing a folk-religion made up of arbitrary taboos inherited from the hinterlands of the Volga steppes, liberally laced with more than a dollop of holier-than-thouism.

The *Jewish* law governing food and drink on *Yom Kippur* provides for conduct diametrically opposite to that displayed by our unfriendly *rebbetsin*. The Talmud (Yoma, 83a, ss.), as I read it,

teaches that if someone is seized by pronounced dizziness or nausea, which they believe to be induced by lack of food or drink, it is obligatory to provide them with whatever food may be immediately available even if it be unclean or belongs to the sacrifice of the Temple.

The Mishna requires for example that the elders of the synagogue follow the advice of a physician. The Talmud reverses this decision and evolves a fascinating if evanescent civil libertarian concept called "the knowledge of the heart," to wit: that each person really knows what is best for him. To the extent that our knowledge of the symptoms rests on the subjective appreciations of the sufferer, we will rely on him for the cure, as well.

Suffice it to say that under even the more rigorous *Mishnaic* ruling, people are allowed to drink prudent amounts of water (the measure given is, whatever your cheeks will hold). But a man with a medical problem is forbidden to abstain. To the contrary, the rabbis tell us, he must eat or drink until *he* says that he feels better.

Visiting the Sick

The apex of the pyramid of Jewish values is occupied by a class of good works *(gemilut chasadim)*, whereby people are called upon to imitate and replicate specific acts of mercy attributed by scripture to the Holy One Himself. These acts include clothing the naked (a gloss of Gen. 3:21), visting the sick and offering hospitality to strangers (Gen. 18), comforting mourners (Gen. 25:11), and burying the dead (Sota 14). They are to be preferred to lesser forms of *tsedakah* because, unlike them, they benefit both the rich and the poor, the living and the dead, the donor and the recipient, and are seen as typifying and reinforcing all that is best in the relationship of a man with his neighbors (Sota 49).

The indispensable Talmudic source on *bikur cholim* is found in B. Nedarim 40, where we are told that, when one of R. Akiba's disciples was taken ill, his classmates declined to visit him. Rabbi Akiba not only went to see the young man but himself attended to his needs, both physical and spiritual, whereupon the boy experienced a dramatic improvement and was soon back at the *yeshiva*. Noting the effect of isolation and lack of social interaction on the sick, R. Akiba laid down the maxim; "Anyone who fails to visit the sick is guilty of murder." While R. Dimai explained: "All those who visit the sick encourage them to live, those who fail in this obligation encourage them to die." Rashi and others comment on the obvious practical benefits of frequent visitors to aid in the care of the sick, while the *Gemara* points out that no opportunity should be lost for imploring God's mercy on the sick person because there can be no true prayer unless it includes petitions for the welfare of others (Jeremiah 7:16).

The place of *tsedakah* in the world of the rabbis is spelled out in the liturgy of the Holy Days: "For *only* by means of (I) re-uniting the soul with God, (II) the service of the heart and (III) the establishment of righteousness is it possible to assuage the severity of God's edict." One establishes righteousness in this world by giving alms for the good of our souls in the next.

So much is this the case that the ancient Hasidim gave alms before permitting sacrifice to be offered to the priests of the Temple, and the rabbis were unfailing in their custom of giving a *pruta* (small coin) to the poor before reciting any prayer whatever, for it is written: "By establishing righteousness I will behold Thy Countenance." (Tur Y.D. 249 Ps. 17:16)

Failure to implement and develop *tsedakah* for the disabled renders the entire community ethically if not ritually unclean. Jews who do not practice *tsedakah* should not bother to pray *or* to study the Torah. By their own callousness they have cut themselves off from all possible knowledge of the Creator and communion with the Most High.

As to the centrality of the disabled in God's plan for Israel, the Psalmist has said it all:

Happy is the man who has compassion for the afflicted.

God will surely save him in time of trouble,

Protect him, give him long life, and secure him in the Land.

Nor will He abandon him to the greed of his enemies;

He will give him strength and fortify him during illness:

Oh Lord, You alone have procured his recovery and returned him to health. (Psalm 41:2-4).

In search of care for the handicapped
Melvin M. Landau

My son has cerebral palsy. He is confined to a wheelchair. While he has many physical limitations, he has above average intelligence. Ten years ago I took him to a Temple Sunday School for enrollment. The principal was reluctant. He said, "He will frighten the other children. There is a TV program on Sunday morning with Jewish content; let him stay home and watch that."

As it turned out, my son did not frighten the other children. But I think he frightened the institution. While he was ultimately admitted, little accommodation was ever made for him. My simple request to keep his classes on the first floor seemed much too complex for the school. The first floor (only three stairs) was for the younger children. The second floor (twenty-three stairs) was for children in wheelchairs! Finally, after a few years, it was established that his home-room would be on the first floor; however, there were always services or other classes or special events which necessitated his being hauled up and down several times each Sunday. In his wheelchair, I dragged him up and down the stairs for five years— until he got too heavy for me to do this with safety. My wife also did some of the hauling. All too often, men and husky adolescents walked past her while she was struggling with the wheelchair, without offering to help.

It is said, *"Si iz schver tsi zein a Yid."* ("It is hard to be a Jew.") It is even harder if you are a disabled Jew. My son identifies himself as a Jew. I wonder— does the Jewish community accept him? I have often wondered about the fate of other Jewish children with similar problems. And more important, what will happen when they are adults— without parents? Will the Jewish community take any interest in them then?

God willing, my son will go to college and learn skills to make himself self-sufficient and independent. But, if not, what then? If he can't get up to the second floor, will they serve him on the first floor?

When Orphaned, How Will They Survive?
There are several hundred disabled Jewish children and young adults in the Chicago area. I have met some of them, and their problems seem worse than my son's.

Susan, a most severely handicapped young woman with barely intelligible speech, spent most of her childhood in a state-run institution, but with indomitable spirit went on to college where she met and married a young gentile, who was not handicapped, thus solving her problem of how to remain alive with dignity.

David is fourteen. He is afraid to grow up. He is afraid that if he gets any bigger, his mother and father will not be able to lift him. He has become very depressed. For the past year he has been starving himself. But he was denied admission to an excellent hospital treatment program for emotionally disturbed children because they do not take wheelchair patients.

Mark, a college graduate, is also so severely disabled that he will not be able to live independently. His parents are growing older; he must soon find an alternative living arrangement.

Andy, another Jewish boy, was struck by a car while riding his bicycle. He suffered brain injury which caused personality changes, and he will need someone to guide him for the rest of his life. He is an only child; his parents are middle-aged and his mother is terminally ill. His father wonders who will assume the responsibility of overseeing his son's welfare when he is gone.

Because the same problem concerns me— I went to the Family and Children's Services Division of the Jewish Federation in Chicago recently to see if they had a Guardianship Service. I asked, "If I manage to provide in my estate enough money to provide for my son's needs, would the Jewish Federation assume the responsibility of seeing that such funds are used for his support? Would they see that someone visits him to know that his needs are being met? That he is living with some semblance of dignity?"

I was told that no such service is available in the Jewish community.

Jewish Residential Facilities Are Needed

Because I am concerned about where disabled adults can live with independence of spirit if not of body, I searched the wider community. There is a Christian residence for approximately fifty young adults at Walworth, Wisconsin, 60 miles north of Chicago. It has a very strong Christian orientation. My Jewish son would not feel at home there.

I joined an organization called Over the Rainbow, whose purpose is to build and maintain residential facilities for handicapped young adults. After four years of struggle, it now has under construction eight specially-designed units in Chicago which will be available to disabled adults who can live independently. But, its members still face the bigger challenge of building a residential facility for their own children. The parents have realized that while getting funds to build a building is a formidable task, it is small in comparison to the more important problem of ensuring continuity of care for their children after they are gone.

I estimate that there must be several thousand physically disabled Jewish young adults in the United States. But I don't really know, nor would I expect you to know. They are largely invisible. Because they are in wheelchairs, their mobility is limited. Many of them have difficulty communicating, so they cannot speak out and make their presence known. Because society in general has not taken them into account, their access is limited; they can't cross streets because of the curbs, they can't get into public buildings because of the stairs. They are often kept at home and apart from the public and each other.

Because of physical barriers they are shut out. Because of attitudinal barriers, they might not be welcome if they could come in. They are separated from each other because of their limited mobility and small numbers. They cannot even form a Jewish handicapped community. This is not to suggest a desire or need for an exclusive community, but the need for a community where there are enough Jews, so that they are not outsiders— enough Jews so that they may continue to identify as Jews and practice Judaism if they desire.

Fear in Place of Compassion

But even as I turn to the Jewish community for help, I wonder— as I have had cause to wonder many times as the parent of a disabled youngster. I wonder about the attitude of Jews toward the disabled, toward those who falter, who fail in the race to achieve. I speculate as to whether many Jews are "turned off" by the spectacle of a young person who clearly has little chance of "making it", who won't be a doctor or a lawyer or a Nobel prize winner.

My son is mainstreamed at the local public high school— the first student in a wheelchair not turned away by the school, because of recent federal legislation. There is a large Jewish population in the school. I have not asked my son whether he has Jewish friends in school. I only know that the friends who have come to visit are gentile. In the summer, he spends two weeks at a camp for handicapped children. Afterwards, he corresponds with some of the counselors. Generally, they are college students. They come to visit him during the year. None of them are Jewish.

Do only gentiles have the obligation of *bikur cholim*? (visiting the sick)

Is there not a Jew who will play chess with my son? Is there no Jew who will visit him in later years to see that his needs are met? Have Jews lost the ability to *"kleib naches"* (take pleasure) from personal involvement with the needy and now are left only with the sterile joy of public giving or professional service?

I write not in the spirit of bitterness or complaint; more to suggest that the Jewish community may be losing its *Yiddishkeit*— its compassion. Is it possible that the principal of my son's Sunday School properly perceived the problem— that Jewish adults (not the children) are frightened of dealing with these different-appearing children and adults? Can it be that we Jews are still striving so hard for acceptance— for assimilation— that we avoid anything that is "deviant," even our own children? Are we so concerned with developing our children's intellects and turning them into achievers that we don't want to bother them with their peers who may not make it?

Second, and more important, I hope that I may stir some of you to action. I would like to find a group of similarly situated parents who have the resources to organize and maintain a residential facility where their children may live out their lives in dignity, with whatever degree of Jewishness they deem appropriate. Or better still, that the Jewish service community recognize the needs of these hidden young people and find the time and the means to serve them, so that the needs of all such Jewish youth may be served without regard to their parents' ability to provide. However, a beginning must be made somewhere.

Homosexuality and the halakhah

David M. Feldman

The halakhah on homosexuality, it would seem, is quite straightforward. The Torah calls it "an abomination" and forbids it categorically. It's an open-and-shut case, and where do you go from there?

Not only is the Torah's legal judgement of homosexuality clear and unequivocal, with the Bible's narrative giving it both the stigma and the name of sodomy, but there is hardly much call for the halakhah to define circumstances or legislate on violations — and hence hardly much room for an article on the subject. While adultery, by contrast, is no less roundly condemned, so much is yet left for the halakhah to formulate — a regimen of rules, for example, to prevent *yihud*, "being alone together" with a married woman. No such precautionary legislation is neces-

sary for homosexuality: "Israel is above suspicion of sodomy or bestiality," says the Talmud and, hence, a man may properly be alone together with another man, even sleep under the same blanket.

The confident Talmudic judgement and its waiver of precautionary rules are relayed in the Codes, from that of Maimonides and onward, except that the formulation in the *Shulhan Arukh* retrieves a dissenting view from the Talmud: "Still," we are told there, "in our countries and in this time temptation is great and it is better to avoid *yihud* with another man." But a major link in the legal chain, the *Bayyit Hadash* of Rabbi Joel Sirkes in 17th century Poland, disagrees: "The law is clear; *yihud* is permitted." And his contemporary and master, Rabbi Solomon Luria, even regards it as religious pretentiousness to follow the stringency recorded in the *Shulhan Arukh*.

Clear, unequivocal and unanimous
The matter of *yihud*, then, is virtually the only area of dispute in a question otherwise sealed by unanimous prohibition. Even Responsa on the subject are scarce — though one of them does expatiate. Written by none other than the sainted Rabbi A.I. Kuk in 1912 — when he was yet only the Rabbi of Jaffa — this Responsum considers the case of a man whose appointment as *shohet* (ritual slaughterer) was challenged. The man was rumored to have been involved in a homosexual act. Now if a *shohet* can be disqualified because of Sabbath violation; if his *shehita* is not to be trusted for reason of laxity in, say, another matter of *kashrut*, then he certainly would disqualify himself were he to violate this clear injunction of the Torah. In analyzing the question in its various parts, Rav Kuk concludes, as it happens, that the *shohet* can be retained in his post simply because the evidence against him was hearsay. Moreover, he says, the man may have already repented. That legal difference on *yihud* now comes in here for an intriguing resolution: The author of the *Shulhan Arukh*, Rav Kuk suggests, had called for a ban on *yihud* "in our countries" — namely Spain and Palestine — where the climate is warm. In warm climates, the tendency or temptation to sin in this manner is greater; but Poland is in a cold area of the world — there, Rabbi Sirkes could discount such temptation, and rule that *yihud* between men is quite all right.

But surely the halakhah must have more to say to us about the act of homosexuality itself. Is the sin so lacking in extenuation or the subject so devoid of nuance?

Repentence reveals a moral stance

Something of extenuation of the sin's severity we see in Rav Kuk's presumption of repentance on the part of the man in question. In a Responsum of a century earlier, Rabbi Haim Palaggi of Turkey had already written at length about presumed repentance in this matter. Which leads us to the heart of our present concern. Repentance is pertinent to homosexuality only if the act is immoral; if it is to be deemed a sickness, repentance is irrelevant. The halakhah and these Responsa, then, in taking a moralistic stance, are merely spelling out the Torah's moral judgement. Furthermore, the halakhah can only be concerned with the behaviorist end-result; even if the homosexual act is impelled by physiological or psychological disturbance, the act remains "an abomination."

By the same behaviorist token, on the other hand, homosexual fantasies — or even homosexual acts other than intercourse — are not yet a violation of the Torah's proscription of *mishkav zakhar* (sexual relations between males). Certainly, for example, the pseudo-homosexuality that Professor Lionel Oveseyer speaks of, whereby homosexual fantasies can actually be no more than deep feelings of admiration for, or emotional dependence upon, another man — certainly this does not come under the Torah's prohibition of an act. This remains the case even were we to transcend mere behaviorism and view the situation in terms of the Talmudic stricture that "thought of sin is worse than the commission of sin" — explained in another context by Maimonides that sinning with the mind or soul, wherewith we are truly human, is worse than sinning with mere body.

The myths of homosexuality

The Gay Liberation movement, of course, rejects the notions both of immorality and of sickness. In a forthcoming book, Michael Kotis, President of the Mattachine Society of Gay Militants, argues that the attitude to homosexuality by "straights" is based on three myths: that homosexuality is a) an illness, b) unnatural, or c) immoral. He rejects the first on the grounds of Kinsey's estimate that 50 percent of American males are "capable of a homosexual response." If so many are sick, or tend toward it, something is basically wrong, he says, with this "illness" theory. In the charge, too, of "unnatural," Kotis sees a "camouflage" for "an early tribal need for workers, hunters, and warriors;" that the anti-homosexual prejudice is essentially the glorification of reproduction as the sole purpose of sexual relation-

ships. And the "immoral" argument is meaningless to him because morality is relative and, better still, moral behavior is that which manifests "selfless, loving concern" for another person. Since homosexual relations between consenting individuals bring joy to them, they are therefore moral.

From the standpoint of Judaism, the "illness" atti-

tude has served as a welcome device with which to enable the Rabbi or Jewish law to be compassionate rather than judgemental. This can be said to accord with the extra-halakhic observation of the Talmud, that "a man does not sin unless he is possessed by a spirit of madness." But the "illness" theory has come under fire from various sources: Gay militants reject it as not only scientifically invalid, but as oppressively paternalistic. George Weinberg's *Society and the Healthy Homosexual* implies that psychiatry is legitimizing continued oppression of homosexuals in order to safeguard the sexual caste system. On the other hand, Thomas Szasz has been militating for years against the notion of illness for most disorders. There is no such thing as mental sickness, he tells us. "We are all a little more or less adjusted to certain norms than the next person." The concept of mental illness is an evil concept; it makes us patronizing and judgemental, and even permits us to institutionalize those whom we judge.

Jewishly — an abomination

Physicians and psychotherapists have their honest differences as to whether homosexuality is an illness, an abnormality, or neither. Some who claim it to be neither have yet traced the etiology of the condition to what they do call sick or improper family relationships or background, and others refer to personality "deficiencies" as either the cause or the result of homosexual tendencies. For our purposes, this debate must be irrelevant. We must deal with the question as a religious one. Our judgement of the Sabbath breaker or idolator has nothing to do with the findings of psychology or medicine. Judaism does declare homosexual indulgence a sin, of which the most and the least healthy are capable. Having said so, we can temper our judgement of the act with compassion for the actor.

Nor is the nature of this sin or its repugnance in the Jewish tradition attributable to what Kotis points to as the second myth, i.e., a primal desire for hunters and warriors. Certainly the context of the Bible gives no support to that explanation. Homosexuality is declared an abomination in the context of other prohibitions — adultery, incest, and bestiality — all of which are quite removed from the question of procreation. (Compare the absurdity, according to Ibn Ezra and others on *Leviticus* 18:20, of contemplating adultery in order to fulfill the mitzvah of "be fruitfull." Compare also the censure, in Talmud and Midrash, of lesbianism.) The prohibition is absolute, although in the Talmud's assignment of "reasons for the prohibition" we find the suggestion that the Hebrew for abomination, *toevah*, can be understood, as by a play on words, to mean *toeh attah bah*, "You go astray because of it." In the Midrash, this play on words has reference to the fact that a homosexual act cannot result in procreation. But another interpretation is that of *Tosafot* and other commentaries to the Talmud, which understand the going astray or wandering as the abandonment by the homosexual of his wife and home. Family life is seen as the prime victim of this aberration. A third

explanation is that offered in *Torah Temimah* of Rabbi Baruch Epstein, to whom the "going astray" is "from the foundations of Creation." Homosexuality defies, to him, the very structure of the anatomy of the sexes, which is manifestly designed for heterosexual relationships.

Halakhicly — an immorality

In my *Birth Control in Jewish Law*, I have sought to demonstrate, in analyzing the discussions of contraception by halakhic authorities in Responsa through the generations. that the various contraceptive devices describe a hierarchy of acceptability. Once contraception is indicated in principle, the method to be used is at issue. Methods which least interfere with the natural course of the sex act are least objectionable for contraception. The integrity of the sex act is not violated by the absence of procreative possibility — such as when the woman is already pregnant or is barren; or even by the absence of procreative intent — such as in oral contraception; but by interference with the heterosexual character of the act. Accordingly, that contraceptive method which is closer in character to homosexuality than to heterosexuality is for that reason objectionable. Homosexuality is akin to Onanism, and as such is repugnant to the halakhic tradition.

Nor, certainly, is the definition of morality as that which manifests "loving concern" for another at all sufficient in the Jewish system. Along with "therapeutic" adultery and other antinomian examples of the surrender of law to emotion or sentiment, homosexual indulgence is immoral, because it violates the Torah's view of man.

The urgency to condemn a moral lapse

I know I was invited to write not only on the halakhic view of homosexuality, but also to reflect on its validity for today. I see homosexuality, in the accepted sense of the term, as a sin, violative of the letter and spirit of the halakhah and of the Jewish instinct and experience — regardless of the findings of psychology or the demands of sexual liberationists. I think that pastoral compassion should, of course, be bestowed on transgressors, and that in this case our human concern ought to go even farther. If, for example, prison conditions are as scandalously conducive to forced or indifferent homosexual compliance (as horrendously detailed in the *Village Voice* and elsewhere), then reform of those conditions — such as by permitting conjugal visitation or otherwise —

should become our activist concern. But, above all, I think we ought unabashedly affirm our moral stance. We need not be ashamed of holding fast to standards in an age of nihilism. We do, after all, more highly regard holiness than freedom as a personal value.

So much of the Jewish sexual code has as its purpose — to the extent that we can speak of the law's purpose — the preservation of the marriage bond and the family unit. As committed Jews, our responsibility in an age of family dissolution is all the more urgent and positive.

Or so I would have written yesterday. Today I see that Jill Johnston has sharpened the issue in an article in *The New York Times Book Review*: "The lesbian and male homosexual by their very existence are a threat to the programs of marriage-family-home that every child is conditioned to believe is 'the true way.' The gay and radical feminist movements join in advocating an end to this oppressive institution..." she writes. This, then, is war, and the battle lines are drawn. If such are the stakes at issue, then even compassion for the transgressor becomes a subversive act, a condonation of a life-style antithetical to the values we seek to uphold.

Appropriate here is another Talmudic reference to the subject — in a passage which seeks to evaluate the decadent heathenism of surrounding society. These heathens might indulge in homosexual liaisons, says the Talmud, but they are not so far gone, or so cynical, as to arrange a marriage contract for the purpose! This remark the great moralistic tract of the 18th century, *Mesillat Yesharim*, applies to the problem of corruption generally: even in the worst degeneration there is a redeeming feature that offers hope — namely, that moral lapses are not made respectable. Not making them respectable is both easier and more urgent when the stakes are so high. □

Worldwide gay jewry, five years together

Anonymous

I migrated from New York City to San Francisco in 1972. My conscious purpose was to go to graduate school of public health for a year — but it became clear to me as the year progressed that my motivation had been not merely academic/professional, but quite personal as well. For by the time the school-year was

over and I had made my decision not to move back to New York, I had started to become an active member — especially in political and social senses — of San Francisco's gay community. (Although "gay" is a silly word for characterization, I'll use it because it has become accepted. "Homosexual" is too clinical and also has too many syllables. Incidentally, when I use the word "gay," unless otherwise qualified, I refer to both women and men.) This included involvement in a small, relatively-informal group called, variously, *Chutzpah* or *Achavah*. The group was comprised primarily of gay men who were Jewish and who somehow wanted to combine these two aspects of their lives. Activities were primarily social, though there was some outreach to the straight Jewish community as well as High Holyday and Passover services.

As time progressed several of us felt the need for a more formally organized and religiously oriented Jewish-gay organization. In 1977, together with a stockbroker and a school teacher, I helped to found Congregation *Sha'ar Zahav*. It rapidly became apparent that *Sha'ar Zahav* was filling a real need. Since that time, *Sha'ar Zahav* has grown to 140 + members, has an average attendance at Friday night services of 75 and has developed a full program of activities in addition to religious services. The Congregation has a rabbi — Rabbi Allen Bennett, an *openly* gay rabbi — and publishes a monthly newsletter — the *Jewish Gaily Forward*. Having served as *Sha'ar Zahav's* co-leader, it's apparent to me that it has had many of the "growing pains" associated with most new congregations, as well as some unique to a synagogue that focuses on lesbian and gay needs: e.g. eliminating the male bias that has existed for so long in synagogue liturgy and leadership.

Why have a Jewish - gay movement?

San Francisco has not been alone in the development of synagogues with an outreach to lesbians and gay men. In more than ten cities in the U.S. and Canada, primarily gay congregations have been established. Recently, *Sha'ar Zahav* hosted the Fifth International Conference of Gay and Lesbian Jews (there are also groups in Israel, France, England and Australia) which provided an opportunity for these groups to meet, discuss mutual problems and just to enjoy being in the company of other gay Jews. More than 200 people attended various workshops and business sessions, the meetings culminating in the organization of an on-going association of gay and lesbian Jews.

Why has this Jewish-gay movement formed — both on local and national levels? What were — and are — the motivations of Jewish gay activists? What have been the unique needs that have been satisfied by the development of these organizations? In answering these questions I present my personal viewpoint, based on my acceptance of my sexual orientation for what it is. I have no intention of presenting any theological or psychological discussion or argument. As far as I'm concerned — and most of my gay sisters and brothers feel the same way — the fact that I'm gay is a given. That's the reality of the way I am; for me to try to be heterosexual would be as un-natural as it would be for a heterosexual to be gay. Being gay is what seems right and comfortable to me. I consider myself fortunate to live in a time and place where I can express my true feelings to myself and others and not hide them the way I would have just a few years ago, let alone in past centuries.

We refuse to be regarded as ''flawed Jews''

In light of these feelings, it's apparent that the traditional Jewish condemnation of homosexuality, on both religious and socio/cultural levels, represents a ''stone wall'' for the gay person who is accepting of her or himself. In assuming that homosexuality is a freely-chosen, perverse life-style (or, at the very least, perverse sexual conduct) traditional Judaism condemns homosexuality as both immoral and a threat to Jewish family life. To the slight extent that a gay person *is* accepted, it's on the basis of that person being a flawed Jew. Religiously: ''Well, if you can't observe 613 *mitzvot*, at least try 612''; culturally: ''*Nebech,* you'd make such a nice wife/husband for a nice Jewish boy/girl.''

We can't accept this partial tolerance. We won't be ''accepted'' — as sinners. To us, being gay is normal. We want to live as complete Jews without compromising our psycho-sexual natures. Despite a degree of acceptance by national and regional organs of Judaism (especially the Reform movement), at the local level we have only been able, until now, to find *full* acceptance in Jewish organizations of our own. A synagogue is more than a place to worship; it should be the focus of a Jewish community. Gays find themselves as less than first-class citizens in most *shuls*. When was the last time *your* rabbi gave a *mazel tov* to Shirley and Sheila on their 10th anniversary? What would be the reaction in *your* temple if David and Joel waltzed together at your annual dinner-dance? Does *your* rabbi offer counseling to same-sex couples? In the several Jewish-gay groups, we are interacting together in a mutually-supportive fashion, integrating our personal and religious/cultural/traditional lives.

The Jewish community must accept us

What of the future? Except for the spectre of right

(left?) wing oppression, gays will increasingly continue to live their lives ''out of the closet.'' (I should parenthetically add here that the religious and political repression that might result from an extremist government is worrisome to both Jews and gays. The parallels between being Jewish in a gentile society and gay in a straight society are striking.) As a group, we're not going to fade away. The Jewish religious and communal establishment will have to come to terms with us, understanding our specific needs and helping us integrate into the larger Jewish community.

The Jewish community of San Francisco has increasingly served as a good example of this awareness and understanding. *Sha'ar Zahav* meets for both its regular religious services as well as various special events in the San Francisco Jewish Community Center. We are participants in the annual fund drive of the Jewish Welfare Federation. Our rabbi is an active member of the Board of Rabbis of Northern California. We consider ourselves, and are regarded as, a part of the community.

In addition to increasing their integration into the broader spectrum of Jewish communal life, gay Jews have other concerns. Liturgical development is continuing. Several of the congregations serving gays have begun to evolve prayers that respond to gay concerns, as well as eliminate (at least in English) references to a male God. Due to our concern for female-male equality, and non-anthropomorphic conception of God we refer to the Eternal One only in the neutral gender.

As with any Jewish community, we must begin to develop programs and services for elderly gays; for our sick members (*Sha'ar Zahav* has an account at the local blood bank; we want to be able to have blood released for our loved ones even if they don't happen to be our legally-wed spouses); for our sisters and brothers who die, frequently at great distance from their families. In all of these areas, we will be interacting with the resources of the local Jewish communal agencies.

Gays in Israel also need our support

Of particular concern to many gay Jews are the problems faced by Israeli gays. As with most Jews, gay Jews have strong personal and ''people-hood'' links with Israel and are, consequently, strong supporters of it. But we are dismayed by the continuing negative attitude towards gays displayed by both the government and society as a whole, an attitude that has prevented many gay Jews from making *aliyah*. When the 3rd International Conference of Gay and Lesbian

Jews (1978) attempted to donate more than 900 trees to the J.N.F. and have a suitable plaque erected, our contribution was refused if either the word ''gay'' or ''lesbian'' was included. Only a ''closeted'' donation was deemed acceptable. That incident took place last year, during the 4th International Conference which was held in Israel — at a hall rented under an innocuous name because the Rabbinate had threatened to remove the *Kashrut* certificate from any establishment that hosted us. Our gay siblings in Israel will continue to need much support from us in the coming years.

Why gay Jews need separate groups

Will there ever come a time when there won't be the necessity for separate gay Jewish groups? Probably not in the foreseeable future. When do you think *your shul* will have, in addition to groups for couples, singles, divorced people, men, women, - - a group for gays? In addition to the present inprobability of it, there are few *shuls* with enough gays willing to openly create a viable group.

Hopefully, there won't be a need in the future for the writer of an article like this to have to remain anonymous to avoid upsetting his family, but there *will* probably be a continuing need for our groups. In addition to the need for mutual support, we have a long way to go to convince many Jews that we didn't choose to be gay; that we won't deny our natures; that we aren't living inherently inmoral lives; and that we won't ''go away.''

As long as there are straight Jews who feel the solution to our ''problem'' is to meet a nice Jewish — (of the opposite sex), there will be a need for *us* to be able to say to a lesbian or gay Jew: ''Come, you'll meet a nice Jewish girl/boy!''

The last seder

Laurence K Milder

Now in the presence of loved ones and friends, we gather for our sacred celebration. It was on this Passover night that centuries ago our ancestors were freed from bondage. God brought them from slavery to freedom, from degradation to joy.

With terrible plagues and mighty deeds that defied nature, God released us from the oppression of

LAURENCE K MILDER *is a rabbinic intern in the New Jersy-West Hudson Valley Council of the Union of American Hebrew Congregations. This was his Senior Sermon delivered at Hebrew Union College-Jewish Institute of Religion.*

our enemies. Therefore, we have continually retold this story on this very night, just as we have continually striven to emulate God and to release all those who suffer in bondage.

Until finally in these recent years, with terrible plagues and mighty deeds that defied nature we have succeeded in emulating even God's destructive power.

Let us recall our history: how we went from freedom: free to live, free to bring forth new generations — to slavery: enslaved to death, enslaved in a dying and decaying world.

First, our leaders balked at making peace. "We cannot sign a treaty," they said, "for our hands are tied, and we are of impeded speech." "Fear not," said our magicians, "for we shall give you the power of God before your enemies. They will not dare to attack us, lest we multiply our signs and marvels, and crush them with our mighty hands, and our outstretched intercontinental arms." Then our leaders said to our magicians, "Produce your marvels." And to demonstrate their might, they took the twenty-megaton bomb they held in their hands, and cast it down, and it turned into a snake.

It is taught that God cursed the snake, saying: "On your belly shall you crawl, and dirt you shall eat . . ." And the nuclear snake ate mountains of dirt, while our leaders cheered. "When our enemies see this," they said, "their hearts will melt, their eyes will melt, their skin will melt."

Then their leaders called upon their magicians, and they cast down their bombs, and they turned into snakes also. And we reasoned, "If Aaron's snake consumed the snakes of the Egyptian magicians, surely we can do the same." Then all sought to build the bomb that would be able to consume the other's first, but none could do it. Nor did our enemies' hearts melt; fear did not deter them, but rather hardened their hearts, as they hardened their missile silos.

Our leaders said to their leaders: "Let *this* people go;" and their leaders said to our leaders: "Let *that* people go." But no one moved.

So our magicians took hold of our bombs and held them over their cities. And when they would not relent, we cursed them: "By this you shall know that we are as mighty as God." And we hurled down thunder and hail and fire, as God had rained down hail upon the land of Egypt, as it says, "The hail was very heavy, fire flashing in its midst, such as had not fallen on the land of Egypt since it had become a nation."

But their magicians did the same to us, hailing down bombs on our cities, destroying everything in a massive firestorm. And because we each sought to consume the other's snake first, we unleashed the snake which did not stop consuming until it had devoured the entire earth.

As each bomb exploded, it was as though the power of the universe had been concentrated into a single point, as the magicians said to Pharaoh, "This is the finger of God!"

Kamah Maalot Raot

"How many destructive paths" are there to a twenty-megaton bomb? If the blast wave had hurled through space people, cars and houses, crushing all but the strongest buildings within twelve miles, but not emitted a thermal pulse, *Dayenu!*

If the thermal pulse of blinding light and intense heat had fried alive people up to twenty-three miles away, but not emitted an electromagnetic pulse, *Dayenu!*

If the electromagnetic pulse sent through power lines, antennas, and railroad tracks had knocked out all electricity, but not emitted lethal radiation, *Dayenu!*

Were it only so that all the terrible destruction of each bomb had been wrought in the instant of its explosion, *Dayenu!*

But it was not so; for long after the bombs had ceased to fall, we still had the radiation. And it was the radiation which started the chain reaction leading to our ultimate enslavement to death.

Radiation transforms the handiwork of God into garbage. It disfigures the body from within. Cells become monsters. For thousands of square miles around each explosion, we died within hours from lethal doses of radiation. Further away, we perished slowly, over weeks, months, years, as our blood turned sour inside us, as our organs rotted from within. And if we escaped these, the snake ate deeper, scrambling our chromosomes for its meal. And we gave birth to mutatons and monsters that were not meant to be brought into the earth.

Ogden Nash once wrote, "In his wisdom/God made the fly/and then forgot/to tell us why." And there are those who say that he made it to survive us, in the end of days. For though the radiation killed the more complex species, the insects were not all killed. And they multiplied and swarmed over the land. And what few simple crops remained were utterly consumed by the legions of swarming things, as it says, "Locusts invaded all the land of Egypt... and they ate up all the grasses of the field and all the fruit of the trees which the hail had left, so that nothing green was left of tree or grass of the field."

Mountains of soot were spewn forth from the inferno, floating in the winds, and returning to earth as fallout, as it says, "Each of you take handfuls of soot from the kiln, and let Moses throw it toward the sky in the sight of Pharaoh. It shall become a fine dust all over the land of Egypt, and cause an inflammation breaking out in boils on man and beast..." And wherever the fallout landed, a contaminating inflammation broke out.

And the fallout contaminated the water, and killed the fish within it. And the rivers and lakes turned putrid so that none could drink from them, as it says, "and the fish in the Nile died. The Nile stank so that the Egyptian could not drink from it."

Even the frogs came out, until they, too, lay piled up in heaps. And the land stank from rotting corpses, as it says, "The frogs died out in the houses, the courtyards, and the fields. And they piled them up in heaps, till the land stank."

Then came the disease-carrying insects, as it says, "Hold out your rod and strike the dust of the earth, and it shall turn to lice throughout the land of Egypt." And epidemics spread throughout the land, killing whole communities that had escaped the bomb and fallout. And though we screamed in agony, there were neither doctors to tend us, nor drugs to ease our pain.

Just as we destroyed the cell, the microcosm of life, so too we eventually destroyed the earth, the macrocosm in which life exists. Our bombs ate away at the protective lining which shields us from the sun, the ozone layer. Whoever ventured outside was blinded by the ultraviolet rays, and so darkness prevailed over humans and animals alike, as it says, "Hold out your arm toward the sky that there may be darkness upon the land of Egypt..." Even the plants, their ability to photosynthesize destroyed by ultra-violet light, would find themselves in their own darkness, and eventually, death.

Elu Eser Makot

"These are the ten plagues" which we have brought upon ourselves through nuclear war:

Fire. Radiation. Blast Wave. Fallout. Contamination. Epidemic. Starvation. Mutation. Ozone Depletion.

Now we who remain, sharing this *Seder* meal, await the final plague— The Death of the Last Born. We have enslaved ourselves, because we acted as if we had the power of God. *Anachnu vlo malach:* "It was us, and not an angel," our hands, and not the hand of God, which brought about the ultimate holocaust. God brings plagues and sets people free. *Eleh adam eyno chen.* "But humans are not the same." For when *we* bring plagues against our enemies, we *enslave,* not only them, but ourselves as well.

Veafilu kulanu chachamim, "*Even though* we were wise," even though we had tested and experimented and knew that the extinction of life was now a possibility that lay in our hands, still we did not dismantle our bombs. *Mah haavodah hazot lachem)* "What's it to you?" we said to our enemies. To you, and not to us, as if our bombs would destroy their part of the world, but not our own. *Ulefi shehotzi et atzumo min haklal, kafar baikar.* "And because we removed ourselves from the world community, we uprooted the root of all life."

When the last living thing is gone, we will have undone all of creation. Our extinction will be the final night. No one will remain to ponder this darkness. *Mah nishtanah halailah hazeh mikol halailot. "How different is this* night from all other nights!" •

The state and the *sukkah*
Arthur Waskow

I have just been through several months of pressure-cooker education on the relations between religion and the state; and I think it is important for the Jewish community to do a conscious re-examination of its knee-jerk reaction on this issue.

Not that knee-jerk reactions are always wrong— sometimes they save lives. But if the surrounding environment has changed without our noticing, the old knee-jerk response may do us in instead of saving us. We need to look around.

ARTHUR WASKOW *is Director of the Shalom Center, on the faculty of the Reconstructionist Rabbinical College and Editor of Menorah.*

My education grew out of the *Sukkat Shalom* campaign. It was initiated by The Shalom Center, the national resource center for Jewish perspectives on preventing nuclear holocaust.

Sukkat Shalom drew on the traditional sense of *Sukkot* as the *time* when the People Israel sacrificed and prayed for peace for all the seventy nations, and on the *sukkah* as the *space* of peace. ("*Ufros alenu sukkat shlomecha*"— "Spread over us the *sukkah* of Your peace," as the evening prayer service says.) We saw the fragile, open-roofed *sukkah* as the perfect symbol of security-through-vulnerability— the inverse of a fallout shelter— the perfect symbol that in the world of impending nuclear holocaust, the only security is *sharing* insecurity— not building more weapons and more walls.

A Jewish Symbol Universally Understood

We felt the *sukkah* to be both a very strong symbol of this message that could be universally understood, and also *our* symbol— that is, a symbol of peace that wells up naturally for Jews who find their caring for peace growing from their engagement with Torah and with Jewish history.

It seemed a far more powerful, and for us, a far more authentic symbol than, say the three-prongs-in-a-circle that is often used by secular nuclear pacifists.

Now— why were we exploring these issues? Because it seemed to us that in the present historic moment, Jewish tradition and Jewish experience require us to bear a message into the public sphere— to say to the broader Jewish world and to American society that at the moment of great danger to the earth, we should keep peace and the prevention of nuclear holocaust as our pre-eminent value.

So— what more obvious? We decided that in order to affect the public sphere, we should carry the symbol of the *sukkah* into the public sphere— specifically, on to Boston Common, Independence Mall, and— above all— Lafayette Park in Washington, D.C., in between the White House and the Soviet Embassy. Why was this "obvious" to us? Because, on public issues, we had always been accustomed to carrying the symbols that moved *us* into the public sphere so that they could move others: lighting *Hanukkah* candles across the street from the Soviet Embassy, dancing on public streets with the Torah on *Simchat Torah,* doing a *Pesach Seder* at Battery Park, wearing *talleisim* at a civil-rights vigil, saying *Kaddish* at a Holocaust Memorial on public land, fasting and reading Lamentations for *Tisha B'Av* on the U.S. Capitol steps and in Lafayette Park.

Facing Jewish Opposition

But this time, to our astonishment, we met criticism and opposition within the Jewish community— not from people who disagreed with our sense of what the tradition teaches about preventing nuclear holocaust, but from people who *agreed* with our views on disarmament, but who invoked "separation of church [*sic*] and state."

What made this moment different? Most important, the fear and tension among many Jews arising from the recent Supreme Court decision upholding the Pawtucket creche, the recent efforts in Congres to pass a Constitutional amendment favoring prayer in public schools, and the recent talk among President Reagan and some strong supporters of his administration about state support for making the United States a religious, even a Christian, country.

And one distinction: The *sukkah*, said the critics, is a *structure*. Different form wearing a *tallis*, lighting a *menorah*, chanting Lemantations. "How is this different from a creche?" They said "How can we oppose the creche and support this?"

But— we answered— this isn't the *state's sukkah*. This *sukkah* is a *critique* of the State, not a creature of the State. *We* will pay for it, *we* will build it, *we* will sit in it, dwell in it, pray in it, speak in it.

Doesn't matter, they said. First of all, we oppose the building of creches on public land even if they are privately paid for and maintained. And secondly, this will *look* like the same thing— even if (as we had intended), you all arrange a twenty-four hour vigil so as to make clear that the *sukkah* is *yours*, not the government's— in a sense, a collective *tallis* that you are all wearing. Maybe, they said, that makes it Constitutional. But it still undercuts our efforts to uphold the separation of state and church.

Compromise Reached

The result of this dialogue was a compromise. We first built a *Sukkat Shalom* on private ground— the George Washington University campus, near the White House— and then on Sunday morning of *Chol Hamoed Sukkot* (the intermediate days of *Sukkat*) we took some of its *s'chach* (thatch) and used it to help roof a *sukkah* that we then

built in Lafayette Park itself. On that Sunday we had a children's program in the new *sukkah* and then held a rally there, at which spoke such notables as Ted Mann, Leonard Fein, Susannah Heschel, leading Reform, Conservative, and Reconstructionist rabbis, and the director of Washington's Jewish Community Council. And then we took this one-day *sukkah* down.

One aggadic comment helped soothe our *neshama* (soul) about this peculiar arrangement— that our "portable" public *sukkah* was like the first *sukkot*, those of our forebears in the wilderness.

For the urgent moment, it was not a bad compromise. But the issues run deeper:

• Is there not a distinction between governmental efforts to control and shape religious life and efforts of religious communities to shape governmental policy on great public issues? Does not the First Amendment forbid the one and encourage the other? When it comes to the use of public property, what is the line between them?

• What are the boundaries? Why a *tallis*, but not a *sukkah*? Or should we oppose all religious devotions in public space?

Must We Be Restricted to Secular Symbols?

• Why should authentic religious symbols that stir people to take public positions not be brought into public space? Elsewhere in Lafayette Park that day, there were tents that had been put up by another religious group as long-term symbols of "Reaganville," criticizing the Reagan administration's disregard for the needs of the poor and homeless. Is not the *sukkah* a Jewish "tent," a poor person's home turned into the symbol of sharing? Why is a secular— or not-so-secular— tent *kosher* for conveying this message, but a *sukkah*, not? Should people who arrive at their political views out of religious conviction abandon their own deepest symbols in that way? Does this not abandon the public arena to sheerest secularism? For Jews, does this mean that we say— for example, to those of us who are passionately committed to ending the nuclear arms race— "Join SANE, or the Freeze Committee— but stay away from Jewish life?"

• Are liberals who are sensitive to pluralism and the religion-state issue trapping themselves into a position where they won't use religious symbols in public, but the right wing *will*? After all, we *lost* the Pawtucket case. Politics and constitutional law are often a game of leapfrog. If the rules have "changed" (or gone back to what they were 30 years ago), how long do we sit on the sidelines and let others play the only game in town, and when do we decide to use the new rules to advance pluralism, liberalism, our own vision of religion?

Perhaps Our Fears Are Outdated

• For example, how dangerous would it be for Christians to put up creches in public spaces as expressions of the religious roots of their own political beliefs, and for Jews to build *sukkot*? Are our fears rooted in an earlier era when we felt both very weak *vis-a-vis* the non-Jews of America, and very weak in regard to our own religious and cultural roots? Has anything changed? (Maybe not!)

• If some of us feel more comfortable in a bland or homogenized-secular culture than we would in one where Judaism, Christianity, Islam, Buddhism, and other religions are intense, vigorous and publicly visible, how does that feeling fit with our fears of assimilation?

• When the Temple still stood, the great Jewish festivals were celebrated *en masse*, in public, and thus had the "political" effect of symbolizing and expresing power. In the Diaspora, when we had no land and no political power, the festival celebrations became dispersed, communal, familial, and unpolitical. But now that Jews— in Israel and in America— have serious political power, should we not again bring the festivals' meanings to bear on public policy by celebrating them in public?

Finally, I think it possible— likely— that a profound and historic shift in the world-views of many people in many different human cultures may be at the root of all these questions. There is a religious Great Reawakening afoot through much of the world. This Reawakening is rooted in deep doubts about modernism— doubts expressed either in regressive, restorationist religious movements that utterly reject modernity like Khomeini's or Kahane's— or in renewal movements like that of Martin Luther King, which try to infuse the better aspects of the modern project into a profound religious vision. For at least the next generation, it is very possible that more and more public discourse on the great public issues— the fate of the earth, the fate of the poor, the fate of freedom— will be cast in religious terms. Indeed, not only the language we use *about* the issues— but more deeply— the very way the public issues are understood, may more and more rise from religious world-views.

If so, I hope the Jewish people will bring its own sense of the wisdom of Torah into the great public arena— rather than either withdrawing from the debate altogether, into a private religion, or relying on a frozen secular modernism as its way of thinking. •

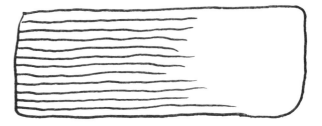

As our community confronts nuclear war
Maurice Lamm

In dealing with so complex, ponderous and passion-filled an issue as a strategic nuclear war, we should first understand that there are *no clear Halachic guidelines for Jews to follow*. It is more a sense of the *Halacha*, a worldview that derives from the sages' treatment of similar or analogous matters.

Let us also establish those points which are commonly agreed upon by the diverse parties to this global debate.

1—Nuclear war is the most horrendous evil ever conceived by any people in the history of the human race.

2—Both super powers now have strategic balance, a rough parity in warheads, delivery systems and accuracy, plus a redundancy ability which enables them to destroy each other many times over.

3—Civilized men must do everything in their power, at all costs and at all times, to prevent that eventuality. I am also convinced that characterizing any of the parties to the debate is pure fiction.

Before we proceed to analyze five specific issues, some general observations about ethics and Judaism are in order. Ethical decisions respond to realities, not disembodied principles. In this sense,

---

MAURICE LAMM *is rabbi-emeritus of Beth Jacob Congregation, Beverly Hills, Ca. This article was abridged from a lengthy analysis of this topic.*

there is no "pure" ethics as there is "pure" reason and "pure science."

In all of Jewish literature until the Middle Ages there is no special tract of systematic ethics. The Bible contains a Book of Proverbs and the Talmud a tractate called "the Ethics of the Fathers," but these are collections of aphorisms, not philosophically reasoned analyses. Such works do not begin to appear until Jews felt the influence of Moslem and later Christian forces. The style of *Halachic* decision, both in its Talmudic form and later in the Responsa, dwells on the realities of a case with all their attending conflicts, on the claims and counterclaims of people and ideas. A decision is issued in terms that are directly appropriate and relevant to the earthly concerns which triggered the problem in the first place.

In Jewish tradition *applied* ethics is fundamental. From it you can abstract a *theory* of ethics. It does not work the other way around.

Such a system cannot easily accommodate a perfectionist ethic. Reality knows proximate, doable goals. For that reason we have the Talmudic formulations of *l'chat'chila*, ideally desirable conditions, and *b'diyavad*, after-the-fact situations, which invoke less-than-ideal results. The process of ethical decision-making involves a calculus of relative values with relative moral weights applied to specific circumstances, and not always capable of being generalized into broad principles applicable to different realities.

The resulting decisions may not be passion-inspiring or heroic, but they do have a tendency to work. The problems of human relations are thus hammered out by careful, balanced, sensitive negotiation, not impassioned sloganeering and pulpit-pounding.

May one ever Press the Button?

Because defense depends on offensive capability, a number of critical ethical problems arise.

1. Is the firing of a nuclear missile morally permissible or not? If its use is not moral, how can the threat to use it be moral? The American Catholic Bishops say quite simply: "If the deed is not moral, the threat cannot be."

The Jewish war ethic, in my view, must part company at this juncture. It is not moral to declare a "no use" policy for nuclear weapons, when that clearly is the only defense available. The Bible, Exodus 22:1-2, refers to a thief who breaks into a home at night and is killed in the process by the homeowner. Not only is the homeowner permitted to retaliate without incurring "'blood-guiltiness," but if he does not strike back, it is considered immoral: "Is his blood redder than yours?" What right do you have to allow yourself to be harmed? This was generalized onto the national level. The defense of the nation is itself the height of morality. Second-strike is the morally responsible position required of every national authority.

I can see no Halachic substantiation, however, on the question of first-use. Even though it is intended for deterring conventional wars, primarily in Europe, the escalation from conventional to nuclear arms is a disproportionate response and appears to contradict every moral postulate of the Just War. It is in no way the defensive act our tradition calls *milchemet mitzvah* (a required war) and it cannot find justification as preventive war when the means of achieving its goal is so massive.

The Threat to Act has a Separate Status

But even if we make no decision on the morality of retaliatory bombing—as the Bishops have not—we must maintain that the threat to respond is unquestionably moral.

The *locus classicus* is Lev. 19:16: "Thou shalt not stand by the blood of thy neighbor." This refers to a pursuer, "A," intending to kill someone, "B." "C" may not merely stand by and make no attempt to stop "A." According to Maimonides, "C" must warn "A" explicitly. And then, even if "A" disregards the warning and does not expressly acknowledge the threat, "C" must intervene by taking appropriate measures, even to the extent of killing "A."

If "A" comes at his prey with a club and threatens not to kill but to break both his legs, "C" may not kill him. That is responding disproportionately—he is taking one's life to protect another's limbs. If he does, he is guilty of murder. Now, what if "C" threatens "A" by warning, "If you break his legs I'll blow your head off?" Is he guilty for threatening "A" ? Not at all. That is a moral act—to deter bodily assault—even though, if he carried out the threat the court might find him guilty of murder.

Similarly, even if we held that that second strike was immoral, the threat which, in fact, today keeps first-strike from happening, is highly moral. It has prevented death; it has kept the peace.

When the Corporate Good Takes Precedence

2. There is a more fundamental ethical question. Is it ever better to fire a nuclear bomb (even in reprisal) and risk death, than surrender and risk the destruction of one's value system? Is not life itself the ultimate value? Jonathan Schell makes a convincing case that it is preferable to live on for another day so as, perhaps, to survive the era of darkness and reconstruct the values we cherish today.

But a more compelling case can be made for the idea that life, physical existence, is not necessarily the "chief value." Parents sacrifice their lives for their child's life, soldiers do so on the field of battle and martyrs achieve a special sanctity.

The value of physical existence versus personal values on a national level is elucidated by a Talmudic ruling. The law holds that *pikuach nefesh docheh et hakol*, "danger to life voids all other observances." On the Sabbath, for example, one must violate every religious observance in order to save a person from being killed, or maimed, or even harmed. But war may be waged on the Sabbath and, in obligatory wars, it *must* be waged. Now war surely will trigger death. But, it is reasoned, war waged for the protection of the people, for national survival, is clearly a superior value.

3. Shall the missiles be directed at military forces only, a counterforce strategy, or at the civilian population, a countervalue strategy, commonly called MAD—Mutually Assured Destruction? Albert Wohlestter, in rejecting countervalue, justly holds that destroying non-combatant centers, is a violation of the Just War theory which does not permit indiscriminate killing. Conversely, Raymond Aron shows that already since World War I the Civilian-combatant distinction has been more or less erased.

A Jewish view must hold that a non-combatant must remain immune to military attack; that countervalue is morally impermissible. The unforgettable savagery of the ancient Amalekites consisted primarily in this—that they brutally attacked the weak and the aged, the unarmed, the women and children. For that they are warred against by God in every generation and symbolically destroyed by Jews every year. So today the Israeli army is duty-bound to implement the principles of *Tohar Haneshek*, "Purity of arms," which forbids soldiers from needlessly harming civilians. There were numerous Israeli casualties in the Yom Kippur War, as in the "Peace For Galilee" War, because "civilians" shot at soldiers from behind babies and women, from out of schools and monasteries.

The Jewish *Jus in Bello*, just war, principle since biblical days insisted on such policies as the "Open Fourth Side," which provided the enemy population with an escape route when their city was besieged. The reason for this was debated by Maimonides and Nachmanides. Nachmanides held that for humanitarian reasons people were encouraged to leave. Maimonides held that it was for military and strategic ones—namely, that if the enemy had no way out of the trap, he would fight more violently and cause more casualties. In the end, Maimonides' theory, too, is humanitarian, if also utilitarian.

In addition, there was never to be rejoicing at the fall of an enemy. They, too, are God's creatures. There are a number of instances spread throughout Midrashic literature which picture God as saddened at the death of His enemies. And it is the Jew's duty to imitate God in having compassion on all His creatures.

Judaism Espouses an Ethic of Realism

But the problem of countervalue is complicated by a persistent confusion as to *who* is properly to be considered a "non-combatant?" In Vietnam, as in Lebanon, and now on the front in the Iraq-Iran War, is a twelve-year-old child with a submachine gun a proper military target? Do you judge by his person or by his function? Another dilemma in countervalue arises in the case when the killing of non-combatants is judged to be a "military necessity," for example, to defeat an aggressor so as to protect one's own civilian population. If a gun emplacement that is menacing a squad of tanks is placed near a hospital, should the tanks resign themselves to death and casualties rather than retaliate? And if they do retaliate, who is to be considered guilty for causing civilian deaths, those who placed the gun or those who fired on them?

In response to these problems generally, one view holds that ethical principles are absolutes and do not alter with different realities. A second holds that ethical principles are only general guidelines which must at all times bow to the larger requirement of military necessity. Yet the Nazi *Kriegraison*, their doctrine of military necessity, justified every expediency perpetrated for any and every nefarious purpose.

A third view, one of moral realism, holds that when two mutually-exclusive ethical principles conflict with one another, the context should influence the decision. But the context must be accurately and honorably interpreted. If it is to be subverted to immoral purposes, it must be forcefully denied on the most elemental grounds.

Thus, there is a clear difference between whether one is targeting a teeming city-square because there are military supplies nearby or whether one is aiming at a munitions dump near which civilians live. The context determines that one is moral, the other immoral. If the context indicates that you may be killed by a twelve-year-old and it cannot be avoided, there is no reason to sacrifice your life. Even the blood of a youngster is not redder than that of an adult. While that is easily misconstrued and often subverted, particularly when, as happens, something needs to be done instantly, making such ethical judgments is one of those necessary contingencies of this tumultuous life.

What if the Force is Limited?

4. A fourth ethical concern is counterforce—the use of tactical nuclear weapons of only several kilotons targeted precisely onto clearly military objectives. The Bishops insist that even such circumscribed nuclear violence will not be able to be limited and ultimately will trigger an escalated massive response. But counterforce objectives are well within the parameters of the Just War concept of the Jewish people. To reject even counterforce strategy is, in effect, to neutralize the power of the deterrent altogether. In addition, there is an ethical value we should not overlook—counterforce might make war once again a professional conflict that military forces wage against one another and civilian populations will not be ravaged.

5. All of these ethical concerns may very well be academic with the development, still in its research stage, of Strategic Defense Initiative, SDI, mislabeled "Star Wars." It is the first defensive strategy in the nuclear age that appears to be viable. Perhaps, with the help of science and technology, human beings will have developed weapons so well that they become useless. Perhaps, by the end of the century, society will bring down the curtain on the final act of a half century of nuclear ballistic missiles.

The Quality of Nuclear Peace

Our expectations for nuclear peace cannot and will not share the expectations of conventional peace—a tranquility that arrives after the cessation of fire. Nuclear peace will always be a time of tension since all sides have the ability to totally destroy the enemy and the ability to produce the bomb will be easily available.

Jews are very much at home with a tension-filled peace. True Isaiah and Micah speak of beating swords into ploughshares, of the wolf living with the lamb. But another Prophet who dreams of the future is Joel. He writes: "*Proclaim ye this among the nations, prepare war;/ Stir up the mighty men;/ Let all the men of war draw near,/ Let them come up./ Beat your ploughshares into swords/ And your pruning-hooks into spears;/ Let the weak say: 'I am strong'.*" (Joel 4:9-10)

The peace prophecy of Isaiah is not contradicted by the war prophecy of Joel. According to the Amora Samuel (Shab. 63a), Isaiah speaks of the future in *Olam Haba*, the Next World, posited by the tradition as totally and qualitatively different from anything we know in *Olam Hazeh*, This World. Joel, however, speaks of the "days of Messiah," a historical vision, a preliminary stage of the glorious future. Joel addresses himself to the first step of the future, and speaks to the Jewish people. Isaiah addresses himself to the final step in the redemption, and speaks to the whole world.

In our unredeemed world we will have to settle for the Joel prophecy, a world of tension, miraculously still capable of being a Messianic era. I pray that the God of the Noahide covenant will shine through His rainbow that hangs in the sky, and may that be the only thing in the sky until the *Mashiach* comes. □

Noah and the ethics of environmentalism

Eric I.B. Beller

In testimony before a Congressional committee earlier this year, Interior Secretary James G. Watt was asked a question about preserving natural resources for future generations. In reply, Watt stated, "I do not know how many future generations we can count on before the Lord returns." This latest exposure of the religious substratum underlying Watt's anti-conservationist policies succeeded in multiplying the outrage of many already concerned over the fate of our coastlines, mountains, and wildlife. President Reagan had found not just any wolf for the chicken coup; he had found one who would sooner bring on the Apocalypse than compromise exploitation of the world's natural resources.

The vociferousness of the environmentalist response goes beyond any immediate material stake. Watt's vexing dogmatism poses not only a practical threat, but an ideological one. In the previous decade, environmentalists pinned back the ears of industry apologists who spoke in the name of progress and profit. Pitted now against an adversary who seems more than ready to invoke Divine will instead, environmentalists fear losing the public's trust and loyalty. As inheritors of a predominantly secular, liberal initiative, they fear drowning in a fundamentalist deluge.

Whether or not these fears prove fully justified, Watt's anti-conservationist rhetoric has achieved one ideological success already— the proclaimed association between religiosity and unfettered resource development has suddenly proven itself quite potent. A second success seems likely— that of leaving the impression that this association is the only one possible, that being religious virtually *means* adopting the Watt platform.

Such a notion must be rejected. It would be divisive and wasteful, indeed, were the environmental movement to do battle over the opposition's new religiosity rather than over its hackneyed platform. The loss would be philosophic as well as strategic. In overlooking or rejecting traditional religious sources, environmentalists would lose access to paradigms of the very ethic they espouse, that of reverence for all life, not just human life. It is time for those of us who believe this most deeply to speak up. I would begin with the story of Noah.

Noah Worked for Survival of All Species

The outlines of Noah's story are well known— the warning, the building of the Ark, the ingathering of the species, the Flood, the reinhabitation of dry land (Genesis 6-9). The story's ethical content receives less attention. Noah's knowledge implies obligation. Forewarned of impending disaster, he must labor not only for self-preservation, but for the survival of all species (Genesis 6:13-21). Lest we deem this task secondary, Nachmanides teaches that Noah was commanded to strive on behalf of the animals as he would for his own life. Each narrative segment ends with the report that Noah acted exactly as bidden, and with complete success.

Taken at all seriously, the story of Noah challenges us to undertake any effort, however immense, that is necessary for the survival of all species. The challenge translates into concrete positions on concrete issues.

Had such a message been heeded two years ago, for instance, Congress would have honored the plain intent of the Endangered Species Act, which, as the Supreme Court had held, was "to halt and reverse the trend toward species extinction, whatever the cost." Instead, Congress ravaged it, first by watering it down, and, when that did not work, by exempting specific projects outright. Now the Act is administered by James Watt. One response of concerned Jewish groups across the country could be to "adopt" local endangered species, to monitor and publicize their fate, and to help organize further efforts to save them.

It should be entirely possible to generate a more detailed and comprehensive environmental platform from the full range of Jewish sources. One forum potentially hospitable to such an endeavor is New Jewish Agenda, which has formed standing committees to work out informed positions across the spectrum of progressive Jewish concerns. At the same time, we must also share our ideas and pool our resources with secular organizations such as the Sierra Club. Mutual awareness and support will lay the groundwork for effective coalition politics later on.

"Who Creates All Varieties of Creatures"

The story of Noah holds other lessons, as well. Perhaps the most basic is that limits and conditions attend the familiar grant in Genesis 1:26 of human dominion over our planet. Prior to *Parshat Noach*, it will be observed, no explicit permission to eat animal flesh appears in the Torah. (see Genesis 1:29.) Rather, it appears for the first time in Genesis 9:3, after the Flood has receded and Noah has completed his labors. One traditional commentary derives from Psalm 128:2, "You shall eat the labor of your hands." As Or Hachaim and Radak relate, Noah gained mastery over the species by working to save them. He had toiled to build the Ark and to provide for each animal's needs during the long confinement on board. By his actions he merited new rights.

We live in a time when proliferating modes of human land use, food production, and industrial development pose a global threat. We have abused our dominion with murderous, epochal effect. Is it too heretical to suggest that our right to eat meat depends on working in our day as Noah did in his to assure the survival of all species?

In our own household, we have answered this question by adding a blessing to our meal-time observances whenever we eat meat, fish, or fowl. (Since we observe *kashrut*, are of limited means, and tend toward the vegetarian, these occasions come less frequently than one might imagine.) The blessing goes as follows:

Baruch Atah Adonai, Eloheinu Melech ha'olam, borei minei beriyot. (Blessed are You, Lord our G-d, Ruler of the universe, Who has created all varieties of creatures.)

We have been making this blessing for two years. We experimented with other formulas, but found this one at once the most powerful and most in keeping with the other *brachot* (blessings) over food. It has repeatedly heightened our sense of awareness of and responsibility toward all life.

A Jewish ethic of environmentalism would not confine itself to activities in the public sphere. Judaism teaches oneness and demands unity. Public and private remain distinct only insofar as the distinction facilitates the performance of *mitzvot*. The deeper theme is the passionate, purposeful integration of good deeds with study and worship. We ought not forget this theme as we venture into the arena of coalition politics.

The Threat and the Promise

Unquestionably, secular environmentalism and its wellspring, ecology, perform an indispensable service in decipering signs of global catastrophe. But the response should steer clear of pitting the secular against the religious. Rather, each can and must lend the other the vividness and strength of its insights. At the same time as we educate ourselves in science, we must tutor our imaginations to lift Noah's Ark from the picture books and must discipline our consciences to measure our conduct earnestly against our forebears'. The way out of the current miasma lies less in a transcendence of traditional teachings than in an enlightened rediscovery and rededication. ★

Family, a religiously mandated ideal
Susan Handelman

"A Jew today," someone wrote, "is anyone who has Jewish grandchildren." The words sting—perhaps more than any others in our painful debates about Jewish identity.

Of course, the definition is only metaphorical. Innumerable Jews are unable to have children; others have chosen not to have them. Many have intermarried; others are unmarried by choice or fate.

And many now openly prefer erotic relationships with members of their own sex. Rare, indeed, is the Jew today who can be certain of having Jewish grandchildren.

But Jewish families have never had it easy. Even in the best circumstances, many might agree with George Burns: "One of the secrets of a long, happy life is having a large family—especially when they live in another city."

It's no news that "alternate lifestyles," assimilation, challenges to traditional Jewish authority, and demographic changes have all ravaged the Jewish family. One now hears the argument that the traditional Jewish emphasis on the family is obsolete because it excludes large numbers of Jews from Jewish life. Some feminists claim that the traditional nuclear family is a repressive, patriarchal institution whose ideology has helped to exclude women from full participation in Jewish institutional life. Homosexuals argue for the validation of their lifestyle. Singles often feel hurt and condescended to by a community which sees them as unfulfilled and not full adults as long as they are unmarried.

The other side argues that the family is the foundation of Jewish life and guarantor of Jewish survival; that the first *mitzvah* is "be fruitful and multiply;" and that attacks on the Jewish family emanate not from a depth of true Jewish commitment and understanding but from an all too American ethic of self-gratification, narcissism and antinomianism. Being Jewish is not to be defined by whatever makes one feel good and self-justified. The lifestyles of Jews should not determine the Jewish style of life.

My aim here is not to engage directly in the difficult issues of Judaism and homosexuality, or the challenges of feminism, or the problems of singles in the Jewish community. But these questions have raised for me a deeper, underlying question: Beyond all the usual platitudes, *why* is the family so important in Judaism?

Demanding Continuity—and More

To define a Jew as someone who has Jewish grandchildren—for all its irony—strikes me as conceptually profound. It defines a Jew in terms of family—but not *immediate* family. It validates not only biological self-reproduction but a spiritual continuance beyond the immediate and across time. The Jew is not defined by how Jewish she or he may "feel," or how many *mitzvot* they may perform, or how much money they give, but their ability to *embody* (literally, in children) and *transmit* Judaism so vitally that these children choose to remain Jewish and are able, in turn, to pass on that spark to their own children. "Three is a *hasaka*," as Jewish tradition says. In other words, only when something is done three times, does it have the element of surety, permanence—can one trust its stability. Grandchildren are the third generation; they confirm the Judaism of the first generation. Transmission requires a biological next generation, but that is not enough; biology is shaped by spirituality, self is pulled towards other, the blindness of the present towards a vision of the future.

This is not to argue that simple survival is what being Jewish is all about. Yet, beyond all the obvious reasons for our contemporary stress on "survival" (the decimation of the Jewish population in the Holocaust, the continuous threats to Israel, declining birthrates and intermarriage), Judaism seems strangely obsessed with this theme and with the idea of family from the beginning. Why?

Our God's Concern with History

The Book of Genesis, for instance, is a book all about families, barren wives, sibling rivalries, destructions by flood and fire, constant threats to the process of transmission and continuity. These themes are narrated in part to demystify nature as an autonomous controlling force and stress the then revolutionary idea that the One God is in control of both nature and history.

And history is meaningful in Jewish thought precisely because God is passionately involved in it, a "God of pathos" as Heschel wrote, not the static, emotionless, ahistorical God of the Greeks. Just as God, the ultimate model, is intensely involved with the quarrels of families from Cain and Abel to the conflicts between the families of nations, so, too, are the biblical heroes and heroines deeply involved—in fact, defined by—the problems of their own families. Families are the great scene of spiritual struggle; both then and now, they are the paradigms of intimate connection and intense ambivalence. Unlike their Greek counterparts, biblical heroes do not attain identity and glory in solitary combat away from their families; their problems are deeply domestic.

It's no accident that the critical test of Abraham was precisely the command to sacrifice his son...and not to be tempted in the wilderness, like Jesus, or have to sacrifice himself. For the son was not his alone, and the crisis was not only personal; it was collective. The call to Abraham was for him to become a great nation; it was not a private covenant with a single person. Judaism, unlike other religions, does not advocate or promise "salvation" to individuals. The covenant is made not with Abraham alone but with all his descendants, the family which was to grow into the nation that Moses led to Sinai. And the revelation at Sinai again was collective, to an entire people, not to individuals.

Is this obsession with family the remnants of primitive tribalism? Is the focus on survival the result of a desert mentality and the tribulations of exile? And what does all this have to do with our modern need for individualism and self-definition?

The Primal Act of Keeping Covenant

The family is central to Judaism, I think, because it is central to Jewish ideas of God, creation, covenant, and history. The biological family reminds us that we, like the world, are created; we are not inevitable, necessary, autonomous. We are an effect of someone else's will—and in the best case—someone's desire to give to an other. We have a history. The creation of another human being echoes and partakes of God's creation of the world—it, too, is a something from nothing, an act of faith and hope...and something else perhaps: as Isaac Bashevis Singer once said, "Humanity could not have gone through all its suffering and problems and crises without a sense of humor. The very fact that we are here shows that our grandparents and parents had a sense of humor."

To refuse to give birth to the next generation is to refuse to continue God's creation, and thus also to refuse to live in history, and thus also to deny the covenant. For covenant is *collective* and *historical.* Torah is a guide and inheritance to a people who were to journey not just in space to the Promised Land—but in *time,* through the travails of history. History—the physical turmoil of this world, of its passions, temptations. "The Torah," as the book of Deuteronomy says in a famous passage, "is not in Heaven." "Every descent," the Jewish mystics say, "is for the purpose of an ascent." The soul's descent into the scrappy physical world, the people's wanderings through the course of history enable a great spiritual blossoming—and thus the Talmud compares the Jewish people to the olive: only when squeezed does it give forth oil.

This world, daily human relationships, are the scene of divine action, by both God and Israel. The world is not an allegory; spirituality is not elsewhere. The Jew is engaged in sanctifying this physical world and mundane historical time. That is why memory is so important to the Jews—it is the sanctifying and linking of past, present and future. In Jewish time, the past remembers the future. Memory, said the Ba'al Shem Tov, is the secret of redemption.

Generation: Jewish Responsibility

And to put it simply—there is no physical future, no history without physical reproduction. The family is the unit that creates life, welcomes and protects it, is intimately involved with it and therefore is the most powerful agent of transmitting personal and collective Jewish memory. That is why there is such an emphasis on "generations" in the Bible, why teaching and learning are so highly valued— because they are acts of transmission to and reception and renewal by the next generation. . .of the heritage, of the gift. The threat to the covenant is that there will be no one, or the wrong one, to carry it on into history. Perhaps that is one of the meanings of the famous midrash that when God was about to give the Torah he asked for guarantors who would keep it—it was not enough for the Jews themselves to pledge to keep it, only when they said, "Our children will be our guarantors," did God agree to reveal it.

Just as the children were pledged before they had any choice in the matter,—the self is not an isolate, autonomous, totally free creation, despite the dogmas of pop American psychology. The family is a covenant. For in the family, we are continuously reminded of, obligated to, intruded upon and pained by, delighted and pleased with—others. We are in constant dialogue—even if it is angry. True, one can divorce a husband or wife. But however severe the alienation may be, a child's biological bond to a parent is indissoluble. As Robert Frost once put it: "Home is the place where, when you have to go there, they have to take you in." In this way, familial relations are a microcosm, training ground, reminder, and enactment of the Jewish people's intimate and tempestuous relation to God; why, after all, are we called the "children" of Israel, the "children of God?" The prophets, of course, exploit the full implications of these metaphors: In the book of Jeremiah, God may angrily "divorce" the Jewish people as his unfaithful "wife" who has played harlot (3:8) but then cries yearningly for their redemption, "Return, O backsliding *children*" (3:14).

The Integrity of Traditional Sex Values

Thus I will speculate that one of the reasons Jewish tradition opposes homosexuality is that there can be no next generation from that kind of union—no biological child; therefore, no history, no future, no covenant. Now of course,—Jewish tradition holds that one who teaches another's child is as if s/he gave birth to that child. And this is a great value—but Judaism, unlike Christianity, does not allegorize away the physical commandments of the Torah and seek salvation in another world. The ideal Jewish saint is not an ascetic, or one who, as in other religions, attains purity by removal from the community, or from the demands of a family, or the physical world. For these struggles are the deepest spiritual struggles. The secrets of the *kabbalah* were to be taught only to married men. And the *Kabbalah* itself describes the various aspects of God's mystical inner being (the configurations of the *sefirot*) in terms of family metaphors, "father, mother, son, daughter."

I once heard a founding member of the Havurah movement discuss why he no longer agreed with the radical revisions made in the language of the *siddur*. The rationale had been to take out the crude and offensive anthropomorphisms and the sexist biases: "God as a King, Father, Warrior, etc." "I have a love/hate relationship with the traditional *siddur*," he said, "but I realized that our most primal and intimate human emotions are evoked by much of this language—especially our relations with our families, and that to expunge this language and these human feelings, as ambivalent and archaic as they may be, is to cut us off from achieving the most intimate relationship with God."

Thus the traditional Jewish advocacy of marriage, child-bearing, and heterosexuality, I think, should not be mistaken for a repressive patriarchy, an intolerance of lifestyles, a primitive tribalism, or outmoded ideology. Now Jewish tradition clearly

teaches that a Jew is a Jew no matter what, that every Jew is holy, and part of the Jewish community. I am in no way arguing for the exclusion of those with alternate views from the Jewish community or synagogue. And I do not want to minimize in any way the personal pain this position my cause to homosexuals, to singles, to the childless—but that pain is not a persuasive argument for change...only for compassion and extra warmth.

Our Jewish Duty was—and is—Clear

The family can indeed be a repressive institution—as can any relationship that is distorted, but I have tried to argue here that the Jewish concept of family is distinctive and absolutely integral to Judaism; it is not reducible to a bourgeois societal arrangement or ''Lifestyle.'' It is deeply theological. One is free to make other choices. But what will be the grounds and values on which those choices are made? For the freedom to make choices should not be confused with the freedom to remake Jewish tradition into one's own image...with only one's present in mind. The ultimate ground of value in Judaism is not the autonomous self, but the personhood bestowed by being in and continuing God's creation and covenant.

Rabbi Michael Brooks once said that having children made him relate to God a lot better.''How so?'' I asked. ''Because now I understand what it is like to create something you have no control over,'' he answered. This is ironic and also very wise. Having children is indeed an aspect of being made in the image of God. For God's creation as an act of God's free will gives us free will and so makes our very actions in history meaningful...and makes the Torah ours, to be renewed in every generation. A child is both oneself and completely *other*. Similarly, in the process of transmission, Torah is the same and other—wholly accepted, and also changed and enlarged through newness of the next generation. As the Talmud says, ''Even the innovations which a brilliant student will one day teach in front of his master were already given at Sinai.'' In this sense, the Latin-American writer Borges said, Jews alone produced grandchildren, whereas in the secular Western tradition of writing and texts, ''The nights of Alexandria, Babylon, Carthage, Memphis have never succeeded in engendering a single grandfather.'' Although no one can guarantee it, it is our obligation to try to make sure that we do have Jewish grandchildren. □

Family or community?

Martha A. Ackelsberg

I find Susan Handelman's piece on the place of families in Judaism profoundly disturbing. In the guise of making a theological argument, she makes a biologically-reductionist claim which takes as a model for all time the specific conditions of the earliest period of Jewish history. In consequence, she ignores the crucial importance of *community* in Jewish history and religious life. I believe, however, that if family has been important in Jewish history, it is as a means toward the creation and preservation of the community. It is the community, then, which ought to be the focus of our concerns; and the question for contemporary Jews should be: what are the ways in which that community may be sustained and strengthened?

Family and the Patriarchs

Susan Handelman's portrait of the centrality of ''the family'' in the life of the patriarchs is certainly a true one. The central concern of the patriarchal narratives in the book of *Genesis* is family. The major triumphs and tensions of the book all focus on essentially domestic intrigues: who will inherit, who will carry the blessings (of God and of the patriarchs themselves)? But family is central in these narratives, I would argue, not because the Bible is trying to teach us about the importance of generational connections, but because, in the early period of the establishment of the people, family was coextensive with community. And it is the community, and not the family, which is to carry the burden of Jewish continuity for the generations to come.

For the image of family, while central in the patriarchal period, is surely *not* the controlling image for the rest of the biblical narratives. Once the tribes settle in Egypt, and, most certainly, once the people stand at Sinai, the central tensions and confrontations are *communal,* not familial. Moses is known not as the ''father'' of the Jewish people, but as the lawgiver, the one who molded them into a community and interceded with God on their behalf. The central conflicts in his life were not familial (certainly not in the domestic sense), but communal. Joshua, Deborah, Isaiah, Jeremiah, Ezra, Nehemiah, Mordecai, Esther, and an entire host of biblical heroes and heroines are accorded that status in our tradition not because of their familial accomplishments, surely not because they generated Jewish grandchildren, but because they made crucial contributions—defined in non-biological ways—to the continuity of the Jewish people.

Community and Continuity

The real issue around which Handelman's arguments about the place of families in Judaism turn is the continuity of the Jewish community/people. What sustains it? What contributes to its growth? Here, as Susan Handelman herself acknowledges, the tradition has been clear: while biological reproduction is important, it is not, and never has been viewed, as the *sole* form of contribution to Jewish continuity. In her words, "Jewish tradition holds that one who teaches another's child is as if s/he gave birth to that child." Yet, in her next sentence she attempts to rob that statement of its force by adding that "Judaism, unlike Christianity, does not allegorize away the physical commandments of the Torah and seek salvation in another world." Is that what it is to devote a life to Jewish teaching and learning? Is that the way we remember Rabbi Akiba, Maimonides, Rashi, Joseph Caro, or any of the other great Jewish teachers and codifiers? Their contribution to the continuity of Jewish tradition and Jewish peoplehood is clear and undebated. Their status as biological producers of Jewish grandchildren seems quite beside the point.

Our own communal/religious history provides us, then, with a variety of models of fulfilled Jewish living, including many models of what we might call "grandparenting" in a non-biological sense. Why should we insist now on the eternal validity of a much more narrow definition—one which identifies being a Jew, or contributing to Jewish survival, with biological reproduction in the context of a heterosexual nuclear family?

Community, Opportunity and Obligation

I firmly agree with Susan Handelman that "the ultimate ground of value in Judaism is not the autonomous self, but the personhood bestowed by being in and continuing God's creation and covenant." But, as I have tried to argue, our tradition does not define our participation in creation and in the covenant solely in terms of the nuclear family. Instead of giving us a theological defense of "the family" in Judaism, Susan Handelman has given us a thoroughly modern defense of the "heterosexual bourgeois nuclear family lifestyle," rooted in a reductionist vision of what constitutes generational continuity. But, as I have argued elsewhere—*Response,* No. 48, Spring 1985— understandings and definitions of what constitutes a family and what obligations its members owe to

one another have changed dramatically over the centuries, in the Jewish community as much as in the secular world. Not only is the vision she offers us much narrower than that which Jewish tradition provides, it is also a profoundly, and unnecessarily, limited view of who is a good Jew.

Her biological analysis is seriously flawed in a number of important respects. On the one hand, *biological* continuity is surely not the only kind of continuity there is: as we have seen, people can contribute to communal continuity in other than biological ways. On the other hand, even in terms of biological continuity, reproduction is surely possible outside the nuclear family context.

To define a Jew as one who produces Jewish grandchildren, in the literal sense in which Handelman clearly means us to apply it, is foolish, if not inconsistent. Many Jews who are childless (whether now or in earlier times) find themselves without children not because they "refuse to give birth to the next generation," but because the circumstances of their lives do not allow them to do so: they may be physically unable to bear children, they may lack the economic means to rear them properly, they may not have appropriate heterosexual partners, they may lack the social supports which would enable them to bear and raise children in the absence of such a partner. Others may have Jewish children, but be unable, despite their best efforts, to guarantee that those children will remain committed Jews and, themselves, have children who will remain committed Jews. Ought we to leave such people feeling they are any the less Jews because they do not have control over the choices of their children and childrens' children?

Covenant, i.e., Inclusive Relationship

Furthermore, even if we turn to generativity in the biological sense, heterosexual nuclear families are not the only contexts in which continuity can be assured. And, with respect to "covenanting," I agree that making long-term commitments to love and care for others is important; Judaism does not share the liberal individualism so characteristic of contemporary U. S. society. But heterosexual nuclear families are not the only contexts in which people can or do covenant, nor are they the only units in or through which people may express love, or long-term care and commitment. As all too many studies unfortunately attest, for many women and children, families are often the last place to go for such nurturance.

A more appropriate definition of what constitutes Jewish continuity would not only relieve the "pain" of exclusion for many such people, it might well make possible their biological contribution to the next generation! For, as it is important to note, while biological reproduction is not the only form of reproduction, it is also the case that not only heterosexual nuclear families give birth to biological children. With a more open attitude on the part of the Jewish community, many of those who are now single or not heterosexually-partnered might well be encouraged, or enabled, to have biological children, and make an effort at generating those grandchildren which Handelman claims to value so fully.

In sum, while I agree that, as Jews, we share an obligation (and, I would see it, an opportunity) to "be fruitful and multiply," to contribute to the continuity and the deepening of our tradition and values, it seems to me foolish and self-defeating to define those obligations in narrowly-biological terms. Our tradition is too rich, the community too varied, to claim that all that matters (or that what matters most) is simple biological reproduction. If there is a theological imperative in Judaism, it demands not the blind reproduction of "families," but that we be "a holy nation." That is not to imply that a concern for reproduction is irrelevant: we must continue to exist if we are to fulfill our religious obligations. But it is to insist that there are many ways to contribute to that continuity, whether biologically or spiritually, outside the framework of the so-called "traditional nuclear family." To deny that diversity is to ignore the lessons of our own history and, it seems to me, to threaten the very continuity of the community and traditions we wish to sustain.

...for the sin of deadening conscience

Samuel H. Dresner

The Roman Catholic Diocese of Brooklyn refused the request of the family of Frank DeCicco, "the reputed mob leader killed by a car bomb," for a public mass before the funeral. This decision was reminiscent of the one made last December when the Archdiocese of New York banned a similar mass for Paul Castellano, the reputed leader of the Gambino mobster family, the most powerful gang family in the nation, who was shot to death in a midtown street.

Do rabbis take similarly courageous stands against powerful Jewish crooks in their own communities? Are Jews denied honors of position or rite in congregations by the rabbi because of immoral behavior? Of course, working for the Catholic Church and not the local church, as the rabbi works for the local synagogue, gives the priest a sense of security and support that most rabbis, by virtue of the more tenuous nature of their position, do not have. Nevertheless...

I have been living in New York for nigh unto a year now, and, though, of course, always aware of the immense Jewish population here—some two and a half million, the largest collection of Jews ever in one place—have never quite understood the overpowering nature of that presence, until personally taking up residence. At the moment, culture and finance and politics are clearly in the Jewish domain. In addition, it would seem that they are, at the moment, running the city as well, from the mayor on down. Now I am not naive enough to believe that there can be politics, in the sense of useable power, without corruption. But this present city corruption has over the past months erupted like some ugly disease precisely among—indeed, almost alone among—Jewish political figures. And that is the reason for my unease.

Manes, Lindenauer, Friedman, Lazar, Turoff, Schwarz, Sofer, Shafran, Leff. The names continue to mount. And these are only the Jewish "sounding" names. Millions of dollars have allegedly been stolen from the tax-payers of New York by those who swore to uphold the law and serve the public. Payoffs, bribes, fraud, destroyed records, and on and on, even a bloody suicide. Only the first stage of the tragedy has been completed; the trials are yet to come. We are assured that this will be a matter of a decade, at least.

One of the threads which tragically runs through this whole sordid mess is that virtually all of the indicted, and even the to-be-indicted, are Jews. They all seem to be about the same age, with the same background—poor immigrant homes on the East Side, Brooklyn or the Bronx—as if they had been part of an insidious club or fraternity. Of course, other cities have their scandals—but Jewish political corruption on such a level! It is difficult to find a parallel. More recently Wall Street has been hit with a series of "insider-trading" scandals, which, like the political scene, seem to involve only Jews. First, a senior investment banker—B. Levine—confessed to illegally trading over a five year period in securities of 54 companies, prior to takeover announcements which then drove their prices up, at a profit of some 13 million dollars stashed away in remote island banks. Wall Street was shaken because, as they put it, "millions of dollars change hands on the utterance of a word. It is all based on trust." Imagine their shock, then, with the indictment of five promising Wall Street professionals—A. Solomon, M. Shapiro, M. David, D. Silverman, and R. Salsbury—all between the ages of 23 and 27, all from the best families, schools and firms, who schemed together in the same racket. "Young, Eager, Indicted" was the way the *N. Y. Times* captioned it. For our purposes, it is not without interest to add that some of the five met at a UJA gathering, and that the indicting evidence came from the host of Mr. Solomon, a fellow arbitrager from his firm, who invited him to a Sabbath evening dinner to meet an eligible young woman, but whom Federal investigators had wired for sound.

No Protest Was Heard

How does the Synagogue respond to Jewish scandal? The answer seems to be—with silence. A heavy, thundering silence. It might be argued, after all, that these are not mafia crime bosses who use machine guns and blow up cars, but merely embezzlers only some of whom have actually been indicted, although suicide does speak rather loudly in favor of guilt in one case.

But how would the Synagogue respond, if they were found guilty and sentenced to long prison terms? Would they suffer any religious embarrassment? Would their funerals be in any way different than if they had been moral pillars of the community? If the effusive eulogy given for the now infamous Queens Borough President and suicide victim, Donald Manes, is any example, the answer would seem to be in the negative. Indeed Synagogues are usually the very last to censor their own Jewish criminals. I recall how, when the

treasurer of a congregation I once knew quite well, was convicted and jailed for a crime, he was dropped from all the communal boards and offices that he held, with one exception—the Synagogue, where he continued to serve as treasurer!

How many sermons have been preached in Queens or the Bronx or even Manhattan or Brooklyn, or the rest of the country for that matter, on the scandal of the New York Jewish politicians? How many editorials have appeared in Jewish papers in New York or elsewhere? How many minutes of the thousands of hours of talmud and other lessons given in the countless New York *yeshivot* have touched on this subject? How many meetings have been called by religious leaders to take council on how to deal with this *Hillul Hashem* and to ask what has happened to the humanity of Jews? How have these children of Jewish immigrants, so gorgeously celebrated at the centennial bash for Miss Liberty, become so expert in breaking rather than keeping the law of the land? Yes, rabbis have been busy denouncing the Sandinistas (or the Contras), Kahane and Kadafi, sundry Democrats (or Republicans), Waldheim, Gorbachev, etc., all the enemies of mankind who are either far away or not our own—preferably both—but not Jews in their own backyard, perhaps in their own congregations.

Rabbis are no Exception

But, you may ask, can we really expect religious leaders to "lead," when they themselves appear to be the subject of growing scandals? One can hardly pick up the paper in New York without flinching from the plethora of rabbis involved in shady deals: a Brooklyn meat wholesaler was fined one million dollars for selling 100,000 pounds of meat as kosher; 74 year old Shneur Zalman Guraryey, a revered name in certain religious Jewish circles, and his son-in-law, Nochum Sternberg—"both identified themselves as rabbis"—were arrested for "cheating the Government of more than $100 million in taxes since 1979." (Those who tremble over a bloodspot in an egg seem unconcerned about a blood spot on a dollar bill); a bearded rabbi masqueraded as a doctor in Borough Park, Brooklyn, specializing in sexual dysfunction, including surgery and less mentionable practices, and has been indicted on "a charge of 23 counts of assault, unauthorized practice of a profession, sexual abuse, reckless endangerment and other charges." Tiferet Yerushalayim Yeshiva, founded and led for decades by a famed talmudist generally considered to be the leading *posek* of our generation, was indicted for illegally laundering money for local stores, which then shared with the Yeshivah their ill-gotten tax savings. The Yeshiva's representatives, when accused of this crime, responded, it is reported, by claiming—incredibly—that with the neighborhood change on the East Side, which saw Jews moving out en masse, there was no other way to pay their bills!

Farrakhan and Larouche have no need to manufacture lies about Jews. All they have to do is read the *New York Times*.

And the Synagogue? It seems to prefer silence. I would wager that the subject of Jewish corruption, political or otherwise, is not the burning subject of Synagogue board meetings, nor even of the Social Action committees of local Synagogues or their national constituencies, since the topic was not an important agenda item at last summer's conventions held by Reform, Conservative, or Orthodox bodies.

The worst shame, observed Abraham Heschel, is when one no longer feels shame. □

...for the sin which we have committed

Walter S. Wurzburger

Many of us have been jolted by the disclosures of the conspicuous role played by Jews in the recent New York City corruption scandals. Naturally, we are embarrassed by a *Chilul Hashem* of such colossal proportions. It is especially painful that, as evidenced by other financial scandals, Jewish participation in white collar crimes is not as rare as one would expect in the light of the high priority which we Jews assign to moral values.

But the situation calls for responses going beyond expressions of anguish or consternation. Whenever suffering comes upon us, so the rabbis of old admonished, we must turn inward and examine our own conduct. As we embark upon this self-scrutiny, we must realize that we bear responsibility not only for our own actions, but also for those of our fellow-Jews, especially in cases where we have not exerted ourselves sufficiently to prevent sinful behavior. Awareness of our responsibility for the actions of our fellow-Jews is so deeply etched into the Jewish psyche that the *Vidui* (the confession of sins) includes references to transgressions that we know we have not committed. The late Justice Frankfurter was so turned off by the practice that he disassociated himself completely from all Jewish religious life. He believed that he could not in good conscience participate in a *Yom*

Kippur service which compromised his integrity since the liturgy contained confession of sins of which he was completely innocent.

The learned judge, however, arrived at his decision by overlooking an important consideration: the confession of sins is in the plural—not the singular. We are implicated in the guilt of our fellow-Jews, because "all of Israel is responsible for one another."

Religious leaders and institutions can hardly avoid sharing a measure of responsibility and blame for the total disdain for moral standards which is so rampant in contemporary society. We may wax eloquent in extolling moral virtues, but a variety of ethnic and financial pressures have combined to bring about a state of affairs, where ethical considerations are shoved into the background. When it comes to the promotion of Israel, religious institutions, or other philanthropic causes, the promoters are frequently interested only in the "bottom line" and are totally indifferent to matters of character or ethical propriety. Our ringing declarations that "the God of Holiness is sanctified through righteousness" will sound hollow, when we prostrate ourselves before the idols of the marketplace and join in the worship of success, power and glamour. There must be a limit to our "realism" which dictates that, in the face of budgetary constraints, we honor those who excel in the art of "making it" over those who "walk in the ways of God" and cultivate moral virtues. Have we forgotten the Biblical precept that "he who praises the *Botze'a* (the exploiter, or perhaps, in accordance with T.B. *Sandhedrin* 6:b, the one who is exclusively preoccupied with profit) commits blasphemy against God"?

Does the End Justify *Any* Means?

Religious leaders must face up to the fact that moral values cannot be inculcated by precept. It is only by providing inspiring models in day to day behavior that ethical teachings can be effectively communicated. The "body language" conveyed by a congregation has far greater impact than the formal abstract teachings it disseminates. Religious institutions must be extremely careful lest by their excessive pragmatism—in the belief that the end justifies any means—they create the impression that moral propriety is totally irrelevant to one's standing in a "holy community."

Our Tradition Commands Forgiveness

To be sure, no one should be ostracized. A "holier than thou" attitude has no place within a religious community. Even convicted criminals deserve our loving concern. We must learn to walk a tightrope between sympathy for offenders and unequivocal condemnation of improper, let alone illegal actions. No easy, absolutist formulations can be adequate to the complexities of the ethical dilemmas we encounter. After all, our religious tradition underscores the importance of forgiveness. Even the *Avaryan*—the individual who categorically rejects the practice of Judaism—is at the onset of *Yom Kippur* welcomed to join with us in worship.

But it is one thing to open our doors and hearts even to a convict, and another to give the impression that we are indifferent even to the most flagrant breaches of moral principles. A difficult balancing act is required. We must resist the temptation to jump to condemn our fellow man, because we can never be in the same situation. Yet we must also, especially in an age of crass materialism, go out of our way to demonstrate our overriding commitment to the ethical values which are generated by our faith in the Living G-d. □

JACOB B. AGUS, *among whose other books is a study of Jewish ethics entitled* The Vision and the Way, *is the rabbi of Beth El Congregation in Baltimore, Md.*

RABBI YONAH FORTNER *is the founder of the Polio Survivors Foundation. He lives in Northridge, CA.* ●

MELVIN M. LANDAU *practices law in Chicago, IL.* ●

DAVID M. FELDMAN *is the rabbi of the Bay Ridge Jewish Center in Brooklyn, and is the author of the forthcoming* Judaism And The Sexual Revolution.

ERIC I.B. BELLER *is currently a prosecutor with the District Attorney of Philadelphia. He has also practiced environmental law.*

SUSAN HANDELMAN *teaches English and Jewish Studies at the University of Maryland and is a* Sh'ma *Contributing Editor.*

MARTHA A. ACKELSBERG *teaches government at Smith College, Northampton, MA.*

SAMUEL H. DRESNER *editor, most recently of Abraham Heschel's studies,* The Circle of the Baal Shem Tov *and a* Sh'ma *Contributing Editor, taught at Hebrew Union College in 1985.*

WALTER S. WURZBURGER, *is rabbi of Congregation Shaaray Tefila, in Lawrence, N. Y.*

AL LORENZ *did the art in this section.*

II

MEETING OUR RESPONSIBILITIES

5.
Women and Judaism

Equal only when obligated

Deborah Miller

There is a general rule of thumb that Jewish women are exempt from positive commands which must be done at a certain time. There are numerous exceptions to the rule, some well known, others less-well-known. There is no question that women are subject to the commands which are not connected with special times, and to the negative commands for special times.

I propose here to deal only with the commands closely related to special times. What is the effect of this differentiation? If women are required only *not* to desacrate Shabbat, only *not* to do any *m'lakhah* on Holy days, only *not* to eat certain foods, only *not* to marry non-Jews, they effectively remain apart from non-Jews. But to the extent that they are not required to do much to *make* themselves Jewish—to pray with (as part of) a minyan; to wear *t'fillin* and *tzitzit;* to learn (and read from) the Torah—to that extent they do nothing of a positive Jewish nature.

Yes, it is true that the effect of observing certain *mitzvot lo-ta aseh* (negative commands), is a positive command, particularly for a woman. If no *hametz,* leaven, may be seen in one's home during Pesah, it is, in effect, a positive command to the woman, that is to clean her house so that it is spotless; and what CHUTZPAH for a man to regard himself as having by himself fulfilled the positive command of *b'dikat hametz* and *biyur hametz!* If no fire may be lit or food prepared on Shabbat, it is the same as a positive command to the woman to get all the cooking done, the lights set, the thermostat set, and so on, before Shabbat begins.

Only jewish associationism

But note that all of these result only in rearranging the usual drudgery of running a household or in a revamping of recipes. There is nothing intrisically Jewish about that rearranging. It is not of a different order of living, as the *mitzvot* of *t'fillin* or aliyah are.

Let us quickly add that of the three "womanly commands"—taking *challah* from large quantities of bread dough, lighting Shabbot and holiday candles and *nidah* (separation during menstruation), two are to be done by men (if they bake bread of if they live without mother or wife), and one requires a husband's cooperation. Strictly speaking, they do *not* belong exclusively to one sex.

What does this do to the view a Jewish woman has of Judaism? I'm afraid that it results in Jewish associationism, a mere secularity. That is a view that Jewish people needn't do anything Jewish to remain Jewish; as long as they socialize, play basketball, bowl and play mah-jong together, the Jewish people will continue. Jewish culture and education and religion are unnecessary.

If we are going to refute that idea for the whole Jewish population, we have to refute it for the Jewish woman, and replace humdrum activities done in the name of religion with Jewish activities which represent positive Jewish values.

An end to separate and unequal

Trude Weiss-Rosmarin

"The implications of Women's Liberation give us no cause for complacency," thus James S. Diamond (Sh'ma 1/17). However the contributors to *Sh'ma*'s issue on marriage and sex are *very* "complacent" with respect to the *real* problems of Jewish women vis-à-vis *Halakha* and the mores and customs it molded and molds. They ignore that Jewish law *dis*enfranchises women, especially wives.

Indeed, the Rabbis of the Talmud, and their predecessors and their successors, were chivalrous. And, "like nice guys who finish last," they were mindful of women's sexual needs. However they did not serve their ladies, as they were bidden to serve God, without expecting a reward. The reward was *male* children. The quotations from *Iggeret Hakodesh* and *Leshon Hasidim,* which enthuse Zalman S. Schacter and Arnold J. Wolf are based on *Berakhot* 60a: "If the husband ejaculates first, she will bear a daughter; if the wife emits her semen first, she will bear a son." This follows upon the instruction that, after intercourse, a husband should pray, for three days, that his wife should conceive; from the third to the fortieth day he should implore God's mercy that the child be a male. To be sure, "the world cannot exist without males and females; yet happy is he whose children are males and woe to him who has daughters."

Does the ketubah protect?

Being chivalrous, the Sages were protective of women; hence the *Ketubah,* the contractual promise-and-obligation of the husband to support his wife, accord her marital rights, and provide for her in case of death or divorce. However while husband and wife must live together without a *Ketubah* (in case the original one gets lost, a new one must be written), the marriage is NOT legalized by the *Ketubah* but by the groom's declaration to the bride, "Verily, you are set apart for me with this ring, according to the laws of Moses and Israel." This declaration *precedes* the reading of the *Ketubah*—it does not follow upon it, as in Rabbi Schacter's article.

There is no implication here of any "intention of the law," as Rabbi Schacter thinks that, by virtue of *Kiddushin,* "the bride and groom contract to live by the laws of the Torah, as the rabbis defined it." Likewise, the principle that he who sets for himself a woman apart as his wife does so *al da'at hakhamin* (by the legal *consent* of the sages) refers exclusively to the *halakhic* matters of the marriage ceremony and the *halakhic* eligibility of bride and groom—not to anything else.

The *Ketubah's hundred zuzim* of alimony are irrelevant today. But there is no *halakhic* obstacle to substitute American currency in a suitable amount for the *hundred zuzim* and incorporate *any conditions* the couple may wish to add. Any and everything may be stipulated in a *Ketubah,* provided it gives the place and date of the marriage, contains the promise of the groom to provide for his wife in the manner of Jewish husbands and, this is very important, is properly witnessed, in accordance with the *halakhic* rules of witnessing.

The jewish double standard

The real problem and the source of the *unfreedom* of Jewish wives is not the *ketubah* but the double standard of the *Halakha* which accords to males complete sexual freedom (except with *Jewish* wives and virgins) while denying any kind of freedom to *Agunot,* deserted wives "chanined" to a marriage which is no longer a marriage.

The case of Israel's *mamzerim,* currently in the news, Hanoch and Miriam Langer, proves the inequity of the Jewish laws of marriage and divorce. The premise of Jewish divorce law is that the wife is the property of the husband. Only he, and not a rabbi or rabbinical court—can divorce her. If he refuses to do so or disappears by malice or due to the force of circumstances, the wife can never remarry. She remains an *Agunah*—"chained" forever to the husband, even if he, as is frequently the case today, has remarried in a civil court. If she does remarry during her husband's life and without having received a *get,* she is an adulteress and her children born of the "adulterous" union are *mamzerim.* The mother of Hanoch and Miriam Langer came to Israel during World War II. She assumed that her first husband, a Polish Christian who had converted to Judaism, had perished in the war and holocaust—and she remarried. Years later, the first husband, who had survived came to Israel. This made the present Mrs. Langer and "adulteress" and her children *mamzerim.* The Israel Rabbinate declared that she was still the wife of her first husband when she remarried (Jewish law does not recognized presumptive death) and thus she violated the Seventh Commandment.

Concubinage is not an answer

Concubinage is typical of male chauvinism. It affords the male the comforts and satisfactions of marriage without any obligations. The *pile gesh is* not "a common law wife." In post-biblical times she was a *mistress* and the solace of Ashkenazi husbands after Rabbenu Gershom's prohibition of bigamy and polygamy for Jews living in Christian countries. Rabbi Schacter's opinion that "concubinage would free us paradoxically to treat the couple like *menschen* again" would be amusing, if the implications were not so serious.

In concubinage the woman is even less a *mensch* than she is as a wife. She may be "dismissed" (of course she, too, can "dismiss" her lover) any time. As males are known to tire sooner than women of the same sexual fare and change to another diet, even when it means messy divorce proceedings and social and professional ostracism, "mutual covenanting," in which Rabbi Schacter sets great store, do not mean a thing when the couple who when they were in love could sleep on a bed narrow as the edge of a sword but, after love has vanished, find a bed sixty ells wide too small (sanhedrin 7a).

As for Rabbi Schacter's suggestion that rabbis should give "couples as many options as possible" for the marriage ceremony, *rabbis are altogether not needed for sealing a Jewish marriage*. All that is required is a *Huppah,* the *Ketubah,* two witnesses (*a minyan is desirable but not obligatory*), the bride and the groom with a ring (or an article of value to give the bride).

The problem which *should* "give us no cause for complacency" is the *un*freedom of Jewish women, and especially wives, under Jewish law, being subject to the fate of *Agunah,* being declared unfit to serve as a witness, to vote or be voted for, and to be subject to numerous other legal disabilities.

Women in a minyan: the change demeans

Miriam Shapiro

In the Middle Ages, there lived a woman for whom I bear a particular affection, not only because her name was Miriam Shapiro. She was an erudite scholar who taught Rabbinical students. However, her students never saw her — true to the standards of modesty of her day, she lectured from behind a curtain.

She was not alone. There have been many 'liberated' women in Jewish history: we have documented cases of women prophets, scholars, even *Chassidic* Rebbes. I was intrigued by the question, "Why did these women never ask for an *aliyah* or to be included in a *minyan?*" It was certainly not because they needed their consciousness raised — they were ready to defend their rights in other areas.

As I read more and more, I began to see that not having an *aliyah* was not a sign of inequality. Equality was just not the issue. Rather, women were free from certain

rituals which had to be performed at a set time. They were not held less equal, but on the contrary, our Sages felt that *what women did was important.* The women understood this and did not see their status and dignity flowing from the ritual of the synagogue. They knew that the structure of Judaism rested on many pillars: the home, the synagogue, scholarship, *mitzvot* — to name a few. All were important.

In the American Jewish community today, only one of these pillars, the synagogue, is functioning at all adequately, perhaps because the Christian society in which we live is principally church-oriented. The synagogue, however, cannot bear the burden alone, nor was it ever designed to. The future of Judaism requires that the other pillars begin to bear some of their weight. As we increase the role of women in the synagogue, we increase the strain on the one limping institution we have.

What women should be asking for is a return of the status and dignity that was once ours. Why then has the thrust of the feminist movement been into the synagogue? I have slowly come to the conclusion that we have been sold a bill of goods.

Integrated but unequal

For example, the Conservative Movement rightly congratulates itself on the integrated education it gives to its children: boys and girls study together on an equal basis. Neither studies any subject that the other does not. However, after I made a recent study of textbooks in use in the afternoon schools, the congratulations rang a little hollow in my ears. While boys and girls may *study* the texts together, the *education* is not an integrated one, for the texts are aimed only at the boys.

For instance, any textbook, no matter how abridged, contains the story of how Sarah laughed when informed that she might give birth at ninety. In no text could I find the immediately preceding chapter in the *Torah,* in which Abraham laughs first and is therefore told to name his son Isaac. Here we also find Abraham willing to settle for Ishmael as inheritor, but being told emphatically that the child must be Sarah's as well as his. Our children are taught a distorted view of the story in which only Sarah lacks perfect faith.

In our history courses on every level, we teach that at the destruction of the Temple, the synagogue arose as the institution to fill the void. Prayer took the place of sacrifice. But that is only half the story. The fact that the table at home is likened to the Temple Altar is typically ignored. All the ritual surrounding the table, e.g. handwashing, salting of bread, and most of all, *Kashrut,* is reminiscent of the Temple Altar. Our students never learn that if one seeks the laws of *Kashrut* in the *Talmud,* one must look under the heading of sacrifices. Here again, only part of the story is told so that those rituals which are traditionally in man's province come out looking as all there is to Judaism.

We have raised a generation of girls who as adult Jews want only to be men because we have taught them that men are better and that what men do is best. We climax their education with a *Bat-Mitzvah* that, rather than being creative, is merely a poor imitation of a *Bar-Mitzvah.* We cheat our girls of their heritage; no wonder they want to be as boys. The ultimate in Male chauvinism is to define equality for a woman as doing what a man does. In the area of ritual, it is not Judaism but the distortions of American Jewish society that make women unequal. Let us make the corrections in the proper place.

When exemption does not mean exclusion
I am reminded of the struggle of the Blacks in the early 1960's to be exactly like Whites. They soon recognized that being equal does not require giving up one's own identity. Now the slogan is "Black is Beautiful." My slogan is the same, "Jewish Womanhood is Beautiful."

Our Sages recognized the uniqueness of Jewish womanhood and exempted women from most time-tied affirmative *mitzvot.* A woman must pray every day, but she need not do so at a set time. A man must recite the *Sh'ma* and the *Sh'moneh Esreh* during specific time intervals of the day. While a man may be just as busy as a woman, he is not exempted from the time requirement. A woman is not exempt because she is *busy,* but because creating a Jewish home is a religious obligation.

The other side of the coin of the recent R.A. decision on women and the *minyan* is that the person who may be counted for a *minyan* may be called on to complete a *minyan* when necessary. And indeed in some synagogues women may find that they have been conned into comprising the *minyan.* Jewish tradition tells me that woman's role was too important for this requirement — the Law Committee lowers my position by telling me that I am *not* important enough to be exempt. They compound this insult by telling me that they are now raising me to equality.

An evasion of more serious issues
I cannot resist the opportunity to speculate a little as to why the Law Committee did so. It is a rather well-known fact that the place where our movement is weakest is in the development of a concerned and observant laity. While the Rabbis are debating whether Woman should be counted for a *minyan,* in synagogue after synagogue, there is danger of having no *minyan* at all. Attendance has not picked up markedly in those synagogues which have long practiced what the R.A. has recently sanctioned nor has adherence to *mitzvot.* The truth of the matter is that most congregants couldn't care less — neither prayer nor *mitzvot* are of particular importance in their lives. Could it be that by debating these issues, the Rabbis are avoiding the more difficult issues on which the future of our movement lies? As a Conservative Jew, I have enough confidence in these Rabbis to feel that only good would come to our movement and to Judaism if they would turn to the real issues.

Recently, I taught at a U.S.Y. encampment in which Rabbi Blumenthal's *teshuvah* (responsa) on *aliyah* for Women was part of the source material. As I attempted to explain it, one boy raised his hand and said, "Excuse me, I don't understand. What is an *aliyah?" This* is our problem.

Who's afraid of an aliyah?
Peninnah Schram

As a little girl, I remember sitting in the main part of our synagogue next to my father, the Cantor of an Orthodox synagogue, in a seat facing the Congregation. Since I was the Cantor's daughter, no one insisted I join the women upstairs in the balcony. I can still remember how happy and proud I was to be downstairs, next to the *bimah,* next to *my* father — but also with the rest of the men in the Congregation. I felt important being there because that was "where the action was" — where the important activities of the day (*Shabbat* or holidays) took place. I could see everything close up — the high priests as they covered themselves with their *taletim* and lifting their arms high up from underneath forming a strange shape that, at that moment, did not seem human . . . I could "kiss" the *Torah* as it went by

. . . I could see the old men take snuff, and spit into the spittoons. It was an exciting and a happy time for me.

I rarely questioned anything about the status of women in Jewish life because, whenever I did ask if I could join in or why this was so, I was told in a matter-of-fact way, "A woman can't" . . . or "A woman doesn't have to" . . . or "This is not a place for a woman." I accepted unquestioningly and merely enjoyed my "special" privilege all the more. Whenever I went back to the balcony to sit with my mother, I felt "out of it." At that time I would constantly be annoyed at the talking and socializing that went on all around me. It seemed to me that the women came to synagogue only to see their friends and show off their clothes. While the greetings of *"Gut Yom Tov"* or *"Gut Shabbos"* were beautiful, why didn't they then concentrate on praying or being quiet? I was puzzled by this confusion.

I was especially angry and became adept at giving "dirty looks" when they talked while my father was "praying with all his heart." It seemed that the women were not as serious as the men. Now that I look back at the scene, can you blame them? The women wouldn't even reach out to touch the *Torah!* I went to the *cheder* with the boys together and I learned all the prayers and davening. I could even lead the *Sh'moneh Esray* better than most of the boys; but I was allowed to sing it only in class as practice. Yet, I still did not question why I couldn't participate more in the actual service. That was the way it was.

Discovering an opportunity

Suddenly, as an adult, I found myself surrounded by a whole new concept of Judaism and the woman's role in the religion: Reconstructionism. This discovery coincided with a new awareness of myself as a woman in society, and that the independence I had found could be part of my religion too. I was very excited to learn that a woman at *The Society for the Advancement of Judaism* was counted as part of a *minyan* (and not just in a *minyan* of women for a women's congregation). She could fully participate and have an *aliyah* — and that the *Bat-Mitzvah* takes place on Saturday morning, just like a *Bar-Mitzvah*. Revolutionary — radical — *meshuge;* or democratic and right — my head whirled. I couldn't wait to get my first *aliyah*. I became a member, enrolled my children in the Hebrew School and started attending services on Saturdays and Holidays.

The Synagogue sent me a letter of welcome and invited me, as a new member, to present myself at services so I could be assigned an *aliyah*. Several Saturdays went by, and I realized how emotional I got at the thought of going to the *Torah* for an *aliyah*. When it was the *Yohrtzeit* for my father, I thought to myself, what better way than to have an *aliyah* in his memory. He would have been proud of me and I think, in many ways, pleased. He was very modern in much of his thinking but bound by orthodoxy as his way of life.

I arrived in synagogue and I suddenly relaized I could not utter those words of request for an *aliyah*. Why? I sat trying to understand my resistance, my fear, my inability to make the commitment. I was not in the habit. Yes, that was certainly one reason, no doubt. I had never done it before. I also was sure I would cry when I got up to the *Torah* — the daughter in her father's place. I realized my feelings were in such a turmoil that I was afraid I would make a fool of myself if I went up.

I allowed one year to go by and then one day, my friend's son called to tell me that he was having his *Bar-Mitzvah* and would I take an *aliyah*? My head whirled, my heart beat fast and I could feel myself mechanically saying "Yes," knowing that I had a commitment and then I would have to go ahead with my promise. He asked me if I knew the prayer, as his mother was having difficulty with it. I assured him I knew it very well; indeed, as I rehearsed the prayer, the melody and words came out perfectly, thanks to the repetition practiced in my childhood.

Consummation of a dream

If I had been making my debut in a leading role on Broadway, I could not have been more excited. The day arrived — and I was told I had the fourth *aliyah*. I sat in synagogue and waited, going over the prayer in my head — but not really sure what would happen when I would open my mouth on the bimah.

Time seemed suspended. Then they called for #4 in Hebrew, I took a deep breath to calm myself down, got up from my seat, walked up the three steps, shook hands with the Rabbi — big smile — the very look of assurance — nodded to the Cantor and touched the *Torah* at the place indicated so as to bring the word to my lips — and began. The first words came out loud and clear. During the response, I looked at the *Bar-Mitzvah* boy and winked. He looked relieved and happy. O.K. I went on. I looked at the *Torah* and at the beautiful lettering while the Cantor read the portion. I was proud to be a Jew! I was thrilled to see the words of the *Torah* so close up and to be following the reading from the actual *Torah*. It seemed, at that moment, that there was nothing more beautiful than those words. I felt love in my whole *n'shome*. Then I made the closing *bracha* and I shook hands with the people standing around the *bimah* and went back to my seat — floating on a cloud.

When I sat down my hands started to shake and my heart pounded so loudly I was sure everyone around me could hear it. I had had my first *aliyah*. I could never be the same. I had shared with my father and my forebears an age-old tradition and ritual. I was not just a Jewish woman — but a Jew with all the rights, privileges and obligations. I was not the same person when I left the synagogue that day as when I had entered it.

From behind the mechitzah
Joseph C. Kaplan

For more than 33 years and until just a few months ago, it would have been impossible for me to write an article with the above title. My wife could have done so, as could my mother, my grandmothers, my sister, my aunts and even my daughters—but not I. I never sat behind a *mechitzah* in *shul*; I never *davened* or listened to the reading of the Torah cut off from the center *bimah* at which these activities take place. Never, that is, until the *bat mitzvah* of my niece, Amanda Rosen, which was celebrated this past *Simchat Torah* at the Lincoln Square Synagogue Women's Service.

The *bat mitzvah* ceremony itself was beautiful and exhilarating. Amanda looked radiant, as did her mother and grandmothers who escorted her as she was called to the Torah. She flawlessly recited the blessings and chanted both the Torah portion and *Haftarah* clearly and melodically. Our family and friends beamed as we joyfully accepted the *mazel tovs* that were heaped upon us all.

But for me (and I daresay for other male family members and friends), this *simcha* had special significance. For in order to allow the entire family to observe Amanda's performance, the Women's Service, for the first time, erected a *mechitzah* behind which men could sit and view the proceedings. Thus we were given a unique opportunity to watch a traditional prayer service from a new and different prespective.

The Disconnectedness of the Experience

How did I feel in this new location? Joyous, elated and proud, yet distanced, isolated and disconnected. The first three were my feelings as an uncle; the latter three my emotions as a male Jew. For the first time I was merely an observer of public prayer; it was impossible, and indeed forbidden, for me to fully participate. I could only look and not do, only answer and not be involved. For the first time there was no possibility of my leading the service, reading the Torah, having an *aliyah,* receiving a *kibud* (honor), or assisting in the running of the service.

As a religious experience, therefore, my attendance at the *bat mitzvah*, or more accurately the Women's Service, was a cold one; for me, it lacked the warmth that a *Simchat Torah* service, or indeed almost any *t'filah b'tzibur* (communal prayer), usually engenders. There was a decreased sense of inclusion in the one People of Isreal; a feeling of remoteness rather than unity. On certain levels, my personal religious antennae were dulled rather than sharpened. I could not help but feel that this was not my service, it was theirs; they were conducting prayers for themselves and not for me.

And who was this "they?" It was my friends, wife, daughters, mother-in-law, sisters-in-law and nieces; it was people who are among those closest and dearest to me. But because of the *mechitzah*—separating us into doers and observers and thereby creating active and passive roles—a community of people who before and after the service felt as one were transformed into an "us" and a "they."

It is interesting to examine how "they" acted. I knew from past comments that some of the women did not enjoy being relegated to the *ezrat nashim* (women's area); that they found sitting behind a *mechitzah* difficult, an impediment, rather than an aid, to their prayers. It would not have been unreasonable, therefore, had they, after sitting behind *mechitzot* for so many years, erected one for the men which was high and uncomfortable just to "show them how it feels" or simply because that was what they were used to. But such was not the case. This *mechitzah* was one which offered the men an unobstructed view of the service; its top reached only the minimally acceptable height; it was located in front of the room near the *bimah*; it was as unobtrusive as a *mechitzah* could be.

Caring for Those Behind the Mechitzah

I do not believe that this was mere happenstance, nor do I believe that the decision was made simply out of friendship, even though close bonds of friendship exist. Rather, I believe that these women, because of their past experience, have developed a true sensitivity to the issues involved. They wanted us to be comfortable, wanted us to be as much a part of the service as physically possible given the *mechitzah*. Unlike many men, they deeply cared about the feelings of those who sat behind the *mechitzah*; they were, in a sense, on our side.

I must admit that I have always been considered somewhat of a "liberal" within the Orthodox community in which I was raised and of which I consider myself a staunch member. As such, I have been especially vocal about the problems of women's issues *vis-a-vis* the *halacha*. I have been a long time supporter of the Women's Service which was established against fierce and powerful opposition, written about the need to institute the ceremony of *simchat bat* upon the birth of a daughter, advocated equal education for girls in *yeshivot*, strongly opposed suggestions to raise *mechitzot*, studied the legal issue of the inequality of women with respect to *get* (divorce), and struggled for increased participation of women within the synagogue power structure. While I have not always been successful, I have never given up the cause.

Yet now I feel that I can do more than actively support these positions on an intellectual basis; I can begin to empathize with those women who are dissatisfied. And, when the need arises again, as it probably will, to do battle against a higher *mechitzah*, I will join the women opposing such a move with a greater understanding of the intensity of their feelings; when disagreements arise over the need to teach Torah to girls as it's taught to boys or over the advisability of instituting rituals for *bat mitzvah*, I will close my eyes and hear Amanda's lovely voice ringing in my ears. I can then join the fray with renewed vigor, and with the knowledge that these questions are of critical importance.

The old order has returned; on the *Shabbat* following the *bat mitzvah* I again took my seat on the other side of the *mechitzah*. But things were not the same as before. Those few minutes behind the *mechitzah* had altered, in more ways than one, my view and my vision. ★

We need women conservative rabbis

Harold M. Schulweis

After Chancellor Gerson Cohen's measured and persuasive presentation of the Rabbinical Assembly Commission's report on the ordination of women, I was convinced that the decision was all over but the counting. But then, in the corri-dors of the Century Plaza, I was caught up in a small circle of colleagues still intensely debating the issue. One of the advocates of women's ordination argued his position using terms like "equality," "liberation" and "moral fairness." But he was quickly informed by one of his erudite colleagues that such categories were not pertinent to the making of a *halachic* decision. To allow such extra-*halachic* arguments (from morality) would threaten the whole structure of *halachah* and reflect adversely upon the Law-giver himself. (See David Weiss Halivni's article "Can a Religious Law be Immoral" in the recent Kelman *Festschrift, Perspectives on Jews and Judaism.)*

But he then went on to maintain his *halachic* opposition to the Commission reports with arguments of emasculation, fadism, the divisiveness within the Conservative movement which such a decision might create, the interpretation such a vote may carry with the laity who would likely see it as the Reform-ation of Conservative Judaism, etc. His arguments were interesting. But were they *halachic?*

Surely they were not less pragmatic, socio-psychological or moral than the other side. For that matter, were the Talmudic Sages who over-ruled the precedent allowing women the right to be called for an *aliyah* not using extra-*halachic* arguments? Is their concern, *kavod hatzibur,* the respect of the congregation, an argument from sociology or *halachah?* And are those who use *kavod hatzibur* to ritually enfranchise women less entitled to use such an argument?

The mini-debate in the corridors was symptomatic of an uncertainty as to what is properly entailed by "the *halachic* process." The disagreements were not over pro- or con- *halachic* ideologies but over the understanding of the very character of *halachah*. What have *halachic* arguments traditionally included and what should they include? Are moral arguments pertinent in the *halachic* process or are they to be dismissed as humanistic, relativistic, articulations? Deeper attention to Jewish scholarship and the wisdom associated with Conservative Judaism's commitment to history have much to contribute to strengthen the resolve and courage of the rabbinate.

Women's Ordination Is Not A Fad
The briefest examination of the literature and decisions of the Conservative movement in the

past two decades evidences the expenditure of an inordinate amount of intellect and energy addressed to the role of Jewish women in our religious community. A review of the decisions of the Conservative Law Committee these last decades indicates that the issue of ordination before the Rabbinical Assembly is not some casual or abrupt intrusion into the stream of Conservative Jewish thought. It is consistent with its earlier decisions to enfranchise Jewish women in the religious community, e.g., the calling of women to the Torah, the counting of women in the *minyan,* the allowance of the marriage of Jewish divorcees and proselytes to Jews who trace their lineage to the tribe of Levi, the elimination of the embarrassment of *chalitzah* (the ceremony cancelling a Levirate marriage), etc. So the claims which argue for women's ordination are not faddist eccentricities. The proposal is a natural development of cumulative historical forces within the Conservative movement and is a logical outcome of the movement's creative adaptation of customs of another era to new situations and moral expectations.

Rabbis and laity have long taken to heart the intellectual and devotional claims of Jewish women so marvelously described by Solomon Schechter in his essay, "Women in Temple and Synagogue," (*Studies in Judaism,* first series). In a carefully judicious statement in that article, Schechter wrote, regarding the opinion of Rabbi Eliezer recorded in the *Mishnah* which prohibits women from studying Torah, "But justified as the advice of Rabbi Eliezer may have been *in his own time,* it was rather unfortunate that later generations continued to take it as the guiding principle for the education of their children." Rabbis of a still later generation would surely not be well advised to perpetuate that unfortunate counsel.

Tradition is not Monolithic

Tradition is not of one piece. Ben Azzai's judgement that one is obligated to teach his daughter Torah is at least as valid a precedent to call upon as Rabbi Eliezer's contrary position. The opinions of some of the rabbis of the *Talmud* that characterized women as garrulous, gluttonous, light-hearted, ostentatious, miserly are individual opinions which may readily be contrasted to other rabbinic judgements which perceived women as intelligent, moral, sensitive, compassionate, modest, and honorable (*Encyclopedia Talmudit,* art. *Ishah).*

Noteworthy and admirable is the recent decision of the Orthodox Stern College for Women in New York to introduce intensive courses in Talmudic studies for women, a course of studies introduced by none other than Rabbi J.B. Soloveitchik who offered its introductory Talmudic *shiur* (lesson). And all this from Orthodox leaders, and contrary to the judgements of Rabbi Eliezer, the Rambam and the Baal ha-Turim.

The related issue of women's ordination similarly is not over *halachah* or tradition, but concerns which part of the tradition we choose to lean upon and which criteria for selection we employ. Chancellor Cohen has articulated the criterion of creative tradition, whose principle of selectivity is found in "the healthy appropriation of new forces and ideas for the sake of our own growth and enrichment." To pin the denial of women to function as rabbis on the tradition would malign the very tradition which is so often cited for its innovative ingenuity and ability to transform or abandon customs shown to be inimical to the well-being of the Jewish people.

Women Rabbis Will Add Talent To The Pool

Contemporary Jewish leadership owes the Jewish community more than a reiteration of the litany of Jewish sorrows and failures: Jewish young people who mix-marry, who are attracted to conversionary cults and are indifferent if not hostile to Jewish life. Given the terrifying fact that over 80 per cent of Jewish scholars, rabbis, and full-time students of Torah, have been destroyed by the Holocaust, rabbinic leaders have a moral obligation to call upon the untapped energy of our daughters who seek to serve the Jewish community religiously. As a teacher at the University of Judaism I have taught many of these daughters who come from excellent Conservative Jewish backgrounds and who have been inspired by their experience at Camp Ramah and Hebrew High Schools and their synagogues and who are now compelled to turn to non-Conservative rabbinic institutions because of the exclusionary policy of the Jewish Theological Seminary.

Some changes in Jewish life are opposed because they threaten to diminish, shrivel and exclude Jewish energies. But the admission of qualified women who seek to study at the feet of the masters of our tradition and to translate their learning into teaching and spiritual leadership promises to add, increase and include irreplaceable talent in our midst. Neither traditional moral wisdom nor contemporary pragmatic sense can sustain the exclusion of women from their rightful role in the community.

The same tired arguments which have greeted every positive creative addition to Jewish life by the Conservative movement will emerge again. People argue that the movement will discourage men from Jewish religious life. But history testifies that men did not leave medicine or law or politics when women entered these professions. Men did not lose interest in politics when women received their suffrage in 1920. The *Bat Mitzvah* did not eliminate the significance of the *Bar Mitzvah.* The admission of women to the boards of directors of congregations with voice and vote did not render those councils effete. The wives and mothers are as instrumental in bringing husbands and children into the synagogue and its life as are the latter in bringing women into the life of the synagogue.

The Halachic Process Must Stay Vital

The argument that the Conservative movement would be split were it to affirm the ordination of women is an old form of intimidation. Such neophobic threats have been heard throughout the career of the Conservative movement and have not prevailed. The threat to the movement does not come from the foresight of its creative *halachah* but from a spiritual anemia which casts doubt upon its vitality and sense of purpose. If Conservative Judaism is to sustain its credibility as a world movement, it must continue to demonstrate that the *halachic* process works and that historical understanding of Judaism is not a cloistered erudition but one which helps contemporary leaders make decisions which will strengthen the Jewish people and its faith. The nerve of Conservative Judaism lies in its fidelity to the life-affirming adaptability of the Jewish tradition. That loyalty does not confuse "immutability with immobility" (Louis Ginzberg).

Beyond the issue of women's rabbinic ordination lies the question of the character of a movement which has repeatedly been described by its attachment to history. "More than either Orthodoxy or Reform, it /Conservative Judaism/ professes genuine reverence for history, not only for tradition, but institutions" (Salo Baron, "The Enduring Heritage" in *Great Ages and Ideas of the Jewish People.).* The massive research of the scholars of the Conservative movement, including such intellectual figures as Louis Ginzberg, Hayyim Chernowitz, Louis Finkelstein, Saul Lieberman, has taught its rabbinic and lay students that tradition reflects the changing needs and aspirations of the living people; that no law, custom or opinion is immaculately conceived; that rabbinic decisions in all ages do not emerge out of an intellectual, political, social or economic vacuum, that the genius of the *halachic* process lies in its sensitivity to new situations, and in its courage and wisdom to respond to the needs of the living organism — *am Yisrael.* Gerson Cohen has demonstrated that the great exegetes of every generation "have been able to take a core, reinterpret it and retain its authenticity through *change* and thereby through *contemporary relevance"* (*The Blessings of Assimilation in Jewish History,* 1973, italics his). Solomon Schechter's critique of the ahistorical approach to Jewish tradition was made to oppose the "phonograph-like authority which spends its time reproducing the voice of others without an opinion of its own, without originality, without initiative and discretion" (from *Guideposts to Judaism,* Jacob Agus).

If Jewish scholarship is to be respected, its deeply learned books must be lived. Jewish scholarship has consequences. Our understanding of the past helps us to understand the present. Rabbis in the past made choices and made tradition in accordance with their perception of Jewish faith and ethics and the compelling needs of their constituents. Rabbis in the present can do no less. It is helpful to remember that the past too was once the present.

Women rabbis as a death sign

Pinchas Stolper

The Conservative Movement's move to ordain women brought no hue and cry from Orthodoxy. Why the silence? Still another radical step by Conservative Judaism to break with the mainstream of historical Judaism and abandon an additional requirement of tradition would have brought a spate of articles and outcries twenty years ago.

Orthodox silence derives from the fact that, as a movement, Conservative Judaism is no longer taken seriously. It has long ceased to be a factor in Jewish religious life. The defection of large number of Jews from Orthodoxy to Conservatism stopped a long time ago and today the movement is in the opposite direction. When the sons and daughters of Conservative rabbis seek to find the reality of their religious heritage, they invariably become *baalei teshuva,* accept the Orthodox way of life, and enter Orthodox educational institutions and communities. Otherwise, they do what most members of Conservative congregations have long since done, — abandon Judaism in all but name.

This new Conservative move is seen by the Orthodox community as a gimmick, rather than a genuine effort to bring women into the rabbinate, and a tacit admission that Conservatism is in fact a declining movement. For the Conservative movement, the ordination of women will be a public announcement that they can no longer attract enough men to fill their solitary, small New York Seminary which has not grown in student numbers for nearly thirty years, though it is the one institution in the world ordaining Conservative rabbis. Each year, only twenty or so men are ordained though there are more than 100 Conservative synagogues in urgent need of rabbis. Its total rabbinic student body is approximately two hundred, a sad showing for a movement which claims to represent 52% of synagogue affiliated American Jews. The flow of rabbis from Orthodox sources accepting Conservative rabbinical positions has slowed to a trickle.

Orthodoxy Is Undergoing A Revival

These statistics make a mockery of Conservatism's pretenses at being a serious religious movement and bode ill for its future. It is quite apparent that the momentum of the Conservative "Movement" in Judaism has fizzled, and that no one is any longer really interested. The Conservative movement does not have one popular religious leader whose name would evoke a response; whose method, approach, philosophy or leadership are widely known and respected. There is not one Conservative name which has achieved a following approaching any one of a dozen Orthodox leaders such as Rabbi Joseph Soloveitchik, Rabbi Moshe Feinstein, The Lubavitcher Rebbe, Reb Yaakov Kaminetsky, Rabbi Isaac Hutner, — among others.

In contrast to the austere sterility of the Conservative "Movement", the pursuit of Torah study on its highest levels is undergoing an unprecedented revival in the Orthodox community. At least ninety-five percent of the young men pursuing Talmudic studies in the United States are enrolled in Orthodox institutions. The American and Canadian cities which boast Orthodox rabbinical colleges span the continent, covering almost every major city with a significant Jewish population.

In all, there are in excess of seven thousand students pursuing Talmudic studies on the college and post-graduate level in the United States under Orthodox auspices; and a few thousand more Americans are studying in Israel. This represents an unprecedented explosion of commitment, scholarship and youthful idealism. In ten years there will not be a major American city without an Orthodox graduate, *Kollel* faculty. The solitary comparable Conservative rabbinical seminary, and the solitary Reform rabbinical institution in the United States make a sad showing when contrasted to Orthodoxy with its vast network of over eighty four institutions.

Reform-Conservative Distinctions Will Blur

Admittedly, some of the Orthodox institutions are small or recently established. But as they take firm root with each passing year, they become the rallying point for the positive forces in that community and the generator of whatever hopes exist for the survival of an educated, literate Judaism in their respective communities. In time, the dedicated young scholars of the senior *yeshivot* elicit the admiration and support of the entire Jewish community, Orthodox, Conservative and Reform, generating a Jewish revival in Orthodox terms throughout the community.

The Conservative call for women rabbis will serve to do little more than widen its continuing breech with traditional Judaism, and will further obliterate the distinction between the Reform and Conservative movements in this country. While they have just awakened to the role of women in the synagogue and Jewish society, the Orthodox community in America opened its first school to provide women with an appropriate Jewish education over forty years ago. Today, there are scores of Orthodox educational institutions for women throughout the country with thousands of students, including many schools on the college level, in addition to seven college-level institutions in Israel serving American women.

We Cannot Compromise Our Tradition

The experience of the Reform Movement, which has ordained women rabbis for several years, has not been successful. None of the ordained women hold their own pulpit exclusively, and one has become disillusioned and left the rabbinate. A few weeks ago, Sally Preisand, the first reformed "rabbi" resigned because she was unable to go beyond the "associate rabbi" level. Women who choose to become "rabbis" find themselves dissatisfied once they have achieved their goal, because the phenomenon stems from a basic misunderstanding of the woman's role in the synagogue and Judaism. On the other hand, the graduates of Orthodoxy's women's institutions as a rule find deep satisfaction in the roles provided for them throughout the Orthodox Jewish community.

Although the dynamic growth and resurgence of an Orthodoxy emerging triumphant is everywhere in evidence, we dare not gloat. The tragedy of the large Conservative and Reformed communities torn from their Torah roots, declining and withering by every significant yardstick, is appalling. No one doubts that there are thousands of Conservative and even Reform Jews who are sensitive to the authentic and the real, who love Torah and tradition, and who are deeply concerned with Jewish survival. They must be asked to re-think and re-evaluate the disastrous failure of the defeatist course their movements are pursuing in America. The way to perpetuate Judaism is not to adopt non-Jewish fads, or to attempt to attract non-Jews through inter-marriage, but to make a radical about face by returning to authentic tradition. A religion which subsists on gimmickry can not long survive — a synagogue served by a woman rabbi is probably a synagogue that will close its doors in less than twenty years. The compromises of the Conservative leadership not only deny the reality of Torah, in the long run they simply do not work, even on their own terms. The only synagogues which are packed with young people in this country are Orthodox synagogues, and the schools which attract young intellectuals in ever swelling numbers are the Orthodox schools. In the end, the way that *works,* that guarantees Jewish survival and revival, which insures a thriving community, which effectively resists the inroads of assimilation and inner rot, is the way that is historic and authentic.

If the demographers and sociologists are correct it will not be long before American Orthodoxy emerges as the majority movement in American Jewish life. The way things are heading Orthodoxy's ranks will be swelled by many who abandoned the cathedrals of Conservatism for the more modest, but more honest and authentic synagogues of American Orthodoxy.

Anna o., bertha p., jewish feminist
Nina Beth Cardin

This is the one hundredth anniversary of Bertha Pappenheim's entry into treatment with Sigmund Freud. As the first person treated by the modern psychoanalytic method, Bertha has achieved renown as Anna O. This anniversary has prompted Sh'ma to take a look at Bertha Pappenheim from a contemporary perspective.

Known to the world of psychology as Sigmund Freud's Anna O., Bertha Pappenheim in many ways epitomizes Jewish women throughout the ages: faceless, nameless mothers, wives and daughters, known for their utility to men, stripped of their chosen contributions. For Bertha, her sickness and self-administered cure became her history; her life was reduced to a mental malady, overshadowing the later powerful role she was to play in Jewish history in general and Jewish women's history in particular. However, through the resourceful and impeccable scholarship of researchers such as Marion Kaplan (whose impressive book on Bertha Pappenheim and the German-Jewish Feminist Movement which she founded is required reading), we can begin to reclaim and redeem the other side of Anna O.

No strong historical evidence exists which directly links the German-Jewish feminist movement in the first third of this century to the American Jewish feminist movement in the last third. To all appearances, the two movements grew spontaneously and independently out of the secular feminist activities of their day. Still, in strategy, goals, piety and dedication the modern Jewish feminist movement can learn much from the erstwhile movement's founder, Bertha Pappenheim.

Bertha was a devout Jew and ardent feminist. She knew that one belief could inform and give shape to the other; that Jewish women need not choose between feminism and Judaism, rejecting fulfillment in one area for satisfaction in the other. She dedicated her life to articulating and actualizing this symbiosis.

Can one be both a Jew and a feminist?

Jewish feminists today face this identical challenge. The very term "Jewish feminism" is considered an oxymoron by some. Today's Jewish feminists are striving to define a reconciliation of these two aspects of themselves, with more or less support from the general Jewish community. Some strive for equality throughout the Jewish world: home, synagogue, and community; some choose a bifurcated role: equality in the community, traditional separation in the synagogue and a personalized coupling of the two modes in the home. Whereas Bertha and her co-workers easily defined a woman's place and embraced their distinctiveness within, but sought equality beyond, that area, today's Jewish women have a more profound struggle. They are struggling to define their private space, where equality with men is meaningless, and the public space, where equality is essential. It is this definition, this drawing of lines, which underlies all issues of the Jewish feminist movement.

For Bertha, feminism was a two-pronged struggle to be fought in the streets and in the board rooms. In the street, she and her organization helped save innocent girls from the ignoble lairs of Jewish pimps on the hunt; created girls' clubs to teach religion and piety to the uneducated; established training schools to give women job skills. In the board room, where she was often a woman alone, Bertha fought for women's equal representation, women's vote and women's voice.

Privilege coupled with responsibility

From her we learn that modern Jewish feminism must likewise be fought on two fronts; on individual and communal levels, in Jewish law and Jewish lore. Women must become equal partners in federations (as both lay leaders and professionals), in synagogues and in major Jewish organizations, as well as in the home, in scholarship and in contributions, both spiritual and financial. Bertha never spoke of rights, but of duties to be fulfilled and privileges to be won. While our moral perspective forces us to talk about rights and morality, we nonetheless must learn that duties and obligations come with those rights. A woman should not demand ritual equality in the synagogue yet ignore ritual at home. To demand an *aliyah* on *Shabbat* morning without having lit candles the night before weakens feminism's moral stance. Likewise, men and women who object to women's ritual equality yet do not themselves observe *mitzvot*, have forfeited their moral vote. In addition, larger salaries mean larger financial contributions. Women still need to learn how to be comfortable with the responsibility, and the clout, of larger gifts.

Bertha Pappenheim was admirable for her diligence and constancy. Jewish feminism was her cause, not only her belief. She moved it and fashioned it. She never tired of working for it, and never gave it up. She never forgot that she was the rare woman who "made it" in the man's world, and that others depended on her to fight for them.

Women's organizations: a feminist need

Today, there is a tendency to forget the urgency of the cause, to pay lip service to it only, or to tire of it altogether, especially among those women who have made it, or those men who have fought so long for it. Women rabbis and women leaders, national and local, professional and volunteer, need to remember the cause, to realign themselves with it, and to resist the urge to abandon it. These leaders must show that feminism is still an issue of concern to the entire community, both men and women; that the problems of Jewish day-care, Jewish education, reform in Jewish divorce laws, women's representation in Jewish organizations, ritual innovation, the future of the family and the like are Jewish issues which have not yet been satisfactorily resolved and must be addressed by the entire community.

Still and all, Bertha Pappenheim knew that she could not successfully push Jewish feminism without a full organization of women behind her. Women were and are, after all, feminism's prime movers and women needed a place to be together constructively, a place where they could form alliances and networks, a place where they could support, inspire and encourage each other.

Today, sisterhoods, women's organizations and women's auxiliaries are taking stock and studying their goals, composition and effectiveness. They must determine when and where separate organizations are needed, for psychological, preparatory, social, logistical and economic reasons, and when they are not. Despite the attractiveness of integration, women's organizations must resist the urge to merge when merging means a diminution of power, and a loss of leadership positions. Jewish women's organizations can boast of having been creative and courageous enough to tackle unpopular causes and sponsor unpopular programs before the rest of the Jewish community dared. Yet, not all the existing organizational duplication is necessary. It needs to be determined when such redundancy is wasteful, and simply a convenient tactic to keep women down and out.

Judaism needs Jewish feminists

Bertha knew, as we know today, that Jewish feminism could reinvigorate Judaism; that Jewish women's talents were being under-utilized and their energies wasted.

Bertha was dismayed when Jewish women sought to throw their lot with the secular feminist movement, giving Judaism up for lost. She knew that Jewish women played a crucial role in transmitting the ideals and love of Judaism to the next generation, and that without their active involvement, Judaism would be weakened and impoverished.

Likewise, today, Judaism sees many of its finest daughters turning to the secular world for fulfillment, with only a marginal attachment to Judaism. Jewish feminism offers some hope for bringing them home. It has helped open leadership positions to women in the Jewish community. It has helped produce creative interpretation of biblical text (leading to an understanding of our Matriarchs from a woman's point of view), egalitarian **havurot**, innovative ritual, and renewed wide-spread interest in traditional legal texts. All of these result in part from Jewish feminism's struggle for legitimacy. And all have, in one way or another, enriched the broader Jewish community as well.

A negative lesson should also be learned from Bertha. Famous Jewish women generally fall into one of two categories: mothers and non-mothers; or more broadly, family women or non-family women. Sarah, Rebecca, Rachel and Leah, Hannah and the like are the former; Bertha, Lily Montagu, Henrietta Szold, Golda Meir (in her own way), Deborah and Judith are the latter. Judaism to this very day has advocates who state that family and jobs are incompatible.

Families need communal support systems

Although a wedding of family and career is not easy, Jewish women have been doing it throughout the ages, with the benefit of various alternative support systems. Today, as often in the past, there is no choice. For the most part, neither family nor job/career is negotiable, for whatever the myriad of reasons. Given that, Judaism must not say, ''Choose,'' for the choice is bound to hurt everyone. Rather, the Jewish community today must establish viable, flexible, manageable support systems for parents, both father and mother, and schedule public/volunteer events with the family in mind. It is not only proper; it is wise. Without such aid, those who presently have difficulty juggling family and career, and those who spend thousands of dollars a year on private full-time baby-sitters will have no time and no money for Jewish communal organizations.

One more lesson is worth mentioning: women must educate themselves in all areas of Judaica and in the process, redeem their past, and influence their future. Bertha, for example, translated into German such favorites as *The Memoirs of Gluckl of Hamelin*, and *Tsena Urenah*, a popular commentary on the Bible written primarily for women.

Today, we know that much of Jewish women's history has been ignored. Much work needs to be done to reclaim and redeem not only the outstanding Jewish women who are lost to us today (as Bertha almost was), but the common Jewish woman as well. Historians need to be mindful of the fact that Jewish history encompasses all Jews. The new trend toward social history goes a long way to do just that.

Likewise, women must study the traditional Jewish texts, both so that they might gain a sense of respect and understanding denied them all these years, and bring new perspectives and insights to the hallowed field of rabbinics. Only by being partners in scholarship can women truly hope to appreciate the tradition and to reshape it beneficially.

Integrating mikveh and modernity
Blu Greenberg

Why do I observe *niddah* and go to the *mikveh*? It would be less than honest of me to say anything other than I do so because I am commanded; because it is a *mitzvah de'oraita*. Were I not so commanded by Jewish law, the primary values that guide my life, I surely would not have invented such a rigorous routine. The flesh is weak and no lofty scheme imaginable could have made me tough enough to observe *niddah*. All of this is true for my husband as well, for neither of us could adhere unilaterally; such observance of *niddah* in a marriage would be reduced to a contest each month without this mutual understanding and acceptance of *halacha*.

But wait! There is a certain sweetness for me derived precisely from that sense of *mitzvah*. As I go about my business at the *mikveh*, I often savor that feeling that I am doing exactly what Jewish women have done for 20 or 30 centuries; not only a matter of keeping the chain going but also one of self-definition: that is how they defined themselves as Jewish women and as part of the community; that is how I define myself. While we really don't know how *karet* (punishment by cutting off the soul from one's people) manifests itself, I often feel my reward for observing certain *mitzvot* is the opposite of *karet*--a merging of my soul with the eternal soul of the Jewish people. However vague my understanding, however feeble my attempts at its articulation, this emotional pay-off for me is very real.

Acceptance of the *mitzvah*, then, is the base; the attendant sensations of 'community', 'Jewish womanhood', and 'chain of tradition' are the embellishments. There is, however, more to it than that. I also feel that *niddah* serves a function in an interpersonal relationship, in fact, a whole range of functions appropriate to the ebb and flow of life in its many stages of growth.

Role of niddah in adult life-cycle

Some examples: In early marriage, when passion and romance dominate, *niddah* allows and encourages a man and woman to develop other techniques of communication. Not every peak emotion may be expressed through sex; nor can every newly married spat be settled in bed. One also learns quickly that sex cannot be used as a reward or punishment. If sex is being regulated by a force 'out there', it becomes less a matter of one or the other partner controlling or manipulating.

In the second stage--young children, tired mothers, over-extended, upwardly mobile fathers with well documented discrepancies between male and female sex drives--*niddah* is an arbitrarily imposed refresher period. At the very least, it's less of a rejection than the old "I have a headache" routine. While sex is not, of course, out of favor during these young family years, statistics do show that it is a period of less frequency and less energy. Thus, shrinking the period of availability reduces the likelihood of "You're never in the mood when I am" recriminations.

Moreover, by regulating the off-times it rather directly synchronizes the on-times. While no law can exactly program desire, there is probably a better chance of the meshing of expectations amongst couples who observe *niddah*. I would guess that middle-aged, long married couples who observe *niddah* have more sex than their counterparts who do not observe. All of this ought not be confused with the widespread problem of routinization of sex. Purity-of-the-family marriage manuals notwithstanding, observance of *niddah* constitutes neither a routinization of sex nor a cure for that condition. In fact, although tradition has legislated sex as an obligation on the night of *t'vilah*, approximately two-thirds of the women I interviewed indicated this was not practiced.

In the third stage, as a woman approaches menopause, *niddah* and *mikveh* bring to her a monthly appreciation of her continuing ability to be fertile. I wonder whether a woman who has observed *mikveh* all her life feels a heightened sense of loss at menopause...

Finally, and in all of these stages, *niddah* generates a different sense of self for a woman, a feeling of self autonomy, of being her own person. Some women can generate these feelings out of their own ego strength; for those to whom it is not innate or instinctive, *niddah* is a catalyst to this consciousness.

These benefits aside, there are a number of things the community can do in the way of education and refinement.

How to reform these mitzvot

1. *Niddah-mikveh* should be re-appropriated in the context of a woman's *mitzvah*. Now that women are calling for greater inclusion in tradition, the first step is to educate them to those *mitzvot* which already do exist. There's nothing wrong with using feminist categories for that task.

2. Clean up some of the negative language, like unclean, and some of the horrendous and primitive threats I've seen, such as children conceived during a *niddah's* intercourse will be born leprous, armless, blind, etc. That doesn't impress people who prefer to take on new obligations out of love and not terror. Moreover, while much of the contemporary literature does stress the *kedushah* (holiness) of marriage and family purity, the new literature should emphasize the holiness of sex itself.

3. Perhaps some of the contemporary needs of women such as the often neglected monthly breast examination or the annual Pap smear or gynecological check up, can be grafted onto *niddah*, giving it new meaning and more important, saving lives in the process.

4. Many communities, in an effort to stem the tide of rising divorce, are offering Jewish Marriage Encounter and sex therapy programs. *Niddah* as a technique ought to be an integral part of these programs.

5. At certain stages in life, and for certain people, no sex for almost half the month is just too much. Perhaps there ought to be a *halachic* reconsideration of the Biblical time span appropriate to certain biological stages. I think that many more Jewish couples at this time of return to ritual and tradition would seriously consider the obervance of *niddah* were it limited to the seven day period prescribed by Biblical law.

Niddah for brides and singles

6. Particularly where brides are concerned, and on the assumption that we still place value on virginity until marriage, the distinction between menstrual blood and blood of the hymen ought to be made. Starting off with eleven days of abstinence is maybe not the best way to engender healthy attitudes about the joys of sex in marriage--and perhaps it is a trial that too many fail.

7. Regarding pre-marital sex: without going into the complex *halachic*, moral, and social issues, at the very least, one must acknowledge that it is not uncommon in these times. Given that fact, unmarried sexual partners observing *niddah* and *mikveh* could learn the following:

a) There is more to their relationship than sex, and if there isn't, then perhaps their sex is an abuse.

b) Real relationships mean commitment and sacrifice, and immediate gratification is an unrealistic expectation in enduring human relationships--a good preparation for real marriage.

c) *Niddah* would help single men and women to distinguish between promiscuous and authentic sexual relationships. Even logistically, one cannot 'sleep around'--male or female--if the laws of *niddah* are observed.

An intimate mitzvah, a personal choice

8. One of the interesting things that turned up in my research of modern Orthodox women is that very few couples strictly observe the associated laws of *negiah* which forbids all physical contact. Moreover, each couple seemed to have drawn the line differently, with an enormous range, thus revealing a great deal of 'personal packaging' in this very personal *mitzvah*. As one who respects the *mitzvah* and *niddah*, but also as a student of history who understands that after the *churban* the emphasis quite naturally shifted from *tu'mat niddah* (separation for reasons of ritual impurity) to *issur niddah* (proscription of sexual relations), I find the tremendous emphasis on *negiah* excessive and onerous and would suggest that the *halacha* reflect more confidence in its faithful; one who observes *niddah* will not jump into bed the moment flesh of a loved one is pressed.

In conclusion, if I may be permitted a theological indiscretion: my acceptance of a scheme of reward and punishment--this world or next--notwithstanding, I simply cannot drum up the feeling that those Jewish couples who fail to observe *niddah* are sinners. What is more, I feel that my life and my marriage would have been blessed even had I not observed these *mitzvot*, for I see many happy marriages without *niddah* and some horrid ones with; I see the blessings of healthy children from non-*halachic* sexual unions and the children of the pious afflicted.

Yet all things considered, the laws of *niddah* have added a dimension to my life with my husband that has made it a bit more complex, a bit richer, a bit more special. And since it's those small margins that make the real difference in life, I consider the effort to have been worthwhile.

Mikveh is not a viable mitzvah for me

Laura Geller

I am a religious woman. As I write that sentence I am aware that many people will misunderstand and assume that I am an Orthodox woman. I am not Orthodox. I learn, I pray, I wrestle with Torah --I take Jewish tradition seriously. I struggle with *mitzvot*, observing those that fill my life with holiness and rejecting those which cut me off from an experience of holiness.

I have chosen not to observe *taharat hamishpacha* because it does not connect me with an experience of holiness. The idea of family purity as our tradition defines it seems to belong to another era of Jewish life, an era categorized by roles prescribed for men and women that no longer seem appropriate. While I understand that *tumah* doesn't really mean 'uncleanness' or 'impurity,' I believe that there is a fundamental fear of menstruation involved in rituals connected to *taharat hamishpacha*. That fear might have made sense in connection with a biblical blood taboo; it doesn't make sense in the world in which I live. But the problem isn't only that it doesn't make sense; rather it extends to the fact that menstrual taboos are responsible for real damage to Jewish women's views of themselves and their bodies. I have met many women who learned nothing about Torah except that they could not touch the Torah because they menstruate. As adults, when they are told that that is simply folklore, it is already too late. Their sense of themselves as 'inferior' Jews has already permeated their relationship to tradition and to their own bodies.

Are menstrual taboos the Torah we teach?

Let me give one example. Several years ago, at a *Simchat Torah* celebration, a young woman became very involved in the dancing and rejoicing. Towards the end of services, she ran out of the synagogue crying uncontrollably. I went out after her to find out what was wrong. Tearfully she explained, "I have ruined it for everyone. I was so excited; I felt close to Torah. For the first time in my life I felt that I could have a relationship to Torah and to Jewish study. I became so involved with the excitement of being close to Torah that I forgot I was having my period. I feel so awful -- I 'trafed up' the Torah. I ruined it for everybody. I never should have come tonight."

Nothing I said to this young woman could take away her feeling that she had done something terrible. She is certainly not alone in feeling that because she menstruates she cannot fully participate in Jewish experience. For many women that feeling leads to one of two possible conclusions: either she will feel alienated from Jewish experience or she will feel embarrassed by menstruation. Neither response leads to a healthy involvement with Jewish tradition and Jewish community.

I have talked with several women who argue that *taharat hamishpacha* provides a healthy framework for their sexual relationships. One woman explained that regular abstention from sexual intercourse has forced her and her husband to find new ways of communicating and being intimate. Another described how regular periods of abstinence have helped her husband learn not to view her as a sex object and have given her the courage to turn down his sexual advances when she would rather not have sexual intercourse. I respect the decision of these women, but it is not a decision that I choose to make. There are other ways for a man and a woman to learn to communicate and be intimate without being sexual; there are other ways for a woman and a man to learn not to view each other as sex objects. For some women, the artificial imposition of a particular period of time as a time for sexual abstinence is not appropriate; women differ from each other and the timing of their need for sexual intimacy also differs.

Mitzvot should connect Jews to holiness

My decision not to observe *taharat hamishpacha* has not been an easy one. As a religious woman, I am conscious of how difficult the process of spiritual exploration really is. Many of the symbols and ceremonies that connect Jews to sacred time and to holiness were developed by men for men, and therefore it is often difficult for women to know how to respond to them. Often women simply appropriate those symbols that our tradition has labeled 'masculine', arguing that they

came to be regarded as masculine simply because men were the Jews who participated in public prayer and study. For example, I pray with a *tallit* and a *kippah*, not because they are men's 'clothes' but rather because they are the garments that Jews wear during prayer. But even as I appropriate some of those symbols to help me connect to sacred time and holiness, I want to find and embrace the rituals and symbols that our tradition has provided specifically for women, assuming that those rituals help connect me to holiness.

Mikveh is a ritual that I would like to experience. I sense a connection between women and water, a connection expressed in many different cultures. I like the notion of paying attention to a monthly rhythm, a rhythm familiar to all women. The problem with *mikveh* is that in addition to its being a religious symbol, it has also come to be a political symbol.

Mikveh: both personal and political

Let me explain through a personal example. Before I was married I went to the *mikveh*. I chose to go because Jewish women go to the *mikveh* before they are married and I wanted to connect myself with generations of other Jewish women. My experience was mixed, because I hadn't adequately prepared for it. I had forgotten to do the internal checking for traces of blood that is a requirement for *halachic* immersion. Finally it was decided that I could immerse myself in the *mikveh* but that I could not say the blessing out loud because it would have been a *bracha l'vatalah*, a wasted blessing. The experience made me feel inauthentic; I couldn't say the blessing, and in addition, I felt that because I hadn't made a commitment to *taharat hamishpacha* I was pretending to be something that I wasn't. The whole experience made me angry. I'd like to use the *mikveh* on my own terms, as an affirmation of my specialness as a woman, as a link to other women, but as long as the *mikveh* is operated as an Orthodox institution, I don't feel that it is open to me.

I began this essay by saying that I am a religious woman. I am also a Reform rabbi. As a rabbi, the *mikveh* has another meaning for me. *Mikveh* is a ritual of conversion. My requirements for conversion include a lengthy period of study, *mila* (circumcision or the taking of a drop of blood from the remnants of the foreskin) and *t'villah* (ritual immersion). Unfortunately I am not allowed to use the *mikveh* for *t'villah* because I am not an Orthodox rabbi. I take my converts to the ocean. It makes me angry to be denied access to the *mikveh* for conversions when the same people who deny me access often argue that my colleagues' conversions are inauthentic because they don't require *t'villah*.

Ideally the *mikveh* could be a symbol of women's spiritual exploration. Unfortunately it has become a political weapon in the arsenal which fights against the legitimacy of non-Orthodox Judaism.

Feminism: giving birth to a new Judaism
Martha Ackelsberg

Jewish feminists are discovering what many secular feminists have also found: equal access is not enough. Instead of devoting time and energy to gaining access to male roles, it is time to look more directly at Jewish tradition and at the ways in which it does (and does not) take seriously the lives and experiences of Jewish women. The re-creation of Judaism and Jewish life to which that examination leads can have a profound impact on both male and female Jews.

While there have always been those among Jewish feminists who focused their attention on a uniquely feminine spirituality, over the past ten years, the mainstream of Jewish feminism has addressed itself to the issue of gaining access for Jewish women to positions previously open only to males. Thus, early battles focused on counting women in the *minyan* or calling women for *aliyot* within Conservative congregations, training and ordaining women as rabbis, and having women assume positions of responsibility within the Jewish community.

Much progress has been made toward those goals, but much remains to be done. Reform and Reconstructionist rabbinical colleges are graduating more women rabbis each year and congregations are becoming less reluctant to hire those graduates. But the Jewish Theological Seminary still holds out. Women have gained rights to full membership in increasing numbers of synagogues throughout the country, and in many they hold positions of responsibility—even synagogue presidencies. While women are still not fully recognized within major Jewish communal organizations, at least the questions are being raised and pressure is on. Over time, perhaps more slowly than many of us would like—there has been, and will be, change.

Problems of Sexism in Judaism Go Deep
But many Jewish feminists are realizing that even achieving the goal of "equal access" in the ways

described would not be enough. There is more to a feminist analysis of Jewish tradition and practice than simply a claim that women are prevented from doing what men do. In fact, as Cynthia Ozick recently suggested in a provocative article ("Notes Toward Finding the Right Question," *Lilith*, No. 6) problems of sexism within the Jewish tradition are much deeper. To open Jewish practice and communal membership fully to women will involve a transformation of tradition and practice considerably more profound than what we had heretofore envisioned. I want here to share with you the outlines of that new vision, as it developed from a four-day meeting of a small group of committed Jewish feminists struggling to understand "what a Judaism that takes women's experience seriously would look like."

The group—composed of fifteen women, some of whom are rabbinical students, some rabbis, some teachers, some theologians, some doctoral candidates in various Jewish studies fields, and some "activists" within the Jewish community— had one set of concerns in common. We are all Jewish feminists who came together out of a desire that our spiritual concerns be taken seriously within the Jewish community. Each has felt the pain of being feminist and Jewish in a Jewish community which does not fully recognize or appreciate the experience of modern women. We came together in hopes of ending the isolation each of us had felt. In the course of the four days, we all experienced even greater isolation—a recognition that our issues were not the same and our proposed solutions were, at times, quite disparate. But the experience also allowed us to understand that, in a more fundamental sense and despite our differences, we are not alone.

In particular, through our confrontation with issues of spirituality, we realized that if we are to strive for spiritual fulfillment, we must address those obstacles which prevent our full participation, as women, in the Jewish community. A closer look at those obstacles made it clear to all of us that the problems go considerably beyond equal access. They involve a re-thinking of at least four central elements of Jewish life: education, liturgy/spirituality, family, and children.

Inequalities in Jewish Education
1. The lack of full equality between women and men in Judaism is readily apparent in what is taken to be the common core of Jewish education. Jewish feminists have long pointed out that while many teachers—especially at the elementary levels—are women, the majority of administrators of Jewish

education are men. And faculties and students bodies become more male (and male-dominated) as one moves up the ladder of serious Jewish study. But the disparagement of women goes much deeper than the question of who occupies what role in the community—however important that question is. For it is still the case that the history we study in those classrooms is primarily the history of Jewish men. The experience and concerns of women are largely invisible—whether in the study of traditional Jewish texts or in the study of history. Jewish educators, and students of Jewish texts, must begin to ask new questions. What, for example, did women do while men were doing what Jewish historians have told us is ''important''? What was the collective experience of Jewish women? How did this experience differ for individual women? At different points in Jewish history, what effect did the cultural indoctrination of women to seeing their primary function as that of home-maker and mother have on their labor force participation? What would history be like if seen through the eyes of women and ordered by values they define? In short, taking women and women's experience seriously means rethinking the way we study and teach both Jewish history and traditional Jewish texts. There is much we do not know; much more we have not even thought to ask.

Problems of Religious Expression

2. Issues of spirituality and religious expression are, perhaps, the most problematic; for religious expression, if it is to be powerful and honest, must derive from the experiences of those who pray. But experience of the divine is intensely personal. In addition, our ways of describing that experience are quite far from the anthropomorphized expressions of religious experience on which most of the traditional liturgy is based. Traditional Jewish liturgy addresses a patriarchal God, even while Judaism denies an anthropomorphic deity. The language used in that liturgy, the image of God expressed in it, and the relationship between God and the people of Israel conveyed through it are all predicated on sexist assumptions which we can no longer accept.

The problem, obviously, is not simply a ''women's problem.'' Some congregations—attempting to respond to the difficulties both women and men experience in praying to such a God—have attempted non-sexist translations of the traditional Hebrew prayers. But it is necessary to go beyond new translations, to examine the Hebrew liturgy itself and to develop new modes of religious expression which incorporate the femaleness of God and the experiences of female Jews. For some of us, that may mean attempting the mind-boggling task of writing new liturgy. As the proliferation of *Rosh-Hodesh* (new moon) celebrations attests, that route can be a fruitful one. For others, the strategy may be to develop the equivalent of kabbalistic *kavanot* (meditations said before or after some parts of the traditional liturgy) which imbue old words and symbols with dramatically new meanings. But if women—and men—whose consciousnesses are shaped by living in the modern world are to be able to pray, then the form and content of those prayers must begin to respond to the reality of our lives. Beyond what has already been said, that means we ought also to consider the development of a liturgy which can address a genderless, non-personal God.

3. Family structures provide another arena of current difficulty—and of potential new strength. The lives of many of us differ from the Jewish norm of a traditional nuclear family. The Jewish family—as the American family in general—is in crisis. Large numbers of American Jews live their lives apart from such families. But the failure of the Jewish community to recognize that reality makes it difficult, if not impossible, for us to express our spirituality and to participate fully in Jewish community life. How long will our community deny that some people may choose to remain single or to live communally, and that these are valid long-term choices? How long will it be before the Jewish community will recognize the existence of gay Jews? We cannot continue to ignore people who choose to live differently from the norm. Both for the health and growth of the community and for the possibilities of fulfillment for its members, it is imperative that the Jewish community find ways to affirm and support those who are single, those who live communally, those who are single parents, and those who choose to love persons of their own sex.

Issues of Child Raising

4. Children are a concern for all of us. Judaism places a high value on children and their care. It is often stated that the most crucial commandment for Jews is *p'ru ur'vu* (be fruitful and multiply). But the American Jewish community, which speaks often about the importance of giving birth to and raising Jewish children, has rarely recognized the provision of quality child care as a Jewish issue. Nor has it respected the choices of those who decide not to bear children.

Those who choose not to have children deserve the support and respect of the community for their decision. But they should not, as a consequence, be denied the opportunity to develop relationships with young children or to support those who have children. Those who choose to have children—whether they live in traditional family structures or not—need the full support of the community in raising them. Jewish community centers and Jewish organizations should pioneer in providing day-care both for employees and for community children. They should also take a lead in developing flexi-time schedules and shared jobs, and in making paternity leaves available to men. Jewish communities must start thinking about taking our women and our children seriously. If the raising of Jewish children is a communal priority, it must be recognized as a communal responsibility.

None of these issues, of course, is an issue only for women. Nor are they concerns that can be solved if only women address them. The agenda of equal access has not yet been achieved, and it must not be abandoned. There is much that both Jewish women and the Jewish community can gain by according women equal access to positions of responsibility and respect within that community.

But if women are truly to be included in the Jewish community—if that community is to be responsive to and reflective of the needs of all its members—a more fundamental transformation is required. We must move beyond ''equal access'' to a vision which incorporates the diversity of both women's and men's experience in the contemporary world. The task is a large one. It is our hope, in opening this dialogue, to engage the wider community in making this vision a reality.   ☆

Women cannot discuss *halachah*
Abraham N. Zuroff

While it is true that she is a woman, modern, and Orthodox in practice, does she qualify for the title "philosopher of *Halachah*?" It would seem to me that in order to qualify for such a distinguished designation, years of uninterrupted study in both *Halachah* and philosophy are basic. This alone does not suffice, for our sages in Avot 6:6 have delineated the forty-eight ingredients that are essential in achieving mastery of Torah. In a

ABRAHAM N. ZUROFF *teaches Judaic Studies at Yeshiva University.*

tradition that has through the centuries fostered the study of Torah almost exclusively among men there are still few men who qualify for the title of *posek* (a decisor of Jewish Law). One can safely predict that even in the twenty first century there will be no women decisors of *Halachah.* This despite the efforts of the feminist movement and the proliferation of institutes of Torah study for women promoted chiefly by Orthodoxy. It was not mere accident that Rabbi Joseph Soloveitchik's celebrated essay (*Talpioth*, Vol. I No. 3-4) is entitled *"Ish Hahalchah,* the *"Man* of *Halachah."* And so one would be "barking up the wrong tree" in suggesting a dialogue on the nature of *Halachah* in which participants would not qualify— knowledgewise and pietywise. Can one envisage a useful dialogue on Einstein's Theory of Relativity by college students majoring in physics? Competency in *Halachah* is not acquired merely by calling for changes in Jewish law. Even the ability to decipher a Talmudic or Rabbinic text does not qualify one to engage in the rendering of legal decisions. Unequivocal commitment to the divine nature of Torah law, deep understanding of the Halachic process, unswerving loyalty to Torah, and love for tradition are *sine qua nons* for the posek! To suggest otherwise would constitute a travesty of *Halachah.*

Controversy Is Common

Throughout the centuries covering a period of over two thousand years, the hallmark of *Halachah* has been controversy. Every page of Talmudic literature and the entire Responsa literature up to current times are marked by differing opinions. *Halachic* thought and practice are not monolithic in nature. Rabbinical literature is replete with evidence of differing opinions and practices in different communities at different times. The subject of Torah study for women is illustrative of this thesis: Beginning with the *Sifre* (to Deut. 46) which exempts women from the study of Torah, an opinion which the *Mishnaic* sage R. Eliezer (*Sotah* 20a) extends into a prohibition, we find another *Mishnaic* sage Ben Azzai obligating the father to teach his daughter Torah. (A dialogue between such Halachic giants is meaningful and useful). In the Palestinian version, the opinion of R. Eliezer is even more acerbic. In reply to his son's pleas to respond to the Torah questions of an aristocratic woman on economic grounds (he was a Levite and was the beneficiary of tithes annually) he declared: "May the words of Torah be consumed by fire rather than be transmitted to women."

While Jewish tradition supported essentially the thesis of R. Eliezer, it underwent interpretations and emendations, despite its categorical and resolute tone. The Talmud itself considers the statement of R. Eliezer that equates "the study of Torah by women with immorality" as unacceptable and injects a modification disclaiming such parity. In subsequent centuries we confront an array of "changes" if you will, of this position. In the 12th century, Rambam (a true Halachist and philosopher) in his *Mishneh Torah* (Talmud Torah 1:13) differentiates between study of the Oral Law which is always barred to women and the Written Law which is acceptable at least *post factum*. At the end of the 12th century in Germany, R. Judah the Pious (*Sefer Hasidim* 313) bars only the study of Torah in depth and philosophizing about the rationale for the Mitzvot, but obligates women to study the codes in order to know how to fulfill observance of the Sabbath, etc.

A Tradition Of Prohibition

The pendulum swung back by the beginning of the 15th century in Germany when the Maharil (R. Jacob Moellin) in his Responsum 199, bars the formal study of even the Codes and relies on the oral transmission of Halachic information by word of mouth and through the informal question and answer method. In 16th century Poland, R. Moses Isserlis, the decisor of Ashkenazic ritual, insisted that women were obligated to study the laws that pertain specifically to women (Ramah gloss to Y.D. 246). R. Joshua Falk, (Prishah— commentary to Y.D. 246) a disciple of the Ramah, at the end of the 16th century differentiates between the exceptional woman who is permitted to study Torah herself and the average woman who requires instruction, which he prohibits. In the 18th century R. Haim Joseph Azulai, author of more than one hundred books dealing with *Halachah*, philosophy, Kabbalah and history who lived in *Eretz Yisrael* (the land of Israel), Turkey, Egypt and Italy, in his commentary on *Sefer Hasidim* imposed an obligation on the father to teach his daughters the Code of Law, for practical purposes, but once having mastered the information were not permitted to study Torah for the sake of fulfilling the *Mitzvah*, since women had no such requirement. One of the leading sages of the 20th century, R. Israel Meir Hacohen, author of the *Mishnah Brura*, which is the authoritative guidebook of observant Jews throughout the world, explicitly states that the ancient Mishnaic dictum of R. Eliezer does not apply to modern times, when the structure of

the community has undergone so many sociological transformations. In addition, there are other factors that cannot be overlooked such as the independence of the children, who are immune to parental influence and who instead are influenced by the climate prevalent in the universities and the implications thereof. Their studies of Bible, Jewish theology, Ethics of the Fathers, etc. must be taught to them on at least as high a level as their secular studies, in order to preserve their integrity as God fearing and Torah-observing Jews (see *Likkute Halachot Sotah* 21). These sentiments are echoed too in the Responsa *Moznayim Lamishpat* 1:42 of R. Zalman Sorockin, a 20th century leader in Eastern Europe and subsequently in Israel, who emphatically states that our times cannot be compared to the days of yore, when the Code of Jewish Law was supreme in almost every home and scrupulously and punctiliously followed.

Those Who Care Do Not Tamper

I deliberately omitted the opinion of the 19th century leader of German Orthodoxy Rabbi Samson Rafael Hirsch because his philosophy of "Torah with *Derech Eretz*" ("worldliness") was condoned by traditional Orthodoxy only as a temporary accommodation (*Horoat Shaah*) to meet the specific needs of the period, but hardly reflective of genuine, authentic and unadulterated Judaism.

Does this array of Halachic opinion resemble the computer model of the posek? Hardly, but each one does personify the basic essential ingredients required for Halachic leadership and are vested with the authority to offer new insights into the interpretation of Jewish law. How interesting indeed that those to whom *Halachah* is synonymous with life itself, whose every breath is governed by the dictates of Jewish Law and who would make the ultimate sacrifice for its preservation, refrain from tampering with it, while those whose understanding of *Halachah* is at best peripheral are quick to suggest changes.

Interesting but not strange! ●

Under a *tallit* a woman is invisible
Lori Forman

As has often been said, all beginnings are hard. The difficulty of our beginning as the first women in the rabbinic school at the Jewish Theological Seminary is that in our exhilaration we may be

LORI FORMAN *is a rabbinical student at the Jewish Theological Seminary in N.Y.*

too eager to accept male-defined norms as being the norms we must attain to gain acceptance and validity. While it is easy to pattern ourselves after male models of observance and leadership, it is much harder to delve into ourselves and discover expressions of religious forms derived from our experiences as Jewish women.

Admission of women to the rabbinical school has raised the question: should women fulfill the obligations incumbent upon men? Traditionally women are exempt from the majority of these obligations, which are time-bound. It has been suggested that women take on these obligations and in this manner gain equal status with their male counterparts.

The Very Notion of Obligation is Patriarchal

That opinion is based on the legal definition of *chiyuv* which portrays a Jew's relationship with the Divine in terms of specific obligations to be carried out. A transgression of these constitutes an infraction of the law. This traditional understanding of *chiyuv* stems from the biblical characterization of God as a parental God; the Father commanding the Children of Israel to obey His words or suffer the consequences. This *hierarchical* relationship between God and Israel leads to the development of a law in which hierarchical distinctions are institutionalized among the Jews themselves and between Jews and their non-Jewish neighbors. Jewish feminists question this hierarchical model. A Divine-human relationship based on hierarchy results in similar relationships in this world which has led to the oppression of women. Our experience teaches us that there are other ways to organize relationships aside from the imposition of status. Women's experience points to a model of sharing and mutual responsibility. A first step to this end means demythologizing God as "Father." Our inquiry leads us to explore a non-hierarchical understanding of God and our relationship to the Divine. This new understanding will liberate the word *chiyuv* from its legal definition and base it in our own attempts to discern and thereby fulfill God's will in the world.

To Be Accepted, Must Women Act Like Men?

At the Jewish Theological Seminary this year, women who wish to lead the congregation in prayer have been required to don *tallit* and *tefillin*, the traditional garb worn by men during prayer. Women have been accepted into the (formerly male) conservative rabbinate on the condition that we act like men. Rosemary Ruether, a christian feminist theologian, calls such *conditional* acceptance "androcentrism." The clear message of this conditional acceptance is that being a woman is not enough; one must strive to be a man. The requirements that women wear *tallit* and *tefillin* communicates the hope that if women are visually indistinct their presence may not be so obvious and, perhaps, will go unnoticed.

I do not mean to criticize women who choose to adopt these ritual garments as their own, yet I resist educating ourselves and our children to think this is the sole way to gain validity and fill leadership roles. Rather, women must be encouraged to pray, to dialogue with God. Through on-going prayer — individually, in egalitarian *minyanim* and in women's *minyanim* — perhaps we will develop forms that effectively express a woman's relationship with the Divine.

As Ruth Sohn wrote of Miriam standing before the Red Sea: To take the first step/ To sing a new song/ Is to close one's eyes/ and dive/ into unknown waters/ For a moment knowing nothing, risking all/ But then to discover/

Feminist prayer

Marcia Falk

Feminist prayer: it began as a "women's issue." God was always a male, and that didn't seem right—or should I say accurate?—to those of us who weren't. After all, we too had been told that we were created in God's image. When we raised this objection, the defenders of the tradition explained that He wasn't really a "he," and chided us for our literal-mindedness. Still, they steadfastly refused to pray to God as female, even once in a while. So we started experimenting on our own. Instead of *barukh atah adonay* (blessed are you, Lord,) Jewish women in various places began saying *b'rukhah at shekhinah* (blessed are you, Shekhinah). Almost immediately the reaction rang out (from those same defenders of the faith): "*B'rukhah at*? Do you mean 'goddess'? This is paganism!" But, we protested, *Shekhinah* is a good Jewish word, a *traditional* Jewish name for Divinity. Yes, they agreed, *Shekhinah* was *kosher*, so long as we remembered that she wasn't really God, she was just an *aspect* of Him. The real God was *Adonay*. We seemed to be taking our name for God too seriously, as though it were as legitimate as theirs. Or as though theirs was only a name—a metaphor, that is—just like ours; as though they

זֶה הַיּוֹם עָשָׂה ה' נָגִילָה וְנִשְׂמְחָה בוֹ

THIS IS THE DAY THE LORD HAS MADE. LET US BE GLAD & REJOICE IN IT.

psalm 118

didn't really mean "he" when they said "He"; as though they believed what they were telling us when they warned against literal-mindedness.

Knowing, Discovering, Unknowing

That was the first stage, and I wish we could say that it was over. But, although feminist Jews have gone beyond merely substituting female counterparts for the male images in our prayers, we still find ourselves in the often annoying position of having to explain why it is necessary to change the prayers at all. Meanwhile, on our own, when our energy is not drained from explaining and defending what we are doing, we have been delving into the deeper issues that have arisen out of our initial concerns. For example, in objecting to God the King, we found that God the Queen was not a satisfactory alternative. Because, we discovered, Divinity means more to us than a principle of transcendent rule; even power can be imagined as something other than "power-over." So instead we began to talk about empowerment, about Divinity as that which enables us to be our individual selves, and as that which bonds us when we unite as a community.

And more than this—as we have been talking, meeting, praying together, feminist Jews have come to realize that we are many, even as we are part of the One. Our diversity characterizes us as much as anything else, and that is why it is so hard for us to choose a single set of words to represent us, so hard for any one of us to speak for all of us—as articles such as this one sometimes seem to do. What do feminist Jews think about prayer? Almost everything you can think of. And so our prayers, our God-language, must be diverse enough to include and affirm us all. In this sense, perhaps the most crucial feminist insight into prayer-talk has been the realization that one name does not equal one Divinity. The monotheistic vision can *only* be realized through a multiplicity of names and images, a diversity broad enough to include, and thus unite, all of creation.

We Seek the Inclusive One

Inclusivity. This has been a focus of our feminist vision. And unity, a focus of our feminist-Jewish theology. But we are also conscious of our particular story, our journey as part of the community of Israel, as the unwritten half of Jewish history. As feminist Jews, most of us yearn deeply for historical and communal Jewish connections. And so we try, when writing new prayers and creating new ceremonies, to weave them out of Jewish material: the Jewish themes that have nurtured us, the Jewish principles that have guided us, the Jewish structures that have become familiar to us and have made us feel at home.

Contrary to the perception held by some who see us only at the greatest distance—a distance which is most often self-imposed —the truth is that feminist Jews want *in, into the tradition,* not out. As women—the half of humanity most often viewed as "other" in tradition—we have learned that denial of one's identity is a fruitless and suicidal act. We have learned to take the externally-imposed view of ourselves as "other" and replace it with a self-embracing self. So as feminist Jews, we do not reject Jewish tradition, for we recognize that we come from it; we *are* it. Instead, we claim our right to the tradition, our right not just to participate in it as we receive it but to create the terms of participation. Our right not just to have our foremothers included in the prayers but to have their images, *our* images, reflected in the God to whom (or to which) we pray. Our right not just to own Judaism, but to *make it our own.*

And so feminist-Jewish prayer takes many forms, and our words have been varied and various: tentative, courageous, experimental, poetic, prosaic, moving, moving on. My own efforts to create prayer have emerged out of a conjunction of personal desire and community support. I have needed new prayers and I have felt needed. So I write.

Words, Names, Souls, Truths

Recently I was asked to create a blessing for the sixtieth birthday of a Jewish woman who wanted to affirm her stage of life in a Jewish context. She chose to take on a new name—as Abram and Sarai had received new names when they entered a new phase of their lives—a name to signify a new passage, a new aspect of her identity. So I began thinking about names, about how important they have been in Jewish tradition; how we remember our foregoers by their names; how a soul without a name is forgotten; how the many names of Divinity have been repressed, just as women's identities have been repressed and erased from our collective memory. And I decided to celebrate the Divinity in all our names, in all our holy namings. To bless, to sing with human breath, the heart, the soul of all names. For in Hebrew, the soul

(*n'shamah*) is connected to breathing (*n'shimah*). And in Hebrew liturgical tradition, the soul of every living being (*nishmat kol hay*) blesses God. Yes, and the relationship is reciprocal: Divinity inheres in—and thus blesses—the soul of all living things, the soul in every name and the names of all our beings. And as Divinity blesses us with the power of naming, so we sing:

> *Nashir l'nishmat kol shem*
> *ul'shem kol n'shamah.*
>
> Let us sing the soul in every name
> and the names of every soul.*

May Jewish women's prayers continue to abound and increase, and may they increase the power of naming, of claiming identity, for us and for all of Israel.☐

In our continuing effffort to offer a forum for new writers, we are pleased to present the thoughts of DEBORAH MILLER *in this issue.*

TRUDE WEISS ROSMARIN *is the publisher of the Jewish Spectator.*

MIRIAN SHAPIRO, *a social worker, is pursuing graduate studies in Bible and education at the Jewish Theological Seminary in New York.*

PENINNAH SCHRAM *teaches speech and theatre at Stern College in New York City.*

JOSEPH KAPLAN *is a practicing attorney in the New York area.*

PINCHAS STOLPER *directs the work of the Union of Orthodox Jewish Congregations of America.*

NINA BETH CARDIN *is involved with the Jewish Women's Resource Center in New York.*

RABBI LAURA GELLER *is the director of the Hillel Jewish Center at the University of Southern California.*

MARTHA ACKELSBERG *teaches political science at Smith College.*

"Feminist Prayer" is copyright © 1987 by Marcia Falk and reprinted by permission of the author. The blessing that appears in this essay is from Marcia Falk, The Book of Blessings: A Feminist-Jewish Reconstruction of Prayer (Harper & Row, 1989)

ANN ZAIMAN, *of Baltimore, Md. did the art for page 100.*

6.

The Jewish Way of Birth

Birth rituals and jewish daughters

Daniel I. Leifer

We live in an exciting period of Jewish history, a time of creation of new rituals, symbols and myths. Especially exciting are the new birth initiation and dedication rituals for Jewish daughters which have been created. The ceremonies which have come to my attention fall naturally into two groups. The first are *BRIT* ceremonies whose purpose is to initiate a new-born daughter into the holiness of the Covenant of the People of Israel with God. The second are *PIDYON HABAT* ceremonies whose purpose is the redemption and dedication of a first-born daughter. All of these ritual innovations seek to celebrate the birth of a daughter with the same or comparable equality and dignity with which the birth of a son is traditionally celebrated. All of the ceremonies examined are rooted in traditional forms, appropriating ritual formulae and selections from traditional literature. All are innovative, some are radical, i.e., some have created new *brachot*. The ceremonies listed below are considered in this analysis:

Brit ceremonies

1) *"Brit Kedusha:* A Home Ceremony celebrating the birth of a daughter," by Ellen and Dana Charry. *Sister celebrations, Nine Worship Experiences,* edited by Arlene Swidler, Fortress Press, c. 1974, pp 20-26.

Content: Selection from Psalm 98, *Shehechiyanu* blessing for grandparents. Naming formula from *Brit Mila* ceremony. Original prayer of blessing for child and dedication of parents. Blessing over wine. Traditional blessing (Deut. 28:3,6; Num. 6:24-26). *Shehechiyanu* for everyone.

2) "An Orthodox Simchat Bat," by Joseph C. Kaplan. *Sh'ma* 5/90, March 21, 1975, pp 237-8.

Content: Prov - 10:12, Num. 24:5, Gitin, 57a (planting a pine tree for daughter's huppah). *Hagomail* blessing. *Shehechiyanu* blessing. *Drasha. Hannah's Prayer* (Sam. I, 2:1-10). Traditional blessing (Num 6:24-26). Selection from Song of Songs. A *Mi Shebayrach.* Blessing of *Hatov Vehamaytiv.* Blessing over wine. Drashot.

3) *"Brit B'not Yisrael* (Covenant for the Daughters of Israel)." by Rabbis Sandy and Dennis Sasso. *Moment,* Vol. 1, No. 1, May/June 1975, pp 50-51. Earlier version published in *The Jewish Woman: An Anthology, Response,* No. 18, Summer 1973, pp 101-105.

Content: Greeting. Song of Songs Rabbah I:24. Original prayer of dedication of parents. New blessing "... commanded us to initiate our daughter into the Covenant of The People of Israel." Selection from Martin Buber. Naming formula. Mention of Shabbat Covenant parallel to People of Israel Covenant. Exod. 31: 16-17. Blessing: "As she has been brought into the Covenant of our people, so may she grow into a life of *Torah, Chupah,* and good deeds" or "... a life of Torah, service, joy and good deeds." Blessing over wine. *Shehechiyanu* blessing. Traditional blessing (Num 6:24-26) adapted.

Pidyon habat ceremonies

1) *"Kiddush Peter Rehem:* An Alternative to Pidyon HaBen," by Mark S. Golub and Norman Cohen. *CCAR Journal,* Vol. 20, No. 1, Winter 1973, pp 71-78.

Content: Rabbi's Sermon to Parents. Exod. 13:3, 11-12; Num. 8:17; Num. 18:8, 14-16; Num. 3:11-13; Exod 13:1-2. Parents' Pledge and Self-dedication. New blessing "... who causes parents to rejoice with their children." Rabbi's charge to Parents. Parents' response. Father presents 18 silver dollars to Rabbi. Traditional blessing (Num. 6:24-26) by Rabbi. Blessing over wine. *Shehechiyanu* blessing.

2) "On The Birth of a Daughter: Rituals of Birth, Naming and Redemption," by Daniel I. and Myra Leifer. *The Jewish Woman: An Anthology, Response,* No. 18, Summer 1973, pp 91-100.

Content: Seven blessings plus blessing over wine shortly after birth. Naming ceremony in Shul at time of an aliyah for parents (Reconstructionist Sabbath prayerbook pp 498-9) plus *Shehechiyanu* blessing and a Hebrew letter acrostic of child's name composed of selections from Psalm 119. *Pidyon Habat:* Poem. Explanation of ritual. Num. 3:11-13, 18:13-16; Deut. 29:9-14. Song of Songs Rabbah I: 24. Pesikta de R. Kahanna 121a. Traditional liturgy grammatically reworked for a daughter. Setting aside $18 for Tzedakah. New blessing " . . . to bring our daughter into the covenant of The People of Israel." Traditional *Peter Rehem* blessing. New blessing " . . . who makes parents rejoice with their children." *Shehechiyanu* blessing. Conclusion of traditional liturgy and blessings (Gen 24:60, Num 6:24-26). Blessing over wine and *challah*. Godparents take place of Kohen.

3) *"Pidyon Habat* - Redemption of the Firstborn Daughter," by Elaine and Neal Machtiger. Privately circulated.

Content: Essentially the same as Leifer *Pidyon Habat* with difference that Kohen functions in traditional manner. Exhortation and charge by Kohen to Parents. Parents' response of dedication and acceptance of responsibility.

4) *"Pidyon Habat*-Redemption of the Firstborn," by Raphael and Rhoda Zahler. Privately circulated.

Content: Essentially the same as Leifer *Pidyon Habat* with addition of Exod 13:11-15. Change of wording of new covenant blessing from "covenant of The People of Israel" to "into your covenant." Addition of Bob Dylan's "Forever Young."

The structure and focus of birth rituals
A ritual is an ordered series of ceremonial words and actions which effect a change in the status and being of an individual and/or community. Birth rituals are rites of passage; i.e., individuals pass through a liminal period from one state of being to another. In birth rituals the child passes ritually from a state of non-being and non-membership in the community into a status of being and membership in the community. This is effected by name giving, circumcision, redemption and the recital of formulae and blessings. A community is present at birth rituals as the referent group providing legitimation, support and continuity to the ritual changes effected.

The focus is primarily on the child only secondarily on the parents, who effect the ritual. It is the child whose ritual status is changed. In Jewish tradition,

birth rituals are not ceremonies of dedication of the parents. I believe that innovative birth rituals must follow this classic pattern if they are to be effective and meaningful.

All the above considered rituals follow these criteria, except the orthodox *simchat bat.* In this ceremony nothing happens liturgically and ritually to the child, perhaps because of a desire not to break a *halachic* norm by creating a new *b'racha*. There is an innovation here, however, in the appropriation of *hatov vehmaytiv* for the birth of a daughter.

A ritual to be a ritual has to be done at a specific time and place, otherwise it loses its ontological power and effectiveness. All of the rituals under consideration, except the orthodox *simchat bat*, indicate that the ritual is to be performed at a clear and fixed time. The *Brit B'not Yisrael* of the Sassos links the ritual to the first *Shabbat* after the birth of the child. They follow the traditional custom of naming a female child in the synagogue on the *Shabbat* immediately following a birth. I particularly like the *Brit Kedusha* of the Charrys which fixes the date of the ritual at eight days after birth. This makes it equivalent and parallel to the *Brit Mila* of a male child. All the *Pidyon Habat* ceremonies take place at the conclusion of the traditional thirty day period when such redemption rituals occur for male firstborn children.

Symbolizing entrance into the covenant
If innovative birth rituals are to confer equivalent ritual and community status to female as to male children, they must clearly and explicitly state that the female child is brought into the covenant between the People of Israel and God of the Cosmos. This, of course, is nowhere traditionally done for a female child. For true equality there must be some ritual formula equivalent or parallel to the blessing said at the circumcision of a male child, " . . . commanded us to bring our son into the Covenant of Abraham, our Father." Therefore the bold step of breaking with *halachic* norm and creating a new *bracha* is called for in order to give equality to a female child.

In the ritual ceremonies considered, all the *Pidyon Habat* rituals contain such a formulation either as " . . . to bring our daughter into the Covenant of Israel" or " . . . into your Covenant." In the *Brit* ceremonies, only that of the Sassos contains that *bracha*. While it is understandable that Joseph Kaplan would not want to create a new *bracha* in his orthodox *Simchat Bat*, it is curious that the Charry *Brit Kedusha* does not contain such a blessing; indeed this ritual never uses the word *brit* in a liturgical sense. Kaplan, though stating that parents should sanctify a daughter's birth and her becoming part of Israel's Covenant with God, does not liturgically utilize the concept *brit*.

The confusion of ritual symbols

In her article in the *Response* magazine on "The Jewish Woman: An Anthology," Sandy Eisenberg Sasso states that the Sabbath is "an appropriately meaningful sign around which to develop covental birth ceremonies for a girl" (page 104). She has carried out that linkage of the Sabbath covenant with the covenant of the Jewish People for a female child in several passages of her *Brit B'not Yisrael* ceremony. However, she is aware that this linkage is problematic for she says "there exists only one problem in utilizing the Sabbath as the symbol of covenantal commitments for girls. Whereas circumcision is unique to girls, the Sabbath is a weekly sign of which the whole community partakes." *(Ibid.)*

I do not think her argument convincing and find the linkage disturbing. Even if the Sabbath "embraces special feminine imagery," it is structurally confusing to link the Covenant of the Sabbath with the Covenant of the People of Israel for female children. These Covenants are not equivalent to one another. Each has different liturgical, physical and ceremonial symbols.

The focus shifts from child to parent

In traditional birth rituals it has been the actual performance of the ritual on the person of the child by the parent in the presence of the legitimizing community that expressed the dedication of the parents to care for and Jewishly rear their male offspring. The explicitness with which many of these new birth ceremonies emphasized the dedication of the parent to the nurturing and Jewish education of their female child is a radical new element. It signifies a ritual movement away from the child to the parent. Several of the ceremonies considered here, some more so than others, are less a ritual happening to the child than a ceremony of dedication of the parent. To the extent to which this is the case I believe that these rituals miss the point, i.e., a ritual method for effecting change of status and being at the liminal points of the life cycle. I believe these rituals reveal the growing trend towards privatism and individualism as opposed to community identification which characterizes our times.

Hopes for the child's fulfilment

The traditional ceremonies expressed the hope that as the male child entered the covenant and attained redemption so it would be God's will that "he attained the blessings of Torah, marriage and a life of good deeds." Shall the hope for life's fulfillment for a female child be exactly equivalent to the hope for a male? Or is the hope for both female and male to be different than that of the traditional expression.

Almost all of the rituals considered here continue to express the traditional hope. Only the *Brit B'not Yisrael* by the Sassos contains an alternate reading "as she has been brought into the Covenant of our People so may she grow into a life of Torah, service, joy and good deeds." I believe that Sasso is correct in stating that the traditional prayer "negates the sanctity and significance of the life of a single man or woman, indicating that such life is not yet complete. Throughout Jewish tradition, there has been no place for either single men or women. In light of present society, a change in attitude towards single persons must occur." (op. cit., page 105).

Redemption of the first-born

All of the *Pidyon Habat* ceremonies, except that of Golub and Cohen, retain the emphasis that the child that first opens, frees and redeems the womb of its mother belongs to God. I believe that Golub and Cohen have incorrectly understood the concept of redemption, focusing upon the role of the Kohen rather than that of God. By replacing the concept of redemption by the idea of the sanctification of the first born, they have radically changed the nature of this ritual, making it more a dedication of the child than a rite of passage. I believe that a religious awareness of the source of life demands a ritual redemption

Women have a special place in jewish tradition

of that life from God. This *Kidush Peter Rehem* ceremony is an interesting example of the loss of vitality and acceptability of rites of passage in favor of the less intense and more diffuse ceremonies of dedication. This shift is also an indicator of secularization of rituals, because it changes the focus from God who effects ritual changes upon human beings to human beings who dedicate and offer up themselves or something which belongs to them to God.

Guidelines and conclusions
Looking back at our own ritual creation and at these birth ceremonies, I asked myself what would I do differently if I were now about to have a first female child. I would want to have a *Brit B'not Yisrael* ceremony combining what I believe to be the virtues of the Sasso and Charry rituals. I would want to give special emphasis to the place of our matriarch Sarah as a model and symbol for a female child. *Midrashic* literature provides a rich treasure of appropriate selections. I would insist that this *Brit B'not* take place on the eighth day. This ceremony would be in addition to the traditional naming ceremony of a female child in the synagogue on *Shabbat*. I believe this ceremony to be ritually appropriate because it introduces the child into the community of the People of Israel. Indeed, I would recommend that this custom of synagogue naming be extended to male children as an addition to the *Brit Milah*. In addition, I am even more convinced than ever of the ritual necessity for a *Peter Rehem-Pidyon Habat* ceremony for female children which follows the traditional structure and liturgical formulae.

Innovation within halachah for daughters
Sharon and Joseph Kaplan

Daniel I. Leifer, in his article "Birth Rituals and Jewish Daughters" (*Sh'ma,* 6/111), has brought together, to our knowledge for the first time, a substantial number of the ceremonies being performed today upon the birth of a daughter, including the *simchat bat* ceremony we devised. His outline and analysis of those ceremonies is an important step in their integration into Jewish religious life. That outline and analysis, however, call for some comment both generally as to the ceremonies involved, and more particularly, in connection with some of his statements about our *simchat bat.*

First, it is interesting to note that Mr. Leifer, who performed a *pidyon habat* type ceremony for his first daughter, wonders, at the end of his article, what he would do differently "if (he) were now to have a first female child." The omission of the question of what he would do now if he had a *second* female child is indicative of a serious flaw in the *pidyon habat* type ceremony: what does one do for second (or third etc.) daughters in a ceremony which is appropriate only for first children? This problem does not exist in a *simchat bat* type ceremony; in fact, just a few weeks ago we celebrated a *simchat bat* upon the birth of our second daughter Na'amit Miriam (Daniele Melinda). This type of ceremony, not based on either the traditional *pidyon haben* or male *brit* (though, as discussed below, it is similar to this ceremony in theme), continues to be appropriate even as the family size increases.

The birth ritual should be specifically for a girl
On a deeper level, though, this issue indicates the dangers in taking a male ceremony and adapting it for use by females. First, certain inappropriate forms and procedures are thus foisted upon the ceremony, where none need be. Second, and even more important, one of the most meaningful aspects of a religious ceremony on the birth of a daughter, especially to Orthodox Jews, is the fact that one has the rare opportunity to innovate within a *halachic* framework. Simply adapting from a male ceremony diminishes the ability to innovate.

Moreover, this concept applies also to the timing of a *simchat bat.* Why be tied down to the eighth day (when many mothers are still not at their physical best, and thus cannot fully appreciate and enjoy their daughter's becoming part of the Covenant), or to the thirtieth day (when some of the initial indescribable excitement on the appearance of a brand new human being has worn off), or to *Shabbat* (when many traditionally observant friends and relatives who do not travel on that day would have to be excluded)? Why not pick a new day, as we did, specifically related to *simchat bat?* We did not choose the first Sunday two weeks after our daughters' births at random. Rather, the two week period is derived from an identical period mentioned in the Torah (Lev. 12:5) relating to the birth of a daughter, and Sunday was chosen so our daughters could be joined by as many of their friends and relatives as possible, without the outside time pressure of work as is unfortunately present at many a male *brit.* Again, the timing of the ceremony is a use of tradition (coupled with convenience), based not on male ceremonies, but on traditions applying specifically to females.

Innovation within the framework of tradition
We also take exception to Mr. Leifer's statement that in our ceremony "nothing happens liturgically and ritually to the child." While he is entirely correct in assuming our "desire not to break a *halachic* norm by creating a new *b'racha*," he ignores the *mi sheberach* by one grandfather, the priestly blessings by the other grandfather, and certain explanatory material recited at the ceremony which, together with the blessing of *hatov vehamativ*, "liturgically use the concept of *brit*." Since there is no need *per se* for a *b'racha* in such a situation (as, for example, no *b'racha* is needed when a boy reaches the age of *bar mitzvah*), we decided not to invent one. We did not, however, neglect to make it clear that through this ceremony, our daughters were entering into the Covenant of the People of Israel.

We feel somewhat schizophrenic, arguing on the one hand for freedom and innovation (with respect to the general form and timing of the ceremony), and on the other hand for adherence to tradition (in not creating a new *b'racha*). But that type of attitude perhaps best defines what modern Orthodox Jews (a term we do not like but use in lieu of a better one) go through in their quest for tradition in today's world. In this quest, we have found our answer, at least to the question of how to react to and treat the birth of a daughter. We hope others will follow the lead of Nina Freedman (*Sh'ma*, 6/111) and grapple with the question of what to do when that daughter enters Jewish womanhood, so that in ten years, when that issue is relevant to us, the ground will have already been broken.

The symbolism in innovative rituals
Judith Bleich

Preoccupation and concern with the development of meaningful rituals and liturgical materials often reflect a sincere, at times passionate, desire to give expression to deeply-rooted religious feelings. Perhaps some attempts to create new ceremonies and liturgical forms may be viewed as a manifestation of this spirit. However, all too frequently, the suggested rituals raise basic theological questions and, ironically, despite the sincerity of their authors, prove to be embarrassingly inappropriate when presented as a new link in the chain of authentic Jewish tradition.

Without entering into the issue of whether or not it is permissible to formulate new blessings (a question which from the perspective of *halachah* [Jewish law] would clearly be answered in the negative), a fundamental observation should be made with regard to any newly-evolved ritual. It is unlikely that proponents of any intellectual or religious trend within the contemporary Jewish community would seek to foster the adoption of a religious ceremonial associated with non-Jewish traditions. Such practices are proscribed by virtue of the biblical admonition: "And you shall not walk in their statutes" (Lev. 18:3). In any event, a conscious aping of non-Jewish tradition would presumably be repugnant to adherents of any branch of Judaism in our day.

Bearing this point in mind, it is instructive to examine two recent suggestions for ceremonials with which to celebrate the birth of a baby girl which, it may be argued— one to a greater degree, one to a lesser degree— do not commend themselves as suitable rituals for any Jewish group.

Immersion is an Unacceptable Ritual
In a quest to provide a substitute ceremony for the *brit milah* (circumcision ritual) for parents of baby girls, some individuals have advocated a new rite— an observance which was given a measure of publicity by its inclusion in the second volume of the popular *Jewish Catalog*. The ceremony involves the bodily immersion in water of the infant girl. Ostensibly, the ritual is patterned on the concept of immersion in a *mikveh* (ritual bath) a ritual closely associated with women in Jewish law and lore. Objections to this suggestion have been raised on the grounds that it is an incongruous rite when introduced at the time of birth and one which is more relevant to puberty than to infancy. Astonishingly, a far more basic objection has not been articulated: immersion of infants is not a new ritual. It is one which has been practiced for centuries. It is simply a matter of identifying the ritual by proper nomenclature. This particular ritual is known as baptism, not as *mikveh*. Baptism is regarded as a hallowed practice among Christians. Surely, however, there could be no ritual less befitting to mark the birth of a Jewish baby girl.

JUDITH BLEICH *teaches Judaic studies at Touro College.*

A somewhat less objectionable, but nonetheless anomalous, proposal for a novel ceremony to mark the birth of a baby girl was presented by a group of nine women in the April-May 1983 issue of *Menorah*. This ceremony is a rite of passage called Covenant of Washing or *Brit Rehitzah*. The ceremony involves the washing of the baby girl's feet in a small bowl followed by recitation of prayers and blessings. It is suggested that washing of the feet is a meaningful symbolic ritual of welcome for the newly-born Jewish girl for two reasons. In the first place, it is emphasized, the Bible speaks of a covenant made with Noah after the flood in addition to the covenant with Abraham. "Surely we would want to welcome the baby girl into that [Noah's] covenant as well, a covenant that potentially involves all of humanity." In the second place, feet washing is seen as reminiscent of an incident described in the Bible. "Someone remembered," the authors note, "that when Abraham was recovering from his circumcision, he was visited by three angels of the Lord... Abraham greeted these strangers with the gracious Middle Eastern sign of hospitality— he gave them water to wash their feet. What better way, then, for us to welcome new members in the family of people and the family of Jews?"

Washing Feet and Idolators

These remarks prompt two responses:

"Someone remembered" the biblical narrative, and, apparently, someone perused the sources and selected for use in the liturgy a remark from the *Midrash*, *Bereshit Rabba* 48:10, regarding Abraham's reward. Did no one, however, remember the exegetical comments of Rashi, *ad locum*? Rashi notes that Abraham offered the visitors water to wash their feet because Abraham "thought that they were Arabs who bow down to the dust of their feet, and he was meticulous not to bring idol-worship into his house." According to Rashi's exegesis, Abraham, not yet aware of the visitors' true identity, thought they were idol-worshippers and therefore insisted that they wash their feet immediately in order scrupulously to avoid bringing anything connected with idolatry into his house. By contrast, Lot, Rashi adds, was not particular in this regard and, unlike Abraham, offered his guests lodging before mentioning washing of the feet (see Gen. 19:2). Rashi's comments, as well as the similar midrashic observation, *Yalkut Shim'oni*, Gen. 18, are obviously based upon the talmudic passage (cited verbatim in the *Midrash*), *Baba Metzi'a* 86b: "They said to him, 'Do you suspect us of being like Arabs who

worship the dust on their feet?'" In light of these sources, washing of the feet hardly appears to be a suitable manner in which to welcome a new member of the family of Jews. *Kli Yakor*, commenting on Gen. 18:4, voices astonishment at Rashi's interpretation and notes that it is strange to assume that dust is forbidden because of the foolish notions of idolators. Just as idolators cannot render the sun forbidden, *Kli Yakor* argues, they cannot render the dust off bounds. *Kli Yakor* accordingly interprets Abraham's request homiletically and asserts that water is symbolic of purity and thus Abraham was attempting to influence the idolators to repent by giving them waters of purification. According to this latter interpretation as well, the water is offered to idolators. However, in the opinion of *Kli Yakor*, the purpose is not to wash away the physical evidence of idolatry but to symbolize the need for purification.

It should be noted that one does find mention of feet washing as a Jewish ritual in entirely different contexts. The *kohanim* washed both hands and feet prior to performing the divine service (see Ex. 30:19-21). In later times there is reference (*Shabbat* 50b and Maimonides, *Mishneh Torah*, *Hilkhot Tefillah* 4:3) to the practice of washing the feet prior to the *shaharit* prayers. Normative Jewish law does not posit this requirement.

Which Covenant Takes Precedence?

It is indeed true that Judaism posits the existence of a covenant made with Noah after the flood and embracing all of humanity— the children of Noah. Judaism teaches that the Noachide Code binds all mankind to observance of fundamental ethical and religious norms. However, in the case of the people of Israel the covenant of Noah is superceded by the covenant of Sinai. Jews are not known as "children of Noah," but as "children of the covenant— *b'nai brit*," individuals bound by the Sinaitic Code. Should, then, Jewish girls be singled out and relegated to participation in the more minimal covenant of Noah, even though this covenant does indeed potentially involve all of humanity? It would appear to be far more proper to welcome Jewish infant girls into the particularistic covenant of Judaism and to join their fate with that of a people which prides itself on its distinction: "For He has not assigned our portion like theirs, nor our lot like all their multitude."

Liturgical creativity requires vigilance on the part of all who wish to avoid the pitfalls of alien concepts and foreign traditions. The concern with ritual and the desire to give expression to religious aspirations are laudatory. But, as committed Jews, when we call out, "My soul yearns, yea pines for the courts of the Lord; my heart and my flesh sing for joy unto the living God," we must strive to assure that our prayers and our ceremonies are appropriate expressions for Jews, suitable for those "who dwell in Your house" and befitting for Jews who long to "appear before God in Zion." (Ps. 84:3, 5 and 8.) ●

Day schools and the jewish birth rate

Sharon Strassfeld

What I really want to do is begin this article with a yelp of pain. I've just read the four hundredth article in six months on the latest issue to absorb the attention of the Jewish community: the declining Jewish birth rate, and frankly I'm mad. No doubt the Lord, in His infinite wisdom considers it worthwhile to cause hordes of sociologists, psychologists and Jewish communal workers to descend upon us bringing their own particular theories as offerings upon the altar of Why-they're-not making-babies-anymore.

Frankly, I would suppose ingenuity to have exhausted itself in speculation that 1) Couples are not having children because they're too selfish to make the sacrifice of having children, 2) Couples are not having children because the Women's Movement decreed that women need no longer feel it their duty to bear children, 3) Couples are not having children because there *are* no more couples. Everybody's divorced.

There are two other reasons nobody ever offers—presumably because they would shift at least some of the responsibility from couples and the Women's Movement and place it where it better belongs. These are: 1) We are all of us, increasingly, concerned about the economy. Wildly escalating inflation coupled with a serious recession frighten us. Some of us are afraid we can't *afford* to raise more Jewishly literate children. 2) The two-income two-profession family is here. What the Women's Movement hasn't decreed, the economy has. And the Jewish community has no investment in infant and

early childhood day care. None. In New York City there is no Jewish institution which provides infant day care (although if you check out the churches around you'll discover just who got into this particular act early). Furthermore, on the Upper West Side (not so incidentally the place in Manhattan where the largest number of young Jewish couples reside) the Jewish community has been hard at work closing down as many Jewish nursery schools as it can, and those that are left are frequently amateurish attempts at best.

High Education Costs a Serious Factor

The New York Federation last year sponsored a symposium on Zero Population Growth and Jewish Survival. At that symposium Blu Greenberg, (who after five children has certainly done *her* fair share for the Jewish birth rate) suggested that the cost of Jewish education is a serious factor in deterring young Jewish couples from having more children. Her suggestion was met with patent disbelief. And yet, many of us in the room who were of child-bearing age all spoke to the fact on that occasion publicly and again later among ourselves maintaining that such financial considerations do concern us. The plain truth is that it costs about $2500 a year to send a child to day school. If two children go to day school, that's $5000 of after-taxes money. Which means, if you are in the fortieth tax percentile, your children's day school tuitions account for $7000 of your salary.

Further, Jewish summer camps now average some $1200 per summer per child. Multiply by two children and you'll find yourself being relieved of $2400 a year or more than $2800 of salary.

While it's true that one doesn't necessarily figure out the financial ramifications of having the first and even the second child, once does indeed consider carefully the additional financial burden that having a third child would create. If you are already spending $10,000 of your gross salary to send two children to day school and summer camp, the total sum of what you have to earn to feed, clothe and house the four of you is quite large.

Jewish Community Reaction

How does the Jewish community react? The American Jewish Congress recently chalked up another victory in their fight to insure that no tax credit be granted parents who send their children to private schools. The American Jewish Committee has long held the same opinion. Incredible? Not at all. The Jewish community decided, long ago, that it is within its own best interests

SHARON AND MICHAEL STRASSFELD *edited* The Jewish Catalogs.

to insure the continued separation of church and state. Accordingly the Jewish community supplies funds to organizations who spend these funds making sure that such separation continues in its present form.

Both these organizations maintain that they are not opposed to day school education. They are merely intent on preventing government support of day school education. The net result of their efforts, however, has always been to penalize those parents who choose to send their children to day school. Frankly, I would find it much easier to believe that these organizations support day school education were they each to make available one thousand day school scholarships each year. Or, alternatively, were they to provide subsidies for day school teachers' salaries each year.

Instead the Jewish community allows these organizations to spend their money on an agenda that is, whether it wants to be or not, destructive to the day school movement. It is possible that I do not fully understand the legal, social or constitutional issues involved in providing tax benefits to parents who send their children to private schools. If someone can make a convincing argument that the behavior we now exhibit is not suicidal, I should be delighted to hear it. So far as I am concerned however, I am willing to risk the consequences of government infringement in this area so that we may accrue the benefits that government could provide us.

Jewish Education for Free

Beyond this, however, I have yet another agenda. Since I believe it is in the best interests of the Jewish community to produce literate Jewish adults, I have come to believe it is in the best interests of the Jewish community to provide free Jewish education. In other words, I would propose that we consider seriously the arguments put forth here when the United States decided to provide free public school education. The theory was that the community would be better served if decisions were made by literate adults. And the best way to insure that we have literate Jewish adults is to establish a free compulsory system of Jewish education.

I would, then, propose the following: The Jewish community ought to set up a model program in one city (no, let's *not* study the problem; in this case, study can only amount to speculation since, despite what people may tell you or even think about the issue, having a baby is quite personal enough to make the study about it an exercise in futility). For a period of ten years, the Jewish community would guarantee a free Jewish education through high school to every Jewish child born.

The community would underwrite the cost of the entire program and would couple it with one other component. For the same period of time, the Jewish community would set up infant and early childhood day-care centers which would be open from 8:30-5:30 Monday through Friday, staffed by the best-trained professionals available, and open to Jewish children at costs that were at least competitive with, if not somewhat below, other similar programs.

At the end of the ten year pilot program, we would then have to analyze a fairly simple equation. Given the demographic and sociological factors involved, and based on the testimony of those Jewish parents whose children participated in the experiment, did the Jewish birth rate rise? Interesting corollary issues to investigate are whether the Jews involved in the experiment were more sensitive to the needs/problems of the Jewish community, whether the parents felt that participation in the program put them more in touch with the Jewish community, etc.

Two Possible Objections

I hear in the back rows of my theater the disgruntled rumblings of those who feel that it is not quantity we need in the Jewish community but quality—a generation of Jews; no matter how small, who care passionately for and are committed to the Jewish community. I also hear those seated immediately to the right of those back rows who believe that it is not the responsibility of the Jewish community to subsidize parents who want to "go out and work."

To both groups I say right. You are right that we need quality Jews, and it is certainly *not* the responsibility of the Jewish community to subsidize those who want to work. BUT, there is a point of diminution below which there is no longer any point in talking about quality. We may rapidly be approaching that point.

And while it is not the responsibility of the Jewish community to support working parents, the plain truth is, to get what you want, you sometimes have to inadvertently provide a side benefit that you hadn't meant to provide. If you want to find out whether community support systems will make it easier for people to have children, you have to, inadvertently, it is true, support their ability to maintain two careers.

Is it worth the time, effort and money of the Jewish community to experiment with such proposals? That depends, on how serious we are about our domestic problems—on whether there is any Jewish agency with the mandate and vision to tackle such a fundamental Jewish problem—on whether we can wean ourselves away from our compulsion to talk about an issue just long enough for us to try to do something for a change. I for one hope the answers to these questions are yes. Otherwise I know my fate will be to suffer a sense of resignation and deep resentment as I spend the next few years listening to academic analyses and learned discourses on why I'm not making more Jewish babies.★

DANIEL I. LEIFER *works with Jewish students at the University of Chicago through the Hillel Foundation.*

JOSEPH KAPLAN *is a lawyer in New York.*

SHARON KAPLAN *is a social psychologist.*

7.
The Ethics of Life and Death

Abortion—we need halachic creativity

Blu Greenberg

My stomach tightens at the thought of getting involved in a controversy over abortion, even with myself. Emotionally, theologically, as a Jew, and most of all as a mother who is daily nurtured by the sights and sounds of her children, I am opposed to abortion. And yet, the other facets of unwanted pregnancy are inescapable — fatigued and harassed parents; the shame of rape; the premature end of youth because of a foolish mistake; the degradation and danger of coat-hanger abortion; and not the least, the overwhelming and exclusive claim a child makes on a woman's life for many of her strongest years.

But one is forced to make choices. Because everything in life is a trade-off and all decisions, *halachic* and otherwise, are made with competing claims in mind (this I believe to be an underlying concept of *sheelot* and *teshuvot*), I must tenuously come down on the side of legal abortions. Furthermore, I would challange my Orthodox community to broaden its interpretation of the *halacha* concerning abortion, so that as a community we would support liberalized, legal abortion. We should do this with regrets perhaps; and with grave reservations; but we should do it with a sense of urgency to inform our people and society at large with our own value system. To permit abortion as a medical option, yet to educate and infuse society with a transcending perspective might help a searching society to internalize an ethic which incorporates a sense of the preciousness of human relationships and life itself.

Let us consider, in turn, the three arguments used by the anti-abortion elements in the Jewish community.

1. What it could lead to. Although the notion of *siyag*, "a fence about the Torah" is powerful and necessary,

and gives full credence to an understanding of human nature as it basically is, I don't believe that abortion will necessarily lead to eugenics and euthanasia, nor that prohibiting abortion would guarantee their elimination. And part of the responsibility of the *halachic* community is not to say that it will, but to be ever watchful that it won't. Sweden liberalized its abortion laws many years ago, yet Germany, without a long history of legalized abortion, conceived of and executed the Aryan master race plan and the Mengele medical experiments.

2. The overwhelmingly negative halachic tradition. In reviewing the literature, — say David Feldman's *Birth Control and Jewish Law* — the section on abortion — a comprehensive and insightful review of the data; also Fred Rosner and J. David Bleich in *Tradition,* Winter, 1968, two good summaries in shorter form, it appears that there are a number of different strands, some lenient and some strict.

We can't ignore today's situation

On the whole, the traditional Jewish view of abortion has been more lenient than the traditional Christian view; yet even where it was permitted it was only in cases of therapeutic abortion — where there existed a grave threat to the life or health of the mother. With very few exceptions, the health of the fetus was not a valid reason for abortion; even in those minority opinions validating abortion for malformed fetuses, such as in the thalidomide cases, the rabbinic decisions were based on the threat to the mother's health, and not on considerations of the potential suffering of the child.

However, the issue today is not therapeutic abortion but *abortion on demand.*

There are very few responsa dealing with abortion based on personal, economic, or family planning reasons. This can be understood historically: a) in Jewish communities in pre modern times, even birth control was carefully restricted and the procreative function was high on the mitzvah list. b) in our times, when most Jews opt to have one or two children and when the issue of abortion has assumed national importance, most Jews do not look to rabbinic leadership for decisions in these areas. Even more startling, within the modern orthodox community, most women do not ask rabbis for *teshuvot* on such issues. Traditional couples, just like their Catholic counterparts, have long since made their personal and independent decisions on birth control even before the *halachically* permissible pill. There are very few families with eight or ten children.

Despite the lack of precedents for what we call "abortion on demand," one obvious way to maintain some integrity within the halachic framework would be to broaden the interpretation of therapeutic abortion — to extend the principle of precedence of the mother's actual life and health to include serious regard for the quality of life as well. There exist in the halachic literature some precious few precedents where exactly that has been done. In the 19th and 20th century, there have been some *teshuvot* permitting abortion in cases of rape of a married woman; in cases where carrying full term would cause extended suffering to the mother; or, as mentioned above, in the minority decisions on malformed fetuses.

Therefore I could conceive of a halachic stance which would say that abortion is to be avoided for all the traditional and theological reasons. Yet the circumstances under which it would be permissible would be widened. These might include the need to support self and/or husband through school; the need for time for a marriage to stabilize; overwhelming responsibilities to other children; and so forth. Then abortion should be seen as a sad necessity rather than an evil. Many *mitzvot* are interdependent; they are functions of the several conditions they regulate.

Abortion is not a method of birth-control

3. *The implied devaluation of human life.* The problem with easy abortion is that it can become simply a means of birth control and run the risk of lack of seriousness re the mystery and miracle of human conception and birth. However, to date it has not been shown to do so. Bronx abortion clinic records for 1973 indicate the contrary; only 5% of 2001 abortions were repeats. But with lower costs and greater availability, this development could easily take place.

I understood this when I read of the strike of nurses in a large Baltimore hospital. They could not take the continual sight of aborted fetuses piled high in the bins of the abortion theater. The image that followed in my mind was the heaps of corpses which numbed the allied inspection teams in Auschwitz, 1945, and which numbs the Jewish people forever. It is the ultimate desecration of the images of God. Here truly is the dialectic in the abortion issue with which one must come to grips. But how? How retain the *halachah's* reverence for life? One way is simply that the sanctions for abortion — or against it — be done within some sort of total theological framework which take conception and birth very seriously and which has as its value source God and community. This is the reverse of how abortion decisions are most often made today. It will take courage for religious leaders to say that *in certain instances* abortion is the higher morality if one operates with the overall principles of *tzelem Elokim,* the image of God, and *kibud habriyot,* the dignity of God's creatures—principles which are sometimes lost in the myriad of *halachot* developed to express these theological priorities.

Halacha could be expanded

Some examples: In the last two centuries the grounds for abortion were extended by Rabbis Emden, Waldenberg and Weinberg to include the mother's psychological health. Thus too, Rabbi Yitzchak Oelbaum ruled for abortion where the danger was not to the pregnant mother but to the nursing sibling whose health might be affected if the mother's milk were to dry up. Those *teshuvot* could support new rulings which would encompass such variables as physical strength, stress, even delay in child raising for purposes of family planning or a career.

"V'chai bahem" (the principle "and live through them") could conceivably be applied to permit a Tay-Sach's or deformed fetus to be aborted. Here the dignity of *tzelem Elokim* must be interpreted not as opposing abortion (lest it lead to dehumanization) but rather in light of what hell this image of God and his/her parents will have to suffer when the child inexorably decays and dies at four years of age. It is true that some children with deformities are more loved than perfect specimens. Yet institutions are full of malformed children who eke out a miserable life and whose parents have deep wells of guilt. In this situation, forced birth is the "dehumanizing" experience.

Beyond these situations, halachic leaders should not be fearful of extending the *halachah* to create a better meshing of personal needs with traditional dictates. This doesn't mean that *halachah* must legitimate itself by simply saying "yes." Rather, by saying "yes" under a variety of circumstances, its value judgments of "no" will also be taken more seriously.

The fact that the *Gemara* conceived of a fetus as water until the 40th day can also be used to widen the grounds for abortion. One responsibility then would be to support research for earlier methods of detection. It goes without saying that the halachic community should investigate and develop better methods of contraception, and wider education on birth control. Some additional responsibilities would be the establishment of adoption agencies, continued vigilance and monitoring of the effects of legal abortion lest abuses arise, greater communal sharing of responsibility in raising children, greater sex education and responsibility for one's sexual life.

All this need not simply turn into a situation of abortion "no" — but in this case, a grudging "yes". The emphasis should be: having children is not anything to be taken for granted or taken lightly. And the Jewish people in particular needs to expand its birthrate and replenish themselves after Auschwitz and after four wars in Israel, even as we seriously attend to the question generally of world overpopulation. No one should be coerced into having a child; rather, the case for children is made — and this is a valid and important option in a society where the reverse messages are currently more popular.

The abortion issue is also a symptom
Such forthright ethico-*halachic* leadership might well encourage more Jews — even those who consider themselves observant of Jewish law — to take seriously the *halachah* as a moral force in their lives. Unfortunately it has been reduced to observance of ritual, while ethical, social, sexual decisions are more susceptible to T.V. advertising messages. By the same token the responsibility lies upon those on the fringes or within the community *to ask* the questions. The responsa literature did not grow in a vacuum.

Abortion is, in fact, a symptom of two larger problems: First, a society which establishes the value of goods over relationships. We try to hide the existential truths of human existence with pills, goods, junk and even sexual ecstacy. I have nothing against ease and comforts nor even delusions of self-import but as a society we border on the selfish.

Secondly, the clamor for abortion points up to the way women feel about their role in society and their constriction of options as a result of motherhood. Consider the notion which many feminists have made central to their pro-abortion claims, the right to control "their own bodies." I disagree with this focus. It is simply too narrow a conception when facing the miracle of life-creation. It is also too narcissistic. Furthermore, it releases men from responsibility, both from sexual responsibility and from child raising, thereby reinforcing the sexist models which it seeks to undermine. On the other hand, moral theologians ought to attend to the climate of disabilities and inequities regarding women, these exist in life in general and in the Jewish community, in particular. If nothing is done the situation may yet foment into a final crisis with rejection of child birth and child raising as the expression of dissatisfaction.

Hand in hand with greater *halachic* responsibility and flexibility regarding abortion should be a critique of the society which currently reduces human concerns to such issues. Along with this must come some moral guidance on how a whole society can begin to pull itself up by its boot straps and integrate those values which underly a pose of reverence for life itself.

A critique of brickner on abortion
J. David Bleich

I appeared before the Senate Subcommittee on Constitutional Amendments as a representative of the Rabbinical Council of America for the purpose of presenting the views of traditional Judaism with regard to the emotionally charged issue of abortion. I felt then, and continue to feel, that there exist two misconceptions which must be dispelled. To this end I sought to emphasize that:
1) Permissiveness with regard to the destruction of fetal life is a fundamental moral issue rather than a specifically religious or uniquely sectarian question.
2) Judaism does *not* view abortion as a private matter between a woman and her physician. The destruction of a fetus is viewed by *Halachah* with utmost gravity.

It is precisely because of the repeated distortions of the teachings of traditional Judaism in appearances before legislative bodies and the attendant coverage by the media that an authentic presentation of these views before such forums has become imperative. Throughout the public airing of the pros and cons concerning abortion legislation the impression has been created that for Jews abortion poses no moral dilemma. This, most emphatically, is not so. Any individual or group may choose to accept or reject the teachings of traditional Judaism — It is to that end that G-d endowed us with *bechirah* (free will). But distortion of the teachings of traditional Judaism on this or any other matter is intellectually dishonest and, when undertaken for purposes of molding both the legislative process and public opinion, becomes a matter of ethical concern.

Testifying on behalf of the Union of American Hebrew Congregations, Balfour Brickner rested his case against legislative restrictions upon indiscriminate abortion on two points:
1) A negative stance with regard to abortion must be the fruit of a parochial religous conviction. Since the objections are sectarian in nature, any attempt to invoke the police power of the state in support of this position is a violation of the principle of separation of church and state and of the philosophy underlying the establishment clause of the first amendment.
2) Judaism — as Balfour Brickner sees it — really has nothing against the destruction of fetal life.

Religion does influence legislation
The first argument betrays a lack of sensitivity for nuances of constitutional law. The courts have consistently ruled that the establishment clause is simply a corollary to the free exercise clause. Government cannot constitutionally restrict forms of worship, interfere with ritual or in any way limit the "free exercise" of religion. By the same token it cannot mandate any form of worship, prescribe rituals for its citizenry or in any way promote one denomination over another.

The question of the legislative promotion of moral conduct is another matter entirely. Every religion professes moral beliefs and not even a confirmed atheist would claim that any given valid moral position is of diminished ethical value because it is embodied in the tenets of a particular faith. It is not at all difficult to show religious influences in the legislative acceptance of certain moral views. Polygamy is an obvious case in point. Monogamy is at once a moral and religious desideratum in Western society. Polygamy was banned in our country primarily because it is an insult to our moral sensitivity — a sensitivity cultivated under the influence of Western religion. Despite the constitutional questions which it presented, legislation banning polygamy was upheld by the Supreme Court in *Davis V. Beason,* 133 U.S. 33. More recently, in *McGowan v. Maryland,* 366 U.S. 442 (1961), the Court found that: ". . . the 'Establishment' Clause does not ban federal or state regulation of conduct whose reason or effect merely happens to coincide or harmonize with the tenets of some or all religions . . . Thus, for temporal purposes, murder is

illegal. And the fact that this agrees with the dictates of the Judaeo-Christian religions while it may disagree with others does not invalidate the regulation."

Can the state dictate personal morality?
This, of course, leads to a number of other questions. If religious sanction is not the ultimate authority in the determination of moral values how may one distinguish between authentic and inauthentic moral values? The religionist has no difficulty defining morality, but what criteria are used by the humanist in arriving at a definition? The answers to such questions are what ethics and ethical theory are all about. For purposes of our discussion the salient point is that regardless of the presence or absence of traceable historical influences pointing to the presence of religious teaching in the formulation of moral values such values do acquire a status independent of the religious traditions from which they stem. A quite strong case can be, and indeed has been made for the anti-abortion position without invocation of sectarian doctrine. And, finally, it should be noted that the Supreme Court in its much publicized decision overturning Texas' abortion statue did *not* find such legislation to be an infringement of the first amendment.

But we have succeeded only in pushing the question back one step. Does the state have the constitutional right to legislate in the area of personal morality? Homosexuality and deviant sexual practices between consenting adults are certainly areas in which statutes of this nature are still on the books. The constitutionality of such statutes was recently reaffirmed by the California Court of Appeals in *People v. Baldwin,* 112 Cal. Retpr. 290 (1974). Nonetheless, in a growing number of cases the courts have come to view legislation in the area of private morality as an infringement of the right to privacy and of the due process clause of the fourteenth amendment (again, for emphasis, not of the first amendment) and have tended to strike down such legislation unless the concomitant presence of some "compelling state interest" can be demonstrated. The Court chose not to view the preservation of prenatal life, at least until the final trimester of pregnancy, to be a "compelling" state interest and hence regarded a decision to terminate pregnancy as a purely personal matter.

The fetus has a juridical personality
But is destruction of the fetus indeed a purely private matter? Here we come to the crux of the legal problem. In its recent decision the Supreme Court expressed

the view that a fetus is not entitled to protection of law because it is not a person. "If this suggestion of personhood is established," reads the majority opinion in *Roe v. Wade*, "...the fetus' right to life is then guaranteed by the [Fourteenth] Amendment." Some years ago a prominent attorney ingeniously argued that animals are not persons and hence are not covered by the general welfare clause. It follows, he claimed, that statutory safeguards against cruelty to animals are unconstitutional. To my knowledge, no legal scholar has taken this argument seriously. Now we find ourselves in a rather anomolous situation: an animal is a "person" within the constitutional meaning of the term, but a fetus is not. The proposed constitutional amendment which has been so vehemently decried is essentially no more than an exercise in constitutional semantics. The definition of the term "person" would be unequivocally defined to include a fetus.

This leads us headlong into Brickner's error with regard to the main issue: How *does* Judaism regard the fetus? Does a fetus have a "juridical personality" of its own? Contrary to Brickner's negative assertion, in the Jewish legal system, a fetus does have a juridical personality. Under Jewish law a fetus may acquire property. Physical contact with an aborted fetus results in the very same defilement caused by contact with a human corpse. The Sabbath and the Day of Atonement must be violated in order to preserve the life of the fetus. Parenthetically, as Professor Paul Ramsey pointed out in his testimony before the Senate Subcommittee, the courts themselves have ruled in other contexts that an unborn child is entitled to protection of law. See *Raleight Fitkin-Paul Morgan Memorial Hospital v. Anders,* 201 A2d 537, 42N.J.421 (1964), in which Chief Justice Weintraub wrote for a unanimous court, "We are satisfied that the unborn child is entitled to the law's protection and that an appropriate order should be made to insure blood transfusions to the mother."

Feticide can lead to infanticide
Brickner obfuscates the Jewish position by stating: "Jewish law is quite clear in its statement that an embryo is not reckoned a viable living thing (in Hebrew, a *bar kayyama*) until thirty days after its birth. One is not obliged to observe the laws of mourning for an expelled fetus. As a matter of fact, the laws of mourning, etc. are not applicable for a child who does not survive until his thirtieth day."

Some time ago an eminent scientist and Nobel laureate, Dr. James Watson, made the startling proposal that "birth" be defined not as parturition or emergence of the baby from the womb but as occurring some seventy-two hours after this event. Since the baby is not yet "born," in the event that it is found to be physically or mentally defective it could be destroyed with impunity up to the moment of "birth." As a result of lexicographical sleight of hand infanticide (within seventy-hours of parturition) would be relabeled as feticide; since abortion no longer carries with it opprobrium unwanted babies could be readily (and morally!) disposed of in this manner.

If we are to take Brickner's argument seriously and follow it to its logical conclusion it should follow that, in the Jewish tradition, there is no reason why a baby cannot be destroyed until it is thirty days old! After all it is not reckoned a "viable living thing (in Hebrew, a *bar kayyama*)." Proof of the pudding: mourning need not be observed!

Brickner unwittingly stumbled into this error and the attendant *reductio ad absurdum* because he failed to realize that the law which he cites simply does not reflect a halachic definition of the developmental stage at which an embryo undergoes a metamorphosis and becomes a person. The law in question expresses an entirely different consideration. There is no prescribed mourning for the loss of a child which has not been carried to term. Mourning is mandated only when there is the potential for at least minimal survival. *Halachah* assumes that mortality during the first thirty days of life is due to premature birth and serves as an indication that the infant was not viable. Can one logically infer from such *halachot* that a newly born infant may be destroyed? Or that a fetus may wilfully be destroyed?

"Nefesh" does not mean "person"
Indeed, the renowned R. Elijah Mizrachi in his supercommentary on Rashi, Exodus 21:12, declares that, in theory, wilful destruction of the fetus is a capital crime because fetal life and human life are qualitatively one and the same. In practice, feticide does not entail the death penalty because it cannot be established with certainty that any given fetus has the potential for survival and hence for technical reasons capital punishment cannot be administered.

At the root of the confusion is a proper understanding of the term *"nefesh."* Brickner tells us, "In Judaism the fetus in the womb is not a person (*lav nefesh hu*).'' It is quite correct to say that Judaism does not prescribe capital punishment for feticide because the fetus is not a *"nefesh."* But the term *"nefesh"* does not mean "person." Judaism does not prescribe capital punishment for a *treifah* (rough translation: a person suffering from a fatal abnormality, congenital or acquired, of a vital organ) because a *treifah* is not deemed to be a *nefesh*. Does that mean that a *treifah* is not a person? Certainly not! What it does mean is that *Halachah* recognizes degrees of viability as characterized by clearly delineated physical criteria and excludes from *capital* punishment the taking of certain clearly defined categories of human life. The wanton taking of the life of a *treifah* or of a fetus is nonetheless a criminal act. The term *"nefesh"* simply does not mean "person"; its translation by that term may suffice for colloquial purposes but it is hardly a precise equivalent. Biblical terms are often narrow, precise, technical terms. *Nefesh* is such a term. While R. Joseph Trani and R. Jacob Emden do indeed advance different considerations for prohibiting abortion such authoritative sources as Rambam and *Shulchan Aruch* clearly view the fetus as a "person" and base the prohibition against feticide squarely upon the fetus' status as such.

The mother's life has precedence over the fetus'
Brickner presents a string of Mishnaic and Talmudic quotations and concludes by saying, "However, nowhere does it state that killing the fetus by premature artificial termination of pregnancy is prohibited." In truth, Brickner has himself quoted the *locus classicus* of that prohibition. The *Mishnah, Oholot* 7:6, declares that when "hard travail" of labor endangers the life of the mother an embryotomy may be performed and the fetus be extracted limb by limb. The justificatory reasoning is incorporated in the text of the *Mishnah* in the explanatory phrase, "for her [the mother's] life has precedence over its [the fetus'] life." It requires no great exegetic skill to deduce that when the compelling reason of preservation of maternal life is not present the fetus cannot justifiably be destroyed. Those few authorities who sanction destruction of the fetus for lesser causes were indeed hard put to propound a more limited interpretation of this *Mishnah*.
Furthermore (and perhaps of greater importance to the specific issue at hand) Brickner fails to be mindful of the fact that the *Talmud* expressly teaches that feticide *is* a capital crime under Noachidic law. *Sanhedrin* 57b renders Genesis 9:6 as "He who sheds the blood

of a man within a man, his blood shall be shed." "Who is 'a man within a man'? queries the *Gemara*. "This is a fetus in its mother's womb." For the children of Noah a fetus is clearly a *nefesh* even according to Brickner's use of the term.

Brickner's statement with regard to the "plethora of evidence from Judaism recognizing the legality of abortion" is simply false. To suggest, as Brickner does, that abortion is a Jewishly acceptable, nay laudable, form of population control and family planning is a travesty of Jewish teaching. Particularly vexing is the innuendo in the statement which reads: "The reasons traditional Judaism generally prohibits abortion despite the rabbinic literature permitting abortion [sic!] are complex and diverse." For some "complex and diverse" reasons, unknown to me but presumably known to Brickner, traditional Judaism has chosen to distort the *Halachah*. One may present one's personal views and those of liberal Judaism as forcefully and as eloquently as one is able; conceivably one may even argue that they are in keeping, if not with the letter of the law, with the spirit of Judaic values. But surely one should be mindful not to misrepresent Talmudic law or to impugn the posture of rabbinic Judaism.

Rabbinical duty is to guide morality
Traditionally, for good reasons or for bad, Orthodox Jewry has not sought to publicize its position on public issues, much less to foist its views upon the civil legislatures. Of late, there has been a subtle but discernible shift in policy. Orthodox spokesmen have begun to advance their views for the edification of the general public. This has occurred in part because of a growing concern lest fellow Jews be misled in terms of their own personal conduct, particularly in instances when antithetical opinions have been advanced in the name of Jewish morality. However, of no less significance are grave misgivings with regard to the general permissive moral climate and the erosion of the sanctity with which Western society has always regarded human life. In response to a question by Senator Bayh I stressed that I appeared before the Subcommittee not in the role of a lobbyist but in the role of a teacher, as an exponent of Jewish ethical teaching. It is the function of a rabbi, and of the Rabbinical Council as a national body of rabbis, to provide moral guidance. The manner in which this is to be translated into law is a matter between legislators and their consciences.

116

A critique of bleich on abortion

Balfour Brickner

While I have great respect for the rabbinic scholarship of my colleague Rabbi J. David Bleich, I maintain that neither the Biblical nor the rabbinic tradition support the impression left by his testimony last March before the Bayh sub-committee, that Judaism supports the views of persons like Senators Buckley, Helms and others. They claim that the fetus is a "person" (full human being) from the moment of conception and that to permit abortion under any circumstances is to commit murder. This view is not in accord with Judaic teachings. Nothing Rabbi Bleich has written seems to refute my initial statement — ". . . . that Jewish law does not consider a fetus 'a person.' Jewish law agrees with the majority opinion of those on the Supreme Court who, in their January 22nd, 1973 decision stated:
The Constitution does not define "person" in so many words. The use of the word is such that it has application only postnatally.
The unborn have never been recognized in the law as persons in the whole sense."

Judaism permits abortion. Let us state that clearly and simply. I defy anyone to refute that statement. In the opening paragraph in his fine article on the subject in *Tradition* Rabbi Bleich recognizes and admits this:

While Judaism has always sanctioned therapeutic abortion in at least limited circumstances, the pertinent halachic discussions are permeated with a spirit of humility reflecting an attitude of awe and reverence before the profound mystery of existence and sanctity of individual human life.

No quarrel!

Moreover, I concur with the sentiment expressed in the last part of the above quoted paragraph of Rabbi Bleich. I said as much in my testimony stating, "while Jewish law teaches a reverent and responsible attitude to the question of abortion, reasons affecting basic life and health may sanction or even require abortion." (see page 6 of my testimony) The point is not whether Judaism gives its sanction reluctantly — the point is that *it gives the sanction* under certain conditions. The destruction of a fetus may be viewed in Judaism "with utmost gravity" (Rabbi Bleich's phrase) but that is not a *prohibition* against the de-

struction of a fetus. What is at stake now in America is not the matter of "reluctance" or "gravity". What is at stake now is the possibility of a constitutional amendment being enacted here which would *prohibit* abortions based on the idea that a fetus is a "person" with full human rights from the moment of conception, thus making abortion an act of murder. Make no mistake; those "compulsory pregnancy" people agitating for a change in the present statutes have one ultimate goal in mind — the abolition of abortion as a morally-accepted legally obtainable act. It is inconceivable to me that any branch of Judaism would lend its support to such an effort especially when the *Halacha* does not support such a posture either directly or through the process of rabbinic deduction.

Evidence shows that abortion is permitted

The central issue in the entire discussion is whether or not Judaism regards the fetus as a person — a full human being from the moment of conception. If it does, then anyone electing to have an abortion would indeed be guilty of murder. But Judaism does *not* so describe the fetus. To the contrary, a fetus is not considered a person: *"lav nefesh hu."* Commenting on the classic *Mishnah* text (*Ohalot* 7.6) Rashi writes: "As long as the child did not come out into the world *it is not called a living being* and *it is therefore permissible to take its life* in order to save the life of its mother. Once the head of the child has come out the child may not be harmed because it is considered as fully born, and one life may not be taken to save another." On different but equally compelling grounds, Maimonides came to the same conclusion that a fetus is not a person. In his *Mishnah Torah* Chapter 4, paragraph 1, he writes:

If one assaults a woman, even unintentionally, and her child is born prematurely, he must pay the value of the child to the husband and the compensation for injury and pain to the woman.

Elsewhere he deals with the issue from the argument of "pursuit" and comes to the same conclusion —

There also is a negative precept: not to have compassion on the life of a pursuer. Therefore the sages ruled (regarding) a pregnant woman in hard travail that it is permitted to dismember the fetus in her womb . . . "
(*Hilkhot Rotzeach* 1.9)

Most interpreters of the Maimonidean reference agree

that it is an argument in support of the right to therapeutic abortion.

A similar declaration is found in Karo's *Shulchan Aruch* (Chapter 423, par. 1).

In neither instance is concern expressed for the status of the fetus. It is considered to be part of the mother and belongs jointly to her and her husband and thus damages must be paid for its premature death. However, and this is important, the one who was responsible is not culpable for murder since the unborn fetus is not considered a person. There seems to be little argument from Jewish rabbinic sources that an unborn fetus (for whatever reasons) is not considered a person (a *nefesh*) until it has been born. The fetus is regarded as part of the mother's body and not a separate being until it begins to emerge from the womb during parturition. In fact, until forty days after conception the fertilized egg is considered "mere fluid."

The fetus is not a *nefesh*
Rabbi Bleich recognizes that the fetus is not a living person according to Jewish law and reluctantly admits this in his article —

There are however other authorities who deem the destruction of a fetus to be unrelated to the taking of human life, but nevertheless forbidden on extraneous grounds. (page 77)

These "extraneous grounds" to which he refers in no way alter the basic assertion that Judaism does not prescribe capital punishment for feticide because the fetus is not a "*nefesh*" — a person. Perhaps "*nefesh*" does not mean person. Then what does it mean? In his *Tradition* article Rabbi Bleich writes: "Since, however, a fetus is not accounted as being a full-fledged nefesh or 'life' . . . " (page 81). Is he making a distinction between human "life" and human "person"? If so, "*nefesh*" does mean person. Rabbi David Feldman in his authoritative book "Birth Control and Jewish Law" seems to agree:

A significant Responsum from eastern Europe of the eighteenth century dealt with the matter of B'nai Noah (non-Jews) in its own way, offering us in the process a fine insight for the modern day debate on the 'human' status of the embryo: it is not to be supposed that the Torah would consider the embryo as a person (nefesh) for them (Sons of Noah) but not a person for us. The fetus is not a person for them either; the Torah merely was more severe in its practical ruling in their regard. Hence, therapeutic abortion would be permissible to them, too. Does

the matter then depend on calling the fetus by the name 'person'? (atu bik'riat shem nefesh talya milta') It depends rather on the responsibilities which the Torah has assigned in connection therewith.

To sum up then, abortion is not murder, neither for Israelites nor for 'Sons of Noah.' . . . (Feldman page 261)

This is precisely the point I sought to convey in my original testimony when I stated:

By this reckoning, abortion cannot be considered murder. The basis for this decision is scriptural (Ex. 21.22). Talmudic commentators made the teaching of this Biblical passage quite explicit. They said that only monetary compensation is exacted of him who causes a woman to miscarry. No prohibition is evident from this scriptural passage against destroying the unborn child . . . This concept is reiterated in many different instances and in many different places in rabbinic writing. (page 4 of testimony)

For further examples one may read Feldman (pages 254 and 255) with special attention to the footnotes.

Noachidic law vs. jewish law
Is all this a misrepresentation of Talmudic law and a false posturing of rabbinic Judaism? I say it isn't!

We referred to "Noachide laws" — laws pertaining to non-Jews. Rabbi Bleich used these laws to assert that feticide *is* a capital crime under "Noachidic law." (sic)

Yet, in his major *Tradition* article he quotes extensively from Rabbi Unterman, former Ashkenazic chief rabbi of Israel . . . "R. Unterman draws a conclusion that there is a fundamental distinction between Jewish law and Noachidic law with regard to the assessment of potential life . . . It would appear that the *Halacha* holds them accountable only for *actual* in contradistinction to *potential* life. Accordingly, there is no objection to Noachides aborting . . . within the first forty days of gestation. Since *Halacha* considers that during this initial period the embryo has not as yet developed distinctly recognizable organs or an independent circulatory system it cannot be considered "a man within a man" and hence its destruction does not constitute murder under the Noachidic dispensation. Rabbi Unterman avers that Nachmandides sanctioned the performance of abortions by Noachides only within this forty day period." (Tradition article on page 85)

Much of Rabbi Bleich's argument is based on a Rabinically interpreted translation of the Biblical verse:

"Who so sheddeth a man's blood, by man shall his blood be shed" (Genesis 9:6).

The *Talmud* records the exposition of R. Yishmael who gives a varient translation/interpretation of this passage which Bleich quotes: "He who sheds the blood of a man *within a man*, his blood shall be shed." R. Yishmael then asks: "what is this 'man in man', and he answers: "It refers to the fetus in its mother's womb." (TB *Sanhedrin* 57b and in the name of R. Hannina, in Gen. *Rabbah* 34, 14) Here one sees a classic example of circular reasoning. In order to prove his point, Bleich uses only the Talmudic rendering which was seemingly created in order to justify the very thought it wished to prove. But, as David Feldman points out in his work:

Some modern scholars hold this exposition to be more sociologic than textually inherent, that it represents a reaction against abuses among the heathen. In views of rampant abortion and infanticide says I. H. Weiss in his history of Jewish tradition, R. Yishmael 'forced' the above exegesis out of the Genesis text to render judgment against the Romans.

It is difficult to accept such a doubtful reference with its even more suspect textual treatment as exemplary of a prohibition against abortion for Jews.

Mental health as a compelling reason

When may an abortion be performed? Are there any compelling reasons that would justify a therapeutic abortion under Jewish Law? Threat to the physical life of the mother is one. So too is the *health* of the mother.

Rabbi Bleich quotes the opinion of Rabbis Jacob Emden, Ben Zion Uriel (late Sephardic Chief Rabbi of Israel), Joseph Trani, Weinberg and others to confirm this conclusion. (see *Tradition*, page 95-96) Rabbi Feldman's book leads to the same conclusion. (see Rabbi Feldman's book p. 284 following)

Can the *mental* health of a woman be a "compelling reason" which might allow a person to have an abortion? The answer seems to be "yes". There are classic responsa dealing with this question, one going back to the 17th century. Rabbi Israel Meir Mizrahi permitted abortion when it was feared that the mother would otherwise suffer an attack of hysteria (*Peri Ha-aretz, Yoreh Deah*, Sec. 21). Rabbi Unterman also rules permissively in this matter in cases of extreme mental anguish. Suicidal tendencies are considered a threat to her life and constitute an adequate

warrant. A ruling in 1913 clarified the issue even more definitively:

Mental health risk has been definitely equated to physical health risk. This woman who is in danger of losing her mental health unless the pregnancy is interrupted, therefore would accordingly qualify. (Resp. L'vushei Mord'khai *H.M. No. 39)* (as quoted in Feldman p. 286)

That the laws of *"pikkuah nefesh"* (danger to life) apply to mental health danger as well as to physical hazard was again reaffirmed in a 1957 Responsum by Rabbi Nathan Friedman of B'nei Brak in his *Netzer Matta'ai* No. 8.

The implications of this attitude are obvious. Many "liberals" have long advocated liberalized abortion laws which would take into account psychological needs of women, as for example women with large families who simply cannot face another pregnancy. Abortion is a technique which should be freely available to women seeking physical and mental health. No sectarian legalism, no civil prohibition should stand in the way of a woman's *right* to that health.

That is why I testified:

I am well aware there are some citizens of this country who hold deep religious convictions which cause them to consider abortion as morally wrong. I do not quarrel with that conviction or with those who hold it. But, I cannot believe that the state has the right to foist through legislation the religious conviction of any one group upon all the citizens of the country . . . not to have the option of abortion would deny full protection under the law to those whose religious conviction does in certain circumstances recognize abortion. (testimony page 7)

Religion should inform not persuade

A state must always be chary about seeking to legislate morality lest it infringe on those rights. While it is true that religion, as one instrument, used to shape ethical values, has the duty to inform and instruct the secular state on what it thinks the state's posture on a given issue ought to be, it does not follow either that this is the only view or that the state has an obligation to heed religion's advice.

Religion is *not* the sole authority in the determination of moral values, and religionists do have difficulty (increasingly so) in defining what is and what is not moral, i.e. the debate over the morality of pre-marital sex, the debate over obscenity laws, the current fracas over the use of certain textbooks in the public schools of West Virginia, etc.

What can honestly be said is that Judaism does indeed permit abortion, certainly during the first 40 days of pregnancy. From 40 days until birth the fetus is not considered a living person (*nefesh*) but is regarded as part of the mother's flesh and aborting it is not considered murder legally. Abortion is permitted by most rabbinic authorities where a medical or psychiatric threat to the mother's life or health exists, though to be sure, it is an action which should be entered into only after the most careful consideration. Judaism looks on abortion with distaste, discourages and tries to restrict it, but it clearly permits it and permission is what is at issue in the current debate now raging in America.

Dignity lies in the struggle for life

J. David Bleich

The tragic case of Karen Ann Quinlan, particularly as tried in the press, presented three critical issues. The first, whether or not Karen should be pronounced dead, was a specious question from the start. It rapidly became evident that Karen Quinlan is alive even according to the most liberal definitions of death. The second question was that of vicarious consent, i.e., may parents authorize withdrawal of treatment? From the legal perspective, proxy consent remains a clouded area; from the perspective of Jewish law, parents have no standing whatsoever in this matter. The obligations which exist with regard to treatment of the sick are autonomous in nature and are not at all contingent upon the desire of parents, or for that matter, of the patient. Judge Muir's statement, ". . . the only cases where a parent has standing to pursue a constitutional right on behalf of an infant are those involving continuing life styles," is quite consistent with Jewish ethics. The third question was by far the most crucial: Does anyone have the right to choose death over life? Since the New Jersey Supreme Court had already ruled in a unanimous opinion that no one has a "right" to die, Judge Muir's decision was a foregone conclusion. His decision was but a procedural prologue to a reexamination of this fundamental question by the N. J. appeals court and perhaps ultimately by the federal courts as well. It is this question which will be debated in the months, and perhaps years, to come.

In judaism, life is a basic and absolute good
It is quite true that man has the power to prolong life far beyond the point at which it ceases to be either productive or pleasurable. Not infrequently, the patient, if capable of expressing his desires and allowed to follow his own inclinations, would opt for termination of a life which has become a burden both to others and to himself. Judaism, however, teaches that man does not enjoy the right of self-determination with regard to questions of life and death. Generations ago our Sages wrote, "Against your will you live; against your will you die." While conventionally understood as underscoring the irony that a baby wishes to be born no more than an adult wishes to die, these words today take on new meaning. They may be taken quite literally as an eloquent summary of the Jewish view with regard to both euthanasia and the withholding of life-sustaining treatment. Judaism has always taught that life, no less than death, is involuntary. Only the Creator who bestows the gift of life may relieve man of that life even when it has become a burden rather than a blessing.

In the Jewish tradition the value with which human life is regarded is maximized far beyond the value placed upon human life either in the Christian tradition or in Anglo-Saxon common law. In Jewish law and moral teaching life is a supreme value and its preservation takes precedence over virtually all other considerations. Human life is not regarded as a good to be preserved as a condition of other values, but as an absolute basic and precious good in its own stead. Even life accompanied by suffering is regarded as being preferable to death. (See *Sotah* 20a.)

We cannot judge the quality of life to be preserved
Man does not possess absolute title to his life or his body. He is charged with preserving, dignifying, and hallowing that life. He is obliged to seek food and sustenance in order to safeguard the life he has been granted; when falling victim to illness or disease he is obliged to seek a cure in order to sustain life. Never is he called upon to determine whether life is worth living; that is a question over which G-d remains sole arbiter.

Judaism denies man the right to make judgments with regard to quality of life. The category of *pikuach ne-*

fesh (preservation of life) extends to human life of every description and classification including the feeble-minded, the mentally deranged and, yes, even a person in a so-called vegetative state. Sabbath laws and the like are suspended on behalf of such persons even though there may be no chance for them ever to serve either G-d or fellow man. The *mitzvah* of saving a life is neither enhanced nor diminished by virtue of the quality of the life preserved.

All means, except the experimental, must be used
Distinctions between natural and artificial means, between ordinary and extraordinary procedures, and between non-heroic and heroic measures recur within the Catholic tradition, but no precisely parallel categories exist within Jewish law. Judaism knows no such distinctions and indeed the very vocabulary employed in drawing such distinctions is foreign to rabbinic literature. Rambam in his *Commentary on the Mishnah, Pesachim* 4:9, draws a cogent parallel between food and medication. G-d created food and water; we are obliged to use them in staving off hunger and thirst. G-d created drugs and medicaments and endowed man with the intelligence necessary to discover their medicinal properties; we are obliged to use them in warding off illness and disease. Similarly, G-d provided the materials and the technology which make possible catheters, intravenous infusions, and respirators; we are obliged to use them in order to prolong life.

Judaism does recognize situations in which certain forms of medical intervention are not mandatory. This is so not because such procedures involve expense, inconvenience, or hardship, but because they are not part of an accepted therapeutic protocol. The obligation to heal is limited to the use of a *refuah bedukah,* drugs and procedures of demonstrated efficacy. (See R. Ya'akov Emden, *Mor u-Ketziah* 338.) Man must use the full range of benefits made available by science; but he is not obliged to experiment with untried and unproven measures. Nor is he obliged to avail himself of therapeutic measures which are in themselves hazardous in the hope of effecting a complete cure. Even *chayyei sha'ah,* a short, transitory period of existence, is of such inestimable value that man is not obliged to gamble with precious moments of life, even in the hope of achieving health and longevity.

The exception: the patient in the throes of death
The physician's duty does *not* end when he is in-

capable of restoring the lost health of his patient. The obligation, "and you shall restore it to him" (Deuteronomy 22:2) refers, in its medical context, not simply to the restoration of health but to the restoration of even a single moment of life. Again, Sabbath laws, etc., are suspended even when it is known with certainty that human medicine offers no hope of a cure or restoration to health. Ritual obligations and restrictions are suspended as long as there is the possibility that life may be prolonged even for a matter of moments.

The sole exception to these principles which *halakhah* recognizes is the case of a *goses,* a moribund patient actually in the midst of death throes. The physiological criteria indicative of such a condition must be spelled out with care. (See Rema, *Even ha-Ezer* 121:7 and *Choshen Mishpat* 221:2). It is surely clear that a patient whose life may be prolonged for weeks and even months is not yet moribund; the death process has not yet started to commence and hence the patient is not a *goses.* The halakhic provisions governing care of a *goses* may most emphatically not be applied to all who are terminally ill.

True dignity lies in the struggle to sustain life
Although man must persist in his efforts to prolong life he may, nevertheless, express human needs and concerns through the medium of prayer. There is no contradiction whatsoever between acting upon an existing obligation and pleading to be relieved of further responsibility. Man may beseech G-d to relieve him from divinely imposed obligations when they appear to exceed human endurance. But the ultimate decision is G-d's and G-d's alone. There are times when G-d's answer to prayer is in the negative. But this, too, is an answer.

The coining of the phrase "death with dignity" by advocates of passive euthanasia was a stroke of genius. Opponents of such practices are immediately disarmed. Everyone respects "rights" and no one decries "dignity." Yet, while repeated use of a glib phrase by the press and media may influence attitudes, the coining of a cliche is not the same as making a case. Is sickness or frailty, however tragic, really an indignity? Is the struggle for life, in any form, an indignity? Is it not specious to insinuate that the attempt to sustain life is aught but the expression of the highest regard for the precious nature of the gift of life and of the *dignity* in which it is held?

When a life is no life — the right to die

Bernard S. Raskas

The right to die is an issue which has been circulating in the corridors of hospitals and nursing homes for years. In cases like that of Karen Quinlan, the basic question that confronts us is this: Do we have the right to terminate extreme measures of life-support, and thus permit the individual to die in peace?

We must weigh the quality of life preserved
Physicians enter medicine with a pro-life bias and this is good. The Talmud underwrites this attitude with the statement (*Ketubot* 19a): "There is nothing that stands before the saving of a life." This is as it should be. However, with technical progress in the care of the sick and the dying comes a number of problems and a need to reexamine traditional presuppositions, concepts, and procedures. Clinical death has customarily been defined in terms of cessation of heartbeat, respiration, and reflexes. But the fact is that the death of the brain, or more nearly neocortex death, marks the end of human consciousness and despite its cessation, bodily functions can and do go on. That is to say, the center for thought, memory, and self-consciousness can be completely and irreversibly ended, while the heartbeat and respiration are artificially maintained through machinery and drugs.

When this occurs and the capacity for higher mental functions, for reflective consciousness, ceases, then, it is fair to say, human life ceases. This is now a dead human being living in a "vegetative" existence. The body may be existing but there is no living person; it makes no sense to keep the body alive while the center of human consciousness has irreversibly run its course.

In this aspect of the matter the Jewish tradition, as I interpret it, has an insight to offer. *Pikuach nefesh,* means "to save a life" or literally, "revive a soul." The *nefesh* is usually translated as "soul," but this is not quite accurate. *Nefesh* means personhood, individual integrity, and wholeness of life. Now if a person who has brain damage cannot recite a *b'rachah,* a blessing, to praise God, or is unable to perform a *mitzvah* to help a fellow man, then that individual has no *nefesh,* no personhood. There is no need for *pikuach nefesh* for there is no soul or individual integrity to save. There is only a vegetable. This being so, should we not cease bodily support and permit the remains to return to their natural state? Moreover, would it not be an act of *rachmones,* compassion, to spare the family the expense and the suffering and anguish until a cardiac arrest or a super infection destroys the vegetative drives? The heart, the conscience, and the mind answer these questions in the affirmative.

When death is inevitable, nature should proceed
But is this not euthanasia? The Bible is absolutely clear that euthanasia is forbidden. In Exodus 23:7 it is written, "The innocent and just person you shall not put to death." However, there is a clear distinction between actively killing and "allowing to die" as all moral theologians know. Euthanasia is the employment of some direct means to shorten the life of a patient. On the other hand, I am suggesting that when death is inevitable all the heroic means of treatment should be discontinued and only natural means should be employed.

It is a moral obligation to maintain life by all ordinary means, but there is no obligation to use extraordinary means. Ordinary means are actions which do not cause grave hardship to the patient and which offer a reasonable hope of success. Ordinary or natural means of pursuing life include normal nursing care, feeding by mouth, giving fluids by mouth, the relief of pain, insomnia, and mental anguish. Extraordinary means are means which involve great expense, inconvenience, or hardship and which, at the same time, offer no reasonable expectation of success or of benefit. Extraordinary means are not likely to cure, they are unlikely to reverse the dying process, and they are repugnant to the family who see the patient as a machine kept alive merely by mechanical connections.

By removing these devices are we not playing God? To the contrary. We may very well ask, when a patient has entered the dying process and we artificially prolong life beyond its natural state, if we are not then playing God? Ought we not "let nature take its course"?

Death with dignity and humaneness
It is instructive to read in the *Shulchan Aruch,* The Jewish Code of Law, the proper care that is to be given to the *goses,* the mortally ill patient (*Yoreh Deah* 339). One is forbidden to interfere with the natural dying process. Great care must be taken to respect the untouched order of events to permit the

body to gradually spend itself. The patient should be allowed to die naturally, in dignity, and with the proper decorum. This is the Jewish way. It is also the human way, for as Shakespeare wrote in *King Henry VI,* "Disturb him not, let him pass peaceably."

This, then, leads us to consider the terminally ill patient who is conscious, rational, well aware of his or her condition, who requests that extraordinary measures of life support be withdrawn. Does a person who is mortally ill have the right to refuse extreme forms of treatment? The Talmud states emphatically (*Gittin* 13a): "The instruction of a person on his death bed has the same force as a written document formally handed over." Is it wrong for a mortally ill patient to refuse heroic measures and place himself in the hands of God and naturally accept the dying process? Today, the dying patient is so frequently surrounded by oxygen hoses, nasal tubes, catheters, intravenous needles, and other gadgets that he or she looks like some complicated experimental animal. When death is inevitable is this to be preferred over a death with dignity and humaneness?

The decision must be the family's to make

The real problem here is not dealing with the death of the patient but facing up to our own feelings about death. Until recently, death was a forbidden subject. Now the newspapers, the radio, television, universities, and popular forums are discussing openly and freely the concept of death. From a Jewish point of view, death has always been treated in a natural manner with great openness and honesty. Jewish thinking, traditions, and rituals surrounding death and ghetto life faced death with thorough honesty. Admittedly, there is the pain of separation, the anguish of a loss, the resultant guilt, and the difficult mourning and grieving process. However, when handled properly the therapy of traditional practices are most supportive. And religious faith is a great consolation. The fact is that the "agony of dying" is only in the minds of the survivors. Nature has a process which gradually diminishes the dying patient's feelings and once death has occurred the anxiety of "not knowing" is overcome. The process of dying itself in most cases prepares us for a peaceful death.

Who should make the final decision in the matter of termination of life support? The physician, the patient, if able, the family, and a spiritual counselor if requested. I do not believe this belongs in the law courts because no law will cover all instances. Although there is much we have in common, no two people die in the same exact way and every situation has special emotional, social, and other factors that have to be weighed carefully and cautiously. All we can say is that we should respect whatever decision is made by the appropriate persons.

Jewish law permits natural death

Seymour Siegel

In July, 1971, Mrs. Carmen Martinez, a 72-year-old Cuban woman living in Florida, was dying of a disease that destroyed her red blood cells. Medical science could not provide a cure, but could prolong the dying process. This involved continuous tranfusions. "Please don't torture me any more," she begged. The case went to court and the judge ruled that the "torture" be stopped. (For a discussion of this case see Robert Veatch, *Death, Dying and the Biological Revolution,* p. 116)

Mrs. Martinez was not permitted to commit suicide. This would clearly be against the law. But she had the right, according to the judge, to refuse treatment and "not to be tortured." She was given the opportunity to determine the method of her treatment.

This case has become a landmark in the history of the legal rights of patients. It affirms the right of the person to participate in how he should be treated.

The California statute under discussion is entitled A Natural Death Act. The title given to the act is significant. It is not called a "Bill to Enable Death with Dignity." I agree with Professor Paul Ramsey (*Commonweal,* September 20, 1974) and Doctor Trude Weiss-Rosmarin (*Jewish Spectator,* Winter, 1974) that the widespread "chatter that tells us again and again fables about death with dignity" is not true to the human condition. Though death is inevitable, it is the enemy of life. It is by definition an event bearing with it tragedy and pain. To speak about it as something that is dignified is "chatter." I am happy that the California legislators did not use the phrase "death with dignity."

The California statute is not called "A Statute for Legalized Euthanasia." This would mean that we are legitimating the putting to death of individuals who are sick and incompetent.

The statute is entitled a Bill for Natural Death, giving the opportunity to individuals to have a say "in the rendering of their own medical care" and recognizes "the notion of prolonging the death of patients already at death's door provides nothing medically necessary or beneficial to the patient." That is, of course, if the patient believes this to be the case.

The will: loose, restrictive, or just unnecessary?
All other bills had within them loose language which made abuse likely. The safeguards included in the California statute protects those in nursing homes (by requiring an ombudsman to counter-sign the Living Will); gives adequate opportunity for revocation, limits the time of effectiveness, and limits the applicability of the instructions only "to mechanical or other artificial means to sustain, restore or supplant a vital function where death is imminent whether or not life-sustaining procedures are used." This seems to be adequate to prevent abuses. The legislative process which went into the formulation of the bill is described in detail by Michael Garland in the Hastings Center Report for October, 1976. It is interesting to note that some legislators advised the Governor to veto the bill because it was *too* restrictive. Professors Richard McMormick and Andre Helleghers of the Kennedy Institute for Bioethics, in an article published in *America,* oppose the legislation because they believe it to be unnecessary since patients, family, and physicians are "presently free to exercise their respective prerogatives and responsibilities without legislation." They are opposed to the California Statute because it would then force doctors to subject people without Living Wills to treatment that they should not get. These distinguished Catholic ethicists believe that we need more protection from over-zealous doctors who will use everything available, even when it is not necessary. By protecting only those who have the Will, we will be leaving those who do not have it to be at the mercy of machines which serve only to prolong their death. This is a novel argument. It serves, however, to point up the dilemma that is posed by the use of procedures which do not really serve the patient, which should be the primary consideration.

Living up to the doctor's mandate to heal
The California statute points to a basic ethical issue: what is the task of the physician toward his patient? It would seem that the doctor's main concern should be the welfare of the patient who has put his fate into the healer's hands. The talmudic admonition "he shall cause him to be thoroughly healed . . . from here we derive permission for the physician to heal" gives the medical professional the right to "heal" (*lerapot*). The verb *rpa*, according to Preuss (*Biblisch-talmudische medizin,* p. 33) comes from an older root meaning to soothe, to lighten a burden, to bring succour to a fellow human being. Therefore, the doctor has to do what is best for the sufferer. That is why the doctor is told not always to tell the truth to a person suffering from grave illness, lest he make the patient's situation worse. In using medical procedures and treatments, the doctor should do what is best for the patient. It is clear that where death is imminent and where the procedure cannot bring a cure or even significant amelioration of pain, that what is best for the individual (especially if he expresses his opinion through a will) is to allow him to die naturally.

In regard to the care of hopelessly ill patients a distinction should be made between *optimal* care and *maximal* care. The distinction is suggested by a report published in the August 12, 1976 issue of the *New England Journal of Medicine.* Optimal care is that kind of care which is the best available method to help the patient. Maximal care means the use of every possible procedure available in the armory of medical technology even though there will be little or no benefit to the patient. We have the duty to prolong life, not to prolong death. The ethical approach, it would seem to me, is to determine what is best for the sufferer — not merely to use all methods that might exist. The patient, under the California statute, has the opportunity to express his own preference as to what is best for him. Therefore, it has a very good outcome and should be supported.

The question may be asked whether the Living Will is not a form of suicide. From the pont of view of common sense, suicide is the willful taking of one's own life. Jewish law is very insistent on the presence of *willfulness,* which is defined as a philosophical disgust with life. This is a denial of providence. (For a full discussion of the issue of suicide in Jewish law see David Novak, *Law and Theology in Judaism,* Chapter 9). By allowing death to come when it is imminent a person is hardly denying providence. He is permitting God's judgment to take its effect, without the intervention of useless, artificial means.

A jewish living will is in keeping with tradition
One could ask, "Isn't every moment of life precious

whether sustained by artificial means or not?" Judaism is a religion of life. However, the mere functioning of physical systems is not the ultimate good. We do value martyrdom for the sake of faith. We do call people who are heroic in war, good people, even when they themselves die in the process. Life is a good as long as it is given to us. However, we do have a right to let death come and take it away when it has been ordained that this should happen.

There are well-known passages in the traditional literature which permit a person who is on his death bed to be allowed to die 'naturally.' The most famous of these passages is in the Code of Rabbi Joseph Caro (based on an earlier source in the Sefer Chasidim). "If there is something that causes a delay in the exit of the soul, as for example, if near to his house there is a sound of pounding as one is pounding wood, or there is salt on his tongue, and these delay the soul's leaving the body, it is permitted to remove them, because there is no direct act involved, only the removal of an obstacle." (the Ramah in Yoreh De'ah, 339:2)

What the Living Will makes possible is the giving of the privilege to the patient himself to stop those things "that delay the soul's leaving the body."

There should be a specifically Jewish Living Will drawn up. This will would include some of the features of the ethical wills collected by Israel Abrahams and instructions as to how the burial should take place, proper mourning procedures, etc. The Committee on Jewish Law and Standards of the Rabbinical Assembly is now at work formulating such a Jewish Living Will.

The developments of medical technology have caused problems which our ancestors could hardly have foreseen. We must not forget, in our loyalty to the tradition, the welfare of the suffering patient who, when the Giver of Life has proclaimed the end of his earthly existence, should be allowed to die in spite of our machines.

Torah ethics prohibit natural death

Moshe D. Tendler

The withdrawal of life-support systems from terminally ill patients has been given legal approval in the California Natural Death Act of 1976. Similar bills based on the patient's legal right to instruct his physician concerning the use of life-sustaining treatments are now pending in New York and New Jersey. The latter state, long in the limelight on this issue because of the Quinlan case, adopted in January 1977, a system based on the recommendations of a "prognosis committee," whereby a decision to cease all support system can be made in the absence of patient directives. These bills and guidelines make ethical and legal assumptions to validate their conclusions. What are these ethical assumptions and what validity do they have when evaluated by the objective yardstick of Torah ethics?

1) *Assumption One:* There is a "natural" limit to human life other than death. The "artificial" prolongation of human life beyond these limits by means of modern medical technology is neither necessary nor desirable.

Evaluation: There is validity to the assumption that medical intervention be limited to life prolongation and not death postponement. But can anyone draw sharp lines of demarcation between the two clinical states? How terminal must the patient be before he be really terminal? When is it "unnecessary" or "not beneficial" to the patient (viz. sec 7186) If we are committed to the fundamental concept of the infinite worth of human life, then a piece of infinity is infinity! Excluding the very real problem of "triage" or the finite resources of society, there is no patient-oriented reason other than *assumption two* to differentiate between the care to be given the terminally ill patient and that given the one with cure prognosis.

2) *Assumption Two:* Such artificial prolongation can cause unnecessary pain and loss of patient dignity.

Evaluation: "Dying with dignity" is an ill-conceived slogan, nothing more. Death with dignity is the end result of a dignified life style. In itself, death is a truly undignified behavior. If those attending the dying patient behave in sensitive, dignified fashion, no indignity other than that of death itself is involved.

A treatment modality that prolongs or accentuates pain without hope of cure is indeed to be questioned on ethical, moral grounds. If the patient chooses to continue treatment, despite the discomfort it causes or prolongs, he is entitled to the full support of the health profession. If he requests the discontinuance of therapy, emphasizing his inability to cope with his

pain-filled existence, the absence of any real hope for cure makes this request binding on all who minister to him. (Talmudic precedent can be found in *Avoda Zara* 18a. See also *Ketuboth* 104a).

Obviously this consideration is valid only in the conscious patient, not in the patient in deep coma. Such a patient is a burden on others but not to himself. The decision to withdraw life-support mechanisms can only be made by equating terminal illness with death; the imminent with the actual. What dangers lurk in such an assumption! Can active euthanasia be far behind?

Living wills set a dangerous ethical precedent
3) *Assumption Three:* "Adult persons have the fundamental right to control decisions relating to their own medical care."

Evaluation: Does such a right exist? I think not! The right to suicide or even self-mutilation is denied to an individual in all ethical systems associated with the dominant religions of Western civilization. As discussed in *Assumption two,* pain — physical or psychic — may be a significant factor in permitting passive self-euthanasia by the conscious terminal patient, but this is not relevant to the comatose patient. This denial of the right of self-destruction has been extended by case law, to compel blood transfusions even when the patient's refusal was based on religious principles. The living will thus has little ethical validity in the absence of intractable pain or when the patient is in coma.

4) *General concerns:* The scale-up from personal ethics to social legislation introduces many new concerns that require careful evaluation.

A) *The domino theory* in social ethics: *Living Will* legislation may bring active euthansia a step closer to social acceptance, just as abortion legislation has made passive euthanasia legislation more palatable.

B) *The confidence quotient:* The bill specifies that the attending physician or any employee of the health facility caring for the patient cannot witness the "living will." Why? The courts fear that unscrupulous, mercenary interests may endanger the life of the patient. How sure can we be that the terminal illness diagnosis and prognosis be free of all taint of personal advantage and is truly altruistic?

C) *Ethical aesthetics:* Is there a proper claim on the finite resources of our society and its medical community when life support mechanisms are being maintained without hope of cure? Surely such a claim is valid in a society rich enough to spend massive sums on nonsense fads, commercial sports, or highway beautification programs. Must highway aesthetics be given priority over ethical aesthetics? If continuation of life support systems after the point of no return, will emphasize our commitment to the infinite worth of man and prevent the callus that forms on the soul when a "plug is pulled," it is money well spent. God forbid, that we ever reach the time when true triage must be practiced, with "God committees" deciding who gets the respirator or kidney dialysis equipment and lives, and who dies.

Torah ethics boasts of 3500 years of testing and confirming its validity as a code of conduct fit for man created in God's image. Its evaluations may well serve the needs of all who make up the complex mix of American society.

How small a blemish desanctifies life?
H. Allen Gardner

Ruben was born healthy and beautiful. Now, at three years of age, he is waiting to die. During these three years he has deteriorated neurologically, first losing his ability to sit up, then becoming spastic, listless and unresponsive to his surroundings. By one year he was blind, and six months later he began having the first of occasional seizures and occasional bouts of pneumonia. He lies in his bed emaciated and still, and will be dead shortly. He has Tay-Sachs disease.

Mother is pregnant again. The family knows that Tay-Sachs disease is inherited, and that once an affected child has been born the risk of it happening again will be 25% for each pregnancy. They also know it can be detected before mid-pregnancy by amniocentesis and that if the fetus has the illness a therapeutic abortion is possible. This would prevent the birth of an infant with a severe illness.

Almost every family in this situation chooses amniocentesis and abortion. Why? Because the effects of Tay-Sachs disease on the child are devastating: an inexorable downhill course and an inevitable death by four years of age. And the effects on the family who must care for him or her are equally upsetting. I am very sympathetic to this choice and so are most other people.

The Problems Posed by Down's Syndrome

Let me take another situation. This time there was no long wait before the clinical signs were apparent. At the moment of birth there was little doubt Rachel had Down's syndrome. Rachel was slow in acquiring physical skills (sitting, walking, toilet training) and was mentally retarded (I.Q. of 40). Caring for her became a problem as the whole social pattern of the family necessitated re-adjustment. Special schooling had to be organized, with transportation. It was difficult to find housekeepers when holidays were planned. There was also the reluctance to have anyone but very close friends into the house. The family was frankly embarrassed by her retardation and her appearance.

On the other hand, Rachel was happy and friendly. She tried to be helpful as much as possible by making beds and setting the table. She responded enthusiastically to encouragement and praise. In many respects, despite the burden of her mental retardation, she was a joy to have around. At twelve years of age she developed leukemia (a not infrequent concomitant of Down's syndrome) and died.

Now, mother is again pregnant. The risk of having another child with Down's syndrome is at least 1/100 and perhaps greater. She is determined to have amniocentesis and an abortion if the fetus is affected. But why? Certainly not for the sake of the child. Ruben, as we have seen, suffered from convulsions and neurological deterioration detrimental to himself, an inevitable consequence of his Tay-Sachs disease. This terrible deterioration does not occur with Down's syndrome, and even the leukemia is still an uncommon occurrence. It seems to me the pregnancy will be terminated for the sake of the family who feel the burden of raising a mentally retarded child is beyond them. Is this right or is this selfish? Is embarrassment or the inconvenience of schooling or vacations a sufficient burden to terminate a life?

Bringing the Discussion to Religious School

This is only one of the problems I have been exploring over the past six years with grade 9 students at Holy Blossom Temple Religious School. These children are young and naive, too young, one may argue, to be exposed to congenitally abnormal children or thrust into the center of prenatal monitoring of developing infants. Yet the mother of one student had undergone amniocentesis for detection of Down's syndrome so perhaps we should not assume our childrens' unpreparedness. Their discussions are fresh and lively, and their conclusions are familiar: abortion is justified to preserve the health and well being of the mother and family. If the parents in such a dilemma were to consult their rabbi, this is the guide which would be used in counselling. Occasionally, a student argues that abortion is never justified because the sanctity of life and the right of life, including fetal life, overrides all considerations.

It is my experience that very very few couples who have been told an abnormal child is gestating consult their spiritual leader (Catholics could anticipate what the advice would be). Therefore the decision to abort or not to abort would have to emanate from each family's personal set of values. What are these and where do they come from? This exploration constitutes a second thrust of my course. One may agree that aborting a Tay-Sachs fetus, albeit distressing, is justifiable for the sake of the child and the family. Aborting a Down's syndrome fetus is acceptable to most people because of the effects on the family. The movie ''Best Boy'' offers some insights. After 52 years of caring for her severely mentally retarded son, Philli's mother, says ''If God wanted to punish anyone, He should give them a mentally retarded child.'' That's powerful. (This movie is a must if you wish to pursue this subject).

Deciding What the Serious Criteria are

How does one determine the effects of a handicapped child on the family? Is the financial position of the family important? Their position in the community? Their perception of themselves as a family unit? If you do not believe in abortion there is no problem to ponder. If you do not think of the fetus as alive, the questions are rhetorical. Most patients, however, are very disturbed by the situation and some are upset for month after aborting a severely affected child. Just about all, however, abort. I personally think the fetus is alive; expendable in serious circumstances, but still alive. Most patients I see agree with that statement. The task for each of us therefore, is to define for ourselves the word ''serious''. My approach to this exploration of personal values is to examine and work through various situations I have already encountered or can anticipate encountering with my patients. As you can see, I begin with very serious disorders about which there is little (except diehard) disagreement, and gradually reduce the disability or bring in qualifying circumstances to alter the basic situation. Let us then continue.

What would be your response to the discovery of a fetus with a cleft lip and palate? It is certainly distressing to care for and comfort this child through the required reconstructive surgery. But the results are really very good with minimal facial disfigurement. Is this situation serious enough not to have that child at all, but to abort it, and try again?

The same chromosome analysis on amniotic fluid cells performed to detect Down's syndrome may reveal some other abnormality instead. Klinefelter's syndrome affects males. There may be mild mental retardation, perhaps some behavior problems, and always infertility. Turner's syndrome occurs in girls. They have no ovaries, and therefore no menstrual periods and are infertile. They are also short. I have seen quite a few girls with Turner's syndrome who have been through university, and one is a medical specialist. Would you abort this fetus? Would you abort the boy with an extra Y chromosome-the so called XYY syndrome, ''so-called'' because there appears to be *no* consistent syndrome at all? In fact, data from chromosome studies on newborn males suggest there are many quite normal men with XYY never ascertained because there is nothing wrong with them. What is the smallest blemish which would warrant your decision to abort your baby?

Duchenne muscular dystrophy affects fifty percent of a carrier mother's sons. Aborting all boys means that fifty percent of the aborted boys would have been normal. Hemophilia has a similar inheritance and diagnostic

pattern. Does this less serious disorder now warrant aborting all males? What if fetoscopy showed a large birth mark? Would this be serious or trivial?

How Small a Blemish?

How does that couple, or you, decide the ''right'' course of action when mother is carrying twins-only one of which has Tay-Sachs disease, while the other is normal? The alternative to continuing the pregnancy is to abort both. What if first twin instead of having Tay-Sachs disease has Down's syndrome? What if it has a cleft lip? What is the smallest blemish in one twin that would warrant terminating the life of the other as well? Twins are born with a frequency of one in eighty births, a relatively common occurrence.

As I look at the types of decisions people must make I sigh with relief that my family is complete. However, I still live in this society. I teach in it, I am expected to respond to it, perhaps support it, and certainly through my perceptions of it guide my children through it. You are in this position as well. How do we prepare our youngsters not only to make but to live with these choices and still maintain those personal qualities of humanity expected of Jews? How do we help them develop values which will enable them to cope with situations unheard of a generation ago?

I attempt to answer this question through my grade 9 minicourse. Gently, I hope, I acquaint these students with the reality of congenital handicaps (2-3% of all newborn children) and explore with them the biologic mechanisms which go away during embryology. We discuss the methods presently available to monitor pregnancies and the alternatives for dealing with abnormal results. There is no correct answer so everyone's participation is valid. And if someone changes his mind after talking to the first person he meets after class, I am delighted as it means the lesson has not been lost or forgotten. In fact I have found that I have reached not only the children but their parents as well.

Let me conclude with a true story. The couple came to our amniocentesis clinic because they had two sons at home with X-linked severe mental retardation i.e. carried by the females but manifested only in males. Amniocentesis would tell the mother whether she was carrying a boy or a girl. The couple felt they could not care for a third mentally retarded child and would abort any boy knowing there was a fifty percent chance the boy would be normal. All of us, with them, were desperately praying for a girl to give them at least one normal child to raise. Pre-amniocentesis work-up showed she was carrying twins. Amniocentesis was performed on both amniotic sacs; one contained a girl who would be intellectually normal, the other a boy who had a fifty percent chance of being severely retarded. What personal values do you and your family have to deal with this situation? What decision would you make? The couple decided to abort the pregnancy, and the mother then went on to have a tubal ligation.

(The articles on the Baby M case below were written before the judge's decision had been rendered. -E. B. B.)

The ethics of surrogate motherhood
Marc Gellman

One Monday morning in rabbinical school, Steve Malinger came to me with a story from his student pulpit in a place he called "Shmini Atzeret," West Virginia. During his combined kindergarten through 12th grade Religious School class he was trying to teach the story of how King Solomon had decided between two women both claiming to be the mother of the same baby. Steve was always creative so he had two little muppets act the parts of the two mothers, and an older boy the part of the wise king. He even provided a baby doll for this high midrashic drama. At the climactic point when King Solomon orders the baby cut in half, and the real mother is to withdraw her claim out of compassion, thus proving her true maternity, the little girl who was supposed to be playing the real mother looked at the baby doll and said, "I'll take the head."

Sometimes things just don't work out. The Sterns and the Whiteheads must surely know that feeling now. My ethical starting point in this landmark case cum media circus is simple and unanalyzed *rochmonus* for these two families and this baby. How sad and sleazy it is that these folk and their families are being subjected to public scrutiny and humiliation because they both love the same baby too much. A baby who was to bring joy has brought agony. Beyond all the ethical issues, I wish the Sterns and the Whiteheads surcease from their public trauma, and I wish for little Baby M a life where she has more than an initial for a name.

Legal Procedure and Doing Justly

Beyond compassion, I come to frustration at what seems to be the willingness of the judge in Hackensack to try this case as if it were just another custody battle. The established rules and prece-

dents of who would be a better parent for a child born of a once married and now divorced father and mother, are being imposed upon a case where the father and mother were never married, never divorced, and never cohabited. Perhaps the law must always narrow its horizons and fit unique cases into past precedents (Jewish law is in the same position in evaluating this case), but for me the overwhelmingly important question is not who gets this baby, but whether such babies ought to be born. How bewildering and sad that in the surrogate motherhood case in Hackensack, the ethics of surrogate motherhood will not be judged.

Despite the efforts of Mary Beth Whitehead's attorneys, the court seems to want to avoid judging the ethics of the contract in favor of judging the psychological fitness of the contending families, and this, I fear, has introduced class prejudices which virtually assure that Mary Beth Whitehead will lose. But bourgeois comforts and class privilege are not reasons to ignore the power of the mother/child bond, a bond which the courts seem willing to honor in other rulings and which is basic to Judaism. Indeed, Judaism knows nothing of surrogate mothers, only mothers, and to force this mother to give up the baby she now wants, because of a contract she was too poor and ignorant to refuse, is unjust.

At Issue: Not the Mother but the Practice

Of course there are good reasons, reasons which are not tainted by class prejudice, to award custody of a child to the biological father. To take away Bill Stern's daughter who was once placed in his arms is also unjust, but in this no win situation, the reasons to take Baby M away from her mother must be more than cultural and aesthetic. The fact that she apparently does not play patty cake too well or does not sit on the floor with her baby are ridiculous prejudices, not reasons. The real and proven danger of child abuse, the propensity to violence, the refusal to love and nurture, these would be good reasons to award the child to the Sterns, but Mary Beth Whitehead, from the reports in the press, seems to be primarily guilty of not being too bright, not having enough money, and being married to a garbage man who may occasionally drink too much. In a conflict with an educated and articulate scientist and an accomplished pediatrician who listen to Mozart, Mary Beth Whitehead doesn't have a chance.

But this is not Hackensack, and I am not that judge, and in the end I cannot believe, I will not believe, that one can buy a baby like one buys a refrigerator. Though I have no doubts that surrogate motherhood contracts will continue, I have grave doubts as to whether they should. The first objection to surrogate motherhood, and by far the most basic, is that it is an unnecessary and morally problematic alternative to adoption. Providing a home to an already living homeless child is a high and heroic mitzvah. We read in Meg. 13a, *Hamegadel yatom v'y'toma b'toch veito k'ilu yaldah,* "Who ever raises an orphan in his home is like the one who bore it." The question is not why not allow surrogate motherhood but why not adopt? About the same time the Baby M case reached the papers, there was also a story about the orphan children who are being warehoused in New York City hospitals with no one to even touch them during the course of a day. If these babies did not exist, if adoption was not just difficult (which it surely is) but impossible (which it surely is not), then a case might be made for surrogate motherhood. But not in this world. The need of unwanted babies to be wanted is of greater moral moment than the egotistical need of a person to see his chromosomes live on.

Jewish Law does not Warrant such Risks

Secondly, surrogate motherhood exposes the contracted mother to the risks of pregnancy without justifying those risks. The Jewish prohibition against risk taking is derived from the fourth chapter of Deuteronomy, *v'nishmartem m'od l'nafshoteichem,* "guard your lives carefully." The rabbinic elaboration of this biblical law basically prohibits risking your health or life if there is no *mitzvah* which justifies the risk (MT, *hilchot rotzeiach* 11:4-5 and the Rema to *Yoreh Deah* 116:5). Pregnancy, no matter how routine, presents real risk to the pregnant woman, risks which are justified if she is bearing her own child and thus helping her husband to fulfill the *mitzvah* of *pru ur'vu* "be fruitful and multiply." But Mary Beth Whitehead is under no *chiyuv,* no obligation, to fulfill the commandment of procreation for the Sterns and thus she has put herself at risk for no good reason.

Of course there was a reason that Mary Beth Whitehead was willing to undertake this risk and that reason may have been altruism, as she asserts, or it may have been money. If it was altruism, she certainly has the right to change her mind for no one can be compelled to do a kindness of this sort. If it was the money, then we see a far more serious reason to oppose surrogate motherhood as an exploitation of poor women.

The $10,000 Mary Beth Whitehead was to be paid is less like a wage than a "stumbling block before the blind." Such surrogate services are *oshek,* exploited labor; even if a fee is paid for it, the transaction makes a person's body for sale. Whether this is technically slavery, it smacks of crude class oppression in which poor women become vessels for the needs of the rich, commodities for sale at the market price. Suk. 29b, speaking about *oshek,* reminds us that it is better to do a little good with what is yours than to do much good by exploiting that which belongs to others; and Mary Beth Whitehead's body is not a tool.

Is there no limit to what can be bought and sold? We would not enforce a contract for prostitution. We would not defend the purchase of a kidney or a heart from a living donor. How can we begin to consider regulating the contracts for baby farming?

There are No True Jewish Precedents Here

I have heard it said, "Hagar was a surrogate mother for Abraham and Sarah, Bilah and Zilpah surrogate mothers for Jacob. Why cannot Judaism accept Mary Beth Whitehead as a part of this same tradition?" (Indeed there is an organization which arranges surrogate motherhood contracts called "The Hagar Institute.")

We must understand that ancient world. These biblical women were in no sense surrogate mothers who were to bear their children, and then fade away. They were additional wives! They were a part of a polygamous family structure, *amot* who had status and rights and prerogatives. There is no similarity to this contractual demand that a woman bear a child and then walk away. Hagar was cast into the desert with Ishmael.

Furthermore, the Torah is quite candid in admitting that these relationships did not work out. Hagar and Sarah could not live together, and the children of Bilah and Zilpah, and Leah hated the children of the favorite wife Rachel. Rabbenu Gershom, who settled this issue with his medieval *takanah* forbidding polygamy, was responding to more than social pressures. The sanctity of family life requires a single husband and single wife.

Finally, who is to protect these babies when the contract is breached? In the reverse of the Baby M case, what happens when neither the biological father or the mother wants the baby? Are deformed or retarded babies to be considered defective merchandise? And when the person contracting with the surrogate mother is not married, or living in

וחסדי מאתך לא ימוש

My lovingkindness shall never depart from you.

ISAIAH 54:10

undesirable circumstances, or dies before the birth, who is to step in and say, "I love this child and I will speak for her!" What greater testimony could there be to the alienation of labor in our time than a woman who takes money to give birth to a baby she wants to give away?

What world is this? Perhaps in her tardy change of heart Mary Beth Whitehead has found her heart and taught us all of the enduring power of the bond of blood and milk and love between a mother and her baby. The double tragedy of this case is that Baby M's father and mother cannot both win her, and that surely there will be other such cases.

☐

The ethics of baby m's custody

Seymour Siegel

Perhaps no child has come into the world with so much fame and public notice—at least in recent years—as the one we know as Baby M. Everyone now knows of her origins and is aware of the dispute surrounding her parentage. I would contend that the baby belongs to the Sterns, the parents who have supplied the father's seed. The reasons for this are as follows:

Firstly, in all cases where there is artificial insemination, the resulting child should go to the natural father. This validation is rooted in Jewish law and even in mythical tradition as I read them. (See, e.g., the data compactly summarized in *Jewish Bioethics,* Rosner & Bleich, eds., in Rosner's article on artificial insemination, p.111.) If not, the father in question would be guilty of adultery. The fact that historically our people have not taken this to be the case, proves that the very act of artificial

insemination points to the giver of the seed as being crucial. This notion is furthered by the views of Rabbi Moshe Feinstein as recorded in *Iggerot Moshe* and by the authorities cited in the first volume of *Noam.*

The second consideration is that the surrogate mother made an agreement to bear the child with informed consent. There have been questions about the validity of this agreement, but these questions do not seem to hold up under criticism. Mrs. Whitehead had borne children even before this incident, and thus knew the resulting bonding that takes place upon the experience of motherhood.

Our society rests on the expectation that contracts made in good faith will be honored. Otherwise, the cement that holds together our civilization would be immeasurably weakened.

Another consideration is derived from the fact that our tradition looks with favor upon those who wish to escape their seemingly destined infertility by resorting to the novel methods developed by medical technology. This is part of a very positive value placed on the engendering of children. The bible suggests that nature may be manipulated to glean positive results—such as parenthood, when the natural means of conception prove fruitless. Nature is there to be "used" for man's benefit and welfare, not to be fatalistically accepted.

I hope that those who take Jewish law into account are inclined to honor the view of Mrs. Stern. The weight of the evidence, therefore, points towards the Sterns to be the final parents of Baby M. Finally, I hope that our legislators and courts take note of the ramifications of this episode, fully codify the procedures of surrogate motherhood—to alleviate any future doubt. ☐

Determining when we have gone too far

David M. Feldman

In a sense, the halakhic issues are the least of it in the Baby M case. References, in talmudic and post-talmudic literature, to pregnancy without cohabitation are cited in the Responsa as basis for legal determination of legitimacy, paternity/maternity status, and the like.

True, Rabbi Yehudah Leib Zirelsohn, Rabbi Ovadya Hadaya and other authorities have written that artificial insemination of a married woman with donor sperm is an act of adultery, rendering the offspring illegitimate. True, too, that Rabbi

Eliezer Waldenberg declares artificial insemination by donor (AID) to be akin to adultery and a practice to be disallowed. But others take a more "romantic" view of the matter, declaring that adultery implies a violation of the marriage vows, a forbidden intimacy rather than a clinical procedure. Rabbi Benzion Uziel and Rabbi Mosheh Feinstein have said as much, and *pos'kim* such as Rabbis Schwadron, Baumol and Wolkin concur.

This means, in the "pro-natalist" Jewish system—wherein the mandate to heal also includes the mandate to overcome infertility—recourse to artificial insemination where alternatives are unavailable is not ruled out. It has a number of problems, of course, such as access to the identity of the donor in order to avoid even unintentional incest; the offspring here should not marry a half-brother or half-sister. Aside from other such technical problems, the shattering of family bonds makes recourse to this procedure the least desirable of alternatives. Though it seems preferable to simple adoption, in that at least the mother has genetic input, it brings in tow a series of other legal and human complications.

The Special Complications of Surrogacy

These complications are aggravated with surrogate motherhood, as opposed to AID for a couple with an infertile husband. Again, the halakhic issues are amenable to solution: even taking the stricter stand, declaring Baby M illegitimate in no way compromises Mr. Stern's paternity. An illegitimate child, after the fact of course, fulfills the *mitzvah* of "be fruitful" and the child owes him *kibbud av*, parental honor. He is fully the father—but so is Mary Beth Whitehead fully the mother. She is not a "surrogate" at all, unless perhaps a surrogate wife. In addition to giving genetic endowment, she also carried the child—another misnomer: she did much more than "carry"—by giving her full-term womb and nurture. Maternal and paternal status are unequivocal in this case, leaving the equally troublesome issues of contract and custody.

The case has not yet been adjudicated as of this date, but the court's focus implies that the contract is not in itself acceptable. Just as a contract for illegal gambling or any contract against the law or public order need not be enforced, a contract against the Torah, or against the woman's natural biological maternal status, can do nothing to change that status. It remains a contract about custody, which is best left to the judgment of the court.

I often think of the talmudic passage that seeks and finds another reason for the biblical provision that a woman after childbirth must bring a sin-offering to the Sanctuary. The prosaic reason is obvious: a man or a woman must bring an offering to mark the completion of the purification period after physical discharges. But the Talmud offers a deeper reason: childbirth pain is severe; in pain she must have taken a vow never again to enter into pregnancy; the child is born and in her joy she forgets both the pain and the vow; she forgets to have her vow formally nullified; that's why she brings the sin-offering! The woman before birth, or during birth, is not the same as the woman after birth. Especially having experienced the bonding attachment that comes with nursing, or, as some are testifying, in the birth process itself, how can she be held to an agreement made beforehand? The case, moreover, includes an agreement about a third party, who, if the case continues much longer, will be able to make her own contract about where she wants to be.

The Unacceptable Results of Surrogacy

Continuing along these lines of the facetious, the custody conundrum invites more facetiousness in order to isolate the issues. The biblical precedent of Jacob has been adduced, only, I think, to highlight its inapplicability. There was neither artificial insemination or the exchange of money in the Genesis story; more important, there was no custody question. Jacob, Leah and Rachel, and Bilhah and Zilpah and all their children lived together in one household. No Solomon needed to have them sliced up or given away. Hence, if the "best interests of the child" are indeed to be pursued, my two tongue-in-cheek suggestions have been either that Mr. Stern marry Mrs. Whitehead, or that the Sterns and the Whiteheads move into a duplex together! Today I read that an expert proposed to the court that joint custody is, regrettably, the only right solution, no worse than joint custody for hostile, divorced parents.

Halakhah leaves much of custody determination to the *shikkul ha-da'at*, the prudential disposition, of the judge. Whichever way he turns, there will be a problem for child, for parents, for siblings. The most significant outcome of the trial in Hackensack is that these issues and problems have surfaced, and that Mrs. Whitehead, herself, pleads for the surrogacy arrangement to be disallowed in the future. This is what the Wannock Commission in London concluded two years ago: other advances in reproductive technology are acceptable, but surrogacy leads to too many social and human complications. England's Chief Rabbi readily agreed, reiterating his moral condemnation of hiring a woman's body for this purpose. Other dimensions of psychological detriment are also coming to the surface, such as the anxieties of siblings who may feel threatened with similar negotiability, or implied pressure on nonbarren women to accommodate their friends. This is what rabbinic authorities meant when they said: even if technical adultery and illegitimacy are not involved, the family bond is shattered.

The family bond involves *yichus* in the best sense of that word. It means knowing one's parents and feeling the spiritual dimension of lineage, of advancing their values and aspirations, of giving and taking pride in family nurture and association. The issues raised by surrogate motherhood pose a clash between two desirable goals, procreation and family. The first should be pursued through alternatives that do not destroy the second. □

Infertility management: cure or ill?

Moshe D. Tendler

Therapy for infertility has become a sensitive balance for weighing the relative importance of rights, duties, and privileges in conflict. These include the right of a husband and wife to procreate; the rights of a fetus or pre-embryo to life; the interest of society in preserving its ethical foundations; and the hard reality that scarce resources must be allocated amongst many worthy projects, thus pitting many goods against each other. It is indeed ironic, in light of the Judaeo-biblical heritage that provides the ethical foundation for much of Western civilization, that the right *not* to procreate is more clearly accepted within the legal framework of America's society than the right to procreate using non-coital techniques.

The Natural and the Nature of Man

The allure of the natural has never been stronger. The artificial is equated with the abnormal and even the amoral. Therefore many sterility management techniques that apply the magnificent advances in reproductive biology of this decade have been declared illicit by the Catholic church. (Doctrinal statement: "Instruction on respect for human life in its origin and on the dignity of procreation." March 10, 1986.) Even when the more obvious moral concerns do not apply, such as pre-embryo wastage, masturbation or third party intru-

sion into the conjugal relationship, the disjointing of the sex act from the procreation process is considered illicit because it "deprives human procreation of the dignity which is proper and co-natural to it."

The Judaeo-biblical tradition does not concur with this concern for the "co-natural." The natural is not a good, but merely an ecological niche or a social state early in the development of human society. In Genesis 1:28 we learn that "G-d blessed them and said to them be fruitful and multiply, fill the earth and *master it*." There is a dual command in this verse. The first is to have children, to procreate. The second is to become an active participant, a contributor to the molding of the world to suit the needs of humankind. This active interventionist role encompasses the pursuit of all

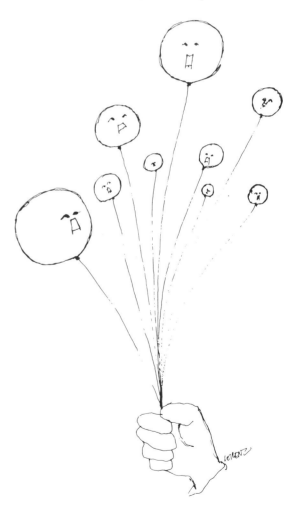

knowledge for the betterment of mankind. We are obligated, by divine decree, to lift the veils off the hiding face of nature. The non-natural is no more than man's fulfillment of this divine command.

We are Required to Heal

To heal the sick is a biblical imperative. (Ex. 21:19; Deut. 22:2; Lev. 19:17) Infertility is viewed as an illness akin to other non-physiological conditions. Biblical language underscores the severity of this illness. When Rachel appealed to Jacob for help (Gen. 30:18) she cried out "Give me children or else I die." The cure of so significant an illness justifies the assumption of some modicum of risk to the patient, as well as the sensitive concern of those who can offer help. This risk, however, is often shared by the fetus and the concern of the health professional must often encompass whole family and social groupings.

The Ethical Import of Embryo Transfer

The transfer of an autologous embryo, as in the IVF (in vitro fertilization) technique using sperm from the husband, and egg from the wife, is in itself free of serious ethical issues. Indeed, until the recent blanket disapproval by the Vatican of almost all techniques used in infertility management, it was assumed that a consensus existed among ethicists of all faiths, to approve autologous embryo transplants. From the Judaeo-biblical heritage, these techniques conform with the Divine instruction to master the physical and biological world by lifting another veil from the face of nature. The oligospermic husband, the wife with blocked Fallopian tubes, can now be given the opportunity of having children whose cells contain their own hereditary material.

The ethical issues raised by this protocol apply to many other procedures used in infertility management. They are: a) risk to mother; b) risk to fetus; c) semen procurement: of special concern for Jewish Orthodox patients; d) egg retrieval and disposal—pre-embryo wastage. The detailed evaluation of each of these issues is beyond the scope of this paper.

Those who are guided by the moral and ethical principles of traditional Judaism must consult with their rabbi. Usually he will refer them to a colleague specially trained to apply the immutable laws of our Torah to the complex issues raised by the rapid progress of science and technology.

Surrogate and Incubator Mothers

These are modified adoptive modalities not designed to cure the illness of infertility. As such, they introduce a new illness, a societal pathology or social iatrogenesis. In surrogate motherhood, the old solution to a barren wife—to take another wife, is now accomplished by renting another wife's uterus. While a monogamous relationship with the infertile wife is maintained, another woman contributes her genes and her gestational input to the birth of a child to be raised by the barren wife.

If the surrogate is a married woman, the solution for the infertile couple requires the intrusion of a third party—the sperm of husband 1—into the private, intimate, relationship of couple 2. Concerns for the psychological impact on couple 2, religious concerns for adultery, bastardy and consanguinity, must be addressed. This is not a curative modality. It substitutes illness for illness, pathology involving many for the pathology of one woman.

This hiring of a "breeder-bleeder" mother, is particularly offensive when viewed as enslavement or exploitation of the poor by the wealthy. In organ transplantation, laws or hospital regulation forbid the purchasing of a kidney to save someone's life. Is the renting of the uterus; the payment for someone to assume the risks and discomforts of pregnancy and parturition any less heinous?

The impact on the concept of "family" is also of great concern. A woman, unwilling to endure the physical demands of pregnancy, can hire an incubator mother, to gestate a stranger's egg fertilized by a strange husband. Frivolous motivations soon become socially acceptable. An infertile couple can obtain a donor egg from woman A, have it fertilized by sperm purchased from a sperm bank, B, hire incubator mother C to gestate the embryo. The resultant child will become the progeny of Mr. & Mrs. D & E. What happens to the "flesh and blood" bond that is the glue of family obligation and support?

Surely a scenario can be proposed in which all participants have only the most altruistic motivations. Such unique, rare circumstances can be responded to in accord with the traditional methodology of rabbinic responsum. The realities of this new adoptive modality are such as to require society to legislate against surrogate and incubator motherhood as violating the sensibilities of a free, democratic, people.

Throughout human history, there has been tension between the "trees of the garden from which you may eat," and the "tree of knowledge" forbidden to man. Even the "bleeder-breeder" mother was known to earliest societies [Gen. 4:19]. The survival of our society as one in which the human maintains his infinite worth, depends on intellectual integrity, and a commitment to personal and societal ethics as defined by the Judaeo-rabbinic tradition of the Jewish people. □

BERNARD S. RASKAS *serves as rabbi at Temple of Aaron, Saint Paul, Minnesota.*

SEYMOUR SIEGEL *teaches Jewish theology and ethics at the Jewish Theological Seminary and is a founding Contributing Editor of Sh'ma. We are particularly grateful to him for communicating his views to us though recuperating from a recent illness. We wish him a speedy and full recovery.*

MOSHE D. TENDLER *teaches Talmudic law and biology at Yeshiva University and heads the Rabbinical Council of America Bioethics Commission.*

MARC GELLMAN *is rabbi of Temple Beth Torah, Dix Hills, N.Y.*

H. ALLEN GARDNER *is the Head of Cytogenetics, Department of Pathology at Toronto General Hospital.*

DAVID M. FELDMAN *is rabbi of Teaneck Jewish Center and author recently of* Health and Medicine in the Jewish Tradition.

PEGGY H. DAVIS *letters and illuminates calligraphic work in Hebrew, Yiddish, English and Russian in Minneapolis, MN.*

8.
Race and Class

Self-interest is a mitzvah

Ronald Millstein

Until recently, I was the Reform rabbi in Laurelton, Queens and I still live in Laurelton. Laurelton is a middle-class home-owning community with a mixture of Jewish, Black and Italian ethnic groups with Jews still predominating and Blacks coming up fast. If integration could be made to work anywhere, it had its best chance in Laurelton. We have the advantages of a small neighborhood, private home-owners who really like their community and do not want to move, excellent leadership and community organization. And we do not have to contend with the disadvanteges of poverty, welfare and the anonymity of apartment house dwellers. My former Temple, as an act of faith in the continuity of the Jewish community and as an act of faith in the idea that a racially integrated community could be made viable and long-lasting, erected a new $300,000 building. I don't have to tell the readers of this magazine that words come free and easy, but deeds, especially the building of a new structure, is a serious act for a congregation.

For a few years, beginning in 1963, the leadership in the community, including myself, campaigned to educate the residents "not to panic" at the sight of a Black face and a Black homeowner. *We succeeded.* There was no panic. Integration proceeded with a normal and even less than normal turnover of homes. We stopped the blockbusters and held the local real estate industry to a standoff. Things went reasonably well for some years. The new Black homeowners were accepted on the block and in the community organizations. Not surprisingly, they took good care of their property and still do. Our goal of establishing a stabilized, integrated community—one in which both whites and Blacks were moving in and out—this goal appeared possible of achievement.

The beginning of the end
Then, in 1968, came the Kennedy and King assassinations, riots and demonstrations of all kinds, the N.Y.C. public school teachers' strike and the rise of Black power. The mood of the country and the city turned ugly. Integration was no longer an ideal towards which decent men were to strive. Never mind. In Laurelton, we persisted and still persist. But we discovered two things—two things that Jews would *not* accept. They would not accept the increasingly difficult public school situation and they will not accept the recent surge in burglaries, muggings and purse snatchings. Are our Black middle class neighbors at fault? Certainly not! Many moved to Laurelton hoping to find better schools (read schools with large numbers of highly motivated Jewish students) and relief from the crime culture of their former ghetto neighborhoods. They are, of course, also victims of crime.

But, alas and alack, there is a large Black underclass whose existance cannot be denied or pooh-poohed away. Many are alienated from society. They care not for school and rip-offs are a way of life. They prey upon their own Black middle class and upon the Jews among whom the Black middle class lives. Thus, being culturally unable to accept problem-infested schools, and unwilling to live in fear of limb and property, the Jewish family reluctantly moves away. And we witness the beginning of the end of a strong Jewish community.

If all this is so in Laurelton, how much more so in Forest Hills, Rabbi Kirshblum's pieties (Sh'ma 2/21) notwithstanding!

Facing the reality situation
He stated in effect, that as *Jews* we *cannot* oppose low income housing in Jewish communities. It would be immoral to do so. He is *right*—on an abstract, theoretical, philosophical level. But in all issues of morality and ethics, we have to judge the

practical, the real effects, the consequences of a particular course of action. As Rabbi Kirshblum knows as well as I do, Jewish ethics and the Jewish law based upon those ethics is not an abstract system. It judges real-life situations and balances rights and wrongs—or one *right* against another *right*. In the situation under discussion, it may be immoral to oppose the low income projects, but it would be an even *greater immorality* to permit the withering away and eventual destruction of the Jewish communities of Queens. Furthermore, the minority-group residents of these low income projects will *not* benefit from the disintegration of the surrounding Jewish communities. They will be no better off than before. Thus, the benefits accruing to them will be of a short term and rather dubious nature, while the harm done to the already existing Jewish communities will be long-lasting, even permanent—as was the case in other boroughs.

In conclusion, Rabbi Kirshblum and the liberal universalists among us may be right in a generalized sort of way—but the QJCC, representing the total interests of the Jewish community in Queens *is even more right*. In Jewish ethics, which incorporates legitimate self-interest as well as universal concerns, preservation of the Jewish community is one of the *highest* values. According to the Torah, "Love thy neighbor as thy self" does not mean to love him *more* than yourself. And as Hillel said: "If I am not for myself, who will be for me? And if not now, when?"

Homelessness, *tzedakah* and *kedusha*
Margaret Holub

In November of 1984, when the Federal government made Job Training Partnership Act funds available to retrain unemployed recession victims, the Los Angeles county Supervisors came up with an innovative use for the money. Rather than setting up CETA-like job training programs, as the fund had intended, the Supervisors cancelled the County welfare of all 14,000 indigent people classified as employable and used the new funds for them. The new program, by the county's own admission, ran like this: letters were sent to all 14,000 people telling them that their welfare was

MARGARET HOLUB *is a rabbinical student at HUC-JIR in New York.*

cancelled and that they had to come at a specified time to enroll in a new program that had no office, no caseworkers, no phones, no procedure for issuing checks and virtually no job training component at all. 6,000 people got lost in the shuffle. They didn't get their monthly checks, couldn't pay rent and were evicted from their skid row hotels. By the County's own figures, all 6,000 of these people were made homeless. They were never reinstated.

That was exactly the plan. The Supervisors had instigated this program deliberately to shake people off the welfare rolls, regardless of their need. They stated this intention brazenly to the press. As soon as the initial chaos began to lessen and fewer people were getting shaken loose, new and equally impossible regulations were sent down— designed, the county again admitted, to keep the number of so-called terminations at around 2,000 per month. The program continued in this fashion until a combination of litigation, public outcry and its own staggering inefficiency closed it down in July.

Homelessness is Deliberately Produced

In this instance my County was using its intelligence and its resources to deliberately make people homeless. They knew what "terminations" meant. They wrote plans to keep the level of terminations artificially high; they were aggressive in implementing these plans and shameless in defending them. I have worked for years on Skid Row, always before out of a basically religious motivation which saw homeless people as unfortunates and my work as *tzedakah*. My encounter with the JTPA program told me, and finally convinced me, that homelessness has nothing to do with fortune. It is an economic and racial weapon waged against the most defenseless members of our society by the best equipped and strongest members of the public and private sectors joined together in a war against poor people. Homeslessness is a human defoliant.

Providing Shelter is not charity-work

Another exmaple: in Phoenix the Mayor and the City Council have funded a "bums go home" campaign featuring billboards and bumper stickers showing a person sleeping on a bench with a red slash through him.

These policies are not accidents; they cost money and they take planning, public approval and enthusiastic execution. Nor is it any accident that these aggressive programs which exacerbate homelessness are appearing at the same time that the demographic profile of the homeless person is moving agonizingly towards young, strong Black or Latino men who were working two years ago—articulate, shocked, angry young men— the very people least attractive to those people who see food and shelter as charity and government benefit as handouts. Food and shelter are not charity, and providing homes for the homeless is not a *tzedakah* project. It is a battle, and it forces us straight to the heart, or to the black hole where a heart should be, of American life. Working with the homeless is intellectually and emotionally dangerous, nothing to be relegated to the youth group. In the language of our tradition, the homeless are prophets.

A few comments are in order, then, on homelessness as a Jewish issue. There are indeed homeless Jews; by all accounts the numbers are growing. Many are elderly, but many are not. Jewish Family Service reports an enormous influx of homeless and destitute clients as well as some puzzlement about what to do with them. Kosher food pantries are swamped, and the few Jewish shelters are, like all shelters, always full. Orthodox enclaves like Crown Heights have vast pockets of real poverty within them. Synagogues all over America are discussing what to do when homeless people come to their office begging for money.

Some Jews Cause Homelessness

There are also Jewish slum landlords, Jewish doctors who won't treat welfare patients or who make their practices *de facto* inaccessible to them, Jewish factory owners who don't pay their workers a living wage, Jewish developers and financiers who invest in luxury construction without regard for the displacement of low income tenants in its wake, Jews who support public policies which cut back subsistence benefits to poor people, such as California's Proposition 41, Jews who support and profit from "trickle-down" economic policies which leave poor people languishing while waiting for the goods to trickle down. These Jews and their non-Jewish counterparts make people homeless.

Both sides of the spectrum raise Jewish issues. I worked on a case in which a Jewish landlord illegally evicted a tenant from a skid row flophouse to the streets. The landlord was sued in Small Claims Court and was fined $1,500. He evaded payment, and, in the course of my investigations to collect the fine for our client, I learned not only that this landlord owns slum property all over the worst parts of Los Angeles but that he had donated $25,000 to the Jewish Federation that year. I am not sure what should be done about this man and his tainted money; but he seems as much at the heart of any Jewish discussion of homelessness as does the homeless Jew sleeping under Venice pier.

Jewish congregations are beginning to shelter homeless people, and local federations are beginning to give money for shelter projects, and this is good. But it tends to obscure a larger question: when the social action committee goes to the temple board, or the local interfaith group goes to the local Federation for support of a shelter project, how are the people who will decide profiting from homelessness?

Encountering Holiness On the Edge

Let me finish with what will seem like a digression but is actually the heart and soul of the whole matter for me. In the years that I have lived and worked on Skid Row I have met some people engaged in an emotional and spiritual struggle the extent of which I have experienced nowhere else in my life. For a homeless person in the midst of his or her extraordinary hardship to remain or become caring, articulate, politically active, attractive, funny, or in touch, to me is heroic. No one succeeds all the time, but I know some emotional heroes, people endeavoring heart and soul to be human beings in an inhuman place. Nothing is holier than that effort, no piece of ground more holy than the park where they sleep. The work which I have chosen, which has brought me close to them, has entailed some risks and has left me more exhausted and bitter than I would like to be. But it is a place where, more than anywhere else in my life, I have come close to *kedusha*. At the extended edge of humanity must be the frontier of divinity. People of all faiths and people who profess no faith at all report this kind of experience when they travel out to the edge of human cruelty and human pain. They come back and say that they saw something sacred there and that somehow they have been touched and changed by the encounter.

My hopes, then: I hope that more nights of shelter will be made available in more synagogues, that campaigns against benefit cutbacks will flourish, that thousands of letters and phone calls will be received by every public official about these issues. I hope that *hachnasat orchim* (welcoming guests) will be taught in religious schools and that youth group members will be encouraged to visit soup kitchens and shelters. I hope that all sorts of projects to shelter homeless people will be conceived, supported and done well.

When the gift horse has rotten teeth

I also hope, or think I hope, that the Jewish community will begin to consider disapproving of the most flagrant business and political practices which increase the numbers and the suffering of the homeless, even when they are done by Jews. Dare I hope that one day that Los Angeles landlord's $25,000 contribution will be turned soundly back to him as the blood money that it is?

Even more, and more personally, I hope that here and there some Jews will individually elect, without waiting to be appointed, to go much closer to the edge, to be overwhelmed by the darkness and the light of the presence of the homeless, that they will take greater risks than we might ask of a congregation or a Federation, and that they will be moved and changed by their work. I cannot prescribe exactly what the content of that work or those risks should be; it is exactly the nature of this kind of individual action that one looks a homeless person in the eye and finds a personal response. With my imagination and the colleagues I have been blessed to find, I have done a little and I want to do more. And I hope to be far exceeded in imagination, grit and success by other Jews who are also pulled on by the holy human struggle of the poorest people in our country. •

How we became slum landlords

In the April 19th issue of *Sh'ma* (15/292), Margaret Holub wrote, "Dare I hope, that one day that Los Angeles [slum] landlord's $25,000 contribution [to the Jewish community] will be turned soundly back to him as the blood money that it is?" There are two sides to every story. Here is the landlord's side:

One can become a slum landlord in one of several ways. An area may be ripe for redevelopment and a developer may buy a block of buildings with hope of building a hotel near the new train station, convention or shopping mall. In doing so, he may inherit a slum dwelling or two. That happened to us once. We did do an illegal eviction on that property. It was a house. The woman who sold it to us had rented rooms in the house to ten tenants. None of them had leases and we didn't have any of their proper names. She moved out

after the sale but the ten unnamed tenants refused to move and refused to pay us rent. We started legal proceedings. It was like grabbing quicksilver. We would serve an eviction notice (cost $12) to John Smith, only to find that John Smith was no longer there or that the person we thought was John Smith was really Bill Jones. Meanwhile, it was against the law to turn off the utilities in a building which was occupied. So we were paying utilities and not collecting rent. This could have gone on for many months and cost us much rent, time, money out of pocket and aggravation. Instead, we hired two goons to go into the building, state that they had rented it and wanted everyone out. One of the "tenants" called the police. The police came, understood the situation and decided legality did not always equal justice. They watched the "tenants" pour out of the building bag and baggage. They recognized one of them as a wanted felon and arrested him on the spot.

Our Tenants Destroyed Our Building

Another way a person might acquire slum property is in the hope of rejuvenating it. We did that once. We installed window air conditioners, laid sod, put screens on all the windows and doors, installed playground equipment for the children and furnished a recreation room with ping pong, billiard tables, and card tables. We paved the parking lot and assigned spaces. The tenants did not want to use the parking lot. They wanted their cars parked right outide their bedroom windows so they could hear if, at night, one of their neighbors was siphoning gas or stealing their tires. Children and dogs dug in the sod, leaving large holes. In the rainy season, the tenants took off the screens from their doors and windows to cover these holes so they would not have to walk in mud from their cars to their apartments. In the summer they complained that they had no screens. The air conditioners disappeared as did the playground and recreation equipment. We wound up putting barbed wire around the tree trunks because for some reason they would peel the bark off the trees.

A person might own a slum building because, when he bought it the neighborhood was not a slum but subsequently deteriorated. This happened to us. There were rats in the halls. We didn't put them there. They came from the garbage the tenants put in the hall. There were broken windows. We didn't break them. The plumbing was always clogged. We didn't clog it.

The plumbers who were willing to go to these buildings charged more and more and would only go in teams of two. Sometimes there was no heat because the thermostats were broken. The managers (we had many) were incompetent alcoholics. Who else would live in that building? One manager was held hostage at gun point for six hours in a police auction. He quit without notice. There are broken doors. Often an irate husband will put his fist through a door to get at his wife. Many tenants lose or forget their keys and would just as soon break a door or window as find some other solution.

We own much other property besides the slum dwellings. That's our livelihood. It's difficult to keep track of the problems of each tenant. We've made mistakes and misjudged; but please don't forget our side of the story.

We donate much money to Jewish charities. We are heavily involved in the Jewish community in many ways. That is our way of life. You might, in a fit of righteousness, refund our donations. You might be doing a serious disservice to us and to the Jewish community. •

We are one—with the haitians!
Judea B. Miller

The contrast on that bright Monday morning made the sight even more appalling. The luxury homes and condominiums along the resplendent beach of unsoiled sand overlooked corpses strewn along the water edge. These were Haitians who lost their lives responding to the invitation on our Statue of Liberty: give me your tired; your poor; your huddled masses yearning to breathe free air.

Near the start of the Second World War there were desperate groups of Jews who tried to flee for their lives to some land, anywhere, where they would be safe. On the seas were pathetic, unseaworthy boats which sometimes made their way to what was hoped to be safe shores. But always they were sent back to sure death at the hands of the Nazis. Boats like the *S.S. St. Louis* were sent back from the shores of Florida. The United

States Coast Guard made sure these desperate refugees did not violate our sacred shores.

But there were other boats, some whose names may never be known because they were battered to pieces by the sea. One such boat was the *S.S. Struma* which in February, 1942 had gotten out of Rumania. It made its way to freedom only to have its desperate passengers forbidden to land in Turkey. The boat was towed out to sea by the tugboat of that "neutral" nation and then was beaten to pieces by the waves, with 769 passengers drowned.

One would have thought that the conscience of the world should have learned something from these atrocities that were allowed to happen by innocent by-standers.

On that Monday we saw that nothing has been learned. A boatload of desperate Haitian refugees were drowned off the beaches of Florida. Those fortunate enough to survive the rigors of the sea in their tiny boats are either sent back to further persecution and abject poverty and often death in Haiti—or are interned like criminals in remote concentration camps scattered around the country. Do we not ever learn from history? [Will not the conscience of humanity ever become humane?] ★

We are one—with japanese-americans!
Eugene B. Borowitz

The solidarity of Jews with all other ethnic minorities in America was confirmed to me when I read of John J. McCloy's testimony to the Congressional Commission on Wartime Relocation and Internment of Civilians—essentially, the Japanese, during World War II. I did not see a transcript of his remarks but only the version of them that appeared in the *N.Y. Times*, thus far without objection.

Mr. McCloy was one of the key government officials who oversaw the relocation, but has long since left government. Unlike some of his colleagues in that program, he still defends it as really for the Japanese-Americans' own good. They found "a healthier and more advantageous environment [in the internment camps] than they would have on the West Coast." They were not "unduly subjected to the distress of the war" since it "caused disruption in all our lives." Besides, he described conditions there as "very pleasant."

Thus far we have only the banality of bureaucratic evil.

But what aroused my Jewish sensibilities was Mr. McCloy's cause. He came to the Commission to caution it, says the *Times*, "not to advocate policies that might someday prevent the forcible relocation of other American citizens because of ethnic background." If you don't let us do it to the Japs, how will we be able to do it in the future to…well, I suppose, whomever we come to think is an enemy of the state.

To Speak Out Against Bigotry

McCloy is right. If we don't let it happen to the Japanese then it won't legally be possible to do it to anyone else. So if other ethnic groups abandon the Japanese they open themselves up to similar treatment. Nisei civil rights may not be very high on the Jewish list of survival priorities but to ignore them is to imperil our survival. We have had the courage openly and visibly to fight our President and his understanding of American interests in the Middle East. All the more reason then why some of our energy must always be devoted to assuring the rights of dissident, troublesome, disliked or otherwise provocative citizens. We know painfully what it means not to have rights but only the privilege of residence. We have special incentive, then, to make the struggle for civil rights a permanent, active part of our Jewish agenda. And for that, sporadic arousal only when Jewish interests are immediately at stake, is no substitute.

John J. McCloy was no hack official. He was U.S. High Commissioner in Germany after World War II, and chairman of, variously, the Chase Manhattan Bank, The Ford Foundation, and the Council on Foreign Relations, as well as one-time president of the World Bank. When calculated bigotry speaks with such clout, it is no wonder minorities need the protection of law. ★

JUDEA B. MILLER *is rabbi of Temple B'rith Kodesh in Rochester, N.Y.*

RONALD MILLSTEIN *is the rabbi of Temple Israel of Jamaica, Holliswood, New York.*

9

American Jews and American Politics

On saving all, not some, soviet jews

Jacob B. Agus

It is time to examine our basic presuppositions in regard to the Jews of the Soviet Union. A massive propaganda apparatus has been created under the slogan, "let my people go," or "let them live, *or* let them leave." We operate on the assumption that what we do and say *affects* the policy of the Soviet government, since we do share some humanist principles in common. However, we cannot *control* the reactions of the Soviets to our efforts. I see a clear and present danger that the campaign for freedom of emigration may result in a progressive deterioration of the economic and cultural status of Soviet Jews to the point of their being reduced to "hewers of wood and drawers of water."

The campaign may be conducted either within the context of the rights of Soviet Jews, or on the supposition that Jews qua Jews cannot form part of Soviet society. While initially the campaign was kept within the limits of the first assumption, there are now signs of a shift to the second axiom, a shift that is fraught with the gravest consequences to the well-being and life of our brethren.

A dangerous shift in emphasis
Signs of such a shift are, for example, the continual parading of Jewish emigrés at public meetings, as exhibits of the incompatibility of Jewishness and Soviet life. Publicity was given to the following exchange between a Russian official and an emigrant to Israel. The Official — "Why should I add a soldier to Dayan's army?" — The emigrant — "Would you rather keep a fifth-columnist in your midst?" Other emigres are not so explicit, but the policy of centering attention on them inevitably fosters the notion that Jewish identity is inimical to and inconsistent with life in the Soviet world.

This notion is likely to be reinforced by the escalating rhetoric and the zest of "activism" that are so characteristic of a mass-movement.

Let us be clear about the possible results of this latter approach.

If we convince the Soviet government that Jews are candidates for emigration to the camps of their enemies, it is likely to deny young Jews any opportunities for education and training. It takes roughly a decade to train young people in the professions and management positions, where Jews are now highly represented. Consider what the denial of opportunities for a decade can do to a whole generation! Or are we interested only in "saving" those who wish to join the state of Israel, since the others, by far the vast majority, are candidates for "assimilation?" Are we unconcerned about "assimilated" Jews? What does being "assimilated" mean? How far is the distance from Russian assimilated Jews to the similar species in America or elsewhere in the free world? — Yet, many of our most respected leaders live on the boundary of total assimilation, in every sense of the word. We should remember the warning of the sainted "Hafetz Hayim" — that in our own lives we should be concerned with our own spiritual values, but when we deal with the lives of others, we should give primary consideration to their physical needs.

Full citizenship for soviet jews
I see the specter of the Herzlian thesis in the present campaign — namely, the attempt to solve "the Jewish problem" by a clean surgical operation, separating the nationalists by emigration to the Jewish state and consigning the rest to total assimilation. In the life of a large, well-educated community, no such separation is possible. We know "that all Israelites are responsible for one another." The "liquidation" of Soviet Jewry cannot be carried out in the same way as that of Iraqian or Yemenite Jewry.

We can continue to insist on the right of Jews to emigrate, either to Israel or to other lands, on the basis of principles acknowledged by Soviet society — the right of each person to leave his native land, emigrate to another country and return, if he so desires, a right included in the U. N. Declaration of Human Rights; the right of people to seek the unification of their families; the right of people to seek ethnic, cultural and religious fulfillment. These rights are closely related to other rights of which Russian Jewry is presently deprived — the right of publishing books and magazines on topics of Jewish interests (only one monthly is now being printed), the right to supplement the education of their children, the right to foster Jewish learning and culture on all levels. Such rights do not controvert Soviet principles; they are available in other Communist lands; they were previously available, in some degree, within the U. S. S. R. as well.

Judaism is apolitical

The thesis underlying this approach is the proposition that Judaism is a cultural-religious heritage that is independent of the push and pull of international politics. The loyalties imbedded in the Jewish tradition and transmitted through its educational-cultural-religious institutions do not detract from the loyalty Jews owe to the land in which they are citizens. Judaism is far more than Israel-centeredness.

Naturally, this position would be far more plausible, if the state of Israel had been "neutral," or "non-aligned." By the same token, our position in the United States would have been adversely affected, if Israel had joined the ranks of the so called "popular democracies." We must not forget that the U. S. S. R. accepts and favors the continued existence of Israel. Still, our two-thousand year Diaspora was predicated on the principle of Jewishness being compatible with diverse political loyalties. And this principle must be upheld, for political alignments are perpetually shifting, while Jewish life cannot but be steady and continuous.

Assimilation is not the threat

Russian Jewry is far too massive and highly cultured to disappear by way of assimilation. On the contrary, apart from the occasional prodding of antisemitism, Jewish awareness is likely to be kept up by the momentum of a great tradition and the stimulus of Jewish life in other countries. A people, deeply self-conscious, cannot be taught to forget its heritage. The very attempt to do so is certain to be counter-productive.

To write, as a recent author does, of the prospective disappearance of Soviet Jewry within twenty-five years is potentially absurd. As to the course of events in de-

cades and centuries, who can speak with certainty of the distant future? The time is likely to come when intellectual-cultural freedom will be revived in the Soviet world. At that time, too, Judaism in Russia will emerge reborn. In Russia, as throughout the world, the cause of Judaism is more dependent on the cause of intellectual-cultural freedom than on the shifting winds of international politics.

I call upon the rabbis and community-leaders to be mindful of the distinction between the two ways of appealing to the Soviet government — the one on the basis of Jewish life in the Soviet Union, the other on the basis of Jewish life *outside* the Soviet Union. The right slogan is, "let them live *and*, let those who so desire leave." The campaign to "save Soviet Jewry" must not be turned into a campaign to save the few activists, while the masses are stifled spiritually, and, *chas v'shalom*, ("heaven forbid") suppressed socially.

Addenda

What are the principles that should govern the campaign to secure public opinion in behalf of Soviet Jewry?

First, mass-demonstrations, even non-violent ones, depend on over-generalizations and sloganeering; they generate a mood in which the intemperate and the violent flourish. Violent rhetoric, dispensed by mass-media, produce violent incidnets. Such efforts should be avoided, except when a specific situation calls for it.

Second, appeals should be directed to public bodies for endorsement of resolutions that are carefully worded — such public bodies as unions, associations of journalists, of professionals, of clergymen, of academic personalities. These appeals should focus on specific complaints and demands.

Third, in respect of the rights of Jewish people within the Soviet Union, an effort should be made to mobilize the help of similarly concerned groups. Judaism is not the only religion that is stifled. Catholics, Baptists, Lutherans and Greek Orthodox people have similar complaints, even if there are degrees in hell.

Fourth, well-known intellectuals should be mobilized for a public trial, in which the denial of Jewish rights, as well as other manifestations of tyranny would be expounded, toward the end of challenging the Soviet Union to expand the range of freedom for all its citizens. The basis for such a trial is the proposition that we are all our brother's keepers, and any restriction on individual freedom is a threat to peace.

We must see the smoke behind the silence

Norman E. Frimer

No section of American Judaism has been as sorely scarred by the Holocaust as the Orthodox. Not only is its theology still deeply faith-centered (and the attack on theodicy is clear); but no other group is familially as close to the horrors of Chelmno and Ponary. Many of its people did not come to American shores until the '40s, literally, in Biblical terms, as brands miraculously plucked from the consuming fire. And for them the searing memories of their inexplicable survival continues to throb with poignancy and pain just below the surface.

Such a traumatic experience could not help but father a new — or renewed — *Weltanschauung* (world-view) for Jewish living. Three of its facets are, with some exceptions, evident within the mind set of contemporary Orthodox leadership, especially of the Yeshiva and Chassidic "worlds."

The context of orthodox quietism

1. The classical distrust for the nations of the world, so concretely expressed by some of the sages of the Talmud in their interpretation of the words "V'chesed l'umim chatat," — "even the kindness of the nations is (replete with) sin," was dramatically confirmed for this generation as well. How else could one interpret the silent complicity, and at times active treachery, of the Western World while six million died.

2. The politics of the world was largely in the hands of brute, pagan power devoid of genuine moral concern and human consideration. Overt human interests were but rhetorical trappings for covert national and inter-national self-interest. Consequently in such a world of *golus* (exile) — a word to be taken in its most profound implications, Jews as a corporate entity ought to be guided by the ancient scriptural wisdom of "behold (it is) a people dwelling alone, not to reckon itself among other peoples." The exception was to be only in matters that impinge on particularistic Jewish needs. Then might it become a question of group survival. Otherwise, the strategy was to live "in" but not necessarily "with."

3. The absolute redemptive faith and trust which modern society has vested in secular political movements and social instruments must be placed under serious historic and religious critique — and worse.

The demonic forces latent in these humanistic "idols" were still being ignored even though they had found their most potent and savage thrust not among primitive peoples but amidst the most civilized nation of the world. What greater demonstration therefore that high culture, progressive social thought and free institutions were in themselves no match for the explosive barbarism which constantly lurks in the Torah-less and God-less soul! Such admirable and noble "wisdom of the Nations" is exploited by satanic men only to achieve more efficient crematoria of consumption.

It is the writer's personal contention that only within such a historic context of fear, distrust and withdrawal can Orthodoxy's pervasive silence on social issues be adequately and fairly explained. To level charges of moral insensitivity or personal timidity without such understanding, converts criticism into sheer cavil, a sterile if not puerile exercise at best. For were a grave challenge, God forbid, to confront normative Judaism from the outside there is little doubt that the *gedolim* ("great ones" — the recognized *halakhic* authorities) like their forbears would be unhesitatingly ready even for the eventuality of *Kiddush Hashem* (martyrdom to sanctify God's name). However, in those spheres normally designated as political and social, they hesitate to presume publicly on God's providence and much less on Western society's much-prated liberal tolerance. For repeatedly has it been weighed in the balances and been found tragically wanting.

The need for caution

This presumed explanation might also make clear the refusal to date by these same *gedolim* to sanction and encourage the tactics of protest and demonstration even against the oppression of fellow-Jews in the U.S.S.R. In fact, Lubavitch is reputed to have proscribed such militancy for its adherents, urging instead the tested ways of quiet diplomatic and behind-the-scenes intercession. Do not take risks of inciting the wolves, goes the popular Yiddish adage, lest their anger result in even greater peril to man.

This is the ethos which has given birth to a policy of corporate orthodox non-participation in the issues of Vietnam and the like. What one feels or thinks privately can be and should be expressed in the ballot box. A Jewish public pronouncement is too risky especially when offered by a recognized *halakhic* authority whose position-statements command as well as demand. The day of accountability might not be too far off and the tomorrows of such headline-making may well be too costly for "klal Yisroel" (the entire Jewish people). Responsible leaders therefore dare not take such hazards in a beleaguered social order.

To be sure, many of the new and emergent lay and rabbinic leaders have begun to move away from this position of powerlessness. Their bold statements and vigorous actions speak for a new view on the diaspora. The U.S.A. is different they affirm and the Orthodox community too must move into the mainstream of life despite its undeniable risks. For to do otherwise would serve truly to compound that very risk. Yet, surprisingly, careful observation demonstrates that even this newly found militancy is not so radically different. It still seeks legitimacy and refuge primarily within the framework of authentic Jewish issue and concern.

Re-evaluation, but from a new perspective
Let it be very clear that this analysis is not an attempt to adjudicate between these two views. The time is not yet ripe for such a verdict. Moreover, a fundamental re-evaluation of the sagacity of Orthodoxy's approach to America's social concerns is certainly timely and worthwhile. The public debate generated by Henry Siegman's soul-searching "attack" is long overdue. What is aimed at, however, is the invalidation and elimination of his moral rhetoric and the puristic moral judgments this rhetoric implies. The lessons of the Holocaust and of the long painful history of European Jewish experience dare not be ignored. Consequently, let one take strong exception to the classical *Weltanschauung* of the *golus*-mind regarding the gentile world, as well as the social strategy which rationally flows from it. But all that has little to do with primary ethical sensitivity or religious empathy for the Vietnamese, the Biafrans or the like. It does have to do with the consequence suffered and conclusions drawn from empirical first-hand (rather than intellectual second-hand) experience with the nations of the world.

With that in mind, one might still refuse to buy a perspective which concludes that the world has been surrendered to the forces of the satanic. But neither can one, with personal or intellectual impunity, place oneself at the side of the angels – no matter how liberal or democratic their winged posture. For while modern sophisticated men may have ceased to believe

in the existence of a netherworld of the "other side", contemporary orthodox Jews – and many others too – can testify from their own lives and that of their kindred families to the brutal reality of its power and destructiveness.

But we are commanded not to be silent
Saul J. Berman

The quietistic inwardness which Wyschogrod attempts to propogate as a tenet of his Orthodoxy is substantiated neither by reference to the *gedolim* he cites, nor by reference to tzaddikim (chasidic leaders). Silent suffering may have some ultimate redemptive impact, but it is a privilege granted only to the few who can rest assured of the impact of their mere compassion. The silence of the *tzaddik* is not a model to be emulated by his followers but is rather his unique form of actively seeking the attainment of his plea. His hidden suffering may be as potent as the physician's medication, but it is for him to suffer and for the physician to prescribe medication.

Likewise, *gedolim* are activists in the realm in which their activity may be most productive of human fulfillment, within the four cubits of the *halakha*.

If Rabbi Moshe Feinstein needs no lessons in active compassion, the bulk of Orthodox Jewry may. If "it is not permitted to love suffering humanity more than . . . the Lubavitcher Rebbe," it is still permissible to manifest love for them in different ways. The *gedolim* and *tzaddikim* may be engaged in relieving suffering, through their halakhic creativity or through their effective entreaties, but can the same be said of the communities which they lead?

An alternative to withdrawal
It is pointless to attempt to refute Wyschogrod's theological proposition that the sole responsibility of the Jewish people to the world is to study Torah and raise a new generation of Jews. Withdrawal has been an effective defense mechanism and at times the only course open to the Jewish community. Nor is there a lack of quotable Jewish sources to substantiate the position.

However it is also possible to propound an alternative model, premised on the "priestly" function of the Jewish people, which would demand an active engagement with the problems of the entire world. This alternative would presume that the law revealed to the Jewish people was ultimately the means to perfection of all of mankind and could therefore be used as the yardstick by which Jewish measurements of all human behavior was to be undertaken.

The consequence of this perspective would be a charge substantially more serious than that levelled by Siegman, and broader in its applicability. Not only Orthodox leadership, but Jewish leadership generally has failed to bring to bear the uniquely Jewish perspectives of our tradition on the critical moral issues of our day. Rabbinic and lay Jewish organizations fail in their responsibilities when they issue statements founded in knee-jerk liberalism instead of Torah values.

It is embarrassing to see Siegman marshal an attack on Orthodox silence on Vietnam without making the *halakhic* case for the immorality of the war. It is ever more disappointing to see Golub's total capitualation to non-Jewish values in his broadside against the "cruelty" of *halakha.* Is he indeed totally ignorant of the competing Jewish moral interests which gave rise to the laws which he so glibly denominates as merciless?

A unique morality which must be extended
On the whole I would be compelled to agree with Siegman and Golub only to the extent that the Orthodox community has been verbally and behaviorally unresponsive to the human suffering of Vietnam, Biafra and Bangla Desh. But this failure to respond to distant devastation has not produced resignation as to the pain of members of the Jewish community itself. I have yet to discover a community, be it middle America or counter-culture, in which the human needs of its own members are as avidly cared for as in the Orthodox community. We have successfully withstood the pressures toward indifference and resignation which are so tragically present in America's treatment of her poor, her aged and her disadvantaged.

The wellsprings of mercy in the Orthodox community are as deep as ever; they have, however, been drawn from primarily for Jewish needs, and that is at once its glory and its shame. It behooves Orthodox leadership to cease being so defensive as to be unable to admit the shortcomings of our own community. Much can and should be done to sensitize the Orthodox community to its responsiblities to the outside world.

But the starting point of that process can be neither Wyschogrod's apologetics for the status quo, nor Siegman's and Golub's denial of the ethical sense of the Orthodox community. A proper beginning must be a new understanding of Jewish obligation and its interpretation in the light of the unique qualities of Jewish morality.

Watergate must not mean passivity
Seymour Siegel

Eugene Borowitz admirably points out the futility and harm done to our social fabric and to our souls by verbal over-kill (*Sh'ma* 3/56). When exaggeration dominates discourse (for example, when the Chairman of the Watergate Committee says that our current troubles are a worse tragedy than the Civil War), then the judicious person might best keep quiet. This is good advice.

It is also good advice to look to the institutions in which we are all involved so that water-gate-type actions be avoided. We all know that cover-ups, deception, and enemies' lists are part of almost all institutions — business, governmental, and even religious.

However, some words of criticism must be spoken. Eugene Borowitz believes that we live in a "foul age" and therefore, the usual type of social action is useless and even immoral. What has brought about these doleful meditations? The answer, of course, — the Watergate revelations.

It is a fundamental error to believe that our own "age" is worse than previous ones. It is a curious conceit of most people to believe that their time is worse than all previous times. But is it true? Is this administration, for example, even if it is guilty of all that is alleged (which is by no means certain) worse than the Roosevelt administration which stood by while six million died? Is it worse, to look back to ancient times, than the reign of King David when the ruler was an adulterer and a murderer, surrounded by evil counselors? The answer is obviously "no." Our ancestors did not withdraw because the times were bad.

It is a fundamental error of those who indulge in moralizing to believe that valid political action can only take place in an atmosphere of complete political purity. This is the point made over and over again by Reinhold Niebuhr. (It is, incidentally, ironic and

146

tragic that the insights of this great thinker have been forgotten so quickly). The prophet Samuel pointed out long ago that inherent in the political process is corruption and sin. Politics involves the pursuit of power, and power (even its pursuit) inevitably corrupts. Does this mean withdrawal into private purity? Obviously not! It means that moralists are always needed to restore balance; to puncture self-righteousness, and to call for improvement.

Bringing good out of evil

Furthermore, it is important to remember that good can be done even through the instrument of flawed men. The help of Mayor Daley, for example, was sought by all the democratic candidates — and one does not dismiss the good of the Kennedy administration because the Mayor of Chicago might have rigged the election of 1960. The Chairman of the Watergate Committee, who is lionized by so many, has been defending segregation during all his political life; and an important member of the Committee, Herman Talmadge was one of the main rabble-rousers against civil rights. If we insist on complete flawlessness in our political leaders, we will have no political leaders. Perfectionism is the bane of moralists and makes them useless in the real world. Again Reinhold Niebuhr could instruct us in times such as these.

What then should be done?

First, I would submit that we should maintain a sense of balance. Here Eugene Borowitz (perhaps against his will) agrees with President Nixon. To wring our hands about the end of democracy; to call America *Amerika,* to invoke Hitler and his minions as fitting parallels to our present leaders will do more harm than good. It will blind us to the real problems and the real possibilities. Let our institutions, especially the judiciary, ferret out those who did wrong.

Furthermore, let us be fair to those who have been accused. This, too, is a high moral responsibility. Let us abandon double standards, giving the benefit of the doubt to those whom we approve and believing every allegation about those whom we disdain. Let us lobby for better laws and more vigilance so that the type of abuses which have been uncovered might be avoided in the future.

Most of all, let us get on with the business of the country; acting like mature people who know that the world is not perfect (least of all, we ourselves), but that in an imperfect world there is still a great deal to be done.

Do i owe israel support of nixon?

Jonathan Groner

How would the impeachment or resignation of the President affect the future of Israel, and therefore, how are we as Jews to respond to calls for either?

It is clear that if the removal of Richard Nixon would directly endanger Israel's security — for example, if a Fulbright stood to succeed him — we would have to support Nixon and swallow our revulsion. Similarly, if somehow Israel's survival were not bound up with American arms and economic support, we could express our disgust at the present administration without compunction. The truth is somewhere between these extremes. Because of the inevitable instability that would result from impeachment or resignation of the President, perhaps because of a potential White House reaction against outspoken Jewish opposition to the President continuing in office, there is some risk of disadvantage to Israel. Not certain destruction, I think it fair to say, but some disadvantage. The question thus becomes, How much risk to Israel, if any, are we willing to accept in order to express our outrage at what seem clearly to be immoral, criminal, and repressive men and acts?

When the question is phrased in this way, without the usual rhetoric of "the very life or death of Israel and the Jewish people," it can at least be dealt with. I care very deeply about Israel, but as a Jewish human being, I also care very deeply about the survival of freedom and the rule of law in America. These commitments are both absolute and relative. They are absolute when they are being radically tested: when Israel is actually in danger of destruction or when fascism is actually imminent here. They are both relative in lesser situations, and can then be balanced against each other. From this non-absolutist viewpoint, there is an excellent case that the potential risk to freedom and justice in America if we do not speak out against the President outweighs a hypothetical disadvantage to Israel. A serious and committed Jew can take this position in good conscience, while remaining constantly vigilant for a radical threat to Israel which would call for his absolute commitment.

In almost all other significant matters it is perfectly respectable for a person to make distinctions and to respond in a measured way; but, for completely understandable reasons, many supporters of Israel react to the present issue only in an absolute fashion. Is it too much for them to understand that theirs is not the only possible Jewish position?

Church and state: a reassessment
Seymour Siegel

A state without the means of some change is without the means of its conservation–
Edmond Burke, 1790.

A very popular error, having the courage of one's convictions; rather it is a matter of having the courage for an attack on one's convictions–
F. Nietzche.

The problem of the extent of the assistance by government of religion-related private schools again looms large. The docket of the Supreme Court contains several cases concerning the constitutionality of state statutes extending some form of aid to such schools. These cases involve the payment of state funds to teachers of secular subjects in non-public schools; state aid for supplementary educational materials; and for other forms of assistance. The cases to be decided also involve federal construction grants to church related colleges and universities for buildings which do not include religious facilities. Several political campaigns, notably the race for governor of Michigan, involved issues of state aid to private schools. It is clear, that this matter is again coming to a crisis. As usual, American Jewish organizations, notably the American Jewish Congress, have been involved in the litigations on the side of the strict separationists. Probably most of the defense and civil liberties agencies within the American Jewish community (and perhaps outside of it, since so many of the supporters of groups such as the Ameri ca n Civil Liberties Union seem to be Jewish) are fighting to uphold the notion that the governments—federal, state and local—should not extend assistance to private schools, especially religiously-oriented ones.

It has been considered one of the givens of American Jewish life that the Jewish community, speaking through its agencies, would be on the side of the strict separationists. However, there are signs that this once solid front is not holding. There is a growing feeling, not limited to the Orthodox, that whatever were the good reasons for this stance in the past, it does not serve Jewish interests today.

One is for up; two is for down.
Three is for girth; four is for birth.
Five is for sleep; six for belief?

Thus, our religious umbrella organization, the Synagogue Council, which requires unanimity for any official position, has not been able to arrive at a stand. There is increasing disquiet within the constituent organizations of the Conservative movement. At the last meeting of its Commission on Social Action there was a spirited debate about the question with strong voices heard on each side. And something is said of change within the Jewish community, when both candidates for governor in New York in the last election directed statements toward them, promising to urge the state to assist private schools.

The case for revisionism
I am one of the number who believe the time has come for the Jewish community to revise its stand on this question and to support the public officials who are in favor of state aid to all schools, including parochial schools, day schools, and *yeshivot*.

I am not competent, of course, to discuss the constitutional question which will be decided in the courts. However, as has been frequently pointed out, the Jewish community is not rigorously separationist. It does accept the notion of the government paying chaplains in the army and in state-supported institutions; has fought for the continuation of the tax exemption for religious facilities (which, of course, represents an indirect government subsidy) and has received manifold benefits from the state in many ways. It is clear that the so-called wall of separation between church and state is more like a hedge, where if you really want to, or have to, it is not too difficult to get through.

There are good reasons, in my judgment, to support efforts to ease the financial burden of those who are providing their children with alternative education. They are founded on the growing interest in the day school within all the segments of the Jewish community. The Orthodox have thrown most of their educational eggs into the basket of integral education. There is more and more realization in the Conservative movement that the strengthening of the Solomon Schechter Day School movement is essential for the maintenance of religious life. Even the Reform movement, once positively antagonistic, seems to be opening such schools, recognizing that they are vital to Jewish survival. So Jewish parents are now more sympathetic to the plight of Catholic parents. They have been claiming that without government aid for their parochial schools they were carrying a double load of taxation and that the special financial burden of supporting children in church-related institutions constituted, in effect, a threat to their religious freedom.

The latter argument is of some interest. It says: the guarantee of the free exercise of religion is endangered if parents who, as a matter of conscience, wish to educate their children according to the tenets of their faith, are taxed so heavily that the economic burden makes the practice of their religion prohibitive. This, by the way, was the argument of Justice Stewart who ruled that the Sabbath closing laws could be modified in favor of those who did not observe Sunday as their day of rest. It must be remembered also that according to the American system (in contrast to the continental view) it is not the state which is the primary educator of the young but the parents. The state acts *in loco parentis* providing services which the parents cannot themselves provide. The state does not have a monopoly on education. This was defined by the Supreme Court in 1925 (Pierce vs. Society of Sisters) which declared unconstitutional a statute of the state of Oregon requiring parents to send their children to public schools only. Therefore, parochial schools, yeshivot, and other church-related institutions are a means by which the parent exercises his conscience. He should not be so penalized for this that the free exercise of religion become impossible. In past years, Jewish parents, as a matter of personal distance, tended to be unsympathetic to this argument. Now that they are in the situation they can see the cogency of the argument that the parochial schools perform an important social function and therefore merit some financial support from the state.

But what of our love for public schools?
A telling argument against aid to church-related schools is that such assistance would wreck the public school system. We Jews owe a great deal to the public school system. It was the chief agency of Americanization of the immigrant and made possible, in large measure, the stunning success of the American Jewish community in the economic, cultural and political spheres. However, it would be folly not to realize that both the ethnic communities in America and the public school have changed. It is clear that most Jews are *born* American and they have to *become* Jews, in contrast to our parents' generation when they were *born* Jews and had to *become* Americans. There is a good deal that plagues our public schools. Much has been written about the malaise affecting them. Homogenizing Americans is not our problem. Constructive pluralism is. If we are to attain it, as many options as possible should be left open for parents and their children in the educational enterprise.

One of the more promising new ideas in this area has been the so-called "voucher plan". According to this scheme, every parent would receive from the state a voicher in the amount of the per capita expenditure for education. He could use this voucher wherever he wished. He could send his child to a public school, a religiously-oriented school, or any other institution of his choice and present his voucher for payment. The virtue of this plan would be to give to the parent an opportunity to choose the kind of schooling he wished his child to have, under government enforcement of minimum standards, of course. This plan has been supported by conservatives such as Professor Milton Friedman of the University of Chicago

as well as radicals such as Edgar Friedenberg and Paul Goodman. It would help parents who wish to have a religiously-oriented education for their children and most especially ghetto parents who feel that the public school short-changes their children.

Whether the voucher plan is the best plan or not what is clear is that the future of education in the country depends on the breaking of monopoly of one type of organization and outlook on the educational process. Competition from alternative systems would spur the public school to improve itself and thus further the education of all. It is frequently charged that such schemes would only increase racial segregation. This could be legally prohibited by banning the use of vouchers in any school in which racial tests were being used. In any case, what is being said here is that the health of the nation and the vigor of the educational enterprise of the country would not be vitiated by supporting private education, but would rather be strengthened.

The changing function of religion

There is still another consideration conducive to change. Jewish civil rights and human rights were won in Europe usually under regimes which were "secular" and "laic". It was usually the "religious" governments which were reactionary and active in denying Jewish rights. There, the anti-clericalist parties were the ones which championed Jewish rights. "Religion" meant Christianity and Christianity meant Jew hatred and the teaching of contempt. This was especially true in reference to Catholicism which held sway in Eastern Europe and in parts of Central Europe. So the Jew has come to oppose the incursion of religion into the life of the state.

This European experience, it seems to me, is still reflected in the opposition of Jewish bodies to any breach in the wall of separation of Church and State. Whatever was the truth of this feeling in the 19th century, it no longer is true today. Both the "religious" and the "secular" forces have changed radically. The reformation of both branches of Christianity, their attempts to purge themselves of anti-Jewish bias, and their changed view of themselves is one of the crucial cultural events of our times for Jews. On the other hand the secular forces usually finding expression in movements of radicalism and left ideologies have by and large not been friendly to Jews and Judaism. I am asserting that today, we have far more to lose as Jews when religion wanes, especially Christianity, than when it is strengthened. This is especially true because if the state aids church-related schools it will also aid yeshivot and day schools.

We should not keep our gaze backward. The notion of the separation of Church and State which was championed so vigorously by such thinkers as Spinoza and Mendelsohn reflected their justified fears that a "religious"

150

state would exclude the Jew. But in pluralistic America where there are constitutional guarantees against the establishment of any *one* religion and where the prevailing ethos ordains that Judaism is one of the "three religions of democracy" the strengthening of parochial schools would not endanger the Jewish status as a full citizen. What endangers Judaism is ignorance and an all-pervasive secularism. To fail to recognize this change in the cultural climate and to hold on to positions better suited for other times is folly. Peter Viereck, professor of Yale, has perceptively remarked that anti-Catholicism is the anti-semi-of the liberals. It would be dishonest not to admit that a good deal of the opposition to state aid stems from the undeniable fact that the main beneficiaries would be the Catholics.

We, the people, deserve help

Today, I am arguing, such prejudice is intolerable and state aid would be good for the Jewish community and for the general welfare. So it would serve us better if Jewish organizations were to promote government help, insofar as our constitution allows it, rather than fight against it. Realistically, of course, even if the state were to be generous to religious schools this would not completely remove the burden now borne by parents of children in yeshivot and day schools. But even some help is important. This should not, of course, absolve the dispensers of Jewish communal funds from helping our educational efforts to the best of their ability.

I do not question the integrity and the ability of our agencies who have taken such a vigorous stance on the question of Church and State. I do think that they served us well in the past. However, conditions have changed and the Jewish community has changed. Today, it would seem to me more prudent and more true to Judaism to urge our states and local authorities to recognize that education must be supported wherever it is being fostered – both in private and public schools.

Sanctuary is a jewish issue

Charles Feinberg

On February 19, 1984, Beth Israel Center, along with three Church groups, declared Sanctuary. We took responsibility for Ruheligo and Maria Gonza-lez and their four young children. Ruheligo and Maria had fled Guatemala after eight family members, including Ruheligo's father, step-mother, and two year old brother, disappeared. Ruheligo's father had been warned not to attend a rally sponsored by a labor union. Yet the whole family had been out of work for a very long time. Ruheligo's father did attend; shortly afterward he and his family disappeared. Ruheligo believes soldiers arrested his family and murdered them. He does not know this for sure. They have been missing for almost four years.

I became interested in Sanctuary when a dear friend came back from the Texas border with tales of Central American Refugees and their suffering. That Central Americans have suffered terribly, I could accept. That our own Government seemed to compound their suffering, I had a hard time accepting. Yet as I listened to my friend's stories of what goes on at the border, as I looked at her slides of her experience, I could not help be moved.

The Law and the Refugees

I began looking at the facts that our own Government acknowledges. In 1980 the Congress passed an Immigration Bill. This was the last bill on Immigration passed by any recent Congress. In this legislation Congress for the first time established a non-political definition of a refugee. A refugee is defined as any person: *Owing to well-founded fear of being persecuted for reasons of race, religion, nationality, membership of a particular social group, or political opinion, is outside the country of his nationality and is unable or unwilling to avail himself of the protection of that country; or who, not having a nationality and being outside the country of his formal habitual residence is unable or owing to such fear, is unwilling to return to it.*

Moreover, the United Nations Convention on Refugees (to which the United States is a signatory nation) provides: *That no Contracting State shall expel or return a refugee in any manner whatsoever to the frontiers of territories where his life or freedom would be threatened on account of his race, religion, nationality, membership of a particular social group or political opinion.*

The refugees who flee the violence of Central America are fleeing because their lives are in danger. Because of some opinion they hold, because of some act they did, they have been threatened with expulsion, torture, or death. Some, like Ruheligo and Maria, have seen their families disappear and have understood the message. At that point, many decide to give up what they have and they flee. The journey they embark on is fraught with danger. If they are lucky, they make it to the United States border.

The Impenetrable Paper Barrier

Many of them are arrested at the border by officers of the Immigration and Naturalization Service (INS). They are locked up in prisons, called "detention centers." The conditions in these prisons are poor if not terrible. Usually they have little money. If they are lucky, the INS will inform them that they can apply for asylum. It takes months if not years for an application to be processed. In order to leave these "detention centers" a refugee has to post bail bond of $1500 to $4500. Most refugees do not have the money. Thus a refugee faces a difficult choice: either to sit in jail or be deported.

Many refugees are not even informed they have the right to apply for asylum. If they apply for asylum, and if they are able to post the money for bail, the application is first sent to the State Department of review. It is here that the politicization of refugees begins in earnest. The State Department can hold on to an application for a very long time. Many times an application is not really reviewed: the same form letter is sent to hundreds of refugees. The statistics speak for themselves: In 1984 13,373 refugees from El Salvador applied for asylum. 328 were granted asylum; 13,045 were not granted asylum. The American Jewish Committee has reported that close to 250,000 refugees were granted asylum in 1980. In 1985 the Government will admit no more than 70,000. While our Government accepts refugees from Poland and Afghanistan by a ratio of 2 to 1, it accepts refugees from El Salvador by a ratio of 40 to 1.

When Everyone Suffers no one is a Refugee

Our Government refuses to accept Salvadorans or Guatemalans as refugees. On February 3, 1985, the *New York Times* reported the following case of a Salvadoran teacher: *who had petitioned for asylum, maintaining that because he had participated in the Salvadoran teachers' union, he had been arrested and tortured with acid, and a brother had been kidnapped, tortured and decapitated. His petition was supported by doctors for Amnesty International...and the service (INS) did not contest the Salvadoran's assertions.* Yet the Government

turned down this man's petition, based on this curious reasoning: *The problems of the applicant and his family members do not stem from persecution but from civil strife which has torn El Salvador apart over the past five to nine years. The tragedy of El Salvador is that the suffering, the armed kidnapping, and other excesses are not confined to one particular group, but are endured and perpetuated by all.*

No one from El Salvador can be a refugee because so many suffer. Such is the "logic" of the INS. There is nothing in the Immigration Act that indicates that only one group has to suffer in order for its members to be refugees. Nor is it clear how civil strife and persecution are mutually exclusive terms.

As I began to study and understand this evidence, I realized that this was an issue I could not easily evade.

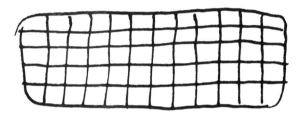

Applying our Beliefs to this Issue

Sanctuary challenges us on whether we believe the God of Israel is the Creator of all creation. The rabbis ask why God didn't create many people as He created many animals at once? The rabbis answer that the Torah teaches in this case that we all have one father and one mother. Ultimately, we are responsible for other human beings, no matter who they are. And everyone who saves a life is as if he creates a whole world. By giving sanctuary we become partners with God in Creation.

Sanctuary also challenges us to be faithful to the teaching of Exodus. Central American refugees are strangers in our midst. They truly are weak in the face of violence and oppression at home and in the face of the hard-heartedness of American officials. They need our protection. Refugees have been on the Jewish Agenda for centuries if not millenia. But it is only in this century that the whole world turned its back on Jewish refugees. Today, we hear the same arguments and evasions that were pronounced then. Then, our Government said we had no jobs for Jewish refugees; or that Jewish refugees would take jobs away from Americans. Today, our Government says the same thing about Central Americans. We know what the consequence of our indifference was in 1938, when after the fiasco of the Evian Conference on refugees, the Nazis realized that no one cared what happpened to European Jewry. We do not know what will be the consequence of our indifference today. But surely, by being silent in the face of oppression, we become accomplices. For these reasons let us consider the moral argument for offering sanctuary and for supporting the Sanctuary Movement. □

NORMAN E. FRIMER *coordinates Hillel activities in the greater New York area.*

SAUL J. BERMAN *teaches Judaic Studies at Stern College for Women in New York City.*

JACOB B. AGUS *is the rabbi of Beth El Congregation in Baltimore, Maryland and teaches Jewish Thought at Temple University.*

JONATHAN GRONER *was a Sh'ma Fellow in 1973.*

CHARLES FEINBERG *is Rabbi of Beth Israel Center, Madison, Wi.*

10.

American Jews and the State of Israel

My zionist dilemmas: two recent cases

Balfour Brickner

Years ago things were simpler. I could love God, serve the United States and be a Zionist all at the same time. Today nothing integrates easily. Herewith two recent experiences in loyalty leading to intense personal conflict.

The first agony came just after the Jordanian-guerilla war began. A radical Jewish friend phoned from Washington. He had heard the U. S. was about to intervene and thought it disastrous. He was rounding up goyish names for a protest. Would I take the lead in collecting Jewish names.

Once again I could see myself at odds with the American Jewish community. And the Israelis would also descend upon me. Why rock the boat now? Hadn't Golda and Nixon just concluded one of the most celebrated love fests in the annals of Israeli-U.S. relations? Undoubtedly, what was good for America had to be good for Israel. And, if the United States decided to intervene to protect its citizens, what right did anyone have to object? Besides, this was a case of Arabs killing Arabs. How could that be anything but "good for the Jews?"

The issue might have been simple for the ordinary American Jew who, at the instruction of most national Jewish agencies over the past coupleof years, had often been taught to swallow his anger at the administration. But not for those who, despite their love of Israel, had long and loudly protested their country's intervention into the Vietnamese civil war. Was the Jordanian situation any different? And what if the U.S. either dragged or pushed Israel into Jordan with her. Neither

was it beyond imagining Hussein silently welcoming a few Israeli Phantoms over northern Jordan to blast Syrian tanks, an action which would later be explained to the world as a self-defensive response to Syrian aggression. Imagine the weapon such an action would place in the hands of those who at every available opportunity chant about Israel imperialism.

The suffering begins

My dilemma was real. An American army of 12,000 was being alerted in Germany and South Carolina and the 6th fleet in the Mediterranean was being deployed to do more than save a few hundred Americans. After all, the International Red Cross was already working on that job. As for what the hucksters might shout—well, they're always shouting anyway so to hell with them. How could I ever again publicly protest against our immorality in Vietnam if I didn't protest a similar immorality in Jordan?

But was the immorality similar? I am not a pacifist. Pacifists see intervention in dimensions of moral absolutism. I do not. U.S. intervention in Vietnam is wrong, not because it is always wrong but because in Vietnam we are an aggressive intervenor on the side of one party in a civil war. Our intervention in Jordan could have been wrong for the same reason only the Syrian intervention had changed the situation from a Jordanian civil war to a war of national defense. The violation of a recognized international border legitimatized U.S. involvement on the side of Hussein. The 17th parallel dividing South from North Vietnam is not such a border, so that is a different case. Clearly, those who would take a negative view of U. S. intervention into the Jordanian situation must base it on other grounds than analogy to Vietnam: that it is unwise and has too many risks, viz. a Soviet response. That swayed me. But my response was now practical, not moral. I wondered whether I was fooling myself. I didn't know. I did know I had learned from situation-ethics that the situation cannot be left out of an ethical decision.

I began to wonder what American Jews who support Israel but are absolutists against intervention would say about U. S. intervention to protect Israel from a united Arab-Russian attack. I was glad I wasn't that rigid. Not knowing when intervention might be right isn't comfortable. I hurt plenty after that phone call.

Practically speaking, what happened was that I adopted a non-interventionist posture based on a pragmatic evaluation. It would not be good *at this time*. When I called my friend back he seemed to understand but, in talking, he threw me into turmoil a second time, asking how I would feel if Hussein overwhelmed the guerillas. Ouch.

Again the alternatives are traumatic
Establishment type Zionists and Israelis have been supporting the Hashemite monarchy. They constantly say that a sovereign nation can negotiate only with another sovereign nation. Since the Palestinian groups are certainly not an established government, Israel cannot negotiate with them. It was Golda Meir who repudiated the notion of a separate Palestinian entity when she so glibly remarked: "A Palestinian—what's a Palestinian? I, too, was once a Palestinian!"

The logic of this position loses cogency with each passing day. Witness the surprising student support for Nahum Goldmann when, last spring, he wanted to accept Nasser's invitation to talk. Witness the growing, though admittedly still small, support for Israeli doves like Shlomo Avineri, Yaakov Talmon, Ernst Simon, Arieh Eliav and others. But the cruelest paradox is that though Israelis, despite their emergency, freely debate what attitude to take to the Palestinians, in America merely to raise the issue is to risk being branded a heretic or an enemy of the Jews.

Someone more concerned with ethics than organizational discipline, has shown me a confidential memo that one national organization sent to its regional offices. It warned its constituents against becoming involved with an Israeli, a member of the Knesset, no less, who was coming on a tour to this country. Why?

Because, in the words of the memo: "He advocates the abolition of Zionist ideology in Israel, its institutions and traditional Jewish aspirations." Which means, as the memo continues "He is against any incorporation or annexation of the administered territory and is against the establishment of Jewish settlements in administered areas until peace is achieved... he advocates that all Arab refugees be given the choice between repatriation or compensation." Should not the settlement question, such as the recent move by a group of Orthodox Jews to Hebron, be debated? Is the compensation alternative so heretical? In 1954 Michael Comay, then Israel's Ambassador to the U.N., offered a measure of compensation. In 1958, Abba Eban did the same and reiterated it in his Nine Point Peace Proposal of October 1968.

The memo admits that this Israeli dove has repeatedly stated a) his committment to the continued existence of the State of Israel, b) his opposition to Al Fatah, and c) his opposition to any Israeli withdrawal from territories until peace is established. Nonetheless, it urges no contact with him.

Civil Liberties for whom?
This is a particularly disgusting example of the kind of "adhere-to-the-party-line" approach which has become standard in the American Jewish community and which has caused many thinking Jews to turn away from its organizations. How can we take seriously their call for free speech in every other facet of American life when they themselves deny it? The day for this kind of blindness is over. The Middle East cannot afford to go again to the brink to which the Palestinians in their extreme of frustration brought it during two fateful weeks in September. The Palestinians may have lost the military shoot-out but just as the NLF won their right to sit at the Paris peace talk table, so the Palestinians have probably made good their demand to be a part of whatever negotiations finally take place between Israel and the Arab world. It was their frustration which drove them to the barbaric extremes of plane hi-jacking and the murderous military escapade from which they emerged so mauled. Unless they are accorded some recognition now, the world can anticipate that they will re-group and have an-

other go at it. Uri Avnery is right when he writes: "We Israelis have been the activating force in the Middle East for the last three generations. We have been the victors, militarily at least, of three wars. Now, I believe, it is up to us to take the initiative and the first step toward peace—a view which makes me sound heretical in Israel...If no solution is found soon, the guerilla war of organizations like Al Fatah will start a vicious circle of its own, a steep spiral of terror and counter terror, killing and retaliation, sabotage and mass deportations, which will bring undreamed of miseries to the Palestinian people. It will poison the atmosphere and generate a nightmare that will make peace impossible in our lifetime, turning Israel into an armed and beleaguered camp forever, bringing the Arab march toward progress to a complete standstill..." One who agrees with this position is no less a lover of Israel for so agreeing than one who does not. Indeed, to fail to see the truth of these words may do a greater disservice to Israel than can be imagined.

Making the inevitable practical

It may sound strange but it might have been better for Israel had the Palestinians won. When they had the burdens of restoring Jordan to viability, it would have made it possible for Israel, American Jews and the world to discount their inflammatory rhetoric about driving Israel into the sea. No one believed that the Arabs could do this when they were powerless; fewer would believe their boastings once they were masters of a nation and plagued with all the problems attendant to such a position. Even after they had settled their internal chaos and the rhetoric again escalated Russia could be expected, behind the scenes, to keep things from reaching a critical point. Russia may want to keep things seething but even she is leary of them boiling over.

I agree with those radical Jewish youths who talk about the necessity of Israel's recognizing the Palestinians. But they are wrong when they identify the militant Palestinians as true revolutionaries and thus much to be admired. This September's events should have made the falsity of such an equation painfully clear. The actions of the National Front for the Liberation of Palestine have revealed them to be gangsters. That they may end up having helped their people win recognition does not make them less criminal or their crimes less reprehensible. To say less, is to badly confuse means and ends. To try to defend them is to try to legitimatize every defiance of international law and to make an unquestioned virtue out of bloody civil strife. Many of these same Jewish radicals are always trying to tar Israel with the brush of imperialism. Is not that charge now more properly evoked against Syria or, for that matter, even against the Palestinians themselves?

I have learned from these experiences that I live in a special sort of exile. I love the State of Israel but I cannot stand some of the tactics of its supporters. I think moral imperatives can and must govern more of our political life but I am repelled by the self-hate and self-delusion of some of the people who try to take civic morality most seriously. I am sure there are many other American Jews wandering in this no-man's-land but mostly I feel very lonely.

Will israel become zion?

Arnold Jacob Wolf

The downing of the Libyan airplane was not so much an international incident as a symbol of what Israel has begun to become. Not, despite her fanatical enemies, a conventional, power-mad imperialism; but rather a frightened and thus, inevitably, trigger-happy, besieged yet somehow also haughty, developing nation. Is this what a hundred years of Zionism has led to: more danger to Jews than in the *golah* itself, more recklessness and violence than in all of our long diaspora history?

Zionism, as I understand it, meant and means primarily the end of subservience to other men's determination. It meant the fulfillment of God's promise (*Lev.* 26) to "break the bonds of your yoke and make you walk upright," *kom'miyut.* Zionism promised and promises a new, organic authenticity, a Jewish life lived out of inner standards, in dialogue with Jewish sources, speaking the Hebrew language, without the circumlocutions and the evasions of all our fearful ghettos. Zionism opposed and opposes that comfortable liberalism which substitutes premature utopianism for patient Jewish messianism and which asks us to become part of the nations instead of a nation dwelling alone. Zionism opposed and opposes that Orthodox petrifaction which treated the *halakhah* as a fortress to be defended and not a life to be lived.

Zionism also opposed and opposes Christian denigration of Jews and of Judaism, the brutal repression by those who were not entirely sure that their Messiah had come and had, therefore, to throttle us whose Messiah was always yet to come. Zionism refuted Pauline Christianity for which hope meant always the distant, other-worldliness of the *parousia,* and the irrelevant comfort of the *eschaaton.* Zionism refuted Christian *agape* which, seeking to love the neighbor better than oneself, ended by requiring that he become oneself. Zionism attacked the *ecclesia,* the church triumphant, which demanded that all men become her children and that all men worship the man she called God. Zionism refuted Christian *pistis,* a faith in dogma, doctrine and salvific paradigms, an individualistic belief in an incarnate God, without Law, without community and without toleration.

The achievements of zionism
Against Christian claims, Zionism reasserted perennial Jewish values: the holy understood as the secular under God; faith as faithfulness, Israel as the truly chosen people; the "way" of Torah as a disciplined, commanded life; history as the promises of God unfolding in the lives of men. Zionism looked back to traditional Jewish self-understanding, to the prophecy of Zechariah that even the pots and pans in the new Jerusalem would be "holy to *Adonai,*" to rabbinic service of God through commandments and communal discipline. Revolutionary Zionists like Hess and A.D. Gordon and Rav Kuk and Martin Buber superbly refracted these traditional Jewish norms until they shone forth with a profoundly innovative communitarianism in the *kibbutz,* and a brave new Exodus from lands where Jews could no longer live or could not live like Jews. The conquest of the Land and the conquest of labor and the conquest of self-hating atavisms were all achievements of Zionism as the authentic and unique national movement of the Jewish people everywhere.

Much has been achieved: more pride and more scholarship, more unity and more stability than could have been predicted from the early history of European Zionism. Exiles have been gathered, including many who had forgotten that Jews *are* exiles, no matter how comfortable their lives. The Jewish state is a fact, ineluctable and glorious, but it is not and

may never be the Zion desiterated by the Movement or foreshadowed by the Tradition.

The disappointments of Zion
There has been in Israel a steady retreat from socialist and religious egalitarianism. The *kibbutz* is isolated and diminished and, if it is the glory of our propaganda, it is also a vulnerable island in a sea of capitalist encroachment — and now knows it is. Where Pro-Palestinian Zionism was open, the State of Israel has become triumphalist and often also expansionist. The mood of its people coincides all too nearly with the program the Movement for a Greater Israel. Percentages of party representation remain the same as they were a half century ago in the European Congresses, a stunning indicator of cooptation and congealed constituencies. Despite the fact that the population has become increasingly Eastern and strikingly young, governance by coterie, even by *landsmanschaften,* continues unmodified and unlamented. New groups and new ideas are harder to discover or to support than they ever were in the historical Zionist movement.

Israel colonizes the "administered" territories without regard to international Law or to the rights of the indigenous Palestinian nationality. Israel forces go deep into Egypt or Lebanon — sometimes to ferret out spies and terrorists, but often to carpet-bomb wholly innocent Arab neighbors. Few Israeli soldiers die now (thank God!) but, as in Viet-Nam, its pilots can rain death from skies which they and they alone control.

Zionism opposed Orthodox unilaterialism, but in the Jewish state, Orthodoxy is enpowered, entrenched, established and corrupt. While deeply traditional Jews like Yeshiah Leibovitz and Professor Urbach denounce clericalism in its Jewish, un-Jewish form, the Orthodox establishment continues its veto over free, religious expression by Israeli Jews, and blindly contributes to the militarism of many religious citizens.

Old temptations corrupt anew
Zionism spoke movingly of *kibush avodah* (the dignity of work) but, increasingly, in the Jewish state, hard work is done by Arab hirelings and by volunteer Americans who enjoy getting their hands dirty for awhile — and this even in socialist *kibbutzim.* It did not take Ben Aharon to see ahead a Jewish Rhodesia with the end of the Zionist dream of dignity and self-realization through labor, a dream curiously enough now sweeping lands of affluence and pollution while a

poorer Israel sets its sights on consumption and ridicules any ecological concern. Did Zionism mean to create an American-style super-market on the Mediterranean built by Arab masons and carpenters?

The power and strategy of the military is both open and deeply threatening to the Zionist ideal. Generals are kings, and ex-generals run the country; they raise an Amin in Uganda who then drives their own and other people out; they conscript children of the East to man their patrols and defend their swollen borders; they use up resources desperately needed for education and for housing and for health, while refusing any move that might lead to *detente;* they recognize the Thieu regime on its very deathbed. The Russians are practically gone from an Egypt which offers to recognize Israel, but Israeli generals are still waiting for the phone to ring. The United Nations and the Friends and some of our best senators from the United States are painted as enemies of the Jews, thus inevitably alienating young Jews who still believe in peace and work for it, even in the Middle East.

Jabotinsky, the life-long *bête noire* of the Zionist movement is now posthumously rehabilitated, to become a Hero of the Jewish State with his name on a hundred street signs and his face on thousands of stamps. Violence, repudiated by the Zionist leadership, at least until Weizmann, is defended subtly by Eliezer Schweid and blatantly by *Gahal,* until the repression of whole populations in Gaza or the downing of a civilian aircraft is seen as defensible by all and glorious by some. Israel sends to America not her scholars or her farmers or her singers, but generals and strategists, as if the Six Day War were her finest hour and *Tsahal* (the Israeli Army) her greatest accomplishment.

A prophetic indictment
The decline of the Dayan family symbolizes the swift decline of the Zionist ideal. A classical *halutz* (pioneer) grandfather; a brilliant and self-assertive general for a son; a grandson and daughter who are jet-setters and beautiful people. One need not wonder what Shmuel Dayan would say about his grandchildren's sophisticated decadence, but the view from present-day Israel of what the generations portend is far more obscure.

A downed plane is not itself a mark of anything; a single example proves nothing. But examples seem to converge and to indict. Israel may be the Jewish state; it is not now and perhaps can never be Zion, the Zion of scripture or the Zion of the Movement, in Moses

Hess' words "the historic ideal of our people, none other than the reign of God on earth." But what Israel will become depends on other than the will of men, even men who call themselves Jews. "That which cometh into your minds shall not be at all. You say: we will be like other nations, like the families of other countries. As I live, says God, with fury poured out shall I rule over you."

The israelis and us, the new distance
Eugene B. Borowitz

Like everyone else in recent weeks, I have tried to do things for the State of Israel. I've been transferring *Sh'ma* funds to an Israeli bank; demonstrating against the P. L. O. at the U. N.; and, like everyone else, wishing there were more I could usefully do.

One thing I can do — must do — is think about what is going on. The tremendous turnout for the U.N. demonstration was a sign of the extraordinary solidarity American Jews have with the State of Israel. But we should not be deceived by it. At the same time, below the surface, I am convinced a new distance has opened up between us. This is not an easy matter to discuss for the alienation has been largely unconscious and the grounds for my judgment are highly subjective. Moreover, the very notion is repugnant: what could be less "good for the Jews?" Yet I believe it politically prudent and morally necessary to try to bring this psychic undertow to our attention lest we not know how we may most usefully work together in the difficult months ahead.

One major source of our American Jewish disillusionment is the recognition that we cannot do as much for the Israelis as we had thought we could. True, our monetary response to the *Yom Kippur* War far exceeded our already generous giving during the Six Day War. Yet accompanying that pride is the shock that ultimately, our fund-raising does not mean very much. Three weeks or so of war cost, by some estimates, seven or eight billion dollars. The Israeli economy suffered badly during the full mobilization, and has remained crippled during the subsequent periodic call-up of reservists. Total all the costs and the sums involved are staggering. Cynics suggest that though the Arabs may not be able to defeat the Israelis militarily they might through a series of even ineffectual wars bankrupt the State of Israel.

Monetary sacrifice is not the answer

In this financial context, our U.J.A. donations and bond purchases are small change. They are necessary, even indispensable, but nowhere near decisive. If we raised another $100,000,000 a year for the U.J.A. or if, by sacrifice, we managed to double our present advanced level of giving, it would not begin to pay for the *Yom Kippur* War. If there were another war — God preserve us! — the financial needs would be utterly beyond us. So, even as checks are made out in gratifying amounts, many donors ask themselves how long these emergency demands will continue and how vital it is to the existence of the State of Israel for them to press themselves for another hundred or thousand dollars or more.

Without doubt our selfishness is also a factor here. Like all Americans, we are not as well-off as we were a few years ago. American Jews have not been impoverished, but it was easier to be generous when we were richer and confident of growth. Selfishly motivated or not, we can see that the State of Israel is far from being the creation of our "charity". Like all other nations its needs are overwhelmingly dependent on international fiscal arrangements and the growth of its internal economy.

The same pattern is found in the political realm. Our activity was impassioned, sustained and successful. The Arab cause won little public support. Our telegrams and demonstrations made it possible for our lobbyists to emphasize that almost every Jew felt personally concerned about American support for the State of Israel. The overwhelming majority of both houses of Congress remained staunchly devoted to the thesis that American interests closely matched Israeli needs. Such was our triumph.

Realizing israel's dependence on the U.S.

Yet the very political achievement has given rise to an unanticipated disquiet. We now realize that the State of Israel is radically dependent upon the United States, but we have also learned that American Jewish political power is highly limited. The more unexpected blow fell as we saw how illusory is the independence of the State of Israel. Without the American air-lift of arms and material, the Israelis could not have prosecuted the Yom Kippur War to its militarily successful conclusion. (Some commentators insist, it simply could not have gone on fighting much longer without the supplies.) In all the world the State of Israel has no effective power to rely on other than

the United States. No wonder Mr. Nixon's offer of aid to Egypt for the peaceful development of atomic energy caused dismay in many Israeli circles. Suddenly we must face up to the possibility that, in the Middle East, U.S. politics may change. American national interests might well seem best served by a more "even-handed" policy, one which, though it did not sacrifice the State of Israel, put it more substantially at the mercy of its neighbors. We have seen greater American shifts in international affairs — with China and the detente with Russia. Realpolitik means simply that the United States will pursue its national interests regardless of what was said last year about friends and foes.

Should America, confident of Israeli dependence, play up to the Arab nations, there are serious limits to what American Jewry could do to change such a policy. While we are an unusually useful and valuable minority group, our "clout" rests on little hard basis. Our success with regard to Soviet emigration was less an exhibition of Jewish power than of our being able to latch onto American anti-Soviet sentiment. We have few votes, though we cast most of them, and our political contributions while disproportionate are hardly indispensable. We are a significant power only in the politics of the great urban areas and we have extraordinary numbers and contacts in cultural and academic circles. That is about all. It would not amount to much should there be a shift in the American sense of where the best interests of the nation lay. And except for a clear-cut threat to the viability of the State of Israel, we can now see that American Jews could not afford to risk such power as they have in strong opposition to what was generally regarded as the American interest. That was the thoroughly depressing possibility which we learned about during the Arab oil embargo.

Losing a link with our old jewish past

A similar sort of disillusionment arises from our discovery that, for its part, there is much we had expected which the State of Israel cannot do for us. Again the issue would not arise but for the success which makes us the incredibly enriched beneficiaries of the State of Israel. This is the inalienable premise from which our present tentative alienation proceeds. In part we were unprepared that the Israelis should turn out to be as human — that is, as fallible and petty — as the rest of us. They who continually warned us to be on guard against the American anti-semitic attacks we said we could not see coming, refused to believe the Arabs would attack them. They who preached to us of the importance of Diaspora solidarity behind the State of Israel in its time of emergency could barely put together a government. Particularly their handling of the "Who is a Jew?" question has resulted in a loss of dignity for all sides. Much of this came home to us when we lost almost all of the figures in the Israeli government with whom we identified. Dayan and Eban spoke to aspects of our Jewish souls. And while it may be a blessing to the Israelis that the old immigrant generation, Golda Meir, Pinhas Sapir and their like, have finally made way for a Sabra government, we have lost a tie with our own East European Jewish past. In the old-timers we American Jews could see what our parents or grandparents would have been like had they immigrated to Palestine. What we share Jewishly with the new men of native Israeli secular Zionism, the present cabinet, is not immediately evident. Thus, Zalman Shazar, the previous president of Israel was a Jewish educator, who invited leading figures in Israeli society to study classic Jewish texts with him and to join him in *davenning* in the synagogue he had built as part of the new official residence of the President. Ephraim Katzir, the present incumbent, is an accomplished physical scientist, with broad social sympathies and, by reputation, a person of high moral stature. He has splendid human qualifications for a president. Yet to our American sensibilities something seems lacking from what we had imagined of the chief symbol of the Jewish State.

The nixon pressure widened the gap
Yet nothing has so begun to set a distance between us as our different reactions to Richard Nixon. In their gratitude to him for the air-lift of American arms Israelis, by and large, refused to see much significance in the Watergate scandals. Rather they asked us — indeed they did not have much asking to do; we knew what they wanted of us — they asked us to avoid giving any antagonism to their benefactor. And we did that. To my knowledge, no major Jewish organization, even in the presence of overwhelming majority moral indignation at President Nixon's conduct, passed a resolution calling for his impeachment. We faithfully followed the Israeli lead here. We put their needs ahead of our own — but it is clear to me that this act of ethnic discipline came at a high price. Richard Nixon as political leader and personality was sufficiently repugnant in 1972 so that despite the pressures exerted by our organizational spokesmen and the call of some of our intellectual leaders to vote for him, approximately 60% of American Jews voted for McGovern. Today, most of that group feel events have vindicated their judgment

then. They are not alone in their moral revulsion. Again and again I have run into Jews who voted for Nixon who felt betrayed by their erstwhile champion. What troubles us is not the legal issue of whether Nixon technically deserved to be impeached or whether under the special procedures of such a decision he deserved to be found guilty of "high crimes and misdemeanors." We have seen too many people of power use legal technicalities to outwit justice to be deeply moved by such juridic flim-flam. For most of us American Jews the soul of Judaism is its ethics and our problem with Richard Nixon was his morality. With our society increasingly indifferent to, sometimes in rebellion against, the great Jewish and humane values, we needed a president who would set something of an example in decency, someone who would "bring us together" as persons and as a society. Instead, Richard Nixon was a classic model of the decline of American character. And we, as a Jewish community, one which prides itself on its emphasis on moral concern, had to keep quiet in the face of such a situation. Out of love for the State of Israel we met this moral provocation with silence.

Self-restraint was no virtue
No American Jew ever imagined that loyalty to our Israeli kinfolk would require of us so demeaning a stance. We are traumatized by the experience — and not because we think we are saints. The indecency here was so blatant even we knew we should act — but for the sake of the State of Israel we could not. That has been our pain.

I believe many American Jews have been deeply touched by what the Israelis demanded of them in this past year; doubly so, because most Israelis seem unaware of how much moral self-restraint they asked of American Jewry. When one day, we are able to admit what happened to us in this period, when American Jewry is free enough again to face and discuss these matters, I do not see how it can find itself in quite the same close, unquestioned relationship to the State of Israel as existed before the Yom Kippur War.

The root of the present disenchantment is surely our previous unrealistic expectations of ourselves and the Israelis. Now these illusions are falling away. Mature statehood has put the decisive level of action for the existence and development of the State of Israel into governmental and not private hands. And the State of Israel turns out to be tiny in area, poor in resources, financially troubled, faction-ridden and utterly human in its conduct. I suppose, with the arrogance that often comes with insight, we should have always known these truths. But mostly our leaders and our organizational personnel have thought it unwise to face them. They have regularly been by-passed by stirring references to our suffering or our accomplishments. Now, history has made itself felt among us and a shock wave of realism has shaken many American Jews.

The Zionism of illusion needs to be replaced with a Zionism of ambiguity. Much of what we must now regularly do may not achieve great or good results and much of Israeli policy may be or seem to be humanly counter-productive. Politics breeds uncertainties out of the complexities of social conflict and the antagonisms of the battle for power. Our present Jewish problem is how to sustain a high sense of Jewish responsibility to the State of Israel when our decisions must regularly come in a context of ambivalence and the results of our action, taken with the best of intention, are as likely to leave us sinful as righteous.

Zionism secularized messianism

Even on a secular level I think it possible to argue that a commitment to Jewish existence inevitably requires such social responsibility despite its uncertain outcome. For myself, however, what is happening to us cannot be understood without reference to the religious dimensions of the problem. The Zionist movement proudly proclaimed itself the contemporary representation of Jewish messianism. It secularized an eschatological doctrine of faith into a movement of political nationalism. But as we now see often happens with such secular transformations of religion, what has been eliminated in content is often existentially retained. That is, the secularist relates to his institution or group in a religious way. The difficulty is that secularized activities, emptied of all transcendental reference, are ultimately unworthy of man's ultimate concern. In the initial stages of their success we are given reason to believe that they are equal to the problems of humanity. As time progresses, we are forced to acknowledge their serious limitations. One special pain of the twentieth century has been the recurrence of such disillusion. From Marx to Freud to education to participatory politics we have been whipsawed between optimism and despair so many times that it is difficult to believe that there is anything left worth believing in. Such is the consequence of the fallacy of misplaced faith. What we Jews are going through today is the desacralization of Zionism. The excessive faith we had placed in it will no longer hold – but we cannot stand surrendering our illusions.

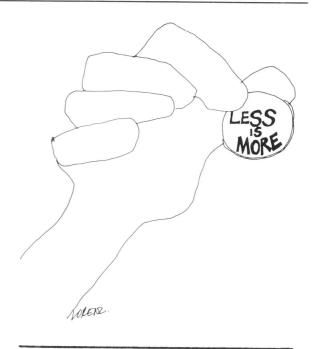

Zionism must arise from the covenant

We have a number of options out of which we might properly re-sacralize our Zionism, not as a refurbished and hence ultimately self-refuting secularism, but as an aspect of religious faith. The Covenant is made with the people of Israel and with individual Jews as members of that people. The corporate destiny of the Jewish people is best fulfilled today in the existence of a Jewish state. Thus every believing Jew is ineluctably involved with it. At the same time Jewish belief makes clear the distance between God and the Jewish State. No reasonably informed Jew could ever confuse where perfection is to be sought. To be sure, this means that the State of Israel is regularly to be criticized in terms of the transcendent demands God makes of the Jews. Yet for that very reason — because we then know that Israeli government and politics and social affairs are utterly human — we will not be disillusioned by Israeli performance (or our own) though we may often be disappointed. And our duty to support the State of Israel, amidst all the newly acknowledged ambiguities of history, remains unshaken by this or that Israeli failing. The Covenant is lived out precisely amid the tricky affairs of humankind, in the markets, the businesses, the family conflicts, the social tensions which shape the contours of human destiny. We do our Jewish duty there though the Messiah tarry. We do the right as best we can now, knowing that perfection awaits the Messiah's coming. We Jews live in a strange mix of obligation and hope, and thus, though we remain in the midst of history, we survive and ultimately redeem it.

The new zionism of the diaspora

Richard N. Levy

Jews have the capacity, somehow, to turn awful events into benefits. The U.N. General Assembly, which almost thirty years before had given international recognition to the fruition of Zionism, has now declared it to be a racist movement. But rather than becoming despondent, Israelis and other Jews around the world, who for almost thirty years had been arguing whether Zionism still had any meaning once a Jewish state was established, suddenly found that the old word still had some power in her after all. The U.N. proclaimed to Jews: The Zionists among you are racists. The Jews responded: In that case, every Jew will declare he is a Zionist. November 10, 1975, may be the day when what was once propaganda became truth: Jews and Zionists are, in fact synonymous.

Zionism is central to jewish messianic hopes
The U.N. debate had a certain revelatory quality for us. It is not unheard of these days, even in liberal Orthodox circles, to affirm that certain dramatic events in contemporary history may reveal a new aspect of the will of God and the *mitzvot* He desires for His people. Whatever the varied political rationales for their vote, the majority of the General Assembly affirmed that Jews have no right to a state of their own (Zionism), because such a state necessarily excludes the rights and national needs of other peoples, particularly Palestinian Arabs (*ergo,* racism). That every national movement desires to change a minority into a majority was deemed irrelevant; the U.N. was saying that Jews have no right to be a majority.

The rage which most Jews felt upon hearing of that vote reflected how widespread is the conviction even of uninvolved Jews in the Diaspora that we have every right to be a majority, and to create a nation-state in whatever image we choose. More than that, knowledgeable Jews are aware that for a Jew to go along with the General Assembly would be ultimately to deny the basis of the Jewish hope: that one day there will arise a Messiah (or a messianic age) in a land and a society where the principles of Jewish law and values will govern. To say that Jews may never be

a majority is to deny that the Jewish messianic hope will ever be fulfilled.

That hope was denied before, of course, in the tormented years when early Zionists could not be taken seriously by other nations or other Jews. But anyone who believes that history reflects the hand of God cannot but affirm that the existence of the state of Israel is part of the divine fulfillment of the promise to the patriarchs and to Israel, their seed, that a Jewish progeny and a Jewish land would be established. For the nations of the world to deny that Jews have a right to a state of their own is, in 1975, a theological denial of the working of God in the universe. If it is a choice between the nations of the world and God, most Jews know where their vote must go.

A jew affirms both the people and land

How can a Jew be a Zionist if he does not believe that the state of Israel is the only center of the Jewish people? To say that to be a Jew is to be a Zionist does not mean, however, that one must be Herzl's kind of Zionist, or Ben Gurion's kind, or even Achad Ha'am's or Rav Kuk's kind. To say that to be a Jew is to affirm the necessity of a Jewish state is not to say that being Jewish is fulfilled in the existence of a Jewish state; it is to say that in 1975 the existence of a Jewish state is part of the fulfillment of being a Jew. It is important to remember that Zionists chose Palestine as their homeland in place of Argentina or Uganda (or Kenya) because *Eretz Yisrael* was the focus of the Jew's messianic yearnings and prayings from the first century of this era. *Eretz Yisrael* has been a holy land because we believed that it was on its highest height, on the Temple Mount, that the God of all the universe chose a site in which human beings could have the closest physical relationship possible to a God who transcended all physical sites. A people holy because its members lived by times in which they and God had encountered each other believed itself doubly blessed because God had chosen not only special times but a special place — the Holy of Holies — where space and time could be transcended, and corporeal humans and incorporeal God could meet. The holiness of that place spread out to the city and the land around it, and we have prayed for the restoration of the place, the city, and the land even as the people remained alive, continuing to meet with God in time though we could not in place.

To be a Jew, therefore, is to affirm the existence of the Jewish people, which preserves holy times of meeting, and of the Jewish land, which preserves the holy place of meeting. God covenanted with Abraham that He would ensure both His temporal presence with the people and His physical presence at the place; a Jew who partakes of that covenant should affirm both the people and the place. But to affirm the existence of the people is to affirm their existence wherever they live, for they preserve the holy times of God and Israel wherever they live. Jews in the Diaspora have profoundly deepened the sense of holy time by living out that time among many other cultures and religions, who are also children of God; our presence in the Diaspora must also be seen as the working out of the divine hand, enabling us to season the holy time Jews have enjoyed in their own land with the different aspects of festivals revealed in the intermingling of Jews with Christians, Moslems, and the non-religious in Spain, Europe, Araby, and the Americas.

The diaspora also has a messianic role to play
To say that Diaspora reflects the hand of God is also to say that it has value in and of itself. One of the dangers of political Zionism is that it threatens to undercut the messianic aspect of Judaism, suggesting that the Jewish state as it exists today is all that Jews need hope for. The profundity of being Jewish has always lain in part on our suspension between polarities: affirming the present and yearning for the future; celebrating holy time and praying for holy space. The state of Israel as it exists today is not a perfect state; to declare it faultless is both to commit idolatry and to deny the messianic dream. Necessary as the state is, it must always be subject to a messianic critique, as should every other state; and it is the duty of Jews to critique it in whatever country they live because the state is part of their destiny as Jews. But the Diaspora is also a part of their destiny as Jews, and if one believes that the Messiah will come only when human beings have paved the way, then part of the reason we are in the diaspora may well be to do our part in Judaizing the societies among which we live sufficiently to prepare the way for the Messiah to enter the world. That the state of Israel has always existed side by side with the Diaspora distinguishes it from other (though not all other) nationalist movements; that it was created as the political arm of a messianic dream distinguishes it even more. Unlike the nationalisms of many other peoples, Zionists could never deny that there was a world outside their own which they had to take into account — a human world and the World

to Come. Cognizance of the human world means that the Jewish state is but one center of the Jewish people; the Diaspora is another. Cognizance of the human world also means what it meant to political Zionists in 1947 when they agreed to the U.N. Partition Plan — namely that Palestine must accommodate Arab national needs as well as Jewish ones, or Jewish national needs will continue to be frustrated as they are today, by terrorism, the continued threat of war, and the international affront of the General Assembly resolution. Cognizance that a Jewish state exists over against the World to Come means that Jews all over the world have an obligation to work for that world in whatever land they live, and particularly to desire that the groundwork for the Messiah's arrival upon the Mount of Olives should be laid as firmly as possible in the state where that mount stands. To suspend judgment on the actions of the state, to cease to work for peace between that state and its neighbors, is to be false to the real situation of the Jewish people.

Diaspora zionism and the search for peace
If this does not sound exactly like political Zionism, or religious Zionism, or cultural Zionism, perhaps on November 10, 1975 a new kind of Zionism was created — Diaspora Zionism. Diaspora Zionism recognizes the legitimacy of Jewish national, religious, and cultural existence in its own land and among the nations of the world, in lands where Jews are a minority and in the one land where they have a right to be a majority. Diaspora Zionism recognizes that time and space are equally important in the realization of the Jewish people, that the needs and demands of this world must always be balanced by the dreams and standards of the World to Come. Diaspora Zionism recognizes that every people throughout the world created by the God who scattered us is entitled to actualize itself that it might reach its own messianic potential, so long as it recognizes the same rights for its brother and sister peoples around the globe.

It would clearly be tragic if the General Assembly resolution leads to a movement to dismantle the United Nations, or to resist any more moves for peace with Arab states and for recognition of just national rights — a state if need be — for the Palestinians. It is the U.N. Security Council, after all, which laid the groundwork for negotiations between Israel and the Arabs, and which is policing the truce between Israel and her neighbors. And without the General Assembly, there would be little opportunity for Israeli diplomats even to meet their opposite numbers in other parts of the world. It is important also to remember that the United States and Europe have not always been in the right when they stood on opposite sides of issues from the smaller countries. Some check on the will of the great powers is still desirable.

As for the need to continue the search for a peaceful settlement — who after all these wars could deny it? Not the true political Zionist, who desires a Jewish state that Jews might live in safety. Not the true cultural Zionist, who desires that Israel have the breathing space truly to become a center of Jewish art and music. Not the true religious Zionist, who knows how much the exigencies of a state of siege interfere with the creation of an halachic, messianic state in holy space. And certainly not the true Diaspora Zionist, who has only now been able to say that he or she is a Zionist too, aware that only when the Diaspora and *Eretz Yisrael* together are upbuilt can the hopes of political, cultural, and religious Zionism really be fulfilled.

Racism, the unavoidable national sin

Henry Schwarzschild

The November 10 United Nations resolution terming Zionism a species of racism came with stunning ill grace, considering its source. Have so many pots ever called so few kettles black? For Rabbi Richard Levy, as for most of those who were heard reacting with proper outrage at the resolution, there is no discussion of the merits, no debate on substance, no refutation of the charge. There is merely a cry of solidarity with Israel and an outpouring of historical analogies with the 1930's. Now there is also an effort to snatch a "benefit" from the jaws of an "awful event."

The benefit that Rabbi Levy sees flowing from the U.N. vote is the slogan proclaimed by the American Zionist establishment that "every Jew is now a Zionist." The coincidence with the anniversary of the *Kristallnacht* evidently suggested the problematic parallel with Robert Weltsch's enjoinder to German Jewry *"Tragt ihn mit Stolz, den gelben Fleck!"* ("Wear the Yellow Star with pride!") But the slogan claims too much, and Rabbi Levy seems to know it, for he demands so little from it. If Zionism were merely the affirmation of the worth and necessity of the Jewish state and the Jewish people, there would have been little reason to argue for almost thirty

years about the meaning of the term. By diluting the ideological strength of the word, he hopes to make it palatable to one and all.

Zionism is essentially political nationalism
The essence of Zionism, in the history of modern Jewish political thought, has been: The Jewish State as The Solution to The Jewish Question. It has meant that Jews, dispersed, oppressed, insecure, dependent upon their host governments, would find physical security in their own nation-state. All other considerations, normalization of Jewish economics and psychics, re-establishment of *ur-halakhic* norms, revitalization of the Hebrew language and of Jewish culture, experimentation with new social arrangements, were superstructural.

The debate over the rights of the indigenous Arab population in the Holy Land, a debate as old as modern Zionism itself, has been carried on with varying degrees of concern and realism. Rabbi Levy is not far from the normative tone of that debate in defining the terms of the Jewish nation state as (a) consisting of a Jewish majority, (b) that majority creating a nation-state "in whatever image we choose," and (c) excluding the rights and national needs of minority

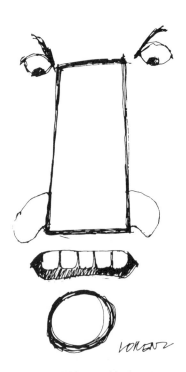

*I'm not mad at anybody.
I'm a U. N. Ambassador*

populations. Add to this the halakhic definition of the Jewish people by matrilineal descent (with exceptions that are statistically and politically insignificant), the conceptual assumption ("a land and a society where the principles of Jewish law and values will govern"), and the constitutional implementation (e.g. the Law of Return), and one would suppose that the charge of racism is at least worthy of rebuttal rather than dismissal.

Racism is inherent to ethnic nation-states

Ethnic nationalism, far from being the outdated 19th century notion that liberals and radicals of the century between 1850 and 1950 thought it was, remains the most potent force in the earth's political arrangements. The ethnic nation-state is by its nature exclusionary vis-a-vis other ethnicities. (The United States, as a state, was created *ex nihilo* rather than on the basis of a pre-existent nation, but even this did not preserve us from anti-American Indian, anti-Oriental and anti-African racisms. Many of the new post-colonial states are multi-tribal rather than ethnic; that hasn't helped either, witness Uganda.) The insistence by ethnic nations upon being in the majority in their state, upon creating the state in whatever image they choose, and upon letting ethnic-national values predominate in it, is the functional equivalent of racism. The 1960's taught us that we are all children of the 19th and 20th centuries: *Nous sommes tous des racistes* (We are all racists). It merely remains for us to acknowledge and deal with this part of our natural inheritance. If racism is a sin, it may not be one that an ethnic nation-state or its ideology can avoid, since it is built into its very definition and nature. Ethnic nation-states, indeed, are prone to many other sins as well. Perhaps it is necessary to make some hard choices.

The noblest liberal illusion is that all self-interests harmonize. But the "actualization of one people's messianic potential" (presumably "in whatever image it chooses") may cause sharp conflict with other peoples actualizing theirs. Indeed, the very phrase conjures up *jihad*, Crusades, *mission civilisatrice,* white man's burden, *Lebensraum,* and The American Century, none of them a paradigm of messianic peace.

We must support israel, but we are not all zionists

The General Assembly action, hypocritical and craven as it was, found more nations abstaining or voting-in the minority than have in recent times evinced any support for Israel. Much more commonly, the United States has been Israel's sole friend, and one of increasingly doubtful reliability at that. For Israel, a country of 3½ million, surrounded by a hostility that it has done too little to diminish, the survival of its people must be a higher priority than the actualization of its messianic potential. The Jewish national need for survival may perhaps be frustrated by more than Rabbi Levy's peculiarly disingenuous triad of terrorism, threat of war, and the U.N. resolution. What if the Jewish nation-state frustrates that need for Jewish survival because it impedes the actualization of the Arabs' messianic potential? That *would* be sauce for the gander!

The particularist eschatologist in Rabbi Levy has the Messiah arise in a Jewish land; the universalist eschatologist in him expects the Messiah from a Judaized diaspora. At the present historical reading, messianic hopes had perhaps best concentrate on his/her arrival upon God's utter desperation at the failure to Judaize either Israel or the diaspora.

The safety of the *yishuv* is of the most central and intense concern to every Jew who was able to say *"shehecheyanu"* in 1948. But nowhere (as we are ceaselessly told by Israel and its messengers) are Jews in greater danger of genocidal extinction than in Israel. The Jewish state, conceived as the *solution* to the Jewish problem, has become *the* Jewish problem. That melancholy irony proclaims the absolute end of Zionism.

In defining all Jews as Zionists, Rabbi Levy makes a dubious virtue out of a non-existent necessity. It is not necessary (nor possible) for us to be Zionists. It is impossible for us not to be *hoveve zion* (those who cherish Zion). It is only terribly hard for us to be Jews *baz'man hazeh* (in our time).

For dissent on israeli policy — part 1

Eugene B. Borowitz

(In June I was invited to address the annual meeting of the Synagogue Council of America to help open a discussion on American Jewish criticism of Israeli policies. A few days later I was asked to fulfill the same role at a meeting on the same theme by the Conference of Presidents of Major Jewish Organizations. The response to my first presentation elicited a somewhat different argument in the second speech.

The transcription of what I said to the Synagogue Council, slightly revised, is given below. The talk to the Presidents' Conference will appear in the following issue of Sh'ma. *While I do not normally permit myself to take up so much space and only in our first volume have I ever appeared in two issues running, I think this topic significant enough to merit this departure from custom. Your comments on this matter, particularly your dissent from my attitudes on dissent, are herewith warmly solicited.* — E.B.B.)

I am here to speak for no organization and I represent no institution, though I think the opinions I shall present reflect much of what is going on in the minds of many thoughtful Jews. I am not here to advocate an absolute right to Jewish dissent. There are two limitations I accept on this matter. First, I think critical views worthy of attention particularly when they come from people who are demonstrably loyal Jews, that is, people who have sent letters and telegrams on behalf of Israel, who have attended rallies, maintain organizational memberships, make pledges to Israeli causes, pay them, and, in my book, are also preferably educated, believing and, in some way, observant Jews. I think there are many such dissenters in our community. Second, a time of "clear and present danger," such as a war, is not the appropriate time for large-scale policy discussions. Of course, the question will immediately be raised as to whether, in effect, we are not now in such a time and I will discuss this matter below.

One of the difficulties in discussing this topic is its mixture of theory — religious, moral and political — and practicality. The former cannot be avoided but the latter must bear the weight of our attention.

Theoretically, it would seem, the fullest possible discussion and airing of dissent is desirable. In a moment we shall ask if that is practical but first, let me make a concise statement of the theory. In Judaism the right to disagree and argue, even about the most seriously held matters, is a cherished one. Morally, the right to think for oneself, to state one's opinions and participate in self-government is a sign of maturity and adulthood. Politically, we are trained in, are the beneficiaries of, and devoted to democratic procedures, and these call for the open airing and discussion of differences. In recent decades the Jewish community has increasingly recognized the power of these motives to open discussion. From the domination of our community by *shtadlanim* (the well-connected) we have come to more democratic organization and representation. From community fund distribution by oligarchy we have come to relatively democratic procedures. From the domination of social issues by the liberal point of view, specifically on the issues of day school and abortion, we now have a general acceptance of pluralistic opinion in the Jewish community. In other words, we have, over a period of decades come to the point where we practice the value called democratic pluralism — but with one exception: affairs concerning the State of Israel. It is obviously something of a communal anomaly to call for openness in discussion on everything but not to do so with regard to the State of Israel. Moreover, it is an interesting irony that for many years it was the Zionists and the intensely Jewish members of our community who led the fight for democracy, but who now insist that with the regard to the State of Israel it has serious limits.

The seven arguments used against dissent
As a result of all this the arguments against allowing for dissent on matters relative to the State of Israel are, on the whole, not theoretical, but practical. People argue that the theory calling for discussion is right but it does not apply in this instance and for seven reasons: 1. This is essentially a practical matter and theoretical considerations, deserve little weight. 2. Most American Jews, professors, rabbis and lay people, don't know enough on this topic to speak responsibly. 3. Only the government of the State of Israel knows what is best for the State of Israel. 4. Since the Israelis have to live with the decisions, they alone should make the decisions. 5. In any case, this is a special issue since the survival of the State of Israel and perhaps the whole of the Jewish people is involved. 6. One who cannot see this is repeating the errors of the Holocaust period. 7. If despite all this one must speak, it should be done quietly and within accepted community channels.

I would like to speak briefly to each of these seven points and then make an additional point of my own, relative, I think, to this particular body (the Synagogue Council of America).

First as to this being essentially a practical matter, it seems to me that neither Judaism nor general morality allows for such a distinction. It is precisely in social and political matters that we believers need to apply what we believe. Indeed, that is mostly what the Bible is about, theo-political situations in Martin Buber's elegant coinage. Moreover, to try to keep dissent smothered as much as possible for pragmatic reasons is counter-productive. In the contemporary social situation people are suspicious of leadership and don't trust it. Not allowing people to debate, being unwilling to recognize that there is legitimate difference of opinion, is a special sign that a leader is weak and unworthy of trust. Practically, failure to debate alternatives in advance leaves people unprepared for changes. In politics these changes can come with extraordinary suddenness — and then people are badly shaken up because they didn't realize that this was even within the realm of consideration. I suggest we American Jews are unprepared, either for a possible settlement with regard to the West Bank which gives it back; or a change of government, and the acceptance of the *Likud, Gush Emunim* policy of the annexation of the West Bank; or if, as I gather from various hints, Rabbi Joseph Baer Soloveitchik has indicated that peace could be more important than territory, should *Likud* come into power we would expect that the West Bank would be annexed only *Mafdal* (the Religious party) might then back away, and we would be utterly unprepared because these possibilities simply had not been discussed. Pragmatically, the reason for thoroughly airing alternatives is to enable us better to accept later decisions.

Who knows what is best for the State of Israel?
Second, as to most American Jews not knowing enough, I certainly agree that everyone doesn't know enough to discuss this matter or very many other matters, intelligently. But one reason we don't know enough is that we are not getting the various alternatives opened up to us. I do not know how many people in a position of leadership are thoroughly familiar with *Likud's* position on the West Bank, or of *Eretz Yisrael Hashlemah* (the Whole Land organization), or of Mapam with regard to giving greater recognition to Palestinian rights. The reason that we're not intellectually prepared to enter the discussion is because we have not been given adequate guidance in this regard. It is also true that not everyone is ill-informed, and not all the reasonably informed people agree. But on the question of the value of dissent, on this issue, and the criticism of the State of Israel, for example, I would follow the positive opinion of Prof. Hans Morgenthau whose right to a judgment on this matter is quite clear.

Third, as to only the Israeli government knowing what is best for the State of Israel, I think that it is generally true. One should dissent from the State of Israel position only on critical issues. But one must also resist the idea that government always knows best. Our post-Watergate views with regard to government, all governments, now the House of Representatives as well as the Executive branch, make us skeptical of all people in power. Israelis are human — they are not beyond mistakes. They have made blunders and have engaged in self-protection. Indeed, as they, unfortunately, would be the first to say, their government too has known malfeasance and scandal. Specifically at this moment to put one's trust in government policies and never criticize it, is not to admit the reality, that the present Israeli government is weak and badly divided from within. Moreover, it is not clear what the relationship of the Rabin government is to its citizenry and to its real desires. Therefore, only to follow government policy right now is unwise. In fact, it seems to me, there are often issues well worth arguing. When a few years ago the State of Israel gave us its hints or more than that, that we should oppose the Koch Bill to admit 50,000 Russian Jews on special visas to the United States, I think the Government of Israel was wrong, and needed to be resisted. I think the Government of Israel was wrong when it thought that what was good for Israel was good for the United States and quietly pushed the candidacy of Nixon.

For the Israelis sake and ours we need a change.
It is clear to me why the Government of Israel would avoid encouraging U.S. Jews to debate their policies and prefer a continuous show of unanimity. They've got enough trouble. To educate us and to carry us along is a terrible burden, I admit. But the effects of

The arms budget debate: positive

this sort of Israeli leadership on us is bad for two specific reasons. First, for what it does to us as people. It makes us schizoid — democratic in everything, open and arguing, but on one subject suddenly not allowed to use our intelligence and conscience. Or we may say it infantilizes us. We become like children waiting for daddy or mommy to tell us what is good for us rather than being allowed to use our own minds — and this with regard to something terribly important to us. Secondly, this sort of leadership by the State of Israel is politically unwise for it tends to devalue the protests we make. If we always jump when somebody picks up a phone in the Israeli Consulate then our activity is discounted in advance. For example, I think most people took our delegation to President Ford with regard to transport planes to Egypt as a charade on both sides. Simply to follow the Israeli Government in every case is not good for either of us.

Moreover, there is presently a serious question regarding the government's position and Israeli feelings generally concerning the West Bank. The recent *Gush Emunim* march provoked many anxieties. Will the Rabin government be able to hold to its present policy in view of the pressures it is under? Who will win the next election and what will the next government of the State of Israel be like? Then, too, the Arab elections and West Bank riots dispelled our myth that the Arabs had never had it so good as when the Israelis were able to occupy their territory and bring them as many benefits as in fact they have. In other words, there are serious questions about the present government and the relation of that government to the future of the State of Israel and that is why we need more discussion rather than simply to follow the government line.

The question is not decisions but voicing opinions
Fourth as to only Israelis making the decisions about the future, that is absolutely correct. They alone can and should make the decisions about their own State. But that does not mean that we must keep quiet. We have argued with regard to the Soviet Union, that world opinion is a factor and that therefore the opinions of people around the world need to be expressed. Therefore our opinions and that of the United States with regard to Israeli actions also need to be expressed. Moreover, the Israelis keep telling us that we are one Jewish people. In fact, what they do in their decisions will affect us and they want our support, not only for the decisions but for all the future. Hence, we should be entitled to think through our opinions in open dis-

cussion with one another and voice our views. To be sure, they must make the decisions and do what they think best, but we should be allowed not only to talk, but to learn from them and let them know how we see their various alternatives. It is very important for us to recognize that it isn't as if all the Israelis have one point of view on political matters. They themselves are divided. We Americans who want to talk about these matters are only picking up options that in the State of Israel are part of the conversation of every citizen. We should think through with *Gush Emunim* and *Likud* what we are willing to sacrifice to take and hold the West Bank. We should consider with Yigal Yadin under what circumstances we might be willing to talk to Arafat. We should be in a position of debating back and forth with Lova Eliav to what extent it is necessary for us to recognize Palestinian rights. American Jews are not creating issues — the issues are there and every government knows this. If they're doing their homework they also have a good sense of the variety of what U.S. Jews are thinking, despite the facade of solidarity, the press releases and our use of *The New York Times* as the newspaper of record for the American Jewish community. The State of Israel will be better prepared in small part and we will be better prepared in large part for their eventual decisions if we can argue over the options now.

Survival as the code word for silencing critics
Fifth, as for this being a matter of the survival of the State of Israel or the Jewish people, indeed I'd agree, in the face of clear and present danger, survival would be a reason for keeping quiet. But the word "survival" cannot simply be taken at face value. It should not be made a code word for "shut up." For 20-some years now "survival" has been used to silence all criticism about the State of Israel within the American Jewish community. I recall clearly how, nearly two decades ago, when the Central Conference of American Rabbis at its Atlantic City Convention debated a resolution on the State of Israel, the word was passed that we should vote it down because it was bad for the State of Israel. One can't keep saying "survival" every time an issue comes up for decades and still expect people to listen. Indeed, the words "survival" and "national security" have been abused by all governments. When somebody says "national security" and "survival" today, one thinks of Nixon and the break-in in Ellsberg's psychiatrist's office. There is certainly at least substantial difference of opinion as to whether

the term "survival" has a literal relationship to current political-social issues. It is a matter of simple historical data that the State of Israel did survive without the West Bank. Without it again it might still go on to survive. I do not think it utterly unreasonable to suggest that the people of Israel has survived and can survive with even a somewhat goegraphically limited State of Israel. I do not advocate these positions at the moment. I only point out that such matters are at least worth discussing, so that the word "survival" cannot mean an absence of discussion. In my opinion, Jewish, moral and political reasons suggest that our survival has a better chance when there is more intelligent debate rather than less.

Are dissenters aiding the enemies of the Jews?

Sixth, as to our not repeating the errors of the Holocaust period, I think that is a perfectly legitimate and worthy concern. We American Jews want our leaders to guard us. We want them not to cooperate with our enemies. We want them if they are going to make a mistake to err on the side of over-sensitivity. But that doesn't mean that we want them to gag us. Not every critic of Israeli policy is an anti-Semite. Very many of them are Israelis. Debate on some issues would make clear how seriously we take the fundamental agreement about which we don't debate, namely that the State of Israel must live and flourish. I think it is terribly important to distinguish between areas of flexibility and fundamental principle. And I point out to you what using "Holocaust" as a gag rule to shut up critics has done to the word, emptying it of some of its serious and sanctified associations.

Seventh, as to dissent being quiet and within channels I think it reasonable to measure the effect of the medium one uses for one's dissent, and to be responsible for an appropriate choice of forum. Some limited things I think can be accomplished within the community. Thus a recent statement of 100 varied American Jews with regard to the *Kadum* settlement was published in Israel, not in the United States. The limit of this kind of within-the-community activities has to be recognized immediately, namely, American Jewish organizations are dominated by the State of Israel and its welfare. They follow its lead. Indeed, they over-react. They sometimes don't even wait for hints from the Israeli Embassy. Take the recent case of the Mexican boycott. Our organizational leaders were so eager to show their militance that when the Israelis reversed policy on us, we were embarrassed because we could not back-track without looking silly. Moreover, because our organizations are so deeply committed to the State of Israel, there is a problem of dissent in their midst being truly effective. It is quickly co-opted and handled within the power process. I suggest that it is the feeling that dissent is not being recognized by the establishment that creates new organizations. That happened a few years ago with the Jewish Defense League; it happened with the Anti-Poverty group. I suggest to you, facetiously to be sure, but nonetheless seriously, that *Breira* is a creation of American Jewish community leadership.

Dissent is real — what shall we do with it?

The real problem is what shall be done with the feeling of dissent which now truly exists? Stonewalling has

The arms budget debate: negative

not worked well and it doesn't look like a good policy for the future. It will only create more disagreement. Maybe we can get away with some token dissent, just enough to allow the mood to pass without substantially altering things. I think that's probably the most likely policy and depending on what happens it may work out. But I believe that it would be far better leadership to take over and sponsor dissent. Let the establishment set up high level debates of Jewish differences of opinion concerning the State of Israel, its government, its problems, its potential courses of action. There would probably be some short-range loss since there's probably more dissent than most of us imagine. But I think there would be a great long-range gain. It would destroy the dissent issue in our community and it would educate us for the future possible actions of the State.

One last comment, particularly for religious leaders. Should not something be done to set limits to the co-optation of religious life to serve the national needs of the State of Israel? We gave Yom Kippur away for bonds, which perhaps we can justify though it is an investment not a charity and we take interest from fellow Jews. Then we are told that *Shavuot* Sunday ought to be used for Federation mobilization day. And the UJA suggests through its Rabbinical Council that we get congregations to agree to get 100% pledging with the congregation then taking the responsibility of collecting the pledges people do not pay. Note, there is no disclosure to the general community as to how United Jewish Appeal funds to the State of Israel are used and there is no democratic community control over those funds. It is the only place in the Jewish community where you don't know and can't know. Synagogues are asked to be this servile. Worse, as to having 100% campaigns for UJA pledges, may I remind you that we don't have anything like that for any one or all of the ten commandments! A campaign for 100% observance of any directly religious matter in our congregation isn't even a possibility, yet fund-raising for overseas relief can claim this sort of devotion from us.

This is not a matter of being anti-Israel. It is an effort to admit the continuing displacement of Torah by nationalism claiming to be *mitzvah*. I think my even raising this question will disturb you. Any sign of independence in our community is immediately considered *trefah* (unclean). I suggest that this mood, that you can't even raise such an issue, is wrong for

human beings in general and Jews in particular. It is a major indication to me of why we need a more independent stand, one which will not just tolerate, but which will sponsor positive dissent.

Israel — public debate is irresponsible
Geoffrey Wigoder

In a way by sending you any response I am committing myself to a certain acceptance of your basic thesis. *(Sh'ma 6/116-117)* If I accepted the premise that Israeli issues should not be discussed by American Jews, I would have to accept that Israelis have no say in internal quarrels between you and the U.S. Jewish establishment. And truth to tell, I do have the feeling that in the words of the foreman of the jury in the "You Don't Have To Be Jewish" record — "We shouldn't mix in."

Nevertheless, I will permit myself certain reactions starting with my negative vibrations to your use of the terms "dissent" and "dissenters" to describe the position you say you stand for. You state "We only want to think through for ourselves matters regularly debated in the State of Israel," in other words the right to express democratic criticism of certain aspects of the policy of the Israel Government. Although semantically speaking you may be justified in calling this dissent, the fact is that a "dissenter" has become a loaded word, especially in its most familiar connotation relating to Protestantism. It implies a *kopher be-ikkar* (apostate) and would perhaps be appropriate for those Jews who deny the validity of the State of Israel. But if it is to be applied to everyone who does not accept all aspects of government policy, then nearly everyone in the State of Israel is a dissenter. It reminds me of the use of the term "Black Panther" by the Israeli-Morroccan group protesting social conditions: it was chosen to shock. I am suspicious of an intellectual protest utilizing emotive words to achieve an effect.

Don't act from a diaspora perspective
While sympathizing with the above-mentioned principle you seek to establish, I am worried by aspects of its application. The strength (and sometimes the weakness) of Zionism from its inception lay in its democracy. All vital issues relating not only to the world but to developments in the *yishuv* (Jewish community in Palestine) were open for all to argue.

When Weizmann brought the non-Zionists into the Agency, he was willing for them to have a say, although his colleagues in Palestine were less than happy about this. Today, when virtually the whole Jewish world has become Zionist in the broadest (and, I think, basic) sense, it is natural that all problems of Zionism and of Israel should be open for discussion. The tendency to stifle discussion and to present an over-roseate picture is counterproductive, especially in view of the burgeoning intellectualism of the Jewish communities and the all-pervasive impact of mass-media. Issues exercising Israelis are familiar to the world at large and form legitimate subjects for concern among all Jews. Indeed part of the problem in integrating immigrants has sometimes been the result of the distortedly optimistic picture they have received prior to settling.

However it is one thing to discuss issues and another to attempt to influence directly the policy of the Israeli Government. The situation today is not the same as it was before 1948. The factor of sovereignty is crucial and the Government of Israel, for better or worse, democratically represents the people of Israel and must not be subjected to policy pressures from world Jewry. That was the point made by Ben-Gurion vis-a-vis Abba Hillel Silver shortly after the establishment of the State. And the fact remains that notwithstanding all open communications, things do look different from here. To give a personal example, I remember that when I was a student at Oxford in 1946, some of us were attracted by the concept of a bi-national state and considered voting in the Zionist Congress elections of that year for Hashomer Hatzair because of its espousal of that policy. In the end our dislike of Marxism led us not to support them. But when I came to live in Israel in 1949, I saw in retrospect that we had been living in cloud-cuckoo-land. Seen from the harsh reality of life here, the wooliness of many liberal attitudes was forced in on us, and I could not help being alarmed by my own *chutzpa* in trying to judge a vital issue from distant ivory towers.

Speak, but don't put pressure on israel

My feeling is that it is perfectly legitimate for you, if you so desire, to try and project your views to the Israeli population and to identify and link up with any like-minded group here, just as Poalei Zion link up with the Israel Party, religious groups with Mizrachi, or General Zionists with Gahal or the Inde-

pendent Liberal Party. What is not legitimate is for any of these groups outside Israel to try and force the hand of the Israeli Government. Even more potentially alarming would be attempts by Jewish individuals or groups to seek to influence the U.S. Government to undermine official policies of Israel. I pray you may never have to choose between American interests and Israel's interests, and should such an eventuality *has va-halila* (God forbid) arise, that you will adopt dignified precedents, such as the stand of British Jewry in 1945-48 and French Jewry in 1967. Meanwhile I am sorry the word "survival" turns you off and makes you think of Nixon and Ellsberg. I am not quite so blasé. I have been living with it for 27 years and today it looms even larger than in the past.

I have just attended a seminar on Zionism held under the auspices of President Katzir. Michael Walzer of Harvard and Julius Gould of Nottingham University both — like you — described the troubled minds of intellectuals regarding Israel's Middle East policy. President Gottschalk of Hebrew Union College, in opposing them, used the family metaphor — you don't go around criticizing your wife (or at any rate you shouldn't). Of course this is an over-simplification, and is no new argument to you. Yet it has a valid application. By all means discuss the issues facing Israel — this is healthy — but do not try and influence general public opinion in your country in the hope that in this way you can bring them to put pressure on us. I strongly object to those groups who resort to the general press under such circumstances. You correctly say that the media will in any case pick up fundamental points that are being hotly debated. But this is not the same as *initiating* such debates in the media and often thereby blowing up issues out of all proportion.

Other issues may also be discussed — carefully

Finally, after reading your two speeches, I am concerned at the narrowness of your expressed interest in Israel issues. The only subject you bring up (repeatedly) is the West Bank. Of course, this is basic, but it is only one of many problems bothering us here in Israel. Why don't you mention the quality of life in Israel with its effect on *aliya* (immigration) and *yerida*? (emigration) What about economic policies? What about labor and capitalism? What about sociological issues and culture? I know you are concerned with the subject of non-establishment religion, but why don't you make an issue of that on which you are a *bar-samcha?* (authority) Why zero in solely on the West Bank? I do agree that you are entitled to equal time with the Lubavicher. In a way your positions are parallel, although on different sides of the Green Line. The Lubavicher Rebbe expresses his support for settlement in the West Bank and encourages those who follow him in U.S. Jewry and in Israel to support such settlement. But fair is fair — he sticks within his context. You are surely entitled to the same consideration and freedom — and the same context.

Doubtless my views are much closer to yours than to those of the Lubavicher. But I do not want my government's policy to be in any way subject to direct pressure by you or him or any such group. I am as concerned as you with policies that have been adopted and that might be adopted. I would be delighted if you would follow the precedent of Meir Kahane and come and try to influence us from within. But if not, I side with the views you quote of Golda Meir and Prof. Avineri encouraging full and frank discussion within a Jewish context of all issues facing Israel, assuming of course that there is a basic commitment to Israel's survival (excuse the expression) and the recognition that we are, after all, two sides of the same cohen.

Zeev jabotinsky: 100 years
Daniel J. Elazar

Who says politics have no influence on intellectual life? Would there be serious public commemoration of the 100th birthday of Zeev Jabotinsky had it not been for the fact that the Likud won the election in Israel in 1977? Not likely. For thirty years and more, Jabotinsky was one of those non-persons in Israel and the Jewish world of the kind which abound in the contemporary world as a result of political fortune. The ruling Labour Party made him a non-person for the same reasons that it portrayed Menachem Begin and his supporters as uncivilized fascists— it is easier to beat the opposition by painting it as irrelevant, intolerable and non-existent, until it is too strong to be dismissed. Now Jabotinsky is rehabilitated, at least sufficiently to pay him some mind. Perhaps the most important lesson of his rehabilitation is that we should not allow such things to happen. The importance of Jabotinsky or any other public figure must be judged by less partisan criteria.

What of Jabotinsky himself? An important fact about him was that he was right. That is to say, in almost every position he took, he was far more right than wrong in his understanding of hard realities and Jewish necessities. The second most pronounced characteristic was that for many reasons it was usually impossible to act upon his diagnoses. That is not to say the Jewish people should not have tried to act upon them. One of the reasons that it was impossible to act was that the Jews were not yet ready to exercise the will necessary to do so.

In relatively circumscribed matters, such as the creation of the Jewish Legion in World War I, Jabotinsky and a few others could act alone and secure the desired result. Today all Jews celebrate that effort. When it was a question of forecasting the imminent destruction of European Jewry and the necessity for a mass migration to *Eretz Israel*, then it was not something that could be done by a few people operating alone; the whole of the Jewish people had to be convinced and this proved to be impossible. Jabotinsky was right but his solution was never implemented; the Holocaust was the result. When Jabotinsky forecast that it would take military action for the Jews to gain and hold their state, Jewish liberals and socialists recoiled in horror and refused to believe. Once again he was right, not pleasant, but right.

Following in Jabotinsky's Footsteps
In many respects, the heirs of Jabotinsky have continued in the Jabotinsky tradition. When Menachem Begin resigned from Israel's wall-to-wall coalition government in 1970 at the time of the cease-fire which ended the War of Attrition, to protest the Egyptians' immediate violation of the cease-fire by bringing up their missiles to the edge of the Suez Canal, and demanded that Israel take action, he was right and was proven right three years later in the *Yom Kippur* War. (I know we should not talk about these things today because it is not nice, but as Jabotinsky teaches, there is right, and there is nice, and we should not confuse the two.) But perhaps his being right was "inoperative" because of American pressures on Israel to accept the cease-fire even as it was being violated.

So, too, with the settlements in Judea and Samaria. The need for a Jewish presence in those territories for national and security reasons is rightly perceived. Being in the government, there was an opportunity for Jabotinsky's heirs to exercise the will necessary to operate on their perceptions which so many declared to be unimplementable even if right in principle. Not every aspect of its settlement policy need be accepted as wise to come to this conclusion. The outcome of this effort is as yet uncertain, but at least this time we have a chance to try to be right, and to make the right operational. For this, Jabotinsky would have been grateful.

Need for Jewish/Western Alliance

People who follow such matters are well aware of Jabotinsky's teachings regarding the impending demise of European Jewry, the necessity for military effort to establish the state, and the desirability of a Jewish state in the whole of historic *Eretz Israel*. But there are two other teachings of Jabotinsky's which retain great relevance for us. One is the necessity that the Jewish people be allied with the West. Jabotinsky saw an intimate connection between Jewish and Western civilization. More than that, he saw that in the geo-politics of the 20th century world, the Jews' hope lay with whatever great power would lead the West. In his time, Great Britain was the focus of his attentions but the principle was more than simply an anglophile one. Begin's solidly pro-American stance continues this strain in Jabotinsky's teaching.

Jabotinsky also recognized the importance of religious belief in the shaping of a people. No less secular than his socialist Zionist enemies, he did not make their mistake of seeking to promote secularism. Rather, he sought to develop a Jewish civil religion which would retain certain beliefs and ceremonial forms, particularly the public ones, and integrate them in the service of national goals. Menachem Begin's public religiosity is very much in the spirit of Jabotinsky's civil religion. Such a civil religion is not, in my opinion, adequate for Jews but it is certainly better than the secularism which it is seeking to replace.

In fact, Jabotinsky forecast what would be the trend among Israeli leaders, including those in the Labour camp, and increasingly among diaspora leaders as well, namely a definition of being Jewish that is basically political in character but which seeks to rest upon religious foundations that synthesize traditional religious expressions with the political goals to which they are committed— in other words, a civil religion. Judaism lends itself to civil religion because in some respects all of Judaism embodies a civil dimension, although it would be unfair to characterize *halachic* or Pharasaic Judaism as designed for civil purposes; rather it is the other way around. Saduccean religion was more in the way of a civil religion and Jabotinsky's thinking represents a first contribution to the revival of Saduccean Judaism in our times, which elsewhere I have argued is part of the true normalization of the Jewish people.

Increasingly, it is becoming clear that Jabotinsky was

indeed a giant in the Jewish national revival. Unfortunately for him and for the Jewish people, his genius was in foreseeing events long before others. He flowered before his time and all of us are poorer because we could not keep pace with him.

Facing the possibility of a third exile
Marian Henriquez Neudel

I have long believed that "thinking the unthinkable" is the last refuge of intellectual machismo. I take no pleasure in finding myself doing it. I do not look forward to the events projected in this article. I dread them at least as much as does anyone who reads it, and would give much to be proved wrong by future history. Specifically, I am referring to the theological and political potential for a Third Exile.

To examine that potential, it is first necessary to look at the theological weight now borne by the State of Israel. To the early secular Zionists, and to the Reconstructionists, the founding of the State was unquestionably a quasi-messianic event. To many orthodox groups it was, on the contrary, a human usurpation of the messianic function. Today, some Hasidim and groups such as Neturei Karta still hold this latter position. In fact, Neturei Karta has extended "official" recognition to the PLO as the rightful government of the land on which Israel stands.

Most other religious groups take positions somewhere in between. The Reform movement, seeing the Messiah as an event or an era rather than a person, has not felt officially obliged to identify that event with any part of our recent history. The Conservative movement and most orthodox groups are explicitly supportive of the State, but give it no official theological function.

All of this theological caution is utterly irrelevant to the gut feelings of the average Jew—of whatever religious or political persuasion—on the street. Whether the term "messianic" itself means anything to the given individual, Israel is seen in messianic terms by almost all of us. It comes as close as any historical event can to giving meaning to six million otherwise incomprehensible deaths. It comes as close as any historical event can to healing the basic insecurity of the Jew hopelessly outnumbered in a non-Jewish (and often anti-Jewish) world. The fact that the official theological categories have not yet caught up to this reality is the theologians' problem.

Blinded By Messianism

Because of this deep-seated, unspoken, messianic

Zionism, we have been reluctant to look at the State of Israel in the light *either* of modern political reality *or* of the biblical dialectic in which the people of Israel and the land of Israel first became the state of Israel. That curious duality is at the very root of the modern State's existence, brought into being as it was both by an armed struggle of self-determination against a vast but exhausted empire, and by a gesture of belated contrition by the nations of the world for having allowed the Holocaust to happen.

Because of that unconscious messianism, representatives of the Israeli government, and its advocates, can say—often in virtually the same breath—both "Israel is entitled to behave like [i.e., as badly as] the other nations of the world" *and* "Israel has a unique divinely-given mission in world history." Indeed, most of us do not boggle at demanding for Israel both the privileges that go with a divinely ordained mission without the corresponding obligations, and the opportunities for self-aggrandizement available to a "nation like other nations" without the risks other nations run in taking advantage of those opportunities. Israel need not behave with the caution which other nations use in assessing their self-interest—because God will protect us. And Israel need not behave in accordance with the covenant whereby the Land was given to us in the first place—because that would be inconsistent with modern political reality.

That double ostrich game is even less constructive now than it was 15 years ago. If, as the secular Zionists and the orthodox claim to believe, the modern Israeli state is a nation like other nations, it had better face the fact that the nations it is *most* like are *small* nations, not superpowers. Like any small nation today, it can determine its own destiny only to the extent that it either does not tread on the toes of the superpowers, or has allies to protect it when it does. It had better also face the reality that, of the available allies in the world, the United States may be (given its dependence on Arab oil, and the continued influence of anti-Semitism in the State Department) among the least reliable. In the long run, Israel's best chance for security may lie with the nations of Eastern and Western Europe, or even with the Third World, in a technology-for-oil swap, improbable as that may seem to us now.

The Covenant Has Two Sides

And if, on the other hand, Israel exists today because of a miracle, a gift from God to the Jewish people, then that gift was presumably given subject to the same strictures whose violation is traditionally seen as the cause of the First and Second Exiles. The *Mishnah* states that the First Temple was destroyed by reason of

bloodshed, immorality, and idolatry, and the Second for causeless hatred and malevolence. Jeremiah's understanding of the covenant of the Land is: "...if you thoroughly execute justice between a person and his neighbor; if you do not oppress the stranger, the fatherless, and the widow, and do not shed innocent blood in this place, nor walk after other gods to your hurt; then will I cause you to dwell in this place, in the land that I gave to your fathers for ever and ever...will you steal, murder, and commit adultery, and swear falsely, and offer to Baal, and walk after other gods...? I will cast you out of my sight." (Jer. 7:5-7, 9, 15) For a human being to demand of Israel a higher standard of behavior than is expected of other nation-states may be unfair, anti-Semitic, or self-hating. But if God demands it, are we who have accepted the gift in any position to refuse the conditions under which it was given?

That is not an idle question. The treatment of Arabs and oriental Jews in Israel may well qualify as oppression of our brothers and sisters and of strangers in our midst. The annexation of more and more of the land won in the 1967 war brings an ever-increasing number of those strangers into our midst, and breeds tensions that make it increasingly difficult to avoid oppressing them and still maintain political stability. The often violent disputes between different orthodox groups, and between orthodox and secularist Jews may well constitute causeless hatred. The relentless exploitation of the Israeli environment, to a degree not even imaginable in the Biblical era, when the *shabbats* for the land were first imposed, may well be a prelude to the same sort of involuntary fallowness of which the Torah warns us (Lev. 26:34-5). Even idolatry, remote as that may seem to us, is perhaps not beyond or behind us. It is hard to know what else to call the recent pronouncement of a right-wing rabbi that every grain of sand in the Sinai is as holy as the Torah.

Israeli's Existence Is Not Guaranteed

Let us be honest with ourselves. Either we accept Israel as a gift and a miracle—in which case we must accept also the possibility of losing it as it was lost twice before, for violations of the conditions of the gift—or we see it as a political fact, a nation like other nations—in which case the Israeli government will have to be either stronger, smarter, richer, or luckier than those of other states in that area to survive.

Either way, we must accept that there are no guarantees. We must accept that the stakes are both higher and lower than we normally think: higher, because a Third Exile *is* a possibility, and lower, because if (God forbid) it happens, it need *not* mean the destruction of the Jewish people as a whole.

Given that the average life span of governments in the turbulent part of the world in which Israel lies is 200-400 years, and that that average has been getting noticeably shorter in this century, we must still accept the possibility of what is now unthinkable to us. *Only* by accepting that possibility can we take realistic steps to increase the likelihood of Israel's continued survival, from the perspective of either religious imperative or political reality.

The shame of american jewry
Eugene B. Borowitz

(Erev Shabat Shuvah, just before the Sabbath of Repentance.)

This has been the second most shameful week in the history of American Jewry. The first occurred decades ago when our leaders had indications of the Final Solution and kept silent. This week, after the massacres at Sabra and Shatila, silence would have been a lesser moral lapse than what our non-dove "leaders" did say. Despite each day's mounting evidence of Israeli responsibility, collusion and complicity, they persisted in denials and evasions, in hair-splitting and side-stepping, and, the last refuge of the high-minded, calls for more information. Only the most odious comparisons will do for such behavior. It uncannily recapitulated what the "decent" anti-Semites used to say when confronted by the early evidence of the Holocaust.

The only moral hero of this week was William Safire, the conservative columnist of the *New York Times*. Alone of all the Jewish supporters of the Israeli invasion of Lebanon he did not waffle. He had conscience enough to know when ethical demands outweigh political and ethnic responsibilities, and he said so with no dodging. Our Jewish institutional leaders had long assured us each time they supported the Israelis despite their excesses, that they certainly had not issued the Israelis a blank check. Sabra and Shatila apparently did not overdraw their backing for this Israeli administration. One can only wonder now what would.

The Cost of Faulty Priorities

For all its knowledge of Torah, the rabbinate generally has not displayed greater moral sensitivity. If my informal survey of *Rosh Hashanah* sermons is indicative, our "spiritual leaders" are so invested in group loyalty and nationalism that even inside the synagogue on the Day of Judgment they cannot bear to criticize the State of Israel's government. Since *yom tov*, British Jewry has had the stirring example of Chief

Rabbi Immanuel Jakobovits' unequivocal, public denunciation of Israeli guilt. American Jews have had to settle for rabbinical voices calling for an impartial investigation. In the meantime, our ears still ring with sermons about the books of Joshua and Judges, exhortations to political realism, insistence that the State of Israel be judged only like all other states and pronouncements that one ought not play by moral rules in an immoral world—uttered while the massacres were going on.

All of us must share in the shame that has fallen on our people this week. By insisting a united front was our greatest American Jewish good, we may have convinced the Israeli leadership that they could do anything they wished and still count on us to lobby Congress for whatever they want. By effectively stifling dissent among us, we have not prepared American Jews for the possibility that one day a public protest against an Israeli act or policy might become necessary. By smearing every critic as self-hating, self-seeking or worse, we have inhibited our leaders from recognizing a Jewish moral crisis, much less standing up to it and saying, no matter who heard, that we oppose governments whose acts outrage the conscience of any decent human being.

Avoiding the Repetition Compulsion

Henry Schwarzschild (*Sh'ma* 12/236, Sept. 3, 1982) was wrong when he said that the invasion of Lebanon marked a turning point in Jewish history. It turned out merely to be "business as usual." But I agree that the massacres at Sabra and Shatila must profoundly alter the relations between American Jewry and the State of Israel if Judaism is to survive as anything more than tribalism.

We must now be rid of our old ideology which subordinated all of Judaism to ethnicity. Judaism does *not* need a political entity in the Land of Israel to survive worldwide. A State of Israel that can conspire with Phalangist thugs is *not* a proper response to the Holocaust. And we are *not* one people if that means condoning blatantly immoral Israeli acts.

I have not given up my membership in any of the "major American Jewish organizations" and I propose this year, as every year, to pay my increased pledge to my Federation (though I certainly intend to earmark my donation). But neither of these social instrumentalities nearly represents my understanding of Judaism or my Jewish priorities.

I fear that within a few weeks our communal structure will once again reassert itself and we shall be engulfed in a campaign of white-washing and cover-up. Our first duty then will be to reject the thesis that the reality of anti-Semitism entitles us to gloss over Jewish sinfulness.

We need to go on to vote against all resolutions which seek unanimity by avoiding genuine issues. We ought to challenge the undemocratic maneuver of the American Zionist organizations—including, surprisingly, Hadassah—who helped call off elections for the forthcoming World Zionist Congress, thus effectively denying proper representation to tens of thousands of new Reform and Conservative religious Zionists. And we ought to insist that our Federations make available to us locally the reports that their leaders receive about the actual distribution in the State of Israel of that portion of our U.J.A. funds which go there. Most of us only know that we are doing *Tzedakah*. We haven't any idea what sorts of institutions or causes are the main beneficiaries of our help—or whether, if we knew as much about them as about our American Jewish organizations, we would consider these priorities reasonable.

Positively, the time has come to acknowledge that nothing is more important for the survival of Jews and Judaism than the rounding-out and implementation of an American Jewish piety. Ethical as well as Zionist, spiritual as well as cerebral, everyday as well as *Shabatdik*, pluralistic as befits this environment and the diversity of human temperament, it will make the service of God unequivocally our highest Jewish priority. There never should have been any question about that.

Choosing to commit the sin of silence
Simcha Kraus

There is a well known *halacha* in Tractate *Sanhedrin* which states that when, in a capital case, all of the judges agree that the defendant is guilty, he is released. The reason for this seemingly strange *halacha* is that when an entire *Sanhedrin*, all the judges, cannot find virtue in the accused— if there isn't one who is able to find a redeeming factor— there is something lacking in the judicial process. It is impossible, taught the Rabbis, for matters to be so simple, so black and white, that no one, amongst the judges, can find a mitigating circumstance.

Rabbi Eugene Borowitz, in his passionate denunciation of the "shame of American Jewry," (*Sh'ma* 12/239) wonders why Jewish leaders spoke out in defense of Israel, instead of forcefully protesting against the government of Israel for its role in the Beirut massacre.

SIMCHA KRAUS *is Rabbi of Young Israel of Hillcrest, Queens, New York.*

Perhaps the answer may be found in the fact that the *whole* world arose to condemn Israel. Without exception, before all the facts were in, the *Sanhedrin* of world opinion unanimously arose to condemn Israel. And when this happens there must be something wrong.

Let us be honest. What transpired in Shatila and Sabra was a tragedy. It was a tragedy of immense proportions. It was something of which every Jew, who identifies as such, should be ashamed and contrite and heartbroken.

But did the events in Beirut warrant the outcry, the denunciation, the unanimous condemnation that followed? Did the protests not come too fast and too furious? Did not the world protest too loudly at this event in comparison with other events of equal magnitude? Should not this over-response lead a thinking person, and particularly a thinking Jew, to question the motives and sincerity of the protest? Perhaps the world is concerned with a different agenda.

Rabbi Abraham Chein cites a wonderful *Midrash*: After Cain killed Abel all the animals and birds of the world assembled to avenge Abel from the hands of Cain. God glanced at this assemblage and recognized the serpent amongst them. "He who would kill Cain will be punished", God said. In this convening of the animal *Sanhedrin*, God understood that the serpent wanted to avenge Abel. But God realized that the serpent's concern was not so much the blood of Abel who was dead, but rather the blood of Cain, who was still alive.

True Concern For the Victims?

What I sensed in this unanimous outcry by the various governments, the media, etc., against the Beirut massacre, was not the concern for the victims who were dead. It was rather, a concern about the government of Israel, the stewardship of Prime Minister Begin, indeed, the existence of Israel itself.

Let me briefly document, albeit in sketchy form, my point.

Item: Just a few days after the Beirut massacre, the *New York Times* had a special pull-out section detailing every hour of the massacre, in minute detail. This can be called good journalism. Except that when one remembers that in Cambodia, millions of people were butchered without the *Times* publishing such a section, one wonders why this case had such priority rating.

Item: Just a few weeks ago (Oct. 12th), the *Times*

reported a story of a massacre in Guatemala. The story concerned 300 men, women and children, who were massacred by the *armed forces* of Guatemala. Somehow this story found itself respectfully hidden on page 3A. For some reason it did not warrant the headlines on the front page which were reserved for Shatila and Sabra.

Item: Also buried on page 3A was a report by Amnesty International that since March, 2600 people— men, women and children— have been massacred in Guatemala. In other words, an average of 325 people a month. That is Shatila and Sabra eight times over. I fail to note the great outcry of protest. I fail to see, anywhere, great remorse, contrition and self-flagellation. Here, presumably, the world *Sanhedrin* sees more mitigating circumstances.

The action of the Jewish leadership is likened by Rabbi Borowitz to the silence during the Holocaust period. It is now but a month after the events in Beirut. Already, an Israeli commission of inquiry has begun the task of investigating what transpired. Israelis, by the thousands, staged protests. The Israeli media was terribly critical of the whole affair. Can you imagine how many Jews would have been saved if 400,000 Jews would have marched on Washington in 1942?

I am Guilty of Ethnic Chauvinism

"We must now be rid of our old ideology which subordinated Judaism to ethnicity," writes Rabbi Borowitz. Certainly there is more to *Yahadut* (Judaism) than ethnicity. There is *Torah*. There is the love of *Eretz Yisrael*. But is it too much to ask of rabbis and communal spokesmen that in a case of *legitimate* doubt, they at least withhold negative judgment, when it comes to *acheinu bnai yisrael*, (Our brothers, the children of Israel) until the facts are clear. I do not know about others, but for myself, in the current mood, in the current climate of blatant and open anti-Semitism, when the whole animal *Sanhedrin* is willing to condemn Israel at the slightest pretext, I plead guilty to this old, outdated ethnic chauvinism. I will not and cannot join this chorus of condemnation before all the facts are in.

Rabbi Borowitz further states: "Judaism does *not* need a political entity in the land of Israel to survive world wide. A state of Israel that can conspire with Phalangist thugs is *not* a proper response to the Holocaust. And we are not one people if that means condoning blatantly immoral acts."

Let us assume, *arguendo*, that the Israeli leadership, including Prime Minister Begin, knew about the events from the very beginning. Let us assume this worst of all scenarios. Is this statement of Rabbi Borowitz warranted? Does Rabbi Borowitz not confuse the government of Israel with the State of Israel? Does Rabbi Borowitz really mean that, because of Beirut, the State of Israel has lost its right to exist? Have all the events since 1948 lost their redeeming value? Are they to be wiped off the record because of Beirut? Is the very legitimacy of the State of Israel to be judged by this event alone? Further: the whole chain of events that led to Israeli "cooperation with Phalangist thugs", i.e. the safety of the northern borders— is that not to be taken into consideration before condemning Israeli policy? Is the blood of Jewish men, women and children any less red than the blood of Palestinians?

Rabbi Borowitz frames his remarks in the powerful imagery of *teshuva* (repentance). His words demand a response from the same frame of reference. The Rabbis in the *Midrash*, commenting on Reuven's remorse and contrition over the fact that he failed to prevent the sin perpetrated against Joseph by his brothers, said that Reuven was the first to "open with *Teshuva*." Reuven, in other words, was the first person to repent. The question is obvious. Adam before him had sinned and repented. Cain had sinned and repented. What does the *Midrash* mean with the statement that Reuven was the first person to "do" *Teshuva?*

Repenting For a Mitzvah

Rabbi Menachem Mendl of Kotzk provides us with a profound insight. Adam committed a *sin* and repented. Cain, murdering Abel, knew that his act was *sinful* and therefore repented. *They* established the principle that there exists repentance for *sins*. But with Reuven it was different. Reuven, Rashi informs us, could not save his brother because, at the time of the sale, he had been immersed in "fasting and sackloth," i.e., *teshuva* for having tampered with his father's private life. For in his zeal to perform the *mitzvah* of honoring his mother he had moved Leah's bed into Yaakov's tent after Rachel's death. Hence, we see that the *teshuva* (repentance) on the part of Reuven was qualitatively different from the acts of repentance associated with Adam and Cain. For Reuven repented for having performed a *mitzvah*. Reuven was the first to recognize that, at times, *teshuva* is necessary for the very act of performing an apparent *mitzvah*.

It has become fashionable, of late, to engage in the *mitzvah* of *tochacha* (reproof)— to criticize Israel and Israeli policies. More and more people are jumping on this bandwagon. Somehow *tochacha* attracts many people. The wildness and ferocity of this onslaught is difficult to explain. Except for the fact that, perhaps, people are greatly interested in the performance of *mitzvot*.

For myself, I would rather not perform this *mitzvah*. In a period when the unanimous *Sanhedrin* of world opinion is so slanted against Israel; when the serpents of the world lie in wait for every opportunity to kick us; when, to use Dr. Norman Lamm's phrase, "media pogroms" are everyday occurrences; I would rather commit the *averah* (transgression) of silence. For that, I can at least do *teshuva*. I still don't know how to do *teshuva* for the *mitzvah* of criticizing Israel when it finds itself in such an unprecedented *et tzarah* (time of trouble). ●

A letter to fahtma

Rachel Adler

Dear Fahtma,

I have long been dreading this day. No friendship between an Arab psychiatrist and a Jewish psychotherapist could take place in a political vacuum, but we who are both religious, feminists, politically sensitive, never sought to conduct our friendship apolitically. Since the beginning, we have engaged in a bi-level dialogue: person to person and people to people. That is why our bond is so strong. We are always conscious of being reunited cousins from the same feuding family. So it was painful but not unexpected when you told me a few weeks ago that two of your relatives had been killed in the Israeli bombing of Southern Lebanon. I have always feared that someone one of us loved would be destroyed by the other's people. How quiet, how tight-lipped you were when you said to me, "I am trying to remember that you are my friend Rachel, and I love you."

It is painful to me to be complicit in those deaths, and I believe that I am. Jews are accountable for their behavior collectively; that is inherent in the covenant at Sinai. That is why I cannot refrain

RACHEL ADLER *lives in Minneapolis, Mn.*

from having opinions about the actions of Israel's army or government, although some would call this intrusive on the part of a diaspora Jew. It seems to me that anything I will have to own in collective confession on *Yom Kippur* is my business.

Your relatives' deaths are my business. They are heavy on my conscience. I open my newspaper to pictures of bodies half buried in rubble or sprawled on pavements and pray they are not people you knew. Every new bombing fills me with dread. I hate acknowledging them to you, but it is crazy between us if I don't. When you come to work, I scan your face. Pallor and puffy eyes mean a late night call from overseas and more to mourn.

I Am Ashamed

I do not need to repeat truths we presuppose: that I am a Zionist, committed to Israel's survival, or that equally inexcusable deeds have been done by Palestinians. We have been through these things; they are not justifications. My people have done your people a great wrong, and I am ashamed. Ashamed of the bombings of villages, ashamed of the soldiers breaking into the warehouses, mixing together the sugar, the flour, the salt to create hunger for your people, ashamed of the random seizures and interrogations not only in Lebanon but on the West Bank, where your people are routinely treated disrespectfully and unjustly by mine.

It has come to the point where I cannot recall the victimization of my people without confronting the parallels with yours. I remember Kishinev and read about Gush Emunin pogroms on the West Bank. I recall Streicher and notice newspaper caricatures of beaked and evilly smirking Arabs, and then feel in my own body your indignation, your shame, your terror for yourself and your little girls. I am aware of the pain of exile, the longing for the Land and know that you experience it with me. Wherever I touch my pain, Fahtma, I find yours beside it.

If a *tikkun*, a repair, is to be made, I know we must make it together. Here is all I know so far about my part: I promise to inform myself about current events and not to hide in my ignorance, to listen without defensiveness to your reality and to communicate mine without blaming, to protest senseless violence, to seek political ways to work for peace. Finally I want you to know, Fahtma, that after you told me of their deaths, I began saying *Kaddish* for those in your family, who are also my family, who died in the bombing of Lebanon.□

On withdrawing from Sh'ma

Henry Schwarzschild

This is my resignation from the Editorial Advisory Board of *Sh'ma*.

The contributions from me that you have published over the years have been few in number and less than earth-shaking in import, and you are therefore not deprived of a great editorial asset. In any case, my resignation has almost nothing to do with my relationship to *Sh'ma* as such. It is the consequence of a very much superordinated reorientation by me of my relationship to the Jewish community in the largest sense. Let me explain as best I can.

For a generation now, I have been deeply troubled by the chauvinistic assumptions and repressive effects of Israeli nationalism. I have experienced the War on Lebanon of the past few weeks as a turning point in Jewish history and consciousness exceeded in importance perhaps only by the End of the Second Commonwealth and the Holocaust. I have resisted the inference for over thirty years, but the War on Lebanon has now made clear to me that the resumption of political power by the Jewish people after two thousand years of diaspora has been a tragedy of historical dimensions. The State of Israel has demanded recognition as the modern political incarnation of the Jewish people. To grant that is to betray the Jewish tradition.

The State of Israel and its supporters have probably been right all along in arguing that political power comes at the price of the normal detritus of the nation state, such as Jewish criminals, prostitutes, and generals. They may also be right in asserting that the War on Lebanon is the sort of thing a Jewish state has to do to survive. I am not disposed to await the outcome of debates by politicians and theologians on whether the threat from the Palestine Liberation Organization was sufficiently clear and present to justify the killing of so many Lebanese and Palestinian men, women, and children, or only so many. I will not avoid an unambiguous response to the Israeli army's turning West Beirut into another Warsaw Ghetto.

I now conclude and avow that the price of a Jewish state is, to me, Jewishly unacceptable and that the existence of this (or any similar) Jewish ethnic-religious nation state is a Jewish, i.e. a human and moral, disaster and

HENRY SCHWARZSCHILD *directs the project on capital punishment for the A.C.L.U.*

violates every remaining value for which Judaism and Jews might exist in history. The lethal military triumphalism and corrosive racism that inheres in the State and in its supporters (both there and here) are profoundly abhorrent to me. So is the message that now goes forth to the nations of the world that the Jewish people claim the right to impose a holocaust on others in order to preserve its State.

For several decades, I have supported those minority forces in and for the State that wanted to salvage the values of peace and social justice that the Jewish tradition commands. The "blitzkrieg" in Lebanon, terrifying and Teutonic in its ruthlessness, shows how vain those hopes have been.

I now renounce the State of Israel, disavow any political connection or emotional obligation to it, and declare myself its enemy. I retain, of course, the same deep concern for its inhabitants, Jewish, Arab, and other, that I hold for all humankind.

I remain a member of the Jewish people - indeed, I have no other inner identity. But the State of Israel has now also triumphed over the Jewish people and its history, for the time being at least. I deem it possible that the State, morally bankrupted and mortally endangered by its victories, will prove essential to the survival of the Jewish people and that it may likely take the Jewish people with it to eventual extinction. Yet I believe that the death of the Jewish people would not be inherently more tragic than the death of the Palestinian people that Israel and its supporters evidently seek or at least accept as the cost of the "security" of the State of Israel. The price of the millennial survival of the Jewish people has been high; I did not think the point was to make others pay it. That moral scandal intolerably assaults the accumulated values of Jewish history and tradition.

If those be the places where the State of Israel chooses to stand, I cannot stand with it. I therefore resign all connections with Jewish political and public institutions that will not radically oppose the State and its claim to Jewish legitimacy. *Sh'ma* is one of those. ●

The agony of our jewish hellenists

Meir Kahane

The clearly agonized attack by Eric Yoffie (*Sh'ma*, 13/252) on statements and articles by religious Israelis whom he labels "anti-Jewish, anti-Zionist and an affront to the entire Jewish people" brings to mind earlier agony on the part of westernized Jews. In his *A History of Zionism*, Walter Laqueur wrote concerning the Jews of the Emancipation:

"Much of the (Jewish) apologetic literature concentrated on refuting anti-Semitic attacks on the Jewish religion, but in this respect the Jewish liberals were on shakier ground than they realized. The anti-Semites rediscovered the *Talmud* and the *Shulchan Aruch*, whereas the Jews had just about managed to forget them. Educated Jews of that generation genuinely believed that 'their religion had always taught universalist ethics' (Y. Katz), and the general Jewish public was genuinely astonished and outraged when it realized that this just was not so and that the *Talmud* included sayings and injunctions which made strange reading in the modern context."

The difference between the agonized Jews of the nineteenth century and those of Rabbi Yoffie's persuasion is, of course, that the former mounted the barricades against the non-Jews whereas the latter are forced to contend with fellow-Jews who insist on quoting from Jewish sources. The common denominator is, however, clear: The Jewish Hellenists of the last century and those of our time are faced with the truly agonizing and tortuous fact that authentic Judaism holds to fundamental views that are truly contradictory of western, liberal concepts. And since they and Rabbi Yoffie (who speaks for them) are essentially products of the gentilized western world of the non-Jew, they are faced with the too-terrible choice of either facing up to the contradiction and choosing one, while rejecting the other, or finding some method of deliberately counterfeiting a "Judaism" that emerges as a circumcized version of gentile westernism.

Modern Hellenists Use Theological Fraud

As one very well expects, few of the modern-day Hellenists are courageous enough to opt for truth. As their forefathers were chastised by Elijah ("How long do you halt between two opinions. . .") they choose the easy way of theological fraud, preferring to attack the individuals who cleave to the painful authenticity rather than admitting to their own betrayal of Judaism.

One can do little about Rabbi Yoffie's own predelliction for western concepts. Given the Divine decision to grant man free will, each of us is free to choose falsehood but those of us who

are both perceptive and honest in our Judaism cannot permit the prostitution of Judaism. Either the Lord of Baal, but surely not the coexistence of the *shaatnez* (intermixing). And certainly not the sanctification of the profane, the elevation of darkness that is now to be called light, the rabbinical stamp of *kashrut* on the swine of gentilization, the purification of the creeping things in a myriad of ways.

Judaism Contradicts Western Ideas

Anguish, indignation, outcry, protest and, ultimately, vilification can never be substitutes for, or replies to, the truth that Judaism stands, again and again, on the opposite side of basic concepts from western civilization. To Rabbi Yoffie these are the things that are basic and true: democracy, equality, tolerance, et al. But "My thoughts are not your thoughts, neither are My ways your ways, saith the Lord." (Isaiah 55:8).

Democracy? When, with the Assyrians surrounding Jerusalem and offering to spare the lives of the Jews if they surrendered, the citizens of Jerusalem opted by 130,000 to 110,000 to go with the party of Shebna the Scribe which advocated surrender ("Surrender Now," perhaps? and King Hezekiah wondered if he was not supposed to follow the rule of "to follow the majority," the rabbis of the Talmud describe the reply of Isaiah: "Say you not a confederacy to all that the people say is a confederacy' (Isaiah 8:12). Meaning, it is a confederacy of the wicked and a confederacy of the wicked is not counted." (Sanhedrin 26a).

No government, no king, no majority has the right, in the eyes of Judaism, to elect to go against Jewish Law. Maimonides, quoting from the Talmud (Sanhedrin 49a), states: "If one disregards an order of the king because he is engrossed in *mitzvot* he is free from sin for when faced with the words of the Master (God) and the words of the servant (the king) the words of the Master take precedence. *And there is no need to say that if the king ordered Him to negate a mitzvah that He does not listen to Him.*" (Hilchot Melachim 3:9).

Halacha is Not Democratic

No earthly, temporal government has any relevance to the actions of the Jews when its orders and regulations are contrary to Torah law. There is no democarcy for Jews in any sense of a majority being permitted to freely choose to go contrary to Torah law. And in the words of the Talmud: "Take a staff and strike them on their heads. One spokesman for a generation and not two."

Is this any way for a democratic way of life to speak? Of course not, and Judaism has never been a democratic form of society.

Equality for Jews and gentile? Indeed. If the Torah declares, "Thou shalt not place a stranger over you who is not a fellow Jew" (Deuteronomy 17:15), and Maimonides rules: "And not only as king but it is forbidden to appoint them to any authority in Israel," what does one say to the principle of equal rights for all, regardless of religion, etc.?

And shall we who worship at the altar of Jefferson, the Reform Democrats and Voltaire as interpreted by Teddy Kennedy, shout for joy over the fact that the non-Jew who wishes to live in the Land of Israel must give up his idolatry with its victimless crime and accept the payment of tribute and servitude (See Deuteronomy 20:11; *Sifre*, ibid; and Radak (David Kimchi) on Joshua 9)? And what will Rabbi Yoffie, who is so indignant with present-day religious scholars, say to a Maimonides who describes the servitude of the non-Jew seeking to live in the Land of Israel: "And servitude means they shall not raise their head in Israel and they shall be under our domination and never be appointed to a position of authority over Jews." (Hilchot Melachim 6:1).

Killing The Amalekites is a Mitzvah

And leaving aside for the moment the question of whether any nation today falls into the category of Amalek or the seven Canaanite nations, the question that I pose to the Yoffies of the Jewish world of indignation is:

If you were faced today with the reality of an actual Amaleki and Canaanite individual would you, therefore, perform the *mitzvah* of killing him (as is enunciated by Maimonides, the Chinuch and all other commentators on the place of this commandment in our time)? If unhappy over those who say that Arabs are in the juridical shoes of Amalek would you kill one who *is*, theoretically, proven to be a pure-blooded Amalekite? And what kind of ethical person is a Jew who prays in a temple whose ark holds a Torah scroll that advocates genocide against nations?

And what of the Jewish tradition to precede the Grace after Meals with the weekday reading of Psalm 137 which concludes with the following outrageous verses: "O daughter of Babylon that art about to be destroyed, happy shall he be that repayeth thee as thou hast served us. Happy shall he be that taketh and dasheth thy little ones against the rock." One can only stand in dismay at the words of David who is, we are told by Jewish tradition, the forefather of the Messiah.

Time and space both limit a veritable book (which I am in the midst of writing) concerning the endless sources of Jewish law and tradition that are at odds with western civilization and the Hellenism of Rabi Yoffie. A Pinchas who is given the Lord's eternal covenant of peace for having interfered with the peaceful fornication of a Jew and gentile and who is praised for having "made atonement for the children of Israel." (Numbers 25). And the *Midrash* there (Tanhuma) declares: "Did Pinchas then bring a sacrifice that the Torah uses the word 'atonement' concerning him? Rather it is to teach that he who sheds the blood of the wicked is counted as one who has brought a sacrifice."

And the vengeance that all Hellenists know is *verboten* is dealt with in the Psalms with, "Let the righteous rejoice for he has witnessed vengeance..."

Choose: God or Baal

And finally, let us put an end to the pitiful broken reed waved by the agonized who hoist the Talmudic parable of God refusing to allow the angels to sing praise as the Egyptians died. True enough. But the fact remains that even as the Almighty grieves for the failure of the work of His hands (the Egyptians, the Nazis, what-have-you), at that very moment he proceeds to drown them and whatever went on in heaven had no relevance to the Children of Israel who *did* sing joyful praise as it is written: "Then did Moses and the Children of Israel sing this song unto the Lord..." (Exodus 15)

The lesson is clear. Rabbi Yoffie has a problem. All the Yoffies have a problem. Judaism differs fundamentally from western civilization and Rabbi Yoffie is a westerner, not an idealogical Judaist. He has a choice: either to be honest and accept the yoke of Judaism, of Heaven, and bow his neck and western concepts beneath it, or to forthrightly reject Judaism and admit it publicly. For that is indeed his quarrel—not with some Orthodox scholars, but with the Judaism that is Biblical and Talmudic and that existed from Sinai until the present day.

Let honest intellectuals cease defaming and namecalling. Let them openly debate the issues (and is not name-calling the last refuge of non-thinkers?). Rabbi Yoffie must choose: if the Lord, let him bow to Him; if Baal, let him opt for idolatry. But let the two never be confused and let the swine be clearly labeled unclean. •

The end of zionist ideology?
Mitchell Cohen

"Tell me your honor, how am I to understand this, that you write about 'light, light, light' while I feel the dark in every part of my soul?" Yosef Hayim Brenner to Rav Kook.

For Zionists dismayed by the direction of Israel in the Begin era, it is time for some hard thinking and tough questions. Even apart from its manifestations in Israeli-Arab relations, there is a profound malaise within Zionism— a malaise with roots deeper than the fortunes and policies of the current government in Jerusalem. To borrow a phrase from Hannah Arendt, Zionism no longer thinks what it is doing. It congratulates itself incessantly for its many (and very real) accomplishments. It does not try to understand its own limits and possibilities in today's world and prefers to rely on old lifeless formula and an elaborate institutional network to safeguard its future, pretending that this institutional network is a popular movement of the Jewish people. For Zionism to survive as something with value, it must begin an internal dialogue unafraid of the conclusions that might be reached. It must think itself.

Historical movements neither appear nor sustain themselves *ex nihilo*. Conditions, generally of conflict, provide the soil for their growth. In the golden age of Zionist thought (roughly the half century after 1881), real conditions gave the impetus to political ideas. Self-scrutiny of the Jewish people was the essence of Zionism. Zionism attempted to think the condition of the Diaspora and propose an alternative. Thus as long as there is a Diaspora, the *raison d'etre* of Zionism exists.

Current Zionism is Contentless
The existence of a *raison d'etre*, however, does not guarantee the continued existence of a movement. By and large, post-state Zionism is an uncritical Zionism, a non-thinking Zionism with nothing to say to Diaspora Jews about their *own* lives; we have instead an Israeli nationalism on one hand, and a support movement in the *Golah*

(exile) for the Jewish state on the other. This is an easy Zionism, especially for American Jews, because it has no need to pose difficult *Zionist* questions about the nature of life in the *Golah*. This contentless Zionism permits fixation on the *formal* (though, of course, unquestionably necessary) aspect of Zionism, the State *qua* State. Questions about means and ends, indeed the very effort to define ends, are disparaged as "ideological bickering," leftovers from another age and another continent. After all, it is better to be "pragmatic" like good Americans.

One aspect of American political culture is a self-congratulatory enthusiasm for being "non-ideological." This was crystallized in the "End of Ideology" thesis propounded by various social and political scientists in the 1950's. Briefly (and broadly) the assertion was that the end of ideology was upon us because the advanced West could resolve all major problems within the existing systems, thus allowing everybody to be happily integrated. Hence if we can properly manipulate the means (e.g., the American political and social systems), we need ask no real questions about political and social ends. In this technocratic outlook, the means became the end; as Alasdair MacIntyre has pointed out, the "End of Ideology" argument was an ideology itself. We add: an ideology of the status quo masquerading as pragmatism.

For the American *Golah*, where Zionism as a critique of Jewish reality was never taken too seriously, a similar end of Zionist ideology poses no problem. Indeed, it was Zionist ideology that was the problem. What better exemplifies this than Brandeis' famous rationalization that to be better Americans we have to be better Jews and to be better Jews we have to be Zionists. If Zionism is a critique of *galut* (exile) reality, it is self-evident that it makes American identity problematic.

The Relationship Between Means And Ends
Mainstream American Zionism has always been that of Brandeis; it speaks of the State which American Zionists support but not of the relations between means and ends. Means and ends may be conceptually distinguished but are in reality always mutually determining. Their interrelation was at the heart of the division between left and right within Zionism. Jabotinsky's attack on the rising power of the Zionist Socialists in the 1920's and 1930's was based on a statist vision of nationalism, the goal of Zionism was a state, pure

and simple. The national endeavor ought not to be "polluted" by foreign, divisive elements such as socialism and the question of social classes. "In Zionism and in Palestine," he wrote in 1931, "you are but a puppet dangling from a wire and playing a prescribed part, and the hand that pulls that wire is called— the State in building."

Such a formulation, of course, begs the question of what a state is. A technical means of protection and organization? A tool of oppression? An arena for the the expression of various forms of life? Are the institutions and tools of a state, e.g., government, army, police, embodiments of human realization?

Jabotinsky *reified* the State; he made it a thing unto itself, the be-all and end-all. Hence the Labor Zionist reply to Jabotinsky, articulated in particular by Ben Gurion at the time, was that means and ends could not be separated; any national movement, including Zionism, could be good or bad depending on the social reality it creates.

If social vision is subordinated, the means, however, become the be-all and end-all... And Zionism becomes an ideology of statism whose focus is the Jewish State rather than the liberation of the Jewish people. In short, it becomes an ideology of means masquerading as a pragmatic nationalism. Ironically, Ben Gurion himself came to embrace something like this— it might be argued that in this regard he became his opposite, Jabotinsky. In pursuing his policy of *"mamlakhtiyut"* ("statism" or *"etatism"*) as Prime Minister, Ben Gurion sought to subordinate all institutions, including those of the Labor movement (the *kibbutzim*, the Histadrut) to the State and its exigencies. Statism, colored with a foggy messianism, replaced socialism in his political vocabulary, and while much of the Labor leadership still spoke of socialism, it increasingly became statist as well. Israel may be the only historical example of a socialist movement nationalizing its own institutions and, by this, undermining itself.

Compromise For The Sake of Coalition

Take, for instance, the question of education. During the Mandate, labor, religious and general Zionists each maintained their own school systems. *Mamlakhtiyut* dictated one, state-run system; but for the sake of his coalition with the religious parties, Ben Gurion satisfied himself

with merging only the general and labor systems and continuing a separate religious one. In 1953, the year before the merger, 43.4% of Israeli students attended the labor schools as opposed to 19.1% in the religious and 27.1% in the general "trends" (as they were called). In other words, Labor yielded a critical means by which to socialize young Israelis into its value system. No doubt many in Mapai thought that their dominance in the government would guarantee the infusion of Labor ideals in national education. In retrospect, we can see how wrong they were.

Indeed, three decades later the Zionist right wing, long the apostles of fetishizing the state, came to power and gave their coalition partner, the National Religious Party, the portfolio for Education and Culture. Zvulun Hammer, a religious and not a "pure" nationalist, has sought, albeit with caution, to enhance the religious content of the curriculum of the secular state schools which he oversees along with the religious ones. Labor, in the meanwhile, is dominated by statist technocrats and finds itself not only in opposition but bewildered and unsure of its own vision and goals.

The State Has Become An End In Itself

Israeli and American Zionisms have met where the means become all and ends— ideology— are negated. What this ultimately signifies is the triumph of right wing Zionism— a triumph, if the above analysis is correct, prepared by the Labor Zionists. With this triumph the State *qua* State becomes an object of worship, nationalism runs rampant, and there is no place for a critical Zionism. The promotion of *aliyah* today exemplifies what this implies: how often are American Jews told to move to Israel "because it is good for the State" (i.e. American Jews are a means to the end of the State), rather than because *aliyah* responds to dilemmas to their *own* lives (in which case, the State is a means, and only a means, for the well-being of the Jewish people)? The two approaches represent difference between a statist Zionism and a humanist Zionism.

Ahad Ha'am once wrote an essay entitled "Anticipations and Survivals" in whcih he tells us that in each age there exist beliefs that are out of step with their times, hidden in "watertight compartments" in the minds of a few, with no practical effect. These are "survivals" lacking the conditions which originally nurtured them, and their contemporary appearance of life "is illusory: it is no real life of motion and activity, but the passive life of an old man whose 'moisture is gone and his natural force abated'."

Alongside "survivals" there are "anticipations"— ideas yet in their youth, alive (like "survivals") in a world that doesn't understand them. Writing in 1892, Ahad Ha'am saw the Return to Zion as a "survival" which, given the right developments, could flourish as new life, and become as a soul to a body. For there is hope for both "anticipations" and "survivals," he insisted, as long as they have a breath in them.

Zionism is Nearly Lifeless

The Zionist world today is composed of bodies without souls, institutions with red tape in their veins; their appearance of life is illusory as demonstrated by the surreal world of the Zionist Congress held this past December. (How many delegates returned to the *Golah complaining* that there was too much "politics" at the Congress? Better to be "pragmatic.")

A vibrant, critical Zionism is but a survival today, somewhere in watertight compartments in the minds of a few. Shall it suffocate or break out and breathe? Here then is one task for thinking Zionists: an intellectual guerrilla war against the Zionism of today. Before Zionism's future lies the question of finding a form of itself relevant to the conditions of the times. In the era of Beginesque triumphalism this is to ask: can the survival become an anticipation too— an old-new soul giving rebirth to a decaying body? ●

Orthodoxy must reject rabbi meir kahane

Yitzchok Adlerstein

After making careful study of unscrupulous marketplace practices, Rabbi Yochanan ben Zakai found himself between Scylla and Charybdis, rather than in his native Jerusalem. "If I describe them, other deceitful vendors will learn from them. If I remain silent, the unscrupulous will conclude that Torah scholars are not perceptive of the machinations of the wicked...." (B.B.89b)

The Orthodox community finds itself in a similar bind regarding Rabbi Meir Kahane, who often points to Orthodox thought to justify his views. On the one hand, critics of Orthodoxy are keeping busy enough without traditional Jews helping them sharpen their poison quills. And, however distasteful the tone of his rhetoric, we do find many of Rabbi Kahane's points unarguable. Western democracy overlaps, but does not coincide with,

Torah values. Torah law *should* become the law of the State, preserving our peoplehood by binding the Divine to all areas of human conduct, including the waging of war and limiting sexual partners to our own people.

On the other hand, silence woud imply that we lack the perspicacity to firmly reject all that Rabbi Kahane preaches that is thoroughly foreign to Torah thought. When the good name of Judaism and its people is continually assaulted, silence cannot be maintained. "When G-d's name is desecrated, considerations of human honor are set aside." (Er.63a)

The Duty to Avoid Chilul Hashem

The Torah does much of its moralizing through vignettes. Some of these deal with conflicts between legitimate Jewish rights and non-Jewish moral sensitivities, even when unjustified from our perspective.

After initial victories at Jericho and Ai, fear of the conquering Jewish armies led the ancient Gibeonites to try desperately to save themselves. Emissaries were sent to Joshua, disguised as travelers from some distant land, to arrange a pact of mutual protection. The Jews had been instructed not to enter into a covenant with the indigenous peoples of Canaan. Through a ruse, the Gibeonites overcame the incredulity of their interrogators, and a treaty was drafted. G-d was not consulted. (Joshua 9:14)

When they learned the truth, the people were infuriated. They had been deceived, taken. Joshua, however, refused to repudiate the agreement. Legally, morally, ethically, the agreement wasn't worth the parchment it was written on. But others wouldn't understand legal subtleties. They would think that Jews failed to honor their solemn word, that the "voice of Jacob" was one of deception and untruth. And what they thought did make a difference to Joshua, although these were the very same people who were being ejected from the land because of their moral degeneracy. He knew that the character of G-d Himself would be scrutinized through the actions of His proxies, His chosen people. The Jewish mission of bringing Divine enlightenment and morality to the land could not be compromised or diluted, even in the eyes of the heathen.

Several days later, the Gibeonites were attacked and Joshua committed the lives of Jewish soldiers to defend the terms of a sham treaty. It is precisely at this time that, according to the Talmud, G-d miraculously reversed the laws of nature, stilled the march of the setting sun, and allowed additional hours for the Jewish triumph to occur.

In 1948, the Arab population of Israel was guaranteed rights of citizenship and due process. Those who offered those rights did not consult G-d, Rabbi Kahane, or Torah law. They were not appointed by world Jewry, but they were, in the eyes of the non-Jewish world, the voice of the Jewish conscience. Can anyone glibly dismiss the *chilul Hashem* (desecration of G-d's name) that repudiating such rights would cause?

How we Must Use Our Power over Gentiles

Numerous laws of redemption are set forth near the end of Leviticus. One of them deals with a Jew bent under the weight of penury, who sells his freedom for a few years to a non-Jew, or worse yet, into the custodial service of an idolatrous temple. His survival as a committed Jew is imperiled, at best. His plight is an embarrassment to his brethren who did not provide for him; watching him decorate his master's Christmas tree or its pagan precursor is a thorn in the side of national pride.

One would expect that the Torah would allow all sorts of extraordinary and extralegal means to alleviate the spiritual danger to this unfortunate soul. It could recommend kidnapping. It could legislate the contract out of existence. (It could even have the non-Jew deported to some other country, where millions of his cousins reside!)

What the Torah calls for is a very different response. "He shall make an exact reckoning with the buyer." (Lev. 25:50) The non-Jew is, in fact, forced to divest himself of his Jewish servant. The Torah insists, though, that restitution be made forthrightly and with integrity. Any tendency to take ethical short-cuts is quashed. Vigilante action to win the Jew's freedom, even negotiating a ransom price not entirely "fair" to the Gentile's interest, are ruled out. (B.K.113b)

It is clear from the Talmud's context that the Torah's response is addressed to those who have the ability to impose whatever solution they wish upon the non-Jew. If this were not the case, the forced divestiture would be nothing but wishful thinking (cf. Maimonides, Hil. Gen. 7:8). But here again, our moral right, our national pride, our political power, are all limited by a greater consideration—how the Gentile world will react.

The Place of Gentiles in the Holy Land

The discussion thus far has assumed some merit in Rabbi Kahane's assumption of a halachic mandate to rid the Land of non-Jews. In fact, Rabbi Kahane confuses the ancient, degenerate Canaanites (who have long disappeared) with all non-Jews. Judaism is not xenophobic; it extends the right of residence to non-Jewish inhabitants who subscribe to the fundamental principles of decency and humanity called the Noachide Laws (Ravad, Is. Biah 14:8 and Kesef Mishneh, Av. Koch. 10:6). "Its ways are the ways of pleasantness" (Prov. 3:17). Halachic literature abounds in affirmation of minority rights of non-idolatrous peoples in Israel.

Rabbi Kahane is certainly entitled to his halachic opinion, if he can defend it. But given the grandstanding he practices, there comes a point where his opinion becomes the imposition of an image of Torah Judaism upon everyone, including his dissenters. Surely Rabbi Kahane is aware that not all opinions are equally weighted, and the heftier questions are to be left to greater authorities (*Shulkhan Arukh*, Y.D. 242:11). And he cannot point to a single major halachic decisor (he certainly cannot claim to be one himself!) who supports his contentions.

To be charitable, let us assume that much of what Rabbi Kahane says is meant to entice the Israeli electorate, and not for implementation. Unfortunately, the devastating effect of his rhetoric on Jews in and out of Israel is not minimized. By taking pot-shots at the sensitivities of the entire non-Jewish world like some reckless cowboy, Jewish lives are endangered everywhere. And brandishing G-d Himself as his six-gun is just plain poor theology. G-d *does* stand behind His people, but they cannot force His hand to produce miracles, neither on the battlefield, nor in the world of *realpolitik*.

It should come as no surprise that Rabbi Elazar M. Shach, unofficial mentor of both Agudah and Shas, recently instructed all Knesset members under his control to dissociate themselves from any and all legislation introduced by Kach, even where they completely support the legislative intent of such bills. Rabbi Kahane's attitude of "the devil with the *goyim*" must be abhorred and rejected. And not for the protection of our small interests, but for the sake of G-d's good name. □

Formative experiences in my jewishness

Seymour Melman

I am a child of the Great Depression. Born in 1917 and raised in a Yiddish-speaking household of Russian-Polish parents and grandparents, my childhood years were also affected by the upward economic mobility of my father, a pharmacist in the East Bronx, who had reached the U.S. as a 17-

year-old fugitive from the Czar's police. But he, like millions of others, was vulnerable to investments that failed. Within our own family the prospect of economic well-being was transformed into a nightmare of marginal existence. By age fifteen I saw the Great Depression blighting the working people and lower middle-class populations of that neighborhood. Unemployment and evictions of families—huddled with their household goods on the sidewalks—were commonplace. Bank failures destroyed modest savings.

No explanation for all this was offered in my public schools. Capitalism had a business cycle, and President Hoover intoned that "Prosperity is just around the corner." But where was that corner? The despair that shrouded the community was more meaningfully addressed on street corners, at political meetings, and in the widely read leftist literature. The lesson to me was that my schools had little to offer by way of explaining the most important conditions of life.

My interest in the condition of Jews was shaped by my parents' and grandparents' accounts of their lives in Europe, and also by my studies in Jewish history in the rather good curriculum of the Hebrew school that I attended after public-school hours. The minority status of Jews and its accompanying weaknesses were brought home to me in the classic works of Theodore Herzl, Pinsker, Ahad-Haam, and particularly Ber Borochov. The historic pattern of Jewish vulnerability to scapegoating was clear and made visible by the rising fascist movements in Europe and the development of fascist organizations in the United States. The lesson to me was that the Zionist idea of changing the minority position of Jews by self-government and occupational normalization was attractive as a scheme for directly altering the core condition of Jewish vulnerability. We regarded a clear view of, and opposition by Jews to, the fascist movements as indispensable for dealing with the position of Jews in our time. At the same time we were critical of the military buildup that had been started in the U.S. during the latter 1930s. For we were suspicious of the motives and policies of the U.S. government as giving little or no evidence of opposition to fascist movements in Europe and elsewhere. The U.S. government's policies during the Spanish Civil War confirmed our worst suspicions.

During the year 1939-40 I was an Avukah Fellow, living in a *kibbutz* in Palestine and traveling about the country. It was an extraordinary time, the first year of World War II. I was exposed to the full range of ideas and institutions of the very dynamic Jewish community of Palestine.

The Realities of Zionist Politics

When a student colleague and I left Palestine in the spring of 1940, we were thoroughly searched by the British authorities, interrogated at some length, and suffered confiscation of various papers and photographs, notably those showing Jews and Arabs in some joint activity. An open police file seemed to contain photocopies of all our correspondence. Of greatest concern to me was that the authorities not discover political papers that were concealed in the bindings of some books as well as a certain cannister of film. The latter had newsreel film of the Jewish revolt in all the main cities against the British rules severely restricting further Jewish immigration and forbidding the purchase of land by Jews. The film was to bring the news to the U.S. and bypass British censorship.

We delivered these films to one of the Labor Zionist headquarters in New York where they were promptly destroyed. The reason was soon made apparent during a visit to Justice Louis Brandeis to report our observations in Palestine. Justice Brandeis responded that he felt the Palestinian Jews had lost their heads in protesting as forcefully as they did. He regarded it as absolutely essential that both Roosevelt and Churchill be accorded unqualified support by all Jews as an indispensable requirement for achieving the destruction of the Nazi power.

Brandeis' approach and policy analysis made a strong impression on me and my Zionist friends. In our view, unqualified, carte-blanche support to Roosevelt and Churchill was unthinkable in view of the U.S. and British role in facilitating Franco's victory over the Spanish Republican government by an arms embargo. They would possibly act against the German and Italian fascists, but with methods that suited their political world view, not ours.

For me the lesson of this encounter was fundamental and durable.

Reactions to the Holocaust

The years 1945 to 1948 brought a marked change in the way my parents and closest family viewed the position of Jews and my own political activities. Since I was a teenager, my parents, my father in particular, had regarded "Seymour's activities" with a certain amusement, a youthful enthusiasm that he would overcome as he came to maturity and sought a proper place in the world.

In response to the Holocaust, the horrendous news and photographs of the extermination camps, my family, like others of their generation, were overwhelmed with guilt—unspoken—for their brothers, sisters, aunts and uncles and cousins. Suddenly their long obsession with "making it" in America was paralleled by an obsession to support the most far-out activities and movements that declared themselves for rescuing the Jews of Europe or for transporting them to Palestine, or for battling the British for the grant of a Jewish state. So these men and women who had thought of Zionism as some sort of idealistic, esoteric, and farfetched goal transformed into militant activists who used the Holocaust as a rationalization for supporting the fascist wing of the Jewish community in Israel, led by Menachem Begin. The end justified the means.

The founding of the Jewish State in 1948 was seen as a political defeat by me and many of my friends. We judged that a nationalist Israel would confront a rivalry without foreseeable end with Arab nationalist counterparts.

Late in 1948 I was invited to give an educational talk to a Hashomer Hatzair youth group in Brooklyn on the history of Zionism in the U.S. I did that, with emphasis on the internal politics of the Zionists and how that correlated with occupational and social class. At the close of the talk I referred, briefly, to the role that Jewish leaders played during World War II. Jewish leaders were trapped into the function of shielding Roosevelt and Churchill as they participated in holding back information on what might have been done to save many Jews from the extermination program.

A few days later I was on the receiving end of shrill denunciations on the telephone from U.S. representatives of Israel's Hashomer Hatzair: how dare you say such things about our leaders? I stated that every point I had made was based upon solid evidence and I offered to make this known to the group at a further meeting. That meeting was cancelled. Then the cancelled meeting was reinstated, and this time I delivered a substantial account of the history of negotiations with German leaders and the American and British governments bearing on possible exit of Jews from Europe during World War II; and the policies of England and the United States that frustrated all the proposals that were made for rescuing some substantial part of the Jews of Europe from the Nazi murder machine.

For the next fifteen years after that long evening, I did not receive a piece of mail from any Jewish organization. I have never favored conspiracy theories. But it seemed that in making this modest and unreported analysis before a rather small group in Brooklyn, I had touched a nerve on an enormously sensitive issue. There was a massive reluctance among people concerned with the fate of Jews at that time to concede that political decisions by Jewish leaders during World War II had played a part.

Surprising Turns in America and Israel

During the early 1950s I found myself, several times over, doing a task that had surrealist quality. The McCarthyism plague had struck a number of classmates and friends from City College days, as various military-serving laboratories and other government organizations discharged, wholesale, staff members whose qualification for discharge was that they had obtained an academic degree from City College. So there I was, several times over, ridiculing the idea that these men, long known to me, could have been either Communist ideologists or Communist dupes or in any way willingly hostile to the security of the United States.

Appearance before these loyalty review boards was a horrendous experience. Though not a lawyer and not fine-tuned to the niceties of testimony before such groups, I was fully sensitive to the idea that I was participating in a proceeding where innocence rather than guilt had to be proved. If I was a credible witness before these boards, it was probably owing to combined circumstances: having known these people for many years; having been a national officer of the student Zionist federation; having served in the U.S. Army; and finally being an instructor at Columbia University.

In 1956 I took responsibility for conducting a wide-ranging investigation that reported on the methods that could be used for carrying out a workable inspection system to control compliance with international disarmament treaties. This work required detailed studies on the methods of secret military operations and secret arms production systems. One of my students at the time was Moshe Kelman, a hero of the Palmach, who was well connected with the Israeli Army. A few months later I arrived in Tel Aviv for a two-week crash course on secret military operations and production systems (which later turned out to be the same as guerilla warfare).

The officers of the Israeli Army were brimming over with confidence after their victory against Egyptian armies in 1956. After completing my studies with them, I tried to turn the lesson around and suggest that dedicated Arab nationalists could one day have the full capability of turning the art of secret military operations against them. There wasn't much of an audience for those ideas. The lesson for me was that arrogant nationalism helps to blind people from coherent understanding of realities.

Continuing the Struggle for Justice

During the long political struggle occasioned by the U.S. War in Vietnam there were many opportunities for joint work with Rabbi Abraham Heschel. I remember that in 1966 I called on the executive committee of Clergy and Laity Concerned to suggest preparation of a study on U.S. war crimes in Vietnam, thereby making a powerful moral case against the government's war. The representative from the American Jewish Committee quickly stated that this study should be put in the hands of Herman Kahn at the Hudson Institute. I was astounded to hear such a suggestion from anyone in that group and so was Heschel, who didn't lose any seconds before rescuing that project from oblivion.

In June, 1984, in the company of nine other colleagues (economists, engineers, and scientists) I helped to conduct the first U.S.-Soviet Symposium on Conversion from Military to Civilian Economy; held in Moscow and to be followed by a meeting in the United States. These discussions laid bare a crucial feature of both the United States and the Soviet Union. Both countries are in the grip of military-industrial complexes, varying in style and detailed history but requiring that both societies develop ways to change over from military to civilian work as an indispensable condition for effecting a real reversal of the dreadful arms race. On reviewing the course of events that preceded the conduct of this symposium, I am persuaded that I had brought to bear for this important purpose the whole array of knowledge and values that I had accumulated over many years.

For Jewish nationalists of liberal persuasion the emergence of militant Zionist extremism in Israel and America creates a crisis of values: will the liberals be prepared to stand against their fellow nationalists who now champion the sort of rightist fanaticism that is the hallmark of fascist movements?

For me the lesson is clear: it is a moral obligation of Jews who value human life, personal and political freedom, political democracy, human decencies, and a peaceful, productive future for the Jews of Israel and everywhere else to give support in every available way to the people and parties in Israel and in the United States who stand against the ultranationalist, authoritarian, militarist, and clericalist-fundamentalist tendencies in Jewish life who know that there is no military solution, and who bend every effort toward achieving a peaceful settlement of the Israeli-Palestinian conflict that has warped the quality of so much of Jewish life during the last forty years. □

Eugene B. Borowitz, like all other Editors of this journal, speaks only for himself when he writes in these pages. ●

MARIAN HENRIQUEZ NEUDEL is an attorney in Chicago doing environmental work for a government agency. (Sh'ma received the above article in May, a month before the Israel Defense Force entered Lebanon). ●

GEOFFREY WIGODER *is the editor-in-chief of the* Encyclopedia Judaica *and a frequent contributor to* The Jerusalem Post.

Rabbi Meir Kahane asked to be identified as a Jew who lives in Israel.

In somewhat different form, Richard Levy's article appeared first in Ha'am, *the Jewish student journal at U.C.L.A.*

YITZCHOK ADLERSTEIN *directs the Jewish Studies program at Yeshiva University of Los Angeles.*

SEYMOUR MELMAN *teaches economics in the Engineering-School of Columbia University and this article is radically abridged from his address on receiving the Abraham Joshua Heschel Peace Award from The Jewish Peace Fellowship.*

III

THE PUZZLES AND FASCINATIONS OF JEWISH LIFE

11

The Varieties of Jewish Experience

Should 'g-d' exist?

Menachem Kellner

Does the *Halakhah* demand the use of expressions like 'G-d' and 'L-rd' instead of their fully-spelled equivalents?

In *Deuteronomy* 12: 3-4 we read: "And ye shall break down their altars (i.e., those of the idolaters) and dash in pieces their pillars, and burn their Asherim with fire; and the graven images of their gods ye shall hew down; and ye shall destroy their name out of that place. You shall not do so unto the Lord your God." On this latter verse the *Sifri* quotes Rabbi Ishmael as having said: "From whence (do we learn) that he who erases one letter from the name (of God) transgresses a negative commandment? It is written: '. . . and ye shall destroy their name out of that place. You shall not do so unto the Lord your God.' " Nachmanides, commenting on this verse, likens the erasure of God's name to the destruction of the altar in the Temple. This, if nothing else, demonstrates the seriousness of the issue.

These verses are the source for the custom under discussion. Since we are not allowed to erase (one letter from) God's name, we may not write it on anything which is likely to be destroyed: for example, the pages of *Sh'ma*. This conclusion is correct; the use to which it is commonly put, however, is warranted by neither *Halakhah* nor logic.

The *Gemara* (*Shebu'oth*, 35a, bottom) says: "There are Names which may be erased, and there are Names which may not be erased. These are the names which may not be erased: . . . (there follows a list of names) . . . — these may not be erased; but *the Great, the Mighty, the Revered, the Strong, the Powerful, the Potent, the Merciful and Gracious, the Long Suffering, the One Abounding in Kindness* (etc.) — these may be erased."

Maimonides (*Yad, Hilchot Yesodei Hatorah,* 6: 1-2) asserts: "Anyone who destroys any one of the holy and pure names by which the Holy One, Blessed be He, is called, is flogged. This is the law of the Torah. For, (as) it is said of idolators, '. . . and ye shall destroy their name out of that place. You shall not do so unto the Lord, your God.' And the seven names are . . . (there follows a list of seven names) . . . anyone who erases even one letter of these seven is flogged." In *Halachah* 5 he continues: "All other appellations with which we praise the Holy One, Blessed be He, such as . . . (there follows a long list of names such as *the Gracious One, the Merciful One,* etc.) . . . they are like all other Holy Writ and it is permitted to erase them." R. Yosef Caro, in the *Shulhan Aruch* (*Yorah Deah,* 276: 9) concurs with Maimonides in asserting that the prohibition of erasing God's name applies only to seven particular Hebrew names. (Caro's list of names differs slightly from that of Maimonides; see the comment of the *Turei Zahav, ad. loc.*)

What's in a name?

It should be abundantly clear, then, that according to the *Halakhah*, there are seven distinct *Hebrew* names of God which may not be erased. *Seven and no more.* (Some *Halakhic* authorities even deny that the erasure prohibition extends to transliterations of these seven names. See, for example, the *Hidushei Ra'ak* on the *Shulhan Aruch, ad. loc.*)

There is no *Halakhic* basis, then, for extending the prohibition of erasing God's names to expressions like 'God' (or even to Hebrew expressions, like *'Harahum'* — the Merciful One), nor is there any logical reason for so doing. The Torah warns us against destroying the *name* of God. In the strict sense, 'God' is not the *name* of the Holy One, Blessed be He. 'God' is used to name that Being whom we call 'Creator,' 'Lord,' etc., but is not His *name*. We can use an expression to uniquely describe some entity without that expression becoming the name of the entity so described. Thus, the expression, 'first editor of *Sh'ma*' names Eugene Borowitz without being his *name*. Similarly, we use expressions like 'God,' 'Creator,' etc., to denote the Holy One, Blessed be He, but these expressions are not His *name*. To determine these names we must consult the Torah, not accepted English usage.

Not only is 'God' not the name of the Holy One, Blessed be He, but it can be used to denote Allah, the Father of Jesus, Krishna, etc. Furthermore, the expression 'god' denotes, or can be used to denote, a near infinite number of deities whom it would be blasphemous to associate in anyway with the Holy One, Blessed be He.

Probably because it is basically un*Halakhic* and illogical, contemporary Orthodox usage of terms used to denote the Holy One, Blessed be He, is inconsistent, too. If 'G-d' is correct, why not 'the H-ly -ne, Bl-ss-d be H-' or 'O-r F-th-r, O-r K-ng'? Would not Pascal's phrase, so dear to pulpit rabbis, have to be corrected to "G-d of Abraham, Isaac, and Joseph, not God of the philosophers"?

Allow me, then, to plead for logic, moderation, and, above all, respect for the *Halakhah* among my fellow Jews. Perhaps then we can truly join together in praising the name of the Lord.

A dash of respect

J. David Bleich

"Everything is dependent on *mazal* (luck) even the Scroll of Law in the ark." For reasons which the rational mind cannot always fathom some *mitzvot,* some forms of meticulousness in observance, some expressions of piety are luckier than others. Some evoke approbation even among the non-observant; others become the subject of derision even among the ostensibly devout. For some strange reason the practice of not writing out the name of G-d has aroused quite vigorous negative feelings. Why? Is it because some are rankled by what they (mistakenly) believe to be mass *am aratzut* (ignorance)? Does the attitude stem from a sense of embarrassment at public display of such "quaint" Jewish ways? Or is it simply a manifestation of the unfortunate tendency even among the observant to ridicule any particular practice to which one does not subscribe?

Menachem Kellner seems to be genuinely unaware of the authoritative sources for this practice and his comments are indeed well intended. While *Sh'ma* is hardly the forum for a technical *halakhic* discussion, the matter

can be cast in its proper light only by an examination of the relevant sources. The Gemara, *Shevu'ot* 35a, states that it is forbidden to erase the name of G-d, and for that reason care is taken not to write the Divine Name upon any document or paper which might be destroyed. *Megillat Ta'anit* 7a and the Gemara *Rosh Hashanah* 18b report that during the Hasmonean period promissory notes bore the legend "In such and such year in the reign of Yochanan, High Priest of the most high G-d." The Sages, upon hearing of this innovation exclaimed: "Tomorrow the debtor will repay his debt with the result that the note will be cast away with the refuse!" Accordingly, they abrogated the practice and declared the day on which they did so to be a holiday. On the basis of this source Rema, *Yoreh De'ah* 276:13, rules that the name of G-d may be written out in full in printed works which presumably will be treated with respect but that it is forbidden to write the Divine Name in correspondence or other forms of writing which are likely to be discarded heedlessly.

G-d's name: handle with care
The prohibition against obliterating the name of G-d is limited to the specifically enumerated Divine Names which possess intrinsic sanctity. Other cognomens are regarded as adjectival descriptions rather than as names of the Deity and as such are not included in the prohibition against erasure. Both Shakh, *Yoreh De'ah* 179:11, and R. Akiva Eger, *Yoreh De'ah* 276:9, state definitively that the name of G-d occurring in languages other than Hebrew is regarded as a cognomen with reference to the prohibition against erasure.

Although the prohibition against erasure is not applicable, proper respect must nevertheless be paid to the name of G-d even when it occurs in languages other than Hebrew. *Nedarim* 7b states: "Every place where the unnecessary mention of the Divine Name is found, there poverty is to be found." This is deduced from the biblical verse " . . . in every place where I cause My name to be

mentioned I will come unto thee and bless thee" (Exodus 20:21), indicating that the pronouncement of the Divine Name in a sacred manner is rewarded with blessing and prosperity. From this the converse is also deduced, viz., that the pronouncement of the Divine Name in vain leads to poverty.

Two renowned authorities, R. Jonathan Eibschutz, *Urim ve-Tumim* 27:2, and R. Ya'akov of Lissa, *Netivot ha-Mishpat* 27:2, maintain that reverence must also be accorded to written occurrences of the Divine Name whether in Hebrew or in the vernacular. Both scholars decried even the use of the French *adieu* (the root meaning of which is 'with G-d') in written communications because of the dishonor of the Divine Name resulting from careless disposal of such correspondence. *Arukh ha-Shulchan, Choshen Mishpat* 27:3, is most emphatic in condemnation of heedless use of the name of G-d in the vernacular. For a distinction between the term G-d, which in this context is regarded even in translation as the proper name of the Deity, and adjectival cognomens the reader may consult R. Moses Feinstein, *Igrot Mosheh, Yoreh De'ah* I, no. 172.

From generation to generation

Religiously motivated forms of conduct practised by devout Jews over a span of generations are but seldom without a firm basis. Our Sages long ago counseled in this regard, "Even if they are not prophets, they are the sons of prophets." The columnists of the London *Jewish Chronicle* who for years have been inveighing in caustic tones against the manner in which their coreligionists spell the name of G-d not only err in their preconceptions but fail to realize that such time-hallowed customs acquire a meaning and significance of their own. The Jew who inserts a dash in spelling the Divine Name is filled with an all-pervasive sense of the immanence of the Almighty. His action demonstrates that he feels no inhibition in expressing his reverence for the Divine in all aspects of his daily life. Whether or not one chooses to adopt this practice, whether one regards it as well-grounded or as ill-founded, the usage G-d should, at the very minimum, command a dash of respect.

"Jew" as defamation in the dictionary
David B. Guralnik

In 1969, Marcus Shloimovitz, a textile merchant of Manchester, England, and a member of the Board of Deputies of British Jews, filed a class libel suit against Clarendon Press, publishers of the famed *Oxford English Dictionary* (for short, OED), the famous thirteen-volume repository of the English language. In his suit, Shloimovitz charged that the entry for the word *Jew* in that work contained the following defamatory noun definition: "a person of Hebrew race; an Israelite. . . as applied to a grasping or extortionate money-lender or usurer, or a trader who drives hard bargains or deals craftily," as well as a verb definition: "to cheat or overreach, in a way attributed to Jewish traders or usurers." Shloimovitz indicated that he was not claiming damages, but was "seeking an injunction to stop this defamation of Jewish character" by a correction in the appropriate volume of a forthcoming supplement to the dictionary.

The suit moved slowly through the British legal system, finally being scheduled for a hearing by the High Court on July 5, 1973. During the four intervening years, the Clarendon Press refused to make any public statement about the charge of the suit. On June 10, 1973, an item appeared in the *Sunday Times* of London reporting a speech given to the Philological Society at Oxford by the editor of the OED, Robert Burchfield. In his talk, according to the *Times,* Burchfield took a stand "against politicians, nationalists, religious bigots, and zealous hordes." In effect, he said that the OED had no intention of altering the definition of *Jew* except, perhaps, to add an explanation of how these usages came about. Burchfield used the occasion to "caution icily against 'Guralnikism,' a word denoting the modern equivalent of bowdlerism whose etymology derives from one David B. Guralnik, editor-in-chief of *Webster's New World Dictionary,* Second College Edition 1970." The report went on to state that "Guralnik deemed that words like *dago, kike, wog* and *wop* should be excluded." The article made no reference whatsoever to the pending libel suit.

Defining the obscenities

As the less-than-honored eponym of that Burchfield coinage, I must here explain our practices, past and present, in this connection. In the first College Edition of *Webster's New World Dictionary* (1953), we followed the prevailing dictionary custom of including common terms of racial and ethnic opprobrium, except that we alone carefully noted the derogatory and offensive nature of each such term. For example, for the use of *Jew* as a verb, we added: "vulgar and offensive expression, in allusion to methods attributed to Jewish merchants by anti-Semites." In the years following the publication of that work, I had reason to doubt the wisdom of our decision. Letters from users of the dictionary showed that some misapprehended the adjectives in such a note as that at *nigger* ("a vulgar, offensive term of hostility and contempt, as used by Negrophobes") as applying to the victim of the epithet rather than to the term itself. And despite my regular quotation of Montefiore's dictum that the dictionary should not be blamed for a recorded usage any more than a thermometer should be blamed for a fever, I found myself wondering whether the very inclusion of such terms in the dictionary, with or without notation, did not, in fact, lend respectability to them and tend to perpetuate their usage.

During the planning conferences for the Second College Edition in 1963, staff and consultants debated the question of whether or not to include the so-called obscenities, the taboo English terms dealing with sex and excretion, which were only just then beginning to surface in some publications but had not yet reached the present flood stage. It was decided that the objection to such terms which still prevailed in many quarters, especially in schools, made it unwise to risk the ban that would keep the dictionary out of the hands of students for whom it had been primarily prepared. Having made that decision to exercise our prerogative of selection in one area, I then proposed that we take the next logical step and dispense with those true obscenities, the terms of racial and ethnic opprobrium. After some discussion, it was agreed that we were well within the limits of our lexicographical responsibilities to ignore these terms, which, as I later pointed out in my Foreword to the book, were appearing in print with decreasing frequency these days.

I met Robert Burchfield at a lexicographical conference in 1972, at which time he chided me for our failure to include the taboo sexual terms. I explained the thinking behind our decision and called his attention to my statement in the Foreword. At that time he made no reference to our concomitant decision on the racist terms, nor did he reply to my question about why it took the OED over one hundred years to decide to enter the taboo terms, for which the Oxford editors had long been amply supplied with citations going back to the fourteenth century and earlier.

An explanation is offered
Upon reading the report of Burchfield's speech to the Philological Society, I promptly dispatched a letter to the London *Times*, in which I outlined the principles of vocabulary selection for a desk dictionary of limited scope. On the basis of our own citational evidence, I disputed Burchfield's contention that the use of *Jew* as a verb is frequently met up with in print these days, adding that H.L. Mencken had written in 1945 that the verb, by that date, "seldom appears in any save frankly anti-Semitic writings." I then went on to offer gratuitously my views on how I would handle pejorative terms in a vast, "unabridged" work, such as the OED:

I would, of course, enter all terms for which I have sufficient citational evidence. I would also make certain that the record of usage was complete and that, for example, the verb "to jew" was properly identified as the offensive term that it is, to spare an innocent but insensitive user of it from a social gaffe. I would not treat such a term as dago *as it is dealt with in the OED. The original entry (Vol. III): "U. S. . . . A name originally given in the south-western section of the United States to a man of Spanish parentage; now extended to include Spaniards, Portuguese, and Italians in general." And the expansion in Volume I of the recently published Supplement: "For U. S. read slang (orig. U. S.) . . . (Now a disparaging term for any (sic) foreigner) . . . 2. the Spanish or Italian Language." No indication of opprobrium on the part of the user, except as applied to "any foreigner," and no indication of the offense that could be taken by the reader. In effect, a term that might properly be used in such a sentence as "The* Divine Comedy *was the first major work written in Dago."*

I would not define Jew *as: "A person of Hebrew race," for although I, like most of my lexicographical colleagues, am neither anthropologist nor sociologist, I am sufficiently well-read to know that the Jews are not a race, despite observations to the contrary by such as Houston Stewart Chamberlain and Alfred Rosenberg.*

The *Times* regretted that it would not "have space available in the Letters page to publish it (my letter)." One does not, *khas vesholom*, make space available to criticism of a national institution. The *New York Times,* whose ox was not being gored, printed in its entirety a shorter version of the letter, which I had sent to them.

On July 5, 1974, High Court Justice Sir Reginald Goff dismissed the suit against Clarendon Press on the legalistic grounds that no personal damage or actionable offense against Shloimovitz was done by the dictionary listings. The defamatory matter should and must be construed as a reference to him as an individual. Sir Reginald added with majestic benevolence, in what must rank among the leading bench fatuities of British jurisprudence, "It must, of course, be absolutely apparent to everybody — and I am happy to say this in open court, that there are many fine persons who are Jewish by birth or creed, persons of utmost integrity, honesty, reputation, skill, and ability." And then in a burst of generosity, "If there be Jews, and no doubt there are, who do not in fact measure up to that standard, there are many people not Jews who are just as bad or worse, and there are many non-Jews to whom these derogatory words could very properly be applied."

'To jew' or not 'to jew'
Shloimovitz said he would not carry the case to the Court of Appeal, but would leave the matter to public opinion. Clarendon Press promised not to collect the court costs awarded against Shloimovitz.

But that is not really the end of the matter. Shortly after the publicity attending the OED court case, I received from a correspondent a reproduction of a letter appearing in *The Chicago Tribune* on March 13, 1872, from G. & C. Merriam, publishers of the Merriam-Webster dictionaries in Springfield, Mass. The letter was in reply to a complaint from a Mr. Solomons (note the coincidence — Solomons is the English equivalent of the Slavic Shloimovitz) about the inclusion of a verb *jew,* "to cheat or defraud; swindle" as unjust and unsanctioned by good usage. The publishers conceded that his complaint was justified; that, in fact, a search of earlier British dictionaries reveals no record of such a usage; that they "do not recall ever seeing it employed in literary composition;" that "we fear it must have been drawn from Worcester, where we first find it;" and that it was their intention to drop the term from future editions of the dictionary.

Joseph Worcester was the editor of an American dictionary competing with the Merriam's in the middle of the 19th century. It is a fact that no citations for a verb *to Jew* have yet been uncovered antedating its appearance in Worcester. Is it possible that my fears about the influence of dictionaries are well-founded and that we have here the instance of a usage not only promulgated by dictionaries but actually initiated by one? More research is clearly called for.

A postscript: the current offering of the G. & C.

Merriam Co. includes the verb *to Jew,* as do all other dictionaries of that scope, with the exception of *Webster's New World Dictionary,* Second College Edition.

Why is there no german refugee novel?

Julia Hirsch

A colleague at Brooklyn College recently urged me to volunteer as "literature resource person" for a new, interdisciplinary course on twentieth-century migration to the United States. The suggestion appealed to me. Here was an historical event of which I had some personal knowledge. My childhood had been spent in New York, in the 1940s, with German refugee parents who had bred into me an incurable nostalgia for a Europe I would never truly know, and which had already been shattered beyond restoration. I contacted the chairman of the course. But after reflecting on the syllabus he sent me I realized that the principal literary analogues for the sociological materials it contained dealt with the American experience of Eastern Jewry, whose number has exceeded that of any other Jewish immigration to the United States; for there is at present no imaginative account of refugees like my parents and their Upper West Side circle.

But why is it? Numbers alone are not an adequate explanation. Did not men like my father (the last male of a Prussian-Jewish entrepreneurial family) or his cousins (physicians who knew Classical German, Latin and Greek poetry by heart) have sensibilities? Did not their wives (connoisseurs of fine china, singers of *lieder*) have taste? Could not their ample literacy have charted the rippings and tearings brought about by their own displacement? Nagging questions: for their kind yielded interpretive artists (Bruno Walter, Otto Klemperer); men of pure and social science (Einstein; Erich Fromm); countless professional intellectuals: but no poets, dramatists or novelists who wrote about refugee experience.

Thomas Mann, Jewish by marriage, wrote essentially about the Old World, not the New. But it is quality of migration, not the number of migrants, which is significant here.

The Eastern Jew, by his very act of migration, began his participation in the American myth of success. By travelling steerage — grim *rite de passage* — he was enacting an aquatic Turner thesis, and beginning his career as a Mosaic Horatio Alger. At every turn into the New World he was living a favorite American theme.

In europe they knew their place

But for the German, Belgian and Dutch refugees among whom I grew up in America, despite verbal homages to FDR and LaGuardia, was a falling off. (The contrast I am suggesting between Eastern and Western immigrants is the subject of Donald Kent's study of *The Refugee Intellectual*). In Europe they had had class, prestige, a place within the Gentile community; and within their own, venerable, Jewish culture. In Europe they had already arrived: nothing in the New World could duplicate that achievement. There was no place within American society to which they could rise which would *transcend* the status they had already achieved in Berlin or Antwerp or Amsterdam.

And yet the Western European refugee was, in external ways, far better suited to the realities of American life. Not only did his high level of literacy help him to penetrate the various systems with which the new immigrant had to cope (currency regulations, employment agencies, educational institutions) but his propensity for precision, decorum and punctuality enabled him to master the most pressing contingencies of life: "first papers", housing, schooling for the children. At the same time, the richness of New York, with its department stores and public libraries and concert halls, awaited his well-groomed appetite for the sophisticated pleasures of life which he, with his affinity for "international culture", was better primed to enjoy than was his shtetl counterpart. But ultimately none of these faculties gave much lasting comfort to those who had them. On all sides life in America constituted a decline. A particularly witty cousin of my father, a woman who read English voraciously and favored Jane Austen, declared that "Woolworth supplies the refugee with all his needs, and whatever Woolworth doesn't have, the refugee has no business wanting." What sort of consolation was that if one had been used to dining off Hutschenreuter and Rosenthal?

America not only represented a material decline, but put a final seal on emotion. The stiff upper lip of the Anglos is prevalent as well among the Saxons, and it tends to calcify under stress. The Eastern Jew had brought with him to the New World a folklore of humor, tales and practises which gave him a secure and comforting mode of expression: it helped him to maintain and reconstitute within the New World a sense of community. Eastern Europe had given rise to the great mystics of Jewish tradition and to the charismatic founders of Chasidism. Eastern Jewry had already demonstrated a singular genius for self-expression and spiritual insight which merely reasserted itself in the New World. It is not difficult to understand why Eastern Jewry became a subject for literature; nor why the content of its culture infected the American imagination.

Contrasting the east and west

But my parents' circle had no such expressive resources. They merely dug deeper into their skills for quantification, measurement and punctuality; and sought solace in the appreciation of art rather than its creation. They took English lessons (with far less humor than Hyman Kaplan); they joined choruses. They established medical practices and set up businesses; and formed the core faculty of the New School. They seemed to repeat in the New World the behavior of those German immigrants to Palestine who had acquired the derisive nickname "Yaeke" (derived, I have been told, from "Jacke" for jacket) because they had kept to European dress and procedures even in the frontier torridity of the Jewish Homeland. For me the contrast between East and West was crystallized on occasional Friday evenings when a certain Mr. Shmulewitz came to visit my parents. I do not know how they met: but Mr. Shmulewitz — who spoke a thick and musical Yiddish — came from Poland, and for hours he regaled my parents with anecdotes of shtetl life. By the end of the evening the three of them were in tears. Mr. Shmulewitz wept for his own fate; my parents grieved for a metaphor of theirs. My parents knew where in New York to locate a Rembrandt or a good Panama hat: Mr. Shmulewitz had the gift both of self— and Jewish expression which had carried the essential, emotive qualities of his past into his present.

Mr. Shmulewitz was not ashamed of using the same language and idiom he had spoken in Poland. My parents and other native German-speakers rigorously avoided using the language in which they were eminently articulate and subtle. They wanted above all to dissociate themselves from Hitler. German might be used behind closed doors (among intimate friends or in the heat of a family fight) but it was not to be used in public. Official uneasiness among American Jews and Gentiles alike as to whether

German Jews were truly "Germans" or "Jews" (an attitude documented in detail by Zosa Szajkowski in the *American Jewish Historical Quarterly* of December 1971) vindicated their scruples. But their linguistic restraint was not only political. It represented as well the drastic expunging of analytical and expressive capacities, a sort of self-immolation, partly therapeutic (it was best not to say too well how expulsion and migration really felt), partly penitential (those who had been part of the culture which could in its extremities produce Hitler required silencing). Out of this expressive impasse no literary *art* could arise. (The one literary invention – still in operation – of this generation of immigrants, was *Aufbau*, a weekly newspaper which also sponsored a social club.)

Neither american nor jewish
And there was perhaps no need to notice this denial of self-expression: New York offered refugees many dodges from it. Here were so many little havens of European taste and achievement: fragile mirages amid which one forgot to brood over one's sense of loss or alienation; or else even daydreamed about an eventual, postwar return. Polite conversation over *kafe und kuchen* could truly be achieved at Schrafft's or the Croyden Coffee Shop. My mother took me to Frick Collection concerts on Sunday afternoons, wearing one silk stocking of her own, and one borrowed from a (refugee) friend: but what did that really matter as long as we listened to Arthur Schnabel or Wanda Landowska? For all the private, petty degradations of America, Europe stood by even here to bring comfort: it was too present for one to sense a keen and irrefutable break. The meaning and scope of migration remained nebulous, a sort of disagreeable allergy, like poison ivy. It was neither a Sophoclean experience, which crushed and maimed, nor a comedy in which mistaken identities and subterfuges yield to festive clarity and reconciliation.

And yet all of these ambiguities have been embodied in literature: not the literature of Jewish migration to America, but of the displacement of American Gentiles in Europe. My parents' melancholy contempt for American *things* (saddle shoes, slang, chewing gum) was an inversion of the excessive awe towards Europe of Henry James' travellers; or the moral weariness of Hemingway's expatriates. My parents' mood was that of Prufrock in whom biological lassitude and cultural satiety had fused. How

paradoxical that their state of mind should be contained in American and Gentile literature. Was this the final irony of their status? Mr. Shmulewitz and his tales have spun themselves into daily American consciousness and have achieved aesthetic fulfillment. Who has not heard of *Fiddler on the Roof,* or confessed a fondness for Levy's rye bread, regardless of race, color, or creed. But my parents' migration and that of their circle was never completed: it never created its own idiom or form. The immigrants of my parents' circle play no literary part in the history of American migration. They are merely a species of universal exile, neither uniquely American, nor exclusively Jewish.

Small town jewry: a rabbi's perspective
Barry Marks

"Cultural shock" is no longer a remote or empty bit of sociological jargon. It is a concept readily comprehensible to me on the basis of my personal experience. Raised in the solidly Jewish enclave of northwest Baltimore – self-styled *Yerushalayim d'America* – and trained for the rabbinate on the Upper West Side of Manhattan, I have spent the last 5½ years in three different communities in Central Illinois – a flat terrain of corn, soybeans, Bible-Belt Protestantism and staunch Republicanism. In an area stretching 120 miles across the state from east to west, approximately 5,000 Jews make their home, largely within the six urban centers of the region – Danville, Champaign-Urbana, Bloomington-Normal, Peoria, Decatur and Springfield. These are towns ranging in size from 40,000 to 120,000 with Jewish communities of 250 to 2,000.

I have been on the "pulpit" end of Jewish life in two of these communities – Danville and, currently, Springfield. In Champaign-Urbana, where I sandwiched in a year and a half of law study between my two pulpit experiences, I found myself largely on the "pew" side of Jewish life – at the local Hillel, although I did work part-time for the Religious School of Champaign's Reform congregation. The experience has been alternately rewarding, interesting, challenging and frustrating. I can almost intuitively grasp the meaning of Jacob Katz's comment about the estate managers, proprietors of crossroads inns, and other isolated Jews of medieval Poland; living in remote hamlets and villages — away from the towns with their established structures of Jewish life *(Kehilla,* synagogue, *heder, yeshiva)* — these Jews continued to regard urban Judaism as normative and experienced a "two-fold sense of *Galut",* exiled not only from Homeland and political sovereignty but also from the mainstream of Diaspora Jewish life.

Even a small town can seem like a metropolis
In actuality, perceptions of size are quite relative. Springfield, with twice the general community and six times the Jewish population of Danville, seems more of a medium-sized town than a small one. Peoria, to Easterners a symbol of small-town Middle America, actually has the feel of a big city, Jewishly and otherwise. Its Orthodox synagogue has a *mikveh,* a Hebrew Day School, and a flourishing daily *minyan* — all lacking in Springfield. Even that rarest of commodities — Kosher meat — is available in Peoria at the community-subsidized butcher shop. While Peoria, in the light of my recent experience, seems like a Jewish metropolis, the new, young associate rabbi there — Pittsburgh-born and fresh out of *yeshiva* — is experiencing "cultural shock". Can he maintain his strictly traditional convictions and life-style in the face of realities that run counter to all of his previous experience and training?
Jewish life, even in the small town, is replete with surprises — particularly in the stories and experiences of the people one meets. Who would imagine in Danville, Illinois a wise and gentle *Litvak,* formerly a prosperous lumber merchant before the Soviets expropriated his business, who had been personally acquainted with such luminaries as the Chafetz Chaim and Reb Chaim Ozer Grodzinski? Or a German-born chemist with 23 patents to his credit and a profound knowledge of philosophy and the humanities? Both of these men have now gone to their eternal rest, and the community is all the poorer for their passing.

Voluntarism is both the blessing and curse of small-town Jewish life. In the absence of extensive professional staff or such features of big-city Judaism as the Kosher caterer or Jewish funeral director, personal participation is heightened. We have a *Chevra Kadisha* (Burial Society) at our Temple, and departed members are washed and shrouded by fellow congregants. Although violations of both the letter and spirit of traditional *avelut* (mourning) abound, at least in this crucial respect *chesed shel emet* (genuine righteousness) is practiced. *Oneg Shabbat* and *seudot mitzvah*

(mitzvah of inviting guest to dine) are prepared by members, families celebrating a *simcha,* and friends. This makes for increased participation and involvement but raises delicate questions regarding *kashrut.* Working for days on end in the Temple Kitchen to prepare a *Bar Mitzvah* luncheon is inconvenient, to say the least. But bringing in food prepared in a non-observant home raises the hackles of traditionalists in the community.

The rabbi's job doesn't end at the pulpit
Where voluntarism ultimately fails is in the field of education. Rarely do the qualities of Jewish knowledge, pedagogical skill and willingness to sacrifice sleep or leisure pursuits on Sunday mornings all co-exist within the same individual. The modest wage which we pay our teachers is rarely a crucial factor in the prospective instructor's decision to teach or not.

The small-town rabbi is jack-of-all-trades (and hopefully master of some). In addition to the usual preaching and pastoral tasks, I am *chazan* (except on High Holidays when a professional is hired, and I am demoted to *ba'al shachrit)* (leader of morning prayers), week-day Hebrew teacher, *ba'al kore, (Torah* reader), *Bar Mitzvah* instructor, and co-editor of the bulletin. On occasion, I even lock the doors and shut off lights and heat following a Temple function. A word to the prospective small-town rabbi: learn the quality of *chutzpah,* know how to delegate authority.

I am also an unofficial *shaliach* (representative) to the Christian religious community. A good deal of curiosity about Judaism exists within the more liberal churches of the Bible Belt. Church groups attend our Friday evening services frequently. Vacation Bible School students are brought for tours of the synagogue on sunny summer mornings. And I find myself lecturing and preaching in a wide variety of Protestant and Catholic settings. In part, this phenomenon is to be explained as a belated and welcome desire to come to terms with the Jewish roots of Christianity.

Kinship by blood or marriage is a basic fact of the small-town Jewish community. Two cousins from western Pennsylvania came to Danville to seek new economic opportunities during the Depression. Their descendants today constitute nearly 20% of the community. The Springfield situation is more complex. Virtually all of the "old-timers" are related to each other in a far-ranging network of in-group marriages —

machatunimschaft (relatives through marriage). It took me six months to master the pattern of relationships; and my wife still warns me not to indulge my weakness for *l'shon hara* (gossip) lest I unwittingly slander someone's second cousin or brother-in-law in his presence.

Reformers and traditionalists argue here too
A high rate of intermarriage is another fundamental reality of small-town Jewish life, even within our Conservative (formerly Orthodox) congregation. Fortunately, my Orthodox predecessors were not rigid or unbending in regard to conversion requirements, and some of our most devoted and loyal members are *gerim* (converts). Our most dedicated worker — without whom the whole structure of volunteer effort would crumble — is a former Catholic, of Italian ancestry. Every one of the three weddings I have officiated at in the past year involved a conversion to Judaism, and the pattern seems likely to continue.

The Reform-Traditional schism has been deeply and bitterly felt within our communities. In one town, reformers and traditionalists tried co-existing under the same roof but quarreled bitterly over who would *davven* upstairs and who downstairs. The congregation, now housed in a new and modern edifice is today solidly within the Reform camp. Champaign's traditionalists — largely tenured faculty members at the University of Illinois with an Eastern big-city background — affiliate with the Reform congregation and send their children to its Sunday and Hebrew schools, but they prefer to worship on *Shabbat* and Holidays with the Conservative students at Hillel. Springfield and Peoria are the only communities within the area which still have two congregations. A proposal for merger of the two Springfield temples was vetoed by extremists on both sides. That was 20 years ago. Relations between the two Temples are much better today, although competition is still keen for the affiliation of newcomers to town. A merger would most likely be rejected today — not because of the ideological or social considerations so crucial in the past, but because of institutional investment. Our 15-year old sanctuary was constructed at great financial and emotional cost, and we are hardly ready to submerge our laboriously-acquired identity in a new, unified entity.

Hardship is the reality for a small-town jew
Kashrut in Springfield is a real problem. Delicatessen items are available at the supermarket, but fresh beef and poultry must be obtained from Chicago (200 miles) or St. Louis (100 miles). For the kosher family lacking a home freezer or the funds to purchase meat in huge volume, the rather tedious trip along Interstate 55 becomes a necessary part of one's routine.

Shabbat morning worship is equally problematical. To my knowledge, none of the area Reform synagogues has a Saturday service except when a *Bar Mitzvah* is scheduled. In Springfield, *minyans* for *Shabbat* morning are scrapped together by phoning members during the week and inviting them to participate. Some four or five come regularly on *Shabbat* morning, whether summoned or not; they find the worship meaningful and enjoy the reading of the *parsha*, even when — in the absence of a *minyan* — it is read from a printed *chumash* rather than a scroll.

The reinvigorating effect of newcomers to the community — State employees working in this, the state capital; or faculty members at Sangamon State University or Southern Illinois University's School of Medicine — has already been ably documented in the columns of this publication. What troubles me is the transient nature of this new Jewish migration. I've seen a good deal of mobility in the past year — families barely established in Springfield on the move once again. The situation may become more stable in years to come. For the present, many of our newcomers — particularly those with roots in Chicago or St. Louis — still identify primarily with their former communities and spend one or more weekends a month out of town.

I imply no criticism of the "old-timers". They have worked hard to build and maintain the institution. Years of "voluntarism" have tired them out, and they look to the young to assume some of the burdens.

If Springfield's problem is stability, Danville's is the more basic issue of survival. The most active segment of the Danville community is now in the 40 – 60 age bracket. Danville's Jews are primarily retail merchants in what is essentially an industrial town. The community's children seldom choose to return to Danville following college graduation. The town seems unlikely to attract many new Jewish residents. And even the elders are liable to choose the more hospitable Florida climate over the harsh Midwestern winters, when retirement time arrives.

Will the jew be strengthened or weakened here

The small-town rabbi faces a dilemma. One's influence and ability to effect necessary changes are proportional to the length of one's service to the congregation. Very often, the mere presence of a rabbi, no matter who he is or what his qualifications, has a unifying and catalytic effect on the small community. Moreover, the small-town rabbi knows that when he leaves, a successor will not be readily found.

But what of my longings for a Kosher meat market on the corner, a *Shabbat* morning minyan that assembles itself without coaxing and a bookstore where I can browse over *seforim*, rather than order over the telephone?

What of our infant son, initiated into the Covenant of Abraham by a *mohel* who travelled in from St. Louis for the occasion? Will he be a better Jew for having to work harder at it? Will his perception of the non-Jewish environment, all the more evident in the small town, strengthen or weaken his attachment to Judaism? When he reaches high school age, how will he react to his Jewish contemporaries, for whom Friday night is football or basketball night? What can his parents do in the absence of an observant peer group, such as a Hebrew Day School might provide? None of these questions are original. Small town Jews have been asking them for many years. If I leave them unanswered, this is because in contemplating both the potential and the perils of small-town Jewish life the basic issues are still unresolved in my own mind.

An instructive failure for sh'ma

Joel Soffin

Imagine yourself as a Jewish economist or an economic Judaicist. Think of the possibilities! You could resolve the crisis of the world economies. You could make economics value-ful (or maybe value-able). You could teach the world the lessons of Judaism, the inspired economic ideas of the rabbis.

We at *Sh'ma* were intrigued by these possibilities and sent requests for articles to Nobel prize winners, economics professors, Talmudists and students. The result: an unwritten issue on the "Jewish contribution" to the solution of our economic problems. Why was this so? Is it Jews or Judaism which has nothing to say about our complex world?

Let's look at the responses more closely. One Nobel prize winner wrote: "Through years of active research and teaching on economic problems, I have . . . refrained from making judgments — limiting my work and publications to statistical analyses of quantitative data." What a concise summary of the position of many economists that their "science" is strictly objective and value-free. It is seen in much the same light as the computer upon which it relies so heavily: neutral. Numbers and statistics do not carry value judgments, nor do their manipulators.

But is this indeed the case? Consider for a moment the simple but significant example of unemployment data. Definitions play a critical role in deciding who is unemployed, for we must first determine what it means to "actively seek employment." Only those people who fit into this category are relevant. Our current definition excludes those workers who have temporarily stopped looking for new jobs. It is as if they simply disappeared. This puts a downward bias, in human terms if not in strictly economic terms, on our statistics and reduces the weight given to solving the problem of unemployment in the face of increasing inflation. The data are not neutral. The assumptions that are imbedded in their collection do influence our decisions. I doubt if there is such a thing as purely objective economic research, but it seems to provide a convenient ideological smoke-screen behind which economists may hide.

Economics and judaism: does one relate to the other

Then there was the response of the *Talmud* student. "I do think that traditional *halachic* and *Talmudic* discussion did not consider macroeconomic activity or problems in the way we do today," he wrote, "and therefore some of these problems are difficult to resolve with care." This statement is most certainly true and it probably goes a long way toward explaining the absence of any serious application of *Talmudic* insights to the problems of our economy. Yet, one cannot help but wonder whether "difficult to resolve with care" is not the *Talmudists'* smokescreen. Each *Shabbat* thousands of rabbis preach about the relevance of Judaism to the whole range of present day issues. Great too is the number of Judaicists who agree with their feelings. But where are the Jewish scholars who will show us in a most careful way what the message of Judaism actually is? Don't any of them find our economic distress an area of high priority for Jewish input? In the back of my mind there is the haunting feeling that their silence may be telling us that Judaism has nothing to say after all!

If economists see themselves as value-free, neutral technicians who leave the value judgments to easily influenced political leaders, must not the scholars of religion rise to fill in the gap, or forever hide in the safe world of ancient history? The problem is a serious one for the future credibility of our religious leaders and institutions depends, in no small measure, on the substantiation of the claim that Judaism speaks to our world in all of its complexity. Social scientists and Judaica specialists must find the time to work together to determine just what the values of our tradition imply in terms of our economic behavior as individuals and as a nation. The time will come when the answers found in *The Jewish Catalog* will no longer suffice as the grounding for anyone's Jewishness.

In search of a new intelligentsia

Michael Nutkiewicz

Much effort is spent in the United States and Israel worrying about Jewish destiny and planning the survival of Jewish life. Jewish survival is usually analyzed in demographic terms: the rate of intermarriage and assimilation, or in speculation about the possible rise of an anti-Semitism which could lead to the physical destruction fo Jews.

I want to suggest, however, that the future of Jewish life in the United States, Israel, and other countries depends on the emergence of a Jewish intelligentsia. I am not using the term "intellectual" with snobbish intent. The intellectual is not defined by formal education but by a passion for Jewish culture and literature expressed through the literary contributions of journals, artistry, scholastic work, and, if possible, the formation of intellectual "salons."

It is clear from Jewish history that only the tradition of genuine Jewish scholarship — in its widest sense — has succeeded in perpetuating Jews and Judaica. Those concerned with intermarriage and assimilation obscure the more fundamental problem — the need for contributions of the Jewish intelligentsia. During one of the most productive and richest periods of Jewish history — Medieval Spain under Islam — mass assimilation and conversion were commonplace, as well as an immersion in secular study. The survival of the

MICHAEL NUTKIEWICZ *treaches religious studies at the University of Missouri in Columbia, MI.*

brilliant legal, literary, and philosophic products of Spanish Jewry was not connected to demographic factors but to the willingness of a "saving remnant" to preserve and continue Jewish learning. Jewish learning was passed to northern Europe through a handful of intellectuals (mainly translators) in southern France. The problem has never been the number of Jews, but rather, assuring interest in preserving and continuing Jewish learning.

Older Models of Jewish Creativity

As important as "defense agencies" are to Jewish life, the obsession with measuring and charting the level of anti-Semitism also misses the mark. Freedom has not always led to cultural contributions to a particular society. In sixteenth-century Poland, Jews enjoyed privileges and relatively little persecution yet were culturally alien and isolated from the larger society. They were regarded by the Poles and, more significantly, by themselves as Germans living in a lower culture. In Italy, by contrast, Jews lived in Ghetto conditions as a persecuted minority; nevertheless, they participated fully in the Renaissance. The conclusion clearly is that the stimulus to creative Jewish participation in a society's culture does not always depend upon the Jews' political or social status but may depend on their cultural integration and upon the extent to which Jews subjectively feel themselves alienated from their surroundings.

The Jewish intellectual, it seems to me, must also be acquainted with the totality of serious Jewish expression without dogmatically insisting on any particular interpretation of Judaism. Whatever their interpretation, Orthodox and Liberal Judaism share the same cultural and intellectual background. Jewish history is neither a smooth continuity with the past nor a series of discontinuities or revolutions. Originality must be expressed in the language of past traditions; on the other hand, Jews must guard against idealizing the past (either through a historical theology or uninformed sentiment). The intellectual cannot dogmatically insist on any particular interpretation of Judaism.

I do not presently see creative Jewish elites or literate communities emerging from the youth of either Israel or the United States. We have models of the intellectual: the late historian Irving Howe, the writers and editors of the *Menorah Journal* (1915-1962), a virtual American Jewish salon of intellectuals, and the international Yiddish circle whose works appear in the journal in Israel, the *Goldene Keyt*. Their contributions exhibit an incredible range of Jewish knowledge and an intimacy with things Jewish. These intellectuals (of course there are more), however, are by and large from an older generation, and I do not see their replacement from among younger Jews (now in their 20's and 30's). I am concerned about this void. We need an intelligentsia which will leave a creative legacy to future generations; moreover, that intelligentsia must have a critical audience, one which is familiar with a wide range of literary, historical, and philosophical Jewish issues.

Sources of Renewed Creativity

Building a new Jewish intelligentsia and an audience which is Jewishly literate is a slow process but it is imperative that it be done. The *havurah* movement could be a format for this intellectual revitalization in the United States but in practice has not realized its full potential. Members are too passive and the *havurot's* function tends to be social. The group may bring in occasional speakers or hold *shabbatons* once or twice a year. While these steps are in the right direction, *havurot* in general are not intellectually oriented. Jewish studies programs at universities may offer the range and format for serious cultural and intellectual work, yet if the values of the community do not encourage such intellectual pursuits it will be difficult to convince young people who are concerned with jobs and their future financial security that there is a value in majoring in Jewish studies or filling their electives with Jewish studies courses. In the United States, federations may have to rethink their priorities in allocating limited funds both to Israel and at home. Perhaps Americans would more easily agree to keep their money at home if federations offered incentives for the Jewish arts and culture as well as insisted on quality educational programs at the local level. Further, we rely on the Jewish "professional" for choices which should be made at the local level. The professionalization of Jewish life in the United States has virtually taken the decision making about education, *tzedakah* and family from the local community.

Learning to Draw from Common Roots

There are still mentors from whom we can learn and with whom our youth may possibly feel an intellectual kinship. It is our reponsibility to tap these sources. Our educators must have a larger vision of Jewish literacy. Orthodox training should reach into the richly textured literary world of secularism (as did the Jews of medieval Spain and Renaissance Italy), and should consider the halachic and philosophical works of Reform and Conservative rabbis and thinkers; secularlists and religiously liberal Jews should not be afraid to immerse themselves with past tradition, expecially the classical sources. Unfortunately, the trend here and in Israel is toward polarization: the clashes between Orthodox and secular Jews in Israel, and the vehement written and even physical attacks of Hasidism on the Conservative movement in Israel are the most obvious manifestations of this polarity. Though we share a common heritage, there exists incommensurate interpretations between particular expressions of that heritage; these differences, however, must be tolerated.

I do not envision or suggest a new synthesis between particular Jewish traditions. The most important factor for the survival of Jewish life is the ability to travel comfortably between the literature and tradition of the two poles of Jewish expression, religious and cultural. Jewish survival entails the willingness to study and the ability to find others who are similarly motivated. A community of Jews articulate and imbued with Jewish learning—the new intelligentsia—will certainly withstand, as it has in the past, any challenge to its survival. •

The office chanukah party

Pat Delaney

It began when a friend and I got into a discussion about the "problem of Christmas" and how as Jews it is easy to succumb to the celebration of this day through participation in festivities which, albeit secularized beyond recognition, are nonetheless a remembrance of and rejoicing in the birth of Jesus as God incarnate. I know the rationalizations to which we (the modern counterparts of the Hellenizing Jews) resort. "How can we deprive the children of Santa and the tree?" "Christmas is really American and not religious." "The people on my job and friends will ostracize me if I do not give or actively participate in a Christmas party." The crucial question for Jews at the time of the Maccabees is still with us today, namely, how to be a complete, active citizen of the larger society without compromising our Jewishness.

We decided that each day in my office, during afternoon break time, 4 p.m., we would observe

Chanukah by publicly lighting the candles and saying the blessings. I work for an agency of the New York City government and, as one would expect, the staff is very diverse. The agency is permitted a yearly Christmas party which is held in the manner typical of all such affairs. We invited staff from the entire building to participate or observe. I was subsequently told that there had never been a *Chanukah* observance in any office or branch of my agency which any staff members could recall.

Our Little Oil Burned Long and Bright

Great events can be sparked in simple ways and it was my friend's gift of two boxes of *Chanukah* candles and his quick printing of the announcements which really created what I believe is going to become a lasting tradition. Monday, the second day of *Chanukah* was the first day of our festival observance. I had no idea how many, if any, people would decide to join us but at the last minute I decided to have a dozen jelly donuts and a bottle of wine ready for a celebration. Shortly before 4:00 p.m., thirty-five to forty people had gathered outside my office. Many of them were then strangers to us. The group was eclectic and included Jews in traditional attire, others in jeans. We had young and old, men and women, from all levels of the agency hierarchy, Christians as well as Jews.

At 4:00 p.m. I lit the candles and read the blessings in both Hebrew and English. I cannot describe the spirit of comraderie, joy, and pride which was apparent in the words and eyes of the group. Our group was truly united. Individuals lingered and chatted with others they had probably passed in halls and elevators for years without so much as a "hello." Line and administrative staff, traditionalists and universalists and agnostics were at least temporarily united by this experience. We explained the story of *Chanukah* and answered questions and at the end invited everyone to come back. I found myself receiving numerous hugs and handshakes. People thanked me for "what I had done for them" and told me "how proud and Jewish they felt." It was not what I had done but the spirit which we had created together.

Joyous Self-respect Is Contagious

Tuesday was unbelievable. Starting at 9:15 in the morning, the food and wine began to arrive. Throughout the day my new friends came to me with pastry, candy, and nuts for the celebration.

Contributions had never been solicited or suggested. This continued throughout the week. I supplied paper goods, office space and some food for a few non-Jewish "regulars" who I discovered were on restrictive diets. It had really happened. It was an affirmation and proclamation by the Jewish staff as an entity. I insisted that subsequent candle blessings be said by a different person each day in order to spread the honors. Each day the group grew as others were lured by the enthusiasm of their co-workers. It never lasted beyond a half-hour. The religious element was always paramount, the partying was moderate — subdued and second to the blessings.

These elements evoked amazement, respect, and commendation from the non-Jewish staff who compared it to the "goings on" at other office parties held at the agency. Each day was special and unique. One day we had seventy home-made *latkes,* on another, baked cookies. On Thursday a traditional friend brought and lit his oil *menorah* and, having filled it too full, had to remain after hours and wait for it to burn down. On Friday a group of mostly non-Jewish clerical workers were so moved by our celebration that they bought a *menorah* and asked me to light and bless the candles. The *menorah* was placed on a beautifully decorated table next to the table that was occupied by the Christmas tree.

Friday was the last day of our office observance. Shortly after 9:00 a.m., I was presented with a large and beautifully braided *challah* along with the usual array of goodies. I knew that our Friday group would be smaller since several would be departing early to prepare for the Sabbath. Yet, they came with gifts in the morning and others called me or came down to wish me a *gut yontif* and *shabbat shalom* before leaving for the weekend. I wanted this last day to be extra special, so in addition to the regular candle blessings I read the *Al Hanissim* prayer. My friend then led the group in the *kiddush* and the *motzi* over the *challah.* The group lingered a little longer than usual. We talked about what the celebration had meant to each of us, how good and proud we all felt, about the new wonderful and unlikely friendships we had formed and other ways we could keep this sense of unity and *am yisrael chai* alive throughout the year.

Yes, this year I experienced Chanukah.

The mental health needs of the pious

Leon Gersten (as told to Adina Mishkoff)

(While Orthodox and Chassidic Jews readily seek medical assistance for physical problems, it has been difficult to get them to seek treatment for psychological problems. As an Orthodox psychologist who is active in the Orthodox and Chassidic communities, primarily in Boro Park (Brooklyn), Dr. Gersten, in a recent interview, discussed the attitudes of members of these communities towards mental health. The following has been condensed from that interview.)

There has always been a recognition that Orthodox and Chassidic people had some difficulty relating to the established mental health profession as a source of psychological help. Their reluctance to seek help can be divided basically into two types of reasons — religious and communal.

First there are fears that seeking help would undermine their religious values. There is the feeling that if you'd be a little more religious and try a little harder then you wouldn't have psychological problems. Associated with this factor is a fear that the mental health worker would not really understand their problems in the context of what their values and goals are. This is somewhat justified since there are situations where a therapist has confused religion with pathology and neurosis. Dealing with Orthodox workers helps solve this latter problem, eliminating terminological misunderstandings. Since people with problems usually incorporate the religion as part of the symptomotology, it is very important for the therapist to be able to differentiate. With a thorough background and knowledge of what Judaism expects and demands, and the implications of certain laws, it is easier to help the person see through the defenses.

For example, I saw one husband who told me that when he got married he bought old furniture even though he had a lot of money. The idea was that he believed it was better to give the money to *"tzedakah"* (charity) than to spend it on new furniture. So, one has to make the judgment whether this was the expression of his high level of religiosity or basically a reflection of extreme stinginess and inability to spend money and enjoy life. Orthodox clinicians can help see what the patient does with the *Halachah.* If this is classified immediately as a defense — that it's not really a

question of the person being religious — obviously you're going to approach it differently than if it's a question of genuine religiosity, if someone's at a very high level, extremely *frum* in a balanced way. People who have this tremendous genuine drive do a lot of things that the average person would not do. Buying old furniture is not the action of an average Orthodox person — you have to be on a higher *"madregah;"* (level) but if you're not, it means that what you're driven by is not authentic religion. And these are the sorts of differentiations an Orthodox clinician can help make.

Therapy Carries Communal Stigma

The other type of fear is the "communal" one: The Orthodox and Chassidic communities, be they in Boro Park, Crown Heights or Williamsburg, are very close-knit groups, each member feeling responsible to and for his neighbor. While going to Orthodox workers might make religious explanations and differentiations easier, there is also the fear that, in a small community like Boro Park, when staff members also come from within the community, they will be recognized. The idea of seeking psychological approaches to problems is still regarded as undesirable — there is a tremendous stigma attached to it, interfering with a person's reputation and communal standing. Psychological approaches tend to emphasize the individual psychological needs rather than the overall responsibility to family, community and God, more a focus on 'self.' To some extent this might be perceived as not having the proper attitudes towards life. There is also the basic (and not completely distorted) theory that mental illness and emotional problems come from genetic factors so that once a family member is believed to have a problem, there's the suspicion that others in the family might have it also, affecting the family's standing the community, especially in regard to potential *shidduchim* (matches.)

The Maimonides Community Mental Health Center's Community Service Center is a branch of the Medical Center but at a separate location, in part so as not to have the 'hospital,' 'psychiatric' stigma associated with it. On the other hand, it is in the center of the Orthodox Boro Park community, staffed by community members, thus creating the possibility that someone coming in for help might be recognized. (The fact that workers naturally hold all visits and activities in strict confidence is not immediately considered by the patients).

The privately-run Interborough Developmental consultation Center near Prospect Park, also in Brooklyn, is the first licensed mental health clinic under Orthodox auspices. I helped found the clinic, opened mainly to serve those Orthodox and Chassidic people who seek psychological help with clinicians who can understand their problems and who either live outside the "catchment area" served by Maimonides or simply want to go to a clinic not near their community where they might be recognized. The main problem, though, is that because of all the above-mentioned fears, traveling the extra distance often adds to the resistance of those not highly motivated to go to begin with.

Who are those that do come, why do they seek help, and what type of help do they seek?

Many Problems Are Child-Related

An important job at the Maimonides Mental Health Center and at Interborough is outreach to community schools and *yeshivot.* Since teachers usually become aware quite early of problems children might be having relating to others in an objective, non-familial situation, the workers try to make teachers and rabbis familiar with the Centers' services and encourage them to recommend either of the centers to parents of problem children. There is more of an acceptance in terms of dealing with children coming for evaluation to try and find out what the problem is; this is often the result of pressure from the school. If parents hear suggestions from a *rebbe* or teacher, they're more likely to try to come for help.

Most of our caseload is related in one way or another to children. If the teacher thinks the child needs help s/he will tell the parent; it is then up to the parent to bring the child in. With children, the problem is usually related to what's going on in the family, so unless the parents are difficult and irresponsible and avoid contact with the therapist, usually they become involved in some direct counseling as well.

The question, however, becomes, how do parents *deal* with the problem, where does the problem come from and what is reinforcing the problem? The reason why we don't have much more success with children is because usually we have trouble changing what's going on in the family,

or the personalities of the parents. Children are much more amenable to change because their problems have not yet become part of their character, embedded in their whole personality; it's still more reactive to pressures from the outside. But when they come to us we usually don't have much control over the pressures that are creating the problems, i.e., the family situation.

Clients Prefer Short-Term Therapy

Most of the Chassidic population will come for help only when the problems are extremely severe and when they're faced with psychotic breakdowns or severe depression. Otherwise, for adjustment-type and minor, neurotic problems, there is still a great reluctance to come. The large part of adult treatment is short-term, dealing with immediate obvious problems. The tendency is that with children and family problems, when things ease up and pressures slacken, the therapy is terminated. If someone comes in for individual therapy, to 'figure themselves out,' so to speak, and not just responding to an immediate pressure, then there is a chance the therapy could be of longer duration. But there are very few among the ultra-Orthodox and Chassidic who decide to undergo or continue in therapy simply to figure themselves out.

In seeking short-term treatment rather than the introspective, analytic approach, medication is often used to solve immediate stress problems. This associates psychological treatment with the more accepted medical treatment and is somewhat of an incentive for the Chassid to seek help. Using medication to solve an immediate problem avoids the need to concentrate on oneself, to examine one's bad *machshavos* (thoughts). Generally, through religion, one tries to get away from bad thoughts and displace them with good deeds and thoughts. Since in therapy one zeroes in on one's deep-rooted problems instead of avoiding them, this long-term analytical therapy is generally avoided.

The medication may not solve the problems that they actually have, though, i.e., not relating well to the children or spouse, but if we feel medication will help with interpersonal relations, we give it to them. Coming back for further psychological treatment is always left up to the patient, since no one can tell them to come back or not, as is always the case in therapy. All the therapist can do is say, "I think this would be highly advisable;

if you're not going to continue, in all likelihood the problem is not going to go away." The only thing we can do is share with them the realistic possibilities.

Women Are More Likely To Seek Treatment

Women are more likely to accept treatment than men, both for their children's problems and their own which usually involve depression and some reaction to a difficult situation. They sometimes come with general marital problems, but this is hardly a trend for most women. Indirectly, it is possible that women are making more demands and expectation levels are higher, but there are complicating factors like their getting married earlier. Women expect more now and are not willing simply to settle for whatever life has to offer. This is one reason why there are more divorces — maybe they *do* want more personal gratification from the relationship as a result of what's going on in the world around them. However, I feel the modern Orthodox woman has been influenced by these factors more than Chassidic women. Because of their more acute feelings of peer reactions, it is very uncommon among Chassidim for the husband to agree to come. He is usually overpowered by the exaggerated fear, the extreme self-consciousness and sensitivity, about his role, and would be horrified at the idea of being seen, thus avoiding stepping into a place like this. The whole *mar'it ayin* concept, what people would think and/or say, is an actual problem here, and it's a disadvantage, because of this factor, being located right in the community, with community people here.

The Centers Strive To Be Flexible

Sometimes the wife will then decide that if the husband doesn't want to deal with the marital problem she might as well see what she can get out of this experience herself, in terms of making her stronger to deal with the pressures of raising the children and dealing with the husband. Occasionally the wife requests that the husband not know she is seeking treatment, but we usually discourage this since it would only create guilt and additional anxiety. I had a recent situation where the mother didn't want the father to know that the child was coming in for treatment. I said that under those circumstances I would *not* agree to see the child because I felt that to get the child into the middle of this secrecy would not be too helpful; any benefit derived from therapy would be nullified. In most cases, especially if the wife

has a little determination, the husband will usually go along. There was a woman who, after being told by her husband that he forbade her to come, just picked herself up and continued coming anyway, despite his threats to leave her if she did.

If various conditions make it impossible for a person to come to the Centers for help, we can usually make accommodations. We're very flexible in terms of making home visits; if a family doesn't want to come, we may go to the home to do the treatment, on a regular basis if necessary. I've seen one couple in treatment where the husband refuses to come in for fear of being seen. We registered them under a pseudonym and even a pseudo-address (or, in some cases, a relative's) since they were extremely sensitive about being identified. But this is an extreme case, which does indicate, however, that we are willing to make adjustments if these troubled families would seek help.

In summary, let me add that our services are limited by the human resources available since there are other demands on these resources. Both Centers *will* continue, but whether their services will expand, even if demand warrants it, is a question, since we are limited both in time and manpower. But we do serve an important function in that we seek to help people who otherwise would not be seen.

I am a pencil; where are all the pens?
Melanie B. Shimoff

Clinical psychologist Dr. Reuben E. Gross once asked the participants of a workshop for Orthodox Jewish singles to write a paragraph beginning with the sentence, "I am a pencil." "I am a pencil," one woman began. "Where are all the pens?

In her simple rejoinder, this woman expressed the unbearable agony that single people are frequently intimately acquainted with. Living in the midst of Manhattan's West Side, I have rarely seen people "having too much fun to marry." Rather, I meet lonely men and women desperately reaching out to others in an effort to find and sustain human contact. Often they fail. The common denominator of their existence is the uncertainly that singles who would like to marry all live with, the uneasy, unarticulated question of their lives, "When will this all end?"

While social rules seem to have disappeared in a society where women have achieved economic and social parity, and while even the men in my circle agree that there are more quality women around than men, I am convinced that demography and sociology are merely excuses, not reasons, that many of my peers remained unjoined by the holy vows of matrimony. Like Dan Dorfman, I am neither a mental health practitioner nor a researcher on living single. Yet I have observed that the behavior of single adults is often consciously and/or unconsciously motivated by the interplay of two psychological forces: the fear of commitment and the pain of loneliness.

It is impossible to underestimate the effect of the ''Culture of Narcissism'' on our psyches. We live in an age where ''I'' is the most important word in our vocabularies. The array of psychological self help books for bruised egos is dazzling: we can learn how to live alone and love it, get divorced creatively, say no to other people, and love thy-self before and above all others. Self has become the primary concern of our lives. As Dorfman points out, even U.C.L.A. assures us we can become caring partners and retain our egos and full identities.

Domination by the Ego

But in a world dominated by ''I'', there is no room for ''we.'' We have assured ourselves that our egos will remain unhurt, our inner secrets untouched by another human, at the cost of our ability to become more than superficially involved with other people. Living in our protected, ego-centric world, we are now witnessing the results of our psychological isolation: higher divorce rates, relationships that seemed ''hot and heavy'' breaking up, a steep rise in the number of people who say they want to get married but who remain single in their late 20's, 30's, and even 40's. We seem to have decided that the stakes are so high and the unknown too vast to risk our fragile egos in such potentially devasting endeavors as relationships.

This dynamic can be termed ''the fear of commitment'' and it is expressed in many forms. For some, it is an attachment to career. How many times has the statement, ''When I finish med. school (law school, business school, graduate school, etc.), I'll get married'' been heard? ''I can't afford it now'' is the excuse, but the truth is closer to ''I don't want to devote the time and energy necessary to succeed.'' Others haven't found the right person yet. They are willing to wait forever for Mr. or Ms. Right to come along. Still others find themselves dating the same person for years with no change in the relationship;

their friends never go out with the same person more than twice.

However, it is possible to overcome this fear. For the terror that commitment engenders lies on one side of a psychological gradient; on the other is an equally intense pain, the result of the profound loneliness that a person who has not found his/her helpmate feels. The pain expresses itself in many ways, from depression and suicide in the extreme to the diffuse feeling that ''something is missing in my life.''

The commitment/loneliness gradient operates in much the same way as the classical model of approach/avoidance conflicts. The approach/avoidance model illustrates the tendency to avoid a coveted goal even as one approaches it. As the goal draws nearer, both the desire to reach it (approach) and to run from it (avoid) become greater. Only when one conquers the avoidance mechanism can the goal be attained. In our terms, this means that as one strives to overcome the pain caused by loneliness, fear of the commitment necessary for a successful relationship becomes stronger. The goal can be reached only when one is mentally and emotionally prepared to make the last, final jump.

When to Change Directions?

The crucial questions, of course, are when and how. When is one ready and how does one know? Alas, there are no clear answers or I could market the solution like old time patent medicines. It appears that people are able to move when one or more of their defenses against loneliness breaks down. It can be a milestone birthday, a change in career status, or watching your friend's children grow up. For some, the crucial moment comes when one's peers get married. I have seen many of my male friends get engaged, usually to women they've known only for a short time, only weeks or months after their roommates or best friends announce their intentions to wed. It is as if they have lost a support system in their lives and now must confront a new reality. (I have rarely seen the same thing happen with women, probably a reflection of the greater freedom men enjoy to be assertive in relationships.)

More often than ''when,'' people I meet are concerned with the ''how.'' ''How will I know?'' is asked by otherwise logical men and women who assume that Prince or Princess Charming will one day sweep him or her off his/her feet. Since nobody rides white horses anymore, everyone is looking for new signs. But ''how'' follows ''when'' in this case; when one is ready to change his/her life, the next person looks a lot more ''right.''

The last question I always seem to hear is, "What do I do now that I'm ready to make this commitment?" This final query should be the easiest for people to answer themselves, for the essence of loving is allowing another person inside one's space. For all its real and exaggerated romanticism, love is possible only when two people learn to compromise, to move over and allow their partners to grow within the relationship. Love comes when "we" is just as important as "I", when pens and pencils find each other, accept their differences and tie their common fate together. ★

How i met my wife
William Wallen

I hereby certify that my wife, Harriet, has read this account and she agrees that all the events described therein are true.

In January, 1978, *Sh'ma* published an article that I had written at their request entitled "Memoirs of a Nice Jewish Boy." In the article I recounted how, by virtue of my upbringing, Phi Beta Kappa key, and law school diploma, I had been designated a "Nice Jewish Boy", and was thus supposed to find and marry the corresponding "Nice Jewish Girl." Soon after the article appeared, an astounding thing happened: female readers of the article, who felt they met my definition of "Nice Jewish Girl", began writing to me via *Sh'ma*. Every week or so, an envelope would arrive from Port Washington, and inside it would be several polite letters of introduction. This episode in my life I now call my "Mr. Lonely Hearts" period, and someday I will tell you about it, but that's not why I'm writing now.

In the fall of 1979, while the "Mr. Lonely Hearts" letters were still arriving, my friend Ralph gave me his opinion. "Look, Willie," he said, "rather than publish these rambling lamentations about your eligibility but lack of prospects, which are really no more than thinly disguised advertisements for yourself, why don't you *do* something about it? Go to Israel."

"Israel?" "Yes, Israel," Ralph replied. "This summer I took a three-week tour of Israel. We had a guide and pretty decent accommodations, and we went everywhere from Eilat to Metullah. And, might I add, everyone in the tour group had to be between 22 and 27, and out of about 30 tourists, a least 20 were women."

I thought about it for a long moment. "Sign me up!" I replied.

At the El Al departure terminal, while waiting out the standard five-hour delay, a representative of the tour operator handed me a list of the members of the group. I scanned its contents, and suddenly I drew in my breath, my hands began to tremble, and the building seemed suffused with a golden light.

I was having a genuine Religious Experience.

Slowly I extended my right index finger and began to count. The tally: Thirty-nine participants in the tour group: seven men, 32 women.

I looked heavenward and smiled with deep satisfaction. A lifelong question had been finally answered, and with certainty. God exists, I thought. Not only that, but He answers prayer, too.

On the first day of the tour, in Jerusalem, Reuven, the tour guide, announced that he wanted to do something to bind the group together, and so instructed the bus driver to take us to the Silwan Tunnel. The Tunnel, he explained, was excavated by King David to bring water into the walled city, from the spring which was outside the wall. During summer, the water was only ankle deep, and one could walk through it and emerge inside the Old City. As we descended into its opening, single file, Reuven handed each of us a lighted candle, which was to be our only light inside. A skinny girl in cut-off denim shorts, Harriet from Massachusetts, was in front of me in the line.

The walk through the Silwan Tunnel took about twenty minutes, and, looking back, was probably the single most significant event in my life. Most of the time the ceiling of the Tunnel was too low for me to stand up straight, and so I had to walk hunched over, holding my candle straight in front of me. For twenty minutes, all I could see was the few feet in front of me that the candle illumined. My view, from my hunched-over position for those twenty minutes, was thus restricted to Harriet from Massachusetts in front of me, or more precisely, her cut-off denim shorts. At the end of the twenty minutes, as we emerged into sunlight, I felt like we were old friends.

That day at lunch I sat down next to Harriet from Massachusetts and perused the front of her, from the waist up. She was wearing a bright red T-shirt that bore the legend "Smith College Centennial 1875-1975: A Century of Women on Top." The T-shirt did not deter me from what I wanted to say.

"Hi, I'm Bill from New Jersey, and I was behind you in the Tunnel today, and . . . . well. . . uh. . . how do you take to really sexist, male chauvinist remarks? "It depends what they are", she said, puzzled. "Why?" "Well, you see," I stammered, "I was walking behind you in the Tunnel today, and. . . er. . . I couldn't stand up straight most of the time, and so I was bent over, and . . . . well, all there was to see was what the candle lit up in front of me, and well . . . . considering my posture, that was your rear end, and . . . so that's all I looked at for twenty minutes, and I just wany you to know that. . . you have a real nice *tush*." She flushed.

On Thursday evening of that week, I asked around the tour group for some volunteers to accompany me from the restaurant where we had gathered to the little park at Montefiore's wind-mill, where I was going to photograph the Old City at night. Only Harriet from Massachusetts came forward. At the park, as I fiddled with my camera, I thought of my father and grandparents, all gone, and their parents and grandparents, and ancestors I never knew or even knew existed, and felt a deep sense of accomplishment. I had com-pleted their journey. For generations, on holy days and in times of persecution, they had longed to stand where I was, in their own city, and feel the security and calmness that emanated from the golden light of that steadfast wall. I was the first of the lines of the Wallens and the Galinskys to make it to Jerusalem. It was my privilege to see what they could only imagine. I took a photograph, to save it.

"Hey, Harriet," I asked a week later in Tiberias, "have you ever read a small publication called *Sh'ma*" "Yes." "Did you by chance happen to read an issue that was dedicated to singles?" She thought a moment. "I think a friend showed it to me. All I remember was an article in which some guy described himself as a terrific catch, because he was a lawyer and had a Phi Beta Kappa key."

"Really!" "Yeah. I thought he was obnoxious."

The former Harriet Zelermyer of Salem, Massachusetts, and I were married on July 12, 1981 at Temple Emanuel in Marblehead, Massachusetts. She wore a chiffon gown and a veil, and I wore a rented tuxedo and my father's cuff links, but not my Phi Beta Kappa key. The photograph of the Old City at night sits on a shelf in the den of our home in Yardley, Pennsylvania. •

209

Should a jew sell guns?

J. David Bleich

Mr. Isaac Goldstein, Proprietor
Rocky's Pawn Shop
Elm Street
Dallas, Texas

Dear Mr. Goldstein:

Time Magazine reports that you are giving serious consideration to discontinuing the sale of handguns in your establishment. No doubt, the recent attempt upon the life of President Reagan is prompting such soulsearching not only on your part, as proprietor of the store which sold that particular gun, but on the part of countless other gun dealers as well. Permit me to draw your attention to one aspect of Jewish teaching which should figure prominently in such deliberations.

Maimonides (*Hilkhot Rotzeah* 12:12, paraphrasing *Avodah Zarah* 15b) declares: ''It is forbidden to sell heathens weapons of war. Nor is it permitted to sharpen their spears, or to sell them knives, manacles, iron chains, bears, lions or any object which can endanger the public; but it is permitted to sell them shields which are only for defence.''

Mr. Goldstein, a sticker on the door of your shop reads, ''Guns Don't Cause Crime Any More Than Flies Cause Garbage.'' Maimonides disagrees emphatically. In explaining the premise upon which this provision of Jewish law is based, Maimonides tells us that in selling arms to a heathen ''one strengthens the hands of an evil-doer and *causes him to transgress*'' and ''anyone who causes one who is blind with regard to a matter to stumble -- or one who strengthens the hand of a person who is blind and does not see the path of truth because of the desire of his heart violates a negative precept as it is stated, ''You shall not put a stumbling block before the blind.''

This precept was understood by the Sages as an admonition designed to protect not only the physically blind, but the intellectually and morally blind as well. A Jew is forbidden to take advantage of another person's lack of awareness in a way which causes harm to that person or to others. The Torah forbids us to mislead the blind and thereby cause them to stumble.

We are forbidden to give the uninformed misinformation or poor advice; we are forbidden to prey upon, or pander to, the predilections of the morally blind.

These restrictions are part of Torah and accepted by Jews because such is the divine command, but they also happen to make good sense. Let me tell you a story.

Everyone remembers the assassination of Martin Luther King. Some, but probably not many, will remember the shooting of Martin Luther King's mother some time afterward. It is an event I am not likely to forget, not because of the event itself, but because of an incident which occurred subsequently.

A short time after the shooting, my wife and I were sitting in a cafe in Prague. A young, highly intelligent medical student struck up a conversation with us. As he began to feel comfortable in our company, he leaned across the table and, in a conspiratorial tone, asked why American intelligence had sought the death of Mrs. King. I hastened to assure him that Mrs. King was a very private person, not involved in political affairs, and that it was highly unlikely that anyone beyond her immediate circle of family and friends had been more than dimly aware of her existence. Moreover, there was cause to believe that the man responsible for her shooting was mentally incompetent.

Our young friend was incredulous. I assumed that he suspected a plot to be lurking behind every headline. No, he assured me, he understood well enough that in the West not everything is controlled by the government. But this incident must have been government-directed, came the clincher to the argument, because otherwise how would the assassin have come into possession of a gun!

We had come to Prague via Vienna. In Vienna, but several kilometers away, we stayed in a hotel off the *Graben on Dorotheergasse*. The street was rather narrow and easily overlooked. Returning from our outings, we recognized the turn by means of a large neon sign outside a store on the corner. The sign was embiazoned with but a single word—*"Waffen."* The young man's reaction to my account of how handguns are freely available in many western nations was that either I must be a weaver of fancy tales or else Western society is plumb crazy!

The ease with which handguns can be acquired in some Western countries is simply incomprehensible to persons who live in a more circumscribed environment. To them this is not a sign of the freedom of the West,

of which they are jealous and which they would replicate if they but could, but of an irrationality of which they wish no part.

Jewish law recognizes that indiscriminate sale of weapons cannot fail to endanger the public. The daily newspaper confirms this deepseated distrust far more often than is necessary. As the bearers of an ageless moral code Jews ought to be in the vanguard of those seeking to impress upon our legislators that handguns are indeed "stumbling blocks" which must not fall into the hands of the "blind." Criminals do commit crimes and it is precisely because "morally blind" criminals are disposed to crime that Judaism teaches that it is forbidden to provide them with the tools of their trade.

Yes, Mr. Goldstein, flies do not cause garbage, but garbage does attract flies. Guns may or may not cause crime, but crimes of violence cannot be committed without tools of violence. Self-restraint in the sale of weapons is a small enough price to pay for even marginal enhancement of public safety.

Sincerely yours,
J. David Bleich

Jewish life in a federal prison camp
Stephen M.

Allenwood is a federal institution. In the vernacular of the Bureau of Prisons, it is a Federal Prison Camp, a minimum-security, no-fence, no-guard-tower installation. It is located right outside of Williamsport, Pa. equidistant from New York, Philadelphia, and Washington, D.C. The called-for population is 374, but overcrowding has resulted in a present population of 500, which will be passed shortly with no end in sight. I "self-surrendered" (a procedure whereby one arrives at the institution one is to be incarcerated in and walks in, the theory being that this procedure avoids staying in local jails on the way to Federal ones, thus saving money and avoiding bad conditions) in the fall of 1980. The first thing that struck me when I entered my dormitory (Allenwood has four separate units divided into eight dormitories) was the manner in which I was made welcome. I was shown to my cubicle and

Mr. M. requested that his last name not be used in print.

given juice, tea, soap and other essential items until I could go to the commissary and obtain my own. Most of this was done by Herb B., my dorm's Jewish Welcome Wagon. In each dorm, I was told there was at least one Jewish inmate who acted as a welcome wagon to the incoming Jewish inmates. Herb did not terminate his services with just juice; he took me around the camp, introduced me to other members of the congregation and showed me the ropes.

I soon discovered that the Jewish population of Allenwood was a well organized congregation. There were Friday night and Saturday morning services, along with a kosher food service. On the *Yontifs*, (holidays) a group of Lubavitcher rabbis came, conducted services, and distributed *Yontif* snacks. The Jewish population at that time was approximately ten percent of the camp; unfortunately, it has since risen to better than fifteen percent.

The services were an attempt to reach all facets of Jewish religious worship. They were conducted in English and Hebrew and whenever we ran short of someone who could read the Torah in Hebrew Saturday morning, a new recruit would miraculously appear. Friday night there was a large turnout, inspired no doubt by the distribution of at least three bagels per man. We had a steady bagel *benchers* club. Saturday morning was another story. For a while it was difficult to obtain a *minyan*, (10 men) but soon after I arrived, the situation stabilized and we didn't have that problem for almost a year. The community was a tight-knit one, always looking out for one another. Men who had never gone to *shul* in their lives attended services, enjoyed it and encouraged newcomers to become involved. We tried to get the best jobs in the camp for one another, and ran an "old boys" network that continues to this day.

Keeping Kosher and Studying Torah

The perennial problem was the kosher kitchen: keeping it kosher and keeping the separate trays and utensils kosher. Since the professional kitchen staff stayed out of the kosher kitchen, it was used to cook contraband which was invariably non-kosher and resulted in periodic *toiveling* (koshering) of the kitchen. The majority of the congregation, while not keeping kosher at home, respected the balance who did, and did not put *traif* (non-kosher) on their plates, etc., but some did and this resulted in arguments with the staff and the rest of the congregation. Quite a few of

the Jews here are here only because there is a kosher kitchen and its demise would lead to harsher incarceration for some; with this and other factors in mind, periodically there is a drive to keep kosher. It is, I am afraid, a task that will have to be done every six months or conditions will get out of hand.

There is a Catholic priest and Protestant chaplain assigned here. The chaplain looks after our religious needs when the "contract" rabbi is not here. The contract rabbi is paid pursuant to a contract for so many hours in the camp. When I arrived, the rabbi came to the camp once a week in the afternoon and usually approved men to eat on the "kosher line" and was available if one had any religious problems. I had very little contact with him and his work. He was discharged last spring over an issue I have never been privy to and a search was made for a new rabbi.

During the winter of 1980-1981, an Orthodox Jew was here for two months and suggested that we organize a Torah class. When he left, he sent in a set of Rashi's commentaries for use in such a class. I had never studied Torah in my life, but for obscure reasons was put in charge of the class. I prepared by reading Rashi on the week's *parsha* (Torah portion) and prepared some comments. When the class started, I was asked, why not start at the beginning of the Torah? And so we did. The class had about ten people, most of them never having studied Torah previously. Time flew by and the class was over. The following week we were up to fifteen Jews and one Orthodox priest (Russian or Greek, he never said which) and attendance never faltered. We owed a lot to Paul L., who had belonged to an adult study group and who was our mentor in the early days. To be sure, we drifted on to every conceivable subject and roamed far and wide from the text, but as an intellectual exercise it was significant. (When I would call a friend of mine all I could talk about was the class and the weekly discussions; the fire took hold and I looked forward to coming home and continuing.) My rabbi helped out by sending me a set of Rashi, and the new translation of the Bible. The new rabbi was Norman Singer, from Williamsport, and as soon as he heard we had a Torah class he arranged to come in one night a week and teach it. Not only is attendance up, but we are starting a class in conversational Hebrew. He has united us and certainly been more than a "contract" rabbi.

Jewish Identity Strengthened

Life here as a Jew has not always been smooth. Last spring the authorities felt that the kosher line was presenting too many problems, so they decided to integrate it into the main feeding line and one was supposed to present a card identifying himself as a Jew and then receive his kosher tray. Nothing could have united our community more than this. We were prepared to wear armbands (yellow with the star of David) to make identification easier, but hours before the cards were to be issued, the superintendent called it off. Somehow it's never far away, is it? I wonder what Meir Kahane would have thought of all of this, since it was his lawsuit that started the kosher kitchen in the first place. I cannot say enough about the Lubavitchers. They come and bring joy and happiness with them. They never preach, but talk to us as fellow Jews. To give up the most sacred days of the year to be with us is something that none of us will ever forget nor fail to remember when we send them money. (I might add that they never ask, it is done on a voluntary basis).

At the present time the congregation is alive and well and, as I said, unfortunately growing. We have had our disagreements, but in the main we have clung together and reinforced our Jewishness. In some ways the services in the dining room, the conference room and the gym have more meaning than in most ornate and pleasing synagogues. Last year's *seder* (Passover feast) for my family and myself (families attended the first *seder* and over a hundred people were present) had more meaning and substance than the "usual" one did. This feeling was not mine alone, and is reflected in this year's decision to have a special family *seder* on Saturday night, to insure maximum attendance.

I certainly never wanted to come here (no one does), but my sense of why I am a Jew and what is a Jew has certainly expanded and I believe the same is true for most of the congregation. God certainly moves in strange and mysterious ways. ●

Adulthood: an age for turning

Arnold Jacob Wolf

The term *baal t'shuvah* can mean many things. It means a repentant sinner, a former evil-doer who has gone straight; it means simply a less-observant or non-obser-

vant Jew who has become (more) observant. The latter term applies to me. I have in the last year or so tried to observe the *Halakah* more or less strictly, keeping *kashrut* and *Shabbat* with care for the details of traditional observance. I do not, for instance, ride, write or answer the telephone on the Sabbath any more, though I cannot (yet?) say that I observe *Shabbat* like Rabbi Moshe Feinstein. In the sense that I have recovered a good many traditional, *halakhic* norms I am, I guess, a repentant Jew.

Which is not to say that I was previously a bad Jew, or a non-Jew. For me Sabbath and Holy Days, commandment and custom always meant a great deal. I observed at least what my family has for several generations, adding a few obligations through several recent decades. My grandmother, for instance who was born in Cleveland before the Civil War, never in her life ate *hazir,* although she had never even heard that shell fish were forbidden. She did not sew or wash clothes on Saturday, though she drove to services and used the phone (after it was invented, of course) without any sense of violating Jewish law. To judge by my own family, Reform Judaism had apocopated Jewish *halakah,* but never acted as if there were no law. We felt that Jews must observe the laws of our religion, but we did not know all of the traditional formulations, and perhaps did not want to know. I suppose we thought of traditional Jews as the fanatical wing of our religious group, but we never felt we belonged to a different people or another faith than theirs.

Halakah: the jew's distinctive jewel

My uncle and teacher, Rabbi Felix Levy of Chicago, spent much of his life urging that Reform Judaism recover *halakah* if it was to remain authentically Jewish. In what has always seemed to me an unanswerable position, he identified anti-nomianism as Pauline and insisted that any kind of religious Jews at all simply had to observe traditional law or forfeit their essential *differentia.* Personally, he was moderately and for most of his life increasingly, observant, though at his most rigorous he hardly practiced more than many Conservative Jews do. But he was unmistakable in his position that obedience to the *halakah* is the *conditio sine qua non* of being a Jew, or at least a religious Jew.

Influenced strongly by him and by the writing of Franz Rosenzweig, I wrote in a *Commentary* symposium some years ago that we were all walking along Jew Street on which we found a number of jewels (commandments) of various sizes and shapes. Those we could pick up we *had* to pick up. There should be no guilt for what we were unable (not merely unwilling) to appropriate, but failing to pick up a commandment we could was wrong. This is, I believe, neither precisely a Reform nor an Orthodox position, but one congenial to a good many of us who think that all such labels are odious, especially after the destruction of our European brothers without regard to their sectarian affiliations. In any case, it tries to be a theology for Jews on their way back.

Several Reform Jewish assertions are denied by my model. There can be now, as Eugene Borowitz has taught many of us, no principle above Judaism by which Judaism can be judged. Reform Jews often decided what to obey by reference to Kantian norms or to the aesthetics of the Central European bourgeoisie. In America, obedience often depended on whether or not the law separated us from our non-Jewish compatriots, on whether or not it helped us move up the American ladder. Convenience, conformity and attractiveness to a non-Jewish *ethos,* become the marks of acceptability. In my view, there can no longer be any standard not itself Jewish by which one can decide whether or not to perform a traditional Jewish act.

Correcting the errors of classical reform
In the second place, whatever is left of Reform biblicism must be overcome. In my Reform Jewish family, *Kashrut* meant Biblical *kashrut*; commandments often menat the Ten Commandments, never the 613. For many Reform Jews, Isaiah is normative, though it is hard to say exactly what he demanded, but *Baba Kamma,* even had it been studied, was not. Officially, and unofficially, Reform Judaism committed itself to the Bible as standard, thus taking a position with Luther

or the Karaites, against all of Judaism since the Pharisees. For us new Jews the standard is not the Bible but The Tradition as a whole.

The slogan of Reform, and not merely Reform Judaism, has been "Judaism as Ethical Monotheism." In the late twentieth century both of these terms have turned problematic. It seems to us harder to be ethical than it did a hundred years ago, and "monotheism" seems to us an Hellenic term for something far richer and more complex, authentic Judaism. God is, of course, one, but for us the *Sh'ma* is not only a credo, but a task; *tefillin,* morning and evening recitation, *tallit,* the whole panoply of obligation connected with "monotheism" but more connected with our own questions and our own quest.

So I had abandoned much of the baggage of Classical Reform some even that my family had kept, however doubting its usefulness. But I was still living, more or less, like a Reform Jew. I was serving a Reform Congregation and that, I felt, meant living in a way mostly congruent with my community's. But I desired and still desire to work with all kinds of Jews, to be free to live a more intense Jewish experience than suburban liberalism permits. So I came to Yale Hillel and to a new intimacy with the dilemmas and glories of the *halakah.* It was a case of put your money where your mouth is! I felt that I could no longer advocate tradition without tasting more of it for myself. I became an experimental *baal t'shuvah.*

The disappointments of being an orthodox jew
My experiment is not an unqualified success — at least not yet. Whatever I hoped for in accepting more traditional Jewish life, and I can no longer quite recall what it was, my dreams have not come true.

I do not like myself, particularly in my new *persona* of Orthodox Jew. As Adin Steinsalz, the great Israeli scholar and himself a *baal T'shuvah,* said here: when I look in the mirror in the morning I do not like the face I see. Said Steinsaltz: it is the face of those I used to despise, and now that face is mine. For me, the transition to observant Jew has not made me (yet?) a more likeable or more decent person. In the short run at least, I think it has often worked quite the other way. I find myself very proud of my new commitments, using them to avoid some difficult old ones, political and personal alike. In short, I am what some Reform Jews call all Orthodox Jews: a hypocrite. I do not perform the commandments for the sake of Heaven, at least not often, but for the sake of my image and self-

L'shana tovah tikatayva v'taychataymu

image. Keeping *kosher* has not made me more disciplined or kind; it has reinforced certain narcissistic and compulsive aspects of my character. I am not a better husband or father or teacher or friend; I am only a more observant Jew. Is that enough, or am I doing something basic and doing it wrong?

I find that I invariably emphasize negative over positive commandments. I am oppressively aware of what I cannot do on *Shabbat,* so that the day becomes not joyous and devout, but clouded over by fear of doing the wrong thing. *Kashrut* has not made our family table an altar but, more often a court-room or a debating society. Some of this, obviously, reflects the inevitable anxiety of the neophyte, but I see a good many more seasoned observant Jews who also seem to be doing more and enjoying it less. On the other hand, the very difficulty of the *halakah* seems to me part of its essential usefulness. If I had been flying after a few months of obedience to the Torah, I would have thought myself fatuous or self-hypnotized, In a curious way, I am glad that it is not much fun yet, though whether that betokens my native masochism or is inevitable in learning a new way of life, I am not certain.

I find myself emphasizing the commandments between man and God as against those between man and man. I sweat out the ritual more than the ethical, though my post-Reform position tells me that there is no ultimate distinction between the two; I feel hypocritical in this case, too. While Cambodia and Watergate exploded last summer, I was worried about *kashering* a knife or talking to a kid with a problem on Saturday. I read (in Jonathan Eybeschutz, as a matter of fact) that the confessional of *Yom Kippur* does not even mention ritual infractions because God is concerned on the Great White Fast Day only with what we have done to help or hurt our fellowman. Would I be able to talk to Him only about what I had been eating or how I said my prayers? I am punctilious about (at least some) of my sins of commission, but I have little time to think about the vast areas that I skip because I don't have the time or will to pay attention. It is easy to know when you use the wrong knife, but not when you hurt a friend. My knives are still kosher (I hope), but I am beginning to worry more about my tongue, my hands and my heart, again.

Potential evils of orthodox living
Out of this phenomenology of "repentance" emerges certain new tasks. I do not propose to retreat to a classical nineteenth century ethicism, but am seeking a twentieth century post-liberal ethical alternative.

The halakah never was and cannot now be a substitute for compassion or for simple humanity. The hardest thing about becoming an Orthodox Jew, said Rabbi Steinsaltz, is living with Orthodox Jews. (The same is true, of course, about living with Reform Jews — or, I should guess, with Zen Buddhists, as well). *Kosher* meat means meeting the *Kosher* butchers; *Shabbat* in an Orthodox synagogue means hearing sermons that come very close to racism and are always ethnocentric. Working with the *k'lal* means sharing your fate with people with whom you have had precious little in common, except that which was most important, that both of you are Jews. It is a difficult task to love Jews; it is a harder task to love Jews without also hating Arabs, Blacks or the United Nations. I don't want to pay for my new spiritual goals with the counterfeit tender of reaction or of pride.

Our traditional *s'darim* last *Pesach,* were magnificent in their fullness of tradition. For the first time in my life I had the joy that comes only from doing something in a way you consider right.But my wife had spent days and weeks getting the house and kitchen ready for our Yale *Seder* and that wasn't fair. In my grandmother's time, the "help" did the dirty work; now we cannot count on Black women to do our *mitzvot* for us. Rabbi David Bleich tells me that much of what we sweated out (actually *she* sweated out), we didn't have to do at all. One must learn the Law better than I have, to find the simple, direct way of obedience. I'm sure he is right, but I also think that much Orthodox piety rests on male chauvinist pillars. We *daven* and study and *qvell,* while our wives do the dirty work. Women enslaved in the kitchen cannot validate a *Seder* in which all Jews become free men. For me, learning to do some of what my grandfather thought was women's work, may be harder than to learn to do what he thought was the duty only of an Orthodox Jew. But the New Traditionalism, I believe, requires new commitments, like Women's Liberation, in order to make old ones, like *Pesach,* possible.

The new traditionalism considers all 613
Another new task is the recovery of lost *mitzvot.* There is a lot of concern in the circles I now move in for Sabbath and *kashrut,* but none about even so central a commandment as hospitality. *Hakhnasat orchim* is the task of every Jew. There are voluminous materials about this commandment of welcoming strangers, some of which I studied only because of a course on it I helped teach — in Yale's Divinity School. Most of our synagogues and community organizations studious-

ly ignore the obligation of hospitality, as if it were not one of the precious 613. I suspect there are many such "unknown" commandments. The New Traditionalism must ferret them out, seeking always a link between ritual tasks and human implication. Hermann Cohen was right, I believe, when he taught that the commandments were *all* ethical, and he was surely correct about his principal example, the Sabbath.

We must learn to do old commandments in new ways, or, what is I believe even more important, new commandments in old ways. The liberal ideal of scientific scholarship must be linked to the traditional *mitzvah* of *Talmud Torah*. We university graduates, we scholars and scientists and modern bureaucrats must learn how to learn. We must find out how it is possible to be a traditional Jewish disciple of the wise without sacrificing any of our intellectual integrity or scientific acumen. Old wine in new bottles is tastier than new wine in old bottles ever could be.

Our agenda is long. There is much work to do. The *baal t'shuvah* contributes not only his new enthusiasms and his new loyalty, but also his doubts, his scruples, his fear. In the end, I hope to be no mere repentant "sinner," no mere proud traditionalist, but, at last, a Jew.

The depoliticization of jewish youth

Mark Hurvitz

Young American Jews accepted the New Left criticism of American policies and institutions and great numbers participated in campus leftist activities — many of us identified with the political ideals for which our parents had struggled in the thirties. We were active throughout the period of the Civil Rights Movement, working in the South and challenging the institutions of racism wherever we lived. We were active in the formation of the Free Speech-Movement in Berkeley and took leadership roles in the development of the Anti-war movement across the country. Young Jews from Reform backgrounds whose upbringing had stressed the universal aspects of the prophetic call for social justice also identified with what was then called the "Movement." Participation in these activities was reinforced and encouraged among an even wider number of young Jews when men like Abraham J. Heschel led the marches. Our Jewishness played a great part in sensitizing us to the need for

these activities although frequently we were not aware of the Jewish sources for our concerns.

An independent offspring: a jewish counter-culture
By 1968 the American counter-culture had taken root and the Jewish counter-culture was beginning to develop. We expressed our awareness of the weaknesses of Jewish institutional life in the way our non-Jewish peers challenged American institutions. The beginning of our dissent from the Jewish establishment, and our political rejection by the New Left (over the issue of Zionism after the Six Day War), marked the beginning of a recognition among us that Judaism and Americanism were far from identical. This understanding initiated an awareness of the traditional Jewish problem of living in two cultures. The proper resolution of this problem according to various spokesmen in the organized community was an identification with Judaism and/or Zionism. They maintained that such an identification offered possibilities for the creation of a counter-culture *par excellence*. As participants in the Jewish student movement, we faced continual tension between the secular counter-culture, which had given rise to our existence, and some version of normative Judaism or Zionism.

Since their inception, there has been very little interchange between the Jewish and American counter-cultures. Many young Jews in the counter-culture experimented with drugs and lived in communes like our non-Jewish peers. Assimilationist young Jews in the counter-culture moved deeper into the American ethos while Jewishly oriented Jews in the counter-culture delved deeper into Jewish sources and traditions. We spoke about the same general concepts: seeking spiritual community, a redistribution of power, and national liberation; however, we had different heroes, read different periodicals, listened to different recordings, and watched different movies and TV programs. Rarely did these groups meet or affect one another.

The fact that most Jewishly oriented counter-culture groups became exclusively Jewish seems to reveal a search for Jewish identity among the young people involved. Some Jews who participate in and are part of the mainstream of the American counter-culture are beginning to stress their Jewish identity. Craig Karpel who made his Jewish appéarance at a Bet Din about which he reported in *WIN* recently discussed his emergent Jewish identity in the pages of *Sh'ma* (3/43). Another rare case is that of the non-Jew in the

American counter-culture who begins to explore and study Jewish sources.

When the young need awakening

The leaders of the Jewish student movement developed various responses to the problems we faced in the campus arena, always moving further into Jewish particularism. Today we have come to recognize that the concepts that have meaning for our lives are primarily Jewish. However, our younger brothers and sisters who are beginning to shape their own lives have not experienced our struggles. Whether or not these younger Jews are concerned about Jewish life, they are making choices without asking the serious questions we did. They are making their decisions without considering the need to balance the universal and the particular that sharpened our awareness of Jewish life. Those who are opting for Judaism are apathetically accepting a generalized majority position within the ideologies and movements in which they were raised, without an awareness of or an attempt to distinguish between the many shades of ideology and practice. Jewish youth leaders must arouse youngsters who may be committed to Jewish life but who respond to Jewish problems on the basis of traditional positions without considering alternatives.

Many of us have come to understand that we must find our answers in America, an America that has developed the means for its redemption as well as for its destruction. Most of us will remain in America, and even the majority of ideologically committed radical Zionists probably do not consider immigration to Israel to be a viable personal alternative. Not only do we live on the fringes of American civilization because of our Jewishness, but our upbringing within America's advanced technological society, and our global perspective based upon that upbringing, places us beyond the pale of Israeli society. American Jews have truly come to a strange crossroads. I am uncomfortable about the choice that I feel is necessary, and I don't know how to decide or act upon the decision I make. We have prepared ourselves to become stateless individuals who can participate in communal associations with like-minded people all over the world.

The American counter-culture has conducted many experiments and has developed many new techniques from which we can learn. Young Jews communicate on a transcontinental level, sharing ideas and maintaining social relationships. Advanced technology and the existence of a strong community in Israel facilitate the establishment of independent and autonomous Jewish communities throughout the world which do not require a particular territory for a base. The "Wandering Jew" was never a negative stereotype to me; we can now make it into a creative identity.

What if shylock were a marrano?

Leo Trepp

It seems to be unlikely that Jewish efforts to have The Merchant of Venice banned from stage and classroom will be truly successful, although the effort is worthwhile. Emphasis might therefore be placed on the reinterpretation of the play, and teachers, as well as producers, be guided to transform it from an indictment of the Jew to an indictment of religious persecution and a call for minority rights. Such reinterpretation of the play may find acceptance, if it strengthens the play itself by resolving inner inconsistencies in the character of the personalities, thus strengthening the play itself. I conceive Shylock as a Marrano, recently arrived from Spain. He has openly confessed his Jewish faith once again. Such casting can be historically defended: the Republic of Venice, badly in need of increased trade with the Levant, granted Marranos the right of residence, permitting and even demanding of them an open espousal of Judaism. By compelling these Marranos to profess their belonging to the Jewish faith and 'nation' openly, the Republic could subject them to special and exorbitant taxes which Jews had to pay for the right of residence and of trade, and could expel them, if they failed to produce.

Shylock is a Marrano. His whole life style shows it. He is aggressive, daring, above all, cunning. He uses ambiguity for the sake of deception. He insists that the law take its course. Marranos had to develop these traits, for only cunning gave them a chance of survival as secret Jews. If they were caught, the law showed no mercy. Shylock cannot help being hateful against Christians. His hatred against them is unrelieved, he has suffered too much. They are out to destroy his 'nation'. Here, in Venice, they will let him live, but only as long as he produces. Money spells survival.

Antonio the merchant, in contrast, belongs to the aristocracy. Generous to his friends, he has frequently lent them money without interest, that they might pay their debts to Shylock. To the Jew this is a Christian plot to undermine his right to live. Without wealth and the production of wealth, he will be cast out of Venice. Shylock sees in Antonio's actions a plot against him and against all Jews. Christians have no feelings; it does not matter to them that the Jew has eyes and hands and organs and emotions. If Christians are crossed, they will avenge themselves, Shylock has firsthand knowledge of their attitude against Jews. Now he has the chance to take revenge on those who have scorned his nation, cooled his friends and heated his enemies. The reaction is logical for a Marrano.

Marrano legacy: jewish father, christian daughter
He loves his daughter Jessica and warns her against joining the revellers at their feasting. Such participation was forbidden Jews, but Shylock has more compelling reasons. Jessica has been brought up in a Christian environment, and Shylock knows that her convictions cannot yet be very strongly Jewish. As it turns out, he is right. (It is interesting that up to 1516 Jews did not have to live in the ghetto, but dwelt among Christians. Subsequently the gates of the ghetto were locked and watched at night, and Jews were forbidden to leave.) When she disappears, he is heartbroken. His friends try to find out where she may be, while he is apprehensive that she may have deserted his faith. He would rather see her dead than an apostate. And he needs his money: in his Christian society he cannot exist without money. This is the curse that 'never fell upon our nation until now': he can continue living without his daughter, but he cannot expect to stay alive without money.

As Marrano, Shylock is an outsider on the Venetian scene, where relationships between Jews and Christians actually were close and frequently very friendly. The agony of the outsider becomes evident at the trial: he must win, he cannot afford leniency. But when he is defeated by the cunning of his Christian adversaries, he has to adjust immediately, and he does. He crawls. He only wishes to retain his money, stating correctly: "You take my house, when you do take the prop that sustains my house, you take my life when you do take the means whereby I live."

This is literally true: without his monetary tribute to the rulers, his right of residence and of existence will be taken from him. He is ordered to become a Christian. It does not surprise him, he has been through all of this before. "I am content." Presumably, he will once again become a Marrano, secretly practicing his faith.

Jessica's conduct equally becomes clear: "I am a daughter to his blood, I am not to his manners . . . I shall end this strife." Up to the time of her father's arrival at Venice, she had been brought up as a Christian society girl, enjoying society's pleasures. Her knowledge of Judaism is minimal, she bears no Jewish name, she has no convictions, no understanding for her father's "manners." She is Jewishly confused and powerfully attracted to the outside world, now even more so, as she has fallen in love. What is "this strife" of which she speaks, if not the inner conflict within herself? Her Christian indoctrination is so strong that she is convinced that the sins of her father and of her mother will no longer be visited upon her, once she is a Christian: "I shall be saved by my husband, he has made me a Christian." Jessica deserts her father not only for the sake of her love, but equally so for the sake of her salvation.

Shylock is a symbol for jews today
Spiritually as well as physically, the Christian majority has corrupted the souls of these Jews by forcing them to deny Jewish ethics, Jewish tradition, and Jewish family love. Portia's great speech on "the quality of mercy" thus becomes an exercise in hypocrisy. Shylock knows it, the audience should know it. It is camouflage behind which hatred, discrimination and oppression are acted out.

Shylock, the Marrano, is the victim of the relentless pressure, exerted by a powerful and hostile majority behind the veil of uprightness. He reveals the agonizing problems faced, not only by Jews, but by many minority groups that may outwardly be equal under the law. He explains the 'immoral conduct' of segments among minorities, which a complacent majority is always ready to castigate, without asking itself about its own complicity in having created it. Shylock equally has something to tell us as Jews: Jewish pride, unaccompanied by meaningful Jewish education and practice, may not be enough to keep a new generation faithful to Judaism; and their defection may not be caused merely by external causes — love of life, falling in love — but by deep inner conflicts resulting from the quest for a meaningful life, for 'salvation'.

As we interpret The Merchant of Venice in this manner, we have to admit that Shakespeare wrote better than he knew. We may also be called upon to re-examine the question of whether it is really such a dangerous play. Perhaps it has something very relevant to say in regard to all minorities, and specifically to Jews.

The jewish way of thinking
Dan Dorfman

We modern Jews have lost something very basic from our tradition and we hardly even notice it. It is a loss more grievous perhaps than the fabled decreases in levels of knowledge and observance, because it is more fundamental. What we have lost is the ability to think like Jews. For we have largely abandoned the distinguishing feature of classic Jewish thought — its profoundly dialectic nature, its determined facility at holding in productive, symbiotic tension conflicting or paradoxical ideas. To our considerable benefit, but our immeasurable loss as well, we have learned to think more like ancient Greeks than like Jews.

Wherever we look in Jewish sources, whatever we examine in Jewish thought, we meet the characteristic dialectic. Dialectic describes both the Jewish world-view and the Jewish thought process, the form and method of Jewish thinking as well as the dynamic content of Jewish ideas.

The classic literature of Scriptural interpretation, the early rabbinic *aggadah* and the medieval commentary, reveals a dialectic form in its embrace of alternative, often contradictory interpretations for the same events and passages. The basic method of legal argumentation in the Talmud — the classic pattern of statement and challenge, of assertion and contradiction — is a dialectic method. The traditional way of Jewish study known as *pilpul*, with its legendary subtle probing and questioning, each answer being met with yet a new question from another angle, is more than mental acrobatics. It is a disciplined method to train minds to appreciate the complex, paradoxical nature of ideas, of reality, of truth.

The Greek way of thinking
This fundamental insight of the form and method of Jewish thinking is the cohesive thread that binds Jewish thought as well. If Jewish ideas teach us nothing else, they teach us that we must accept the truth embodied in the various sides of conflicts, paradoxes, and contradictions in our world if we are to comprehend its reality. It is futile and misleading to try to constrict the rich diversity of life into single, comprehensive explanations.

Thus human beings, in the Jewish conception, are both "little lower than the angels" as well as "dust and ashes" — created in the divine image, gifted with intelligence and moral will, God's co-partner in the rule of the world, yet at the same time finite, temporal, corruptible, rebellious and proud. Human nature is neither wholly benevolent nor basically evil, but a complex mixture of both. Even the "evil impulse" (*yetzer ha-ra*) is understood dialectically — our basic urges draw us into reprehensible acts, but also spark our sensual, creative and productive capacities. Sexuality, viewed by some philosophies as a trancendent good (hedonism) or as an ultimate evil (asceticism), is understood by Judaism to be both a divinely created pleasure and a potentially destructive drive which needs control.

We are not used to perceiving reality in this dialectic way — as an inextricable matrix of opposites and paradoxes. Our way of thought, Western thought, is linear, cumulative, comprehensive in nature. Fact A plus fact B plus fact C leads to conclusion D. The underlying method and motive of ancient Greek/Western thought is the accumulation of successively reinforcing arguments into an all-encompassing generalization. The goal is an explanatory principle containing in its scope the greatest variety of data.

Thought must encompass life's complexity
Jewish thought is radically different. It is fluid, paradoxical, dialectic. It proceeds not by the accumulation of facts and arguments, but by a constantly dynamic probing and questioning. It yields not comprehensive generalizations which seek to homogenize diversity, but rather subtle, many-hued accounts of reality that embrace variety and paradox.

Jewish thought is also more subtle, more sensitive, and even more realistic than what most of us derive from Western thought. That is why, despite all the material benefits and intellectual insights we have from Western culture, our loss may be even more significant.

For the complex, paradoxical perceptions and values of the Jewish tradition are more reliable guides to living than the philosophic one-liners that so often pass for insight in Western thought. They repeatedly force us to remain aware of the variety of factors at work in the ever-changing, always unique situations we face in our lives.

Consider the ethics of honesty, for example. We all grew up being taught things like "honesty is the best policy" and "you must never tell a lie." But we soon realize that this is simply not true and this sets up an uncomfortable dissonance between the value we think we must uphold and the actions we know we must take.

Judaism recognizes that other values come into play and it is therefore not always moral to tell the pure, unvarnished truth. Sometimes we should state only part of the truth, in order to spare someone's feelings (Babylonian Talmud, *Ketubot* 166-17a). Sometimes the truth should be bent a little to prevent strife and friction, to preserve peace (Babylonian Talmud, *Yevamot* 65b).

Let us recover the Jewish dialectic

This may be a more ambiguous and more challenging ethic than a simple "this is right, that is wrong." It is also more appropriate to the complexities of our day to day lives. Each situation we face has its own peculiar combination of considerations, factors, and values that come into play. Hard and fast, writ in stone rules, rigidly applied in all situations, do not yield accurate perceptions or provide reliable guidance. This is the wisdom inherent in the fact that Jewish values developed through a system of case law. General rules, principles, teachings emerge, but we must always consider the particular circumstances of the situation at hand as we decide how we ought to act.

The dialectic, then, underlies the Jewish way of thinking, Jewish perceptions of the world, and Jewish moral guidance. For the sake of both our internal understanding of Judaism and our external approaches to the world, we must recover our sensitivity to this fundamental element of Jewish thought. Our learning and living of Jewish tradition should reinforce awareness of its dialectic nature.

We should, for example, bring out from our intellectual attics the traditional value of *torah l'shma* — open study of Jewish sources, unencumbered by preconceived agendas. This form of study helps to attune minds to the dialectic way of thinking.

We should be scrupulous in exploring and exposing the dialectic poles in Jewish values and concepts. We should no longer teach, for example, that Judaism is the religion of deeds and social justice, while Christianity is a religion of belief and faith or that Judaism accepts human sexuality while Christianity represses it. This kind of approach distorts the internal Jewish dialectic. Judaism teaches faith (*emunah*) as well as action (*mitzvot*) and has both repressive and celebrative aspects to its attitude towards sexuality. It suppresses as well the external dialectic view that authentic Jewish thinking fosters (Christianity has a gospel of deeds which accompanies the gospels of faith; it has developed over the centuries accepting as well as

negative attitudes towards sex).

By stressing the dialectic, we may discover for ourselves a way of thinking and a way of action that is at one and the same time authentically Jewish and perceptively modern.

The logical limits of jewish ecumenism
Shubert Spero

Given the body of beliefs and practices we call Orthodox Judaism, what conditions have to be fulfilled in order for an Orthodox Jew to be able to engage in any sorts of ecumenical activities and still remain consistent with his Orthodox principles?

Condition number one: Reform, Conservative and Orthodox must realize the *asymmetry* of their relationships to their respective Judaisms. By their own definitions, Reform and Conservative understand their Judaism to be developmental, subject to modification and that the mechanism for change is in varying degrees, within the control of their spiritual leadership. However, one of the more persistent beliefs of Orthodoxy is that the Halachic process embodies procedures that are more resistant to human change so that even if Orthodox Rabbis *wanted* to change certain rituals or modify certain beliefs, they could not easily do so. They see themselves more as servants of the process rather than its masters. Reform and Conservative must recognize this asymmetry and not make impossible demands upon the Orthodox or interpret lack of response as recalcitrance, hunger for power or sheer *Sinat chinam* (groundless hatred).

Condition number two: The Orthodox are accused of not having sufficient *ahavat Yisrael*, (love of Israel), Orthodox Jews will give us first-aid oxygen in emergencies and invite us to their homes for *cholent*, but if they are so loving, why do they not accept invitations from *other* Jews to visit *their* homes? The elementary ethical demand is reciprocity. This, Orthodoxy will not give us! The Conservatives accept the Orthodox *get* (divorce) but the Orthodox will not accept a Conservative *get*.

Our dealings with the other cannot always be reciprocal. It depends upon the relationship. The

Shubert Spero is rabbi of Young Israel of Cleveland, Ohio.

(U) will accept Satmar *hashgacha*, (certification of Kashrut) Satmar will not accept the (U) certification. Satmar's principles may be skewed but there is nothing immoral about the situation. This type of imbalance always grows out of the logic of the relationship between the Right and the Left. Interdenominational reciprocity is an unfair and impossible demand.

Suspending Judgment

Condition number three: In order for Orthodox Jews to be able to freely engage in ecumenical activities it is necessary that they adopt a certain psychological perspective that I call the D.D.Z. or the De-Denominationalized Zone. Orthodox Jews must learn to relate to Reform and Conservative in certain settings as taking place in a D.D.Z.— that is to say, we are meeting in a strictly factual world in which I see you as you are and not as I think you ought to be. If you are a Reform rabbi, I neither confirm your rabbinic title nor repudiate it because in this context I am not called upon to do either. You are a rabbinic leader of a Reform congregation. I accept it as a fact with the objectivity of a sociologist. While in the context of the De-Denominationalized Zone, I suspend all intra-Jewish judgments.

Is it right for an Orthodox Jew to engage in such a suspension of judgment? I believe it is. We live in imperfect, pre-Messianic times in which great rabbis have ruled that we can no longer exercise our obligations of *hochiach tochiach*— of rebuking our fellow Jews, of constantly chastizing them and sitting in judgment upon them. This is so because none of *us* is perfect, our motivations are suspect and we have lost the art of *tochacha* (of rebuking our fellows).

Our Claims to Truth Conflict

At this point we come up against a logical limit of Jewish ecumenism. Some people believe the ecumenism requires that I adopt a sort of tolerance of the "three wings" in which I affirm that each branch of Judaism is an *equally* valid version of Judaism, an *equally* correct approach to God, an *equally* legitimate Jewish way of life.

Now, an Orthodox Jew cannot do this—*logically* cannot do this!—because of his understanding of the nature of Orthodox Judaism. For here we are dealing with truth-claims, cognitive beliefs, statements of fact, with propositions that are mutually exclusive so that if one is true the other

must be false and vice versa. Orthodox Jews believe that Judaism requires them to assent unequivocally to certain beliefs, certain cognitive statements; that, for example, "the Torah in our possession is, in its entirety, the word of God." It follows that a rabbi who teaches that it is not is making a false statement.

Therefore in theoretical terms the Orthodox Jew, a la Voltaire, must say: "I believe many of the teachings of Reform and Conservative to be wrong and misleading, but as Jews there are many areas where we can work together."

Traditional Judaism not only includes rituals, theological beliefs, and moral rules, but also functions as a legal system in areas we call civil law. Now what happens when Reform rabbis decide to change the rules in Judaism which involve the status-conferring institutions of the *Halacha*? A Reform rabbi decides that W. is the Jewishly lawfully wedded wife of B. without requiring that W. receive a *get*, a Jewish divorce, from her first husband A. Obviously this is no longer a private matter, a matter of individual conscience which the non-Reform community can ignore. A social fact has been created which may intersect with the non-Reform community. What am I, an Orthodox rabbi to do when the children of W. and B. wish to marry Orthodox individuals? The *halacha* considers the offspring of such a marriage to be *mamzerim* (illegitimate) and forbidden to marry into the Jewish community.

Logic Dictates Our Position

If we are indeed one people and if liberal Jews wished us to continue to be so, didn't they realize they were placing Orthodoxy into an impossible position by unilaterally changing the procedures which confer status? Bear in mind the asymmetry; the logic and not the good will of the situation is such that Reform and Conservative *can* accept Orthodox procedures without violating principle while the Orthodox *cannot* accept Reform and Conservative procedures without violating their religious and legal commitments.

The issue of conversions is the most tragic and anomalous of all. The problem with Reform conversions is not only *who* is doing the conversion or *what* is the nature of the ceremony, but primarily what sort of Judaism have you sold the convert? What beliefs, what practices, what sort of commitment?

What enables me to say to a Reform Jew, "You are my brother," is the fact that he was born a Jew, this according to tradition is the overriding sufficient condition. But now consider this non-Jew who wishes to become Jewish. The biological component of Jewish parentage is not present. Instead we are placing the entire burden of status-conferral, of being born again, of acquiring a new Jewish personality, upon a theological procedure, a set of beliefs, a set of attitudes. But if the ceremony is a Reform one, if the theological procedures are according to Reform *theology*, which differs radically from the tradition, if the set of beliefs that this non-Jew has accepted, the attitudes he has learned, the life style he is to adopt are *not* the traditional Jewish ones—then the *transition* has simply not been made, the difficult and metaphysical change from non-Jew to Jew simply did not take place—because the right ingredients were not used! Change the recipe and you get a different result. How in all fairness can the Reform expect the Orthodox to accept this convert as *Jewish* when their converts are in their entirety, creatures of their theology and the Reform have always known that the Orthodox do not believe in their theology?

Here in the Diaspora, with the growth of the Orthodox community and the increase of *Baalei Tshuva*, (those returning to Judaism) these tragic consequences of denominationalism continue to proliferate in more sad stories, more shocking discoveries, more frustrated relationships. As I have indicated, the only groups, in my judgment, that are in a position by their own understanding to do something about this are the Reform and Conservative. They *can*, if they so desire, for the sake of the unity of *Klal Yisrael*, (the entire Jewish People) bring their procedures for marriage, divorce and conversions into line with the Orthodox.

Ultimately—and here I engage in prognosis—the modern Orthodox even in Israel will learn the ecumenical spirit as I have outlined it here. But there are those built in limits to Jewish ecumenism. Once these are recognized and accepted we can go to work together to achieve the best of all possible Jewish ecumenisms which I am convinced is not inconsiderable and can help to restore some unity to the fractured House of Israel. •

Toward a jewish lingua franca

Irwin Shaw

It was just a hundred years ago that Eliezer Ben Yehuda began his efforts to make spoken Hebrew the official language of the Jewish settlers in *Eretz Yisrael* (the land of Israel).

While great Zionist leaders like Smolenskin and Herzl could envision a Jewish homeland without Hebrew as its mother tongue, and while Orthodox Jews objected to any secular use of Hebrew, Ben Yehuda made spoken Hebrew a national goal. As early as 1879, he spoke of the establishment of a community in *Eretz Yisrael* that would be a focal point for all Jews, so that even those who would remain in the Diaspora would know that "they belonged to a people that dwells in its own land and has its own language and culture."

Ben Yehuda's dream of spoken Hebrew as the language of the Jews of *Eretz Yisrael* has now, of course, been realized. But his broader goal to make Hebrew the *lingua franca* of the Jewish people has not been— nor does it seem likely to be in the foreseeable future.

Why hasn't spoken Hebrew become the common language of world Jewry, despite the fact that many efforts have been made to encourage the learning of Hebrew ion the Diaspora? While there are, clearly, a number of barriers to the achievement of this goal, it is my belief that *the single most serious obstacle is the orthography of modern Israeli Hebrew.*

Earlier Attempts At Reform

When the use of written Hebrew was limited solely to the Bible and the *Siddur* (books that hardly ever changed and that were more "memorized" than read), the language was printed with Tiberian "pointing." In this system, vowels are indicated by dots and other marks located above, in front of and underneath the consonants (the only "real" letters of the alphabet). This system not only requires grammatical expertise in "pointing", but it is also terribly cumbersome to typeset.

With the advent of modern spoken Hebrew and the concomitant publication of daily newspapers, magazines and books in Hebrew, the cost of printing with the Tiberian points became prohibitive. The Israelis found a simple (if procrustean) solu-

IRWIN SHAW *is Executive Director Emeritus of the JCC of Metropolitan Detroit.*

tion to this problem: They merely dropped all the vowel signs. But in solving the problem of printing, they created a more serious problem in reading. As Ze'ev Jabotinsky suggested:

Take a man who studies French: After he has acquired his first 500 or 600 words from his textbooks or from lessons, he takes an easy and interesting book or a daily paper and tries to enrich his knowledge by reading... But where self-study of another language is easy, in Hewbrew it is exceedingly difficult... As long as we have this difference between "letters" and "pointing", we shall have stenography. That, however, is for stenographers, not for the masses of a nation. (*Ha'aretz*, June 28, 1925)

This is the fundamental problem of modern printed Hebrew, and it was recognized as such quite early on by official and semi-official language organizations. They tried to mitigate the problem by introducing a few modifications. For example, they doubled the vowel "yod" to represent the consonant "y", and they doubled the vowel "vav" to represent the consonant "v" (and also, for transliteration, the letter "w").

These and similar modifications have proved to be only moderately helpful, and over the years, many other suggestions were put forth for the adoption of a comprehensive, "one symbol/one sound" system.

One such system would have replaced the Hebrew alphabet entirely, in favor of the Roman alphabet. This was proposed in the 1920's and 1930's by men like Ze'ev Jabotinsky and Ittamar ben Avi (the son of Eliezer ben Yehuda). But the emotional opposition to discarding the Hebrew script was (and remains) too great to overcome, and the approach met with no success.

Most of the other suggestions for orthographic reform involved totally new designs for the Hebrew letters or the addition of new symbols to the existing alphabet. While these proposals were an improvement over the "pointing" system, their adoption would have in every case required a tremendous investment in printing equipment. More important, however, these systems would have required everyone to learn a totally new alphabet. There was therefore never any real possibility that any of them could be adopted.

A Modern Approach to Reform

Hebrew language experts have long been aware of the language's inherent problems, yet few of these experts have been motivated to champion even those improvements that *would* be feasible and that would *not* involve the wholesale transmutation of the alphabet.

What are some of these "correctable" problems? Among them, I would single out three in particular as perhaps the first to be addressed.

Foreign Words or Words of Foreign Derivation. It is most frustrating to try to read (i.e., decipher) an unknown Hebrew word — by applying all the analytical rules for Hebrew grammar — only to find after much wasted effort that it is not a Hebrew word at all, but a foreign word rendered in Hebrew transliteration.

Proper Names and the Adjectives Derived From Them. In English (as in most languages that use a Roman alphabet), proper names are immediately distinguishable because they are capitalized. Since there are no capital letters in Hebrew, the reader-decoder is again thrown off track.

Prefixes. To find the meaning of a word in a dictionary, one must first know how the word is spelled. In Hebrew, this can sometimes be quite difficult because of Hebrew's frequent use of prefixes. Hebrew uses prefixes to express the conjunction "and", the definite article "the", the interrogative indicator, and a number of prepositions such as "in", "to", "from" and so on. There can be three or four such prefixed letters in front of the root word — as in (for example) the word *oo-mey-ha-bayit*, meaning "and from the house," This often makes it difficult for the reader to determine where the prefixes end and the root word (the one he can find in the dictionary) begins.

What can be done to help the beginning-to-intermediate reader of unpointed Hebrew overcome these three hurdles? Actually, a quite practical answer has existed for some time; it simply hasn't been recognized for the powerful, reading-simplification tool that it is.

In 1922, the forerunner agency of the present Academy of the Hebrew Language solved the problem of transliterating consonant sounds that do not not exist in Hebrew simply by adding an apostrophe ("geresh") to an approximate Hebrew letter. Thus, to express the English "j" sound, an apostrophe is added to the Hebrew "gimel"; to express the English "ch" sound (as in "lunch"), an apostrophe is added to the Hebrew "tzadi." What was so delightful about this solution was that it was so easy and clear, and it made use of an already existing and readily available symbol.

Add New Punctuation Symbols

This same approach could be applied to the solution of the three problems I've outlined here, and it ultimately could be systematized into an easily implemented "Augmented Hebrew Orthography" (AHO) that would apply some of the ideas of earlier reformers.

It would be a simple intervention, for example, to precede every foreign word in a Hebrew text with the solidus (/). Every proper noun and the adjectives derived from proper nouns could be preceded by a left-parentheses—"(". And prefixes could be indicated simply by inserting a comma (,) between the prefix letter(s) and the main word; a semi-colon (;) could be used for a prefix normally "pointed" with the "sheva" and located immediately before the main word.

All three of these "solutions" would use symbols already available on present-day typesetting equipment. None would involve any special line-spacing, word-spacing or letter-spacing. None would entail any confusion with the conventional uses of the chosen symbols. And all could be readily and easily assimilated by Hebrew readers at any level of competency.

An additional element of an Augmented Hebrew Orthography would be the use of the colon (:) to indicate certain syllabication. For example, the colon could be used after every non-final letter which (if it were "pointed") would have the "sheva" under it. While this would add a little to word length, it would be a small price to pay for the increased clarity that would result.

An even further extension of the AHO would be the use of the apostrophe after each of the four Hebrew letters whose pronunciation in regular "pointing" would be determined by the "dagesh" (or dot) within the body of the letter—that is, the "bet", the "kaf", the "pay" and the "shuruk." The apostrophe could similarly be used to distinguish the "sin" from the "shin", and—in conjunction with the doubled "vav"—to designate the English "w" sound (as distinguished from the "v" sound in Hebrew.)

Experiments with the kind of Augmented Hebrew Orthography I've described indicate that such a system can significantly simplify and enhance the readability of modern Israeli Hebrew. Of course, an augmented orthography won't guarantee

Hebrew's evolution into a Jewish *lingua franca*. But the absence of such an orthography virtually guarantees that this will never happen. •

London to toronto, personal impressions
Dow Marmur

When we arrived in Canada last summer, a lot of people were talking about a new book called *None Is Too Many*. It is an account by two Jewish historians, Irving Abella and Harold Troper, of Canadian immigration policy towards Jews between 1933 and 1948. Its conclusions are epitomized in the title: Canada's politicians wanted to keep the Jews out of their country at a time when the Jews desperately needed somewhere to go. All kinds of reasons were given for delays and cancellations of permits, but now— under the scrutiny of painstaking research— the truth could be told: it was anti-Semitism; when it came to Jews, even none was too many.

The findings were startling, but not unique to Canada. After all, Bernard Wasserstein had told a similar story in his *Britain and the Jews of Europe 1939-1945* and Martin Gilbert had chartered similar territory in *Auschwitz and the Allies*. Yet neither of those books had stirred Anglo-Jewry the way *None Is Too Many* had upset Canadians.

The difference in reception between essentially similar documentation on the two sides of the Atlantic is significant. Jews in Europe, including Britain, take anti-Semitism for granted and, by and large, learn to accommodate themselves to it. Some even believe that too much protest is counter-productive. North American Jewry, including Canada, is shocked each time it finds evidence of anti-Semitism and often over-reacts. It is determined to make sure that what happened in the 1930's and 1940's does not happen again.

The Different Relation to Israel

For the same reasons, support for Israel is stronger in Canada than in Britain. In fact, it is less than prudent here to express any kind of criticism of Israeli government policies, even if they affect the lives of Diaspora Jews. The argument is that Israel has so many enemies who constantly bombard her politically and militarily that

DOW MARMUR *is the Senior Rabbi of Holy Blossom Temple, in Toronto, Ontario.*

she is entitled to unquestioned and uncritical loyalty from her friends.

But this kind of friendship is superficial. Thus, although vocal and fiscal support for Israel is higher in Canada than it is in Britain, proportionately more British Jews go on *aliyah*. Canadian Jews treat Israel as a symbol and perhaps as an insurance policy, but regard Canada as home. That is why they are so uncritical of Israel and so sensitive to anti-Semitism here.

Yet, Canadian Jews, for all their success in business as well as in political and public life are not rooted in Canadian society. True, it is not that easy to determine what a Canadian identity really means, the way one can decide what it means to be integrated in British society, but even allowing for that, it is remarkable how "ghettoized" Canadian Jews are. It makes British Jews integrated and at ease by comparison.

Those British Jews who are more "integrated" than others usually leave the Jewish community altogether. In Canada, almost the opposite seems to be the case. Apart from the truly Orthodox, those who belong to synagogues are often more assimilated than those who don't. Holocaust survivors from Eastern Europe— of whom there are very few in Britain— rarely join congregations; it is too alien to their way of life.

Their children are different. They feel more at home in the ways of North American middle-class Jewry, and synagogue affiliation is part of it. Since Reform is much more the Jewish Establishment here than in Britain, those who seek their way in, tend to join Reform congregations. The young tend to be more self-confident and mature than their parents.

The Variations in Jewishness
The fact that Reform is part of the Jewish Establishment means that many of Canada's communal leaders belong to Reform congregations. I sat at the dinner table of a distinguished Canadian Jewish leader who is a member of his local Reform congregation. Opposite me was a distinguished Anglo-Jewish leader, probably no more observant than our host, but a member of an Orthodox congregation in Britain. I asked him if he would have been able to attain the position he had in Anglo-Jewry, had he joined his local Reform synagogue. He didn't think so. Neither do I.

A Reform rabbi in Canada, Dr. Gunther Plaut, served as President of the Canadian Jewish Congress. No rabbi, let alone a Reform one, could ever become President of the Board of Deputies of British Jews.

Anglo-Jewry is undoubtedly more observant, more to the "right", than Canadian Jewry, but I don't think that it is more Jewish. There are probably more kosher butchers in Britain per Jewish population unit than in Canada— but there are more good Jewish bookshops in Canada. The standard of Jewish knowledge is higher here, although synagogue affiliation is not. Jewish communal institutions have a high profile in Canada and are hives of activity— but many would be open on *Shabbat* and serve non-kosher food.

If Golders Green, one of the "Jewish" areas of London, has aspirations to be the Jerusalem of Europe— although it has neither the depth nor the piety to achieve it— Toronto is probably more anxious to be the Tel Aviv of North America— and it has the money and the vulgarity to pull it off. It also has almost enough Israelis to populate it.

The difference in outlook is also reflected in synagogue life. One of my major challenges is to fight secularism *within* the synagogue. This secularization expresses itself in scarcity of prayer and observance and in a surfeit of aesthetics and traditional rituals. As a result, in some areas Reform is curiously "left", in others remarkably "right", less religiously observant than in Britain but much more "gut-Jewish." My sense of spiritual alienation is amply compensated for by a sense of being with my people as I knew it in Poland and Russia.

What Should a Rabbi be Doing?
A group in my congregation had a discussion recently as to which of the two "traditional" roles of the rabbi was more in keeping with the needs of the times: that of administrator and public relations person, or that of pastor. When I suggested that, since we were so concerned with tradition, we should start with the rabbi as teacher, I had apparently dropped something of a bombshell. Only a very few of these leaders in the congregation had even thought of the rabbi in this way. In many congregations the teaching is being done by lesser lights or "visiting scholars." In Europe you still expect the rabbi to be the teacher *and* scholar, whether he is Orthodox or Liberal.

The rabbis in North America are confined to their priestly duties, which are curiously secular, or at least intended for secular people. When I declared my intention to follow another pattern, it caused some consternation: Would he want us to be religious? Isn't it enough that he has status and position? People want to enjoy their Jewishness gastronomically and their Judaism vicariously.

But my stance has also evoked enthusiasm. People had forgotten that you could be Reform and yet remain within the traditional orbit of learning and prayer; that it was not enough to pay lip-service to folkways and cash to fund raisers. I am greatly encouraged by the response from the leadership and there are indications that some of those on the periphery might wish to join. Whether the existing institutional structure will tolerate it, remains to be seen. I am full of hope that my European habits will bear some fruit.

The challenge is twofold: on the one hand, to establish a different style of rabbinate and, on the other, to equip the institutions to tolerate the change. The former is easier than the latter. Individuals are receptive to new ideas, whereas organizations are not. But it is also a test for Reform: if it is true to itself, it must allow for change and it must fight rigidity and secularism in its own circles with at least the same vehemence that it fights it in Orthodoxy. I see myself as an emissary from the old world in this struggle. I wonder how the mighty institutional machinery of the new one will respond.

Finding a New and Welcome Home

Happily, there is no reason to fight Orthodoxy, for this is a relatively tolerant community. The fact that Reform has been on the scene first, that it is part of the Establishment and that many, if not most, of the communal leaders belong to Reform or Conservative congregations, makes it impossible for Orthodoxy to have its way as it has in Britain and in Europe. But with an increasing radicalization of Orthodoxy and the ascendance of extreme elements all over the world things may change for the worse and here, too.

In the meantime, Toronto appears as a haven of tolerance. The mother of one of the leaders of my congregation died recently. A leading Orthodox rabbi attended the service in the synagogue (Reform and Conservative congregations often hold funeral services in the synagogues here). Before the service, the same rabbi came to see me in my study to welcome me to Toronto. I cannot imagine any of the *dayanim* of the Orthodox London *Bet Din* doing something similar.

When I was a child in Poland, they often used to ask me whom I loved best, my father or my mother. As a middle-aged rabbi in Canada, I am often asked whether I prefer London or Toronto. The question of today baffles me as much as the question in my childhood used to perplex me.

Comparative evaluation is not possible. I know that what I am today has been shaped by the Leo Baeck College in London, the Reform Synagogues of Great Britain and the two London congregations I served for 21 years. But I also know that what I have been doing in the last six months has been exciting and rewarding. The vitality of American Jewry is infectious.

There used to be an advert in New York: "Dress British— Think Yiddish!" I try to live by it. But I have now also acquired another motto: "Feel British— Act Canadian!" It is, as you Americans would put it, a meaningful and enriching experience. ●

My inner world
Eugene B. Borowitz

I hadn't thought much about my spiritual quest over the years until now.

Much of my Jewish religious life derives from an ambivalent impression of my Ohio childhood. I liked being Jewish. I even enjoyed religious school and going to services. But it exasperated me that my teachers and my rabbi could never explain Judaism in any way that made sense to me. When I discovered philosophy and the social sciences weren't any smarter, I decided to become a rabbi.

Then my ambivalence intensified. I loved the Hebrew Union College in theory but only occasionally in practice. Once again my teachers left me badly disappointed. Along with my two close friends, Arnie Wolf and Steve Schwarzschild, I figured I had better build my own sort of Jewish faith and find my own way of explaining it. And that's what I'm still doing.

A consequent student experiment was critical. I wasn't worried about my intellectual life. That came easily to me. But making personal contact with God was strange to my American upbringing. So I decided to try to learn to pray, not just at the daily college service but by myself. That way there would be no dodging God. Besides, some others of my class and I wanted to be more Jewish. We knew we were modern. What bothered us was how to be Jews. Another lifelong quest. So I tried to learn to pray alone from a prayerbook. I started with the *Union Prayer Book* and worked with it for some years. Later I push-ed my religious growth further by extending my *davening* (praying) through gerrymandered *siddur* (traditional prayerbook) services. Daily prayer has been the bedrock of my Jewish life— and a con-tinual judgment. Let me explain.

Attempting to Link Work and Faith

Early on I decided to pray in my office, to link my work and my faith. Nothing I regularly do is more difficult for me. I find it a terrible trial to pay attention to God when all around me are reminders of things I need to work on. Frequently I discover my *kavanah* (concentration) has broken and I am thinking about one of my projects in-stead of talking to God. I hate that— but it is the fundamental spiritual problem of my life. How do I keep God ahead of all my schemes? How do I subordinate everything I do, especially all the good, Jewish things, to God and what, as best I can figure it out, God wants of me and the Jewish people? In sum, how, in my life, do I make and keep God one?

I do many other Jewish things but I now want to say a word about my other search, the intellectual one. Here I've been fortunate. I've been spared the religious pain of having to surrender early religious beliefs I've later found inadequate. In-stead, much of what I always thought was a good explanation of Judaism has fallen by the way. At the same time, the path I started on as a student— radically theological yet deeply practice-, text- and community-oriented; per-sonalist, not rationalist; richly particularistic without being ghettoizing or a-ethical— now holds a substantial number of our community. Of course, it also helped that I started out more with questions than with certainties. And I have been content to accumulate partial insights and be pa-tient until I gained a more rounded vision.

Sometimes I am troubled that I have not been overwhelmed by the problem of evil. Surely there is enough of it around and we Jews have seen it at its worst. Intellectually, I think my turmoil has been relatively moderate because I never believed God was, in Dick Rubenstein's words, "the ultimate, omnipotent actor in history." It also helped that I did not believe I had to have or was entitled to rational explanations of everything. For an intellectual, I seem to be able to live with a good deal of mystery.

Aware of God's Routine Gifts

Humanly, I simply find I cannot rail at God for long. Here an experience was instructive. In 1953,

on my way to do a funeral, my automobile was hit by a semi-drifter who had borrowed an unin-sured car without brakes. Two days later I was in my naval base hospital with a ruptured kidney. Waiting for it to heal, it occurred to me the rab-bis were right to have a blessing for excretion, so I taught myself the text. Ever since, when my kidneys work or I defecate, I have said it. It does not always mean much to me— but it, more than any of the other blessings I daily say, continually reminds me of what God regularly gives me.

I have also been spared great personal tragedy and physical pain. There has been suffering, to be sure. My family has known cancer of the brain and of the pancreas, two cases of Alzheimer's disease, several instances of coronary artery disease, and disturbing if not incapacitating neuroses. I obviously cannot take *rofe chol basar* (who heals all flesh) at face value, but I remain fundamentally moved by *umafli laasot* (and who works wondrously).

I struggle with many of the things that bother other rabbis. People don't seem to care very much about Judaism. Regardless of my best efforts they do not take it very seriously or find my understan-ding of it very compelling. Despite the occasional life I've touched and the faithful remnant who care, I often feel that, on the human level, my work doesn't really mean very much. It helps when I can remember that God will one day win out even without my success. I found it hard to acknowledge that I was not the Messiah, not even the bringer of the Messianic Age. It is harder still remembering that I am not God.

The Lonely Man of Faith

My greatest spiritual shock has come from the in-tense loneliness I feel as a Jew. My ethical and cultural friends think religion odd. My Jewish companions, the few who are learned and serious, think Reform Judaism intolerably undemanding. I do have the rare good fortune to have Reform col-leagues with whom I can discuss Jewish intellec-tual issues. But we go rather independent ways when it comes to understanding our Judaism, par-ticularly should we ever talk of Jewish faith.

My sense of isolation is intensified by my strong commitment to the notion of Judaism as a com-munity religion. Even desiring a rich Jewish ethnicity makes one an alien to much of American Jewish life. But if one wants to be a self and fulfill oneself in a Jewish community of selves, in Buber's sense, then alienation becomes the com-mon stuff of one's Jewish existence.

I have some partially effective strategies to alleviate my solitariness. I am blessed with a good marriage and kids who still talk to me, and I work hard at keeping it that way. I have a few friends and enjoy a few pleasures. And I try to create community wherever I can. My greatest challenge is to transform my classroom from the rigid, hierarchical one of my school years to one of interpersonal exchange while not sacrificing the demands of Jewish learning. That effort has also given me my greatest rewards. Furthermore, I have the joy of working with colleagues who agree that we must make a serious effort to have our school less an institution than a community. And from time to time we and our students actually bring it into being.

Mostly I have learned a new aspect of Jewish messianism. Of course I hope for justice and look forward to peace. I still aspire to the ultimate vindication of the Jewish people and, through it, of all humanity. But now, too, I long for redemption from the *galut* (exile) of loneliness, for that day when we shall all be one as persons and one in community— for only on that day will God be one in our lives as God, to God, is God. ●

Judaism is my art form
Raymond P. Scheindlin

Theology and theological problems have never occupied a central part of my consciousness, despite lifelong intense involvement in Judaism and despite a rabbinic education. I do not think this is because Judaism lacks a theological dimension or because the curriculum of my rabbinical school was flawed, but rather because of a personality that does not feel strongly the issues with which theology is concerned. I tried for years to think theologically, to explain the Jewish component of my life on either a rational or a mystical-spiritual basis. But at age forty-four, I am finally ready to acknowledge that neither label correctly identifies my inner life.

Morality is no more important a part of my inner life than is theology. I would like to believe that my behavior is fundamentally moral. I do try to face up to lapses in my behavior, to identify and understand my wrong choices in the hope of be-

RAYMOND P. SCHEINDLIN *is Provost of the Jewish Theological Seminary of America, and teaches medieval Hebrew poetry there.*

ing able to avoid repeating them. But I do not believe that the impulse to do this derives from the rabbi in me. There has been so far one occasion in my life when I attributed a moral choice to my Judaism, but in that situation I was one of two Jews in an otherwise non-Jewish environment, and it may have been my isolation that led me to credit the tribe with a choice that was entirely personal. On the whole, I believe that morality is a personality trait.

A Medium for Expressing My Inner Self

Where I really and truly feel Jewish is in my *feelings*. How often I have heard my rabbinical colleagues mock from the pulpit Jews who don't keep kosher, don't go to synagogue, and don't study Torah, but claim to have a Jewish heart. I feel close kinship for these "cardiac Jews," the objects of such rabbinical scorn, for in principle, my Judaism is like theirs, only more involving.

How rich has my "cardiac Judiasm" been for me! It has occupied my intellectual life for decades, filling me with curiosity about our heritage of language, literature, folkways, and history, curiosities which have over the years spilled outwards to the cultures that have influenced Judaism and been influenced by it, and which now, in my fifth decade, I find radiating beyond this circle to analogous aspects of more remote cultures. My interest in our national language, an obsession for most of my life, became the basis of my livelihood, and, what is more important, a means of enriching my use of my native language.

But Judaism has given me something even more precious than an intellectual life. It has given me a means of expression, a substance in which to work the feelings that *are* my inner self, a form in which to pour the undifferentiated, chaotic internal energy only partly put to use by my life with others. It is the area in which raw feeling can find expression. It is an art form.

When I think of Judaism as an art, I do not mean that I collect paintings of families at the *Seder* table and recordings of Hasidic hits. I mean that I perform Judaism as a pianist performs Chopin, reproducing the notes, tempo instructions, dynamic and articulation markings exactly as written in the score, but imbuing them with my own distinctive temperament. I cannot know what Chopin felt when he composed, and if I did I could not summon up *his* feelings to give life to the music. I can only let the score unleash my *own* feelings, and in the dynamic tension between the composer's score and my own personality, make the music come to life.

Words Cannot Express the Feelings

When we say of a musical composition that it is happy or sad, tortured or tranquil, we have said nothing of importance. The exact emotional content of a work of art cannot be adequately expressed in another medium (in this case, language) because the emotions it releases are richer, more intense, and more complex than the form itself. The performer and the participating listener are both individuals who have the capacity of making the connection between the art form and their ineffable inner selves. I am drawing my examples from music because it is the secular art most familiar to me, but I mean these generalizations to apply equally to the other arts, including Judaism.

By analogy, I cannot say of Judaism that it means to me theology, morality, ethnicity, or anything else that can be expressed in another medium. It serves my inner self as a self-sufficient medium of expression. There may sometimes be an occasion to describe the feelings released by Jewish rituals. Then I can speak of joy, exultation, misery, guilt, gratitude, historical identity, and other words that only hint at the true emotion without expressing it. For example, "historical identity" seems to be incongruous with the other items in the above list, since it is a fact, not a feeling; but to me, Jewish ritual unleashes its "feelingness" so that in my Jewish context it is as much feeling as the other items.

Like Art, Judaism Requires Study

Like other art forms, Judaism requires talent and disciplined study, both to perform and to appreciate. I have worked hard at acquiring the skills of my art, and it has repaid my pains. It has also *caused* me some pain, but mostly because I misunderstood it or allowed myself to be oppressed by others' misunderstandings. I love to perform Judaism by studying and teaching Hebrew poetry, reading *Maariv*, reading the Torah in synagogue, acting as *Baal Musaf* (the leader of the Additional Service) in my congregation on the High Holidays, giving my children their *Bar Mitzvah* and *Bat Mitzvah* lessons, etc.

Some of these activities are useful (by reading *Maariv* I find out what is happening in Israel), edifying (studying Hebrew poetry stimulates my thinking), helpful (reading the Torah in my synagogue is a service to the community), or con-

ducive to warm intergenerational relations (*Bar/Bat Mitzvah* lessons), but these are incidental benefits. These activities are my particular life. If I did not know about them I would engage in other activities that are useful, edifying, helpful, and conducive to warm intergenerational relations, as do many others with great success. But then I would be someone else.

In the summer evenings of my teenage years I used to take long walks through my rose-scented suburb, chanting to myself the Psalms and the Song of Songs, sometimes in pious fervor, sometimes in heroic jubilation or adolescent misery. Later I tried to sort out these pious and romantic emotions, but today I gladly let them free to "serve in confusion." Since I have given up trying to arrange and categorize, my inner life has been richer and I have felt whole. ●

Regaining a child from a cult
Marianne Langner Zeitlin

In late June of 1942, four thousand and fifty-one children, wrenched from the arms of their stateless and "denaturalized" parents, were quartered in Drancy prior to being sent to extermination at Auschwitz.

I had reason enough to remember this episode in the past decade, reason enough although I am neither stateless nor denaturalized, and the specter of Nazism, aided by a French puppet government, is supposedly long since dead. I am an American citizen, married to a well-known artist, presumably legally, politically and economically well safeguarded, yet when our son was taken from us while still a student at Prescot College in Arizona, the clock seemed to have been turned back to Holocaust time. The only difference was that he was taken, not by blackbooted policemen using force and torture, but by saffron-garbed mahatmas promising bliss and love everlasting.

The nightmare started for us in the spring of 1973 with a collect phone call when Hillel, our ordinarily articulate and witty son, began muttering about having just been "reborn" and wanting to share the good news with us. When we could finally cut through the preliminaries, we

MARIANNE LANGNER ZEITLIN *lives in Rochester, New York.*

discovered that he had become a devotee of the then fifteen year old Gura Maharaj Ji, the Perfect Master, and a *premie* — a novitiate — or an aspirant- — in the Divine Light Mission. "I've received 'knowledge'," he kept repeating, "and I'm, so blissed out I can't find words."

Helplessly Watching From Afar

Before his conversion, Hillel had been a genuine seeker of religious verification and, like so many of his generation in the wake of the social, political and psychological upheavals of that period, had been particularly vulnerable to the idea of a structured and safe haven with built-in companionship. For over a year he had travelled through Europe and Israel and, what with the advent of the human potential movement all around him, a journey inward must have seemed a logical next step. Helplessly we watched the battle between the Hillel that had been and the Hillel that now was sinking deeper and deeper into the spiritual mire. While his new-found faith initially seemed consistent with his ideals, when he moved into a *premie* commune, more and more sacrifices soon became necessary: the physical, intellectual and emotional scourging of mind and body in order to have but one outlet for relief — the illusion of bliss or Nirvana that comes from prolonged meditation.

With the rise of the assorted cults in the past decade, all this has become an old story — but no less painful to the parents and siblings of the victims for that. Each of us has had somehow to deal with the totalitarianism of the New Right — and because of the religious trappings under which it oeprates, the Kafkaesque spectacle of government and courts upholding the rights of quasi-religious entrepreneurs instead off their pawns. Spiritual chicanery posing as spiritual chic.

We Could Not Imagine Worse

Of course we sought help. When we sought legal help from the American Civil Liberties Union, we were told that under the First Amendment Hillel was entitled to practice any "religion" he wished and at nineteen was no longer a minor under our jurisdiction. When we sought psychiatric help we were told to be "tolerant," to regard our son's "phase" with the objectivity we might use if he were someone else's child. And from well-meaning friends we were told to recite the A.A. prayer [God help me to change what I can and accept what I cannot], to sweat it out, and, above all, to recognize that it could have been worse.

But to us, it couldn't have been worse. What could be worse than watching flesh of your flesh voluntarily enslaving himself in the guise of spiritual surrender? What could be worse than watching the attempted robotization of any human being, let alone one near and dear to you? And because we knew that every cult, including this one, seeks to alienate devotees from their families, we were in a double bind: forced to soft-pedal our opposition for fear of playing into Maharaj Ji's hands.

Although Hillel did leave school when he received *Knowledge,* wanting only to "realize the highest consciousness of god in my soul," we persuaded him to return. Eventually he received a master's degree in social work from Syracuse University. Shortly after he got his first job, he was persuaded to move into an ashram, renounce all worldly pleasures and live a life of poverty, chastity and obedience. Our only solace at this time was that at least he was functioning in the outside world as a psychiatric social worker and as long as he did so there was still part of his brain operating outside of *Mission* control

That solace was to be short-lived. On a visit with Hillel in September of 1979, he announced that he had made application to become an initiator (full-time proselytizer and "Knowledge" dispenser) for Maharaj Ji and would, if accepted, be leaving his profession. As he went on to elaborate on this decision, all we kept thinking was that soon our son would officially help to visit upon others the horror that had been visited upon him and his family.

A Choice of Last Resort

Because my husband and I felt we no longer could live with ourselves if Hillel were to become an initiator, we decided to take action. And the only action left open to us was to attempt to have him deprogrammed.

A thousand fears plagued us. However circumscribed, Hillel still maintained some relationship to us — would we lose him entirely? What faith other than Judaism which he seemed to have rejected could we give him to replace the one he would be losing? What if he should escape?

But, as we weighed the alternative, we concluded we had nothing to lose. What were the legal, social or economic risks compared to literally consigning our son to what we believed was a fate worse than death?

As we went through the necessary cloak-and-dagger arrangements—hiring a deprogrammer, renting an isolated country house (a precaution in case his cult brothers and sisters tried to come and rescue him), arranging for our son to come home for a weekend visitt, etc.—one glimmer of hope lighted our path: the signal we felt Hillel had unconsciously given us by telling us in advance of his intention to become an initiator. At every other stage of his involvement, such as when he received *Knowledge,* moved into the *premie* house, and then to the ashram, we were confronted by *faits accomplis.* Was this advance warning a signal from the submerged Hillel that he wanted "out" and need help? Or was this just another case of parental wishful thinking?

The hunch proved to be accurate: within twenty-four hours after Hillel's arrival home for that fateful weekend, he was deprogrammed, the speed of his recovery aided by his own unconscious desire for several years to free himself of his spiritual fetters.

Now, Deprogramming His Peers

Our Drancy is over now. Hillel is using his first hand experience and hard-won wisdom professionally with remarkable results. Along with Gary Sharf, one of the most eloquent *Moonies* to "come out" of the Unification Church experience, he had founded *Options for Personal Transition (OPT)* a unique cult awareness counselling service and since its inception in 1980 they have been successful in helping over a hundred families to be reunited with their lost children, or, in some cases, lost husband or wife. Ironically, it is in the experience of counselling and deprogramming their former cohorts and peers that they are having an opportunity to fulfill the humanitarian ideals which had lured them into the cults in the first place.

Our personal story had a very happy ending, but for the hundreds of thousands of families of victims still under the cultic yoke the agony remains. Risks in getting exit counselling or deprogramming may be great, but far greater are the risks in not doing so. Therein often lies vegetablehood—mindless, mutilated burned-out husks. Rather than the incomprehensible tolerance with which the government wittingly or unwittingly aids these despots and their pseudo-religious fronts, it ought to be assisting the few counsellors that exist in any way it can, and regard the, by virtue of their unique experiences, as indispensable pioneers on a new psychotherapeutic frontier. At the very least, conservatorships (wherein parents of cultists have the right to place their child under observation by a team of psychiatrists for a period of time) should be made readily and cheaply available. In the wake of the Manson murders, the Guyana suicides, the Synanon rattlesnake, the untold human casualties and their unexplained disappearances, can the urgency be overstated?

Keeping peace at the seder table

Sally Shafton

"Here comes Gram with the matzah ball soup! Aunt Bess will soon be here with the gefilte fish." The kitchen was alive with the sounds of *Pesach.* The *chametz* (leaven) search had been completed the night before, and the table was soon to be set. Each year there was great planning and much anticipation that went into the *Seder* preparation: however, this year, somehow, there was more divisiveness than fulfillment and bonding. Grandma was happy to contribute her culinary effort, but when she was asked to prepare a one minute presentation for the *Seder* on the meaning of the 4 questions to her, she hesitated, then balked.

When the cousins arrived that evening and giggled and laughed as Rachel and Seth asked the four questions in Hebrew and English, there was no Jewish bonding. Aunt Joan and Uncle Bill really were not expectng to read *every* page of the Hagaddah. "Let the kids hunt for the *afikomen* already," said Aunt Joan. But Rachel and Seth's parents had become more strongly identified Jews in the past years. After their second trip to Israel last year, they were looking for more depth and more education not less. So, instead of experiencing joy, the family brought together for this once a year celebration was silently suffering.

Everyone's expectations were different; if there were any hostilities building during the year, this holiday seemed to heighten and exacerbate them. This family could "make it" in their relationships during the rest of the year. Why did *Pesach* and *Seder* result in a gnawing strain, rather than a blending for this and other families? One set of cousins was proud after much practice to have mastered the chanting of the *fir kasches* (four questions) in Hebrew for this year, and the other

SALLY SHAFTON *and her family celebrate Passover in Los Angeles, California.*

230

set of cousins wondered how much money Uncle Ted would give for the finding of the *afikomen*.

A Variety of Expectations Around the Table

Jonathan was twenty-two and in the past year he had re-awakened in himself that exciting feeling for the tradition that he had experienced during his Junior year abroad in Israel. He had attended Friday night services regularly at Hillel, and had become active in the Welfare Fund drive on his campus. He was changing rapidly, but he knew that he would be spending *Seder* with his family, who had not yet moved to another religious place. He wanted very much to be tactful and not hurt his *Zayde* (grandfather) who had led the *Seder* for many years, but he very much wanted to conduct the ritual this year. He decided that it would be rewarding to visit Zayde and to work with him in creating a new type of *Seder* for the whole family. Zayde was receptive to the idea, as long as he could retain control, but at least Jonathan could insert interpretations in many places in the text, and could introduce the joy of the music he had recently learned. He spent considerable time in preparation so that he could bring his family to the place where he wanted them all to be. He assumed that if Zayde went along with his idea, certainly the rest of the family would be agreeable.

The sat down at the table that *Seder* night, and he looked at them with love and enthusiasm. He was certain that his excitement would be contagious. "I don't even need a book," said Aunt Carol. "We'll be eating pretty soon." Jonathan maintained his steadfastness and began to alternate the reading with Zayde. Finally, the side conversation going on between Aunt Carol and cousin Hilda became so distracting that Jonathan had to gently ask them to please follow along. There was much confusion as they all found the correct page, and Jonathan tried again. He had prepared a special presentation on the middle matzah, and by this time it was clear that he and his family were on very different wave lengths. They participated very minimally in group reading, said they could not learn those complicated songs in a minute, and slowly but surely, all of Jonathan's plans disintegrated. The parents began to chide him about "eating already," and of course, the youngsters joined in. This young Jew felt isolated, angry and resentful. He would not remember this evening as a positive Jewish experience in his family history.

Different Backgrounds, Different Needs

All the members of any one family do not identify and observe in the same way and with the same intensity. Yet, each sees himself as an identified Jew. Grandma, who worked very diligently over her matzah ball soup, felt that she was doing her utmost to make *Seder* important. However, her grandchildren, educated in a day school, were not satisfied with gastronomic Judaism. Her children were now wearing *kippot* at the meal, and were keeping a kosher kitchen. Their observance and identity levels had gone in such different directions as to make them a dividing factor, rather than a bonding one. In Jonathan's case, Zayde was willing to grow and change with his grandson, but the aunts, uncles and cousins were looking for something different. All Jews, all observing, and yet emotional turmoil was the result.

There is strength in knowing that other families are suffering from the same malady. No one family need feel isolated and ashamed of what transpires before, during and after *Seder*. It is happening in many Jewish homes, and is probably not a new phenomenon for our people. We have always found strength in diversity. However, who would think that Hillel and Shammai were sitting at our *Seder* tables?

Without being judgmental and destructive we can help ameliorate this condition by first taking an honest and open look at the situation. Most of all, no one should feel alone with this phenomenon, and we must know that within our tradition there is the appreciation for difference and the unity it can achieve, if handled properly. We can begin the process by asking ourselves some key questions. Is not Jewish family nurturing a mutual responsibility? Is it possible for people of greatly differing value structures to be compatible around a *Seder* table? Is there a positive way to manage hostility and disagreement that surrounds that which should be festive and joyous? How can we translate changing roles and relationships into a positive Jewish holiday experience? Even though Grandma has assimilated through her lifetime, isn't it possible for Rachel and Seth to find mutually satisfying Jewish familial experience to share with her?

Reaching for Common Jewish Ground

Perhaps, too, the over-reliance on the structure of the Hagaddah breeds a problem. There may be a need for ease, freedom of conversation and intimacy at this time, and that can be incorporated into the proscribed ritual as well. We need to find a way to make familial differences strengthening and to use the same toleration techniques that we so ably use with friends who do not share our exact value structure.

We also need to think in terms of understanding and trust, rather than in resentment and anger. If all members of the family are encouraged to use their own initiative and creativity in meeting with similar spirit, perhaps some common denominator can be found. Initiative and action can dilute passivity and status quo. The experience together should make a statement about equals, not about powerful vs. powerless. We need to look at family members as they are, and not as that which we would like them to become. Perhaps a clear explanation in advance of the plan for the *Seder*, would eliminate any unrealistic expecations for both hosts and guests. We could ask Aunt Carol "if she would be willing" to do a special reading on the celebration of *Seder* in the Warsaw ghetto. If a message of "growing together" can be transmitted in advance, perhaps cousin Lance will not giggle when cousin Seth chants his four questions.

Judaism has weathered many greater storms than those which are brewing over *gefilte* fish at the *Seder* table. *Pesach* and *Seder* will go on each year in most Jewish homes without fail. However, our goal is to capture the great potential of this family holiday and to make it work for us in a positive way. We must do more than endure the holiday each year with our families. We can be open and honest about the impediments to changing the complexion of the holiday, and in so doing, we will make Gram's matzah balls a lasting and satisfying memory. •

The demise of conservative judaism
David Novak

The demise of Conservative Judaism as a distinctive voice on the contemporary Jewish scene became clearly evident once again in the current debate surrounding the attempted (and failed) move in the Knesset to amend the Law of Return. The Orthodox parties proposed that the current law be specified to include only those "converted halachically" (*giyur ke-halacha*), in addition to

DAVID NOVAK *is rabbi of the Bayswater Jewish Center in Far Rockaway, NY and a contributing editor of Sh'ma.*

native-born Jews. Up until now the law gave the right of immediate Israeli citizenship to anyone who had undergone "conversion" (*hitgyrut*), without further specification. Indeed, in the 1968 Shalit decision, probably the most powerful challenge to the religious connotation of this clause in the law, the late Justice Moshe Silberg cited the Reform rite of conversion as being the minimal criterion of conversion as a religious act (see *Ba'in K'ehad*, Jerusalem, 1982, p. 413). This minimal religious definition was made, according to Silberg, to exclude members of other religions from claiming Jewish identity in Israel based upon cultural affinities alone (*Ibid*,. p. 412). In other words, Silberg affirmed that there is a necessarily religious component in becoming a member of the Jewish people.

It is not at all surprising, then, that Reform Judaism would oppose any change in the wording of the law inasmuch as its conversion procedures, for whatever reasons, have been explicitly accepted by the Israel Supreme Court in a famous test case of this law. It is equally unsurprising that Orthodox Judaism should want this law amended since in its eyes only a conversion conducted according to halachic norms is valid.

Conservatives Took Reform Position

Conservative Judaism, however, was caught in a dilemma. If it had affirmed "halachic conversion," then it would have opted for the Orthodox interpretation of *halacha*, which in the State of Israel at least, invalidates Conservative rabbis from being acceptable members of a rabbinic court (*Bet Din*) having the legal power to accept converts. If, on the other hand, it had rejected "halachic conversion," even in this instance, then it would have recognized the validity of Reform non-halachic conversions *ex post facto*. Instead of attempting to formulate an independent solution of this dilemma, Dr. Gerson Cohen, the chancellor of the Jewish Theological Seminary of America, and Rabbi Alexander Shapiro, the president of the Rabbinical Assembly, joined the leaders of Reform Judaism in a press conference— at the headquarters of Reform Judaism— and expressed common opposition to the proposed amendment. Thus in a confrontation involving the most important item on the contemporary Jewish agenda, namely, who is a Jew, the leaders of Conservative Judaism have now totally capitulated to the Reform position. Indeed, as Chancellor Cohen himself recently stated at a public gathering, "We are all Reform Jews, in a sense" (*Jewish Week*, New York, Sept. 21, 1984).

Nevertheless, had the leaders of Conservative Judaism re-expressed the traditional stance of Conservative Judaism, namely, that *halacha* is *their* norm and that it is not the monopoly of Orthodox Judaism, only to be interpreted and administered by the Orthodox rabbinate, then, it seems to me, they should have done either one of two things.

They Should Have Held Their Ground

On the one hand, they should have affirmed that they accept "halachic conversion" as the only valid form of conversion to Judaism (as the Law Committee of the Rabbinical Assembly— *their* halachic decision-making body— ruled in 1982, adopting a responsum by this author); then they should have selected a case where such an halachically valid Conservative conversion has been rejected by the Israeli Orthodox rabbinate (the only rabbinate recognized in the state of Israel) and sued them in the Israel Supreme Court, forcing them to *show cause* for their rejection. If the case were carefully selected (involving a *Bet Din* of unquestionably observant and learned Conservative rabbis), then it could have been easily shown that the Orthodox rejection of the particular conversion at issue was capricious and partisan, and indefensible on *objective* halachic grounds.

On the other hand, they could have argued on historical grounds (as heirs of the "Historical School" and as a movement led by an historian) that a political definition of a Jew has at times been broader than a strictly halachic one. Especially during periods of Jewish sovereignty, there have been persons who were part of the Jewish polity, who, on strictly halachic grounds, had not been fully integrated into the Jewish people and had been excluded from Jewish marriage and other cultic privileges (see, e.g., Ex. 12:38; Num. 11:4; *Tanhuma:* Ki Tissa, 21; M. *Kidd.* 4.1; also, Philo, *De Vita Mosis*, 1.27; *Sifra:* Emor, ed. Weiss, 104c; *Sifre:* Bamidbar, no. 78). Even among halachically committed Jews there have been problems in terms of marriage one with another (see B. *Yeb.* 14a, 45a). Thus, there is historical precedent for the acceptance of Zionism by all segments of the Jewish people (with the exception of the extreme Orthodox right and the extreme Reform left), based as it is on a universal Jewish consensus about a political definition of "Jewishness," a definition which is broader than a strictly halachic one. This consensus indicates that at the present time politics is a more unifying factor for Jews than *halacha*. However, politics need not obliterate *halacha*. The two can and do coexist together, albeit with great tension. Indeed, this tension between conflicting Jewish identities was recognized by the ancient rabbis and is supposed to last until the coming of the Messiah (see M. *Eduy.*, end). Thus Conservative Judaism should have declared its clear rejection on the non-halachic Reform position on conversion, and *independently* affirmed the different political reality of the Jewish people today (see B. *Kidd.* 66a; P. *Hor.* 47c).

These are the lines of independent argument the leaders of Conservative Judaism could have taken (perhaps there are others too), but the fact is they did not. As such, they publicly showed the superfluousness of their movement. It apparently has no cogent ideology of its own. Conservative Jews have become Reform Jews, *de facto* if not yet *de jure*. Whether or not the Conservative rabbinate and laity will simply fall into line will soon become evident in the days ahead, which by every present indication will see the further demarcation of party lines in contemporary Jewry. In this furthering process of demarcation it is the ambivalent and hypocritical who will be the first to fall by the wayside. ●

Paradox jews
Joanne Greenberg

I belong to a small congregation in Evergreen, Colorado, a foothills suburb near Denver. We are called Beth Evergreen, and when the pious complain of the name, I tell them that it represents us far better than Beth Shalom would. We have more paradox than peace. We have about twenty regular families.

I am one-third of Beth Evergreen's *Bar Mitzveh* preparation staff. Of the parents I see, more than half are married to people who were born into another faith. A sizable proportion of these are unconverted, although I don't know any who actively practice another faith. There may be some who do. Beth Evergreen's services are conducted in the Methodist Church, a *mitzveh* for both parties; their people have been splendid to us.

My sister is married to an unconverted Irish Catholic man and has raised his Protestant children by a former wife along with her Jewish ones by a

233

former husband. My brother-in-law is married to an unconverted Polish Catholic. My prospective daughter-in-law, *alle miles,* as they say, is not Jewish. The pious may rage or whimper; this is the way things are. I am a born Jew married to a born Jew. I am not Orthodox; I am Paradox.

Who We Are, Where We Are

None of us, not one of us in Beth Evergreen, takes his Judaism for granted. No single move is made automatically by any of us, because everything had to be learned from scratch, re-started, made new. We taught ourselves to read Hebrew; we picked things up from this and that source. The people who wanted the congregation as a society club have moved on.

Many of us had run headlong from city congregations that were the mills of the fifties and sixties. They were huge anonymous plaque-oppressive mausoleums where we never heard what went on on the *bimeh* and the female congregation was a furrier's dream. We are more observant than they were; I am more observant than my parents or grandparents were. I had to be; I was the only resource my kids had. My husband, a born Jew, had only negative experiences. He was not a *bar mitzveh,* but now he observes the *Shabbos,* has a *Seder* each year, and made the congregation's ark. His sons were *bar mitzveh.*

The unconverted parents in our congregation are something of a new breed. Maybe they are so accepting because it is no longer shameful to marry a Jew. I often see them at services and I find no difference in their zeal for their children's Jewish education from the born Jewish parents. As we learn more and more Hebrew, as we practice more and more ritual, clothing ourselves and our homes ever more fittingly for worship, I thought we would lose those parents. I was wrong. In two cases, the *non*-Jewish parents, divorced from their Jewish spouses and re-married to Gentiles, continue to bring their children to Hebrew class and *bar mitzveh* preparation. My Orthodox friend says that this is the kind of silver plating that wears thin at the first using. As a Paradox Jew, I know that the Jewish partner would have practiced no Judaism at all if not for the urging of the unconverted one.

True Lovers of Torah do not Slander

We born Jews have a lot to answer for. I asked my sister-in-law and my brother-in-law if they had ever experienced anti-Semitic talk or behavior. My sister-in-law, who is now Mary Greenberg, said that indeed she had. My brother-in-law, Tom Williams, said he had always been around people well-used to the words that made us cringe. Both of them said that while anti-Semitic talk now bothers them deeply, they are far more deeply hurt by the virulence of anti-Gentile talk from Jews. "When they hear the name Greenberg," Mary said, "they feel comfortable about saying things more demeaning and horrible than anything I ever heard *my* people say." Allowing for the surprise she feels and allowing also for the strong identification Mary has to her Polish Catholic past and family, there is still an unexamined fault in our community which should supply several more items in our Yom Kippur *al chet.* Although there is the item on slander, I think it's not specific enough. Half of my Paradox Jewish co-religionists were not non-Jews. They have beloved *mishpucha* who are being vilified by us.

We should remember the shining legacy of Raoul Wallenberg, Andre Trocme, Sugihara, Hans Schindler, and all the many others who stepped into the Holocaust for our sakes, and stop the slander.

We had lost one-third of our own by 1945. Since then, converts have been made to Judaism that we never expected to see. Most of these are Paradox, not Orthodox, Jews, but I feel their presence beside me as I stand for the *amidah* and their whisper comes to me in the smoke of my loss. "We can't be your fathers and mothers, but we have come to stand here with you, Jews also. Until Jews make themselves perfect, Judaism will have to do with us together. Please close your mouths: the family you slander may be mine." □

Some jews among us—akarah

Sherry H. Blumberg

I sit in the synagogue. The time that I have dreaded is about to arrive. I am prepared, I have done all the crying beforehand. There can be few tears left. This is the third year—surely by now I can hear the words and sit still without tears. Now—"*P'ru ur'vu umilu et haaretz.*" God's command to be fruitful and multiply has been given again to our people.

I am an *akarah*—a barren woman. After three years of the latest modern tests and drugs, of artificial inseminations (using my husband's sperm), of long hours in doctors' offices, of humiliating tests and frustrated hopes, and of moments of despair, I am still a barren woman. My husband is healthy; the problem is mine. We have used much of our savings, all of our patience. We have a serious operation to go that gives us a slight chance but may cause a serious risk to my health. I no longer believe in miracles for me (even though modern medicine has worked wonders). I don't see myself as a Sarah or a Hannah who can be granted conception. I would surely offer whatever I could so that my husband could use his healthy sperm to create a child but I've less and less hope that I will be able to conceive or carry that child.

So I sit in the sanctuary as I hear the words of God's command and I feel my emptiness. As my menstrual period comes each month I mourn what could have been. There are no rites nor ceremonies for that feeling time. Only the words *Baruch Dayan Emet* (Blessed be the Judge of Truth—the traditional blessing for evil tidings).

Soon my husband and I will give up the infertility doctors and begin the next frustrating process of adoption. There are few babies, hardly any Jewish babies, and we are too old to go through the "normal channels." We will join the many others who look for children with lawyers, doctors, rabbis and friends. We may have to go to another country. We will spend what we need to spend. We will love any child that comes into our home as our own. I hope that the time will be soon.

What do our Sacred Texts say to Me?

The hardest thing for me is confronting the tradition. There is a stigma about the *akarah*—barrenness is seen as a punishment. It sounds to me that the Barren Woman is one that has sinned or with whom God is displeased. My traditional mind asks, "what did I do?" If my reading of the *p'shat* is correct, then I am being punished. I become angry at God; I scream, cry and find little solace in prayer. I find that there are many times when I cannot call God a "*dayan emet.*" People who do not want children and who abuse children have them so easily; my husband and I who would love and cherish a child, cannot.

And my husband—why is he being punished with me? He could, by Jewish law, seek a divorce. Although in the Mishna (Yebamoth 6:6) it says that it is the man who is commanded to reproduce and not the woman, he was furious with me when I suggested that he seek another wife. Neither of us really wants that solution. We love each other and have a good marriage. So why, I ask, is he being punished?

My rational mind says that my feelings are foolish, based on irrational ideas; the traditional materials and rabbis could not have been so unfeeling. But my feelings are my feelings. I feel the pain of emptiness, the despair of wanting to carry out the *mitzvah* and not being able.

If these feelings are not enough, there are those who say that any couple who does not have at least three children is guilty of adding to the decline of the Jewish population (ergo responsible for the demise of the Jews). When I hear that statement, I freeze. I respond with anger, what I feel is pain. Again, intellectually I know that it is not so, but I feel the numbness in my heart.

When the Saving Act won't Occur

There have been articles like this before, usually written by those who have had a positive result after their long frustration. I am joyful and jealous when I read those articles. For me there may be no positive result. I, and others like me, will have to confront our barrenness—even if we adopt children. Each time the story of Sarah (Gen. 11:30), Rachel (Gen. 29:31), Samson's mother (Judges 13:2) or Hannah (1 Samuel 1-2) is read, I must face my own feelings of being barren, having prayed with all my heart and soul and might. In Isaiah (64:1) the charge is to "Sing O Barren One, That you did not bear, Rejoice and cry aloud... for more are the children of the desolate than the children of the married wife." It is very difficult to take any comfort from these words even if they are appropriate for this time when there are so many problems for our children. It is no easier to read the book of Job (24:21) and discover that the Barren One is devoured by those who rebel against God and the light. I cry out in sorrow and in anger—I have not rebelled.

The hardest moments come, however, as I read in Deuteronomy 7:12-15: *And it shall come to pass, because ye hearken to these ordinances, and keep, and do them, that the Lord thy God shall keep with thee the covenant and the mercy which He swore to thy fathers...there shall not be male or female barren among you.*

Does this mean that through me God will not fulfill the covenant? How does this affect my belief in a loving and caring God? How can I try so hard to keep my part of the covenant when I cannot share in that promise? Why can't I become like the "barren woman to dwell in her house as a joyful mother of children (Ps. 113:9)"?

Faithfulness without Answers

There are no rational answers to these questions, they need none. My faith and belief in the God of Israel will remain strong despite my barrenness. There are too many other miracles of living. I have found ways to serve the Jewish community and insure the perpetuation of Jewish life even if I will always be childless. Yet...

So why write this article? I have tried to alert Jewish care givers, rabbis and communal workers to be sensitive to the things they say to women and men about the requirement to *bear* children (change your words to *raise* children). I have tried to sensitize the reader to this growing problem in the Jewish community. I encourage you to hear honestly the pain and frustration of those involved in the process of infertility testing—the pain is emotional and very often financial (insurance often doesn't cover experimental procedures). Finally, I have tried to help the reader to understand that those congregants or Jews who are experiencing infertility problems may face a crisis of faith when they try to fit into the Jewish community—I still cry when the Biblical portions are read.

In our tradition we praise God for both the joyous times and the painful ones. I, too, must learn to say *Baruch dayan emet* over and over again as these painful moments occur. If my sharing of this part of my life may help one person who feels the same or help give the reader the insight to help another then I can say the blessing with some thankfulness as well as pain. □

Some jews among us—baalat teshuvah

Jinny Roth

There are some benefits to growing up in an almost non-observant home. No Sunday school early Sunday morning, no Hebrew teachers to complain about, and no religious structure to rebel against. I grew up in a home of far too few boundaries. The only thing which allows me to be grateful for this overabundance of freedoms is my passion for Judaism today!

Social action was a vital part of my upbringing. I followed in my father's footsteps marching the line for liberal causes. My political career began at the age of ten handing out anti-Vietnam War leaflets in my community. My dedication was confirmed by the age of twelve when I was tear-gassed in DuPont Square during the 1969 Vietnam morato-

rium March on Washington. Since that time I have been continually involved with many issues. My deepest commitment was to the anti-nuclear movement. I devoted enormous amounts of time to the very active Crabshell Alliance in Seattle. We effectively kept before the public the threat posed by nuclear power and nuclear armament with demonstrations, letter writing campaigns, news releases and acts of civil disobedience.

As a child I was taught to have a questioning mind, and especially not to accept prevalent notions easily. We talked about God in my house. My Dad's gods were the gods of Greek mythology. He could accept the idea of human-like gods, who were above all else, fallible. My grandmother's god was with us; "See you next Sunday, God willing." The voice of Negro spirituals was a part of the home I grew up in. A black woman from North Carolina worked for my parents, and she believed in God. My aunt and uncle who were active members of B'nai B'rith and kept a kosher home were simply crazy. Temple, for my parents, was a place to be avoided after *Bar Mitzvah* lessons, which were unavoidable. My family went to synagogue once or twice a year on the High Holy Days, to be with my grandparents. My parents did their best, which meant being honest about what they did not believe, and choosing to allow us to make our own decisions about religion when we grew up.

The Long Road leads Back to...

I lived, worked and traveled in many different places for some nine years, and returned at the age of 25 to my home and family in New York. When *Rosh Hashana* and *Yom Kippur* came around during my first year back I rejoined the family tradition of attending synagogue services for the holidays. It was the first time I had been in temple for over ten years. During those services I read in the new Union Prayerbook (*Gates of Repentance*) "Cherish your doubts, for doubt is the handmaiden of truth...A belief which may not be questioned binds us to error, for there is incompleteness and imperfection in every belief...let us not fear doubt, but let us rejoice in its help: It is to the wise as a staff to the blind." A religion which would not run from my doubts, one which would welcome my questions, was one I wanted to explore: and it was my own!

After attending those High Holy Day services with my family I began to go to temple on Friday nights, and to light *Shabbos* candles. I wanted to learn. I was exploring with my mind and feeling

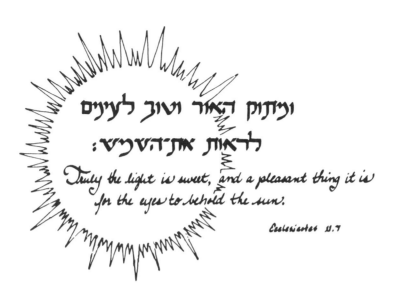

וּמָתוֹק הָאוֹר וְטוֹב לַעֵינַיִם
לִרְאוֹת אֶת־הַשָּׁמֶשׁ׃

*Truly the light is sweet, and a pleasant thing it is
for the eyes to behold the sun.*

Ecclesiastes 11.7

with my heart. I realized it was not important for
me to have all the answers, and to understand exactly why I was "commanded" to light the candles. Rather, I allowed myself the patience to see
if I would experience why the custom had survived
for thousands of years. My patience was worthwhile because I did begin to experience *Shabbos*.

At first the candles were fun and beautiful. Slowly
they grew into their symbolism of joy and peace. I
cherished the peace which settled in my home each
Friday as I lit the candles. They created an atmosphere, a glow in my home which filled me
with warmth. I would read from my prayerbook
and take a few minutes to reflect on the week
which had passed, and to think about the one
which was beginning. *Shabbos* became a special
time in my life, each one, each week.

For me temple became a place to feel at home, to
learn, and to talk to people who were like the relatives I remembered from my childhood. Then I
discovered the most wonderful thing: the basis for
Reform Judaism is education! If I wanted to be a
Reform Jew I was going to have to learn about
Judaism, and make important decisions and
choices. The prospect was, and is, awesome. I
have only traveled a few inches along my journey,
but I have accepted it as my task. It is only on
knowledge that I can build my own Jewish life.

JEANETTE KUVIN OREN *is a calligrapher,
illuminator, and papercutter of Judaic Art
in New Haven, Ct.*

The Revelations of Jewish Study

It did not take long before I began reading about
the Holocaust. I thought that if there was any place
in our history where I might find the secret of belief it would be in accounts from the Holocaust. I
was right and I was wrong. There were those who
disavowed being Jewish as a thing worse than
death, as the Holocaust was for so many people.
And there were those who went to the gas cham-
bers singing the *Sh'ma*. Reading about the Holocaust, and speaking about it with people who lived
through it answered no questions for me. It
presented new ones. I felt what I thought was an
unnatural connection to the experience of the Holocaust. It was crucial for me to have a personal and
victorious response—which was my own Jewishness. I believe what I felt, for the first time, was
the collective spirit of a people. A spirit which
lives in a people, and through a people. This spirit
led me to my first feeling of the presence of God.

I discovered the same feeling in temple. I distinctly
remember the first time I closed my eyes and allowed myself to be absorbed into the Hebrew singing. I felt that the sound I heard at that moment
was the same sound which was heard in Solomon's
Temple. And the same sound heard in synagogues
around the world. That voice connected me to my
past in such a deeply emotional way that it was
startling. Being in synagogue, and sharing prayer,
was the precious time during which I suspend all
other activity and feel the presence of God. It was
during prayer that I allowed myself a few sacred

moments to appreciate being alive. A few sacred moments to appreciate the people and the power to whom I owe my life.

The pain, the evil of the world did not go away. But a new dimension was added. If those of us who are clothed, healthy and secure are to cotinue to assist those who are not, we need a wellspring of nourishment. In the words of Mordecai Kaplan: ''The God idea is not the reasoned allocation of chaos, cruelty, pain and death in some neat logical scheme. It is the passionate refusal of every atom in the human being to be terrified by these ogres. The God idea is not an idea, but the reaction of the entire organism to life.'' I became a humbled human being; seeking the wisdom of those who came before me, looking for truth and for strength in the same places my ancestors did.

Just as a child grows best from security, so I looked to my own history as the secure place from which to grow. The Torah is, after all, my birthright, and I very consciously decided that it would be wise to study its teachings. Choosing to study is to carry Torah through my life as it has been carried through centuries of lives. Rooted by those who are responsible for my being, I am able to go forward.

There are still more questions than answers, thank God! But I have parents who gave me a questioning mind, and I have rabbis who insist that I search for answers. As I proceed, I have *Shabbos* candles to light my way. □

Some jews among us—shikulah

Ruth Segal Bernards

In the Dec. 12th issue of *Sh'ma,* (17/323) there were a number of meaningful and moving articles of Jews who have experienced and coped with anguish and pain. Having experienced a different kind of hurt, I immediately reacted with ''but they left out the *Shikulah* (or the *Shakul*)—the parent who has lost a child.'' It presents still another kind of coping. It will soon be Joel's 12th Yahrzeit, which represents to us 12 years of coping and remembering. We feel a certain sense of pride in having coped and remembered. ''If you didn't know it, you wouldn't know it.'' Because to us coping meant reaffirming life.

Joel was a young man of 22, a senior at Brooklyn College, when he passed away due to a cerebral hemorrhage. In his brief span of life, he himself had to do a good amount of wrestling with physi-

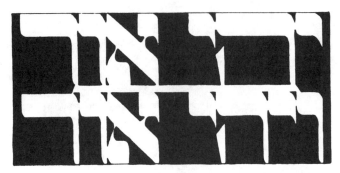

'Let there be light.' And there was light.
Genesis 1.3

cal difficulties. He had a congenital kidney disease, and went through several bouts of surgery, including a transplant. He came through all of the traumas (the congenital illness presented numerous other difficulties, too numerous to mention) with a smile and determination. He was known for his *chedvat chaim* (joy of life). There was nothing too difficult for him and nothing in which he would not participate with joy and gusto, including trips to Israel, sports, studies and hobbies—particularly amateur radio.

Things seemed to be going very well after the transplant, and he had firm plans and hopes ahead of him. With a sure foot, he planned his graduate studies and his future career. It is still a moot question to the doctors as to whether his final death blow was related to his illness or not. But what difference does it make!

Facing the Loss, then Facing Life

I recall my initial words to our daughter, then a sophomore in college, after the hospital called to tell us of Joel's death. In an embrace of father, mother and daughter, I reassured her that life, and the family, would go on.

I read in *Sh'ma* of Nechama Liss Levinson's experience with sitting *Shiva* and had a sense of hearing myself speak. What remarkable *mitzvot*— *Shiva* and *nichum avelim* (comforting mourners). What a reassuring feeling it is to be surrounded with family and friends at this time of total grief. And yes, the best visitors are those who ''stayed on the topic'' as Levinson put it. They were the

JEANETTE KUVIN OREN *is a calligrapher, illuminator, and papercutter of Judaic Art in New Haven, Ct.*

true comforters. Is it not odd that it is the mourner who wishes to speak of his/her loss, of the deceased and of one's feelings, and it is the visitor who mistakenly thinks it is best to distract and speak of everything but the real subject at hand? I will never forget the friend who made a point of coming in the morning, when others might not be around, so that we could speak intimately. She shared with me her experiences with having lost a sister. It was so good to dwell on the real things of that time, about pain and loss, about life and death.

Nor will I forget the special effort made by one couple. They called to say they would be over on Tuesday night. We were a bit puzzled by the necessity of the phone call, since they had already paid more than one *Shiva* visit. It was only when the house suddenly emptied at 7 p.m. did we realize that they did not want us to be alone. It was New Year's Eve.

The second stage of coping was getting back to work. How often have I thought of a song so popular with the early *Chalutzim*—"*HaAvodah Hi Chayenu, Mikol Tzarah, Toshiyenu*"—(Work is our life, it will rescue us from all troubles). The physical pain of heart-ache which I experienced during my drive to school, gradually began to vanish as I faced a classroom of children. Involvement with life issues helped ease the pain of death. It was interesting too, again confirming Levinson's statement of "the discomfort that so many people feel in paying a *shiva* call," that a few of my colleagues couldn't face me, didn't know what to say. It was I, with a sense of determination that life must go on, and also wanting to face the reality of what had happened, who had to break the ice and call them over to speak to me in the faculty room.

The Other Life that Lives in Ours

Another aspect of coping is remembering. Not for a moment did we ever avoid mention of Joel's name. When we speak of experiences with young children, we never hesitate to tell of Joel's *chochmas* as a child. When the subject under discussion may turn to adolescent children, or young adults making their way, we include Joel, just as we do his sister, in our frame of reference.

Yes, of course, we have memorialized Joel with the usual plaques in our synagogue, both here and in Israel, and Prayer Books and *chumashim* given in his memory, but our true monuments to his memory lie elsewhere. They lie in reaffirming and enjoying life to the fullest, much as he did. And by talking about him in a very natural way, thus keep-

ing our memory of him alive. Our formal means of doing this is to read, each *Seder* night the following *midrash on a midrash:*

"It was *Seder* night. We had just completed reading the *Midrash* of the Four Children, when Joel Abba, the son of Shnair Zalman and Ruth, said: '*The four kinds of children do not necessarily mean four different people. They can readily refer to one person at different stages of his/her life. The* She'ayno yoday'a lishol, *the child who does not yet know how to ask, is the infant, as yet unable to articulate. The tam, the simple child, refers to the young, innocent school child who asks simple questions. The Rasha, the wicked child, could be the rebellious teenager, only too eager to remove himself from the established group. The chacham, the wise child, alludes to the young adult who has become a mature personality.*'"

This was Joel's last *Seder* (in 1974). He was taken from us the following December, just as he was taking sure and certain strides on the road to becoming a *chachem.*

He left us a heritage of many warm and wonderful memories, among which is his *midrash* on a *midrash*. We have incorporated it into our *Haggadah* to read each year on *Seder* night.□

Some jews among us—avelah
Nechama Liss-Levinson

Last March, a week before the Passover seder, my father died suddenly from a heart attack. Four months later, after a two year struggle with cancer, my mother died. In less than half a year, the foundations of my world had collapsed and I felt encompassed by the *tohu* and *vohu* of the primeval creation.

During that time period, I also became experienced at sitting *shiva*. As I sat those two long weeks, cradled in the bosom of my remaining family, I often marvelled at the wisdom of G-d's ways as manifested in Jewish law; there were moments of comfort, and even laughter during the seemingly endless grief. I felt moved by the outpouring of family and friends, each giving of himself or herself as they paid a *shiva* visit. And I was aware of a healing sense of consolation I felt after talking with a particular few.

In reviewing those weeks in my mind, I found I was able to elucidate patterns of what was helpful, and what was not, and felt a desire to share my thoughts with others. As I turned the memories of those visits over and over again, what emerged was the discomfort that so many people feel in paying a *shiva* call, in this near encounter with death, in this clear encounter with pain and suffering. I hope that these musings will offer some assistance to those about to embark on such a visit.

Fulfilling the Mitzvah Fully

The best visitors were those who stayed on the topic, that is, the topic of my parents who had died. The greatest gifts I received were the stories which friends and relatives told of my mother and father, lost fragments which were now my eternal treasures. They spoke about incidents, like the tim my father first met another couple forty years ago my dad with his wild hair, bare-footed, and comfortable presence that cemented the relationship. They recalled images, gestures, smiles and fleeting moments, awakened by their articulation. The visitors who brought comfort often shared a piece of who my parents were with them.

Of course, there were others who came, friends of mine, who didn't know my parents, who didn't have memories to share. Those friends helped by allowing me to share my own stories of my parents, of the dresses we purchased for my daughters months before *Rosh Hashana* (even though my mother sensed that she would not live to see them worn), of my memories of my childhood, now flooding my thoughts. They were willing to look at all the photographs I wanted to show them—of my parents at our wedding, of my parents as children, of my parents with the grandchildren, in endless numbers.

Those who offered comfort didn't probe for each detail of their physical death, but were willing to listen if I chose to describe some of those details. People who offered comfort did not offer platitudes. They did not remind me how lucky I was, or compare my situation to theirs or to someone else who had lost their parents at an even earlier age. They did not tell me that this was all part of G-d's eternal plan, and did not tell me to be strong (euphemism for stop crying) for my children's sake.

Of whose Pain are you Thinking?

Good *shiva* visitors were willing to be quiet, were willing to hold my hand, were willing to sit with their own discomfort with my pain. A special few were able to share with me their own painful sense of grieving over the death of a loved one.

Those who were not helpful talked about the weather, what class their children (or my children) had just gotten into, what we had done for the summer, whether or not the children had liked camp, exactly what medications my mother/father had taken (and their side effects), politics, neighborhood gossip, worse tragedies which had happened to other people, and what kind of lunchboxes to buy the kids for school.

Of particular interest was the peculiar attitude some people took towards my children (then aged 4 and 7) who had, along with their cousins, attended the funeral service, and were very present at the *shiva*. Almost no one talked to them about their loss, or about the wonderful memories they had of Bubbles and JoJo—the walks, the gum, the ice cream, the games of checkers, the knitting lessons. . . . Instead, conversations centered around school and summer vacation, as though not talking about it would make the loss go away. Those people who offered to take the children for a few hours of fresh air and friendship offered respite to the adult mourners.

The Pains, the Joy, the Comfort, the Loss

I was exhausted during *shiva*. At times I felt drowned by the numbers of people, and the sheer effort of talking. Good *shiva* visitors need to know when to go home, to realize when the mourners are tired and the hour is late. The person who occupies the chair next to the mourner needs to know that others would also like to occupy it, and needs to move after sharing some time with the mourner.

A few final words on the final few words said when leaving the house of *shiva*. The words, "May you know no more sorrow," rang hollow after my father's death; at the time, my mother was terminally ill. But even after my mother's death, it seemed to me that only my own demise could mean that I would know no more sorrow. After all, isn't that, too, an integral part of one's living? A hug, a reassuring embrace, some tears mutually shed in silence all were helpful. The words of our sages also offered comfort, "May you be comforted amongst the mourners of Zion and Jerusalem." Those words, often recited in Hebrew, caused me to feel part of an eternal, ongoing process of birth and death.

As I write these words, I feel overcome with emotions. I miss my parents. I wish they could proudly read what I have written. . . . And I also feel something which I did not believe at the time of *shiva*, words I did not want to even hear spoken at that point, that is, that the passage of time lessens the intensity, although the chasm can never be filled. □

Some jews among us—yetomah

Rachel Goldstone

There are no models of mourning. People don't know how to mourn and they don't know how to relate to someone who is mourning. It's hard to know what is normal for mourning. When my parents died, within two years of each other, I was 21. As the oldest of five children, I was not alone in dealing with my parents' deaths but I was able to observe the differences and similarities in the way we each responded to the situation. We each experienced it in somewhat different ways because of our age, personality and position in the family. We also shared many common reactions.

One common reaction that each of us went through was anger. We were angry kids with no one to blame. As a Jewish family in a situation of complete chaos, we became more religious. And because we needed religion, God became an easy target for our anger. I had the experience of becoming more religious and more conflicted about religion than ever before in my life.

Despite the tumult of feelings that religion stirred in me, the Jewish traditions of mourning were very helpful. They gave us a structure for mourning and told us how to move through the time stagnant around us. One of the most important traditions is *shiva,* the week of mourning. I was not always nice or in the mood to talk, but I appreciated every person who came through our door. It was not important what people said. Everyone felt awkward and horrible. It was important that the community came to be with us—to mourn for themselves or just to show their support. Our home was a cocoon of safety for that week. People provided food and came to visit, giving us a buffer of time before we had to go back into the world.

And then the Empty Time Stretches Out

Judaism sets aside the whole year for mourning because mourning does not happen quickly. It comes out slowly in little pieces over the first years after the death. I think it is common that people expect you to recover rapidly and are surprised, since you seem to be functioning normally, that many of the issues lurk close to the surface and emerge at stressful times. For me, the mourning after each parent's death was greatly affected by their sickness before their death.

As long as one spends in mourning, I don't know that it is ever over completely. Death leaves a hole that is never filled. Partly I don't want to fill it be-

cause, for me, the sadness is a way of feeling a connection with my parents. I feel closer to them when I am crying because I am remembering them and what I love about them.

In mourning, I found that there were certain things I had to do for myself; there were certain things that we as a family had to do for ourselves. The Jewish community could not help. On the other hand, the Jewish community provided a wealth of support in many practical issues. The rabbi mobilized the community to help with car-pooling my brothers and sisters, to cook meals, to help me with financial advice. The deaths of my parents brought adulthood crashing in and no matter how responsible I had been for myself I did not realize all that my parents had done for me. I was overwhelmed by the responsibility I now had for myself and my family. I felt needy and helpless. Because of this very neediness, it was difficult to ask for help.

The Solace: Those who Insisted on Caring

It was hard to ask for help that I knew I couldn't repay. It was also hard to be grateful. The gratitude I owed people was like a debt that kept growing. I felt ungrateful, but how could I feel grateful in the face of my parents' death? Chicken soup was nice, but it didn't make up for the loss.

I write about this now with the distance of time. When I look back I feel very appreciative of all the support our rabbi and community gave us. I am moved by the families who opened their homes to us and to those who reached out who didn't even know us. It must have been difficult to help us given our anger, our inability to ask for help and our ingratitude in accepting it. I am thankful to everyone who gave in spite of these circumstances.

The involvement of the Jewish community with our family was the double-edged sword that always comes with involvement. When is it too much and when too little? From my experience, I think that the risk of involvement is worth it. My life has been enriched by the people who have taken the risks of caring for and becoming involved with my family. It is Jewish tradition to be with the mourner. It is a good tradition. □

How one jew spends christmas

Andrew M. Sacks

Some time in late October my telephone rang. On the line was Frank Farrell of Trevor's campaign.

Who is Frank, and what is Trevor's campaign? Two years ago an astonished 11 year old boy in an affluent Philadelphia suburb ran to ask his father if people really lived on steam vents in the cold of winter as he had just seen in a television report. His father acknowledged that there were such people. The son insisted they go into center city, Philadelphia with blankets and hot coffee. The father's name was Frank, the son, Trevor, and thus was born Trevor's campaign. Trevor went out each and every night for the next year and a half. (He collected food, blankets, clothes and whatever else was needed.) Together with his family he opened Trevor's Place—a shelter for thirty homeless people.

Trevor's school work suffered. The family was under much stress. Still the effort continued. There were hundreds of people on the street who depended on the loving care Trevor extended to them. But a student must get to his school work. A family must be able to have time to itself. So Trevor and Frank have enlisted volunteers to cook and to serve the food, every day of the week, every day of the year. Even on Christmas.

Frank wanted his family together for Christmas. Volunteers were entitled to have this, their holy day, off. So Frank called me to ask if I would take over on Christmas day. A Jew must feed and clothe the non-Jew who is in need just as he feeds and clothes the Jew in need. This is an obligation spelled out in the Talmud (Gitin) and codified in Jewish law. The reason for helping the non-Jew is also spelled out. The reason is not one of ethics or of a moral responsibility. It is, rather, quite practical, "*mipnei darchei shalom*"—in order to create peace between the community of Jews and non-Jews.

Mipnei darchei shalom I said "yes." But there were other reasons. How many times had I walked by the "street people" and the "bag ladies" indifferent to their plight? Why was it that it was always the Christians (e.g. Salvation Army, the various Catholic shelters) who were out providing one to one care? This gnawed at me. So for the second year in a row I spent December 25 out on the streets of Philadelphia feeding and clothing the non-Jews together with the Jews. Poverty knows no bounds, for on the streets we did find hungry Jews seeking a hot meal.

Friends began to pitch in at once. Eli slipped letters under the doors of his neighbors asking for contributions. Parents and students from Akiba Hebrew Academy offered help. Food began to accumulate. By December 25, with minimal effort we had enough food for 300 people. There were casseroles, soup, fruit and nuts, juice and much more. We had socks, scarves, hats and coats. We had volunteers we turned away, so great was the response.

Seven of us went out. One of the seven was Michael, only 15 years of age. All of us felt the love that Trevor had given us the opportunity to experience. Thus, in a very different way, and for ever so different reasons, December 25 has become for me a day filled with *Kedusha*—a day on which one rabbi, a rabbinical student, a business person, three physical therapists and a high school student participated in the ongoing creation of the world. □

LYNNE AVADENKA, *of Oak Park, Mich., is the artist for this drawing.*

MENACHEM KELLNER *teaches Jewish Studies at William and Mary in Williamsburg, Va.*

LEON GERSTEN *is a staff psychologist at the Maimonides Community Mental Health Center and a clinical supervisor at the Interborough Developmental Consulation Center, both in Brooklyn.*

ADINA MISHKOFF *is a former* Sh'ma *fellow and a professional librarian in industry.*

JOEL SOFFIN *is completing his fourth year as rabbinical student at HUC-JIR and is serving as student rabbi at Temple Emanu-El in Westfield, N.J.*

JULIA HIRSCH *teaches English at Brooklyn College.*

Wiliam Wallen is working on the great American novel and practices law in Jersey City, N.J.

BARRY MARKS *is the rabbi of Congregation Temple Israel, Springfield, Illinois.*

DAN DORFMAN *is the Hillel director at Calfornia State University at Northridge.*

MELANIE B. SHIMOFF, *one of our fellows this year, heads the Department of Synagogue Services and Communal Relations of the Orthodox Union in N.Y.C.*

MARK HURVITZ *studies at U.C.L.A. and edits the Jewish student magazine, DAVKA.*

DAVID B. GURALNIK *is the Editor-in-Chief of* Webster's New World Dictionaries.

LEO TREPP *teaches philosophy and humanities at Napa College in Napa Valley, California.*

PAT DELANEY *works as an administrative social work supervisor.*

JOANNE GREENBERG *writes fiction near Denver, Co.*

SHERRY H. BLUMBERG *teaches education at HUC-JIR, New York. Since writing this article she and her husband David have adopted a son.*

JINNY ROTH *is now a first year rabbinical student at the HUC-JIR, Jerusalem.*

RUTH SEGAL BERNARDS *teaches Jewish Studies at the Educational Center for Retired Adults/14th. St. YMHA in N.Y.*

NECHAMA LISS-LEVINSON *is a psychologist, practicing in Great Neck, N.Y.*

RACHEL GOLDSTONE *is now studying medicine in Los Angeles.*

ANDREW M. SACKS *is rabbi of Congregation Beth Am, Penn Valley, Pa.*

12.
Purim Spiel

Sorry this line isn't on the level but it seemed to me for some time now (Sh'ma 1/11, April 2, 1971) that Commentary has been tilting in one direction.

Commentary

Volume Sixty-eight, Number Five, November 1979

A
Super—
That is a
commentary on a
in this case by
Eugene B. Borowitz

being his strictly personal comments on Julius Weinberg's, "The Trouble with Reform Judaism."

Though we never republish material we knew we'd never find anything funnier than this for Purim (see Sh'ma, 10/182, Nov. 30, 1979.) Fortunately logic came to our aid; considering how many Commentary ex-subscribers and non-readers there are in the inner Jewish community this is as good as publishing it for them for the first time. Being compact, we dote on sticking to the point. Thus we produce only that part of the article where the author made an abrupt detour to get in some whacks at Sh'ma.

That's really unfair. Ever since Alicia Seeger took the galleys away from me our spelling has improved. Issue 4/68, Feb. 22, 1974 was the last one in which our masthead dared include that line which our creative verb, "We print typos which do not obscrue the meaning."

We are not naive. We don't think everyone will make it. What surprises the few of us who are getting close is that people keep arguing with us as they would with anyone else.

Even to liberal Jews, biting the hand is tref. Contributing 8 of our 18 (occasionally) Editors are not now Jewishly employed, but would be happy to have a subsidy if anyone knows a perceptive Jewish agency. Most of our articles come from lay people, unpaid by the community —and certainly

By Vorspan's and Brickner's own admission, not many in the Reform movement have been convinced by their views—except for that group of professional social-activists, rabbis, and laymen who began to gather in the 70's around a new publication, pretentiously named Sh'ma ("Hear," as in "Hear O Israel"), edited and published by Eugene B. Borowitz, a graduate of HUC-JIR and professor of education and theology in the College's New York school.

Sh'ma, printed in a "small-is-beautiful" format (replete with typographical errors intentionally left uncorrected —somewhat of an anomaly for a publication that purports to believe in the perfectibility of man) and keyed to the professionals and cognoscenti among laymen in the Jewish community, offers itself as a kind of ongoing ideological "rap-session." In its pages, the universalists put foward their comments on contemporary Jewish and world affairs, often in a tone of superiority toward the community that pays their salary but (in their view) lacks the intelligence, the foresight, or the moral stature to understand or listen to them, particularly when the advice they offer runs counter to the community's deepest instincts as to what is "good for the Jews." (A number of contributors to

*Or
"Listen," as in
"Can you stop spouting long enough to listen to someone with another Jewish point of view?"*

As Nezikin, the Mishnaic division on damages says (Purma MS), "at least they got your name right."

We got there first! I think I got the idea for our format one day in 1969 when I looked over at my heavy pile of unread Commentarys.

Readers, even our critics think you're special!

TYPO! We do not publish lists, though if Wallace and Walleshinsky want to write for us (at our prices) we'll consider it. Al tikri "universalists" ela "universe of Yids."

"A son a professor, a daughter a doctor, both married to Jews, making lots of

Sh'ma do not share the "New Politics" philosophy of its founder and editor and serve largely as foils for the magazine's basic ideological thrust. A typical issue of Sh'ma might contain excerpts from an Israeli "Black Panthers" Haggadah; an observation by an administrator of the American Civil Liberties Union that "the Jewish state, conceived as the *solution* to the Jewish problem, has become *the* Jewish problem"; interviews by a Reform rabbi and Hillel director with an Egyptian and Israeli in which he discovers the former to be a man of peace and the latter a warmonger; and assorted fusillades against the United Jewish Appeal, the way congregations function, sexism, and as one contributor summed it up, "the horrific vulgarities of Jewish life."

As for Borowitz himself, when he is not busy running a Yom Kippur write-in contest among Sh'ma subscribers for "the most overlooked sin of the American Jewish community," he is demonstrating his self-styled "devotion to the Jewish community, especially its ethics and its spirituality," by attacking the reactionary character of the United States ("the repressiveness lurking behind our society's facade of liberality"); the power-grabbing leadership of the Central Conference of American Rabbis and Hebrew Union College; and assorted other targets — students of the Talmud, Jewish social workers, and teachers — for being concerned with their jobs and livelihoods.

Borowitz's two specialties are moralistic condemnations of the Jewish leadership structure he is an integral part of, and denunciations of Israel that incorporate elements of Classical Reform with 70's New-Left chic. In 1973, a half-year before the Egyptian-Syrian attack on Israel on Yom Kippur, Borowitz used the columns of Sh'ma to chide American Jews for wanting America to be strong in the face of Russian support for the Arabs. After the war, Borowitz posed a number of questions to American Jewry: "Does the war demonstrate," he asked, while prayers were still being recited over the dead in Israel, "once and for all, Israel's priority in our lives; or does it now lead us to the recognition that there must be limits to what Israel can ask of us . . .?" "Taking note of the either/or form of the question, one pained subscriber wrote to Sh'ma: "Is this the time to debate whether we love our mothers less or our fathers more?"*

(Reprinted from Commentary, Nov. 1979 by permission; all rights reserved.)

*In late 1976, Borowitz reproduced in Sh'ma two lengthy diatribes he had delivered on behalf of "thoughtful Jews" to the Synagogue Council of America and to the Conference of Presidents of Major Jewish Organizations on the lack of "dissent" within the organized Jewish community in the United States and on what he considered to be Israel's expansionist foreign policy. As Ben Halpern of Brandeis noted, in a letter solicited by Borowitz: "I find it exceedingly odd that speeches you delivered to both the Synagogue Council and the President's Conference should be printed in evidence of the suppression of your freedom of speech by the local Jewish establishment." Halpern also noted that while the New York Times consistently failed to print his own views on their Op-Ed page, they gave Borowitz's addresses full coverage.

---

week when we're at the condominium in Florida." Personally, I'm ready for it.

See Seymour Siegel's plaintive wail on the next page. As for me, I keep wondering how great a compliment it is to be seen controlling democratic Sh'ma in the way its Editor controls Commentary.

Thanks, Julius. Every once in a while we all need to know we're appreciated.

What a great idea for this Yom Kippur, "the most overlooked merit of the Jewish community." I must admit, though I fancy myself a creative non-Orthodox type, I had never thought of introducing into our Atonement liturgy an Al Zechut. "For the merit which we have accumulated before Thee by . . ."

You mean I could have sent the speeches to Commentary or had one of those brave Jewish organizational magazines publish them and not cost poor Sh'ma the subscribers and contributions it lost?

That turns the knife. The Times paid no attention to my few moments-with-the-machers. In fact, only one of my Sh'ma articles has ever made the Times while Seymour Siegel's have been in twice, getting 6 3/4 column inches more than I — not that someone as ethical and spiritual as I am cares about such things.

---

solicitees. By the way, Sh'ma's deficit-reduction drive begins again April 1 — no fooling!

I knew the Post Office was slow delivering Sh'ma but it looks like they've only gotten to 1976 with . Weinberg's copies. The Panthers were in our second volume, 1972, the next two articles appeared 4 years later. And we haven't attacked the U.J.A. in years; we must be getting soft.

Don't blame me! I once tried writing an intellectual defense of Jewish caterers, going so far as to call them latter-day, low-level Levites — and then one of my Reform reviewers accused me of being a chicken-livered theologian.

My apologies, I didn't know we good Americans were supposed to be proud of things like the F.B.I. trying to goad Martin Luther King into committing suicide.

What happened to the U.A.H.C.? I am an equal-opportunity-critic — or was in 1971.

I categorically deny that my idea of tradition is that the Hebrew Union College goes back to the 1883 custom of beginning ordination banquets with a shrimp cocktail.

And the proof is: my very first article for Sh'ma, was "On Refusing to be Radicalized" (Trial issue No. 2, June 9, 1970).

Mazal tov! I finally have been criticized for coming on too weak. But Jews really hate it when you cite texts inaccurately and I had claimed "common welfare" was in the Constitution and "ethnocentrism" wasn't.

Will you hate me, knowing the truth? Do you appreciate the guilt I live with being a compulsive questioner? Can you believe I was so far gone, they expelled me from A.A. (Askers Anonymous)? Was it so wrong to suggest we might ease our pain by holding dialogues with some obsessive symposiasts? And do you imagine it calmed my Jewish interrogatory needs when our subscriber responded as he did? You think it's easy being a Jew?

Job — kvetch, kvetch, kvetch

Harold S. Kushner

Research into the Book of Job has been hampered by the tendency of scholars to ask the wrong question. They have worried about the ultimately unanswerable question, *"Why does Job suffer?"* instead of the issue which goes to the heart of the book, *"From what illness does Job suffer?"*

In all my studies, I have found only two attempts to deal with this problem, one by Julius Wellhausen in his 880-page tome *Was Ist Hiob's Krankheit Gewesen Worden?* (which I refused to consult on principle, because Wellhausen was an anti-Semite, the book was printed by non-union labor, and I never learned German) and a pamphlet published by the Department of Health, Education and Welfare in Washington entitled *Job-Related Illness* (which was totally irrelevant and showed no evidence of serious Biblical scholarship; no wonder the author published it anonymously.)

But a careful reading of Job yields several valuable clues to the nature of the ailment from which the hero suffers. Thus in 19:17, we read "My breath is offensive to my wife; I am loathsome to my children." Job's problem is bad breath and offensive body odor. In addition, he seems to complain of acne (7:5 – "My skin closes up and then breaks out again"), to which Zophar replies (11:14-15) "If iniquity be in your hand, put it away...Then you will lift up an unblemished face."

HAROLD S. KUSHNER *is rabbi of Temple Israel of Natick, Mass.*

Job Suffers From Modern Ailments

The book describes sympathetically the plight of the man whose dentures do not fit properly in 13:14, "I take...my teeth...in my hand," and warns of the dangers of obesity (15:20, 27) "The wicked man writhes in pain all his days...because he has covered his face with fat and gathered fat upon his loins."

A clear pattern is emerging for the judicious reader. The Book of Job is relevant to modern readers, not solely because Job suffers, but because, like us, he suffers from bad breath, underarm perspiration, acne, loose-fitting dentures and overweight. His problems are truly the problems of Everyman.

It has long been suspected that the Bible was originally presented not as literature to be read, but as drama to be acted out. Is it not reasonable to suspect that the Book of Job originally consisted of commercial messages presented during those dramatic offerings. (Is it entirely coincidence that, in the Hebrew Bible, Job is found right after the stand-up comedy of Proverbs and immediately before the romantic musical number Song of Songs?) Can we not envision a scene in which Job appears, cleaning up the mess in his house after the wind has knocked it over, and cheerfully telling the audience (17:9) "he that has clean hands waxes stronger"?

246

13.
Our Readers Write Us

. . . but others say . . .

A modern jewish dilemma: too much power

"Why be Jewish, today or any other?" asks Joan Koehler in the Movember 5 Sh'ma. Her answer struck a responsive chord in my mind. It *begins*, "Because I prefer the side of the powerless to that of the oppressor." Without discussing whether this is a good reason for being or becoming Jewish, it is undeniable that this is a part, an important part, of Judaism.

The preference for the side of the powerless to that of the oppressor shed some light on the ambivalent feelings of many sincere Jews towards Israel. Where does Israel fit in their moral scheme? As a protector of the oppressed (Jews), or as an oppressor (of Arabs); The leaders of Israel make it clear that Israel is and will continue to be the one country in the world with a Jewish majority. In Israel the Jews are not powerless, they are the people in power.

This fact, unique in modern history, is the opportunity and the dilemma of our time. Is the oppressor—oppressed syndrome inevitable in the majority-minority relationship. Is the dichotomy between the powerless and the opressor the only possible reality? To what extent can Jews in power avoid becoming oppressors?

The Jew who desire personal Aliyah and recognizes this dilemma, what is he to do? If he joins the Jewish majority in Israel, is he merely assuring the oppression of the minority? Must he remain in minority status in the diaspora? (I am talking of those Jews to whom both options are open.) What are his obligations, what his opportunities? Should he go to Israel and strive there to prevent the powerful from becoming oppressors? If he stays away because he believes the task is hopeless, is not his pessimism a self-fulfilling prophecy?

This leading manner in which these questions are posed reveals, perhaps, my own optimistic answers to them.

Lawrence J. Risman
Arlington, Mass.

Halakhah must be responsive to new norms

Rivka Teitz Blau accurately identifies the central problem of the relationship between Jewish women and the *halakhah* (*Sh'ma* 4/63) when she says, "The thrust of the *halakhah* is that the woman is a private modest person whose activities revolve around her family . . . The *halakhah*, being an ethical-legal system, deals with the norm but has room for the exception."

Regretably Mrs. Blau ignores this assessment. For what was once the exception is rapidly becoming the norm and the *halakhah* has not accomodated itself to this change. It is precisely because for an ever increasing percentage of women and for an ever increasing portion of a woman's life span, life revolves around centers other than home and family that even the Jewish woman who starts with a commitment to *halakhah* is in conflict today.

Lifsa Schachter
Bronx, New York

We Must Mix Ability And Yiddishkeit

On the issue of Jewishness and social work skills, I think that Marvin Najberg has missed the point. It is not a question of ability first and *Yiddishkeit* second; rather, the question is how to mix the two together with Jewish communal agencies. If there isn't a strong *Jewish* component to Jewish communal agencies, they have no reason for being and should not be seeking large sums of money from the Jewish community.

Najberg distorts the question when he describes a couple coming for marital counseling to a Jewish Family Service. He says that what they want is professional skill and not a discourse on Jewish views on marriage, otherwise he could send them to a rabbi "if what they are seeking is a Jewish solution." It seems to me that if the couple is simply looking for professional skill, they could go to any trained therapist, not necessarily a Jewish Family Service. If, however, they are looking for skill plus some Jewish understanding of marriage (without lengthy discourses), then perhaps a Jewish Family Service is the right place for them. But if they have to be referred to a rabbi for a Jewish solution, then it seems to me that the Jewish Family Service ought to go out of the marriage counseling business.

Najberg is overly concerned about cost-efficiency in providing social services. It is true that this is an important issue, but there is too much of a business mentality in community allocations, whereby getting the best value for the dollar is the top concern, and the Jewish quality and content of programs is of secondary concern. What previous authors in *Sh'ma* have been arguing is that both quality and cost ought to be given at least equal consideration.

Jewish communal agencies should not be the primary source of enhancing Jewish identity in the community. Synagogues and schools must do their part, and they are the primary sources of strengthening Jewish identity. But Jewish communal agencies should either see their role as at least partially enhancing Jewish identity, or they should remove the Jewish label from their social service agency title.

Ron Kronish
Worcester, Mass.

...but others say about noshrim...

I would like to take issue with your recent publication of Nora Levin's protest against "limiting Russian-Jewish immigration" (*Sh'ma* 12/228).

Ms. Levin mentions freedom of choice. Of course there should be freedom of choice for every Russian Jew. But once he, or she, has arrived in Vienna and been offered a few days of respite, only one choice is to be subsidized - namely Israel. Once a Russian Jew has left Russia he is no longer a refugee and it is entirely up to him whether he wants to live in Germany or Austria or go to Australia or the U.S.A. But if he is looking for Jewish fulfillment for himself and his family then his choice of Israel should be quite obvious and he can look forward to a lot of assistance. But if he wants to be "free", as many Russians declare when asked why they take no part in Jewish activities in the U.S.A., then that freedom of choice should be respected—without subsidies.

If the withdrawal of the title "refugees" will stop $15 million in contributions from the U.S. Government for the accommodation of Russian Jews in this country, then so be it. It is also about time that HIAS recognizes the situation for what it is, after some "friendly persuasion." If, as Ms. Levin indicates, the Russian Jews unwilling to go to Israel will find free rides from non-Jewish agencies for assistance in coming to the U.S.A., good for them. If their Jewishness is that shallow as to open them to missionary influence, let them again exercise their freedom of choice. They will be no loss to the Jewish people.

In brief, I hope HIAS sticks to its guns. Welcome to any Russian Jew who paid his ticket to the U.S.A., went to work here, and joined the Jewish community. He is doing no more than I did when I emigrated to the U.S.A., some 40 years ago, from Nazi Germany. Once here, he should expect no different treatment than any other American Jew.

Martin A. Feldmann
Seattle, Washington

...but others say about jewish intermarriage

A call for an authoratative stand

One of the most important matters before the Jewish community is that of intermarriage. I believe a thorough, rational discussion would be timely, with pros and cons of whether these marriages should be performed by the rabbinate. In fact, it would be desirable to have an authoritative book which should be required reading by anyone considering intermarriage or conversion.

Samuel Alk
Green Bay, Wisc.

Intermarriage between jews

It was interesting to note the opinions stated in a recent issue of Sh'ma concerning intermarriage or mixed marriage. After more than twenty years of marriage, it seems ironical that nearly all such discussions fail to recognize the intermarriage of two Jews. Mine is such a union and has presented unique problems in this vein from time to time.

One of us was raised in a very observant home complete with honored, orthodox grandparents living there. One of us was raised in a home where we acknowledged being Jewish but never affiliated with Judaic causes. In the latter family, both parents were reared in orthodox homes where there was usually a *"Yeshivah bocher"* (a young Yeshivah student being supported by a Jewish family) in residence even though there was not always enough food available. Ours was an intermarriage since one of us didn't mind being Jewish and one of us could not picture life without Judaism.

Surely a situation like ours is much more common than the lack of discussion about it would indicate. How does one partner convince the other that religious affiliation is viable and erudite? How do you convince one partner that the expense of Temple dues and a Hebrew and religious school education is vital during a period when limited income dictates very carefully measured spending? How do you teach the special flavor of a Shabbat or Yom Tov when one partner is too tired to care or put forth any effort? How do you teach children to be observant Jews when there are no others in our larger family?

Marriages like ours can and do work through a good many problems of an interfaith nature, despite the lack of help or understanding of any rabbis with whom we have become acquainted. Eventually one partner learns not to struggle so much with the other partner, but is frequently very difficult to espouse the cause of organized religion when there is no one to help carry the burden of this towering responsibility.

Anonymous

The conversion of a jew to judaism

I had never thought of myself as a convert, nor have I ever attempted to articulate the process of my conversion. However, the autobiographical essays by converted Jews (*Sh'ma* 6/107) prompted me to think of my own development from that of a born Jew through a period of Jewish secularism and finally to a Reform religious Jew.

A child of the 20's and 30's, son of immigrant parents, I was raised in a milieu that encompassed love of *Yiddishkeit*, worker's socialism, a disdain of religion as the proverbial "opiate of the masses" and an agnosticism that bordered on atheism. Momma and Poppa, however, wanted me to strongly identify with Judaism as a people and a culture . . . but not as a religion. There were Jewish books at home but no religious symbols. When the time came, I was sent to a Sholom Aleicheim *shula*, there to learn Jewish history and customs as well as the Yiddish language. I have no childhood recollections of synagogue. I have no memories of Grandparents, for they lived and died in Russia. I had many times been told that they too were non-observant Jews, though they often felt the sting of Cossack pogroms. My life as a secularist Jew and a politically liberal citizen was the mold into which I had been cast.

When my first child was eight, it was time to "Yiddishize" him. The suburban community in which we lived had a young Reform congregation with which it was easy to identify. We sent our youngster but hardly ever went ourselves. At a point soon thereafter it became apparent that we ought not to force him to go while we abstained from attendance. What followed was an occasional Sabbath service which gave way to parental enrollment in adult education and to participation in Social Action projects (which was right up my liberal political alley).

To make the rest of the short story even shorter, I was hooked. My interest had been aroused and my imagination had been captured. The young, attractive, bright and articulate Rabbi, needless to say, played no small part. Though no formal conversion took place, I had surely been converted. From a novitiate layman to knowledgeable congregational leader, I went on to Regional and National participation. I've had the pleasure of teaching study groups and have had the privilege of studying with outstanding Rabbinic leaders. By now our three grown children are products of Reform Judaism and 22 years have passed since our initiation into the movement. We are complete and fulfilled Jews. Who can guess what might have happened to us and to uncounted others like us were it not for Reform Judaism? I daresay a less liberal form of Judaism would never have been able to touch and move us.

Samuel Garfield
New York, New York

...but others say about orthodoxy...

Our Differences Strengthen Us

Jews who linger over the lessons of our history certainly are aware of the unending differences in Jewish life even from our origins. The period of the Monarchy suffered from the arguments of the localists and centerists of the cult. Jerusalem's special place was vindicated not alone by David and Isaiah but also because the localist opposition was destroyed by the Assyrians in 721 B.C.E. The Sadducee base, bound to Roman privilege, was consumed in the flames of 70, even as the Crusades and Inquisition forced Jews out of Western Europe so that the tradition came to be nurtured in the myopic, paranoid atmosphere of the Slavic world. We live at a time when fresh opportunities arise for Jewish differences. We now hear the same type of excoriating expressions cult centerists used against Israelites worshipping at local shrines, Pharisses against Saducees, anti-Maimunists against the *Moreh Nevuchim*. My sincere prayer is that this orthodox-non-orthodox fracas continue for a very long time. *Ahavat Yisrael* has always shown itself through the ages not by the willingness of Jews to agree with each other or even to accept each other, but by our proven unwillingness to destroy one another over those differences. That cruel role was filled by Assyrians, Romans, Crusaders and their like. If my Judaism with its historical-positivism and egalitarianism eschewing the *glatt*-absolutes of others is not where these others wish to *daven*, so be it. I have enough faith to abide their rejection. I also have enough faith in their *Ahavat Yisrael* to know that whatever dangers I face as a Jew will not come from them even as I hope they know that their real problem is not HUC, JTS, or RRC, but the unavoidable possibility of human sin and error and the dangers that yet lurk in that big world out there for all of us.

David J. Jacobs
Quincy, Massachusetts

...but others say about yiddish...

We have Reason, the Will and a Model

In "Yiddish: Decline or Recovery?" (Sh'ma 16/309) David Gold is a bit premature in announcing the death of Yiddish culture. I agree that outside of the Hasidic and Orthodox community (and a handful of Yiddishist families), it is unlikely that Yiddish will survive as the primary, spoken language of large numbers of Jews. But it does not necessarily follow, as Dr. Gold seems to suggest, that Yiddish will cease to be a significant force in modern Jewish life. Quite simply, Yiddish is too important to be forgotten. Can we really expect to know who we are as a people if we ignore the past thousand years of our history?

For almost two thousand years Hebrew was *not* a generally spoken language. But scholars read and debated Hebrew books, and the language in turn rubbed off, exerting its influence on all aspects of Jewish life. Hebrew has become a spoken language, and now it is Yiddish that is the province of students and scholars. But that's no reason for *Kaddish*. Yiddish books are still read, the language is still taught. Just as Hebrew once overflowed from the *kheyder* and the academy into the community, now Yiddish will do the same. Don't despair—Yiddish is too alive, too full of the idiom and wisdom of everyday life, to be safely entombed in academia. As long as Yiddish books are read, either in the original or in translation, they will continue to inform our lives as Jews.

Aaron Lansky
Amherst, Ma.

....but others say about the holocaust....

Don't Rewrite Out the Righteous Gentiles

Eliezer Berkovits' essay on rewriting the History of the Holocaust, (Sh'ma 10/198) seems to me a horrible disservice to his eminent scholarship as well as to me, the reader.

It seems to me, that he continuously and flagrantly confuses two distinctive issues. Who can or will argue with his painful outcry against man's inhumanity to man? Who would want to argue with the 'one' of the event, its *tremendum*, its uniqueness and the silence of the world?

However, I do know, Philip Halley, the writer of *"Lest Innocent Blood Be Shed*, the story of LeChambon — a town where goodness happened (Harper & Row) and to place one single grain of trust in Berkovits' vicious accusations on the motives of truth of Halley's story is a great injustice.

I visited Israel last summer and from there went to Poland to pay homage to its blood soaked earth, precariously holding memories in the wreckage of unspeakable crimes against our martyred people (and yes, 5 million others as well). A rabbi friend gave me a copy of Halley's book and said: "You are running only after death, why not stop by in LeChambon and meet some of the survivors and pay your respect to the uniqueness of life-defeating death." I went not only to LeChambon, but also searched out some of the survivors scattered through France and Italy. I also met Pastor Trocme's widow. Berkovits handles Trocme's deeds in an arrogant, condescending aside. Had he read the book, he would have learned something about the people of Le Chambon that would have, at least, widened *his* view that saving Jews was built on a century old Christian guilt feeling.

My wife was a survivor of Auschwitz and a very late victim of the atrocity. She committed suicide. I spent the war as a spy behind German lines and learned what is involved in knocking on a door — facing the fury of hate and anger, the complexity of bottomless fear or the smile and picture of a human face framed in faith and love, saying: "Yes, come in, come in. Here you will be safe."

All this Rabbi Berkovits wants to sweep away in fear that a recognition of goodness could defeat hatred.

Questions which are important to Jews as to all humanity, pale in his one sided diatribe. Yes, there are sick people who are trying to do just that, but Rabbi Berkovits heard what he wanted to hear and perhaps wrote even something else again.

We do not speak of the righteous gentiles but of "the righteous of the nations." They, so few in number, deserve and need recognition — even, God forbid, had only one single person been saved by the human spark. That spark which has the divine power to break out in flames within — saying "No" to the society so rotten from within. Most of us are content being spectators and silent onlookers. The human monster lies close below a thin veneer of civilization. Anywhere where people can help or hurt each other, in even the smallest way, ethics is happening. "That is a Jewish concern. This is a human concern. And I feel deeply that, though few in number, it is high time that we pay attention and recognize those who risked everything to help a stranger." (Halley)

Rabbi Berkovits confuses badly the enormous number of our dead with the comparatively tiny number of those who found refuge. No one refutes his statement of 'Gentile blamelessness.'' Yet his statement ''A Jew however, facing the question whether to risk his life in order to save a Christian, would be weighed down by the memories of Jewish martyrdom at Christian hands'' — is a direct affront to my sense of the covenant, of my deep sense of what Judaism is all about.

Lastly, when I visited with Pastor Trocme's successor at LeChambon last summer, I asked him: "Pastor, what would you have done, how would you have acted if you would have been the leader of this 'Temple' during the German occupation?" He replied, without hesitation: ''I don't know, I have not been tested.'' Is it not thus with all of us? Jews and Gentiles alike?

Al Ronald
Harrison, N.Y.

Orthodox quietism makes for "understanding"
I have a dear friend whose father was a Lutheran pastor in Germany when Hitler came into power. She told me that when that happened her father instructed her and her mother to cease associating or having anything further to do with their Jewish acquaintances and neighbors.

I confess that when she told me that I was shocked. What could have prompted such a high-minded man — and knowing his daughter and his widow I cannot but assume he was a sensitive and high-minded man — to take such a stand? Was he afraid? Was he concerned with his "tribal" survival?

I did not understand. But now I do. What was at stake was the "spiritual survival" of Lutheranism. Faced with "the choice of being a small ineffective voice and sparing one's people further agony" he opted for silence, for he recognized that silence is a "response to complexity." He was a good Lutheran. As Bainton puts the doctrine: "The state within its own sphere is to be unimpeded by the Church."

I did not understand. But now I do.

Lou H. Silberman
Nashville, Tenn.

. . . but others say about skokie . . .

The Skokie Situation is True Self-defense
I am terribly offended by Michael Robinson's defense of the A.C.L.U. in the Skokie affair. (*Sh'ma* 8/151) Defense of the Nazis, under the guise of the four freedoms, is the equivalent of engaging in a street fight, where your life is threatened, and unilaterally fighting by the Marquis of Queensberry rules. My Jewish theology abhors "turning the other cheek."

Bernard Kaplan, M.D.
Alexandria, Louisiana

After Skokie, the ACLU still deserves our Support
The American Civil Liberties Union is under fire from the Jewish community. The newspapers report thousands of Jews withdrawing their membership — others cutting financial support. It seems to me that this is the time when Jews must rally to the support of that organization which protects the civil liberties which are so essential to the existence of a viable Jewish community in America.

We must remember that there have been times and places where others have considered merely gathering for Jewish worship to be as inimical to their sensibilities as we do the marching of Nazis through Jewish neighborhoods of Skokie, Illinois. Those of us who have been engaged in the struggle for civil rights and for peace in America know that the selective application of the First Amendment is extremely dangerous. We must admire the American Civil Liberties Union for taking a courageous stand in defending an unpopular cause which the staff of the American Civil Liberties Union detests as much as most American Jews do. I do not want to live in America where First Amendment guarantees freedom of speech, press and assembly and worship are not guaranteed. I know the important role in the American Civil Liberties Union in protecting these constitutional provisions. I believe this is a time for an outpouring of our support to American Civil Liberties Union.

Michael A. Robinson
Croton-on-Hudson, New York

Skokie — Visions of the Night
There have been many questions going through my mind about the American Nazi Party's march through the streets of Skokie, Illinois, next month. The first question is why Skokie? The answer to this question is easy. More than 50% of Skokie's 70,000 population are Jewish, and perhaps 7,000 of these Jews are survivors of the death camps. Where else could the swastika cause such a retching reaction?

The second question is an obvious one also. The first Amendment of the Constitution of The United States provides for freedom of speech. In speaking with my lawyer friends the thought is that the First Amendment must be upheld at all costs. This I do not disagree with. The A.C.L.U. has taken this position and so have the courts. But this is a purely legalistic question and I am not a lawyer. However, I do have some knowledge of the Talmud and again I must say that I do not disagree. The point being that the Constitution and its amendments were written for our benefit as well as everybody else's and if we deny one person or group its rights we might as well deny everybody their rights.

The next question is perhaps the most difficult. Can we as Jews, being aware that the box cars are not necessarily part of history, blame our silence solely on the First Amendment? Obviously our "leadership" feels this is true. Each editorial, each article and each conversation I hear leans heavily on this argument. There is also another argument being heard, should we lower ourselves to their (the Nazis) level? By speaking out or having a confrontation do we lower ourselves to the levels of a few crackpots?

Those are the arguments against doing anything. The next question is, can we as Jews afford to be silent again? I firmly believe that the past is only a prologue to the future, guaranteeing what has happened, can and will happen again. Does the march in Skokie mean anything or are they just a few weirdos trying to get attention? Yes, I think these few (40-50) people are trying to grab headlines but the underlying tones, the unseen whisperings are what bother me. As a Jew and a student of history I can not let this gross reminder of the past go by and remain silent. The Zohar (Book of Splendor) says that withholding speech where it is needed is robbery. Can we be silent again, as the world was before, robbing 6 million souls of future generations? Can we remain silent again like our brothers in Europe when the Nazis first started their rumblings? The world has an enormous appetite for the Jew — we can not afford to remain silent. Let the lawyers and courts argue over the First

Amendment for we dare not remain silent, for, God forbid, the cattle cars are waiting — once more.

Elliott J. Allentuck
Washington, D.C.

But others say: seek peace and pursue it

All war is an evil means
Sholom Gold, defending the orthodox Jewish position on the Viet Nam war, writes about the ends and means doctrine. (*Sh'ma* 2/40). He, justifiably, condemns Communism for advocating that the ends justify the means. Buber, too, quoted the Chassidic Rebbe whose interpretation of "justice, justice, shalt thou pursue . . . " was that the double use of justice indicated that the means as well as the ends shall be good. Considering the havoc the United States has created in Viet Nam in pursuit of her goals, aren't we breaking the doctrine too? Can we blame Communism for something we do ourselves, even if the ends differ?

Those who believe in a "just" war, must also believe that the ends justify the means. War is evil. Consequently its use constitutes evil means. Most of us also refuse to face the shocking fact that the violence of the tyrant, and the violence of the man defending his home or country, are equally evil. The consequences of both are the same: the killing of innocents, the creation of long chains of violence and revenge going on for decades, killing more innocents, and the negation of the very foundation of the Torah that justice and righteousness are greater than might. What does victory in any war prove but that guns have prevailed over the issue, rather than right or wrong?

The just alternative: nonviolence
How can a just state be built on the killing of innocents? "Woe to him who builds a town with blood . ." (*Habakkuk.*). The Torah concept of war requires a new interpretation. Like revenge, it belongs in the domain of God, and is not for man's use. The moral law affirms the sanctity of the individual, even the sinner. How much more, the innocent? Gandhi wrote, "The destiny of all men is at stake in the destiny of every man."

Victors may shrug their shoulders at the killing of innocents. "It couldn't be helped." But this does not suffice as an answer for humanity. What's more, victories are always hollow. History is full of the moan

of idealists, who, in pursuit of worthy goals, bloody their hands (of course by necessity) and then agonize because the end is not what they wanted it to be.

The inevitable reply: War is better than submission to a Hitler or extinction. This answer doesn't suffice any more. We needn't choose between Hell A (Hitler) or Hell B (War). There is a third alternative available: nonviolence. During the last thirty years there has been enough theorizing and writing about the idea of nonviolent resistance to evil to fill libraries. It is in this direction that our efforts must lie. Turning to the abyss of war to avoid tyranny, will lead to the destruction of humanity.

Ed Feder
Bronx, N.Y.

Necessity makes strange bed-fellows
Some Jews appear to have forgotten the wisdom contained in the Yiddish adage *Az men darf hoben dem goniff, nehmt men ihm von der t'liah* (if you must have the services of the thief, take him even from the gallows).

I opposed Nixon in 1960 and in 1968. In 1972, I voted for Senator McGovern. With scandals cascading out of the White House, how, then, do I justify my opposition to Nixon's resignation or impeachment? Nixon's swift action in the recent Middle East war. It saved Israel. It did more. It protected American interests. It prevented the extension of Soviet hegemony over a huge area stretching from the Indian Ocean to the Straits of Gibraltar.

Philip L. Lipis
Los Angeles, Cal.

Forest hills: the danger is within us
This is perhaps a very difficult letter for me to write. I am a college student in Maine, raised in the suburbs of N.Y.C., in Queens and Nassau. Talk of Laurelton and Forest Hills. Pretty names, aren't they? A town of laurel, a hillside of pines. Muggings, stabbings, murders, robberies, rapes. . .countless ills of the city. Black—White tension in the community, in the streets.

Come brothers! Yes there is a Jewish people, but it can't exist apart from the Catholics, Muslims and Militants. There are issues deeper than either of us. It goes beyond assuming that when the Black is assimilated he will clean his streets and police himself—teach himself moral pride.

One question, though. Why work to incorporate Blacks and Others into the social system, why not make a better system (if indeed it will be a system at all). Not a Utopia, but a better place where technology works for people. A flawless space shot is vastly more complex than an efficient mass transit system. There can be food for all, KLH stereos if one wishes, if only people stop talking and do something.

We are against a steel re-inforced concrete wall. That's not an excuse, just the acknowledgement of fact.

You ask yourself, "What does the Black want?" He doesn't want anything you have to offer. From now on he will take whatever he wants. You will continue to sit and read, talk, watch – and you will learn no more than you now know. Get up and do something. There is much to worry about, if you just wish to worry.

Be careful, there is an underground just waiting to devour all Jews. It is yourself. It is self-pity. It is pride. It is condescension. It is eliteness. It is inaction.

Edd Glaser
Lewiston, Maine

A critique of the critics

Contrasted to their accustomed high standard of performance, some of *Sh'ma's* Contributing Editors appear to have panicked and taken leave of perspective in reacting to the Yom Kippur War (*Sh'ma* 4/61). For example, Lamm applauds Nixon's support of Israel and shudders at the fantasy of a McGovern presidency. And Siegel in exulting over his courageous rescue of Israel, admonishes us to declare a moratorium on criticism of the President.

Some support and some courage! A Democratic administration led by McGovern, or anybody else, hardly could have done worse than to dangle Israel at the end of a rope for 7 days before initiating the critical resupply effort. It is relaibly reported that there was an American/ Israeli *quid-pro-quo* on the basis of which Israel would refrain from a preemptive strike and the United States would *promptly* and unconditionally resupply Israel's military requirements. Lives and opportunities were lost as a result of the Administration's failure to honor this commitment in its totality.

Another U.S. undertaking in this *quid-pro-quo* reportedly was an assurance that Israel would not be pressured to halt its military operations prematurely. In reversing this commitment, and bludgeoning Israel into an instantaneous and premature acceptance of a cease-fire, Nixon and Kissinger cannot be credited with courageous, to

say nothing of honorable, behavior. And the cost of this reversal to the U.S. and Israel, in terms of Israeli security, the American and Israeli negotiating position in the Middle East, and the prospects for a peace settlement in the best interests of the United States and Israel, is likely to be considerable.

Schwarzschild credits Sadat with proposing a reasonable basis for negotiations, which he condemns the Israeli leadership for rejecting. He should read Sadat in context and not fail to read the fine print. Sadat's reasonable initiatives are formulated in territorial terms – now it is back to the 1947 partition lines – and deliberately neglect the central issue which is the legitimacy of Israel. Sadat's rhetorical retreat from a claim for the unconditional elimination of Israel to a demand for the return to non-existent 1947 lines is a less unconditional, but still an unequivocal formula for Israel's elimination. Small wonder, then, that a political leadership resists a solution which fails to recognize the legitimacy of the political entity for which it is responsible. And as for the Zionist solution, Schwarzschild might less irreverently recall that the first war was fought to establish Israel, and the next three to preserve it.

Finally, there is Levy's gratuitous suggestion that American Jews prod Mrs. Meir more energetically to make peace, coupled with his generous offer of made-in-America models to elevate the quality of Jewish life in Israel. Is it not reasonable to accept that a regime and its constituency, who have more intimately than we experienced lethal threats to their survival, might be better positioned to evaluate the quality of prodding required to assure their survival? They have been telling us and the world for 26 years that genuine peace is the critical ingredient of their survival. Is there any reason not to believe them? And as for American exports to improve other societies, our track record leaves something to be desired. So perhaps we might be less generous and more modest about our capacities, including any presumptions about the quality of Jewish life in Israel.

Elihu Bergman
Lexington, Mass.

but others say about Down's syndrome...

Acceptance and Independence Are Also Goals

My Down's Syndrome son, Myles Levy, was also tutored and had his *Bar Mitzvah*. We must all share these success stories for two very important reasons: first, we must erase the notion that preparing a retarded child for *Bar Mitzvah* is unique or terribly difficult; secondly, by letting the experiences surface, we can expand the possibilities of exactly what some of these children can accomplish!

I wish to take nothing away from Bruce Baron. What he accomplished was beautiful and I can only grin from ear to ear upon reading about his special day.

Myles had his *Bar Mitzvah* December 13, 1980. He too was surrounded by family, friends and teachers - "a four tissue service," as one choir member described it.

Myles, who is classified as educable, and has an IQ in the low 60's, studied the Hebrew letters for one year and then applied himself for another entire year to learn his service in English and Hebrew including a *Torah* portion of eighteen verses (read directly from the holy scrolls) and a *Haftorah* in English.

What we discovered was that learning to read Hebrew was not actually difficult for him. It is very concrete in its rules as compared with English (i.e., pronounce wave, save, cave, have.)

What is necessary, then, is patience, a comfortable space of time to learn (1-2 years) and one-on-one help for fifteen-twenty minutes a day. I truly believe that many retarded youngsters who have some ability to read can learn a fair amount of Hebrew with this formula. Of course, the key ingredient is an eagerness to learn, which obviously both Myles and Bruce had.

The fact that Bruce was in a "Special Sunday School Class" does indicate a classifying and separating of the mentally deficient by his Jewish society.

I have been most proud of my synagogue for mainstreaming Myles in all areas where individual tutoring wasn't necessary. This was important for the other children. Myles is accepted by the entire Sunday School population. It could be that this achievement is more important than *Bar Mitzvah!*

Rabbi Levine's emotional involvement leading to research in Jewish acceptance (or non-acceptance) is very commendable. His eventual realization that we Jews must now work for the total Jewish retarded person in areas of group homes and other educational involvement is almost more than I could have ever hoped to see in print in my lifetime. After all, the bottom line is will Bruce Baron or Myles Levy ever be given a chance to live a Jewish *adult* life away from their relatives? Many of the current group homes and sheltered communities are Christian-oriented because

their churches laid the financial and emotional foundation for their existence!

Where do we start? Actually, Myles's temple started by giving him a job as an aide in a third-grade Sunday School class. This gave him an active role after the "big day." Rabbi Levine's call for conscience, to write *halachot* is also a good start. A reasonable curriculum for a special education Confirmation class is also in order. Why should Myles and Bruce stop with *Bar Mitzvah* when all other children are so strongly encouraged to continue their studies?

Also, all synagogues should, in my opinion, be encouraged to make their building barrier-free, as a statement and visual reminder that all handicapped Jews are welcome.

Lastly, the Jewish organizations in our communities should help create a network among families of the handicapped so they can meet and discuss group homes, sibling relationships, etc. in a Jewish context.

Without ever meeting the Barons, I think I can speak for both families when I say we need Jewish community support desperately for "life after *Bar Mitzvah.*"

Rhona Levy
Flanders, N.J.

. . . but others say about t.v. . . .

Can't T.V. Foster an Honest Jewish Self-Image? Now that the children are back in school, and religious school has formally begun again, we are wrestling with the problem of Jewish identity.

I firmly believe that the television carries just as great or greater an impact on these kids' minds than their school classes, their religious school seminars, or their home lives. Seeing images on the screen and adopting their attitudes or idolizing their life styles has become the "in thing" among pre-adolescents and adolescents. Witness the impact of the "Fonz."

My contention is that the Jewish image on the boob tube is being warped out of all proportion and impressed on these kids' minds, and it makes me more than a little angry.

Consider: Henry Winkler, a first generation Jew whose parents fled the Nazis ends up playing Arthur Fonzarelli, the tough-talking Italian on the *Happy Days* series. Judd Hirsch was cast in the role of *Delvecchio* a cops and robbers series . . . even though there were traces of a definite Yiddish accent in his Italian imitation. Paul Michael Glaser, an admitted escapee from what he calls the "Golden Ghetto" of Brookline and Newton, Massachusetts, plays *Starsky* . . . perhaps the Jewish identity is minimally suggested on the program, but with no great regularity. Mandel Kramer, actor of long standing on daytime serials, plays a French-Canadian, etc.

And then we turn about face to find Mark Russell, the only Jew in the *Kojak* series, except that as the character Saperstein, he obviously isn't a Jew. Note that all the others play exactly what they are: the Savalas brothers as Greeks, Vince Conti as Rizzo, Roger Robinson as a black, etc. In one *Streets of San Francisco* rerun, veteran actor Barry Sullivan played an aging Jew — and did a poor job of it, marring his usually brilliant performance. Recently a crooked detective named Myerson terrorized a plane-load of passengers on a made-for-tv movie. What terrorized me was that the actor was Hugh somebody or other, who as the good Yankee he is, popularized many westerns. In that same film Walter Pidgeon masqueraded as an aging Jewish manufacturer. Ugh.

I would like to know what is wrong with Jews playing Jews? Have we come to the point in assimilation where only non-Jews can play Jewish roles? Sure, there are exceptions — Peter Ustinov did a marvelous job as Gideon a few seasons ago — but I am hitting at the popular series that so many of our kids watch today. There were kids in my class convinced that Henry Winkler was a bona fide Italian.
I think all kids need to see themselves, and the tube is where they pick up a lot of their self-image.

Sharon Hull
Winona, Minnesota

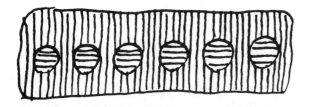

El Al Passengers Are Obnoxious

My wife and I have traveled El Al in 1967, just after the war, 1969, 1971, 1975 and 1978. We have also traveled Korean Air, Japan Air, British Airways, T.W.A., United, American, British Caledonian, French airlines, and Al Italia. Without reservation we wish to say that the service, the service personnel and the treatment on El Al equalled or surpassed that which we encountered on these other air lines in eight separate trans-Atlantic or trans-Pacific flights.

What we have discovered, and certainly our frequency of flight and use of El Al permits us to make this observation, is that the behavior and attitude of Jewish travelers aboard El Al planes ranks with the basest and most despicable we have yet observed. How the personnel of El Al can maintain the service they do and maintain their sanity is beyond my comprehension. The same kind of passengers in American or British planes conduct themselves with whatever dignity and courtesy that one can expect of the inconvenient convenience we call plane travel. Something happens when rational, generally well-behaved individuals get on an El Al flight. Demands are made of the personnel which go beyond reason and decent behavior. Requests to be seated when meals are to be served seem to arouse instincts of erratic movement. Sleep is almost impossible in the cabin, and generally chaos can best describe the atmosphere in an El Al flight out of New York.

We have boarded El Al flights in London, Paris, Rome, and Zurich. The flights were orderly, passengers well behaved and reasonable. Our most recent flight from Lod, one of the first following the strike, began in an atmosphere best compared to the asylum in "Marat Sade." After an hour or so, things quieted down and the remainder of the flight was uneventful. We compared it to our flight six weeks earlier on Austrian Air Lines where the stewards and stewardesses were rude to the point of anti-semitism, where yet frozen meals were served to Jewish passengers, where courtesty and service was not evident.

I would encourage Rabbi Prystowsky to fly other air lines and see what rude service could be.

Hyman Solomon
Los Angeles, Ca.